Constance Young Root.

Mr. William Root
Apt 214
419 Russell Ave
Gaithersburg, MD 20877

West Over the Seas
to the Orient

Ravenholt Family, Formative Years, Life Adventures

Order this book online at www.trafford.com or email orders@trafford.com

Most Trafford titles are also available at major online book retailers.

© Copyright 2009 R.T. Ravenholt.
All rights reserved. No part of this publication may be reproduced, stored in a retrieval system, or transmitted, in any form or by any means, electronic, mechanical, photocopying, recording, or otherwise, without the written prior permission of the author.

Printed in Victoria, BC, Canada.

ISBN: 978-1-4269-1870-4 (SC)

Our mission is to efficiently provide the world's finest, most comprehensive book publishing service, enabling every author to experience success. To find out how to publish your book, your way, and have it available worldwide, visit us online at www.trafford.com

Trafford rev. 12/16/2009

   www.trafford.com

North America & international
toll-free: 1 888 232 4444 (USA & Canada)
phone: 250 383 6864 • fax: 812 355 4082

FOREWORD

ALBERT RAVENHOLT

Sixty-odd years ago, when I first knew him, Albert Ravenholt was a tall, handsome, very bright young war correspondent for the United Press in the China-Burma-India theater of operations. A bit of a loner, he sought sources not mainly from local military headquarters like some other writers but by living and campaigning with Chinese troops in, say, the Salween campaign or by flying on American bomber runs. He also assiduously explored not just military fronts but basic economic, social and political realities in China, Southeast Asia and India.

In the postwar era Albert built a distinguished reputation as a scholarly/journalistic interpreter of Chinese and Asian life. I got to know this at first hand because, fortunately for me, our activities in succeeding decades repeatedly crisscrossed and sometimes merged. We both were fellows of the Institute of Current World Affairs in Asian areas. We both did stints as Asian correspondents of the Chicago Daily News Foreign Service. In the 1950s we collaborated in the launching of the American Universities Field Staff. We both contributed to the Asian interests of John D. Rockefeller 3rd and his family, though on different projects. And we worked with others like John Musser in their substantial Asia-related programs.

Through these decades, right down to the present, my friend Albert proved himself a digger to the roots of the situations and issues he addressed. The articles he wrote in the postwar period, including those reproduced in this book, stand today as cogent interpretations. For half a century he has described the whys and wherefores of Asian conditions, and often crises, in ways going beyond most standard literature.

Albert has always been not just a student of affairs but also an activist. Along with his wife Marjorie he contributed much to the maturing of the Joint Commission on Rural Reconstruction in postwar Taiwan. His creative instincts encouraged the Rockefellers and their Asian associates to establish the Magsaysay Foundation whose awards have become the Nobel prizes of Asia. On farmland he purchased in the Philippines he demonstrated the possibilities of productive agriculture on lateritic soil.

His enthusiasm helped the Asian spread of nitrogen-fixing tree species with their bountiful returns of lumber, fodder, firewood and other by-products. (He also cultivates commercial forest products and vineyards in the United States.)

An extraordinary achiever, Albert has always been a man of high purpose, strong will and absolute integrity. When he has seen overextended power and privilege he has called them by their right names, as the Chiang Kai Sheks of China and the Marcoses of the Philippines learned.

This volume offers Albert's heretofore unavailable biographical history and a broad selection of his Asian articles. They portray a remarkably good man.

August 29, 2004   Phillips Talbot

WEST OVER THE SEAS TO THE ORIENT
Part A
Ravenholt Family, Formative Years, Life Adventures

TABLE OF CONTENTS

Introduction	1
Ravenholts of Wisconsin: their Danish Origins	3
Grand View College and World's Fair	7
West Over the Seas to the Orient	8
Shanghai as World War II Begins	9
Hauling Medical Supplies for the International Red Cross in China	10
United Press War Correspondent in China-Burma-India	13
United Press Bureau Chief for China	22
A Night to Remember: With Mao Tse-tung	24
Albert Ravenholt Marries Marjorie Sevryns in Shanghai	26
Homeward Bound after Seven Years in Asia	27
Fellow of the Institute of Current World Affairs at Harvard	28
West Over the Seas to the Orient Again	29
The Last Half Century: Investigating & Writing on Key Asian Issues.	30
Work and Family Photos	34
The Story of an Immigrant, Anders C. Ravnholt	37
Danish Letter to a Brother	41
Life of Walter S. Rogers, Institute of Current World Affairs	44
Origin of the Magsaysay Awards Foundation for Asia	47
Creation of Foreign Correspondents Club in Chungking	49
Seven World War II Correspondents Visit China in 1985	54
Ho Chi Minh: Revolutionary Extraordinary	55
Miscellaneous Family Letters by Albert	58
Geneva Diplomate Letter to Albert	75
Obituary for Marjorie Severyns Ravenholt	78
Memorable Life of Segundina Lotilla	80
Collage of Family Pictures	82
Albert's Family Leadership	85
Ancestors of Albert Ravenholt	87
Pictures of Albert's Parents	88
Sibling Pictures and Curriculi Vitae	90
Apple Picking Time at Sagemoor	99
Albert Ravenholt's Foremost Publication Titles	104

INTRODUCTION

RETURNING TO THE SCENES of our dairy farm childhood in the West Denmark-Milltown-Luck, Wisconsin community, we nine children of Danish-American parents Ansgar and Kristine Ravnholt were not infrequently asked, "How did it happen that all nine of you made out so well in life?" To which we sometimes mentioned the principal contributing factors of two very intelligent parents, our general good health, the intellectual stimulus of our father Ansgar, the extraordinary mother craft contributions of our mother Kristine, our schooling in Danish at West Denmark (summers) and in English in the Milltown and Luck Public Schools, the exceptional University educational opportunities available to all willing to work hard in the postwar American society, *plus* the outstanding leadership exercised by our eldest brother, Albert.

We were all steeped in the social setting of West Denmark with many relatives of our mother Kristine, the eldest of 11 children of immigrants Niels and Ane Marie Petersen, most of whom lived within a few miles and whose numerous children were our dearest playmates. Fortunately, the Danish Lutheran Church was of the Grundvigian persuasion, emphasizing singing, good works and fellowship more than piety. The Danish Summer School by Little Butternut Lake provided such fine opportunities for singing, swimming, fishing and ball playing while learning something of reading and writing Danish, that it was a memorable pleasure. And the nearby "Gym Hall", an assembly hall with kitchen and eating facilities below, in daily use during summer school, was a popular magnet for all ages on many social occasions, including dances in which the Pastor's family participated. Still vivid in Albert's memory is the large and colorful Jes Smidt painting of "Leif Ericsen Discovers America" which hung in the West Denmark assembly hall through-out our youth - stirring Albert's imagination and wander-lust so powerfully that it may have contributed significantly to his subsequent course - Vest Over Havet til Østen (West Over the Seas to the Orient).

After loss of our homestead farm to bank foreclosure in April 1935, Albert worked for his board and room and essentials with the Chris Birkholm family during 3 years of high school. After high school and a winter at Grand View College in Des Moines, Iowa, he worked at the New York Worlds Fair the summer of 1939, then traveled to California and across the Pacific Ocean as cook on a Swedish freighter to the Orient, continuing on to the Mediterranean Sea, Marseilles, around Africa and back to Shanghai. In 1941-42 he led the trucking of medical supplies for the International Red Cross on the Burma Road and into China's interior not yet occupied by the Japanese; then served as a War Correspondent for the United Press in China-Burma-India, 1942-46, surviving many extraordinary adventures, and continued as a writer and correspondent throughout the Orient during subsequent decades.

We sibs had long anticipated that Albert would write the history of his life experiences - surely of great interest - but he did not. And when in February 2003 he suffered a fall, with advancing dyskinesia, and we realized he never would write his own remarkable history, I proceeded to interview him frequently and intensively during the spring and summer and wrote of the most interesting episodes of his life. Also, being a physician, I got him on an improved regimen of needed prescriptions to enhance his cardiovascular and neurological health; and enlisted the dedicated daily help of his long-time household helper-friend, Segundina

Lotilla, to ensure that he actually took the prescribed drugs regularly. Surprisingly, during the summer and fall months of 2003 his strength and agility greatly improved, with recovery of his remarkable memory of many events since childhood including names and spelling of many Asian acquaintances, events, and places. After each interview my written account of the episode was read by Albert and his suggested changes incorporated into subsequent drafts. Here, then, is our joint account of his life's story.

Reimert and Albert, ages 8 & 14, in 1933

R T Ravenholt, MD, Director, Office of Population, USAID/ Department of State, USA

A V Ravenholt, Foreign Correspondent, Institute of Current World Affairs, Chicago Daily News, AUFS

40 Years Later ---- Together in the Philippines

RAVENHOLTS OF WISCONSIN

BORN SEPTEMBER 9, 1919 to Ansgar and Kristine Ravnholt at their farm home near Milltown, Wisconsin, Albert Victor Ravenholt was a fortunate child. Because their first-born child, Thora, had died of pyloric stenosis at six weeks, his parents were overjoyed that their second child proved to be exceptionally healthy and thriving. He received not only utmost good care from his mother Kristine -- herself the eldest of 11 children and thus well-experienced in child care -- but also from his paternal grandmother Hanne Thestrup Ravnholt, who lived with them until her death in January 1922. Albert's earliest memory from childhood is of being assaulted by a big gander in the farmyard, that bit his ear and dragged and fiercely beat him with its wings until he was rescued by elders.

Well educated in both Danish and English, Albert's parents home-schooled him, mainly in Danish, until he entered Milltown elementary school at age 7. By then he was reading Danish

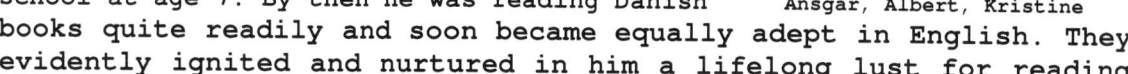
Ansgar, Albert, Kristine

books quite readily and soon became equally adept in English. They evidently ignited and nurtured in him a lifelong lust for reading and learning His education in the Milltown public schools and in the West Denmark parochial school (summers) provided him strong basic capabilities in both languages, and omnivorous readingrapidly expanded his knowledge. Life on the family dairy farm was filled with morning and evening chores and many arduous tasks in the full range of farm and forest activities. Being the eldest of nine

Eiler Halvor Reimert Johanne Albert

surviving children: Albert 1919, Halvor, 1921, Eiler and Johanne (twins) 1923, Reimert, 1925, Otto, 1927, Gerda, 1929, and Agnes and Astrid (twins) 1931, he soon became a great help to his father with many farming operations and also to his overwhelmingly busy mother, helping to care for and lead the younger children. Upon Reimert's birth in 1925 Kristine had five children under the age of six including twins whom Albert from an early age tended while she helped with the milking, worked in the garden, and as otherwise needed. In adolescence he was exceptionally vigorous and enterprising, initiating many projects. During the summer of 1933 Albert and Reimert created and tended a special garden by the poplar grove at onions, parsnips, ground cherries, and melons.

4

RAVENHOLTS OF WISCONSIN

A preceding picture shows them atop corn shocks by the barn, September 1933, ages 14 and 8.

One of Albert's fondest memories of adolescence on "the old farm" is from the snowy winter of 1934; when invited to be a fourth at cards with Uncle Ole Sorensen, Aunt Kirstine and Axel Benedsen, he drove our spirited horses and sleigh there on a frozen moonlit night, returning with hoofs and snow clods flying, harness bells ringing, and northern lights flaring!

Ansgar Ravnholt, a well-educated man with strong theoretical and horticultural interests, ignited and nurtured his son Albert's avid life-long interest in horticultural and agricultural phenomena and practices and in community, national and world affairs. But as Albert passed puberty and rapidly grew to 6 feet 2 inches, he became larger and stronger than his father and increasingly impatient with some of Ansgar's seemingly perverse economic decisions. One such decision that troubled Albert was that when State Highway authorities offered to buy gravel from a hill at the southern edge of Ravnholt farm for reconstruction and paving of the adjacent State Highway 35, Ansgar for sentimental reasons refused to sell the gravel despite desperate economic circumstances. Possibly the offer came too late to save the debt-laden farm created by his parents a half-century earlier and lost to Federal Land Bank foreclosure the next spring. The evening of the day in April 1935 after the sheriff moved the family off the farm to temporary lodging in Balsam Lake Village, Albert went to work for his room and board with kindly neighbors: first with Andrew Jepsen for a month then with Chris and Elnora Birkholm where Albert lived and worked during his three remaining high school years.

These changes greatly challenged Albert and accelerated his educational and developmental opportunities. Andrew Jepsen was an excellent farmer with a fine herd of purebred Guernsey milk cows that Albert enjoyed working with that spring. Chris Birkholm was likewise an exceptionally able and creative man with an excellent herd of 20+ Jersey milk cows and some commercial production of strawberries and raspberries. An accomplished gymnastics teacher at West Denmark and in the Milltown Public Schools, Birkholm worked mainly as a carpenter/builder and did wood carving as a hobby. Because of the range of Birkholm's activities, Albert soon assumed large responsibilities for daily dairy chores (beginning 5:30 AM) of milking, feeding, and barn cleaning, with extensive field work each summer. Breakfast was mainly a large bowl of oatmeal. During his high school years, unable to participate in inter-school athletics because of the inescapable demands of evening chores at Birkholms, he conducted a dairy herd improvement project with monthly weighing of each cow's daily milk production and measurement of butterfat content. He was also active in bee-keeping, orchard care, and 4-H activities -- entering live stock for showing at the annual Polk County Fair. Necessitated by milking of cattle maintained a mile away by Little Butternut Lake during summers, Albert soon began driving Birkholm's 1928 Chevrolet sedan. Birkholm's daughter, Doris, two years older than Albert, was a great help with milking and other chores initially. Having already graduated from high school, she also worked elsewhere and in 1937 went to Chicago to work.

RAVENHOLTS OF WISCONSIN

Physical living circumstances at Birkholms were much more conducive to in-depth study and independent enterprise than at home -- where he shared a bedroom with four brothers and lived in a crowded 11-person household without electricity, radio, or indoor plumbing. At Birkholms, Albert had a bedroom with electric reading lights, radio, and indoor plumbing. Chris and Elnora, and daughters Adelheid and Doris were immediately delighted with the addition of this ready-made and talented "son" to their household and rapidly became enthusiastic supporters of his many creative inquiries and projects. Their beamed-ceiling living room provided a pleasing display of Chris's carvings and Nora's landscape paintings. During the three years Albert was at Birkholms, our family lived nearby on two rental farms. Ansgar worked for the Works Progress Administration (WPA) and we younger sibs did the farming and dairying at home and often helped with milking and berry picking at Birkholms. Family social activities were consolidated at West Denmark - where we gathered for this picture on July 4th, 1935.

Ansgar and Kristine Ravnholt Family, West Denmark, Wisconsin, 4 July 1935
Johanne	Kristine	Ansgar		Albert	Halvor
Gerda	Astrid	Agnes	Eiler	Reimert	Otto

Always a stellar student, Albert daily walked two miles to and from Milltown School. He especially enjoyed his English studies with Miss Dorothy Dunn and his agricultural studies with Mr Earle Sanford. Miss Dunn honed his writing skills. Decades later, at a Milltown High School class reunion, a fellow student recalled sitting behind Albert in Miss

RAVENHOLTS OF WISCONSIN

Dunn's class one day and seeing him -- when called upon to read a required composition -- hold up a blank piece of paper while successfully reading a non-existent composition, which he then quickly wrote-out during the balance of the class period!

In the severe drought summer of 1936, rain fell on June 2nd, our father's birthday; but then no rain fell during 49 days – until July 21st on Agnes's and Astrid's birthday. Suffering from intolerable heat, we sometimes slept on the lawn, suffering mosquitoes. Crops ceased growing, many corn stalks reached only the height of one to two feet, and hay crops yielded very little. We younger boys scrounged for hay wherever we could find it – in ditches along the roadsides of West Denmark and Milltown and from the municipal park, getting barely enough hay for our herd the next winter.

Meanwhile, Chris Birkholm, Eric Smidt, Magnus Jepsen, Albert and several others drove a horse drawn caravan of wagons, mowers, and rakes 40 miles northwest, beyond Grantsburg, to "The Barrens" (now Crex Meadows). Ordinarily these large swamps could not be used for farming because of standing water, but in 1936 the drought dissipated the water so that the swamp grasses could be cut for hay.

They proceded to the farm of a widow lady who had survived the great Hinckley Fire of the 1880s and whose farm buildings were situated in a meadow protected from fire by an encircling fire-brake created by plowing six furrows around the perimeter of the buildings and associated meadow. The Birkholm ensemble worked there three weeks, mowing, raking, hauling and stacking the swamp grasses into three large, 20 by 60 foot, stacks placed within the widow's firebreak. Camping and sleeping by the stacks, Albert thrilled to the nightly howling of wolves and the heavenly displays of stars and streaming lights in the sky. While there, a forest and swamp fire raced toward them driving deer before it and threatening haymaking equipment, so that rapid action by the work crew was necessary to remove and save vital equipment. Fortunately, they harvested enough marsh hay in "The Barrens" that Birkholm's, Smidt's, and Jepsen's livestock survived the following winter, but the poor quality of the hay cut milk production.

Caring for 4 hives of honey bees at Birkholms, and taking out queen cells of a hive in the summer of 1937 to prevent swarming, dozens of bees penetrated a rip in Albert's protective netting outfit, stinging him so fiercely on throat and face that ludicrous swelling altered his appearance a week. He also gained experience in orchard care, grafting varieties of apples.

In October of his senior year Albert traveled to the University of Wisconsin at Madison with Mr Sanford and fellow Ag students. During several days there, he wrote extensive examinations for the Wisconsin Farm Facts Contest - an annual competition for agricultural youth. Even now – 65 years later – he vividly recalls the excitement of the final gathering with thousands of contestants and faculties in the University of Wisconsin Field House, where examination results were announced by a Master of Ceremonies who named each of the top 10 contestants in ascending order of merit; his increasing dejection as the M.C. identified the 10th through the 2nd highest placement winners without calling his name, and his sudden ecstasy when named the winner - "with the highest test score yet attained in Wisconsin" -- for which he received a fine pen and pencil set and much publicity.

Homeward bound, Mr. Sanford commented that no doubt Albert would win additional honors, but rarely if ever would his enjoyment of those honors equal that of winning the Wisconsin Farm Facts Contest. Later in his senior year, he entered and won a national essay contest for high school youth on the nature and significance of the enactment of the United States Northwest Ordinance in 1787 for which he received a cash prize of $300 plus offers of full scholarships to many Big Ten universities. That spring Albert addressed a Farmers Union picnic on "The Key Role of Private Ownership of Land in Determining a Healthy Rural Society", and gave the high school Commencement Address.

Graduating from high school in 1938 midst the severe economic depression, Albert sought work in Minneapolis. Having decided during school to become a foreign correspondent, he chose to learn food preparation skills deemed portably useful in future travels. Proceeding to the Radisson Hotel -- Minneapolis's finest -- he engaged kitchen help in conversation to ascertain what he must do to work there. Learning from them that he must join the Hotel and Restaurant Workers Union of the AFL/CIO, he did this. Becoming acquainted with the Secretary General of the Union, Albert persuaded him to provide a note to the chief chef at the Radisson Hotel recommending him for an apprentice chef position. Thus Albert gained employment for the summer at $12 per week plus meals and acquired a chef's knife and intensive culinary experience.

It was upon returning to Birkholms that September that Albert found the letter -- held during some weeks in anticipation of his return -- informing him of having won the Northwest Ordinance essay competition. Because of the late date and because his father had studied at Grandview College in Des Moines, Iowa, and his mother urged it, Albert decided to go there. His matriculation, however, was delayed until late November by a life-threatening accident while riding about on our horse Daisy visiting relatives at West Denmark before his intended departure for Grandview College at the end of September. Struck by a truck driven by a drunken driver, the horse was killed and Albert suffered such severe trauma to his right lower leg that amputation was considered a likely necessity. But Doctor Raymond Arveson, able family physician in the adjacent town of Frederic, worked so skillfully with potassium permanganate soaks suppressing infection of the extensive lacerations that he managed to save life and limb, and enabled Albert to convalescence at home during October and November. While disabled, Albert organized and directed relatives and friends in a Danish play, "Eventyr paa Fodrejser", performed at West Denmark before he left for Grandview College.

During his year at Grandview College, Albert enjoyed his studies and close associations with students and eminent Danish-American leaders, GVC President S.D. Rodholm, Professor Johannes Knudsen and others. He wrote a history of his paternal grandfather, Anders Christian Ravnholt, "A Story of an Immigrant" which won a prize when published in UNGDOM, October 1939 (Appendix A). He also wrote a brotherly letter to me at Confirmation time At the end of the school year Albert briefly visited family and friends in West Denmark and Luck, Wisconsin, then proceeded to the New York World's Fair. Planning ahead for international travels after the Fair's closure, he stopped at Akron, Ohio, to obtain "Seaman's Papers". Arriving in New York, he visited his father's cousin, Johannes Thestrup, owner of a garden nursery on Long Island -- just where the Verrazano Bridge eventually joined the island. After sleeping in the nursery several nights he rented nearby inexpensive lodging recommended by Thestrup, and had rather long subway commutes to the Fairgrounds.

In Manhattan at a central hiring hall for the World's Fair, he presented his letter of recommendation from the Radisson Hotel French chef and quickly gained employment as steward at the Brass Rail Restaurant, the largest restaurant at the Fair, customarily serving thousands of diners daily. Albert ordinarily worked 6 days weekly, 8:30 AM to 9PM, and routinely ordered huge quantities of chicken and other restaurant groceries plus handling paymaster duties. In New York he attended the wedding of Alvin and Ellen Jepsen who subsequently took over Andrew Jepsen's farm at West Denmark. At the Brass Rail- that ominous summer of 1939 - the chef and some other Workers were German Nazis, resulting in divisive working conditions, exacerbated when Hitler invaded Poland on 1 September. Nevertheless Albert continued working there until Fair closure in mid-October. Then he and John Pizurcki, a fellow worker at the Brass Rail restaurant, hitch-hiked southward, past Washington, DC, until able to hitch rides on trains to New Orleans. Upon arrival in New Orleans Pizurcki became so lonesome for his sweetheart that he turned back to New York. Albert continued alone westward, hitching rides on autos and trains to Los Angeles. After visiting relatives Ingrid and Bill Madsen and Harald and Adelheid Birkholm Sorensen he proceeded to the San Pedro waterfront, seeking oceanic employment. Having joined the Scandinavian Seamen's Union while in Manhattan, Albert was able to pay into "Stu Potten" at the San Pedro hiring hall, which allowed him to eat freely there as long as he was ashore. Meanwhile he and the unemployed seamen slept on benches at the Norwegian Seamen's Church.

Albert at NY World's Fair

Upon arrival at San Pedro, Albert registered as a "Ship's Cook" on the applicant blackboard. Such applicants were required to accept the first opening in their respective category. In the second week he shipped out as First Cook on the MS Agra of the Svenska Øster Asiatic Co. a Swedish vessel bound for the Orient after an early November visit to Portland, Oregon, for a cargo of squared timbers for delivery in Japan. On the trans-Pacific voyage, Albert and a Swedish second cook cooked for 30+ crewmen.

While still in Manhattan, in anticipation of his oceanic travels, Albert had learned some Norwegian and Swedish. On the MS Agra (being fluent in

RAVENHOLTS OF WISCONSIN

Danish) he soon developed a workable knowledge of Swedish. But upon receiving his first pay he was dismayed to find it substantially less than promised. When the Captain made his morning rounds Albert stated his dissatisfaction. The Captain's reply, "Det er kochen's første tur til søs" (It is the cook's first tour at sea), did not mollify him. Hence, later that day when preparing the Captain's favorite fish soup, before the Mess-Boy carried it off to the Captain, Albert added a large spoonful of black pepper.

Soon after delivering the soup to the Captain, the mess-boy excitedly reported back that upon taking a spoonful of the soup the Captain spit it out, exclaiming: "Hvad I Phanning er fehl med soupen?" (What in the Devil is wrong with the soup?) and threw it out the porthole. But on rounds the next morning the Captain assured Albert he need have no further concern about the pay issue!

Reaching Japan just after the New Year, the MS Agra discharged its cargo; then proceeded to Shanghai, Hong Kong, Borneo (refueling at Miri), to Singapore, across the Indian Ocean, a stop at Djiboutie (the Port for Addis Ababa), through the Red Sea and Suez Canal. From Port Said Albert sent cards and letters home. Arriving in Marseille, France, in April 1940, Albert explored the city, the Chateau d'If, and opportunities for joining the French military forces. But the swift collapse of French resistance to the Nazi invasion precluded Albert getting involved. In June when German planes bombed Marseille port shipping, the MS Agra departed, stopping along the SE Coast of Spain for a load of salt, then proceeding down along the West Coast of Africa. In the vicinity of Free Town, Carl (a young Danish second cook, recruited at Marseille), became so seriously ill with fever, vomiting, convulsions and skin lesions that Albert tried to persuade the captain to put in at Free Town for medical care; to which the Captain exclaimed, "Hvis han vil død, saa lad ham død!" (If he will die, then let him die!). Albert tended Carl carefully, massaging his limbs three times daily and Carl gradually recovered. While stopping awhile at the Azores, Albert wrote home.

Rounding the African continent, the MS Agra swung far south of the Cape of Good Hope -- to the "Roaring Forties" (40+ degrees latitude) -- to avoid any submarines lying in wait. The strategy worked well enough that they proceeded uneventfully across the Indian Ocean to Japan. Not permitted to go ashore there, the crew mutinied - just quit working. When the First Mate came asking for a meal, Albert refused; and the mate "blew up the stove." Somehow the crew forced the skipper to put in at Shanghai, where Albert obtained his pay and left the ship. He first moved into the Navy YMCA, but soon moved to the Foreign YMCA where he continued living until he left Shanghai in June 1941. Living mainly on his accumulated pay from the MS Agra, Albert began studying languages with tutors -- Chinese, German, French and Russian. He also became Vice President of a Chinese corporation that winter "because the American General Manager needed another American as a decoration."

On Christmas Eve, Albert "cashed some traveler's checks and went about distributing monies to beggars." Between Christmas and the New Year he and an English friend saw the triumphant German film "Sieg Am Westen" by Leni Riefenstahl at the Kaiser Vilhelm Schule, a four-hour account of the Nurenberg political rallies and the German conquests of Poland, Denmark,

SHANGHAI AS WORLD WAR II BEGAN

Norway, Belgium, Holland and France. The film made a very sobering impression upon them. That winter Albert did some writing, including publication of an article in the China Weekly Review on "The Fall of France." He also did some broadcasts for an English language radio station. Occasionally he went biking and boating outside Shanghai. Soon after moving into the Foreign YMCA, he became good friends with Geog Soderbom, an explorer of Central Asia and Mongolia who had British Intelligence (M16) connections during many years, and had recently escaped from the Japanese in Peking. Soderbom, previously had the Ford dealership for Mongolia, and had sufficient funds. He had led Sven Medin's Central Asian Expedition. A large man, he was substantially taller than Albert and weighed 260 to 280 pounds. He told Albert that in Mongolia the Mongols customarily offered distinguished visitors the sexual favors of their wives.

During the winter of 1940-41, Albert belonged to the "Shanghai Volunteer Corps" and when on duty marched hourly on the bridge over Soochow Creek, meeting Japanese sentries at the middle of the bridge then snapping to attention and marching back. Increasingly aware in the spring of 1941 that the Japanese armies would soon take over Shanghai, Albert (aged 21) met with International Red Cross officials in Shanghai and obtained appointment as "Transportation Inspector" for IRC haulage on the Burma Road with extensions to Central and Northwestern China, headquartered at Kweiyang.

With Associated Press correspondent Walter "Bud" Briggs and equipped with fake credentials as "missionary school teachers" -- obtained through the Foreign YMCA -- they departed Shanghai June 6, 1941 on a Japanese ship bound along the SE China Coast, getting off at Swatou. There Albert and Walter went to the Christian Protestant Mission and were put in contact with a smuggler of lace thread who arranged transport for them on a motorboat up along the coast about 20 miles. The boat then entered an estuary and proceeded among clumps of brackish water trees. Thinking they were beyond the Japanese lines, they were suddenly challenged by an armed Japanese sentry on a pier who signaled them to pull up. Albert was in the bow of their boat with a satchel, which the Japanese pointed to indicating he should open it, which Albert did saying "ohaiyo gozai mas" (good morning). Fortunately, Albert had placed a carton of Lucky Strikes on top in his satchel and indicated to the sentry he could have them. The sentry grasped the cigarettes with alacrity and in doing so gestured to Albert and Bud Briggs to get out of there; which they quickly did and proceeded to an American missionary doctor in Kityang. In discussing his medical practice with Albert that night, the doctor mentioned seeing numbers of throat cancers among male patients, yet none among females, which he attributed to the disparity that on a daily basis the men ate first when the rice was hot and the women ate second when it had cooled off. But we now know it was because the men smoked heavily and the women not at all.

The following day Albert and Briggs proceeded with several other travelers over mountainous terrain and the 4000 foot Sing Sing Guan pass and down to a river. The next day they gained passage on a junk to Meihsien. During subsequent days, they continued onward by junk and truck to Shao-Kuan where they boarded a train to Kwei-lin and continued to Liu-Chou and to Kuei-Yang - capital of Kweichou Province and headquarters of

HAULING MEDICAL SUPPLIES FOR THE RED CROSS IN CHINA

the International Red Cross for Central China. On a nearby hilltop was the Chinese Red Cross headquarters. The road known as "The Burma Road" ran from Lashio to Kunming and onward to Kuei-Yang and to Chungking.

Arriving in Kuei-Yang the last week in June, Walter Briggs independently proceeded to Chungking, while Albert remained in Kuei-yang assuming responsibility for a convoy of six International Red Cross trucks and a staff of two-dozen male Chinese truckers. Two men on each truck, put out chocks to hold the trucks whenever they stopped on hills. Two of the trucks, built in England, had solid rubber tires. Soon, with Albert ordinarily driving the lead truck, they proceeded northward toward Chungking -- seeing the Yangtze River four days later in flood stage and a half-mile wide. At Chungking the river banks narrowed so greatly that at flood stage the river rose more than 100 feet. As they approached the river down a long slope in a queue of 30 trucks, all seeking to ferry across that evening, a Chinese trucker careened wildly past, failed to stop at the ferry, and plunged into the river. Albert worked desperately to get a hawser onto the overturned truck, trying to rescue the driver, but the attempt failed and the man drowned. Because the ferry could take only four trucks at a time, Albert's convoy could not cross that evening; so he walked upstream a ways, got a sampan to ferry him across, then walked 12 km into Chungking -- arriving at dawn just as the Air Raid sirens wailed and Japanese bombers began bombing Chungking. When the bombing ceased, he proceeded to the Canadian Mission Business Agency (CMBA) - through which the International Red Cross for China worked - and got CMBA help in obtaining the Chinese military clearance needed for the convoy trip into NW China.

Proceeding next to the Press Hostel, Albert met a Mr Sadyantz, Russian film distributor for Asia, who invited him to the Russian Embassy that evening for drinks and to view Russian films. There he was introduced to General Vassili Ivanovich Chuikov, commander of the Russian Military Mission to China, who had won distinction earlier at Hankow when Russian fliers defeated attacking Japanese planes. General Chuikov was a large and powerful man and Albert recalls that when shaking hands with him at Chungking he "recognized a soldier's soldier." Recalled to Moscow in 1942, General Chuikov assumed command of the Russian 62nd Army at Stalingrad, helping to defeat the Germans in one of the most momentous battles of World War II.

After three weeks in Chungking, Albert proceeded with the six IRC trucks to Chengtu in Sichwan Province where he delivered medical supplies. A week later they proceeded NW to an Italian Jesuit Mission on the Han Chung plain where he was met most cordially by Bishop Cavelli who upon Albert's arrival shouted to others to "get out our best wines." In addition to medical supplies, Albert brought 400 kilos of sugar (from Sichwan) for the Mission Han Chung. Thus Albert was frequently able to augment IRC haulage with non-medical essentials greatly needed by the missions.

Next the convoy proceeded to Paoji on the Lunghai Railway, where they transferred medical supplies intended for the British Mission Hospital in Sian from their trucks to a train going there. Albert also brought sugar to the British Mission, paid for with money garnered from the "Yellow Fish" -paying passengers riding atop the trucks. When the convoy got to

HAULING MEDICAL SUPPLIES FOR THE RED CROSS IN CHINA

Lunghsien, Albert transferred the IRC goods to pack mules and made a two-day mule trip to the next segment of operational railroad. Sleeping one night in a miserable inn, Albert was severely bitten by bedbugs. They then loaded the medical supplies on a train and traveled 30 miles by train to Luoyang. The train could only run at night because of Japanese artillery covering the railroad running along and above the Yellow River. At Luoyang they delivered medical supplies to the Belgian Jesuit Mission/First Aid Station, which was then ministering to wounded Chinese soldiers. Luoyang was close by the juncture of the Luoyang and Pingdingshan Railroad lines. Albert was able to load the balance of his medical supplies on the south-running train for delivery to points south. The IRC trucks then returned to Baoji, where they were serviced and loaded for a run to Chengtu. In Chengtu, Albert stayed with a Canadian doctor and his wife who had a daughter then studying medicine in Toronto. They insisted she would make a fine wife for Albert!

In September, on Albert's second trip to Han Chung, he again spent a night at the Mission with Bishop Cavelli who had a long white beard and served dinner from inside a U-shaped table. That evening Albert was tipped-off by one of his truck drivers that a spare driver was stealing medicines and other supplies and placing them in his "pugai" (bedroll). The next morning, having proceeded a mile from the Mission, Albert stopped the convoy and ordered the spare driver to place his pugai on the road and open it. As he did so, a hoard of medicines and medical instruments was revealed. Albert seized them, then fired the spare driver.

The convoy next proceeded over a mountain pass to Shwang Shi-Pu and after a night went over another pass to the railroad at Baoji, where they loaded the goods on a train and left the trucks. Proceeding with the goods by rail to the British Mission Hospital at Sian, Albert spent a day with a Scottish doctor in an Out Patient Clinic (OPD) observing his handling of about 40 patients. Most notable was "a peasant woman with 'triple perforation of an eye' from syphilis."

They continued east by rail to Luoyang, where the E-W line crossed the N-S line to Pindingshan. There Albert spent a whole day waiting for the train to proceed. At dark the train went up the mountain, through Tung Kwan Pass and down along and over the Yellow River. For awhile they were exposed to ineffective Japanese artillery fire. At Pingshan they off-loaded the medicines to mules and proceeded 30 miles to their destination, a Belgian Jesuit Mission, after which they retraced their route to Chengtu.

Upon arrival at the missionary depot at the West China Union Universities in Chengtu, Albert learned that the "spare driver" he had discharged for thievery at Han Chung had gone to Chengtu and reported to the depot managers that Albert had been kidnapped and that he had been sent back to collect a ransom for him. The staff of the Chengtu Mission Hospital held a meeting to discuss what to do; and decided not to send a ransom but to hold a prayer meeting for Albert's safe release -- which was done!

> In September, the IRC trucks were heavily loaded with cotton bales at
> Paoji, then transported to Kunming and sold for considerable Chinese
> National currency which Albert delivered to Doctor Robert McClure,

HAULING MEDICAL SUPPLIES FOR THE RED CROSS IN CHINA

Canadian head of the IRC for Free China based in Kwei-Yang. During subsequent months Albert made repeated trips on the road between Kwei-Yang and Kunming, made especially memorable by a difficult five km stretch with 24 turns. On one such trip, as the convoy (with Albert driving the lead truck) reached the bottom of a hill, Chinese soldiers tried to halt them. Fearing banditry, Albert barreled ahead and received a bullet through the truck cab. This aggravated him so much that he returned and upbraided the soldiers for having shot at them, lined them up and sniffed each gun to try to ascertain which soldier had fired at him; until told that the offending soldier had disappeared down the mountainside. They then showed Albert several wounded soldiers on stretchers whom they were desperately trying to get to a place where medical care could be had. Albert took the bolts from their rifles and loaded and transported the two badly wounded soldiers and their comrades to a place where they could receive care.

Chinese roads were almost entirely constructed by manpower -- without heavy equipment -- with large numbers of peasantry engaged in cracking stones for resurfacing the roads. River crossings were made mainly on huge platforms mounted on wide boats. Airfields were leveled by means of huge stone rollers, 9 feet in diameter and 12 feet long, that were pulled by hundreds of coolies. Albert told of one coolie, pulling a stone roller, who slipped, fell under the roller and was killed.

Whenever in Kwei-yang, Albert worked not only with the IRC, but also with the nearby director of the Chinese Red Cross. He soon became acquainted with the director's beautiful and talented Eurasian daughter. A friendly relationship continued during war correspondent years whenever he returned to Kwei-yang.

On December 6th, Albert took a man and wife to the airport at Kunming. They left their two children at the Hotel du Commerce with the understanding that Albert would subsequently transport them to Kwei-Yang and to Chengtu with his next convoy. Albert and Bud Briggs were in Kunming when the Japanese attacked Pearl Harbor on December 7th. On the trip from Kwei-yang to Chengtu, one of the trucks rolled down a mountainside and the help of 200 coolies was needed to haul it back up onto the road. Subsequently the truck lost engine lubrication and suffered burned-out bearings. With the help of a Chinese blacksmith shop, Albert fashioned shortened replacement bearings. He did finally get the couple's two children through to Chengtu.

Hauling a load from Chengtu to Chungking between Christmas and the New Year, Albert let a Charles Fenn ride along to Chungking. They encountered 5 cars stalled along the road and one car stranded in the adjacent rice field - which, it turned out, belonged to the Russian Air Attache. Offering assistance, Albert broke the dike to drain the rice field, and lowered the water table sufficiently that with chains and ropes hitched to the rear axle of the Russian car they towed it up on the road; and earned considerable thanks from the Russians.

International Red Cross (IRC) goods ordinarily were sent by train from Rangoon to Lashio, where Albert with the IRC trucks picked them up and hauled them on the Burma Road to Kunming and many other places in Free China. The 24 truckers were paid regular salaries by the IRC. Albert

HAULING MEDICAL SUPPLIES FOR THE RED CROSS IN CHINA

arranged meals as needed with restaurants along the way - rice, noodles, vegetables, meat - and often arranged for them to sleep nights on the restaurant tables, enabling them to escape bedbugs and rats. One night during his trucking year in China, at a rest stop, having eaten a chocolate bar before going to sleep, he was awakened by a rat on his face nibbling at traces of chocolate by his mouth!

Albert had initially committed to remain with the IRC one year; but in the spring of 1942 when trucking up along the Outer Mongolian Border, he developed severe diarrheal illness - probably amebic dysentery - with severe bowel peristalsis and cramping until he managed to find some Emetine which when injected brought the illness somewhat under control. Albert lost so much weight and strength that in May he decided to leave China and convalesce in India. During his year with the IRC, Albert was not paid a salary but an allowance of $1250 per month in Chinese National Currency. Albert estimates that during 1941-42 he led trucking convoys over roughly 5000 miles of difficult roads in Central and Northern China, and he became familiar with much of that region.

Late in May, accompanied by his Russian friend Mr Sadyantz, Albert flew from Kunming to Calcutta, where he stayed two weeks and had a suit made. He then traveled by rail to Bombay, where he visited bookstores and investigated for the IRC the feasibility of moving goods by road from Bombay to Kabul and on through Kashgar to Chengtu. Finally he flew to Delhi, India, and checked-in at the Cecil Hotel in Old Delhi, where he recuperated during several months -- engaging in a vigorous body-building regimen of daily swimming and biking. He had sufficient travelers checks remaining from the balance of his earnings as a seaman that he lived fairly comfortably at the Cecil. Meanwhile, he became sufficiently acquainted with others that he was offered employment with Time Magazine as a regional researcher and writer. But Bud Briggs told him a job offering greater mobility awaited him at United Press.

In November 1942 Albert gained employment as a War Correspondent for the United Press in the China-Burma-India Theater. He was hired by president Joe Alex Morris in Delhi, with a beginning salary of $85 per week, plus expenses; immediately assigned to cover Indian politics.

An effective writer even during high school, Albert in India honed his writing skills by reading widely and cutting out articles he thought particularly well written, analyzing them and typing them out on a portable Hermes typewriter he purchased. Soon, he was a hard-working U.P. war correspondent writing several articles of 600 to 1200 words weekly that were cabled to UP/NY (collect) after passage by the regional US Military Censor. In January 1943, Albert received accreditation as a U.S. war correspondent, eligible for free travel on any U.S. military conveyance in the CBI Theater.

In India, most of Albert's work was in Delhi, where he covered important Indian meetings and personalities. Government control in India during WWII was shared by the British and Indians. The British maintained influence and authority by assignment of able British colonial officers to work with each princely Indian state. Albert recalls the Chamber of Princes gathering in Delhi during the early months of 1942 *as the most*

UNITED PRESS WAR CORRESPONDENT IN CHINA-BURMA-INDIA

colorful gathering he has ever seen. Questing for news, he occasionally visited officials in the Red Fort, government center for the British Raj.

That winter, during a long conference of the Muslim League in Delhi, Albert became well-acquainted with Mohammed Ali Jinnah, wealthy lawyer and foremost Muslim political leader. When breakfasting with Ali Jinnah in his home on three occasions, an older sister was always present exercising strong influence over him and key Muslim statements on political issues.

Sir Stafford Cripps came to India that winter, seeking to persuade Indian Independence leaders not to oppose and harass the British war effort against the Japanese, perhaps assuring them that Britain would grant India freedom *after* the war.

During some months Albert reported on the build-up of US and British military forces in India needed for an attack on Japanese forces in Burma, he visited the growing number of US supported air and other military installations, especially in the Ramgarh region of Assam. During 1942, as the Japanese armies surged forward in Asia, U.S. Lieutenant General Joseph Stilwell had brought retreating remnants of the 22nd and 38th Divisions from Burma via Imphal to Ramgarh, India.

Whenever in Calcutta, Albert stayed at the Great Eastern Hotel. In February 1943 an amusing incident occurred when the first beer shipment from the U.S. for CBI military forces arrived at Calcutta for trans-shipment to Comilla (now in Bangladesh). The pilot picking up the beer devised a bomb bay floor with 2 by 4 planks in a B25. Loaded with a ton or more of beer, he flew the plane to Comilla at high altitude (20,000+ ft) to chill the beer. Approaching Comilla airport and buzzing the headquarters to announce his arrival with eagerly awaited beer he dived from some height and pulled-up sharply, causing the beer load to break the 2 x 4 scaffold and the bomb bay door and pitching the entire load of beer in a great pile near its intended destination – with many of the cans broached and fizzing. Thereupon impatiently thirsty troops dove into the beer pile snatching and drinking from broken and whole beer cans in a wild orgy of beer drinking, delivered by a very chagrined pilot.

In the spring of 1943, Albert became well-acquainted with General Lewis Pick, recent builder of the great Garrison Dam on the Missouri River in Dakota. He was appointed by President Roosevelt to command the building of the Ledo Road from Assam into Burma and China. Entering North Burma by RAF at Putad, on one occasion, Albert rode an elephant for about 80 miles on the way to Myikyina.

Albert's first bombing run was on a U.S. Air Force B25 plane in March 1943, flying from Comilla to bomb railway bridges in Burma. That spring he flew on a half dozen bombing runs -- mainly on B25s.

Reminiscing about close encounters with disaster as a war correspondent during World War II, Albert remembers most vividly the morning of May 20, 1943, at Panagarh, India, when he boarded a B24 of the 492nd Bomber Squadron, U.S. Army Air Force, loaded with four tons of bombs, to accompany them on a bombing run to Burma. Standing behind the pilot as they barreled down the runway, he shared the crews' sudden desperate

UNITED PRESS WAR CORRESPONDENT IN CHINA-BURMA-INDIA

horror when just as the plane was nearing flying speed, the flight engineer precipitously retracted the nose landing gear and the plane lurched disastrously downward. In a moment believed his last, Albert thought of family and urgent tasks undone. Though the plane left the runway, slewed to the right, and became substantially twisted and otherwise damaged, the bombs did not explode and the entire crew survived with only minor injuries.

In 2003 I entered "A.V. Ravenholt" on the Internet and unexpectedly found a repository for all USAAF and USAF Aircraft Accident Reports, 1918-1955, at "Accident Reports", 1322 West Main St, Millville, New Jersey 08332. From there I obtained the following concise report (with pictures) of the crash of the AAF B24 at Panagarh, India, on 20 May 1943, on which A.V. Ravenholt, war correspondent, was a passenger:

"The subject airplane started a normal take-off. Just as flying speed was being attained and with most of the weight off the gear, the engineer placed the landing gear handle in the "Retract" position without the command of the pilot. The gear functioned in the normal manner with all wheels becoming unlocked but with the nose wheel retracting first. A bump in the runway at this point caused the nose to start down and with no support from the nose wheel it went past the point that insures a positive angle of attack from the wings. This condition forced the nose still farther down out of control. Placing the gear handle in the "down" position held the main gear practically
fully extended, but still unlocked, when the ship was ground-looped to the right, centrifugal force held the left gear extended but caused the right gear to fold out-board". Albert and the entire crew shook awhile and then rejoiced over their narrow escape from eternity. Fortunately, his family at home knew nothing of the accident until much later.

The Sevareid Plane Crash Story

In the summer of 1943, not having heard from Albert during two years, his family and friends were delighted to learn of his existence and whereabouts when his U.P report on the Eric Sevareid plane crash in Burma was widely published in the United States.

It happened thus: Albert was at the U.S. Army Air Force Base in Assam, India, when famed CBS radio commentator Eric Sevareid and a C47 planeload of VIPs on a flight 'over the Hump' from Assam to Kunming, China, crashed. Sevareid and all occupants of the plane except the co-pilot managed to parachute safely into the Burmese jungle. Soon, Albert received a telegram from United Press/New York requesting he cooperate fully with Sevareid in getting out the story of his crash experience.

Learning that a USAAF lieutenant friend in the Air Warning Battalion would be proceeding to the crash site, Albert also learned that he would be carrying a walkie-talkie -- by means of which he could communicate from the jungle to the nearest hill-top air warning post. From there, the story was relayed to Albert in Assam, about 60 miles distant. During two subsequent nights Sevareid with the help of the AF lieutenant talked the story into the walkie-talkie and the transmission was relayed by the nearby hilltop air warning crew to Albert in Assam, who wrote-up the story and sent it to the U.S. Military Censor in Delhi, who passed it on to United Press in New York.

Meanwhile, because it was against regulations for the communications system of the AF Warning System to be used for unofficial messages, Albert mobilized protective action. Knowing that air transport planes were flying over and dropping items to the crash survivors, he arranged for a hot dinner to be prepared in Calcutta, flown by an air transport plane to Assam where Albert got aboard, and proceeded to fly over the Sevareid party walking through the jungle. The dinners were dropped to the Sevareid party while communicating by walkie-talkie. The air crews, were happy to participate in these flights, hoping to get their names mentioned in resultant articles.

Meanwhile, Sinclair McKelway, Public Information Officer for the Air Transport Command, organized a party of correspondents to go meet the Sevareid party. The ATC party, including Albert, flew from Assam to Jorhat Air Base, then started walking through the jungle toward Sevareid. They carried carbines, food for several days, and bedding. Early-on, Albert, having no need to hurry, lagged behind until a Naga Mail Runner came up whom Albert quickly employed to carry half his pack load. Moving rapidly onward, they soon passed the main party, resting beside the trail, and hurried on to the top of a seven thousand foot mountain where they met the Sevareid party. Sending back some Indian bearers to help the ATC party arrive atop the mountain that evening, Ravenholt and Sevareid agreed not to tell the rest of the party that they had already written and sent-out the crash story. The several parties slept on the mountain that night, then walked back to Jorhat, and flew to Assam. There the other correspondents filed their stories with the Assam censor who held the stories up and they were never published. Ten days later the correspondents (including Albert) all flew to Calcutta, where they learned that Albert's Sevareid crash story had been widely published in the United States three weeks earlier -- much to their chagrin and exasperation.

Great Bengal Famine of 1943

Having developed malaria in the summer of 1943, Albert checked into the Great Eastern Hotel in Calcutta and ordered his stored trunk sent to his room. After lunch, walking the streets, he was dismayed to see hundreds of corpses lining the streets. Inquiring the cause and learning that an extensive famine was afflicting adjacent areas of Eastern and Central Bengal, he traveled to the main famine areas and researched and wrote of the causes. Perhaps, we now know, the basic cause may have been an oscillation of the "El Nino" current, because famine was then also occurring in China and Viet Nam. But in Bengal the vicissitudes of crop-reduction weather were compounded by corruption and the speculative purchase and hoarding of grains by officials and others – plus transportation failures. To prevent use by the Japanese invaders, the British had destroyed many of the boats ordinarily used for hauling rice; and both the British and Japanese had commandeered rice stocks. Albert estimated 5 million starvation deaths in Bengal that year, plus 4 million in China and 3 million in Vietnam.

In October 1943, the Japanese invaded the Arakan Peninsula along the Bay of Bengal. During this time, Albert spent a month with the British forces

UNITED PRESS WAR CORRESPONDENT IN CHINA-BURMA-INDIA

at Chittigong, Imphal and Cox's Bazaar. He recalls that when riding a train that left there with British-led Indian troops, he observed the British commander take off his helmut and fill it with water from his canteen, while instructing Albert in essentials of foot care. Subsequently Albert obtained and used sandals woven by Chinese from parachute cords. Wearing these sandals, he waded through rivers and suffered little foot discomfort. Fortunately, he never encountered cobras in Burma.

With Chinese troops of General Joseph Stilwell's Command in Burma.

In India, Stilwell's particular project in 1943 was the build-up and training of a Chinese combat force – the X Force – at Ramgarh, India, with remnant troops of the 22nd and 38th Divisions (9,000) who retreated with him from Burma via Imphal to Ramgarh, India in 1942. Having during 1943 persuaded Generalisimo Chiang Kai-shek to support movement of 45,000 Chinese troops by air over the Hump for training at Ramgarh and eventual use along the North India-North Burma border, Stilwell was impatient to use those troops against the Japanese. During 1943, however, Chiang stalled all Stilwell's proposed initiatives for offensive action with the Chinese troops against the Japanese in Burma. But, finally, on December 18, 1943, after meeting President Roosevelt at Cairo, Generalisimo Chiang Kai-shek gave Stilwell full control over the two trained Chinese Divisions at Ramgarh. These divisions were commanded by two able Chinese generals: the 22nd Division commanded by General Liao Yao-Shang, and the 38th Division commanded by General Sun Li-Jen, graduate of Virginia Military Institute. In Central India, another Chinese division was finishing training. All three divisions totaled 50,000 men. Opposing them in Burma was a comparable number of Japanese troops, dug-in deep.

Leaving Ledo, Assam, in February 1943, attached to the 112th Regiment of the 38th Division, Albert accompanied the movement of the Chinese troops into Burma, along with Frank Martin, Associated Press, and Vic Jurgens of "March of Time" (who had been at Hankow with the Japanese in 1938 when their fliers were beaten by Russian fliers). Walking from Ledo to Tai Gap, they crossed the Pangsaw Pass (5000 feet), and sometimes rode on weapons carriers hauling supplies for Ledo Road construction. When the troops neared Shinbwiyan they encountered a very large python, about 18 feet long and a half-foot thick, which the Chinese soldiers promptly killed, cooked and ate. Albert ate some and says "it tasted like chicken." At Shinbwiyan the Chinese troops had their first fire fight with Japanese troops.

Also near Shinbwiyan, Albert recalls an incident involving lemons: Encountering lemon trees, Albert tied his shirt at the waist and filled his shirt with lemons before returning to camp, where the men slept in hammocks suspended above a split bamboo platform. Somehow in the dark night his lemons got loose on the bamboo platform, startling one of the party into thinking them hand grenades and sounding an alarm causing great commotion. Facilitated by his knowledge of the Chinese language, Albert got along well with the Chinese troops (see photo from the Salween campaign). His relationship was strengthened by his repeatedly obtaining dynamite from road construction officials (who would not give it to the Chinese) and using this to obtain fish for the soldiers from the Hukawng River. At a number of pools, Albert created an explosive parcel by tying

UNITED PRESS WAR CORRESPONDENT IN CHINA-BURMA-INDIA

a hand grenade to sticks of dynamite, attaching a long vine so it could be suddenly pulled down to lower the explosive parcel into the water in time that the explosion occurred under water, killing or stunning the fish. The river water flowed on over a shallow reach and a dozen troops stationed there were able to grab the incapacitated fish and toss them ashore (30 to 40 good sized fish per explosion). The fish not immediately eaten were filleted and sun-dried so that they could be kept for a week or two until eaten.

As the Chinese X-Force proceeded into Burma, General Joseph Stilwell lived with the army part of the time. Albert and Frank Martin, AP Correspondent, usually slept in the same basha (constructed of bamboo and coconut fronds) with Stilwell. Later, Albert learned that Martin had arranged with an Army censor in India to hold-up each of Albert's dispatches to United Press/New York for a week before sending them on - in retaliation for Albert having scooped him on the Sevareid story the previous year. In addition to his two Chinese divisions, Stilwell had Merrill's Marauders and other U.S. army units in close association with his Chinese troops.

Albert recalls several incidents that occurred while with General Stilwell. One evening as he and an A.P. correspondent and General Stilwell were about to hike 9 miles along an indistinct trail to join the 38th Division, the Chinese Commander said he had best give them an escort because there had been a Japanese ambush along that trail the previous day. But Stilwell refused the offer of help and started walking ahead on a dim trail through bamboo forests, with Albert and the A.P. man following. As it was rapidly growing dark, Stilwell repeatedly got off the trail. Each time Albert helped him find it, and Stilwell finally exclaimed in exasperation: "If you can see so goddamn well, Albert, you take the point!"

Another time, when Stilwell decided they would spend some time with the 22nd Division, wearing no insignia of rank they went to a landing where a black regiment was loading cargo on boats for transport on the Chinwin River. As the boat loaded-up, they asked to ride along and climbed aboard. Stilwell sat in the middle of the boat, legs crossed, smoking with a long cigarette holder. As the black American serviceman started the Johnson outboard motor and pushed off, he looked thoughtfully at Stilwell and said, "It sho must be a baad waa, when they sen an ol man like you to fight it!" To which Stilwell made no reply. They went on and spent a day with 22nd Division troops, who had recently caught and slaughtered a Japanese battalion.

In April 1944, after several months with the Chinese armies in Burma, Albert was invited to lunch by General Sun-Li-Gen, Commanding General of the 38th Division and friend of Albert, who asked for a frank appraisal of the performance of the Division in the field. After a moment's reflection Albert said, "If the officers were as eager to fight as the enlisted men, you would have a good army." During much of 1944, while stationed mainly with the U.S. 14th Air Force at Kunming, China, General Claire Chenault commanding, Albert flew as a war correspondent on a B25 Flight. Returning to Guilin air base after Dark from a US air base in East Central China the pilot Lost his way, until Albert helped him gain directional guidance

UNITED PRESS WAR CORRESPONDENT IN CHINA-BURMA-INDIA

by following the railway engine returning to Guilin. Another close call for the correspondents occurred when American-trained Chinese bomber crews under the command of Captain Winston Churchill arrived at the U.S Air Base in Central-East China preparatory to bombing Japanese shipping on the Yangtze River. Albert had thought to accompany that bombing mission, until he discussed the proposed venture with Captain Churchill who strongly recommended he not do so because he thought the group insufficiently well trained.

Harold   Analee Albert Clyde   Gen. Claire   Teddy
Issacs   Jacoby R.   Farnsworth Glen Chenault White
Newsweek Time   U.P.   A.P.   CoS Com.Gen. T&L

Albert then warned his friend Clyde Farnsworth, AP Correspondent, against going on that mission -- which was fortunate because the plane they had planned to accompany was shot down by the Japanese at the Yangtze River.

While with the 14th Air Force in 1944, Albert was asked by Chenault's staff for help in establishing a Vietnamese rescue system by which means the 14th Air Force might better recover U.S. air crews shot down during air battles with the Japanese over Indo China. Having become well-acquainted with Ho Chi Minh in Kunming between fact-gathering trips, Albert recommended him as an honest man able to direct such a mission. He took the Air Force officer and Charles Fenn (then with OSS) to meet Ho Chi Minh, a multilingual cosmopolitan, who had spent years working in London, Paris, and New York. The 14th AF then began supplying Ho Chi Minh with communications equipment, arms and money. An unforeseen by-product of that action was that when the war ended, Ho Chi Minh was in a very advantageous position for establishing his political faction in Vietnam.

A key experience that bolstered Albert's repugnance for Communist doctrine, was an in-depth encounter he had with a very intelligent American Jewish doctor in 1944. A Captain in the 14th Air Force, he had created a free medical clinic in Yenan, at which he treated the Chinese with the understanding that each patient would teach him a new Chinese word. He was also a member of Stilwell's Dixie Mission to the Communist government in Yenan that was then gathering intelligence preparatory to planned U.S. attacks upon Japan. Albert and the Captain met at Chungking airport and had lengthy discussions there, then flew together in a DC 3 to Kunming. During seven hours together the Captain told Albert many details learned from his patients about Mao's re-education of the Chinese cadres, allowing no questioning of his statements.

In the early spring of 1944, Albert and Brooks Atkinson, drama critic for the New York Times, drove from Kunming west on the Burma Road to Paoshan, headquarters of the Chinese Y Force under the Command of Chinese General Way Li Hwang and American General "Pinky" Dorn (who had been at the Peking Chinese Language School with General Stilwell in the 1920s). An offensive campaign was planned by the Y Force against the Japanese army of 3600 troops holding a heavily fortified position on Sung Shan Mountain; that blocked the Burma Road and prevented the U.S. from shipping adequate supplies into China. This Japanese position was their

UNITED PRESS WAR CORRESPONDENT IN CHINA-BURMA-INDIA

foremost advance into West China in 1942. If the Allies succeeded in removing the Japanese forces at this key juncture, U.S traffic could readily move from India on the Ledo (Stilwell) Road to Lashio and on the Burma Road to Kunming and elsewhere in China.

Albert with Chinese troops on Salween River

The terrain along the Salween River was difficult. The nearby gorge was more than a mile deep with a two-hump mountain rising on the western side of the river. Quite rapidly the Chinese forces captured the southern hump, and the U.S. flew in a company of anti-aircraft gunners, sent to hold the southern hump of Sung Shan Mountain and prevent the Japanese from air-dropping to their troops on the northern peak which the Japanese had heavily fortified. The Burma Road switch-backed up the northern mountain, then wound around the northern flank, and continued westward towards Lashio. The introduction of the American anti-aircraft gunners at Sung Shan Mountain was the first instance of U.S. ground troops fighting in China in WWII. Albert wanted to get their story and walked a circuitous route of 35 km up the southern mountain. He did key interviews, stayed a night with the gunners, and the next morning set off on a more direct route straight down toward the base on the Salween. Having gone about one-fourth of the distance, he was startled by the familiar whine of a .25 caliber Japanese sniper's bullet closely missing him. Immediately he dove down the slope, rolled, and leaped out of range. Fortunately not hit, he got back to the suspension bridge of cobbled eight inch width planks suspended 150 feet above the river - and got safely across and back to base.

During the succeeding 90 days, the Chinese troops first attempted frontal assaults on the deeply entrenched Japanese near the top of the northern peak and suffered 7,000 casualties. They then began trenching methodically up the mountainside and at a chosen altitude began tunneling under the main Japanese position. Meanwhile a U.S. explosives expert brought 7200 Kilograms of extra powerful explosives, flown over the Hump, placed strategically under the Japanese position and set to go off at 9AM the following day. In expectation of seeing the explosion, Albert and Harold Issacs, Newsweek correspondent, positioned themselves advantageously by a telescope on an eminence on the east side of the Salween River. At 9:15 AM a tremendous explosion blew off the top of the mountain creating a large crater that was soon occupied by a considerable number of Japanese troops. But the Chinese and American armies demolished them from long range by means of 155 mm howitzer artillery shells. Of the initial Japanese force of 3600 men on Sung Shan Mountain, 10 escaped and 9 were taken prisoner.

This proved to be the climactic battle of the Salween Campaign. During some subsequent days Albert interviewed surviving combatants, including (with the help of interpreters) 14 Korean comfort women. These 14 Korean women, plus 10 who had not survived, had been recruited in Korea by the Japanese with promises of work in textile factories in Japan. But instead of transporting them to Japan the ship took them to Rangoon, Burma, whence they were taken to the Sung Shan installation and forced to sexually service endless numbers of Japanese troops, and do the laundry of the officers. Albert described the women as severely abused and bewildered. Because of suppressive pressures from General Dorn, the story of the Korean comfort women was not then published.

In early November 1944, Albert traveled to Delhi, India, where he moved into "Wengers Flats" with other correspondents including his good friend Til Durdin, NY Times correspondent, and his wife Peggy, who had just done an article on arranged marriages in India for NY Times Magazine. When they met, Peggy said, "Al you ought to get married." To which Albert replied, "There's no one for me to marry." And Peggy said, "There's this woman Marjorie Severyns at OSS who is giving a party soon." Peggy then called Marjorie and said she was bringing Albert. In early December, Albert went to Marjorie's party along with 35 others and had a pleasant, ordinary cocktail party evening.

But some time later, the Maharajah of Patialla, India's top cricket player, invited a number of correspondents to his principality in the Punjab for a long weekend. He sent his magnificent private railway car to Delhi for them; and Albert with Til and Peggy Durdin, Marjorie Severyns, and five others enjoyed traveling to Padialla in rare style. At Padialla they were met by a fleet of Rolls Royces that took them to a palatial guest house. When Albert awoke the next morning, a Sikh bearer stood by his bed extending to Albert a tray with bottles of scotch, bourbon and ice. Albert queried him, "Is this what you serve for chathausery?" (a small tea in bed). The Sikh replied, "I am sorry, sahib, but we thought it is what all Americans want." To which Albert answered, "No thanks." Then shaved and went to breakfast.

The day was occupied by participation in a celebration of the opening of a large "tank" [reservoir] in Padialla. In the evening the Maharajah gave a major banquet, replete with a 16 piece Viennese orchestra and delightful dancing. During those 3 or 4 days at Padialla, Albert became additionally acquainted with Marjorie.

While at Padialla he learned of two maharajahs of neighboring princely states, who on a number of occasions played chess on a tennis-court size "board" with each chess piece represented by a young woman in a distinctively colored sari: pawn, rook, knight, bishop, queen, king. Whichever Maharajah player won a piece got to keep the woman!

After returning to Delhi in the Maharajah's train car, Albert resumed reporting on events in India and Burma. In January he left on a trip with General Frank Merrill, commandant of "Merrill's Marauders. They flew from Delhi in a C47 at about 12,000 ft eastward along the majestic snow covered Himalayas until mid-afternoon, then on to the vicinity of Myitkyina near the Japanese front. Merrill's Marauders (1300 men) were responding to a desperate military situation. Two Chinese divisions had recently mistakenly fought each other, and in the resulting melee the Japanese troops had again entered Myitkyina. Desperately seeking to stem the Japanese advance, General Boatner went to the area hospital and ordered every American soldier patient able to stand and carry a gun out to face the Japanese. For this action, he was reduced in rank to Colonel (but in the Korean War he was again a General).

In late January, Albert was at the Seagrave Hospital in Bhamo. Leaving there in a jeep with other correspondents including Teddy White and Til Durdin, a race developed with several jeeps carrying Generals and other U.S. army officers to see who could reach Lashio and the Burma Road first. The correspondents won and celebrated with a drinking bout. Continuing on the Burma Road toward Kunming, they found and enjoyed hot sulfur baths used by Japanese officers a few days earlier and again engaged in a drinking bout.

In February the headquarters of the OSS (Office of Strategic Services) - also known as the "Oh-So-Social Club" - moved from Delhi to Kunming, and Albert and Marjorie became additionally acquainted. In late February, Albert proceeded to Sian where the U.S. Air Force was building a large air base. During construction they exhumed many ancient terra cotta figures which local entrepreneurs were selling for 25 cents each. Albert bought enough to fill a box several feet in length, which he carried along back to Kunming and left with Marjorie Severyns. She gave several choice pieces to Larry Sichman, curator for a museum in Kansas City, then shipped the balance via APO, intended for Seattle. But the Japanese attacked the ship in the Indian Ocean and sank it, and the Sian terra cotta figurines were never seen again.

Also at Sian, Albert interviewed a Japanese-trained Chinese kamakazi flyer who had somehow gotten away from the Japanese and managed to walk over a mountainous region in Shansi Province until he encountered Nationalist Chinese guerrillas east of the Yellow River. The Nationalists brought him to Sian. Interviewing him intensively during two nights, Albert gained sufficient knowledge of Japanese kamakazi training and operations that he wrote a long article (5 feet of manuscript) reporting this horrendous new Japanese menace. He also learned that the Japanese kamakazi flyers had been attacking U.S. naval vessels aggressively during three months and sinking many warships; but U.S. censors had until then succeeded in preventing any publication of these kamakazi attacks. Returning to Kunming, Albert took his report to Colonel Jesse Williams, A2 (intelligence) officer for the 14th Air Force and laid the report on his desk. Williams read it and said "Albert Ravenholt! I know what you are doing! But I have no orders to stop you." Whereupon he stamped it "Approved by Censor" and Albert cabled it to UP/NY. When published it made headlines throughout the nation and the world - as the Sevareid story had done in 1942 - creating a sensation.

In late March 1945, from a secret U.S. air base in Yunan Province, Albert went on a first flight of U.S. bombers to the Philippines (along with Clyde Farnsworth of the AP, and Lowell Thomas). Approaching Manila they saw blackened and smoking devastation at Corregidor and in much of Manila. By then, U.S. troops had advanced into Manila from the north as far south as Pasig River. During several weeks Albert observed and reported on U.S. troop actions in the Philippines. He also visited the site of the University of the Philippines and saw a presentation of Oscar Hammerstein's "Oklahoma" by the original NYC cast. Next he visited Baguio, where all had been leveled but one church. In Manila he met his good friend Vic Jurgens (March of Time), and helped found the Manila Overseas Press Club.

In May 1945, in Chungking, Albert was invited to lunch with Ambassador Patrick Hurley who kept Albert and another correspondent drinking until luncheon was served at 3PM. Seated at Hurley's right, Albert was startled when Ambassador Hurley said, "Albert, wouldn't it be wonderful if I could get the Nobel Peace Prize for settling the Chinese Civil War?" A sequel to Hurley's preoccupation

UNITED PRESS BUREAU CHIEF FOR CHINA

with striving to win a Nobel Peace Prize occurred in October of that year when Albert was again in Chungking lunching with him and heard the Ambassador speak bitterly of "the scoundrels in the State Department who prevented my getting the Nobel." Hurley subsequently retaliated against those he thought had constrained his Nobel candidacy, by providing names of alleged State Department Communists to Senator Joseph McCarthy's Un-American Activities Committee.

Returning to Kunming, Albert handled many press urgencies. Asked where he was when he learned of the death of President Roosevelt, Albert replied that he had just picked up Marjorie and was driving her to the OSS office in Kunming when they became aware of Chinese coolies wearing black arm bands shouting, "Losefoo ta tsilla!" - Roosevelt is dead! The Chinese, long believing they would gain their freedom when Roosevelt and the United States beat the Japanese, deeply mourned his passing. Albert then proceeded to Chungking and was named United Press Bureau Chief for China, succeeding Walter Rundle. He became immediately busy reporting on Nationalist vs Communist factional struggles for territory and power.

When Albert was Bureau Chief for the United Press for China, he occasionally met Madame Chiang Kai Shek; and he participated in five press conferences organized by the Chinese Ministry of Information. But Albert never had a private session with her as he did with Mao Tse Tung, and Albert was aware that she did not like him - perhaps because she knew he enjoyed a close relationship with General Stillwell, whom they had made persona non grata and expelled from China when he asserted a different view of the Chinese situation than they were touting.

Albert first met Chou-En-Lai at a press conference in Chungking in February 1944, and became cordially acquainted. Cho-En-Lai was then the official Communist Government Representative dealing with the Nationalist Government Representatives in the Chinese Coalition Government, and Albert was a war correspondent for the United Press. After Albert became the United Press Bureau Chief for China in April 1945, they met repeatedly - sharing dinners four or five times at simple Chinese restaurants in Chungking. Ordinarily they conversed in English, and from Chou Albert got a considerable history of actions by the Communists and the Nationalists against the Japanese. Chou was married to a very intelligent woman, educated in China, who sometimes was with them at these dinners but did not eat with them.

Albert closed the United Press office in Chungking in October 1945 and soon opened a United Press Bureau in Hong Kong. Meanwhile Walter Rundle, Vice President of the UP, opened a United Press Bureau in Shanghai after he went home to the U.S. Rundle returned to China in January 1946 when Albert married Marjorie Severyns in Shanghai.

Albert again saw Chou when General George Marshall arrived in China in December 1945 to negotiate an end to the Chinese Civil War. The Chinese Communists made it a condition for entering negotiations that the Chinese Communist General who commanded the new 4th Route Army be present at the negotiations. But while en route from Chungking to Yenan the Chinese General's plane (a U.S. Army Air Corps C47) was "blown-up."

UNITED PRESS BUREAU CHIEF FOR CHINA

In February 1946 when Albert met Chou-En-Lai in Nanking – the last time they met -- Chou said Americans never would have blown up their own plane. Later General Tai Li, Chief of the Nationalist Secret Service (probably responsible for the destruction of the Communist General's plane), was himself blown-up on a plane traveling from Nanking to Shanghai.

Albert remembers Chou-En-Lai as soft spoken, very quick, intellectually astute, delightful conversationalist -- an altogether likeable man with a strong sense of humor. Many years later, in 1985, Albert again met Mrs Chou-En-Lai when he was one of seven WWII War Correspondents from the United States invited to China as guests of the PRC government. They met with Teng-xiaoping and many other officials, and Mesdames Chou-En-Lai and Liu-Hsia-Chi were their co-hosts.

In May 1945, Albert received a cable from Harrison Salisbury -- Albert's boss at United Press/New York – querying him, "Any probability that Shapiro will need maps in your bailiwick?" Because Shapiro was the U.P. correspondent in Moscow, Albert immediately understood Salisbury to be asking, "Are the Russians coming into the Japanese theatre of operations? To which he responded, "Yes, to your such and such, before my birthday. Check with Jones." The UP personnel director, Jones, would have told Salisbury that Albert's birth date was September 9th -- an accurate prognostication of the Russians entry into Manchuria.

That spring, Albert made a trip to Chengtu to see the huge B29 air base being built near there by the Army Corps of Engineers under the command of Colonel Henry Byroad (American Ambassador to the Philippines in the late 1960s). Returning to Chungking, Albert hitched a ride on the same plane with T.V. Soong (Madame Chiang Kai-shek's brother). On another trip to Sichwan Province, Albert visited the "Mass Education Movement" headed by J.Y.C. Yen, about which he wrote and published an extensive article appended hereto.

On August 14, 1945, when Japan surrendered ending World War II, Albert was in Chungking and watched the Chinese "go crazy with joy." Chinese leaders and others in Chungking organized a victory gathering on August 18th in the Legislative Yuan Hall in Chungking with tea and a buffet. All senior Chinese officials, all senior American, British, and Russian officials and military officers, plus war correspondents and others were invited. Ambassador Hurley brought Communist Chairman Mao Tse Tung from Yenan, which had become the Chinese Communist capital after the Long March. Following the victory celebration, Mao held a press conference with media representatives in Chungking with little opportunity for questions. Chinese Nationalist and Communist leaders then issued orders to their respective commands: the Communists ordering their forces north of the Yangtze River toward Manchuria and the Nationalists ordering their forces to the major Chinese cities.

Albert was then United Press Bureau Chief for China. Following the press conference, Chairman Mao's Secretary, Chao Kwan-Hua, arranged a private interview for Albert with Mao Tse Tung. Albert had earlier befriended Chao in Hong Kong, by arranging medical care for him. On this occasion Chao requested Albert that he not tell other correspondents of the private meeting with Mao, forestalling their requests for similar private interview opportunities.

A NIGHT TO REMEMBER: WITH MAO TSE TUNG

Albert's interview with Chairman Mao, in the Communist headquarters building in Chungking, with Chao Kwan-Hua interpreting, began at 9 PM and continued until 3 AM. During that long night, tea was constantly available and they hadone meal. Mao chain-smoked almost constantly. Years later, Chao Kwan-Hua became Foreign Minister of the Peoples Republic of China.

During the interview, Albert probed Mao concerning his formative experiences. Born and raised in Hunan province in a middle class home (which Albert visited), Mao left home because of some troubles with his father, a landlord. Mao was mainly educated at Pei-Ta, the Peking National University. The Chancellor in 1919 to 1945 was Dr Changmonlin, with whom Albert became good friends in Kunming in 1944-45.

Mao came to Peking National University already a Communist. The head of the University library, a Marxist leader of left wing factions, hired Mao to work in the library. After his studies at PNU, Mao returned to Hunan province, his home, and worked as a teacher in a coal mining community where he became involved with organizing the peasants.

Albert said the main thing he learned from Mao that night was an improved understanding of his personality, which Albert found to be mainly limited to what he was doing. They spent some time discussing the Tai-ping Rebellion, which had swept rapidly through China until put down by foreign troops (British). Mao was not a sophisticated Marxist but rather saw himself much like the Buddhist monk who became a bandit chief and overthrew the Ming Dynasty in 1644. The Chinese Communist Party was formed during the 1920s. During the "Long March" Mao was elected Secretary General of the Communist Party at Tsungyi, a small city in northern Kweichou Province. Ordinarily, the Nationalists were "city-based", the Communists "rural-based".

As the antagonism increased between Chiang Kai-shek's Nationalist Government faction and Mao Tse Tung's Communist faction during 1945, Truman sent General George Marshall to Chungking in December to try to ameliorate the situation and develop an effective coalition national government. He struggled mightily with this during a year and a half, but the political factions proved immiscible. Following Marshall's time in China, John Layton Stuart became the American Ambassador to China and served until the Communist takeover in 1949.

On October 1, 1949, Chairman Mao Tse-Tung and Chou En-Lai announced formation of the new government of the Peoples Republic of China; and in December they traveled to Russia for discussions with Chairman Joseph Stalin and others. Mao came away from Moscow disgusted with Stalin and believed that he, Mao, should become the world Communist leader. Ho Chi-Minh and Mao Tse-Tung met once, before Mao became Chairman of China's Communist Party.

Mao was initially pronatalist - claiming "people are capital" - and was slow to recognize the necessity for curbing birth rates and population growth to accelerate development and alleviate poverty. Beginning with its Fourth Five Year Plan in 1970, however, China adopted the same general strategy for its family planning program that we in USAID had two years earlier published and adopted for the U.S. global population/family planning assistance program: making the most effective means of fertility control fully available throughout each country. This program was rapidly implemented with thorough efficiency and accomplished the bulk of China's "demographic transition" during the 1970s. China's very effective birth control program is now a foremost essential element in its rapid, massive economic development program.

In late August, Albert in Chungking was invited with other correspondents to the U.S. military headquarters to await a press release. When settled as an audience, a curtain was withdrawn and a very gaunt General Jonathan Wainwright was revealed, just retrieved from Japanese imprisonment in Manchuria. Albert quickly got the essential facts and exited the room. Seeing a sergeant he knew driving by in a weapons carrier he called to get aboard and had the sergeant drive him to the Press Hostel, where he quickly wrote and sent an article on General Wainwright to the UP/New York, beating the competition. In September, Albert's very good friend, Theodore White, correspondent for Time and Life magazines, told Albert that Henry Luce the publisher, was soon arriving with a man who would be doing a definitive article on China, and that this man needed an assistant knowledgeable about China to accompany him. Albert suggested Marjorie Severyns for the job. Teddy White hired her and thus she became a correspondent for Life Magazine, continuing until Albert and she returned to the United States in June 1946.

After meeting with Ambassador Hurley in Chungking in the autumn of 1945, Albert flew to Kunming where the 14th Air Force was "closing out" its properties. There he managed to obtain two transceivers for the Hong Kong office of the United Press International and took them with him to Hong Kong. They needed reconditioning, for which he obtained the help of experts on a U.S. naval vessel in the harbor who rapidly got the transceivers working well. Not able to pay them for their services, he hosted a very fine Chinese dinner at an excellent restaurant for all those who helped recondition the transceivers. In November at a restaurant in Hong Kong, Albert met Al Larsen, fellow student at Grand View College, then in the U.S. navy. In early December, Albert flew from Hong Kong to Shanghai in a U.S. Naval flying boat. While continuing to work on their respective tasks, Albert and Marjorie soon prepared for their elaborate wedding on January 28, 1946. Marjorie arranged with General Albert Wedemeyer, Far Eastern Theatre Commander, to "give the bride away." The wedding at the Anglican Cathedral was followed by a reception at the French Club – paid for by General Wedemeyer.

Marjorie & Albert-Chungking

MARRIAGE OF ALBERT RAVENHOLT AND MARJORIE SEVERYNS

Mrs Ravenholt (nee Miss Marjorie Severyns) cutting the cake at the reception in Shanghai after her marriage to Mr Albert Victor Ravenholt, of the United Press. The two Generals watching proceedings are Lt General A. C. Wedemeyer, Commanding, China Theatre, and Lt General George Stratemeyer, commanding Air Forces in the China Theatre.

The following day one of General Stratemeyer's pilots flew them to Peking, where they honeymooned in the General's apartment. In Peking, Ambassador Robertson, Minister to China, gave them a large formal dinner as did Marshall Yeh Chien-Ying, Chief of Staff of the Chinese Communist armies. Albert was one of few Americans who had ever visited his home town of Meishien. Then Marjorie returned to her work with Life Magazine in Shanghai, and Albert returned to United Press headquarters in Hong Kong.

Soon Albert went to Canton to observe and report on General George Marshall's negotiations there with Nationalist and Communist leaders – seeking but never achieving an amicable coalition government. A week later Albert traveled to Hanoi, Vietnam, where he stayed at the Metropole Hotel then proceeded to the new Vietnamese Government Center for a meeting with Ho Chi Minh, President of the Revolutionary Government of Vietnam. At a dinner given in his honor, Albert asked the guest on his right, "What are you doing?" To which the Secretary General of the Communist Party of Vietnam replied, "I am developing methods to poison 40,000 French in one night."

HOMEWARD BOUND AFTER SEVEN YEARS IN THE ORIENT

During the spring Albert and Marjorie acquired furniture in preparation for their departure from China. In Hong Kong, Albert went shopping one day with his friend Sarkisian for oriental rugs and in Peking bought a fine old Ming Dynasty rosewood dining room table and chairs that an Air Force friend hauled to Shanghai in a C46. There they were stored for a few months at Broadway Mansions until their departure. The captain of the army transport on which they were returning agreed to transport the set to San Francisco. Departing Shanghai the last week in June, they arrived in San Francisco 3 weeks later. In their war correspondent uniforms Albert and Marjorie then went to the billeting office seeking a hotel accommodation. The billeting officer said it was too bad they were not married because she just had one available room at the St Francis Hotel – no problem!

A few days later, Albert and Marjorie proceeded to Seattle and Sunnyside, Washington, to visit Marjorie's mother. There the cherry harvest was in full swing and Albert decided that some day he would grow cherries. With John Reith, insurance man in Sunnyside, Albert roamed the surrounding countryside visiting farmers known to John Reith, and saw how irrigation worked.

Then Albert and Marjorie proceeded to Wisconsin to visit Albert's family; who intensely longed to see him after his seven year absence. Continuing on to New York in July, Albert checked in with the United Press. Discovering that through the UP he had health insurance, he initiated definitive treatment of his malaria, and continued the treatment for 8 months.

In New York, Albert and Marjorie lived with Annalee Jacoby for two weeks; then proceeded to Detroit and picked up a new Buick automobile that they drove to Wisconsin and Minneapolis. After a week, Marjorie, accompanied by Halvor, drove it to Sunnyside, Washington. Meanwhile Albert returned to New York, where he attended Teddy White's wedding, and lived in the White's apartment while Teddy and bride honeymooned. Albert worked at United Press into August; then, with his long-time friend Bud Briggs, proceeded to Wisconsin and Sunnyside, Washington. They spent the winter of 1946-47 writing a play, "Press Hostel"; but their agent turned it down – saying it was not really a play! While in Sunnyside that winter, Albert became aware -- mainly from the teaching of Mr Bridgeman, a pioneer Yakima Valley wine grape planter in the 1920s -- of the wine grape growing potential of the Columbia and Yakima valleys.

In March 1947, Albert returned to New York and worked as Night Foreign Editor for the United Press for a modest salary which, with the high cost of living in Manhattan, prompted him to look for other career opportunities.

In May he went to Harvard to see about the possibility of getting a Nieman Fellowship upon his return from China a year hence. He met with Louis Lyons, head of the Nieman Fellowship Program; and also with Dick Lauderbach, good friend from Shanghai, who urged Albert to go see Walter Rogers, Director of the Institute of Current World Affairs in New York City. Hence, the next week, after working all night at the U.P., Albert shaved, had a cup of coffee, and phoned Walter Rogers – who immediately invited him to come right up to 522 5th Avenue. Albert entered Roger's

FELLOW OF THE INSTITUTE OF CURRENT WORLD AFFAIRS AT HARVARD

office, introduced himself, and awaited his questions. Rogers asked, "Have you just gone to work for the United Press? To which Albert simply answered, "No." Rogers then asked additional questions, to which Albert responded that before leaving the Orient he was Bureau Chief for the United Press in China and India, and had worked as a war correspondent for the U.P. in China-Burma-India during the war. Chatting until noon, Rogers took Albert to lunch after which they returned to his office and continued their conversation until 5 P.M. Then Albert returned to the night shift at United Press, on 42nd street, east of Broadway, with about 60 employees.

During ensuing days, Albert met repeatedly with Walter Rogers - starting about 9A.M. and meeting through the day, except for the lunch break. Meanwhile, Albert was being prepped to go back to China as Bureau Chief for the U.P. in China and Korea. But Rogers had Albert make out an application for an Institute of Current World Affairs Fellowship that would enable him to go to China for the Institute, as Doak Barnet was doing. Then Walter Rogers had Albert meet with the Institute's Trustees in New York and Chicago; after which he returned to New York, resigned his employment at the United Press and became a Fellow of the Institute of Current World Affairs, duration not specified. Thus Walter Rogers became Albert's chief benefactor.

Albert's first assigned task was to spend the summer visiting 10 universities, learning what each was doing in foreign area studies. He visited the Universities of Michigan, Wisconsin, Minnesota, British Columbia, Washington, Oregon, and Brigham Young University - and wrote a report on each university. (At that time students on the G.I. Bill got $65 per month).

Meanwhile, Rogers, by phone and letters, arranged a "Nieman Associate Fellowship" entry for Albert to Harvard that fall - the same as the Nieman Fellows, except Albert's expenses were paid by the Institute of Current World Affairs. In addition to tuition, the Institute paid Albert $500 per month. In early September, Albert and Marjorie drove east to Luck, Wisconsin and on to Cambridge. When Albert met the Dean of the Harvard Graduate School, he told him, "But I have no undergraduate degree." To which the Dean responded, "We have special arrangements for persons like you."

Albert and Marjorie found an apartment, moved in, and started going to Harvard and Radcliff, respectively. Albert's curriculum focused on Chinese language, written and spoken, Far Eastern history, Chinese history, anthropology, and economics. Marjorie commenced a PhD program in Chinese studies on "The Role of Women in Classical China," At Christmas, Albert and Marjorie traveled to Washington, DC, to visit Marjorie's Aunt Marjorie and her uncle Mr. Davis, a retired Admiral.

Early in 1948 Marjorie left Harvard to go home and help her mother cope with advancing amyotrophic lateral sclerosis, while Albert continued with his studies. During spring weekends, Albert drove about in their Buick exploring New England. Upon the completion of the academic year, he traveled to New York City and Washington, DC, to Wisconsin and to Sunnyside, Washington for the balance of the summer. His joint assignment with the Chicago Daily News was finalized with Basil Walters, Executive Editor.

In September 1948 Albert and Marjorie returned to Shanghai from the United States, and soon established their residence in Peking. But in December 1948, Chiang Kai Shek stepped down as President of China and moved to Taiwan with many of his supporters and with hundreds of millions of dollars in gold. The Vice President of China, who became President when Chiang Kai-shek moved to Taiwan, entered into protracted peace negotiations with Communist representatives in Peking without reliable progress. By April 20, 1949, the Chinese Communists massed 4 million of their soldiers on the north bank of the Yangtze and soon attacked across the river, progressively occupying Nanking, Peking, Shanghai, and Northern China; then moving south, progressively occupying all of China - as described by Albert in the articles that follow.

In 1949-50, during stressful months covering the advances of the Communist armies in China, Albert stayed just one jump ahead of them: from Peking to Nanking, to Shanghai, to Chengtu, to Canton, then to Hong Kong. Meanwhile he suffered a severe exacerbation of osteomyelitis in his right lower leg, a sequelae of his accident in Wisconsin in September 1939. Despite penicillin and other treatment his leg remained considerably swollen, necessitating use of crutches during five months. While a correspondent for the Chicago Daily News Foreign Service, Albert remained a Fellow of the Institute of Current World Affairs. He continued writing for the Chicago Daily News during 20 years.

While Albert was in Nanking in 1949, staying in Hank Lieberman's house, the British captain of HMS Consort came to tea and spoke of things "being rather dull" around there. The following day, the Chinese shot-up the HMS Consort, killing 49 of the crew before the ship got away to Shanghai. Also, the British cruiser HMS London and the destroyer HMS Amethyst were shot-up by the Communists. The Amethyst was beached on the Yangtze shore; but several months later, having made some repairs, it managed to get away to Hong Kong. The USS Hope was at Shanghai, and Albert traveled on it to Hong Kong. His right leg continued badly swollen, and he continued to need crutches during some months. Upon arrival in Hong Kong, he was treated in St Mary's hospital for a time. Where he first met Dr Han Suyin.

A little later Albert's good friends, Eric Chow and his wife organized a dinner party, including Albert and Marjorie and Ian Morrison with Dr Han Suyin. They soon became good friends. Ian Morrison, a foreign correspondent for The London Times, had just returned from covering the "Malaysian Emergency." Dr Han Suyin, an intelligent and attractive Eurasian woman, was born in Henan Province, China, in 1917, of a Chinese railway engineer father and a Belgian mother. In 1938 she married a Kuomintang army officer, P.H. Tang, who served some years as military attache with the Chinese Embassy in London, where Han Suyin received her medical training. P.H. Tang rose to the rank of General and was killed; after which Han Suyin became a practicing clinician in Hong Kong.

Albert and Ian became good friends. The night before Ian was leaving for Korea to report on the Korean War, Albert and Marjorie gave a dinner for him and Han Suyin; and as Ian was leaving he asked Albert to look after

THE LAST HALF CENTURY

Han. Ten days later in the Manila Hotel in the Philippines, Albert read that Ian along with a British and an Indian correspondent had been killed in Korea when their jeep hit a land mine near the front lines. He immediately cabled Han Suyin, offering sympathy and any needed help. Later she wrote and published the very popular novel, "A Many-Splendoured Thing". After the Korean War, she worked in a tuberculosis clinic in Malaya and married Leon Comber, British Intelligence Officer in the Malayan Service; later moving to Lausanne, Switzerland. In 1972, then directing the global population program of the U.S. Agency for International Development, I met and chatted with Han Suyin at a population/family planning conference at the Plaza Hotel in New York City, which she addressed.

In his over-lapping roles during more than three decades as Fellow of the Institute of Current World Affairs, Foreign Correspondent for the Chicago Daily News Foreign Service, and Fellow of the American Universities Field Staff, Albert (and Marjorie) maintained homes in Manila and Seattle while traveling widely in Asia and the United States. Typically during those years, he researched and wrote on issues and topics suggested by the editor of the Chicago Daily News Foreign Service, by the director of the Institute of Current World Affairs, and by the director of the American Universities Field Staff - responding to requests from the faculties of a dozen membership universities - *the University of Alabama, Brown University, California Institute of Technology, Dartmouth College, Harvard University, University of Hawaii, Indiana University, University of Kansas, Louisiana State University, Michigan State University, Tulane University, the University of Wisconsin.*

His many in-depth reports, such as those that follow this account, were published by his employers and widely distributed and read. Typically, Albert and Marjorie worked at and traveled from their base in Manila during two years then returned to their Seattle base for a year, from which Albert made rounds of the AUFS membership universities, lecturing, consulting and writing during a year. After several months of leave, they again moved abroad and repeated the cycle.

In addition to Albert's essential research and writing tasks, his life style enabled him to delve deeply into many other projects, some of a philanthropic and others of a commercial nature. He became well-acquainted with both John D. Rockefeller 3rd and Ramon Magsaysay before and during Magsaysay's presidency; and it happened that soon after Magsaysay died in a plane crash, April 1957, John D. Rockefeller 3rd phoned Albert and invited his suggestions for what memorial might best be created to honor Magsaysay's memory. He invited Albert to come to tea in his town apartment near the United Nations headquarters on his next visit to New York for in-depth discussion of same. I know this sequence of events very surely, because in April 1957 on my way to Washington, DC, from Seattle, I stopped a night with Albert at the Curtis Hotel in Minneapolis. In the morning when the phone rang, I answered it, and it was John D. Rockefeller, wishing to speak with Albert. Albert did give it careful thought, and when in New York City several weeks later at tea with Rockefeller, he suggested a Magsaysay Awards Foundation be created to annually honor Asians *"who through personal creative leadership in their communities had contributed most outstandingly to the development of one or more South East Asian nations"* - somewhat like a Nobel Prize for Asians.

THE LAST HALF CENTURY

Upon Mr Rockefeller's acceptance of the suggested plan for the Magsaysay Awards Foundation, Albert and his wife Marjorie worked with the Philippine national legislature to establish the Foundation, to ensure that the awards would be tax-free in the Philippines, and to create a Secretariat to ensure its successful operation. Each year during three decades, Albert wrote the commendations for each of the five annual recipients of the $50,000 awards. Marjorie Ravenholt worked during those years for the Rockefeller Brothers Fund to ensure that the management of the Magsaysay Foundation achieved its intended purpose. She played a role in the creation of the Rockefeller Endowment for the Awards Foundation by guiding the construction of a 14 story office building and Magsaysay Center on Rojas Blvd with Rockefeller grant money. The rents from this building have since funded the annual awards. Fortunately, during these many years the Ramon Magsaysay Awards gained considerable recognition and stature in Asia.

Beginning in 1954, Albert and John Musser (an heir to the Weyerhauser timber fortune, and director of the General Services Foundation in St Paul, Minnesota) with Frisco San Juan, Thomas Cabili and other leading Filipinos, created a Philippine American Timber Company (PATIC) "aimed at demonstrating optimal forest management for the Philippines" on a 30,000 acre logging concession they obtained on Negros Oriental Island. A reason they were able to get that timber concession was that it then had no access from the sea. This necessitated their building a 44 mile all-weather road from the sea to the concession at 2300 ft altitude; much of which had to be rebuilt after torrential rainstorms. Also, they had to buy much heavy duty construction equipment from the Caterpillar Co - caterpillars, hysters, and other logging equipment. After overcoming many start-up difficulties, PATIC operated profitably during several years - selling logs to Japan -- until Imelda and Ferdinand Marcos became jealous of their success, cancelled their lease, and barred further export. PATIC then built a sawmill and for a time employed several hundred sawmill workers. But the sawmill did not become a profitable venture, because it soon burned, ending the Philippine timber business.

With Mochtar Lubis and several other partners, Albert gained a timber concession in Sumatra, Indonesia. The logging there was largely directed by Albert's good friend Dave Brameld, who had helped with PATIC in the Philippines. Unfortunately, that enterprise never became profitable, losses rising to more than a million dollars before it was discontinued.

In 1953 Albert was the leader and main source of funding for the construction of a substantial new Ravenholt home on the farm overlooking the public golf course at Luck, Wisconsin, as pictured below, where our Mother lived and where we sibs and our families often vacationed.

Also in the 1950s, Albert began investing in Puget Sound real estate in Washington State, and in forest lands near Luck, Wisconsin. He made timely buys of lands that during subsequent years gained greatly in value. On one choice land acquisition on Bainbridge Island near Seattle, Albert invited my ownership participation. During subsequent years, on this property with several partners, we built the Quay Bainbridge Apartments - which have proved a valuable holding during many years.

THE LAST HALF CENTURY

Throughout Albert's life his agricultural, horticultural, and zoological interests have continued strong - witness the Wisconsin Farm Facts Contest while in high school and the in-depth articles on tropical agriculture that follow. Omnivorous reading of agricultural topics continues even into his eighties, with an extensive library including volumes such as the following:

A GARDENER TOUCHED WITH GENIUS: THE LIFE OF LUTHER BURBANK by Peter Dreyer; *THE GRAFTERS HANDBOOK* by R.J. Gerner; *ADVANCES IN FRUIT BREEDING* by Jules Janick and James Moore; *MANUAL OF SUBTROPICAL FRUITS* by Wilson Popenoe; *TROPICAL LEGUMES: RESOURCES FOR THE FUTURE* by Noel Vietmeyer; *PERSIMMON CULTURE IN NEW ZEALAND* by Hirotachi Kitagawa and Paul G. Glucina; *VEGEABLES IN SOUTHEAST ASIA* by G.A.C. Herklots; *TREE CROPS: A PERMANENT AGRICULTURE* by J. Russell Smith; *THE EUCALIPTS* by A.R. Penfold; *WORLD CATTLE (3 Volumes)* by John E. Rouse; *THE CIROLLO: SPANISH CATTLE IN THE AMERICAS* by John E. Rouse; etc.

With a remarkable appetite for acquiring new insights into many aspects of agriculture, horticulture and zoology, Albert belonged during some years to the "Society for the Preservation of Poultry Antiquities." During many years he maintained a large experimental farm on Negros Island, experimenting with diverse crops. Somewhere along the way he began collecting nuts from a prolific, short coconut tree; leased from the owner to obtain the annual yield of nuts for experimental plantings. This went well for a number of years until one brother became so incensed with another brother for taking a substantial portion of the yield of nuts for his own purposes, that finally their father became so aggravated with their squabbling that he chopped the coconut tree down - thus settling their argument and ending Albert's supply. In building his experimental farm, he got involved in building a large water system to provide potable water for a growing village. Asian agricultural colleagues sometimes speak of Albert as the "Toynbee of Asian Agriculture."

Born of deep interest in soil improvements, Albert Ravenholt, John Musser, President of the General Services Foundation in St Paul, MN, and James Brewbaker, Professor of Genetics, College of Agriculture, University of Hawaii, in 1980, started the Nitrogen Fixing Tree Association, headquartered on Oahu. Eventually this organization had members in 112 countries, doing plant explorations and demonstration projects, reported in the article "FAITH GARDENING AND SALT FARMING, Universities Field Staff International 1985.

Marjorie Severyns had grown up in Sunnyside, Washington, and when Albert first visited there upon returning from Asia in 1946 he became fascinated with the prospect of developing an orchard for raising cherries. He also became interested in the production of wine grapes, and learned much from Mr Bridgeman. Who, in earlier years could not develop a profitable wine grape growing enterprise because of then little interest in U.S. wines. Hence he shifted his farm to raising juice grapes (Concord) for the Jewish fortified wine market in California.

In 1966, when living in Sunnyside some months because of Marjorie's surgically-treated illness, Albert went to see three wine grape plantings by Bridgeman, then discussed the idea of a wine grape growing enterprise with his business partner, Alec Bayless; eventuating in their purchase of

THE LAST HALF CENTURY

initial acreage of what became Sagemoor Orchards north of Pasco along the Columbia River. Their initial plantings of wine grapes in 1972 constituted the first such grape growing in the State of Washington since WWII. When these plantings yielded large crops of wine grapes a few years later, Albert and partners suddenly became heavily involved with the marketing of the grapes: at one time selling and trucking grapes all the way to Montreal. Following the fortunate sale of some Bainbridge real estate holdings in 1974, Albert and Alec Bayless and several others substantially expanded Sagemoor Orchards and now grow cherries on approximately 200 acres, wine grapes on another 200 acres, and apples on 200+ additional acres. After large investments and much care during many years, these orchards have become substantially profitable enterprises: in 2003 they yielded 800 tons of cherries, 2200 tons of wine grapes, and 2400 tons of apples. Albert provides continuous horticultural expertise for these ventures and greatly savors being present each year at harvest time. In 2003 they sold grapes to 46 wineries; and some of their best customers now contract for grapes grown on designated sections of Sagemoor Vineyards, pruned to their specifications. Altogether, wine grape raising has flourished in Washington State during the last 40 years, and there are now more than 300 wineries in the State.

Likewise, the Sagemoor cherry orchards have flourished - supplying burgeoning markets in Taiwan, Japan, Hong Kong, Singapore and Bangkok, in addition to extensive sales to East Coast and Midwestern markets. Washington State is the foremost producer of highest quality cherries – Bings and Rainiers -- in the United States and in the world. My wife Betty and I, and other family members, have particularly enjoyed going to Sagemoor Orchards each year just after completion of the commercial harvest of cherries, to glean hundreds of pounds of huge, black, sweet, and very tasty Bing cherries for eating and canning. Albert also maintains a keen technical interest in apple growing, keeping pace with trends away from Red Delicious to Granny Smith, to Fugi, and now to Minnesota Honey Crisp varieties. Annual crops, maintained and marketed by cooperative packing houses, have yeilded thousands of tons of choice fruits for shipments by trainloads across the continent.

Albert's interest in local, state, national, and world political affairs continue strong, though he has never run for public office. Until recently he continued authoring important articles on Asian agriculture and related developments for the Encyclopedia Britannica, Foreign Affairs, and the Institute for Current World Affairs. As "leader of the Ravenholt clan" he has taken a very active interest in the affairs of his sibs and their families and has helped many sibs, nieces and nephews in timely fashion. In 1998, Grandview College gave him an Honorary Doctorate recognizing his distinguished career as writer, correspondent and agriculturist.

During recent years Albert and Reimert and three sisters -- Gerda, Agnes, and Astrid - and our families - have lived in the Seattle area, enjoying innumerable extended family gatherings. Herewith pictures of Albert and Marjorie and other family members. Extensive accounts of our ancestral origins and many family activities are presented on www.ravenholt.com, Ravenholts of Wisconsin/Albert.

Albert interviewing Gen. Claire Chenault

Albert relaxing with book and friends

Groom with Lei and Correspondent

Albert and Marjorie with tropical blooms

Albert gathering agricultural data in Taiwan

Albert bargaining for fruits

Albert in his 40s

Albert in his 50s

Albert in his 80s

Marjorie in her 60s

Johanne   Reimert   Kristine   Eiler   Albert   Otto
Celebrating Mor's 90th Birthday, November 6, 1982, at West Denmark, Wisconsin

Reimert   Agnes   Johanne   Albert   Astrid   Eiler   Halvor   Gerda   Otto
Celebrating the Great Life of Kristine Petersen Ravnholt, November 6, 1892 - September 23, 1986.

Grand View College, Des Moines, Iowa, October 1939

THE STORY OF AN IMMIGRANT

By Albert Ravenholt (From Anders Ravmholt diary writings)

On October 12, 1870, that is on the day he was 24 years old, Anders Christensen Ravnholt stood on the wharf in Copenhagen ready to go on the steamship "Aurora", bound for Kiel. It was with not a few misgivings that he bade farewell to his homeland and faced the great unknown.

Born the oldest in a family of five boys and two girls, his experiences had been those of the average young fellow of his time. Schools were uncommon, but possessing a natural desire for learning, young Anders attended night school, taught by a young teacher, Jensen, from Knudstrup. His teachings were to leave a lifelong impression upon young Anders and later incite him to further his studies. Though books and periodicals were scarce, such as there were, were devoured eagerly. When the one paper did arrive, it happened perchance that the oxen took a turn around the field alone as the young man became enveloped in fantasies of far off places. Our Civil War was at that time in progress and its development was followed with keen enthusiasm. Indeed, his interest in America became so great that after he had served his time at the military infantry camp at Hald, he packed and embarked upon his ventures.

Since there were at that time no ships running directly, he had to go via Kiel to Hamburg, Germany, and thence aboard ship for Grimesby, England. The Franco-German war caused considerable interference with shipping and complicated circumstances somewhat. A number of Germans, taken aboard at Hamburg and also bound for America, entertained on shipboard with all their new wartime songs. At Grimsby they boarded train for Liverpool and from there shipped to New York aboard the ship, "City of Washington". The fourteen-day passage proved uneventful except that Anders witnessed his first funeral at sea. A child of Swedish immigrants had died and the captain summoned all Scandinavians on deck to witness the burial. The wind and waves and sorrowing relatives all lent atmosphere to make the scene very touching as the hole-riddled coffin was shoved overboard and quickly sank in the deep.

Just as it has to so many others, New York, with its thousands of ship masts, immense buildings and bustling traffic, impressed Anders Ravnholt profoundly. Of course, at the time, an immigrant was treated as such, and

THE STORY OF AN IMMIGRANT

great was the sorrow among the women as they watched their treasured trunks haplessly shoved down the gangplank to break open and their contents lost.

After the usual customs inspection, the journey was resumed westward by rail for St. Paul via Cleveland, Toledo, Chicago and Milwaukee. From St. Paul he again continued westward by rail to Wilmar, Minnesota, and from there finished the last lap of his journey behind a team of oxen, with a farmer just returning from town. Here in central Minnesota, Anders had reference to one of the first Danish immigrants to that region, Jens Troelstrup.

With his destination reached, Anders sought employment. The Northern Pacific Railway was being extended westward from St. Paul to Brainerd and, like many other young Danish immigrants, he worked here during the summer, and in winter found employment on surrounding farms. "Birds of a feather flock together" here as well as elsewhere, and young Anders soon became acquainted with a number of contemporaries. One of his newly found friends was in the sorrowful plight of losing his sweetheart in Denmark. She, in the usual fashion, was destined by her parents for another. In his predicament, he petitioned Anders for help, and so well did Anders employ what little literary skill he had achieved that the girl was permitted to wait and eventually marry the one she desired.

By the summer of 1874 the lure of chance proved too much for him and he set out for the new gold mines in Montana. The trip was made on the Union Pacific to Ogden, Utah, and from there north by ox caravan to Helena, Montana. In company with his friend, Hans Jensen, he secured a cabin and set up housekeeping. The West was then still in its wild and wooly stage of development, yet there were two things he never carried with him: a watch and a revolver. Not that he was any kind of conscientious objector, but he merely thought that carrying a gun was inviting trouble. Eventually, the strenuous work in the unhealthy mines plus the bachelor food proved too hard for his health, so in August, 1876, after two years in the mines, he decided to return to Denmark. That trip proved the most adventurous of his life. By this time he had taught himself to read and write English and happily kept a diary of his journey.

The first leg of one hundred and fifty miles from Unionville, Montana, to Fort Benton, on the Missouri River, was made in stage coach. From Fort Benton he had expected to proceed by steamboat; but alas no steamer was there. The next day in company with a Yankee and a German they bought a row boat and proceeded down the Missouri River. That summer witnessed the noted uprising of the Sioux Indians under Chief Sitting Bull, and while in the mines they had heard of General Custer's massacre. So the trip of 198 miles to Cow Island in an open boat was by no means a pleasure jaunt. As they floated down the river, they at times thought they heard Indian war whoops, and at one time, after a particularly anxious moment, Anders sat up and let go a sigh of relief. But the German, not yet feeling entirely secure, knocked him so hard with the stock of his gun that it sent him rolling in the bottom of the boat. Strangely enough, he made it through even with the seventeen hundred dollars he carried on his person.

THE STORY OF AN IMMIGRANT

Arriving at Cow Island, a wait of ten days for a steamer proved futile; so they continued on in the rowboat to Carroll, a distance of 67 miles, and there (after a further wait) took passage on the steamer "Benton" for Bismark, Dakota Territory. While en route he had the experience of watching the buffalo swim the river as the steamer hove to and passengers enjoyed themselves by massacring the buffalo until the river ran red.

From Bismark the journey continued by rail to St Paul and Chicago. Both in St Paul and Chicago, Anders visited museums and theatres, and stopped at Scandinavian hotels whenever the opportunity permitted. The United States was then celebrating its birth at the Philadelphia Centennial Exposition, and with natural curiosity he trouped thither. Six days were spent visiting the exposition, Independence and Carpenter Halls, theatres, museums, and other places of interest. On the second day of November, 1876, he sailed for Liverpool, and returned home via Hull, Hamburg and Kiel to Copenhagen, and finally arriving home in Thorning Sogn on the 26th of November, 1876, after three months of travel. So ended his first experience in America. And now, having had his fling, he was thought ready to settle down.

During the winter of 1877 he attended Askov Folk School, then under the direction of Ludwig Schroder. Askov was one of the folk high schools which at the time were beginning to play an ever more important role in Danish religious and political thought. Since then they have become recognized as the means through which Denmark awoke mentally and resurrected itself. About this time Anders came under the influence of Markus Lund, a minister of remarkable intellect, who preached in his home locality. Apparently he had a preference for October 12, for on that day he married his cousin Inger Johanne Thestrup. The young couple then purchased and settled on his homeplace, Ravnholt Gaard. But by the summer of 1883 his longing for America had again become so strong that, against the advice of relatives, the young couple sold their belongings and left for the United States.

Their first destination in the United States was Ashland, Michigan. But the opportunities there appeared so meager that they decided to go to Elkhorn, Iowa. Unhappily for them, they stopped-over in Grand Rapids, Michigan, where a fair was in progress. Here Anders cashed the bank draft he carried representing their worldly possessions, somewhat above a thousand dollars. While he boarded a street car, someone dislodged his suitcases, and as he stooped to recover the suitcases, someone snatched his billfold from him, and disappeared in the crowd. The police were notified at once but all efforts proved fruitless. Destitute indeed were the straits of the young couple as they stood alone in an unknown world with all their worldly belongings lost. Luckily they held tickets to Atlantic, Iowa. Whither they went. In Elkhorn, through the aid of friends, they got started on 80 acres of virgin prairie. But their debt overhead was so great that the next year they sold out; and attracted by the glowing reports of the country there, they moved to West Denmark, Wisconsin, where they settled - purchasing forested acreage, which they cleared and built a home.

THE STORY OF AN IMMIGRANT

In 1885 a group of Danes banded together and started Wisconsin's first cooperative creamery. Having studied buttermaking in Denmark, Johanne Ravnholt was chosen to run the creamery and Anders was employed to gather the cream and do other hauling. After 5 years they ceased operating the cooperative creamery, and in 1992 started their own "A.C. Ravnholt Danish Creamery", which they operated until 1898.

From the very first, Anders took a keen interest in the religious questions of the time and became an active member of the West Denmark congregation. Discussions appealed to him; though he considered local politics too petty for his consideration, he followed intently political trends here and abroad. In 1899 his longing to again see family and friends in Denmark prompted his return to relive the experiences of his youth. Though he enjoyed his visit, he returned to West Denmark after several months and resumed farming. In 1903 he and family moved to Des Moines, Iowa, the location of the Grandview College and seminary for the synod; and for two years they enjoyed the cultural life centered there. Upon their return to the farm in Wisconsin, he entered again fully into the life at West Denmark with all his old vigor. Nearing the fullness of his years, the returns of a vigorous life were beginning to be his; and in various capacities he participated wherever people of like interests gathered.

During the summer of 1912 Ravnholt suffered a fractured collarbone as he was dragged while trying to arrest a run-away team. And at year's end he began suffering from what proved to be gallstones and cancer, for which he had two operations which did not arrest the cancer. He passed away on May 14th, 1913, and was laid to rest in the tranquil West Denmark cemetery. That is a brief biographical sketch of my grandfather. He lived a turbulent, fast-moving life, deeply affected by his religious and social convictions. With perhaps a little provincialism I can say that I am proud of my grandfather in that he let a keen mental balance dominate his actions. But his importance lies, not so much in what he achieved individually as in the spirit and type of people of which he is at least partially representative, namely, Danish-American immigrants, to whom America owes a far greater debt than she at present realizes.

Anders Christensen Ravnholt
Nearing age 40, Milltown, Wis.

Hj. løkken hele ett[a]
Den 29. Marts 1934

Kære broder Reimert:

Hjertelig tillykke paa din store
dag. Jeg kan nok tænke der gaar dig
mange tanker i hovedet og det burde
der ogsaa. Jeg ønsker jeg selv kunde være
hjemme til den begivenhed. Det er
ligesom konfirmationsdagen betegner en
forandring. Man synes man begyndes at se
paa livet anderledes. Jeg haaber det der
følger efter for dig, maa give alle glæde
og at din gang attid maa være fremad.
Vor families forhold nu om stunder er
langt fra hvad vi ønsker og det ængster mig
meget, men det eneste er at arbejde sammen
og hjælpe til for det vil gøre livet
lykkelig for os alle.

Vi troede vi havde faaet sommer
her i Des Moines og saa vi oftere fik vi
fire tommer sne, men det gaar nok atter
igen. Skole livet her haaber jeg saa
inderlig du en gang maa faa lov til at
deltage i. Jeg føler i det mindste som om
jeg faar meget. Enda ogsaa af stinkbomber,
Vand paa hovedet osv. Den anden
aften havde nogen vædet saa skulle at

fyldte min pude med peber og salt og
sengen med thumbtacks. I Mandags
var jeg ude ved Drake University.
Jeg havde hirt 6 skole hyre hahtredes
unge karle og til Worlds Fair at arbejde,
men nu tog de dem fra University of Chicago.
Saa vidt har jeg ikke taget gymnastik
for benets skyld men jeg tror nok snart
jeg kan begynde. Forleden fik jeg mine
recomendation tilsendt fra min chef, den vil
jeg bruge til foraar i New York. Fra brevet
til Tulle har i vel hørt om turen til
Omaha. Den var ellers morsom skønt vi
ikke fik Europa sat helt i stand. Om morgen
often kommer Esten Aakjær og læser hans
faders digte. Jeg har Tyrue rides af philosophi.
Jeg skal have læseline i often og det er drøje
sager. Nu har jeg ogsaa begyndt at tage
recreational leadership class. Til i morgen
skal vi hver have en folkedans at forklare
di andre. Heri vil du finde in lille
penge sedel som du kan bruge som du onsker
Nu slutter jeg med det bedste haab for din
fremtid og ønsker for familiens vel fard.
Kærlig hilsen
din broder
Albert

45

(A Translation)

```
Grand View College                                    11:30 PM
Des Moines, Iowa                                  29 March 1939
```

Dear Brother Reimert,

Hearty congratulations upon your big day. I can understand your head is filled with many thoughts, as it should be. I wish I could be home for the event. It is as though Confirmation Day implies a fundamental change. It seems one begins to see life differently. I hope that all that follows after for you will give pleasure and that your way always will be forward. Our family's current situation is far from what we would wish and that troubles me greatly, but we must work together and help with all that will make life fortunate for us all.

We thought summer had come to us in Des Moines, then got four inches of snow; but that will soon vanish. The school life here I earnestly hope you, too, may come to know. I feel at least that I am getting a lot here. Also of stink bombs, water dumped on my head, and so forth! The other night some were pleased to fill my pillow with pepper and salt and the bed with thumb tacks. Monday I was out to Drake University. I had heard that they should hire 50 young fellows for work at the World's Fair, but they took them from the University of Chicago. So far I have not taken gymnastics because of my leg but I believe I can soon begin. I just received my Letter of Recommendation from my Chef, which I will use this spring in New York. From my letter to Tulle [Johanne] you have probably heard of the trip to Omaha. That was fun though we did not get Europe entirely done up. Tomorrow evening Eshen Aakjaer is coming to read his father's writings. I have 20 pages of philosophy still to read tonight and that is tough stuff. Now I have also begun to take a recreational leadership class. In the morning each one of us must know a folk dance so as to explain it to the others. Herein you will find a little banknote which you can use as you wish. Now I am closing with best wishes for your future and with wishes for our family's well being.

Dearest Greetings,

your brother,

Albert

A WINTRY WISCONSIN EXCURSION!

Illustrative of how Albert's enterprising spirit often activated the family, in late November 1937 on a bitterly cold and snowy Sunday afternoon (minus 20 degrees) Albert, Eiler and Reimert proceeded with a team of horses and sleigh to the western shore of Little Butternut Lake, a mile distant -- seeking to acquire a stranded rowboat from a southerly stretch of the lake, noticed earlier. Tying the horses along the shore, we proceeded with tools over the recently frozen ice out toward the marooned boat; with me proceeding somewhat aside from Albert and Eiler, hurrying along among clumps of weeds carrying an axe in one hand and a hammer in the other -- until suddenly plunging into a brief stretch without bearing ice, perhaps kept open by aquatic mammals. The shock of my sudden descent into icy water caused me to let go of the axe and hammer; whereas, because I was heavily clothed in thick winter clothing, I did not sink into the water above my shoulders but quickly climbed out onto bearing ice, calling for the others. Then, because we knew how furious Father would be with us for losing the tools, Albert stripped off clothing to his waist and with Eiler and me holding unto his legs he submersed his head and upper body into the lake, feeling for the tools. Surprisingly, the axe was quickly recovered. Then, ignoring the lost hammer, we hurried to the shore and rapidly home, with me running behind the sled to avoid freezing in my wetted condition. There, Mother quickly arranged a pail of hot water for me to warm my legs in. No illness ensued, but we never returned for the boat.

Walter S Rogers, Director, Institute of Current World Affairs

Following their first meeting in May 1947, Albert and Walter Rogers rapidly bonded; with Rogers becoming Albert's chief mentor during the postwar years - helping him gain an ICWA/Nieman Fellowship in Chinese studies at Harvard during a year, to become a Chicago Daily News Foreign Service correspondent, and a founding member of the American Universities Field Staff.

An extraordinarily able and experienced Midwesterner, Walter Rogers was born in Chicago and attended the school in south Chicago that evolved into the University of Chicago. While there he worked as a campus correspondent for Victor Lawson's three Scandinavian newspapers - Danish, Norwegian and Swedish -- which he later combined to create the CHICAGO DAILY NEWS.

While staying on at the University of Chicago to gain his law degree, Rogers also wrote for the Chicago Daily News. The fact that the Northwest Ordinance forbad slavery north of the Ohio River contributed to the great industrial development in and around Chicago during and after the Civil War.

Walter S Rogers, Director, Institute of Current World Affairs

Eli Scripps, a great newspaper tycoon, employed Walter Rogers and Harold Ickes to run the "Day Book" in a square mile of downtown Chicago. Carl Sandberg was a feature writer for that publication. Rogers showed Albert a clipping of an article by Carl Sandberg: "Today I am going to put a rose on the coffin of my friend and go on writing." His friend was a part Indian doctor who devoted his life to striving for decent living conditions in Chicago. Rogers also showed Albert a letter he had received from President Woodrow Wilson, about 1920: "Dear Walter, Your letter of ---- confirms as I've always known you to be, an inveterate friend of progress…."

Rogers was employed by the R.T. Crane Co. as an attorney in the 1890s; thus becoming closely associated with Charles R. Crane who inherited $70 million from his father (R.T. Crane). Walter Rogers and Charles Crane became well acquainted with Woodrow Wilson. When developing Federal Reserve legislation during the teens, President Wilson once asked Rogers help in getting a certain Chicago banker to Washington, DC. Upon his return to Chicago, the banker told Rogers that "The President does not understand banking." But a year later, after having worked repeatedly with the President, the banker said, "President Wilson knows more about banking than any other person in America."

In Geneva just after the war, Rogers became well acquainted with Herbert Hoover as they strove to get the League of Nations established. But it was turned down by the U.S. Senate. A little later, Hoover and Rogers bought the Washington Times newspaper, of which Hoover became the principal owner and Rogers the publisher until 1925 when they had a falling out. Then Rogers with strong financial support from Charles R Crane established the Institute for Current World Affairs (ICWA), which Rogers directed until 1959. When John Hazzard graduated from Harvard Law in 1936, the ICWA sent him to the Moscow Juridical Institute for four years. When he returned to the U.S. in 1940 he became President Roosevelt's principal Russian interpreter and also Number Two in direction of the Lend Lease Program for Russia.

Walter Rogers retired as director of the ICWA in 1959 after 34 years service, and was succeeded by Richard Nolte, a former Fellow of the Institute, who served for 19 years. Nolte, in turn, was succeeded by the current director, Peter Bird Martin, who is also a former Fellow. Hal O'Flaherty, a trustee of the ICWA, was also director of the Chicago Daily News Foreign Service, and during WWII was chief of Naval Intelligence under Secretary Knox. Altogether, after becoming a prime protégé of Walter Rogers, beginning in 1947, Albert consistently enjoyed a remarkably high level of support and access to foremost opportunities in his chosen field of foreign correspondence, mainly dealing with SE Asia. Additionally, his most enduring friendships have been with other Fellows of the ICWA - Phillips Talbot, Thomas Blakemore, Richard Nolte, Peter Martin, and others. Files of Albert Ravenholt-Walter Rogers correspondence during many years are maintained at the Institute of Current World Affairs headquarters in Hanover, NH.

By 1953, Albert had accumulated sufficient funds that he largely paid for the construction of a much improved Ravenholt family home by the golf course near Luck, Wisconsin - where extended family members have enjoyed vacationing during many summers.

ORIGIN AND DEVELOPMENT OF THE MAGSAYSAY AWARDS FOUNDATION

Gainsborough Apts
1017 Minor Avenue
Seattle, Washington 98104

Mr. Donald H. McLean, Jr. 18 October 1976
Room 5600
30 Rockefeller Plaza
New York, N.Y. 10020

Dear Don:

It is good to receive your letter of 6 October 1976 that Marjorie forwarded from Manila; it was waiting here when I returned from lecturing at the University of Hawaii. Your questions about the origins of the Ramon Magsaysay Awards and how the idea and Foundation took shape I will answer as you numbered them.

1. In March 1957 I was lecturing at Harvard University when the plane crashed on the mountainous backbone of Cebu Island that cost the life of President Ramon Magsaysay, another fine friend Senator Tomas Cabili, and others. The week following this tragedy I reported in to our American Universities Field Staff headquarters, then in New York City. I found an invitation from John D. Rockefeller, 3rd, to come to tea at their apartment. After a general discussion of the tragedy and its probable consequences, John said he was thinking of a memorial to Magsaysay and asked for suggestions. The idea of a Nobel-type award in Asia for those individuals who stand up to be counted for the public good had been germinating with me for some time, so it was natural for me to mention it to John. He responded positively and said he wanted to think about it and consult his brothers. John telephoned me at the Curtis Hotel in Minneapolis, Minnesota, when I was enroute to Northfield to lecture at Carelton College. He then requested the memo on the Magsaysay Award idea, of which you now sent me a copy. John explained on the phone that he wanted this memo for discussion with the family and associates and asked that I meet with you upon my return to New York.

2. I first met John when you, he and I had that careful talk concerning your interest in establishing what became the Council on Economic and Cultural Affairs and now is the Agricultural Development Council. This was in New York City and I believe the year was 1954. When John and Blanchette came to Manila -- as I recall it was 1956 -- Marjorie and I had them for dinner with a group of the able and impressive young Filipinos that President Magsaysay had brought into government, including Manny and Connie Manahan and a half a dozen others. We took John and Blanchette on a trip to Central Luzon to see the efforts at land reform and other rural development. We all had a lively breakfast at Malacanang Palace with President and Mrs. Magsaysay. As best I can remember, two of the younger Rockefellers were along. Gerald Wilkinson, and possibly Mariana, joined us for the breakfast.

3. During our telephone conversation between New York and Minneapolis John said he particularly liked the Award idea and we discussed its possible significance in elevating models of positive effort in Asia for young people to emulate. Earlier, when we had tea in New York I had first

suggested to John establishment of a New York Times type of newspaper for Southeast Asia. In our telephone conversation he elaborated on the reasons why he felt this was not appropriate.

4. As mentioned above, the visit with John at his apartment was our first discussion of the idea of the Magsaysay Awards. At the time we talked about the trend toward disillusionment throughout much of Asia, especially among the young, and the vital need for leaders of genuine integrity who were able to help the common "Tao," or peasant, improve his lot through democratic methods. As you know, John had been much involved with Japan. This was a time when in the rest of Asia there was much confusion reflecting the ripple effects of the Chinese Civil War, the Korean War and various rebellions underway in Southeast Asia. The problem we discussed most was the need to enable Asians to find and encourage attention to practical and positive leaders for these struggling new nations.

5. Wolf Ladejinsky came to New York and joined with us for a day of conversation because you and I agreed we needed to try our ideas on someone with sound sense. Wolf had proven himself through his contribution to the land reform that remade rural Japan and Taiwan. When the three of us went down from your office that evening about 6:30 PM and walked out to Sixth Avenue, you may recall Wolf telling us the story of how he used to sell newspapers on that corner during the cold winters of the depression years. He said he watched them building Rockefeller Center then and "used to wonder what kind of people would use those offices up there."

I suggested to you that we invite Ed Lansdale to join us for the same reason we invited Wolf; he had valuable experience and constructive instincts. Also, Ed likewise was my friend. We met first in the Philippines in 1948 when the new Republic was near its nadir and Marjorie and I were en route back to China to cover the Civil War for the Chicago Daily News Foreign Service. Ed only spent a couple of hours with you, Wolf and me and had to leave because of other commitments. So, we outlined the idea of the Awards to Ed and I asked him to let us have a memo on his reaction.

6. Ed Lansdale never was mentioned in any of the discussions that John Rockefeller and I had at his apartment or on the telephone, nor in early talks in his office. Later, when you and I had drafted the paper on the Awards, who would be eligible, how the Awards would be made, etc., you or I mentioned in a talk with John, and possibly later in a talk with Nelson Rockefeller, that we had tried out the ideas on Wolf and Ed, who both responded favorably. Once John had taken the initiative, I felt our problem was to convince the other Rockefeller Brothers that others with substantial experience in Asia thought the Award was practical.

7. The involvement of Ed Lansdale was my idea. I telephoned him in Washington, D.C., asking him to come to New York City that day to sit with Wolf, you and me. You will recall that Wolf and Ed both were ardent admirers of Marjorie, who worked with Wolf in China. They both had insisted you would be better off with her as your traveling partner to Manila to enlist Filipino support and establish the Magsaysay Award Foundation.

ORIGIN AND DEVELOPMENT OF THE MAGSAYSAY AWARDS FOUNDATION

Marjorie came to New York for talks before the two of you left for Manila and I went on to lecture at the universities. I believe the Awards had a far more auspicious beginning because you got Marjorie to go with you and through her enlisted Belen Abreu to resign as Chief Attorney of the Commission on Elections and become the Executive Trustee of the Foundation.

It proved critical that we designed the Foundation so she is Executive Trustee, somewhat after the British system of a managing director. Had her role been that of an executive secretary under a board of trustees, she feels it would have been unworkable; it would never have been possible to maintain the standards of quality in selection of Awardees that are the key to the respect with which the Magsaysay Awards are today viewed throughout most of Asia. Belen, some of her conscientious trustees, and Marjorie with "behind the screen" assistance and friendship, plus flexible collaboration by the good folks in the RFB shop, over two decades of far beyond routine effort have made John Rockefeller's choice of an idea a remarkable reality and one from which we can all take a bit of encouragement.

Peter Johnson said on the phone that he wants to talk with me on background for his writing, which I take as a most convenient opportunity to come to New York City with Marjorie and Belen and see you all. Please write a note to Alan Horton, AUFS, Wheelock House, 4 W. Wheelock Street, Hanover, New Hampshire 03755, confirming that it will be useful for me to be there.

Cordially,   Albert Ravenholt

OVER PACIFIC go Albert Ravenholt of the Daily News Foreign Service, and Mrs. Ravenholt. They are shown about to board a Pan American World Airways System plane in San Francisco bound for the Far East.

From THE CORRESPONDENT   March 1993

Representing a Profession, Not a Mob

The Foreign Correspondents' Club was first founded by a small group of correspondents in Chungking in the spring of 1945. Albert Ravenholt, the last surviving member of that group, recounts the Club's early years in an interview with Ashley Ford.

Last assembly of correspondents at the first FCC site in Chungking in 1945.

WITH THE SECOND WORLD WAR just getting into full swing a fresh-faced young Wisconsin "dairy farm boy" working at the New York World's Fair fretted that the hostilities might pass him by. Not that Albert Ravenholt wanted to take part in the shooting. Rather, he had long seen himself as a "foreign correspondent".

The last-surviving founding member of the Foreign Correspondents' Club was determined to fulfill his dream and shipped out to China where he had a premonition history would soon be in the making.

"I decided I'd not go back to college but had better take off. There was a whole generation of us like that," he recalled in an interview from his Seattle home.

Short on journalistic experience, young Ravenholt was not deterred. Upon arrival in Shanghai he threw himself into learning Mandarin, French and Russian and earned a meager living filing for United Press International and a host of other news outfits.

Why Shanghai? "Shanghai was a very interesting place in those days. It was an international city and was the one place in the world you could go without a passport and a visa "he said. It was a prescient choice.
"We knew the war was coming and another fellow and I decided the time had come to really cover what the Japanese were doing in China," he said.

"We got ourselves some fake documents as missionary school teachers and took a Japanese ship south and smuggled ourselves through the lines at Swatow."

BECOMING A FOREIGN CORRESPONDENT

Eventually he managed to become a transport inspector for the International Red Cross which gave him access to China's interior. Strangely enough China was not yet a "hot story" in the US or anywhere else in the West for that matter. He recalls that UPI and other US media were just not interested in China. That was until Pearl Harbour. "That changed everything," he said. "Overnight they got acutely interested in China. Luckily it was a very cheap place to live."

The still sprightly 74-year-old Ravenholt learned his journalism the old fashioned way by writing for everyone he could. "I did what a lot of us did at that time. I wrote for the *North China Daily News*, the *China Daily News* plus some radio work."

While Ravenholt craved the life of the foreign correspondent even he didn't realize his move was the beginning of a five-decade odyssey that would take him through some of the pivotal battles in the Pacific campaign and China's civil war. His interest still remains in Asia and he continues to split his time between Seattle and the Philippines where he maintains a residence.

Thirty of those years were spent working for the *Chicago Daily News*. A job Ravenholt says, that was a dream for a journalist. "The *Chicago Daily News* was very good to me and they gave me he space to write not just about war but also other developments in Asia such as land and agricultural reform," he said.

Much of his war experience was spent behind enemy lines. He went through eight campaigns with Chinese armies; covered both the Arakan and Imphal campaigns in northern Burma; went behind Japanese lines with Brigadier Orde Wingate on the second Chindit operation in Burma in 1944; reported on the Kachin tribesmen who fought a successful guerilla campaign against the Japanese in north-east Burma armed with 18th century flintlocks; and covered General 'Vinegar Joe' Stilwell's campaign in northern Burma.

Foreign Correspondent corps in the first convoy over the Burma Road.

FOREIGN CORRESPONDENT'S CLUB

Despite a number of close calls Ravenholt managed to come out of the war unscathed. But that is not to say there were not times when he thought his number was up. "Once I crashed on take-off in a B-24 loaded with four-tons of bombs. I was standing behind the pilot and figured this was curtains. Every other bomber that crashed on take-off had blown up but for some reason this one didn't," he said.

Another time he played hide and seek with a Japanese sniper while descending a mountain in southern China on the Burmese border. Ravenholt said: "The Japanese 25-calibre sniper's rifle had a sound that you could never forget."

With the war in Europe coming to an end, Ravenholt found himself in Chungking, in Sichuan province with a small army of other foreign correspondents which formed the nucleus of what is today the FCC (Foreign Correspondents Club).

"It all started in Chungking in the spring of 1945," he said. "Up until that time we (the foreign correspondents) had no organization except for the correspondents from Tass but they stayed away from us. The rest of us lived in a pretty meagre building known as the Press Hostel.

"It was built of woven bamboo plastered with mud and was pretty sparse. We had our own garden of sorts. The hostel was built around a courtyard with our own banana trees." Sparse it certainly was and he recalls that privacy was not exactly readily available. "It was the kind of place where if a couple got together, which was not unknown, you could feel the walls shake," he said.

Ravenholt said that with the war coming to an end in Europe the focus of attention would switch to Asia and the correspondents realized that they had to "get their collective act together. "Up until then, for us at least, the war had been pretty much a holding action except for Burma," he said. "The Correspondents' Association was formed to represent us in dealing with not just the Chinese government but with both the American and British military commands. Up until then it had been every man for himself with all of us scurrying around trying to cover China. It was not very practical."

Ravenholt doesn't remember how many actual founding members there were but he does recall that it cost a hefty US $100 to join. I think, from memory, it was either nine or 10 of us," he said, "it wasn't a social club like it is now. It was a professional club. There were representatives from Reuters, The Daily Telegraph, UPI, Associated Press, CBS and a couple of others whose names or papers I can't remember."

"At that time we expected there would be a landing of American troops at two places on the coast of China, one in the south near the Chinese-Vietnamese border and the other south of Shanghai at a place called Hangchow Bay.

"It was a question of having somebody to represent us in terms of our profession so that we would not be seen as a mob where everyone was fighting with everyone else to get on planes or to important battlefront areas. We also knew we could be at the mercy of the army information people if we didn't have an outfit to represent us. "Then of course there was the matter of censorship and again we realized we would have a better chance of fighting it if we were seen and taken seriously as a journalist organization."

The overriding reason for bringing some organization to the "juno ranks", Ravenholt recalled, "was our concern with getting some facilities where we could send our stories. A story isn't worth anything if you can't get it sent and read."Ravenholt says he can't recall who the Club's first President was, but he did a brief stint as the second President before he had to go off to Kunming.

He returned to Chungking shortly before the Japanese surrendered. "I remember sitting in the local Chinese radio station when the flash came from New York saying the Japanese had surrendered," he said. "That night I watched the city go wild. My god it was a night. I had never seen Chinese behave the way they did that night ... they really celebrated."

It was obvious that following the surrender the press corps would be moving back to Shanghai and the club made its first substantial decision. "A committee of us from the club went to see the Chinese government (Nationalists), and told them that when we got back to the coast we would like to have space for our activities, both living and working," Ravenholt said. The Chinese were amazingly cooperative and Ravenholt's local Shanghai knowledge paid off handsomely.

"The Chinese came up with an astonishing reply to the Club's request," he said.

"They said how would you like the Broadway Mansion? I kicked the guy next to me before anything stupid was said and replied that would be just perfect. "I knew all about Broadway Mansion and it was a real coup for us. It was the largest apartment house in China, 18 stories high and right on Suichow Creek and the Wangpo River. I could hardly believe it when the Chinese amiably told us this would be set aside for the foreign correspondents. It seemed to be too good to be true and it almost was. When we got to Shanghai the US Air Force had started moving into the building and we had a fight with them," Ravenholt recalled.

"We finally compromised. We took the top half of the building from the 13th floor and made the 17th and 18th floors the Club. I can still remember [in 1949] watching the communist advance on the city from the top floor. This might have been the best joint in town but the departing Japanese had stripped the place of radiators making it pretty cold and uncomfortable. The US Air types weren't about to give a bunch of journalists any help either," he said. "When winter came we had to try and scrounge some electric heaters."

Ravenholt said the move back to Shanghai saw the Tass correspondents move into the Club. "In Chungking they didn't live with us and we had very little contact. But all that changed in Shanghai because every month a plane from Moscow would arrive loaded with vodka and other goodies." The Club quickly saw its ranks grow as correspondents who had covered the Pacific War began moving to Shanghai. "Shanghai was something they had only dreamed about," he said. "So we ended up with about 40 correspondents in Broadway Mansion.

"It was about this time the social aspect of the club stated to surface. We had started the thing to fight our battles and make life easier. Now that we had the facilities, we needed transportation, access passes, etc. and the Club became a social centre. That changed it dramatically."

When the Chinese communists started their last major southward offensive across the Yangtze River in April 1949 the Club moved down to Canton before finally moving across the border into Hong Kong. Ravenholt and other colleagues barely escaped intact. "It was an amazing thing to witness," he said. "The communists had 84 armies on the north side of the Yangtze River. Few people realized the extent of the fighting that went on in the Chinese Civil War, or the casualties."

FOREIGN CORRESPONDENT'S CLUB

Ravenholt and the Club had a parting of the ways in Hong Kong. "In 1951 there was some support for me to become President, but a fight developed over whether the place we were occupying on Conduit Road should be purchased or leased."

As he tells it the lease side won and to this day he believes it was the single biggest mistake the Club ever made. "I wanted to buy the place," Ravenholt said. "I even went as far as discussing the matter with the Chinese sugar merchant who owned the place. He had made a lot of money on sugar and was willing to sell it for a modest down payment and the payments would have been a little more than we would have been paying in rent. So when they wouldn't go along with the proposition of buying the place I turned down becoming president. It was a fabulous property and I know I was right."

Ironically, Ravenholt remembers that Hong Kong and its future was being discussed just after the war had ended in the Pacific and firmly believes the British could have secured another lease if they had bothered to try.

"I can remember having a discussion with The *Daily Telegraph* man about it at the time. I can't remember his name but I know he was a great admirer of Clement Attlee, the British Labour leader. I can still remember how delighted he was when Attlee won the election. As soon as Attlee came to power the British decided to give up extra-territoriality," he said. I was writing a story about it and was having a discussion with friends at t1he British embassy in China."

"We talked on the subject at great length. I could not believe Britain was serious in giving up all its territories. So I asked why not renew your lease on Hong Kong. After all the Chinese were euphoric that Britain was giving up all its territorial rights and Britain stood a good chance of renewing its lease on the New Territories. Besides Hong Kong was tiddlywinks to the Chinese at the time anyway." "The answer I got, and I still remember it to this day, is that 1997 was a long way away and besides, it would be too much trouble."

Ashley Ford is an absent member of the FCC and is Pacific Rim correspondent for the Vancouver Provident.

Albert Ravenholt, UP War Correspondent
Albert Ravenholt, UP War Correspondent

Albert Ravenholt, age 80

Albert Ra

SEVEN U.S. WAR CORRESPONDENTS IN CHINA DURING WORLD WAR II
Invited As Guests to the Peoples Republic Of China In 1985

IN MARCH 1985, Albert Ravenholt was one of seven former U.S. War Correspondents in China during World War II* invited by the Peoples Republic of China to visit China for a month as guests of the PRC – "to come see China on a New Path". Deng Xiaoping was then Chairman of the Peoples Republic of China; and the official hostesses for their visit were Madam Chow En-Lai (widow) and Madam Liu Hsiao-chia, wife of the Chairman of the PRC Chung Yang.

Marjorie accompanied Albert to Beijing, where they socialized awhile with other correspondents and wives they had known and worked with during WWII, before the official tour commenced for the correspondents. In Beijing, at the start of the tour, the correspondents met with top level government officials, including Chairman Deng Xiaoping (see photo). Albert "had long been fascinated" by Deng Xiaoping's career: a very intelligent native of Sichwan Province, of short stature, who rose rapidly among the Communist hierarchy. During the climactic Huai Hai battles of the Chinese Civil War in 1949 between the Yellow and Yangtze Rivers, Deng Xiaoping was political commissar of the Second Field Army, with Marshall Liu Po-Chang commanding. Meanwhile Albert was reporting from Nanking on the battles, the faltering Nationalist armies, and the movement of the Nationalist government to Taiwan.

In 1976, upon the deaths of Chow En-Lai and Mao Tse tung, Deng Xiaoping, then Secretary General of the Chinese Communist Party, became Chairman of the Military Affairs Committee and ruler of China. In that capacity, he rapidly returned land ownership to the families from whom taken for creation of the Communes in the "Great Leap Forward" in 1958; and he also took many initiatives toward instituting a market economy –– spurring the great economic developments still continuing.

From Beijing, the correspondents accompanied by four representatives of China's Ministry of Information, flew to Yennan, in Shensi Province –– the Communist headquarters following the "Long March" and during WWII. After which they traveled to Sian (now Xian), capital of the Chin Dynasty that unified China in the 3rd Century B.C.; where they enjoyed seeing thousands of terra cotta figures.

Albert Ravenholt, Deng Xiaoping, Phil Potter

*   With Hank Lieberman, N.Y. Times; Til Durden, N.Y. Times; Phil Potter, Baltimore Sun; Robert Shaplin, Newsweek; George Weller, Chicago Daily News; John Hlavachek, United Press.

From Xian, Albert left the tour group, and rambled independently, mainly by rail, retracing his travels in 1941-42 when hauling medical supplies for the International Red Cross on the Burma Road and widely in Free China. A week later, from Chengtu he traveled by train to Chungking, rejoining the other correspondents for a voyage down the Yangtze River; stopping at points of interest, at Wu Han City, and on to Shanghai. There they again met with top directors of diverse government programs, with Albert being especially interested in the agricultural programs. Altogether, these seven War Correspondents from WWII, were given a most interesting and pleasing view of developments in China, replete with many banquets and much friendly fellowship.

Universities Field Staff International   1985/No. 36 Asia [AR-1=85]

HO CHI MINH: REVOLUTIONARY EXTRAORDINARY
An Obituary

By Albert Ravenholt

THE REVOLUTIONARY LEADERS who so largely reshaped Asia after World War II often loom larger in retrospect than they were in reality. Even Ho Chi Minh, who was a more complex and many-faceted personality than any of his senior Chinese Communist comrades, was a much more human type than histories make him out to have been. Among the several names he used was Nguyen Ai Quoc (Nguyen the Patriot). We first came to know one another in 1944-45 when Ho was in his mid-fifties and I in my mid-twenties. Ho then was an impoverished revolutionary, hiding in China's southernmost provinces of Yunnan and Kwangsi. I was a war correspondent with the United Press, covering the combat fronts of the China Burma India Theater from my base in Kunming. It was there that we met, in the tiny 10 by 16 foot room above an Indo-Chinese restaurant that served Ho as office, conference room and bedroom, when no one else was sitting on the plank platform with a straw mattress where he slept.

Quite often, when I returned from covering the war on one or another front, Ho and I had dinner together and long talks. Always eager to know what I had observed of the fighting against Japan, this tough, frail yet intense Vietnamese nationalist, who liked to smoke American cigarettes, was an engaging conversationalist -- he spoke Chinese, French, English and Russian in addition to Vietnamese. He ate sparingly and had suffered illness, especially malaria. Among modern Asian revolutionaries he was the most widely traveled and sophisticated, with the possible exception of M. N. Roy, the remarkably literate Indian communist. Our conversations were not limited to war and politics. Ho enjoyed recalling what it was like when he worked in the kitchens of London's Carlton Hotel and cooked in some of the better restaurants in Paris after he had first shipped at sea in his early twenties as a galley boy. Like some of us who had "ridden the rods" of railway box cars and lived in hobo jungles during the 1930s, Ho had seen the underside

HO CHI MINH: REVOLUTIONARY EXTRAORDINARY

of American life 20 years earlier, during World War I, and fortified his social anger.

As has been my experience with other revolutionaries before they come to power, Ho was surprisingly candid about his own earlier activities. He gave me the impression that the refusal of the "Big Four" (Vittorio Orlando of Italy, Georges Clemenceau of France, David Lloyd George of England and Woodrow Wilson of the United States), meeting in Versailles for the peace conference, to consider his lonely plea for Vietnam's independence had consequential results. When the French socialists split at the Council of Tours in 1920, Ho was prompted to join with the communists. This brought him to Moscow in 1923, where the Third International was taking shape. And it led him to join forces with the legendary American revolutionary, Michael Borodin, who headed the advisers to Sun Yat-sen in Canton in 1924-25. There Ho first met Chou En-lai, then political commissar, and Yeh Chien-ying, director of military instruction at the Whampoa, Military Academy of which Chiang Kai-shek was the commander. In this South China center of revolutionary fervor Ho trained Vietnamese cadres and sent them home with anti-French literature.

When the Chinese Nationalists and Communists split in 1927 and launched their civil war that lasted intermittently for 22 years until the Red Armies triumphed in 1949, Ho slipped out to Thailand. He found it expedient to shave his head, don the orange robe and take up a begging bowl in the guise of a Buddhist monk. Two years later he moved to Hong Kong to reorganize Vietnamese champions of independence. French intelligence agents discovered his presence and advised the British that per the extradition agreement they also shared with the Dutch in Indonesia, Ho should be arrested and handed over to them. While in the Hong Kong prison Ho was interviewed at length by a Britisher in the Special Branch, who sympathized with Vietnamese aspirations; after warning Ho what was likely to result were he delivered to the French, the Britisher enabled Ho to leave the prison on condition that he depart from the Colony. Ho got out to Shanghai, visited Russia and, after the start of the Sino-Japanese War in 1937, settled in remote Kwangsi Province, near his homeland but out of reach of the French.

France's capitulation to Hitler's conquest in June 1940 and subsequent Japanese military occupation of Indochina, while leaving the Vichyite civilian officials in place, created Ho's great opportunity. With the French weak and discredited, Ho announced creation of the Vietminh -- the date of this joining of nationalists and communists in a common struggle was 19 May 1941, Ho's 51st birthday. The Free French mostly shunned making an alliance with the Vietminh while both the Chinese Nationalists and Communists began giving him modest financial assistance. However Ho's greatest help came first from the U.S. Fourteenth Airforce. In return for helping recover their American pilots and crews downed behind Japanese lines in Indochina, Ho got radios, money and some weapons. When the American Office of Strategic Services in 1945 began preparations for a possible Allied landing in the Tongking Gulf, such assistance became even more generous.

The next time Ho and I talked was in Hanoi in the spring of 1946. Although he was now President of the Democratic Republic of Vietnam, which governed the country south to the 16th parallel, and occupying the imposing palace of the prewar French high commissioner, he was still dressed in his faded cotton bush jacket and wearing his old Chinese cloth shoes. I asked Ho why

HO CHI MINH: REVOLUTIONARY EXTRAORDINARY

he had signed the 6 March 1946 agreements with the French at Fontainbleau outside Paris, under which he agreed to remain with the French Union as conceived by General Charles de Gaulle and to allow the return to North Vietnam of the 14,000 French troops then being awaited. Ho answered that he thought long-term ties with France could prove positive and stated emphatically that it was his only protection from the Chinese — at that time Chinese Nationalist soldiers were disarming the Japanese, as had been specified in the Potsdam Declaration, and also freely looting shops. To my query about his progress in building a Vietnamese army, Ho mentioned recruiting noncommissioned officers from the Yunnan provincial regiments. These troops, often tribesman and loyal to Yunnan leaders, had been disarmed when the American-trained Chinese New First and New Sixth armies moved up the Burma Road after Japan's surrender to strengthen Chiang Xai-shek's Nationalist control in the region.

After about an hour and a half of discussion, when he had hedged several times, I stood up, thanked President Ho and remarked that when a person such as he moved into power he was less at liberty to be candid than before. Ho looked at me as he tugged at his long thin beard and answered with a smile: "I think what you say is true."

April 1946 was an uneasy time in Hanoi, as was also evidenced from conversations with the Revolutionary Journalists Association. Although the 15 August 1945 proclamation of independence had mass support, many issues were unresolved. Using British transport, the French had moved back into Saigon and southern Vietnam. In the north the communists were eliminating, sometimes by intimidation or assassination, the competing nationalist leaders. Ho very much wanted American and other Western recognition of his government and support; that the Far Eastern desk of the U.S. State Department so ignored Vietnam while the opportunity remained to shape the future is indicative of its proclivity for shortsightedness. Ho also wanted a federation of all Indochina, including South Vietnam, Cambodia and Laos.

When General Jacques Leclerc and his troops landed in Haiphong and moved on to Hanoi, suddenly the French colonials who had been hiding emerged and waved flags in anticipation of return to the old colonial order. A succession of weak governments in France proved incapable of standing by their brave wartime promises. The French High Commissioner, Admiral Thierry d'Argenlieu, who had headed the Carmalite Order yet brought along his mistress, seemed determined to restore the prewar system, especially when the Surete began to encroach upon the police functions of Ho's government. By 1947 this led to the open break with the French and their defeat at Dienbienphu in 1954. Actually, Ho's latitude for international maneuver had been exhausted by the end of 1949 when the Chinese Red Armies completed their conquest of the adjoining mainland and could "call in their chips", as they did by providing the artillery that finally defeated the French.

Ho was far too worldly wise, well read and traveled to accept crude Marxism as a valid formula for Vietnam's development. But he was trapped. Leninism — and he knew Lenin personally — when joined with teachings of Marx offered a formula for organizing and managing a revolution that could capture power and harness a people for war, and Ho used this formula. Independence and unification have been achieved but the third of Ho's goals lies ahead: Vietnam has yet to match China's new leadership that looks to pragmatic options for the better life of their people.

MISCELLANEOUS FAMILY CORRESPONDENCE

Here is a miscellaneous collection of Albert's correspondence during postwar decades with family members, professional colleagues, and friends, documenting the broad sweep of his activities and everlasting interest in helping family members in diverse ways, no matter what the problem and location. Albert's leadership and consistent help over many years surely contributed much to the successful careers and lives of his siblings.

C/O U.S. Consulate General, Hong Kong   31 August 1949

Dear Father,

I can understand it is difficult for you to appreciate how your sons can be so tardy about writing letters. But I believe that if you were on the spot in the Far East you would also realize that for someone who has to keep step with events here and report on them there is little opportunity left for writing personal letters of any kind. There is also the difficulty that once the situation has been summed up and put on paper for other purposes it is hard to sit down and rehash it into private correspondence. And yet, I do not want to write inadequate letters.

To give you a fuller appreciation of what is going on in this part of the world I am sending you copies of two newsletters I wrote for the foundation which financed my studies at Harvard University. To write such newsletters in addition to my regular correspondence demands much time and work. I usually choose as the subjects for my letters a particular situation which appears to me to have importance for the future. These newsletters are NOT for publication. But you may find satisfaction in reading them and showing them to Bill and Ingrid and other close relatives. But I think you should limit the readers to those individuals. In the Future I will from time to time send you copies of other letters as a means of answering some of the questions you raise about events in this part of the world. There are no fast and easy answers to those problems and it is important to remember that we are dealing with a country, culture and civilization entirely different from our own.

Since April my work has been hampered by trouble with my right leg. For two months during which I was in Nanking, Shanghai, Canton and Hong Kong, I took daily injections of penicillin and continued to work on crutches. I did not find the required improvement under those conditions and in June entered the Queen Mary Hospital here in Hong Kong. Six weeks of treatment there brought considerable improvement in my leg and I am now able to move about with a cane. However, I am prepared to revert to using crutches any time the leg demands it.

Within a few days I plan to leave for a trip to West China. I expect to visit Chungking, Chengtu and a number of the other places we knew during the war. It will be interesting to see the change over the years and assess present developments and trends. My address will continue to be in care of the U.S. Consulate General here in Hong Kong. Marjorie at the moment is in Taiwan. She is working as Public Information

MISCELLANEOUS FAMILY LETTERS

Officer for the Joint Commission on Rural Reconstruction. It is a joint Sino-American organization concerned

with helping Chinese farmers learn and apply some of the improved methods of agriculture developed in the United States and elsewhere. Unfortunately, because of the civil war their work is now coming to an end. The job has also helped her earn some money toward meeting our heavy expenses involved in keeping her mother with nursing care in a sanitorium.

After Otto has gotten himself well established in Japan, I intend to try and arrange a trip to that country to do some work and visit him. I may delay the trip until his wife comes out if that is in the plans. In the future I intend to be more regular in writing to you of my activities and findings. In the meantime, please know that we think of you.

Your son,   Albert (s)

PS. Hilse Ole, Kirstine og alle de andre, Din Son,

Institute Of Current World Affairs,
522 Fifth Avenue, New York 18, N.Y.

Dear Father   30 May 1951

First of all, let me wish you a happy birthday. My boy hood memories bring to mind the occasion of your birthday as one of the happier days of the year and I hope it will prove so now.

Long before now I had planned to be in California to give you an account in person of my activities, but the pressure of work has so far prevented that. As Gerda mentioned to you, she traveled out to Seattle with me in December when I was taken ill. My trouble apparently resulted from the accumulated strain of the previous several years of work in China and – particularly the pressure of events following the outbreak of the Korean *War* when several of us tried to make known the kind of information which we felt might have prevented the entry of the Chinese Communists into the Korean War. Throughout January I rested and did some writing in Seattle where Marjorie and I had purchased a house in November. Marjorie had spent the month of December fixing and furnishing the house so her mother could be moved in with two nurses and a housekeeper before Christmas.

In February just when I was on the point of leaving Seattle to join Marjorie who had returned to work in Washington, D.C., Mrs. Severyns passed away. She had suffered severely for a long time and I suspect she herself wanted to end her existence on this mortal plane. Marjorie returned from Washington as soon as the plane schedules at the time would

MISCELLANEOUS FAMILY LETTERS

permit after we had informed her that her mother had slept away. We took several weeks following the funeral to straighten out affairs. Marjorie returned to Washington, D.C. and I remained trying unsuccessfully to sell the house where after I went on to Washington after visiting in the Middle West.

Since March I have been absorbed working for our Institute first in Washington, D.C., and later traveling around the country. On behalf of the Institute I have talked to groups of students and faculty at a number of Universities. These included Columbia, Harvard, Brown and Massachusetts Institute of Technology in April. Late last month I traveled to Washington, D.C., to see Marjorie off for Formosa where she arrived on May 1st.

I have now just completed a trip which took me by way of Chicago and Minneapolis to Houston, New Orleans, back through Chicago to Toronto, Ottawa, Montreal and back to Boston where I spent last week. This letter is being written on the Eastern Shore of Maryland where I an spending some time with friends while completing some necessary writing. I have work yet to complete in Washington, D.C., Baltimore, New York and Chicago. Thereafter I am going west to Seattle and down through California enroute back to the Far East. I thought at that time I would like to come and visit. When my time schedule is more certain I will telephone. In the meantime the best address at which to reach me will be in care of Johanne in Minneapolis where I will stop on my way west.

While I was in Minneapolis at the beginning of this month we planted around Johanne's and Ernie's. Ernie and I were offered a 15-foot high basswood tree free by a nursery - if we would dig it up. This we did and also bought some raspberries and a pine to plant around their place. I am anxious now to see whether they grew. There are few things in life which give me as much satisfaction as planting trees which I believe is something I have inherited from you.

I also drove with Halvor and Rosemary, Millie and little Janna to Luck where we bought a picnic lunch and took it to Murdock Lake. I went ahead of the party and started a fire which immediately got out of hand and we spent our should-have-been-picnic fighting the blaze which we eventually brought under control thanks to a fortunate shower of rain. I had hoped we could have planted in a substantial number of small trees this year but the boys were all too busy with their individual projects and exams to take time.

We finally ate lunch at the farm and I was interested to see that the pine trees you planted northwest of the house are growing up fast. Eiler has rented out the house. The land we rented out last fall on conditions which require that the renter apply fertilizer as well as lime to the land. My hope is that even if the farm does not bring in any cash return in excess of taxes it at least will be steadily improved in quality. I would like to see the open piece on the south forty plowed, limed, fertilized and seeded to a good stand of hay and pasture.

My friend with whom I am staying has to hurry into town to see his young daughters last day of school ceremonies. So I will close this now with the best of wishes for the coming year and the hope that you may have many more happy birthdays.

                                    Your son,

                                            Albert

c/o United States Embassy,   26 May 1953
Manila, Philippine Islands

Dear Father,

    As the time approaches for your birthday it brings a flood of boyhood memories; of a Wisconsin spring warming into summer, corn fields beginning to
show with green rows, and relatives and friends coming to visit for coffee, playing horseshoes, good talk and singing. It was always an occasion which I anticipated with excitement, greatly enjoyed and was sorry to see end, when the time came to milk the cows in the evening. Although we now are all so widely dispersed, I hope that this year you may have the warm feeling of good company and friends and relatives at your birthday time. Also I much hope that you may have many more birthdays to come and that we can so arrange affairs that we can again share some of them,

    My work, as usual, keeps me more than busy. During this year in the Far East I will visit Hongkong, Formosa, Jppan and possibly several other countries, but my first concern is to gain a useful insight into events here in the Philippines. I have known these Islands in a passing way before; I visited here briefly when I sailed through before the war, returned as a war correspondent in 1945, and have come back on three other visits prior to this trip, But never before did I spend enough time here to gain a sense of motional exchange with the Filipinos. This time I am discovering the kind of human beings they are 'beneath the surface', and I like them more with each passing experience. Compared to the Chinese or the Indians with their great traditions of civilization and learning the Filipinos lack cultural depth and a high development of the critical faculties of evaluation. Neither the nearly four hundred years of Spanish rule with its heavy emphasis on the introduction of the Catholic Church nor the half century of American administration has fully remade these people. And beneath these cultural overlays the Filipinos are still a Malay people made more ambitious and alert to the rest of the world by American education.

    Much of this is evident in their love for politics. I am enclosing a copy of a report I did recently for the AUFS which examines some of these recent events. You are welcome to show it in the family but it should not be passed to outsiders. I thought you and Uncle Ole might enjoy discussing it.

    I had an opportunity to look briefly inside our own politics recently when I went up to Hongkong to meet Adlai Stevenson and his party. I had been asked to help them gather some of the information they needed and that enabled me to meet with Stevenson and his assistants several times, I flew back to Manila with them and saw them off for

MISCELLANEOUS FAMILY LETTERS

Indo-China, where I was unable to go along because my French visa was delayed.

Stevenson is an exceptionally able and attractive person and he gathers around himself as assistants men of similar quality. The Governor has a humanity rare among the political leaders I have met at home and abroad. I am satisfied that we have witnessed only the beginning of his performance as a national leader in America. Although he and his associates bring to the Democratic Party some high quality talents the job that confronts them in rebuilding the Party in the United States and giving it the Ideas that can be meaningful in terms of the needs of the last half of this century will demand long and painstaking effort. I am increasingly convinced that our old concept of politics and to some extent the organization of our political parties is not adequate to enable us to measure up to the responsibilities for international leadership that now are ours I intend to devote some efforts toward study and writing in this field.

Otto has probably written you as he did me that this spring he planted more than 6,000 trees on the farm at Luck. I hope that next year we can set out an even larger number of trees as we accumulate experience and improved planting methods. In time it should give us two things; a growing timber stand on otherwise nonproductive land and meanwhile Christmas trees that can
be taken out for sale. If we are to extend our tree growing enterprise we will need more land. If you have any suggestions I wish you would pass them on to Otto. You should take some satisfaction from realizing that the ideas you instilled in us as boys regarding the worth of trees and the satisfaction you taught us to take from nature are now bearing fruit.

The mail for the United States closes shortly and I must now take this to the post office. When you have the opportunity to write I would like to hear of your work and learn your address. Meanwhile, I am sending this in care of Les and Nanna. Please give my very best to them and all our other good relatives and friends. And may your days be bright with sunshine, mellow wisdom and humor,

Your son,

Albert

Where Albert Ravenholt and eight brothers and sisters were born and lived until April 1935.

Ansgar Ravnholt riding in farmyard, Milltown, Wisconsin

MISCELLANEOUS FAMILY LETTERS

                                  Litton Apartments, 6-B
                                  1219 L. Guerrero, Ermita
                                  Manila, Philippines
                            (Mail address; c/o U.S.Embassy)

Dear Reimert,   July 27, 1958

In the Science News Letter, Time and most recently through a too short mention n the Saturday Evening Post, I have followed your public health campaign on hospital infection. There is mention recently of a new antibiotic which to this layman appears effective against the disease you have been warning the hospitals to guard against. Does this mean the problem is solved? What is your next focus of research? You will make a far more worthy mark in the long haul by staying home and tending to your scientific investigations than by traveling around the country giving talks even to learned groups--take it from me.

Your letters of June 28d and 22nd were most welcome. Periodically. I become lonesome for my family and such letters give a special pleasure. I am delighted to learn not only about family activities but also the community and friends. It is as well that you did not go to Pakistan-- save that trip until such time as we can make it together. There is much to learn about finding your way about in this corner of the world and you may as well profit from my experience. Marjorie is recently back from better than a month in Pakistan, India, Burma, Thailand and Vietnam. She found Pakistan the least attractive of the lands where she visited and assembled--strictly for your private knowledge--information for the Ramon Magsaysay Awards to be given here come the 31st of August. Its the program on which you may recall that I was working with the Rockefellers last year and in my spare time on this tour to the Philippines it has taken added attention. I have recently written urging John Rockefeller, 3rd. and his attorney, Don MoLean,Jr., to accept the invitations to come, extended to them by the Filipino board who want their presence for the ceremonies. The AUFS headquarters in New York was supposed to send you my reports and I am writing to remind them.

I am glad to know from you that the farm in Luck is proving a pleasant and satisfying home for the family--no one else has written me a word. What has become of Father? Did he go to Denmark or not and Why? What do you mean by Eiler's ventures in Minnesota politics? My suits at home are well packed away and it is difficult to get at them now. But if you will send me more exact information I will have one made out here for Halvor. Since she arrived in Europe I have had one letter from Astrid. Like you I do hope this trip proves thoroughly satisfying. But essentially I do not feel she will find fulfillment without a creatively demanding profession and she has medicine in her being. You are the one who can guide and encourage her to study medicine and I hope you do. I do not know how to reach her in Europe and leave you to take the initiative.

MISCELLANEOUS FAMILY LETTERS

Please do set me straight on Otto. You once made passing mention of his coming to Seattle and he referred to it on his graduation card. But that is all the information I have. What is he doing and are we still required to underwrite him financially as you indicated last spring? I want from Otto promptly a detailed statement of my financial relationship with him and would appreciate your assistance in securing it. As of now I do not know where I stand on this matter and funds will be needed for Astrid as well as for my own purposes. I am delighted that Alex got the ten acres and wish you would get the 20 acres with the old farm to the southwest of it on Bainbridge. But perhaps you had better wait and negotiate with my Filipino tenants after the end of sunny weather this fall.

I sent Alec a check for the Inertia, Inc. payment and hope the cash coming to me from the 25 acres Bill Herdman sold will meet payments for some time on the 80 acres in which I understood you wanted a share.

If the Eisenhower-Dulles team pulls more adventuaes like their most recent one in the Middle East, keep an eye on our Bainbridge farm. In any event fire up the stove to burn off the rust. Hedderly-Smith who owns the 80 acres to the northwest is unfriendly, as you may remember I mentioned. But Berg who lives just across the road is a Dane and cooperative. If the fruit trees are getting dry, please ask Jerry Trask to take care of watering them.

My love to you, Millie and the family.   Albert

A. RAVENHOLT   June 28, 1959
Raffles Hotel, Singapore

Dear Halvor, Eiler, Reimert and Otto,

The other evening as I returned from cabling an article and paid off my taxi in front of the hotel that supplies its guests with this stationary, I was enthusiastically accosted out of the dark. It was my old friend Dr. Alec McFadzean, professor of medicine at the University of Hongkong. He introduced me to hiis companion Dr. Gordon Ransome, the professor of medicine at the university of Malaya, in Singapore. After a bit of urging they gladly joined me for a drink on the hotel's open veranda.

It is customary for Chinese and those who have lived among them to exchange greeting cards when they make a new acquaintance and Dr. Ransome and I did so after we had settled into our chairs. Alec and I had been catching up on each others recent activities when Dr. Ransome interrupted by touching my sleeve and saying, "You know, you and I have the same name. Where did you come from?" After explaining that I grew up on a

MISCELLANEOUS FAMILY LETTERS

Wisconsin farm but now lived on Pudget Sound, I was interrupted by the impatient doctor who wanted to know where our family originated. "'We're Scandinavians," I answered and he smiled. According to the good doctor who evidently has made a hobby study of these matters in his spare time, the names in England and now in America, throughout the Comonwealth, etc. , that begin with Raen, Ran, Rand, Raven, or Ravn, have a common root and trace to the same clan. Most are descended he said from the Danish vikings who invaded England and settled in East Anglia during the nineth century. Others such as our direct ancestors remained longer in Denmark or returned home from their foraging expeditions abroad. The home, some, olph, holt and possibly other endings on the original clan name were appended usually to indicate a holding of land, the spelling having been modified over the centuries. Upon returning to Manila I checked in the Encyclopaedia Britannica and find that Danes under Ragnar Lookbrok's sons Ivarr and Ubbi captured the. kingdom of East Anglia in 870. Their rule was succeeded by that of the Danish king Guthrum. But in 921 the Danes of East Anglia submitted to King Edward the Elder. Now I do not propose that any of us should go out and announce ourselves as relatives eleven centuries removed of Peyton Randolph, President of the first American Congress. But it is intriguing to consider what the clan has been up to since its members began wandering out of Denmark carrying the figure of a raven on their viking standards and coat of arms.

As we parted at the hotel the good doctor remarked, "Remember, it was the fools who could not get along at home that left first." And I countered, "Or those who had more imagination and initiative." Father, mother, and our sisters will probably enjoy this bit of family lore. So I will depend upon each of you to share it, but not with outsiders.

With cordial wishes to each of you,

Albert

AMERICAN PRESIDENT LINES

Aboard S.S. President Wilson
Albert Ravenholt

My dear Reimert, June 14, 1960

Now that I am well into Sandburg's "The Prairie Years" I understand why you felt this was vital reading and appreciate even more your thoughtfulness in prodding me and also the gift of the set. Certainly, as I sort over what these years meant for Lincoln--and nights at sea can be well used for thinking--there is increasing substance to support the contention that only his times alone and certain melancholy traits that encouraged this gave the struggling lawyer that extra dimension of human depth. Where and how in our modern urban life does a man find opportunities for such contemplation? that in our experience can match the encouragement to contemplation of driving in a buggy down a country road one day after the next? We boys are fortunate that our youth had just enough of this being alone with nature so we know what it is all

MISCELLANEOUS FAMILY LETTERS

about. But for the future perhaps we should institutionalize opportunities for doing this. And a farm or cabin in the hills could well serve as an ashram where we could better come to know the value of our own experience, and have fun in the process.

This voyage has been routine to date. There was less time between train and ship in San Francisco the morning of the eighth than I had allowed for since the snip sailed on Daylight Saving Time; Aboard the train for breakfast I met Jack Churchill and wife an attractive and I suspect able couple, he a Littauer graduate at Harvard, who had worked for Senator Morse in Oregon until his presidential primary defeat. Keep him in mind since he might be helpful in Washington. The next morning our ship docked in Los Angeles. I hitched a ride with Les Brown and wife--an attractive band leader-- to their Santa Monica home, rented a Hertz U-Drive car and drove to Pasadena and Cal Tech. Hallett Smith who heads the humanities work there and several of his scholarly associates are considering a project to case US economic aid abroad and I feel this could fruitfully be a joint effort with AUFS. Much good talk with some friendly, first rate people and I stayed the night with David and Nancy Elliott.

Marjorie is working very hard handling both the Rockefeller Brothers Fund work for the Magsaysay Awards and the Century 21 project for whom she has done a superb job in helping enlist participation by such governments as those of Vietnam and Ceylon.

Alec said when I discussed Stavis Bay with him on the phone last night that he understood Father is returning to Los Angeles today. I hope his visit in Seattle proved as restorative as seemed indicated when I left. I would like one copy each of the shoppers published by Alec's friend.

Please send me in Manila three sets of Carl Sandburg's biography of Abraham Lincoln like the one you gave me. These are to be presents for several Filipino friends. My address for the next several weeks will be in care of the American Consulate General, Hongkong. After that I will return to Manila.

My affectionate greetings to you, the family and our good friends.

Albert

MISCELLANEOUS FAMILY LETTERS

Litton Apartments, 6-B,
1219 L. Guerrero, Ermita
Manila, Philippines

19 July 1961

My dear Reimert,

Your good letter written from New York on July 13th has just arrived. It certainly would be a joy to explore Europe together with you, but that will have to wait. Meanwhile, just a word of caution. Until you get the "feel" for a new setting such as you are moving into, go slow and look before you move, be sure of your methods of transportation and the people you depend upon to do things, even in handling your baggage. While appearances may seem amiliar, remember that the premises from which people act may be entirely different than those you are accustomed to expect.

Were I you then I would definitely keep the family at home in the U.S. until the Berlin issue is resolved, since the signs point to the possibility that this time the crisis may be pushed further than before. When you bring them to Europe it would seem to me from this distance that they would be more safely situated in Copenhagen than Paris, although you can best judge this on the spot.

Marjorie and I found enough cash to meet the payment on Inertia, Inc., and sent Alec Bayless a check for the sum with a note to return your advance for me in case it had arrived. Thanks anyway. As regards anything you would want me to do for your children, I would be glad to be of all possible use, but trust that the need will not arise.

It is too early yet to judge whether the logging venture will be a success; I look upon it as a long shot. Meanwhile, we are putting up a few rough buildings on the Negros Cacao Plantation, Ltd., land at Tambo, where the logging company camp also is located. Am also planting various kinds of tropical fruit trees, etc. This is primarily experimental at this stage, but should afford a rural hideaway in the event that urban centers become target areas. It is only 60 miles to Dumaguete which is a quiet, attractive town with a good hospital at Siliman University, a missionary supported institution.

When my book is completed I will make one or two trips to neighboring countries, but this is a presidential election year in the Philippines and we have much to write about. Carl Mydans of Life who is an old friend was here during the MacArthur visit. And now Teddy and Nancy White have just been through on a trip to escape the demands of the success of his new book on the presidency. And I am determined to learn to write as effectively.

Take care of yourself,

Love,   Albert

MISCELLANEOUS FAMILY LETTERS

USS OKLAHOMA CITY
Enroute Keelung, Formosa to Hongkong   9 April 1962

Dear Reimert,

Just a note as we are sailing into Hongkong Harbor after a pleasant cruise from Northeastern Formosa down through the Formosan Strait. This is the flag ship of the U.S. Soventh Fleet, which includes about another 124 naval ships, some 65,000 men, etc. spread from northern Japan to the waters of Southeast Asia. Recently, I was out on amphibious maneuvers with units of this fleet and marines off Mindoro Island in the Western Philippines. Then I made an appointment with vice admiral William Schoech, Commanding US Seventh Fleet, to make a trip with him so there would be time for leisurely talks. After finishing some work in Manila, I flew with the US Airforce from Central Luzon to southern Formosa, took the train to Taipeh in northern Formosa and then boarded this ship in the port of Keelung.

On a trip such as this it gives me time to think and I have been speculating on what you may be doing, trying to visualize you operating and living in Europe and wishing it were possible for me to visit with you there. Originally, I had planned to visit Europe this summer enroute home to the US; next September I am starting again on the university lecture tour. But the amount of work to be done hereabouts, personal ventures to attend to in the Philippines and my concern with seeing the World Fair in Seattle probably will preclude a visit to Europe this time. Just now our ship has sailed through the gate between the rocks that marks the entrance to Hongkong harbor. As the admiral's flag ship we are taking the salute of a US aircraft carrier and perhaps ten smaller US ships that also are in the harbor. Shortly we will tie up alongside and I will go ashore., hoping to find hotel accomodations so I can settLe in and write a series of articles from here.

It is a year ago last January that I was last in Hong Kong. My preoccupation with writing that book for the Asia Society entitled THE PHILIPPINES: A YOUNG REPUBLIC ON THE MOVE and the presidential elections in the Philippines that brought a now administration to power have kept me occupied. Both the AUFS and the Chicago Daily News have been anxious for me to get out and travel, so now that Marjorie has flown back to Seattle to get the Asian participants in the WorldS Fair settled in it seemed an appropriate opportunity to got out and move around.

This letter will need to be completed after I get ashore since we are now tying up alongside the British Naval Dock and I must get packed.

Albert

                              Litton Apartments, 6-B
1219 L. Guerrero, Ermita
Manila, Philippines   6 May 1962

My dear Reimert,

There was so much to do in Hongkong and I was in bed for several days with a bout of loose bowels, that I did not get to finish the letter enclosed which was started as we were finishing the cruise with the flagship of the U.S. Seventh Fleet in the Formosa Straits. My Chicogo Daily News story on that said in essence that Kennedy's place in the history books could depend substantially more on what he did or did not do in the Formosa Straits than upon what happened in the Bay of Pigs off Cuba. This relates to the unquestioned great dissatisfaction on the mainland of China and the Chinese Nationalist announcements on Formosa that the time is getting ripe for them to attempt a return to the mainland. The refugees in Hongkong who had come out from the mainland of China leave me with the impression that a few peasants and former Chinese businessmen under the Communists may see a little hope in Chiang Kai-shek, but the Chinese intellectuals and professionals do not want him back, much as they fear and detest the Communists.

Here in Manila where I arrived aboard one of the American President Line freighters, SS President Madison, I found your note of 7 March with the enclosed copy of your paper read at Detroit and your pleasant card from Marseille. I am glad you enjoyed the south of France and that the children were intrigued with the Chateau D'if. Yes, I do remember well being there in 1940. It was spring and I tried to enlist in the American ambulance corps that was working with the French and British armies behind the Maginot Line. But before my application could go through, Hitler's armies broke through the low countries and moved in on Paris and all French resistance was collapsing. One night we were bombed in the harbor - not our ship but others around - and I stood on deck and watched the firey display of the tracer bullets from the bombing planes and the anti-aircraft guns before deciding it was better to be shielded below by the steel deck plates. I remember the crew coming back aboard telling how several of them had been in a cat house in bed with the girls when the bombing shook the roof so it fell in on them. Before leaving Marseille I bought a suit case full of French liquers some of which in time was carried all the way to west China and the final bottle given to a friend in Kunmming who had been my host. From there we sailed to the southeast coast of Spain, still showing the scars of civil war and then on down the Atlantic coast of Africa. I am sure you found it all much more attractive now.

Have also just found here the note from Halvor reporting the birth of a new daughter, Sue Ellen. I am delighted that he is keeping up the production line at home. But when will you and Millie turn out another of your wonderful products. You know that I depend upon you to make up for me and that requires at least several more.

I will consider it a great favor should you buy for me the two volume work "Traite d'Acupuncture" par Docteur Roger de la Fuye, published by Librairie Ecole Francois, 91 Boulevard Saint-Germain, Paris, second edition 1956. Also, any information you can get from Doctor J. C. de Tymowski, the director of the Centre de Massotherapie chinoise, 62 Rue Saint-Lazare, Paris IXe; M. Georges MARTIN, 16 rue Petel, Paris XVe, or the Secretary of the Societe Francaise d'Acupuncture, 8 Avenue Franklin-Roosevelt, Paris VIIIe, will be appreciated. When you dig up these materials they should be shipped to the U.S. so I can get them there next winter. Please do not let yourself be prejudiced by your views on the arts of the orient. There is much in it that is of interest.

Many of the indications do support Steffanson's observations in his book "Cancer: A Disease of Civilization?" and the book you so kindly secured for me, "Cancer, Nature, Cause and Cure" by Alexander Berglas of the Institute Pasteur, Paris. If I told you the extent of my list of "patients" you probably would shake your head in distress. They include some such as an Asian ambassador to Peking who met me in Hongkong, Pir Ali Muhammed Rashdi of Pakistan, who is interested in related work in their inherited traditions of the healing arts. But best that you say nothing of this to anyone except Otto and when we all are together we can talk it through thoroughly.

I am glad that you saw the Bayanihan Dance Troupe of the Philippines in Paris. They are due in Seattle in July. Now you will appreciate better the products and possibilities of hybrid vigor and know why I believe that the Spanish priests also made a considerable ethnic contribution to the future of this country. When the great Spanish scholar who now is out of favor with Franco, Don Salvador de Madariaga was here last December for the Jose Rizal Centeniary he spoke on this in his "Reflections on Colonialism" mentioning the creative "tension in the blood" that results. And much of our American vitality I am convinced can be traced to just this fact.

In the event that you have not done so already, do buy the March 27th issue of Look magazine and read Bill Worden's articles on politics in the Pacific Northwest. I know that you probably would like to see the Fair. But remember that most of the buildings will still be there when you get home and our mutual interests are of a more permanent nature. Just make certain that you learn everything possible about European politics and keep a file folder of ideas that may later be useful.

How are you fixed for cash? We are buying another 240 acres to add to the plantation at Tambo in Negros. I have been collecting several varieties of dwarf coconuts that bear nuts in three to four years as contrasted with the normal type that bear in seven to eight years and making trial plantings of these. Also, am continuing to plant tropical fruit trees. Meanwhile, we are renting the land to a group that is experimenting with planting castor beans. It gives insignificant income, but does mean that the land is being developed. Castor beans as you may know are poisonous, but the oil has an increasing number of industrial uses, including synthetic fibers. And I reason that eventually if all of these experiments prove less than promising we can plant the area to improved tropical pasture and raise cattle. The Philippines is a major importer of meat and dairy products. One or two of the best recent French publications on tropical agriculture would be handy to have. In Hongkong I met a French couple who had been managing a 12,000 acre rubber plantation in Cambodia. His yields of three tons of rubber per hectare of 2.47 acres is the highest I have heard of with the near selected strains of rubber. That stock in the Malayan rubber plantation I sold when we bought Inertia, Inc., is now quoted at three times the price it was then.

MISCELLANEOUS FAMILY LETTERS

That timber venture continues to absorb all the cash we can find. Will write you when we see how it works out. Meanwhile, I would appreciate if you do not mention to my friends these several interests since it is best to proceed quietly with such matters.

Several friends have been directed to look you up. Emilio Yap's wife Lydia and her mother and god mother will be in Paris this summer and may call upon you. He continues to be a staunch friend and I will appreciate anything you can do for them. Tarzie Vittachi, former editor of the Ceylon Observer and now the Asian Representative of the International Press Institute is going to Europe about now and may look in. He keeps trying to figure me out, much as I enjoy him and I will be curious to learn if you two meet up.

Do take care of yourself and make time for reading.

My love to you, Millie, and the youngsters,   Albert

1302 Seneca Street
Seattle, Washington   19 January 1963

Dear Reimert,

Your welcome letter of January 10th was waiting here when I returned this afternoon from lecturing at California Institute of Technology. Your kind comments about the modest book are appreciated, as are your ideas. Writing is a demanding labor and this is only a beginning, but it has whetted my interest in trying what can be done. I only wish you were here so we could talk through alternatives and fix our aim. The Puget Sound region is much more fun when you are around.

One gets the impression at a distance that you and yours are acquiring a rather high-level and delightful introduction to all that Europe has to offer. But do be cautious, especially when traveling. I was concerned during the holidays when you had written of the projected trip and we had news of the winter storms. I would like to know whether you feel this increasingly comfortable European society will be capable of producing individuals with the moral and physical stamina that leadership requires. Several of my friends who have a depth of experience in Europe and affection for those lands have recently returned, heartened by the evident postwar recovery and
discouraged by a snug reluctance to face and accept a larger responsibility. Your offer to buy us a Mercedes Benz is much appreciated. But at this stage such an expensive car is beyond my ready cash, both as to purchase and the customs duty demanded for import into the Philippines. I am looking here now for a second-hand car dealer that I chanced to meet in the University District, promised to find one that will do.

Regarding Inertia Inc., it does not look practical as something to be done now or a means to raising ready cash. Alec and I have been over there to scout the possibilities. The supermarket has not made another bid and they were the principal cash customer that so far has shown an interest. All sold together the lots might bring an extra $1,000 each above what we paid for them. But this would have to be on contract sale from which we might expect at most 25 percent down and one-half of this would go for real estate commissions.

Ed and Carl seem inclined to sit tight without increasing expenditures and seek to sell lots that can be disposed of at a fair price on the fringe mostly to the west while we keep the group to the east. Alec feels we might put up a well-designed modest apartment house on two or three lots in the name of another corporate entity. But doing so will require buying several lots interspersed among ours which means cash. And then the construction must be financed and managed. I feel Alec's idea is sound when we have cash and time to manage it. Meanwhile, the general project should benefit from the closure of the shipyard which was bought by Sam Clarke and associates. They hope to start a yacht club while Jerry Trask's brother is trying to put in a marina there. Much depends upon the Washington State Ferry System and whether they will install another terminal, etc.

As concerns your payments this year, please write me in New York soonest and indicate whether you want me to get Otto and or Ernie to make these payments. My own cash situation is tight since I not only need to meet obligations here and in the Philippines but am just now trying to find money to buy back the half interest sold several years ago in the Fragaria land. Griff Way had some
forestry people appraise that piece for tree growing and they came out with a figure significantly below the price at which I sold.

So buying them out seems the only sound way of solving the problem even though it costs me both cash and the money I already have paid to the Bureau of Internal Revenue. When I do have the money I want to find a piece of land and join with others to build an apartment house here in Seattle wherein we each can own one.

Enroute south to Cal Tech I stopped for a visit with Paul and Agnes; she is well following a miscarriage. Both are doing nicely although Paul after having made a success of his parish is seeking broader horizons. He has an interest in politics from which Agnes so far has discouraged him and you could help counter this. Certainly, Claifornia is on the way to becoming the bellweather of American politics. Saw Father both Wednesday at Ingrid's and again Thursday when we went over to the Harold Sorensen's for dinner before I took the train. He has his heart set on going to Europe, preferably this summer while you still are there. He suggested flying over and coming back on the ship with you. This, I discouraged, saying you would be busy packing and if he went a visit with you he should come earlier. He would like to be in Denmark in June and early July. I left it that I would write for your views.

Assuming that we can raise the cash for his ticket and his health continues as it now is, this would appear to be the time. Although apparently well, he has faded. Ingrid feels the trip would do him good; it would give him ideas and experiences to live on now that other satisfactions are ebbing. We are much indebted to Bill and Ingrid particularly for being so considerate as they are, and I want to do something for them. Bill dreams of some day having a boat. I mentioned

MISCELLANEOUS FAMILY LETTERS

the possibility that he, you and I might manage one together here on Puget Sound when you return, which appealed to him greatly.

You were most considerate to buy me the Danish book and the two on acupuncture in French. Enclosed is a check for fifty dollars to cover same. This week before leaving for Indiana University I am putting a door and windows in the half basement on Bainbridge Island. Since Marjorie does not want to live over there while I am out of town this probably will remain a camping out place. But for that it should be fun and you and yours can also go over there when you are home.

Your estimate of the Kennedy administration's performance in Europe is one I would value. In Washington DC I saw Ed and Jo and lunched with him and his boss. Among us I do not share Ed's fine enthusiasm for this team, At least as regards Asia, they talk so much better than they do; the Peace Corps is the only major distinction there between this administration and its predecessor. Possibly, I expect too much. But I am certainly glad to have heeded Otto's advice in 1960 and not become entangled in government. There are times when I feel that with our private efforts in the Philippines and neighboring areas our little fraternity accomplishes as much as the government with all of its huge and nearly unused resources. Will your new position at the University here afford you an opportunity to come to the Far East? It would be fun to have you out for a smell of Asia.

Eiler is getting a liberal education in Washington, DC, and whetting his appetite for politics. But clearly money is increasingly essential to such ventures and since we did not inherit or marry such we will first have to make it. So please try and keep your standard of living simple and leave a bit to spare. I know that at a certain stage one may have a yen to indulge oneself. But later you will realize that much you bought was really of little use and the expenditure served primarily as a psychological exercise. Also, luxurious living tends to encourage envy, which is hardly ever useful. There is a most valuable self-discipline that results from deliberately curbing appetites one could satisfy.

Father proudly carries around the fine pictures you sent him and treasures all the consideration shown. We had fun discussing the map from Jutland you sent me and others. While Europe clearly has given you and your family additional perspective I feel you are sound in returning now to the Pacific Northwest. So save your energies and thoughts for what is to be done here. During the holidays we attended a meeting of the Metropolitan Democratic. Club at Stim Bulletts house. Many of your friends asked with interest, when you are returning and I avoided giving a direct answer. But it's evident you have a place here and there is much that awaits our efforts.

Affectionately,   Albert

GENEVA DIPLOMAT
Editor and Publisher J. Pizurki
42 Vermont Parc, Geneva, Switzerland
(John Pizurki was a co-worker with Albert at World's Fair in 1939)

Estimado Companero: 5 May 1970

Delighted! Your letter triggered off a flood of nostalgic memories of the golden haze of my youth. There we were two aspiring Globetrotters of the same Poorman's Richard Halliburton pod. Ah, the exuberance of life when one is 21.

Intermittently, I was able to ferret out peripheral items about you from Commissioner Innoncio Ferrer. Last November, the Madame Chairman of the UN Population Conference here , a female barrister named ?Esposito? from Manila, promised to convey my respects to you. I discovered later that your brother had attended this conference also but had departed before I became aware of his presence here.

Your reference to "a pace that suits one after 50" brought a lump to my throat since it forced me to realize the reality that I am also more than 50. Somehow, I can't visualize you being other than the 21-year-old youth I was privileged to know from the heartland of America (Luck, Wis,) full of hiss and vinegar, on the royal road around the world. Last summer I stood again on the corner of Canal Street and the Bowery, adjacent to Chinatown and searched for the eight clocks which once showed the time in the various areas of the world. They were no longer there. Neither were you but your spirit in my memory was. Recall the elation with which we regarded them in '39, both convinced that the greatest thing in the world was to go out and discover it.? Unlike many of our contemporaries we did just that. I have never come across anyone in my early life who had made such an imprint on me as you had. In you I found a spiritual brother who was as cursed as I was with the curse of the wanderlust. Do you remember the last supper we had on that terrasse that stormy autumn day of '39? You procured two chickens from unauthorized sources as well as the vintage wine. Remember the tenor of our conversation? I recall telling you: "Wonder where we will be 30 years from now?

Update you about myself after our trails separated. VE Day I was assigned to Cornell for a Russian Refresher Course. What a beautiful spot. I recall the winter of '46 at Chanute Field where a newspaper woman friend handed me a UP Telex stating that the famous war correspondent A.R. was marrying a girl from the spook outfit. Subsequently, spent a year at Monterey, California, studying Russian at the Army Language School. Remained on active duty until the Korean War, the duration of which, fortunately, I was assigned to Germany. I came across your article in Foreign Affairs in Frankfurt. Magnifico, companero!

On demobilization I looked about for the Ideal Spot as defined by Plato, an ideal city with not more than 250,000 inhabitants. Geneva fits that definition admirably. Met Thien at the Graduate Institute of International Studies here. Learned more from Thien than I did from any of the professors. My wife is mentioned in the forward of his book since she edited his doctorate. Currently, wife is employed as editor at the World Health Organization. Daughter Berinda, 23, is attending my and Thien's alm mater. Tamara, 21, attends Ecole des Arts Decoratif here -- when I selected the name for my newly born 23 years ago my WASP, racist, Superior in the Army considered it a subversive one. Lara, my joie de vie, attends the Swiss public school, is completely bilingual. (Ever come across Admiral Rickover's book: "The Swiss Schools are Better than Ours")?

Thien must have used deductive logic to arrive at the image he conveyed to you why I hadn't returned to the Land of the Free and Home of the Brave. Primo, I find the nonprofit ambiance of the United Nations Specialized Agencies specifically suited to my personality. Secundo, educating two grown daughters on a university echelon in the States would bankrupt me. Here the costs are about one-tenth of those in USA. But, Amigo, I love the land of my birth. I risked my life for it in two wars and would do it again. I have been searching for the Ideal Spot most of my life. Finally, I found it, in my own back yard. Last year I saw the sunrise over the Blue Knob from my Dad's farm on the crest of the Alleganies. It intoxicated me more than the sunrise I saw from Darjeeling of Mt Everest. My last testament is that if something should happen to me I want my ashes strewn among the mountain laurels over the Blue Knob where I was raised. The reaction of Berinda, the executor of my last testament: "Why pollute the Blue Knob environment?

My guru still remains Henry David Thoreau. Simplify, always simplify your life. I have no vehicle but my daughter does. I carry no watch, but my youngest Lara does. I have never been afraid of the gutter, the experiences of my youth there have taught me the warm places one can find even in the gutter.

Recent feature of mine on "Mao's Mayflies over Albania" was translated in five languages -- striving for Second Strike Nuclear Capability with medium range missiles on six mobile missile sites, etc. Source: Albanian refugees in Montenegro and Macedonia. I learned to speak Serbo-Croat working with Jugs in Pennsylvania coal mines. In the Army, chaperoned the first military mission sent by Tito to the States after the break with Stalin

MISCELLANEOUS FAMILY LETTERS

I note your interest in farming remains unabated. I recall the Future Farmers of America belt buckle you wore when we rode the rods together. Never have I witnessed such expertise, not even among experienced railroad bindle stiffs, as you demonstrated when you lunged at that speeding freight train on that regrettable day of our parting on the banks of the Mississippi.

I believe it was Innoncio who mentioned in August praise your tome on land reform. Thien also referred to it. Thien awards you practically all the credit for the Taiwan Land Reform Scheme. Jacques Marcuse disdains your contribution. This Ignoramus is pawning himself off as a Sinologist during his current lecture tour in your land and mine. I queried the UN Book Store manager here on the number of copies sold of Jacques "Peking Papers". Reply: Four. At the '54 Geneva Conference I tangled with Gunther Stein about the merits of your talent. Both he and Israel Epstein considered you in doctrinaire terms. Is Epstein still in prison? I warned Epstein at the '62 Lao Conference here that Kang Shang would make a scape goat of him one day when it suited his purpose. Edgar Snow is ailing. He just acquired some modest property up the Lake. Shares my high regard for you.

Is it still "Breakfast-in Bed-Ravenholt"? as it was at the Hotel Marina, room 29, 27 years ago, Bearer, Jaldi hai? I was in Delhi several years ago and stayed at our old stamping ground, the Marina. I looked for faces I knew wouldn't be there. I was significantly looking to see yours. Thomas Wolfe was correct, You Cannot Go Back Home Again.

So, Amigo, here we are both of us in the first month of the autumn of our lives. When it finally strikes midnight I want to be in a position to say that I've had no regrets because I had lived.

Por favor, estimado companero, do write. Even though a thousand mountains and rivers separate us, one day you and I will meet again.

Insh'Allah! Salaams to Mensahib
of the OSS.

Ruefully, John

Albert with friend Carl Mydans on shoulders awaiting

return of Gen. MacArthur to the Philippines, 1961

THE SEATTLE TIMES   SATURDAY, MAY 30, 1992

OBITUARY

From Asia To Seattle, People Felt The Presence Of Marjorie Ravenholt

by Dave Birkland
Times staff reporter

FROM SUNNYSIDE, a small farming community near Yakima, Marjorie Severyns Ravenholt's life and interests took her all over the world.

She was a reporter in China for Life Magazine, an intelligence officer during World War II in Asia, an Asian representative for the Seattle's World Fair, as well as a friend and associate of the famous and wealthy Rockefeller family. To name just a few things.

Mrs. Ravenholt, 71, died Monday May 25 in Swedish Hospital from complications following surgery for lung cancer.

"She was in the midst of about as much as you can be," said her husband, Albert Ravenholt, a retired newspaper foreign correspondent, who met his wife while both were working in Asia. They were married Jan. 28, 1946, in Shanghai and had their honeymoon in Peking, now known, as Beijing.

Mrs. Ravenholt had worked with American efforts to try to mediate between the Nationalist and Communist forces who were involved in the Chinese civil war. "It was a hectic time in China in those years," Albert Ravenholt recalled. At that point, he was the bureau chief for United Press International in China.

"I'll always remember that the Chinese Communist army gave us a royal reception because I was the only foreigner who had been to Meishien, the home town of the Chinese Marshal Yen Chien-Ying," Albert Ravenholt recalled.

Betty Ravenholt remembers her sister-in-law for her style and intelligence. "Throughout her life she has continued to be a person who exuded sophistication, both intellectually and personally," she said. "It was a source of great interest and pride for the rest of the family to follow Albert and Marjorie's adventures in life and hear about their friends and acquaintances. We felt through them we were in contact with a much larger world," Betty Ravenholt said, "They were among the intellectual elite of the country," she added.

Mrs. Ravenholt's grandfather settled in the lower Yakima Valley in the Rattlesnake Hills about 1900 after living in California. Mrs. Ravenholt graduated from Sunnyside High School in 1937 and then went to the University of Washington, where she studied political science, international law and history.

In 1940, Mrs. Ravenholt traveled to Japan, China and Korea as an exchange student. While at the UW, Mrs. Ravenholt took an intense interest in Asian affairs, and she came under the influence of the late Dr. Charles Martin, head of the political science department, and Dr. George Taylor, retired, who founded the Far Eastern and Russian institutes at the university, her husband said.

After receiving her degree here in 1941, Mrs. Ravenholt received a fellowship to attend Fletcher School of Law and Diplomacy in Massachusetts, where she received a master's degree in international law and diplomacy. When she graduated from Fletcher, Mrs. Ravenholt went to work for the federal Board of Economic Warfare, which was dedicated to buying up strategic material, such as rubber from Brazil, so it would not fall into the hands of the Axis powers, Albert Ravenholt explained.

After that service, Mrs. Ravenholt joined the Office of Strategic Services, the forerunner of the Central Intelligence Agency. Her duties took her to China, where her job was to help with an analysis of psychological warfare being used against Japan. When the Japanese surrendered, Mrs. Ravenholt went to work for Life magazine.

Mrs. Ravenholt later served on the U.S. Joint Commission on Rural Reconstruction in China, which later transferred to Taiwan. For three decades, Mrs. Ravenholt worked for the Ramon Magsaysay Award Foundation, which was funded by the Rockefeller family. The foundation's awards, which became the equivalent of the Nobel Prize in Asia, have brought recognition and financial encouragement to many of Asia's most creative persons, Albert Ravenholt said. It was named for the Philippine president who died in a plane crash in 1957.

When Seattle was preparing for the World's Fair, Mrs. Ravenholt was recruited by the late Joe Gandy, president of the Seattle World's Fair, to enlist participation by Asian nations. Her work led to some of the most spectacular pavilions at the fair, Albert Ravenholt said.

Besides her husband, Mrs. Ravenholt is survived by numerous Asian and American godchildren as well as many friends and co-workers, both here and abroad.

*Cremation has taken place, and the time and place for memorial services will be announced later. Remembrances are suggested to the University of Washington political-science department.

Marjorie and Albert Celebrating Christmas

SEGUNDINA LOTILLA
Albert's Gourmet Cook and Care Giver Extraordinaire!

THE RAVENHOLT FAMILY was well-aware during earlier years that Albert and Marjorie in the Philippines enjoyed very able help from "Gunding", their Filipina friend, assistant, and gourmet cook. Yet full recognition of her many talents and indispensable role in their lives only came about after she moved to Seattle in the 1980s. Here she helped the Ravenholts establish a reputation for superior cuisine; and after Marjorie's death, in 1992, Gunding stayed on as gourmet cook and mainstay of Albert's household in Seattle, providing indispensable help during challenging years. When Albert's health was in crisis during 2002-3, her household care and conscientious daily supervision of his pharmaco-therapy enabled him to regain much of his former activity and capability. We four siblings and families living in the Seattle area know Gunding as a most esteemed friend and integral family member: always smiling, warmhearted, intelligent, hard-working, generous, and everlastingly helpful.

Born May 2, 1925 in Egana, Panay, Philippines, Gunding survived extreme hardships and many challenges during her youth. Her father, Vidal Lotilla, was a farmer. Her mother, Fe Abutas, a housewife and small business operator, bore six sons and two daughters, of which three died in infancy, a sister died at age 11, and a brother at age 13. Gunding, the fifth-born child, from age seven helped her mother sell fruit and vegetables, but says she was generally "a spoiled brat not knowing how to boil water" until her mother suddenly died when Gunding was eight. That day, Gunding went with her cousin to the river, not knowing her mother was seriously ill. Returning after two hours they found her dead in bed, with no signs of trauma. Gunding, her brother Macario age one, and sister Arsenia age eleven, were left in the care of their father. But several weeks after their mother's death, Arsenia suffered a severe illness. A doctor came and gave her a shot, but soon she was unable to open her mouth to eat or speak. Twenty-seven days after her mother's death Arsenia died [perhaps of tetanus].

Living with their father, during four years Gunding cared for her young brother. But at age twelve her father suddenly developed severe illness and died [perhaps cholera], leaving Gunding and five-year-old Macario alone. A cousin then came and took them to live with him at Iloilo City (97 km distant). There during four years, Gunding learned cooking, sewing, and other skills. With her cousin's family, she worked fetching water, cooking, washing clothes, and cleaning house. She also worked so successfully marketing fruits and vegetables that when 14 and 15 years old, several women wanted their sons to marry her. At the outbreak of the war in 1941, the Japanese bombed Iloilo City, and Gunding and Macario left and returned to Egana. Soon the Japanese beheaded her cousin (a tailor) and bayoneted his pregnant wife. In Egana, Gunding and Macario lived with their cousin's daughter, with whom her father when dying had left an emergency supply of 15 cabans of paddy rice (690 kilos), which Gunding never received. Within months, Gunding and Macario, ages 16 and nine, moved to the mountains with her mother's cousin. "It went okay for a couple weeks until the wife became hostile"; so Gunding and her brother moved to the house of their mother's half-brother, who had three sons and sufficient rice to feed them. Once she was summoned to Philippine Army Headquarters and accused of selling to the Japanese. A friend said Gunding had been reported to the authorities by someone wanting her to work for him without pay. Gunding and her brother then proceeded to the home of another aunt in the mountains, but she, too, had little food for them; so Gunding built her own hut near that of a cousin, where she and Macario lived while she got vegetables and rice for helping with the harvest, and caught fish, crabs and shrimp in the river. But they soon tired of living thus, and went back to Egana Barrio and stayed with relatives. A Japanese soldier came to the house; and as Gunding tried to escape, he said "No, don't run away! Come up, Come up!" Questioning her concerning her family, he said he had a sister her same age in Japan; and he gave her a statement to show the Japanese. He also brought her some food and money; and soon Gunding began buying and selling fruits and vegetables again, continuing with this until the war ended, and beyond.

In 1946, her business going well, Gunding made quite a lot of money. A Philippine army soldier wanted to marry her; but not wishing to marry, she went to Manila and Bulacan where she did housework and sewing. During almost a decade she worked for a succession of wealthy households in Manila, usually as chief cook. In 1955, she was working for a

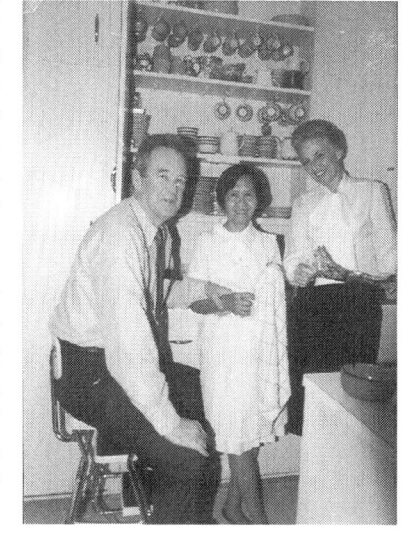

SEGUNDINA LOTILLA

Jensen family living in the Litton apartments, who, leaving for a year in the United States, leased their apartment to Albert and Marjorie Ravenholt. Upon their return the Jensens wanted Gunding to remain with them; but she wished to continue working for Albert and Marjorie, and moved with them to another Litton apartment where she ordinarily did the cooking and much else. In 1972, rotating back to Seattle Albert and Marjorie brought Gunding along, and after several rotations gained the necessary immigration papers that she remained with them in Seattle and is now a U.S. citizen. Now beyond retirement age, she continues working with Albert and frequently sends help to the eleven children of her brother Macario: *Candelaria, Leticia, Henry, Maria Luc, Vidal, Monic Fe, Arsenia, Roberto, Macaria, Marichu, Jackylou, and their 20 children*. With a Phone Card ($5 for 48 minutes), Gunding speaks daily with relatives in the Philippines. When invited to Ravenholt family gatherings in Seattle along with Albert, she invariably insists on contributing a delectable dish for the meal: *Tuna Tempter, Chicken A la Russe, Binacol, Adobo, or a wonderful soup*. Every family needs a Genie like Gunding!

SEGUNDINA LOTILLA, 2003

A COLLAGE OF FAMILY PICTURES

Kristine with Johanne, Eiler, Halvor and Albert, 1924

Halvor   Albert   Johanne Eiler
                      Reimert   1925

                Eiler   Johanne
Halvor   Reimert   Otto   Gerda   Albert
Just before eating the watermelon raised by Reimert in 1933.

Albert with Reimert and Family celebrating Father's Day, 2003

Albert, Johanne, Gerda, Agnes, Astrid, Reimert
At the grave of our parents and sister Thora
West Denmark, Wisconsin, August 2001

A Note On Albert's Family Leadership

Mindful of our rural Danish origins, the distinctive contributions of our parents, the exigencies of depression years, the powerful wartime currents, and emerging opportunities during postwar years, I reflect again on the many ways and times that Albert guided, intervened, and supported the developmental activities of his siblings, even though usually far away and fully engaged in his own challenging career tasks:

- By His Visionary Leadership. As documented in his letters to me, Albert's letters ordinarily drew attention to many far-ranging problems and opportunities, and strove to engage our thoughts and activities in related ways -- as had our father, Ansgar, whose mind and communications often focused on worldly events and problems. But Father's interests were largely theoretical, rhetorical and inoperable; whereas, because of Albert's demonstrated adventurous involvement in mighty events, his perceptions and advisories gained additional currency with us, especially when joined with financial and other assistance. Albert's mind roved worldwide, focusing on interesting and challenging ideas and projects, urging active involvement.

- By Provision of Timely Financial Support. During the war, Albert in Asia, and Halvor working in Hawaii and in the Navy, contributed importantly to our family financial resources - enabling our mother to hold everything together for her growing brood during our father's mental health crisis, requiring hospitalization during two years. In critical ways, Albert helped when needed: While working my way through seven years of pre-med and medical studies at the University of Minnesota, I only borrowed a few hundred dollars from Halvor and Eiler, but upon graduation in 1951, then with a wife and one child and needing an auto to move to San Francisco for my internship. Albert readily loaned me $1000 -- with the stipulation that I repay it after my internship with monthly checks to our younger sisters, Agnes and Astrid, then at Grand View College. Fortunately, Johanne gained federal Nurse Cadet training support during the war; Halvor, Eiler and Otto gained substantial educational support under the G.I. Bill.

- By Enlisting and Supporting Us in Diverse Investment Opportunities. Albert loaned me funds for the purchase of my first home in 1954; and, most importantly, invited my participation as a partner in a real estate purchase in 1957 and in a Quay Bainbridge Apartments development during subsequent years; which has yielded important augmentation of family income during many years. Likewise, Albert generously involved other sibs, nephews and nieces in diverse purchases of land in Wisconsin, Nevada, and Washington State. His resources have always been greater than those of any of his brothers and sisters; mainly because they have generally been burdened with the large costs of raising numerous children. Without children of his own, Albert has many times assisted sibs and their offspring.

- By Assisting Our Parents. During earlier years, Albert and Halvor not only provided financial help to our parents, but Albert

A Note On Albert's Family Leadership

```
provided the leadership and monies for building a much improved family
home on the farm overlooking the golf course at Luck.

It was our great fortune in life, that our eldest brother applied his
remarkable talents to help us all escape poverty and realize our
potential for contributing toward social betterment in our chosen
fields.

Even while recovering from a life-threatening horse-auto accident
during the fall of 1938, Albert organized and directed the
presentation of a Danish play at West Denmark; before proceeding to
Grand View College in Des Moines, Iowa.
```

Cast of Danish Play, "EVENTYR PAA FODREJSE", West Denmark, Nov. 1938

| Anna | Tommy | Georg | Aage | Axel | Marie | Gus | Svend | Johanne | Reuben |
| Henriksen | Laursen | Hansen | Petersen | Benedsen | Hansen | Jensen | Utoft | Ravnholt | Strandskov |

Ancestors of Albert Victor Ravenholt

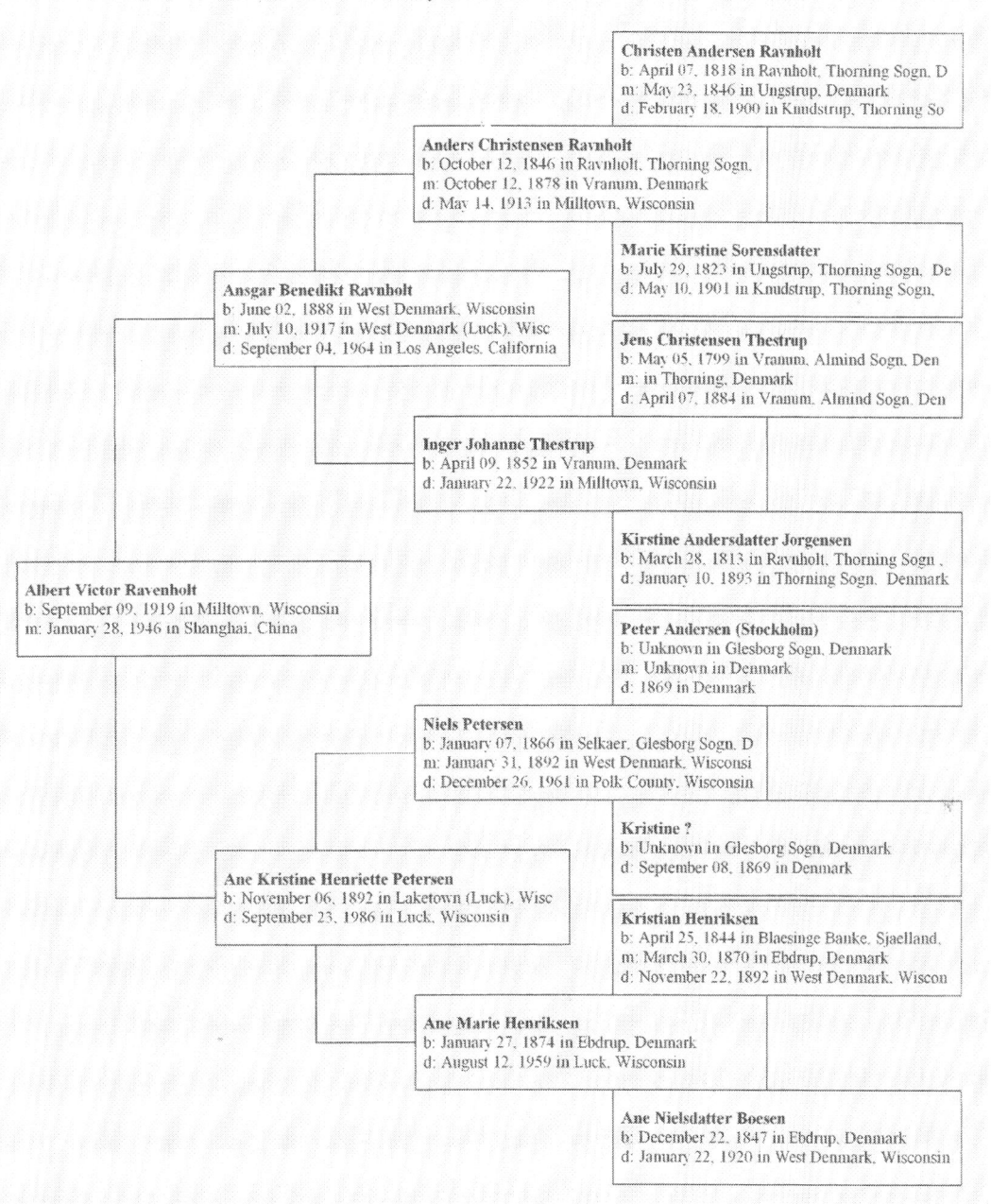

Albert Victor Ravenholt
b: September 09, 1919 in Milltown, Wisconsin
m: January 28, 1946 in Shanghai, China

- **Ansgar Benedikt Ravnholt**
  b: June 02, 1888 in West Denmark, Wisconsin
  m: July 10, 1917 in West Denmark (Luck), Wisc
  d: September 04, 1964 in Los Angeles, California
  - **Anders Christensen Ravnholt**
    b: October 12, 1846 in Ravnholt, Thorning Sogn,
    m: October 12, 1878 in Vranum, Denmark
    d: May 14, 1913 in Milltown, Wisconsin
    - **Christen Andersen Ravnholt**
      b: April 07, 1818 in Ravnholt, Thorning Sogn, D
      m: May 23, 1846 in Ungstrup, Denmark
      d: February 18, 1900 in Knudstrup, Thorning So
    - **Marie Kirstine Sorensdatter**
      b: July 29, 1823 in Ungstrup, Thorning Sogn, De
      d: May 10, 1901 in Knudstrup, Thorning Sogn,
  - **Inger Johanne Thestrup**
    b: April 09, 1852 in Vranum, Denmark
    d: January 22, 1922 in Milltown, Wisconsin
    - **Jens Christensen Thestrup**
      b: May 05, 1799 in Vranum, Almind Sogn, Den
      m: in Thorning, Denmark
      d: April 07, 1884 in Vranum, Almind Sogn, Den
    - **Kirstine Andersdatter Jorgensen**
      b: March 28, 1813 in Ravnholt, Thorning Sogn,
      d: January 10, 1893 in Thorning Sogn, Denmark

- **Ane Kristine Henriette Petersen**
  b: November 06, 1892 in Laketown (Luck), Wisc
  d: September 23, 1986 in Luck, Wisconsin
  - **Niels Petersen**
    b: January 07, 1866 in Selkaer, Glesborg Sogn, D
    m: January 31, 1892 in West Denmark, Wisconsi
    d: December 26, 1961 in Polk County, Wisconsin
    - **Peter Andersen (Stockholm)**
      b: Unknown in Glesborg Sogn, Denmark
      m: Unknown in Denmark
      d: 1869 in Denmark
    - **Kristine ?**
      b: Unknown in Glesborg Sogn, Denmark
      d: September 08, 1869 in Denmark
  - **Ane Marie Henriksen**
    b: January 27, 1874 in Ebdrup, Denmark
    d: August 12, 1959 in Luck, Wisconsin
    - **Kristian Henriksen**
      b: April 25, 1844 in Blaesinge Banke, Sjaelland,
      m: March 30, 1870 in Ebdrup, Denmark
      d: November 22, 1892 in West Denmark, Wiscon
    - **Ane Nielsdatter Boesen**
      b: December 22, 1847 in Ebdrup, Denmark
      d: January 22, 1920 in West Denmark, Wisconsin

**Ane Kristine Henriette Petersen
10 July 1917
Ansgar Benedict Ravnholt**

Ansgar Ravnholt in his 70s

Kristine Petersen Ravnholt in her 70s

ALBERT VICTOR RAVENHOLT

Born 9 September 1919, Ravnholt Farmstead, Milltown, Wisconsin; 2nd child of Ansgar and Kristine Ravnholt

Educational History
Public Schools, Milltown, Wisconsin, 1926-38; Grand View College, Des Moines, Iowa, 1938-39; Fellow, Institute of Current World Affairs, Harvard University, 1947-48 (Chinese studies).

Employment History
Farm hand, Wisconsin, until 1938; Worked as apprentice chef, Radisson Hotel, Minneapolis, MN, summer 1938; Worked as steward, The Brass Rail, New York World's Fair, summer 1939; Chief Cook, MS Agra, Swedish freighter: Los Angeles, California, Shanghai, Philippines, Indonesia, Singapore, Marseilles, Spain, Cape of Good Hope, Shanghai, 1939-40; Convoy leader for International Red Cross trucks transporting medical supplies from Lashio via the Burma Road then widely in China not occupied by the Japanese, 1941-42; United Press war correspondent, China-Burma-India, 1942-45; United Press Bureau Chief: China, India, 1945-46; Institute of Current World Affairs, Harvard University 1947-48; Fellow of the Institute of Current World Affairs, 1947-1984; Foreign correspondent, Chicago Daily News, Southeast Asia, 1948-78; Staff member American Universities Field Staff, Southeast Asia and American Universities, 1952-84; Developer of Patico (Philippine-American Timber Company); Developer of Sagemoor Orchards (cherries, apples, wine grapes), Pasco, Washington; Developer of Quay Bainbridge Apartments, Bainbridge Island, Washington, and other real estate enterprises, Seattle, Washington.

Family History
Married Marjorie Sevryns, 28 January 1946, Shanghai, China.
Marjorie Sevryns, born 23 August 1920 in Sunnyside, Washington, worked many years for the Rockefeller Brothers Fund and the Magsaysay Awards Foundation. She died 25 May 1992 in Seattle.

Albert lives at 1017 Minor Avenue, Seattle, WA 98104

Halvor and Rosemary Ravenholt and Family, 1998

HALVOR BERNHARD RAVENHOLT

Born 12 February 1921, Ravnholt Farmstead, Milltown, Wisconsin; third of ten children of Ansgar and Kristine Ravnholt.

Educational History
Public Schools, Milltown, Wisconsin, 1927-39; Diving training, Pearl Harbor, Hawaii, 1941-42; Underwater Demolition Unit, Seabees, U.S. Navy, 1942-1945; University of Southern California, 1947-48; University of Minnesota, 1948-51, B.S. (soils technology) 1951.

Employment History
Farm and construction worker: Wisconsin, Minnesota, North Dakota, Missouri, Washington, until 1941; Diver, Pearl Harbor, Hawaii, 1941-42; Underwater Demolition Unit, Seabees, U.S. Navy, 1943-46. Served in invasions of the Philippines and Iwo Jima, 1944-45; U.S. Soil Conservation Service, 1951-1990: Owatonna, Minnesota; Thief River Falls, MN; Bemidji, MN; Carrollton, Georgia; Bemidji, MN; Torrington, WY, 1963-1966; Afton, WY 1966-1969; Rock Springs, WY, 1969-1990.

Family History
Married Rosemary Elizabeth Johnson, 18 June 1949, Minneapolis, Minnesota. Children: Jed Vincent, b. 19 September 1954, Thief River Falls, MN; Denise, b. 25 September 1956, Bemidji, MN; Amy Louise, b. 20 March1959, Carrollton, GA; Sue Ellen, b. 11 March 1962, Bemidji, MN; Todd Anthony, b. 24 June 1963, Torrington, WY.Jed m. Katharine Osvald, 1 March 1980, children: Juliana Osvald, Anders Christian, Nicholas Tate; Denise m. Matt Vandeleur, 17 June 1978, divorced 1980; m. Ron Tucker, 1981, children: Daniel Morgan Tucker, 4 January 1982, Joan Tucker; Sue Ellen m. Kenneth "Bob" Tyler, 18 July, children: Andrea, Lynn; K. Tyler deceased in 1994; Sue Ellen M. Charles Gilpin, 1999; Sue Ellen m.Charles Gilpn, 1999. Rosemary died July 3, 1999; Halvor died April 8, 2003

95

EILER CHRISTIAN RAVNHOLT

Born 21 February 1923, Ravnholt Farmstead, Milltown, Wisconsin; 4th of 10 children of Ansgar and Kristine Ravnholt.

Educational History
Public schools, Milltown, West Denmark, and Luck, Wisconsin, 1929-41; Niagara University, Niagara Falls, New York (ASTP), 1943-44; University of Minnesota, Minneapolis, 1946-48, B.S. . (education) 1948; University of Southampton, 1949-50.

Employment History
Farm hand: Wisconsin, Minnesota, North Dakota, until 1941; Shipyard worker, Bremerton, Washington, 1942; U.S. Army, 1943-46; 104th Infantry Division, European Theatre of Operations, 1944-45; High school teacher/principal, Dover, Minnesota, 1948-49; High school teacher/principal, St. Croix Falls, Wisconsin, 1950-52; High School Teacher, Mankato High School, Mankato, Minnesota, 1952-62; Chairman, Blue Earth County Democratic-Farmer-Labor Party, 1960-62; Delegate, Democratic National Convention, 1960; Assistant to Hubert H. Humphrey, U.S. Senator, 1962-64, Vice President of the United States, 1964-68; Administrative Assistant to Daniel Inouye, U.S. Senator, 1969-80; Vice president and Washington representative, Hawaiian Sugar Planters Association, 1980-1995.

Family History
Married Edna Joyce Collis, 23 March 1947, West Denmark, Wisconsin. Children: Elizabeth Collis, b. 22 August 1948, Frederic, Wi; Ann Collis, b. 15 July 1951, Mankato, Mn; Margrethe Collis, b. 15 April 1954, Mankato, Mn; Jane Collis, b. 6 December 1957, Mankato, Mn; Christopher Collis, b. 28 August 1964, Washington, D.C. d. 21 December 1987.

Ann m. Henry Bokelman Jr., 27 August 1970, children: Seth and Jessica.

Jane m. Gary Ellingson, 17 July 1981, children: Jana and Emily .

Margrethe, m. Christopher Hankin, 11 October 1981, children: Erik and Lars.
Elizabeth m. Michael Zipser, 8 May 1982.

Current Address
Eiler Ravnholt   ravnholt@aol.com
850 Butternut Drive, Luck, WI 54853,

Edna, Beth, Ann, Jane, Meg, Chris, Eiler

Paula, Alicia, Ernest, Johanne Fremont /Wedding Ensemble

JOHANNE MARIE RAVENHOLT

Born 21 February 1923, Ravnholt Farmstead, Milltown, Wisconsin; 5th of 10 children of Ansgar and Kristine Ravnholt.

Education History

Public schools, Milltown, West Denmark, and Luck, Wisconsin, 1929-41; Grand View College, Des Moines, Iowa, 1942-43; Fairview Hospital Nursing School, Minneapolis, Minnesota, 1943-46, R.N.; Avila College, Kansas City, Missouri, 1953-55, B.S. (nursing) 1955.

Employment History

Operating Room Nurse, University of Minnesota Hospitals, 1947-50: Head Nurse, Heart Clinic, University of Minnesota Hospitals, 1950-51; Director, Operating Rooms, Research Medical Center, Kansas City, Missouri, 1951-56; Staff nurse, Greater Kansas City Community Blood Center, 1976-present.

Family History

Married Ernest Hoar Fremont, Jr., 27 December 1947, West Denmark, Wisconsin. Children: Paula Marie, b. 24 July 1956, Kansas City, Mo; Alicia Ann, b. 4 February 1959, Kansas City, Mo; married Charles Podraberac, October 31, 1992.

Johanne R Fremont
6647 State Line, Kansas City, MO 64113   jrfremont@msn.com

REIMERT THOROLF RAVENHOLT

Born 9 March 1925, Ravnholt Farmstead, Milltown, Wisconsin, the 6th of 10 children of Ansgar and Kristine Ravnholt.

Educational History
Public schools, Milltown, West Denmark, and Luck, Wisconsin, 1931-43; University of Minnesota, Minneapolis, 1944-51, B.S. 1948, M.B. 1951, M.D. 1952; Rotating intern, U.S. Public Health Service Hospital, San Francisco, California, 1951-52; Epidemic Intelligence Service Officer, National Communicable Disease Center, USPHS, Atlanta, Georgia: Ohio State Health Department, Columbus, Ohio, 1952-53, and Seattle-King County Health Department, Seattle, Washington, 1953-54; University of California (Berkeley), School of Public Health, 1955-56, MPH, 1956.

Employment History
Farm and harvest hand, Wisconsin and North Dakota, until 1943; Surveyor's helper, Engineering Department, Milwaukee, St. Paul, and Pacific Railroad, Minneapolis, Minnesota, 1944-45; Business manager, Students' Cooperative, University of Minnesota, Minneapolis, 1945-48; Senior Assistant Surgeon, U.S. Public Health Service Hospital, San Francisco, California, 1951-52; Director, Epidemiology and Communicable Disease Control Division, Seattle-King County Health Department, Seattle, Washington, 1954-61; Epidemiology Consultant, European Region, U.S. Public Health Service, American Embassy, Paris, France, 1961-63; Associate Professor of Preventive Medicine, School of Medicine, University of Washington, Seattle, 1963-66; Director, Office of Population, U.S. Agency for International Development, Department of State, Washington, D.C., 1966-79; Director, World Health Surveys, Centers for Disease Control, Rockville, Maryland, 1980-82; Assistant Director for Epidemiology and Research, National Institute on Drug Abuse, Rockville, Maryland, 1982-84; Chief, Epidemiology Branch, Office of Epidemiology and Biostatistics, U.S. Food and Drug Administration, Rockville, Maryland, 1984-87; President, Population Health Imperatives, Seattle, 1987-present.

Family History
Married Mildred Froysland, 19 June 1948, Minneapolis, Minnesota. Divorced June 1974. Children: Janna Naru, b. 6 October 1950, Minneapolis, MN.; Mark Viking, b. 2 March 1952, San Francisco, CA; Lisa Kristine, b. 10 December 1954, Seattle, WA.; Dane Victor, b. 8 October 1956, Seattle, WA. Married Betty Butler Howell, 26 September 1981, Kensington, Maryland. Children: Matthew Butler Howell, b. 10 August 1971.

Janna m. James Warren Kent, 10 May 1975, children: Chad Christopher, Ty Dannon; Mark m. Kathleen Pavlich, 4 September 1982, children: Ry Pavlich Ravenholt, Zane Pavlich Ravenholt; Lisa m. Edmund Olaf Belsheim, 8 December 1984, chldren, Sophia Elizabeth Belsheim.
Current Address
3156 E Laurelhurst Dr NE, Seattle, WA 98105,   ravenrt@oz.net

OTTO HAKON RAVENHOLT

Born 17 May 1927, Ravnholt Farmstead, Milltown, Wisconsin; 7th of 10 children of Ansgar and Kristine Ravnholt.

Educational History
Public schools, Milltown, West Denmark, and Luck, Wisconsin, 1933-45; University of Minnesota, 1946-47; Army Language School (Japanese), Monterey, California, 1948-49; University of Minnesota, 1952-58, B.S., 1955, M.D., 1958; Rotating Intern, U,S. Public Health Service Hospital, Seattle, Washington, 1958--59; University of Minnesota, School of Public Health, 1959-60, M.P.H., 1960.

Employment History
Farm and harvest hand, Wisconsin and North Dakota, until 1946; U.S. Army, Counter Intelligence Corps, Japan, 1949-52; Director, Department of Public Health, Topeka, Kansas, 1960-63; Director, Clark County Health District, Las Vegas, Nevada, 1963-1998; Also, concurrently: Coroner, Las Vegas-Clark County, 1963-1988; Director, Department of Human Resources, State of Nevada, 1968; Administrator, Southern Nevada Memorial Hospital, 1973-75.

Family History
Married Marie Forslan, 15 January 1949, Los Angeles, California. Divorced August 1978. Children: Garth Anselm, b. 17 July 1951, Japan; Kim Marie, b. 26 April 1955, Minneapolis, Mn; Dirk Ansgar, b. 19 February 1957, Minneapolis, Mn; Jon Albert., b. 13 May 1965, Boulder City, Nv. Married Barbara Meisner, 13 April 1979, Carson City, Nv, Children; Sherri Lou, Theresa Genevieve, and Stefan Matthew Meisner.

Garth m. Jeanette Beicek, 26 September 1972, children: Jessica Ruth, Gabriel. Kim m. Craig Ringland, 15 November 1978, children: Cara Marie, Kristine Treasure. Dirk m. Cynthia Poleschook, 19 April 1981.

Barbara & Otto in Retirement

Current Address
3224 Antilles Court,
Las Vegas, Nevada 98117   ohravenholt@yahoo.com

Sven   Gerda   Bob   &   Kaj   Bune

GERDA ELINOR RAVNHOLT

Born 5 February 1929, Ravnholt Farmstead, Milltown, Wisconsin; 8th of 10 children of Ansgar and Kristine Ravnholt.

Educational History

Public schools, West Denmark, Milltown, and Luck, Wisconsin, 1935-47; University of Minnesota, 1948-49; Stout Institute, Menomonie, Wisconsin, 1949-52, B.S. (home economics) 1952.

Employment History

Home economics teacher: Public high schools, Quincy, California, 1952-54, Junior-Senior High School, Edina, Minnesota, 1954-55; Shoreline High School, Shoreline, Washington, 1955-59; Edison Technical High School, Seattle, Washington, 1962-63; Garfield High School, Seattle, Washington, 1964-65; Monroe Junior High School, Ballard, Washington, 1965-81; Whitman Junior High School, Seattle, Washington, 1981-85.

Family History

Married Robert William Bune, 5 July 1953, West Denmark, Wisconsin. Children: Kaj Levis, b. 27 November 1959, Seattle, Washington; Svend Eiler, b. 23 April 1963, Seattle, Washington.

Svend Eiler m. Dana Schwartz, 24 August 1985, in Seattle, Washington. Children: Quinn, b. November 8, 1992, Seattle, WA; Spencer b. April 28, 1994, Seattle, Washington.

Kaj m. Mahlon Hanold, September 29, 1990, Kitsap County, Washington. Children. Nils Robert Bune, b. April 25, 1999, Seattle, Washington.

Current Address: 12225 9th NW, Seattle, Washington 98177

Karin, Eric, Ingrid, Lynn, Paul, Agnes Nussle

AGNES ELIZABETH RAVNHOLT

Born 21 July 1931, Ravnholt Farmstead, Milltown, Wisconsin; 9th of 10 children of Ansgar and Kristine Ravnholt.

Educational History
Public schools, Milltown, West Denmark, and Luck, Wisconsin, 1937-49; Grand View College, Des Moines, Iowa, 1949-51; Augustana College, Rock Island, Illinois, 1951-53, B.A. (speech rehabilitation) 1953.

Employment History
Pastor's wife, Lutheran parishes, Tyler, Minnesota; Salinas, California; San Luis Obispo, California; Santa Barbara, California; Lake Tapps, Washington. Public school teacher, Sumner, Washington, 1979-2000.

Family History
Married Paul I. Nussle, 10 July 1954, West Denmark, Wisconsin. Children; Lynn Kristine, b. 12 April 1955, Des Moines, Iowa; Eric Ravnholt, b. 26 April 1957, Tyler, Minnesota; Ingrid Thyra, b. 10 June 1964, Salinas, California; Karin Astrid, b. 18 April 1969, Santa Barbara, California.

Lynn Kristine m. Monte Loren Krog, 27 November 1982. Children: Tor Christian Krog, b. February 2, 1990, Seattle, WA; Kiersten Annette Krog, b. July 15, 1993, Seattle, WA.

Eric Ravnholt m. Jo Anne Borgatze McGee, September 27, 1997, Louisville, KY; Jo Anne was b. November 7, 1959, Kentucky. Son Dalton Raey Alvey, b. December 3, 1992.

Ingrid Thyra m. Chris Lyden, August 23, 1986, Sumner, WA;

Karin Astrid m. Andrew Buchholz, 1992, Sumner, WA, b. September 12, 1970, Kirkland, WA; Ashley Kristine Buchholz, b. November 10, 2000, Sumner, WA; Brooke Janelle Buchholtz, b. April 17, '03

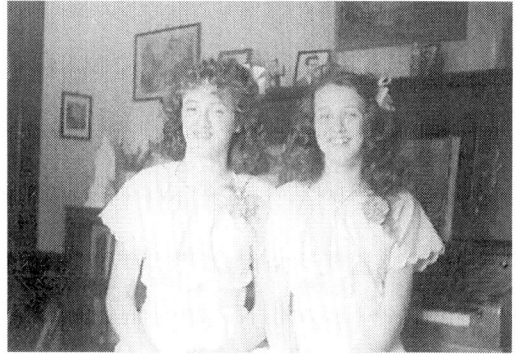

Agnes and Astrid

Agnes R Nussle , 4453 185th Ave. E, Lake Tapps, WA 98391

Astrid   Kristine   Gerda

ASTRID MARGRETHE RAVENHOLT

Born 21 July 1931, Ravnholt Farmstead, Milltown, Wisconsin; 10th of 10 children of Ansgar and Kristine Ravnholt.

Educational History
Public schools, Milltown, West Denmark and Luck, Wisconsin, 1937-49; Grand View College, Des Moines, Iowa, 1949-51, University of Minnesota, Minneapolis, 1951-54, B.S. (nursing) 1954.

Employment History
Adult Psychiatry Nurse, University of Minnesota Hospitals, 1954-55; Polio immunization program, Seattle-King County Health Department, Seattle, Washington, 1955; Child Psychiatry Nurse, University of Minnesota Hospitals, 1956-58; World tour, Europe, Southeast Asia, Pacific, 1958-59; Child Psychiatry Nurse, University of Minnesota Hospitals, 1959; Public school nurse, Salinas, California, 1959-61; Foreign Service nurse, Medical Department, U.S. Department of State: Bamako, Mali, 1961-63; Seoul, South Korea, 1963-65; Rio de Janeiro, Brazil, 1965-66; Vientiane, Laos, 1967; Washington, D.C., 1968-71; Saigon, Vietnam, 1971-73; Lagos, Nigeria, 1974-76; Foreign Service Institute, Washington, D.C., 1976; Rome, Italy, 1976-79; Colombo, Sri Lanka, 1979-81; Tokyo, Japan, 1981-85; Kuwait City, Kuwait, 1985-86; retired from the U.S. Foreign Service, Department of State, 31 May 1986.

Family History

Married Dr Mel Grace, June 13, 1999

Current Address
5051 50th Ave NE
Seattle, WA 98105
206-524-6821

Fugi Apple Picking Time At Sagemoor

WEST OVER THE SEAS TO THE ORIENT

Part B

Albert Ravenholt's Foremost Publications

WHILE RANGING WIDELY IN ASIA during 50+ years, researching and writing on topics of compelling interest for the Institute of Current World Affairs, the Chicago Daily News, and the American Universities Field Staff, Albert wrote many in-depth articles of timely interest to historians and others. Articles listed here, follow immediately below:

```
Table of Contents ---------------------------------------------  104
Report of Communist Takeover of China -------------------------  105
Report from Canton on Dr Hsu Chi-chu and the JCRR--------------  113
Report from Chengtu on Dr Yen and Mass Educational Movement----  121
Report on Taiwan Population Explosion -------------------------  131
Reds Aim to Submerge Religions Under Cold Communist Materialism 137
Communist Destruction of Overseas Chinese Support -------------  139
FORMOSA TODAY. A Comprehensive Report on Taiwan in 1952 -------  146
Adlai Stevenson's Asian Journey -------------------------------  156
The God's Must Go: Communist Attacks on Religious Beliefs -----  162
Peoples Communes: China's Peasants Take the Ultimate Step -----  168
The Chinese Communes: Big Risks for Big Gains -----------------  180
Bitter Peasants Force Easing of China's Farm Plan--------------  190
Red China's Food Crisis----------------------------------------  193
The Human Price of China's Disastrous Food Crisis--------------  204
Red China's Sagging Industry-----------------------------------  214
The New Chinese "Red" Catholic Church--------------------------  224
Feud among the Red Mandarins-----------------------------------  231
Awakening the Land: by Land Reform in Formosa (Taiwan)---------  239
The Red Guards - of the Cultural Revolution--------------------  248
Can One Billion Chinese Feed Themselves?-----------------------  265
Whose Good Earth: Health, Diet, and Food Production in China-   283
The Philippines: Where did we Fail?----------------------------  300
Filipino Birth Rate One of the Highest-------------------------  309
A Note on the Philippines: the Land, the People, the Politics   312
Miracles with New Rice Technology------------------------------  323
Of Ducks and Geese and Pigs for Bangkok------------------------  333
The Philippines: Is Democracy Restored?------------------------  343
Dairy Farming in the Asian Tropics-----------------------------  360
India's Bovine Burden------------------------------------------  369
Man-Land-Productivity Microeconomics in Bali-------------------  382
The Japanese Farmer: Wheat or Rice for the Yen-----------------  394
Who Will Grow the Food for the World Food Bank?----------------  405
Faith Gardening and Salt Farming-------------------------------  417
John Musser Letter to Albert-----------------------------------  427
Seattleites Help Link U.S., Orient-----------------------------  428
```

INSTITUTE OF CURRENT WORLD AFFAIRS
522 5th Avenue, New York 18, NY,
Walter S. Rogers, Executive Director

Albert Ravenholt, Enroute
Shanghai to Hong Kong
28 April 1949

Dear Mr. Rogers:

Events during the last eight days in China may have been the almost inevitable development of conditions that existed before, but they brought into full focus the major political forces at work in this country. As such I think this brief period of Chinese History is worth special attention.

Midnight of April 20th was the deadline set by the Chinese Communists for Nationalist acceptance or rejection of the Red peace terms drafted in Peiping, As the time for talking ran out we could almost feel the tension mount in Nanking. Ever since Chiang Kai-shek was kidnapped at Sian in December 1936, Nationalist and Communist leaders had met for periodic, tortuous discussions of a possible peaceful settlement of China's civil war. Each time when the "talks" broke down the opposing leaders returned to their respective camps and continued in the pattern of life from which they bad come. This time it was different. The Nationalist leaders saw their immediate personal as well as political survival at stake.

The Communist terms which both sides had pledged themselves to keep secret until that night were harsh. They had been drafted during two weeks of negotiation in Peiping and handed to the 'Nationalist peace delegates there on April 15th, In effect, Acting President Li Tsung-jen and his government had to choose during their five days of grace between surrender and facing a full-scale attack by Red Armies which Li and his men knew they lacked the power to hold off for long.

But the Communist peace terms were important in another sense -- they indicated the pattern of rule the Red leaders intended to establish in China, either by negotiation or force. The Communist conditions were known officially as the "Twenty-four Points." They were the detailed means whereby the Communists insisted Mao Tze-tung's eight-point peace proposal announced on January 14, 1949 should be implemented.

Stripped of their verbiage, these Twenty-four Points boiled down *to* four essential demands: (1) An immediate crossing of the Yangtze River by Red Armies; (2) Eventual Communist military occupation of all Nationalist China, with the provinces in the Yangtze Valley to be taken over first; (3) Reorganization of the Nationalist Armies into the Communist Peoples Liberation Armies; (4) Permission for the Nationalist Government to function as a caretaker government which would implement orders from the Communist Revolutionary Military Committee until the new Coalition Government was established. This included a provision that the Nationalist Government would be held responsible for turning over in good order all its physical, financial, military and other assets to the future Coalition Government.

COMMUNIST TAKEOVER OF CHINA

There were other demands of less immediate significance. One required the Nationalists to deliver to the future Coalition Government all treaties and agreements with foreign powers. These would then be "examined" and possibly abrogated or renegotiated. The Constitution was to be abolished, General Okamura and the 260 other Japanese leaders released by the Nationalists "dealt with anew" and land rents and interest reduced, preparatory to a later redistribution of land.

During the weeks of negotiation in Peiping the Communists had agreed to modify only one of Mao's eight terms -- the War Criminal issue. In return for repentance and cooperation the Communists promised "clemency." All who continued to oppose the "cause of the Peoples Liberation" were warned they would be punished. The Communist negotiators reportedly stated they would insist upon "bringing to justice" the Four Families -- Kungs, Soongs, Chiangs, Brothers Chen Li-fu and Chen Kuo-fu -- and some secret service officials. Most of these men are already out of China and the demand in practice would probably have amounted to condemnation and confiscation of their considerable property, along with other large "bureaucratic capital acquired through political prerogatives and plutocratic influence" which the Communists insisted must be handed over to the Coalition Government.

Probably the most important aspect of the negotiations was the Communist refusal to give any guarantees for the future to members of the Kuomintang Party who have participated in the Nationalist Government since late 1946. The Communists only agreed to "propose" to the preparatory committee of the New Political Consultative Conference which is to establish the Coalition Government that the Nanking Government be permitted to send a number of "patriotic elements as representatives" to the Conference,, It was implied during the discussions that members of the Nationalist Government who wished to seek a political future must do so within the framework of Marshal Li Chi-sen's Kuomintang Revolutionary Committee which has already established headquarters in Peiping. The Communist terms were very specific. They lacked the latitude for discussion so common in earlier Chinese politics. Nationalist peace delegates were told that not "one character" of the terms could be changed -- they had either to accept or face the consequences. The rejection of the Communist terms which Li Tsung-jen telegraphed to Peiping on the afternoon of the 20th was in many ways a tragic message. In contrast to the terse Communist demands, it was politely worded. It said in effect that the Nationalist Government could not agree to the conditions proposed and emphasized that in any event the Government was unable to impose acceptance of such terms upon the Nationalist Army. The Nationalist reply, also signed by the Premier, General Ho Ying-chin, asked that more time be allowed for discussions and that in the meantime the Red Armies hold off from their announced objective of pushing south across the Yangtze River.

Acting President Li Tsung-jen and the men around him had known for some time that Chiang Kai-shek and the troops still accepting the Generalissimo's orders would probably refuse to participate in any peace settlement. But as far as I could judge, Li, his premier and cabinet and most of his supporters among the leaders in the Legislative and Control Yuans had hoped they might be able to negotiate an agreement with the Communists which first of all would end the fighting in most of China

COMMUNIST TAKEOVER OF CHINA

with the probable exception of Chekiang, Fukien, the Shanghai area, Taiwan and the Northwest, Thereafter, they evidently hoped to insure that most members of the Nationalist Government could remain and participate as responsible leaders in the future of their country. Many of them thought that if they could assure themselves of a minority representation in the Coalition Government they would be able to temper future Communist policies. Up until very near the end most of these men still thought in terms of some form of geographic division of China which would leave them with local control in a number of provinces. During the three months he served as Acting President in Nanking, Li Tsung-jen sought to further principles which represented, as far as it is possible to judge, the wishes of the great majority of Chinese people in Nationalist areas, Most of those with whom I talked during that time wanted peace. They were convinced the Nationalists had lost the civil war. The question in doubt was the pattern of Communist take-over In his struggle for an "honorable peace, Li, whom many people had discounted when he first came to power as an honest, well intentioned old Kwangsi Province warlord, won a wistful admiration from many groups. Li gained for himself and his government more respect and support than most had expected. His failure to achieve the ultimate goal of a civil war settlement which would have insured a place in the future for many of the men and ideas of the Nationalist Government was due, I think, to fundamental factors beyond the control of Li and the many Chinese leaders who worked with him*

The Communists demonstrated unwillingness to compromise which made it impossible for a government as shaky in its hold on power as Li's to impose any terms it accepted. The Communists had the great preponderance of military and political power which meant they could afford to go slow without endangering their ultimate objectives. Instead, they chose to ram their program through regardless of the cost.

It may never be possible to give a final judgment of Chiang Kai-shek's role during the last three months when he was officially in retirement at his ancestral home near Ghikow in Chekiang Province. But in Nanking it was clear that the Generalissimo did more than any other individual or group to sabotage the Nationalist chances for an acceptable peace settlement. On Chiang's orders almost the entire Nationalist treasury -- roughly $300,000,000 worth of gold bullion and silver -- had been shipped in January to Taiwan and Amoy where it was controlled by the Generalissimo's men. Chiang repeatedly refused to let the Nationalist Government have any part of this reserve -- most of it provided originally by a U.S. loan of gold bullion at the end of the war -- to shore up its crumbling finances, pay troops or slow down the inflation. As a result, the Nationalist government became steadily weaker even while the peace talks were in progress.

Chiang Kai-shek also personally intervened and literally wrecked the Nationalist plan for defense of the Yangtze River. In Nanking I heard generals, who for years had been loyal to Chiang, curse the Generalissimo for destroying their only chance to inflict a temporary defeat on the Red Armies which might have forced more favorable terms from the Communists.

Several weeks ago Chiang by-passed the Nationalist Ministry of Defense and ordered the strongest Nationalist armies under General Tang En-po to evacuate key points along the Yangtze and fall back toward Shanghai, leaving large holes in the line. The Generalissimo also refused to permit the Nationalist Air Force to be brought back from Taiwan. Nationalist military planners estimated that if their air force could have destroyed the Communist river boats and barges it would have set back the Communist offensive by three months. They never had a chance to test their plans. From his Chikow hideout, Chiang also controlled the Nationalist secret police. Their agents either ignored or contradicted orders from Li Tsung-jen's government and created trouble calculated to embarrass the Nationalist peace negotiations.

A third explanation for the failure of the peace efforts can be found in the very nature of modern Chinese society. Li Tsung-jen attempted to organize for political support middle groups between the extreme right and left. From the start his government was opposed by the two most powerful factions within the Kuomintang -- the CC Clique and the Political Science Group. For nearly twenty years the right-wing CC Clique had been the organizational backbone of the Kuomintang. Now, apparently on orders from Chiang Kai-shek, it sabotaged Li's efforts at civil rights reform and government reorganization. The middle class which logically might have supported Li's championship of its ideas, had been largely destroyed by inflation. The years of Chiang Kai-shek's rule had denied these people political experience and they now proved unable to organize to help themselves, The only firm immediate support Li could count upon was provided by his Kwangsi Province partner, General Pai Chung-hsi, who commanded the Nationalist troops in the Hankow area, and local leaders in the Central China provinces. These forces combined with the men working for peace in the Legislative and Control Yuans were unable to muster the necessary power within the time allowed them to give their side a bargaining position.

Shortly after word of Li Tsung-jen's official rejection of the Communist terms had spread through Nanking on the evening of the 20th, we learned from the Ministry of National Defense that the Red Armies had launched a general offensive south across the Yangtze River. The Communists had stated earlier that they would cross the River on or about that date, either to implement the terms of the agreement if the Nationalists accepted or to attack. The Red generals were operating against their own deadline imposed by the May flood rise of the Yangtze.

In mounting their offensive on the 20th, the Communists collided with the British Navy. The sloop, HMS Amethyst, was enroute that morning up the Yangtze from Shanghai to Nanking to deliver supplies to the British Embassy and stand by for emergency evacuation. About 85 airline miles east of Nanking the Amethyst sailed into a barrage of Communist artillery fire, The Amethyst continued upstream and eventually went aground on Rose Island. The Communist gunners, who may originally have mistaken the Amethyst for a Nationalist naval vessel, continued their fire after they must have recognized the British flag. The British destroyer, IBIS Consort, the sloop, HMS Black Swan, and the cruiser, HMS-London all engaged in a running gun battle with Communist batteries on the north bank of the Yangtze while trying to rescue the Amethyst. The British ships sailing in the narrow channel were in an untenable position and took a bad beating from Communist anti-tank guns and heavier fire. It would be interesting to know to what extent the Communist commanders were

COMMUNIST TAKEOVER OF CHINA

influenced in their decision to continue their deadly fire by memories of past actions of British ships in China waters and the knowledge that they had the British ships bracketed at almost the same place where the British Navy sailed in more than a hundred years ago and forced treaty concessions from China.

The offensive which the Red commanders pushed south across the Yangtze River beginning that night was the largest single military operation attempted by Chinese in modern times, Along a 600-mile front on the north bank of the Yangtze more than a million Communist combat troops were in position to jump off. They were organized as three field armies under veteran Communist generals. General Chen Yi, the French-educated Communist commander for East China, had 21 armies in his Second Field Army between the Grand Canal and Nanking, roughly 150 airline miles southwest of Anking. The Communist one-eyed raider, General Liu Po-cheng, had 12 armies in his Second Field Army between Anking and Hankow. North and West of Hankow General Lin Piao had built up his Fourth Field Army with more than 400,000 troops brought down from Manchuria by way of Peiping and Tientsin, For several months all of these armies had collected and built thousands of boats. They had brought down food and ammunition by rail and canal from North China and stockpiled it at key points along the River. Nationalist troops along the south bank of the River numbered between 500,000 and 600,000. During the last three months the Nationalists had carried out a ruthless conscription program and most of the units were up to strength. However, due largely to Chiang Kai-shek's interference, there was no single command and many of the troops were badly demoralized. When the Communist attack came there was almost no resistance along most of the front. Some generals including the commander of the Kiangyin forts on the Yangtze halfway between Nanking and Shanghai turned over without fighting. The troops in front of the major Communist drive between Wuhu and Anking simply retreated or scattered. Within 48 hours the Communists claimed to have Put 300,000 troops across the River. About the same time the Nationalist Ministry of Defense lost contact with an estimated one-third of its troops, The only clear picture of operations came from the Hankow area where the Communists limited their actions to probing General Pai Chung-hsi's defenses.

In Nanking the end which everyone had expected yet hoped somehow to avoid had finally come. Any remaining doubts about Communist intentions were dispelled by the broadcast over the Peiping Radio on the afternoon of the 21st, of a general order by Mao Tze-tung and Chu Teh to Peoples Liberation Armies north of the Yangtze and Red guerrillas south of the River. The Communist troops were ordered to: (1) Advance and annihilate all Kuomintang reactionaries, liberate the whole country and defend the independence and integrity of Chinese territory and sovereignty; (2) Capture all war criminals, particularly Chiang Kai-shek; (3) Sign regional peace agreements with any Nationalists willing to accept the Twenty-four Points; *(4)* Give the Nationalist Government another chance to sign the peace agreement if the Government was still in Nanking after the capital was surrounded,

The Nationalist Government was almost as poorly prepared for the Communist attack as its troops. In a series of hurried conferences, it was decided to evacuate the Executive Yuan to Shanghai and the

COMMUNIST TAKEOVER OF CHINA

Legislative and Control Yuans to Canton, China. National Aviation Corporation was ordered to cancel all commercial flights to aid in the evacuation. Officials who had not already left, hurried to Nanking's two airfields and scrambled aboard the planes that landed and took off at all hours, On the 21st , Chang Chun, who served as Cabinet Minister without portfolio, made a hurried trip to Chikow, reportedly to ask Chiang Kai-shek to either take over as President or stop meddling in political and military affairs and leave China. The next afternoon Acting President Li Toung-jen, Premier Ho Ying-chin General Pai Chung-hsi and Chang Chun held a conference with Chiang Kai-shek near Hangchow. That night Li stopped in Nanking for a hurried visit and then took off again by air for Kweilin, the capital of Kwangsi Province. Li and Pai, run a paternalistic government in Kiangsi that has greater popular support than the government of any other province in Nationalist China and the Acting President has remained there since that flight. His supporters state Li does not intend to come out again as a national leader as long as he only serves as a "cover for Chiang Kai-shek's maneuvers."

The climax in Nanking came on the night between April 22 and 23. About 11 o'clock that evening the Communist troops broke through the so-called Puching Line in front of the Nationalist bridgehead at Pukow across the Yangtze from Nanking. The Nationalist army holding Pukow then scrambled back across the Yangtze in any craft they could grab. There was a final furious two hours of artillery bombardment by both sides and then rather suddenly the firing that had kept most of Nanking awake for three nights stopped.

About three o'clock in the morning the Nanking city government decided to pull out. By nine o'clock all police were gone from the streets and looting was in full swing. There was a curious pattern in this looting -- the first buildings to be ransacked were the former centers of authority such as the garrison headquarters and the central police station. When I first drove by the mayor's residence that morning the looters -- coolies, farmers from the countryside and tradesmen -- were carrying sofas, tables and kitchen utensils down the street I came by again in the middle of the morning and found them carting off the doors and window sills which now were only good for firewood. About the same time the looting spread to the food shops where I saw men dash in, grab a bag of flour or sack of rice and hurry down the street,

Over most of the capital there was a strange hush that morning. Small groups of citizens gathered at the street corners. They weren't particularly excited but looked rather casually at the looters and few large cars of tardy officials fleeing out of the city. Once in a while they glanced up to look for the stray shots that could still be heard throughout the city. The only exceptions were on Nanking's wide main streets where long lines of troops, mules and artillery carts fought for a right-of-way to march out of the city. The troops were still moving as organized units, but they commandeered buses and cars and piled their gear on top of staggering loads of private luggage moving on carts out through Nanking's city gates in the direction of Shanghai.

At the airfield where we bad to wait for our pilot the Chinese planes were leaving with their last loads of files and luggage. The Nationalist troops who had guarded the airfield longer than any other point were then first forming in line and marching off toward the highway leading southeast out of Nanking. After we took off on the next to the last American plane to leave Nanking, we saw the roads south and east of the city crowded with troops, trucks, pedicabs and rickshaws streaming out. The regular Communist troops who entered Nanking the following night met no opposition. They found the Nationalists had dynamited the Nanking railway station -- the most modern in China -- and that looters had set fire to the beautiful Judicial Yuan building so the pattern of decay in Shanghai was a slower continuation of the Nanking debacle. The organs of Government that escaped to the port city as organized units soon dispersed. A number of civilian and military officials resigned. Others, when they learned that the Nationalist military forces were incapable of offering further large-scale resistance, simply took off for Taiwan or South China. The Communist armies after their original speedy drive across the Yangtze moved slowly ahead, encountering no serious opposition. The 18 Red Armies that had crossed the River between Wuhu and Anking pushed toward Hangchow -- a move that would cut Shanghai's land links with South China.

Shanghai is apparently slated for the worst experience in its one hundred years as a modern port. The Communists evidently do not have available now the 65,000 tons of rice flour and other commodities that are required every month to feed the city's roughly six million people. The new rice crop does not become available until mid-summer. If the Communists proceed in the same manner they did in Manchuria they may delay taking the city until they have time to bring food down from the North or even until the new crop is nearly ready. In the meantime the city is living off ECA stocks of food. If these are out off several million people will starve.

The Nationalist financial system is now finished, business is at a stand-still and firms and factories can find only a small portion of the silver money needed to pay their workers. If the EGA-financed fuel oil for the Shanghai Power Company stops coming, most of the city's factories will be forced to close down for lack of power, the tram lines will stop running, it will not be possible to pump out Shanghai's sewage and the telephone system will be limited to a few hours of operation per day, if it functions at all.

Nationalist troops in the Shanghai area are being moved out as fast as they can be loaded on ships. Most of the troops are shipped to Taiwan, although a few boat loads have put in at Amoy and Foochow. The Nationalist commander, General Tang En-po., is "milking" the Shanghai merchants for as many gold bars as he can find -- there are no definite figures for the size of this ransom but I would estimate that it amounts to the equivalent of several million United States dollars. So far the Communist underground has kept out of sight. At the moment their principal concern is with protecting Shanghai's public utilities from Nationalist destruction. The Nationalist Garrison Headquarters has rounded up several thousand suspected Communist sympathizers but they have been unable to get at the real Communist organization.

With the disappearance of the Nationalist Government as a functioning organization Shanghai, like other areas of South China has to live on its own organizational resources. The extent to which these communities provide their own leaders now will do much to decide how well they weather the storm.

>Sincerely,
>
>Albert Ravenholt

Received New York 5/17/49.

INSTITUTE OF CURRENT WORLD AFFAIRS

522   5th Avenue, New York 18, NY,
Walter Rogers, Executive Director

Canton, China
May 23, 1949

Dear Mr. Rogers:

In 1926 when Dr. Hsu Shih-chu was 21 years old, his classmates at the Ningpo Baptist Middle School urged him to leave his studies and come with them to join the revolutionary movement then remaking China. "I refused to go with them," Hsu explains. "I think I saw further than they did. I knew politics could not solve my country's problems – only science could really help."

Today in keeping with that approach to life Hsu is adjusting himself to the new political conditions in his country. Lt the same time lie continues to attempt to-work out solutions to the problem that has absorbed most of the energies of his mature life–how do you begin to provide modern sanitation, public health and similar services for more than 450 million people of whom 85 percent live in rural areas, when, for example, the qualified medical schools in this country produce between 200 and 400 graduates a year?

Hsu looks almost too boyish to have many of the answers. He is slightly built, even for a Chinese. But when he begins to talk he demonstrates an apparently inexhaustible energy which must in part result from his deep sense of dedication to the welfare of ordinary people. As he explains his work and the ideas to be applied, it is hard not to be caught up by the quiet enthusiasm he generates,

At present Hsu is in charge of the work of the rural health committee of the Joint Commission on Rural Reconstruction. JCRR was created as a result of the China Aid Act passed by the U,S. Congress in the spring of 1948. The Act was extended this spring and JCRR was assured of about 15 million dollars to develop its many-sided program in non-Communist areas of China. The headquarters of the Sino-American organization (three of the five commissioners are Chinese and two American) are here in Canton and it is from this base that Hsu has struggled to evolve a program that might promise results under the near chaotic conditions in many of the provinces where lie is able to work.

The brave beginnings which China made in the field of public health before 1937 largely went to pieces during the years of the Sino-Japanese war and the civil war. The Japanese were apparently not interested in public health except for the protection of their own civilian and military personnel and Chinese immediately associated with them, During their occupation of much of China, the Japanese made only occasional attempts to continue the efforts started by the Chinese Government and private Chinese and foreign organizations.

In the areas ruled by the Nationalist Government during the war with Japan and since VJ Day the situation is not much better. On a recent

JOINT COMMISSION ON RURAL RECONSTRUCTION

inspection trip in Chekiang Province, Hsu found the monthly public health budget of a typical hsien or county was only $300 Gold Yuan. The price of a single Chinese newspaper at that time was $1,300 Gold Yuan. In Southern Fukien Province he discovered that the salary of hsien doctors was 60 pounds of rice per month. "In all the hsien I visited I didn't see a single qualified doctor," Hsu said. "Real doctors won't go to the rural areas -- they can't support themselves. Frequently, the men holding the jobs are relatives of the hsien magistrates. Some have no medical training. Others are former army first aid attendants who call themselves 'doctors'."

In most of the hsien Hsu visited the government maintained health center was only a "sign board." The medicine bottles were usually empty. The centers lacked even simple tools such as scales, He found that the literally millions of dollars worth of drugs UNRRA and subsequent relief organizations sent to China had seldom reached local government health stations -- the provincial public health organizations lacked funds to pay for distribution. In instances where drugs had reached local health centers, the "doctors" had frequently sold them either for personal gain or to pay the operating expenses of their organizations. Hsu watched several health centers for five or six hours and "not a single patient came."

Hsu traces the breakdown of the originally inadequate public health system to several factors, The inflation and heavy government expenditure for military purposes left almost no funds for health work. Doctors and nurses who were unable to live on their inadequate salaries left the rural areas to work in private practice in larger cities. The Government's personnel system bred nepotism and the official audit regulations made it impossible for a public-spirited official who still managed to survive to use his limited facilities and supplies effectively. Hsu found a few districts where the health centers operated effectively. They were the hsien where the local government paid the basic salaries of the public health practitioners and the people of the district provided the equipment and medicines and supervised their use.

"These were our findings," Hsu said as he finished the description of his tour. "Now how can we improve the situation?" Without local government support Hsu feels health work in rural areas is impossible. The few qualified private practitioners refuse to leave their city positions to work for nothing. "To get anything accomplished," Hsu adds, we must work with the established organizations, public and private, and try to improve them. There just are not the qualified people available so it would make sense to try and create new organizations to send into the countryside."

As a beginning Hsu and his JCRR colleagues are working on Chung Shan Hsien in Kwangtung Province. In this hsien of 750.,000 people where Sun Yat-sen was born they are testing out an approach which will later be applied in a number of selected "demonstration" hsien in other provinces starting with Kwangsi and Sechuan. Before the program was initiated Hsu insisted the hsien government must pledge itself to spend five to ten percent of its budget for public health. "I tell them,," he said,, "now you do only two things—you tax and you conscript -- and the people hate you. Health work is on the other side and is positive. With the growing

JOINT COMMISSION ON RURAL RECONSTRUCTION

threat of Communist-organized local guerrillas the argument has an effect it might not have otherwise.

Hsu's program requires the local authorities to reestablish a health-center in the market town which is the seat of the hsien government and to set up health stations in each of the districts of which there are usually six or eight in a hsien. "At this particular time," he explains, "a hospital is not necessary. We must concentrate on preventive work. If a hsien can't find a good doctor, we tell them not to try and get one -- use nurses or midwives. The job is organizational and educational. We don't want to emphasize a poor curative service." The third part of the program calls for the creation in each hsien of a public health board composed of teachers, peoples representatives, religious leaders and chamber of commerce representatives. The board becomes the governing body supervising local health work, It handles directly all funds and supplies and approves expenditures. By giving the local board authority, it is possible to dispense with the personnel and delays involved in the present cumbersome official accounting procedure "which in any event is meaningless." It also prevents health work from becoming the exclusive preserve of the local gentry who frequently control the hsien government.

An important part of the project provides that the staff of the hsien health centers and stations be paid a bonus calculated as a percentage of income from their out patient work. The bonus serves as a stimulus to arouse interest in their work and gives a health worker an honest means of earning a living. The agreement with the local authorities also states that the hsien government can not change health personnel without the approval of the local health board -- a form of security from politics that does not now exist.

When a hsien government accepts these conditions, then Hsu and the JCRR organization are willing to come in and help. The sums JCRR invests in the program would appear ridiculously small to westerners but they have proven adequate to starting the wheels of local initiative. The local health board, selected with JCRR participation is given an original grant of US$200 for each hsien health center and US100 for each district health station. This sum is used to purchase minimum equipment which may include whitewash, mosquito netting and furniture. In addition the board is given medical supplies and US30 for the health center and US $15 for each health station to provide a six to twelve month operating budget,

The aim of the program, as Hsu explains it, is to establish a self-supporting (public and private) health service on a lisien level which will be controlled by local people. JCRR purposely adds nothing to the health workers basic government salary paid in rice and permits the local health board to decide the percentage of bonus to be paid from receipts -- rich patients are charged as much as they can afford to pay and the poor are treated free. Hsu thinks one of their biggest jobs will be to train local boards to spend money publicly--a practice that is rare in China. 11thile the boards are learning JCRR maintains a supervisory control. Wherever possible they also assist in mobilizing community support and providing pamphlets and other educational material. Once local initiative is organized. *Hsu is convinced there will be a gradual improvement in the work done even by poorly qualified health workers.

JOINT COMMISSION ON RURAL RECONSTRUCTION

Judged by Western scientific standards the level of health service provided by the program may appear primitive. As Hsu explains it: "We want to cure people where we can, but our real concern is with preventing people from becoming sick and very often that is a question of rooting out ignorance." The illnesses that plague most of China's peasants are relatively few. They include trachoma and other eye infections; skin diseases due largely to lack of sanitation and simple disinfectants; children's diseases including measles and small pox; tuberculosis, dysentery, hookworm, roundworm, malaria, schistosomiasis, kala azar and frequent cases of undernourishment which Hsu says is essentially economic. In Hsu's mind the methods of the JCRR program he now is organizing can be only the beginning of the solution to making the people of China stronger, healthier and happier. For the more long range permanent ideas to meet these needs Hsu draws upon the experiments he and other leaders in the field initiated before the war with Japan interrupted their work in 1937.

The realization of the need for public health and particularly rural health first gained prominence in China during the late 1920's. At that time Peiping Union Medical College began to give special training for work in rural areas. Some of the first experimental work was done in Tinghsien near Peiping where Dr. C.C. Yen and his colleagues developed their mass education techniques. In Tinghsien public health men discovered that the average Chinese spent about forty Chinese cents per year for his health. (The Chinese dollar at the time was valued at from $2.00 to $3.30 for US $1.00) This was the amount of money the average farmer paid out to Chinese herb doctors for their concoctions, that he spent for offerings to the gods. In Tinghsien these man also learned they could provide a modern health service at a cost of about ton cents per capita per year, Such a service included a health center with a 45 bed hospital at each haien seat and a health station staffed by a doctor, a nurse and a midwife in each of the haien's six or more districts. By using the mass education movement, they were able to mobilize voluntary workers from among the students and farmers to report births and deaths, give vaccines and simple first aid, report communicable diseases and keep the villages clean. Hsu feels the principle defeat of the Tinghsien experiment was that the money to finance it all came from the outside, Hsu began to take a leading part in public health work in 1935 when he was 30 years old. That year through the sponsorship of the Rockefeller Foundation he was asked by the Chinese Government to initiate an experimental self-supporting public health system in Kiangning Hsien outside of Nanking. When he started the work, Hsu had only his monthly salary of $200 plus an operating budget provided by the Rockefeller Foundation of $300.

"Kiangning was a very poor hsien listed as third class with a population of 450,000," Hsu explains. "We knew that if we could develop a self-supporting program there we could do it anywhere." Hsu first needed money to finance the work. He said; "There is enough money in each hsien but it disappears." The chief income of a hsien government is from the land tax of which one-half is kept by the hsien and the remainder passed along to the provincial government. The tax collection system Hsu found in Kiangning is typical of the practice in many areas of rural China. When he arrived the annual tax collected by the Hsien totaled $350,000. It was not collected directly by the government but by 100 private tax collectors, These collectors inherited their jobs and the so-called "Red Books" which were kept as family secrets,, Each collector's Red Book listed the owners of land in his tax area, the quality of the land and the tax that person should pay. Hsu said the tax collectors in Kiangning were essentially middle men who usually cooperated with the large land owners. Since the Government did not know (1) the actual acreage of tilled land in the Hsien and (2) the real owner of the land, the collectors in return for bribes frequently let the larger owners off lightly while over-charging the smaller peasants. At the same time the collectors kept a good portion of the tax for themselves.

In cooperation with an aggressive new hsien magistrate, Hsu got the hsien government to order: (1) the registration with the government of all land, listing the owner and his address, (2) abolition of the jobs of the tax collectors, and, (3) the establishment of government tax collection stations throughout the Hsien where each farmer was required to pay his tax in person at the harvest season. A warning was issued which stated that all non-registered land would be confiscated. The tax reform which was implemented with the help of students from the KuomIntang's Central Political College in Nanking raised the hsien revenue for the first year to $1,000,000* Many of the small farmers paid only one sixth as much tax as they were charged the previous year. "Now we had money," Hsu said, "almost more than we could spend."

Hsu next needed to learn something about the people with whom he was working and there were no statistics for Kiangning. He and his colleagues mobilized the local school teachers and students from nearby Nanking and in five days took a complete family by family census: They discovered the Hsien was divided into seven districts which in turn, were made up of 88 townships and village-ships of 4,000 to 8,000 persons each. The average family had five persons. The census which gave Hsu his statistics also served a political end. From then on each family was required to keep a card on its door listing the details of all members of the family. They were told to report within five days all new arrivals, births, etc* Through the use of this system the hsien government caught and killed all bandits. Hsu said the system also permitted the Kuomintang authorities to round up anyone who was politically undesirable.

With a portion of the new tax revenue Hsu built a health center in the hsien seat and a health station in each of the other six districts, Previously, there had not been a single qualified doctor in the hsien. Now they were able to employ four doctors plus nurses and assistants to operate the health center. Each of the six health stations was staffed with one doctor, one public health nurse, one sanitary inspector, two attendants and two servants. In important townships and village-ships Hsu established health sub-stations staffed with a public health nurse, a midwife and an attendant.

Of equal importance Hsu feels was the manner in which he and his colleagues mobilized other members of the community to do health work. In each of the 88 townships and villageships there was an elder's office with an elected head and a paid assistant. Hsu gave each of the elder's assistants a month of special training and then subsidized them to give first aid and vaccinations and see that the streets were kept clean. The hsien had 362 primary schools which were attended by about 50 percent of the children of school age (six to fifteen years). Hsu's assistants placed a first aid box in each school and organized regular morning inspections to make sure hands and necks were clean. If a child came to school with a sore throat, he was sent home. Teachers were taught to treat their students for trachoma and taenia of the scalp. The 44 census police in the hsien were trained to become health police. They were subsidized to keep an accurate record of births and deaths, give vaccinations and check cleanliness and orderliness,

This entire public health system, Hsu found, could be supported at a cost of about ten cents per capita per year or five percent of the hsien budget. He feels that the program in Kiangning Hsien failed to deal with one question "which must go hand in hand with public health -- population control. Workable answers to this fundamental problem in China have not yet been found. Hsu said that because of Sun Yat-sen's teachings the official philosophy of the Kuomintang was opposed to work to limit increases in China's population. He adds that no means have yet been found which will permit the average peasant to practice birth control. The problem, he feels, is essentially economic and involves the entire question of mass education.

The program Hsu and his colleagues established became a model which was visited by governors and magistrates from all over China. In time it was officially adopted as the pattern for other parts of the country. But in many hsien men of Hsu's drive and idealism were lacking. In others landlords entrenched in power blocked the necessary tax and administrative reforms. Kiangning Hsien was heavily damaged during the fighting for Nanking in 1937. Most of the doctors fled inland and Japanese permitted the project to die.

Hsu paid a high personal price for the success of the experiment. In 1933 he had married an American lady doctor who had been one of his teachers at Cheloo Medical School. He feels that she gave him much of the inspiration that made his work possible. One night in October 1935 when she was returning from Nanking to Kiangning Hsien she was robbed and strangled to death by a rickshaw coolie.

In September 1937 after the outbreak of the Sino-Japanese War, Hsu went to America to study at the John Hopkins School of Hygiene and Public Health on a Rockefeller Foundation scholarship. He returned to China the next year and went inland to help with the war effort against Japan. For the next nine years he gave most of his efforts to helping control malaria.

During the late summer of 1938 Hsu gave up his announced engagement to his second wife -- they were finally married the next year -- and for three months fought malaria in the rural areas of Kweichow Province. In large districts harvesting of the crops had stopped because all able-bodied men and women were down with malaria. Hsu walked more than 240 miles through the mountains to distribute his limited stock of 20,000 tablets of quinine. He found one village where no fires were burning.

None of the villagers had eaten for several days because they were all too ill to move. Two weeks later when Hsu left the entire population

JOINT COMMISSION ON RURAL RECONSTRUCTION

lined the street to see him off. He was given the kind of firecracker farewell usually reserved for gods and similar folk.

"People in the big cities are only for themselves," Hsu remarked. "They don't care for the people. Nobody else would go out there to the villages and help the peasants. That's why the Kuomintang was defeated -- "everyone was selfish."

After returning from his tour of the rural areas., Hsu was appointed the dean of a medical officers training class in Public health at Kweiyang. As such, like all other senior officials in China, he was required to take one month of special political training at the Kuomintang Party Central Political Military Training Corps Center in Chungking. Thereafter, he was automatically a member of the Kuomintang. But for Hsu, that month of indoctrination was largely a formality. "We technical persons had no political activities," he said.

In 1939 the Rockefeller Foundation invited Hsu to join their malaria research center in Western Yunnan Province as assistant to the director. After a few months he became acting director and was later given full charge of the work. When the Japanese occupied Western Yunnan in 1942 Hsu evacuated his unit up the Burma Road. The laboratory was reestablished at Koloshan near Chungking and moved to Nanking after V.J. Day. Hsu continued his research, training of anti-malaria officers and experimentation with methods of control until November 1948 when he resigned to work with the Joint Commission on Rural Reconstruction. At that time he refused an offer of a traveling grant from the Rockefeller Foundation to study malaria control and rural health in the U.S., South America, Italy and India. It was a strong temptation for a person such as Hsu who had lived on his meager Chinese Government salary while he worked with the Rockefeller group on malaria control,

Although Hsu is convinced on the basis of his experience that the Joint Commission on Rural Reconstruction is realistically tackling the problems of China on the only level where they can be solved, he is debating in his own mind how long he can afford to remain with the organization. He takes it for granted that the Communist Armies can occupy the remainder of China whenever they chose to do so.

"The China Aid Act which provides the money to finance JCRR should not have the clause that states we can not work in Communist dominated areas,," Hsu said. "We should not care whether the Communists or the Kuomintang occupy the area -- we should help the people wherever we can."

It is for this reason that Hsu is convinced that no matter how constructive the effects of his work for JCRR may be, he must eventually leave the organization. "If JCRR specifically refuses to help the people except in Liuomintang controlled areas, then the Communists must treat all members of the organization like enemies. Then how can I continue to work in my country in the future and help the people?"

Hsu was recently offered another opportunity to accept the Rockefeller traveling grant, But be does not feel it would be right for a Chinese to leave his country at this time. He also feels that he can not be an opportunist and go to work for the Communists -- at least not now,

JOINT COMMISSION ON RURAL RECONSTRUCTION

If JCRR is forced to continue its present policy of only working in the shrinking areas that remain under so-called Nationalist control, than Hsu will probably resign and return to his native province of Chekiang. He was born and raised there in the family of a poor silk worker. Hsu was offered his first real opportunity for a medical education by the foreign doctors then in charge of the Ewa Mai mission hospital in Ningpo. His wife and two daughters are now in Ningpo and he has been offered a post at that hospital. He thinks that by returning there and working with the hospital he may be able to repay them in part for the opportunities they once offered him.

Eventually, Hsu is convinced, he must work with the government in power regardless of its political complexion if he is to "serve the people." Otherwise, he feels he would be forced to limit his efforts to a relatively small group while the need is actually so great. "If the new government is really for the people." Hsu added, "it is their job to find good men. They should then invite me to go to work,"

Sincerely,
Albert Ravenholt

INSTITUTE OF CURRENT WORLD AFFAIRS
522 Fifth Avenue, New York 18, NY,
Walter Rogers, Executive Director

Dear Mr. Rogers: Chengtu, China
14 October 1949

Among China's modern pioneers Dr. James Y. C. Yen has won a special place. The Mass Education Movement that he founded may be superseded by newer and more violent methods of social revolution, But the work of this man who combines a Chinese classical scholar heritage with a very modern American approach to getting things done has influenced many of this country's constructive leaders. For anyone interested in the future development of the world's backward areas there is much to be learned from the experience of Yen and his colleagues.

Now at the age of 56, Yen still magnetizes associates with his enthusiasm for building, his energy and quick pointed wit. He likes to give speeches. He is in the prime of his career although most familiar institutions around him are collapsing. When he explains the circumstances and ideas that have made his life work Yen gesticulates freely and his lean sensitive face suggests the man's combination of devout Chinese Christian and smooth, shrewd organizer.

Yen first got a feel for the lot of his ordinary follow Chinese during his early teens. As the youngest son of a family of scholars and teachers from whom he inherited "boxes and boxes of essays and poems and little else," he was sent to study the new "foreign learning" in a missionary school at Pao Ling in North-Central Szechuan Province. Four times a year he walked the 120 miles over the mountains to his native home in Pa Chung. Most of the men with whom he shared the road were cattle dealers, small traders and coolies who earned their living by carrying loads of salt, tobacco and cloth. At night he joined their discussions while soaking his feet in the common tub of hot water and resting on the bug-ridden straw mats.

Traditional Chinese society had two distinct classes; the literate scholars and officials and the coolies and workmen who lived by their physical labor. Each class had only a superficial idea of life within the other group. As Yen sees it now, it was almost an accident that he, became aware at an early age of the ignorance suffering and poverty of the great majority of his countrymen. "It made quite an impression on me," he said. The fall of the Manchu Mynasty in 1911 found Yen studying at the Chengtu mission college which later became West China Union University. His father had taught the Chinese language to several early missionaries and the youngest son had been the first in his family to accept Christianity. After graduation he taught mathematics and English briefly to others who like himself wanted to learn more about the West and then went on to the University of Hong Kong. But Ten was unhappy with the British policy of giving first opportunities to their own nationals and acted on a friend's suggestion that he continue his studies in the United States. Originally, he set out for Oberlin College but a Yale University graduate on board ship convinced the young Chinese there was a better school in New Haven, Connecticut. Yen arrived there with $80 to his credit.

MASS EDUCATION MOVEMENT

The years at Yale University where he worked his way had great influence upon Yen's later life. As he explains it "In China we were caught in the old society. But at Yale I felt a fish in water. I made the Yale Glee Club. That expression of having finally something particularly appealed to me. I took ex-President Taft's course in Constitutional Law. In China it would have been

unthinkable that the former head of the State should come back to teach in a school. That free democratic spirit at Yale suited me tremendously." When the United States entered the First World War, Yen responded to the call for YMCA workers to go to France with the 200,000 Chinese laborers attached to the Allied Forces. He was assigned to work with 5,000 men. "That was the beginning of my real education" he said.

The workers were mostly coolies from North China. They were assigned to loading railway cars, laying track working in factories and digging trenches. At night when they returned to their barracks these men wanted news about their home country and the War. They also wanted to send letters to their families. And Yen found himself swamped with requests to write 60 to 200 letters a day.

Stimulated by circumstances Yen decided the only solution was to teach these men to read their own news and write their own letters. At a special mass meeting he asked for volunteers who would become his students. When 40 timidly raised their hands, he took them on. Yen wrote his own text books. His instruction emphasized two principles (1) to teach the men something they needed rather than what I as a scholar thought they ought to know," and (2) to make the men apply their now-found knowledge immediately. After four months he gave an examination and found 35 of the original class of 40 were able to read simple news sheets and write their own letters. Yen arranged to climax the course with a graduation exercise where the commanding general handed out diplomas amid applause by several thousand Chinese laborers. He then arranged for the newly educated men to teach their comrades and they in turn each taught another group.

One evening when the head of the "Y" Chinese service in France arrived on an inspection tour he heard Yen's students reciting their lessons aloud. He examined the students by writing characters on the blackboard and was deeply moved at the sight of these coolies trying to learn. A week later he ordered Yen to Paris to organize a similar program for all Chinese laborers along the front. Yen gave a one-week seminar on his methods to 80 Chinese students working with other units and they returned to their camps and began teaching. They also started a Chinese Laborer's Weekly in Paris for distribution among the men.

Yen one day got a letter from a man who had recently learned to read. It read roughly as follow: "Mr. Yen, big teacher: Since you published your newspaper I began to know everything under heaven. But your newspaper is so cheap; it costs only one centime and you may close down soon. Here I give you 365 francs for your paper which I saved during my last three years of labor in France." Yen said it was then he decided to devote his life to educating the millions of men in China who were illiterate.

MASS EDUCATION MOVEMENT

Yen was back in the United States recruiting more college men for the program when the Armistice brought an end to the War. With the work in France at an end he took advantage of an opportunity to do graduate work in Political Science at Princeton University. When he returned to China in 1920, Yen was asked to join the permanent staff of the YMCA. He accepted on condition that he be permitted to start a department of mass education.

After two years of preparatory work during which he wrote the first 1000 character People's Reader, Yen, his wife and their co-workers started the first large anti-illiteracy campaign in the city of Changsha. Interest was aroused with street parades, posters and leaflets. The city was divided into

52 sections where recruiting teams enrolled students aged 10 to 56. Volunteer teachers included college students, professional men and women and officials. The provincial governor gave diplomas to graduates of a four-month course. Thereafter the province was helped to organize its own Mass Education Movement.

Similar campaigns followed in Chefoo, Hangchow, Canton and Hankow. Yen's work was separated from the YMCA and in August 1923 organized as the National Association of the Mass Education Movement with headquarters in Peiping. Associations were started in each province and by 1924 Yen said the MEM had approximately 100,000 voluntary teachers. Prominent Chinese intellectuals such as Chan Shen-tung, Hu Shih and Lin Yu-tang helped prepare texts. Among the most forceful contributors was Chen Tu-hsiu, one of the original founders of the Chinese Communist Party. Madame Hsiung, the wife of a former Chinese premier, became chairman of the MEM while Yen assumed the title of General Director of the organization. The Commercial Press publishing house in Shanghai sold over ten million copies of the first four volumes of the People's Readers plus novels, history and other selections from the People's Literature Series.

In spite of its considerable popularity, the early Mass Education Movement did not to come to grips with China's more fundamental problems. In the larger cities literacy in itself had utility -- there were books and newspapers to read. And a literate man had a better opportunity to improve his livelihood. But this was not true in the countryside where lived about 80 percent of the Chinese people. During the middle 20's the MEM carried out literacy campaigns in two areas of North China of 20 counties each, After farmers learned to read they got what Yen calls "divine discontent." Peasants, who had been poor and filthy for so long they did not realize they were poor and dirty, were grateful because they had learned to read and write but they wanted a better income. MEM workers began to see that unless they helped with rural economic improvement literacy would have little meaning.

Yen and his colleagues made several attempts to help farmers economically by distributing improved seeds. But they soon realized that they did not know enough about the Chinese farmer and his problems to be able to help him. They decided that a "social and human laboratory" was needed to study the problems and develop solutions.

MASS EDUCATION MOVEMENT

From this realization grow the Tinghsien Center which Yen likes to talk about as a pilot plant. Work originally had been started in the area by a local landowner who had returned from study in Japan. But other members of the local gentry blocked his efforts and he took to opium smoking. When this man learned of the MEM, he invited Yen and his colleagues to come and work in the area of Tse Chen Village. Work was started there in 1925 by two MEM specialists, an educational expert and a graduate of Cornell University College of Agriculture, who moved into a corner of the local temple. But, as Yen said, "the chasm between the realities of the Chinese peasant and the old way of learning was like the distance between heaven and earth." At the time there was not a regular agricultural experiment station in all of North China and the two sons with the help of assistants who came later had to develop their own breeds of pigs suited to local needs and select their own improved seed. It took six months of work before the farmers developed enough confidence in the MEM workers to discuss their problems freely. But gradually by actually growing better crops and holding country fairs the specialists aroused the interest of the farmers.

In 1928 Yale University cabled Yen an invitation to return for the 10th reunion of his class and accept an honorary degree. At the suggestion of friends in New York, Yen organized the American Cooperating Committee of the Mass Education Movement. Until that time the MEM had lived on Chinese contributions and sometimes been limited to an annual budget of less than $4,000. Yen now set out boldly to raise funds for the work in China but after six months he still had no money. However, he bad learned it was necessary to interest potential contributors personally in the work. With this new approach he secured nearly half a million dollars in contributions for the MEM from prominent Americans within the next four months.

Yen's return to China in May 1929 coincided with an invitation from the government of Tinghsien, seconded by the local gentry, to make the entire county an experimental and demonstration area.

Headquarters of the NMM were moved from Peiping nearly 150 miles south to the old Tinghsien examination hall. The funds from America enabled the MEM to recruit 65 prominent Chinese, including three ex-college presidents and about 25 graduates of foreign universities who had specialized in such fields as education, agriculture and health. Yen said, "We brought the scholars from the big city to the feet of the people. It was probably the first time in Chinese history that scholars went to the people to study their needs."

As the work of the Mass Education Movement at Tinghsien was established on a firm basis it became possible to approach the study of rural problems and possible solutions more scientifically. Over the next six years the MEM workers learned there were four basic problems facing the great majority of China's millions who live on the land. Yen defines these four as follows: (1) Ignorance and mental stagnation that results in part from illiteracy, (2) Poverty resulting from the farmer's failure to produce more and retain a larger share of production for his own use, (3) Disease that handicaps the farmer as a producer and as a human being, and, (4) Misgovernment. As the work begun in 1925 was expanded the MEM found that no one of these problems could be tackled independently. "We had to work at all of them if we were going to accomplish anything that was fundamental," Yen said.

One of the first problems that demanded solution in Tinghsien was "how to wake up the people." Obviously, no program could be imposed from above and it was necessary to arouse the people's determination to work for them selves so they could carry on alone. The MEM approach to a solution on this level is only one of several that have been developed in China.

Yen feels it was important first of all to give the people the minimum essentials of language, without it farmers were limited to sometimes clumsy and inefficient communication by word of mouth. He explained through the establishment of People's Schools that educated the farmers it was possible to accomplish four basic objectives, (1) To give the people the tools for self-improvement, (2) To bridge the gap between the educated few and the uneducated many and begin breaking down the two class system, (3) To give the educated in the village a following for their ideas and in turn make their scholarship realistic, and, (4) to organize graduates of People's Schools into important alumni associations. These associations became strong village organizations larger than single clan groups. Through these new organizations the people could undertake the common work of continuing to learn and reconstructing the community.

As an illustration of what can be done, Yen mentions the work at Tinghsien. The MEM first started two experimental People's Schools to develop content, techniques and text books for farmers. Next they selected six centrally located villages to demonstrate the findings of the first two schools. Within two and one-half years all 467 villages in the county had established self-supporting schools. Through these it was possible to extend an overall program. All the time, Yen said, "It was necessary to keep in mind that when we work at rural reconstruction the most important thing is to reconstruct the people."

Elsewhere in China other methods have been successful in generating initial confidence, response and awareness of a better life among farmers. During the war rural reconstruction workers in Kiangsi Province arranged inexpensive mass weddings that saved farmers from the indebtedness usually incurred in providing the necessary marriage ceremonies for their children. They followed up later with maternity help. In some areas films and other forms of visual education have been effective in stimulating a now attitude among farmers. Experts have found that in each area it in important to discover the "people's felt needs" and demonstrate an ability to fulfill them. Most specialists agree however that if literacy is not the necessary first "requirement of rural reconstruction" it in an essential part of any fundamental program.

The MEN found by using education as a "handle" they were able to go to work. Illiteracy was attacked through the People's Schools and the "Tao sheng" system of volunteer teachers whose students in turn taught others. An educational campaign wherein children sometimes taught their parents and wives their husbands provided the "social yeast" that developed consciousness of other opportunities.

MASS EDUCATION MOVEMENT

Once farmers had learned to read, it was "natural" for them to find out about improved seeds, fertilizers and pesticides. Through the social unit formed around the schools it was possible to introduce hybrid hogs that added an extra 80 pounds of weight per year and chickens capable of laying twice as many eggs as the local hens. From such beginnings agricultural extension in time developed to cover most fields of farm enterprise. In order to consolidate the gains in production, the MEM found it was also necessary to help the farmers to become better businessmen. This required the organization of cooperatives through which farmers could buy materials and transport and market their produce.

At Tinghsien the MEM was unable to take one of the most necessary steps in overcoming rural poverty -- rent reduction and sale of land to tenants. "We had no army," Yen said. "If we had tried to tamper with the land system the landlords would have cut off our heads. To revise the methods of land control requires strong government action." Yen and his colleagues hoped educated and organized farmers would be able to fight for their own welfare. Failing government enforcement of the land laws then on the books, they thought a beginning toward self ownership could be made by providing tenants with cheap credit.

The MEM was forced to go into public health work to insure that farmers and their families would have the physical capacity to learn and build. "As a basic principle," Yen said, "we never used a doctor where a layman with training could do the work." The first emphasis was placed on preventive medicine and school students and others were mobilized and trained to give vaccinations. They found that through the use of volunteers and by organizing health work as a community enterprise it was possible to provide a surprisingly adequate health service at a cost of ten cents per capita per year. The Tinghsien public health work, wherein a number of outside organizations Most specialists agree however that if literacy is not the necessary first "requirement of rural reconstruction" it is an essential part of any fundamental program. It certainly provided the basic pattern for much of China's later work in that field. (See my letter on Dr. Hsu Shih-chu.)

"Once the people began to be informed to produce a little more and to be healthier, we found it necessary to go into politics." Yen said. "There was the magistrate; corrupt, smoking opium and with relatives on the pay rolls. They collected all kinds of illegal taxes from the farmers and threatened to take away what the people were gaining." About this time--1933--Chiang Kai-shek heard of the health work in Tinghsien and called Yen to Nanking to be his guest for three days. Following Yen's visit with Generalissimo and Madame Chiang the Government enacted a law requiring each province to establish an experimental county. Yen at the same time accepted his first government position, he was named President of the first Institute of Political Reconstruction in Hopei Province. The position empowered Yen to recommend the magistrate to be appointed in the Province's experimental county -- Tinghsien. Yen said "Now, we had to go in ourselves and become students of local government. If it was dishonest and inefficient, then, why?" They found that for centuries the county government had concerned itself almost exclusively with tax collection and law suits. The MEM put "new wine in old bottles" and strengthened or created government departments to assist with agricultural improvement, cooperatives, health and education. To train the people, they started the election of village elders. When the Japanese attacked in 1937 and brought an end to the Tinghsien work, they were just ready to hold the first election for county magistrate.

The Tinghsien work was expensive. in addition to the funds subscribed during Yen's visit to the United States, the MEM was helped with work in its area by grants from the Rockefeller Foundation, the Milbank Memorial Fund and contributions from Overseas Chinese, particularly, in Honolulu. But Tinghsien was a laboratory where more than 200 highly trained men sought to discover new social techniques. Hundreds of men came there from other parts of China to learn the new ideas. From Tinghsien crews of specialists went out to six provinces directing work and stimulating government expenditure for rural reconstruction that eventually totaled about 50,000,000 silver dollars.

Like so much of China's constructive work, the Mass Education Movement was seriously crippled by the war with Japan. In addition to the Tinghsien work the MEM before 1937 had established two experimental and demonstration counties in other areas of China. In Hengshan hsien in Hunan Province and Hsintu hsien in Szechuan Province. When the Japanese attacked most of the Tinghsien personnel were moved to these two areas and headquarters for the MEM established in Changsha. The wartime fate of the MEM suggests some of the reasons why the Nationalist Government crumbled in the years since V.J. Day. Most specialists agree however that if literacy is not the necessary first "requirement of rural reconstruction" it in an essential part of any fundamental program.

In Hunan Province Yen and his colleagues were fortunate in having as governor General Chang Chih-chung, who understood and trusted the MEM. During 1938 and 1939 the MEM participated in retraining local officials. An a result of their work two-thirds of the county magistrates were replaced by new men within a year. Those trained to mobilize the people through rural reconstruction and better government included 5,000 provincial and county officials and 30,000 village heads. Thanks to the pressure of war which made officials bolder and the confidence of the Governor, the MEM helped generate a popular support for the Chinese cause that was partly instrumental in keeping the Japanese out of most of Hunan for six years. But as Ton said, "We got into trouble. The men we helped kick out of office were the relatives of important people." When the Governor left the province after the accidental burning of Changsha in 1939, the MEM was forced to go too. They had learned, however, how to conduct a province-wide re-education of officials.

In Szechuan Province that same year of 1939 General Chang Chun visited the MEM work in Hsintu hsien. He was impressed with their accomplishments in surveying land, reforming the tax system, stamping out banditry and starting the people in the county on the path to reconstruction and recommended to Chiang Kai-shek that the same principles be extended to the entire province. Unfortunately, for the MEM and for China, the news leaked out prematurely. Leaders of the powerful Elder Brothers secret society, bandit chieftans, local gentry and local police whose powers were threatened, surrounded Hsintu city with armed men and demanded that the MEM-appointed county magistrate be surrendered and executed. The magistrate-MEM leader at the time was away in Chengtu undergoing an operation for appendicitis and escaped with his life,. But when the governor of Szechuan in cooperation with the local landed gentry refused to protect the MEM, all work in Hsintu hsien came to a halt.

With most of its field work blocked by war and political reaction, the MEM concentrated from 1940 on upon training men and women for work among farmers. The MEM had found that the greatest bottleneck for any program was the lack of personnel who could really work on a rural level. Even modern Chinese university education was in many respects unrealistic. The young Chinese who studied education, medicine and agriculture were usually the sons of officials, merchants and other city folk. The boy who grew up as a "dirt farmer" rarely got enough education to pass college entrance examinations.

The-Rural Reconstruction College established by the MEM in October 1940 at Hsien Ma Hsiang about 30 miles outside of Chungking was an attempt to meet this need for useful young people. At Tinghsien the MEM had maintained an Institute giving short-term training to college graduates before sending them into the field. The new college, established in old Chinese farm homes among the rice paddies, at first provided a two-year course. During the war in an effort to increase production, remain close to the soil and accomplish the most with limited funds, each member of the faculty was required to grow his own crops. The MEM was not exempt from Kuomintang Secret Police interference and shortly after V. J. Day about 25 students from the College were arrested and later released. Mrs. Tong a Columbia University Teachers College graduate who has made a major contribution to the College, was black-listed by the police at the same time.

In 1945 the College was enlarged to provide a four-year course of study. Of the 51 graduates of the first full-course class in 1948, 45 went to work in the MEM. They were graduates of one of four departments, (1) Rural Education, (2) Sociology and social administration that prepared them to manage cooperatives and assist in local government, 3) Agriculture with special emphasis upon rural extension, and, 4) Hydraulic engineering with particular attention to small-scale irrigation. 41 students are required to take a half year "social internship." This may include supervising cooperatives, managing adult education classes, and working at county administration. This summer 102 undergraduates joined the citrus fly extermination campaign in a nearby county. The college has steadily gained in stature and the 194 freshmen who entered in 1949 were selected from 2,010 applicants. But to operate as a College the school must meet Chinese Government Ministry of Education requirements that place heavy emphasis upon courses of little value in rural work. It has not yet been possible on a sufficient scale to give the sons of real farmers scientific training and send then back to the land. However, establishment of the Rural Reconstruction College has stimulated interest in similar work at other centers of learning.

Yen returned to the United States in 1943 after an absence of 17 years. He visited areas where work similar to his own was in progress and consulted with exports in related fields. As he had done previously, Yen gave much of his time to stimulating am understanding in the United States of the present level of Chinese Society and its possibilities for development..

MASS EDUCATION MOVEMENT

Yen arrived back in China after Japan's surrender and began organizing an extension of the MEM methods. The Third Prefecture of Szechuan Province surrounding Chungking with a population of roughly 5,300,000 was designated as the West China Experimental Area on Rural Reconstruction. Veterans of Tinghsien and men who had gained experience at the Shantung Provincial reconstruction center at Tsoping and in the Chinese Industrial Cooperatives were recruited for the work.

The improved techniques first developed at Tinghsien were gradually extended throughout this area until they are now being implemented in six counties and the special district of Peipei. "Cooperative-school districts" of 180 to 200 families have been organized as the basic unit for rural reconstruction. In each there is a People's School with a full-time adult education worker who selects and trains "Tao Sheng" volunteers. These men in turn teach groups of farmers in their home or wherever convenient. Each district has its agricultural production cooperative. Within some units they have also organized special producers cooperatives that enable families to earn added income during slack farm seasons by weaving and other work. Mass education is stimulated by limiting membership in these cooperatives to persons who meet or work toward certain standards of literacy.

In 1947 after the work in the Third Prefecture was off to a new start Yen returned to the United States. He was convinced that if rural reconstruction were to be done on a scale meaningful for all of China, more funds and technicians were needed as well as government cooperation. And the Chinese Government was sometimes more sensitive to suggestions from the U.S. Government than to ideas proposed by its own citizens. For nearly a year Yen tried to educate members of the U.S. Government to the needs and opportunities for rural work in China. Congress responded to his and other efforts and included a clause in the China Aid Act of 1948 providing up to 10 percent of the $275,000,000 ECA allocation could be used for rural reconstruction. When the Chinese and American Joint Commission on Rural Reconstruction was established on October 1, 1948, to implement this provision, Yen was named one of the five Commissioners.

Since that time Yen has been absorbed in the Commission's work of trying to implement on a broad scale throughout areas of China still under Nationalist control a program of rural reconstruction. Many of the ideas used were developed by the MEM. But civil war and the time limitation imposed by the China Aid Act -- it expires in February 1950 -- made it impossible to initiate on a province-wide scale methods as thorough as those evolved by the MEM. Instead, the JCRR has given technical and financial assistance to local sponsoring agencies to enable them to carry out their individual projects, This includes work in all major fields such as production and distribution of hog cholera vaccine, assisting government-backed land rent reduction programs, building small irrigation systems, establishing local self-supporting health services and extension of Nancy Hall sweet potatoes.

The MEM, classed as a sponsoring agency, is scheduled to receive the equivalent of U.S $1,000,000. Regulations governing the China Aid Act require all funds to be expended by the time the Act expires. This prevented the MEM from making the fullest use of the funds. But it did provide the necessary capital to expand and develop producers' and farmers' cooperatives. This year for the first time hand weavers in Pishan, organized into cooperatives using capital provided through the MEM, were able to compete successfully with big city mills. In terms of rural living this meant that thousands of farmers who otherwise would not have enough food could eat adequately and afford to release their children from work to attend school. The overall program is receiving an added boost this year with the enforcement of the Government's JCRR-assisted 25 percent land rent-reduction law that places much needed additional buying power in the hands of the great proportion of tenant farmers.

With the collapse of the Nationalist Government, Yeng like so many of his constructive minded colleagues, must make a difficult choice. During the last 20 years he repeatedly refused offers of high government positions. He feels that although a man might in name be given great power, actually, a permanent contribution can only be made by building up from the grass roots. If he remains in China now and attempts to adjust his dynamic personality and methods to the Communist approach, it is still questionable whether China's new rulers will really permit him to work. In the past the Communists reacted favorably to much of Yen's work. But they were scornful of the attempts to carry through a peaceful and gradual social revolution. Yen's presence in Washington, D.C., at the time Congress enacted the China Aid Act in 1948 caused the Communist radio to attack him almost daily for about two weeks.

And yet, the alternative for Yen is to cut himself adrift from the mainstream of his own culture and people. If he decides to do this his life may continue to have content in the sense that he sees the development of most of the world's backward areas in the same essential terms. He is convinced it is all part of one enormous problem that can not be ignored by any people or government, even if it is without their own borders.

Sincerely,

Albert Ravenholt

Received New York 11/1/49.

INSTITUTE OF CURRENT WORLD AFFAIRS
522 Fifth Avenue, New York 18, N.Y.
Walter S. Rogers, Executive Director

Albert Ravenholt
c/o U.S. Consulate General
Taipeh, Taiwan

Dear Mr. Rogers: 2 February 1950

In discussion of United States assistance to underdeveloped areas I have seen little mention of the need to consider size and growth of populations in those regions. And yet, all I have learned suggests the pressure of too many people on the land -- now so fundamental to political, economic and cultural developments in this part of the world -- is only a fraction of what we can expect when the benefits of Western sanitation, medicine and the like are made available on a larger scale,

Taiwan offers a startling example of the population growth that comes with certain applications of modern science. If the present "natural" rate of increase continues -- without any significant future influx from the mainland -- it threatens to cancel out efforts at increasing production. Eventually, it will doom the people here to a lower standard of living. This is true in spite of Taiwan's great natural wealth and comparatively high level of technical skills.

When the Dutch colonizers arrived on Taiwan in 1624 it is reported that the Chinese population totaled about 25,000, plus an unknown number of aborigines of proto-Malay stock. After the Manchus conquered Taiwan in 1683 they encouraged immigration, particularly from Fukien and Kwangtung Provinces. By the mid 18th Century the old historical accounts estimated there were about one million persons on the Island.

In 1895 when Taiwan was ceded to Japan under terms of the Treaty of Shimonoseki the population was estimated at somewhat more than two million. James Davidson, the US. Consul here then, reported in 1902 that the Island had a population of 2,730,865. The records of the first complete Japanese census in 1905 listed a population of 3,156,706, During the 50 years of their rule the Japanese virtually barred all immigration from the mainland and permitted only a limited number of their own nationals to settle on Taiwan. Official publications state there were 181,847 Japanese on the Island in 1923. But by 1943 when the last complete Japanese figures were published Taiwan's population numbered 6,585,841 -- it had more than doubled during the 38 years for which accurate statistics are available.

Since the Chinese re-established their administration on Taiwan -- and particularly during the last year -- the question of the Island's population has become a highly controversial political issue, Last May the authorities here took a census and released the official figure of 7,026,883. But, although it is not generally known, the real figure is nearly 10,000,000, including about 600,000 members of the Nationalist Army, Navy and Airforce, their dependants and refugee government officials. The most reliable sources indicate the native Taiwanese now number about 7,250,000, one local newspaper that published the story of the "real population figure" based on leaks from the census bureau was immediately suppressed. The Nationalist Government was anxious to avoid criticism for contributing to the Island's economic ills by bringing in so many mainlanders. A few Chinese nowreach Taiwan by way of Hongkong and others are smuggled in from Chusan and smaller islands along the mainland by the Nationalist Navy. But at least for the time being, Communist conquest of the mainland has halted large scale immigration.

As far as can be learned, the phenomenal growth in population since the establishment of Japanese rule resulted essentially from two developments; (1) Rapid expansion of the Island's agricultural production through the use of more modern methods coincident with the building up of trade and minor industries, and (2) Efficient application of Japanese techniques of sanitation. The first offered food and work for an ever growing population and provided a surplus of raw materials for export to Japan, The second removed many of the checks that had limited the growth of population.

When the Japanese first came to Taiwan hundreds of their officials, technicians and soldiers died of disease and others were invalided home, In 1896 more than 100 newly arrived Japanese died of plague in and around Taipeh. Cholera, malaria and smallpox also were common on the Island at the time. Early accounts mention the high mortality rate among infants, Missionaries at that time sought to combat the widespread practice of infanticide, particularly of girl children. With the exception of two small Christian missionary efforts, medical practice on the Island when the Japanese arrived was limited to the work of Chinese herb doctors.

The Japanese moved rapidly to overcome these obstacles to their exploitation of Taiwan. By 1902 they had established a modern medical school in Taipeh that provided a three-year course for about 70 students. They had opened ten hospitals throughout the Island, plus special centers that treated prostitutes and victims of plague and small pox. Wells had been dug to provide safe water for most of the major cities. The Japanese also gave the birth rate a boost by gradually abolishing the use of opium.

Under the combined stimuli of Japanese legal prohibition and growing economic opportunities, infanticide almost disappeared. The ordinary Taiwanese citizen was-able to feed, clothe and put to work a larger family. This and the Confucian social pressure for numerous descendants helped push up the population curve. For example, orphanages found little to do on Taiwan. Unlike ordinary families on the mainland, the Taiwanese were able and anxious to adopt children left without parents.

These developments had an interesting effect upon the population tables. In 1906 the Japanese reported births on Taiwan for the previous year had numbered 121,067 and deaths 104,749. By 1916 annual births bad risen to 133,717 and deaths dropped to 102,519. In 1921 the Japanese census bureau reported 161,987 babies born the previous year while deaths were down to 91,513.

TAIWAN POPULATION EXPLOSION

Taiwan's population increased even faster after the reorganization of the Japanese administration and the rapid expansion of primary education beginning in 1919. The police were made responsible for reporting infectious diseases, enforcing sanitary measures and supervising periodic Island-wide vaccination programs. The Japanese paid a bounty on rats and established 18 quarantine stations to prevent introduction of diseases from abroad. The educational system barred Taiwanese from advanced work in certain fields and encouraged many to study medicine. Japanese medicine here emphasized curative work and provided modern facilities for the cities where lived the great number of Japanese businessman and administrators. It did not supply extensive hospital care for the rural population.

At the start of the Pacific war these measures had helped produce a birth rate on Taiwan that was more than twice the death rate. In 1941 the Japanese statistics listed births at 42.17 per 1,000 and deaths at 18.37. In 1942 the figures were 41.21 births and 18.37 deaths for every 1,000 of the populations. Several Taiwanese cities were heavily bombed by the U.S. Air Force. The War also deprived Taiwan of imported items such as certain drugs. But the Island has a surplus of food and it appears the population was not greatly affected by the Pacific Conflict.

The arrival of Chinese administrators after V.J. Day was followed by outbreaks of smallpox, cholera and plague. They resulted from the sudden influx of mainland troops and the disintegration of the Island's health services under less able Chinese rule. Chinese specialists, assisted by private and international agencies, were called in. After the corrupt administration of the first Chinese governor, General Chen Yi, was replaced by more able Chinese officialdom in the spring of 1947 these diseases were brought under control.

Following the War the estimated 300,000 Japanese officials, police and civilians here soon were replaced by an even larger number of Chinese mainlanders. The Chinese figures, meanwhile, suggest the native population continued to grow at near its previous rate. For 1947 the local statistics bureau lists 37.92 births and 18.37 deaths per 1,000. In 1948 births were reported to number 31.32 per 1,000 and deaths 12.74. Unsettled conditions that discouraged young people from marrying may account for part of the drop in birth rate. The Chinese have been less efficient that the Japanese in reporting deaths and in some cases have ignored infant mortalities in compiling village statistics. Among the aborigines the Japanese system of controls was not replaced by an equally effective Chinese administration and the total population in the mountain districts has dropped due to widespread malaria, pneumonia, worms and other ailments.

During the last 18 months as the Communists moved south successive waves of refugees flooded into Taiwan, officials who minimize this number may themselves be misled by the fact that so many of the mainlanders entered Taiwan illegally or were brought in as dependents of the Armed Forces. The most reliable sources indicate there are now at least two million Mainlanders on the Island, including the Army, Navy and Airforce, plus garrisons on other islands that are supplied from here. If the Communists conquer Taiwan many of these will undoubtedly, want to return to their mainland homes and relatives. Otherwise, Taiwan must somehow provide for nearly ten million persons and their offspring.

It is the considered opinion of Chinese and American experts who have surveyed Taiwan's resources that there are opportunities here for greatly expanding production. Agricultural and industrial production is now below the highest levels achieved by the Japanese. Provided the military burden is drastically reduced and a larger share of government expenditure is channeled into productive enterprise, an able administration here should be able to duplicate the Japanese accomplishment in time. At present the J.G. White firm of American engineers is employed by ECA to assist the Provincial Government rebuild its industries. The Sino-American Joint Commission on Rural Reconstruction is helping restore the rural economy to its prewar level, They have discovered a number of possibilities for increasing production. The engineers have estimated that if the Island's total annual output of rice bran from milling were processed, it could yield about 25,000 tons of edible oil - a critical commodity that now must be imported. Increased development of' hydro-electric power, irrigation, timber resources and chemical fertilizers from local raw materials could all contribute to greater production. But in time the population curve, if it continues at its present pace, would wreck any chances of creating on this Island the kind of life that permits a realization of the individual's "human potential."

A few Chinese and foreign leaders here are now becoming aware of the implications of this population increase. So far they have been unable to do much about it. But their ideas and suggested "solutions" may be of interest to planners concerned with other areas as well as those interested in the future of Taiwan.

One interesting approach to the problem was suggested to me by V.S. de Beausset, an American chemical engineer from Grosse Ile, Michigan, who is advising the Provincial Government on industrial problems. As a result of his experience In India and here, de Beausset is convinced the plans followed inindustrializing "backward" areas can have an important effect upon the population growth.

With a few exceptions, the pattern of industrialization in Asia to date has attempted to reproduce the centralized industrial plants of the West, But the methods and means of the farmers, and particularly the growers of rice, have not enabled them to mechanize production. Wet culture rice growing under methods now in use in Asia generally produces higher annual yields per acre than the mechanized methods developed in the United States -- partly because it is possible by transplanting the rice seedlings to start a second crop before the first is harvested.

This method demands at planting and harvest seasons a very high proportion of human labor to the land cultivated, In most areas of Asia this has meant that as labor was attracted by new industry into the growing cities the continued need for farm hands during the crucial seasons encouraged the bearing of more offspring. As a result of experiments de Beausset has found it is possible to so plan most modern industry that it can release the majority of the labor force for work on the land during the few weeks required for planting and harvesting, and still maintain an efficient operation. In working out these ideas de

TAIWAN POPULATION EXPLOSION

Beausset found the principle of the pilot plant in the United States useful.

The development of home and handicraft industries in some areas of Asia has helped absorb surplus farm labor during slack seasons. In some areas this happened after the "population jump" brought on by industrialization. In any ease it did not take the farmer mentally into the industrial age with all that implies in values and social objectives.

Doctors and others who have studied Taiwan's population problem feel this question of social values is of extreme importance. To the average Taiwanese the "good life" still means having plenty to eat and many children. Under the Japanese they learned to want rubber shoes, bicycles and flashlights in addition to simple clothing. But the average Taiwanese never got the vision of a higher level of living, intellectual and material. As one Chinese doctor expressed it: "Unless they learn to want more than food and children, there will come a time when they can't have both of those and then there will be trouble."

In the urban centers there is a desire for education which might serve to delay marriage and center attention upon other social objectives. But a high proportion of openings for students have been reserved for mainlanders and the present schools can not meet the demand. I know several young Taiwanese who have repeatedly taken entrance examinations for colleges and the Taiwan University and failed to be admitted. In time many give up hope and in response to parental pressure get married and begin raising a family,

In the countryside it is still true that the principal recreation available to an ordinary farmer and his wife is sexual intercourse, The few U.S. films and similar attractions that have been offered in rural areas have brought in large crowds. Outlying villages offered to pay the USIS to send out more films. The experts are convinced that extensive use of films and radio could go far toward arousing an awareness of another way of living,

Eventually, any serious attempt to limit population growth must help a family that wants to do so to avoid having more children. Many of the relatively well-educated Mainlanders who flocked to Taiwan are anxious not to be burdened with large families. But most do not know where to go for guidance. The JCRR has considered providing educational material on the implications of population growth to interested groups. But to date they have hesitated to act for fear of repercussions among Catholic groups in the United States and local Chinese leaders who feel that somehow discussions of a woman's menstrual cycle are crude.

One of the more promising opportunities for dealing with the problem of population control may present itself if and when the now province-wide health service is established. The Japanese achieved their high level of health through regimentation. Now a few Chinese leaders are working hard to replace that method with a system of personal and public concern for general health that emphasizes preventive medicine. One of the greatest obstacles is the number of Taiwanese doctors whose medical knowledge is at least ten years out of date. Many of these have now become politicians.

TAIWAN POPULATION EXPLOSION

The new health system is to be based upon a corps of some 3,000 home-visiting public health nurses, The first class of 30 nurses is now being trained. Unlike the doctors trained under the Japanese, these nurses should have the intimate contact with rural folk that would enable them to give acceptable advice. The program is handicapped for lack of funds. The public health men I talked with would like to have back copies of American medical publications. They would also welcome an opportunity to send about ten of their nurses and doctors to the United States for advanced public health training -- it is difficult for them to break the habits instilled by the Japanese.

All of these possibilities are only incidental to a vigorous official acceptance of the need to deal realistically with the problem of too many people. At least until the political situation on Taiwan is stabilized, either by Communist conquest or clear indications that the Island will continue under its present rulers for a long time, other matters probably will take precedence. But unless the population problem is met in time efforts at increasing production can provide only stop-gap social and economic relief for the people on Taiwan.

I would like to include a comment made to me in West China by a veteran missionary doctor. He had questioned many Chinese women when they reached menopause on their number of pregnancies. The average number was 18 but some had gone through 23 and 24. Several admitted they had taken the lives of their own new-born infants. As this doctor summed it up: "The choice for these Chinese women from ordinary families has nothing to do with whether or not they like the idea of birth control. It is a question of using infanticide or more civilized methods for limiting their families to the number they can feed."

Sincerely,

Albert Ravenholt

Received New York 2/16/50.

Chicago Daily News Foreign Service   January 2, 1951

Reds Aim to Submerge Religions
Under Cold Communist Materialism

by ALBERT RAVENHOLT

HONG KONG,
January 2, 1951

One of the greatest missionary efforts in the history of Christendom is ending as the Communists oust the last of the foreigners who brought the teachings of Christ to China. This grim exodus of foreign missionaries coincides with the severest trial the Chinese Christian churches ever have known.

If the Christian faith now fades out in China as it did once centuries ago, indications are that other religions also will be submerged by the cold materialism of the Communists. But Christianity's survival doctrines of the Red dictator are a choice of standards.

The first Christian missionaries went to China in the 7th Century. But the early Christian communities in China died out in the 14th Century, for reasons unknown to modern historians. About four century's ago the Jesuits took up the challenge and re-entered the field.

When British and other Western warships and troops brought the Emperors to terms and opened China to trade roughly a century ago, protestant missionaries joined in the Christian effort.

At the start of the 20th Century foreign missionaries spread throughout China. The setback they suffered during the anti-foreign Boxer Rebellion of 1900 soon was overcome. The Protestants entered their "golden period" after the First World War, when they had more than 6,000 foreign missionaries in China, many Europeans included.

These represented most of the major Protestant denominations and included many Europeans, although British, Canadian and American churches provided most of the support. Thirteen Christian colleges and universities were built, in addition to numerous primary and middle schools. While Protestants often worked with the newly educated urban groups that prospered on foreign trade and manufacturing, Catholic missionairies in the past century and a half concentrated on Cbina's rural folk. The Catholics built three universities, 189 middle schools and several thousand prayer and primary schools in addition to some hospitals.

At the height of their missionary efforts after the Second World War, Catholic priests, brothers, sisters, and lay missionaries numbered about 7,000. And the Catholics brought an estimated 3,000,000 into their churches.

Today Communist China's rulers are engineering the destruction of the Catholic Church wherever it fails to become an instrument of their regime. The persecution of the church was intensified after the

REDS AIM TO SUBMERGE RELIGIONS

"Chinese Peopl e's Volunteers" crossed the Yalu River in October, 1950. Some missionaries simply have been expelled. Others who were imprisoned experienced brain-washing and forced Communist indoctrination. **Missionaries often have been accused of murder and beaten.** Sometimes they were stoned by crowds incited to condemn them. The known dead include one archbishop and three bishops who perished in jail. Many Flee to Hongkong. This forced exodus has brought more than 4,500 Catholic missionaries to Hongkong. Only about 300 foreign Catholic missionaries are in China now, The Catholics often were slow to train Chinese priests to staff their churches. The comparatively limited Chinese clergy has been subjected to intense persecution. Perhaps 100 Chinese, priests have died in prison or been executed, usually after hysterical public trials. Chinese priests in jail are estimated to number between 300 and 400.Great pressure is directed on the Chinese priests to force them into the "National" or Catholic Reformed Church, sponsored by the Communist, government.

However, priests who have left China believe there is substantial support for the Reformed Church in only one fifth of the dioceses. Communist officials bluntly told some foreign missionaries they have embarked upon a 20year program to wipe out the Catholic Church.

Severing relations between Chinese Catholics and Rome is only the first step. Chinese Protestants who wish to practice their religion openly must become energetic supporters of Mao Tse-tung's "People's democratic dictatorship." The present struggle in China promises an almost classic test of whether spiritual values can be subverted by a hostile, state - supported materialistic creed employing most of the powerful modern propaganda weapons.

Communist conquest of the mainland four years ago found the Protestant churches depending largely upon Chinese leadership. This was the result of experience gained during the revolution in 1926-27, which brought the Nationalist government to power, and the war with Japan, when churches run by Chinese usually survived. It also reflected the approach of Protestant missionaries to their work. While foreign Catholics In China usually expected to live out their lives there in the service of their faith, foreign Protestants aimed to train Chinese replacements to take over the work.

Although there were more than 4,000 Protestant missionaries in China at the height of postwar efforts, this number had been reduced by one half when the Red armies swept across the land in 1949.

The few foreign Protestants who were caught by the Communist-organized "anti-imperialist, hate-America campaigns" suffered and sometimes died in the same prisons as the Catholics. Foreign Protestant missionaries now left in China number less than 20. About half of these are under house arrest and others are too old to leave. The government has taken over all Christian universities, colleges, middle schools, primary schools and hospitals.

INSTITUTE OF CURRENT WORLD AFFAIRS

522 Fifth Avenue, New York 18, NY
Walter S. Rogers, Director

Hong Kong
20 November 1951

COMMUNIST DESTRUCTION OF OVERSEAS CHINESE SUPPORT

Dear Mr. Rogers:

WITHIN RECENT MONTHS the Chinese Communists have made a major political blunder -- they have alienated millions of Overseas Chinese whom they planned to use to enhance their power at home and abroad. The Communists have accomplished this by letting their revolution run wild in the ancestral communities of the Overseas Chinese. The development suggests important flaws in the organizational machinery of China's new rulers. It has created an opportunity for forces opposing the Communists that is at present not used to any substantial degree.

The Overseas Chinese have performed a significant role in modern Chinese History. During the last 100 years, as population pressures in South China's coastal provinces forced Chinese to migrate abroad, they settled in most major cities of the world. There are no complete statistics on the number of Chinese now resident abroad. It is estimated that in North and South America they number several hundred thousand. The largest communities have grown up in rich, under-developed Southeast Asia, where Chinese merchants had maintained settlements for several centuries. At present the Chinese in Southeast Asia total about ten million. This includes more than three million Chinese resident in Thailand, more than two million in Indonesia and nearly three million who are settled in Malaya and Singapore. There are also large Chinese communities in the Philippines, Burma, Indo-China and Borneo.

Chinese who settled abroad often engaged in enterprises that involved a minimum of competition with local citizens, such as the hand laundry and Chinese restaurant business in America. Throughout Southeast Asia they proved to be more aggressive and commercial minded than the native inhabitants. Although the Chinese often started as coolies, in such booming cities as Singapore at the turn of the Century, many soon acquired wealth. They opened shops and trading firms and started rice mills, tin mines and rubber plantations.

As they developed their communities abroad, however, the Chinese maintained close ties with their ancestral homes. When the men left China to seek opportunity abroad, the women often remained at home. Some of the men sent for their wives when they could afford to do so. Others followed the accepted custom and took a younger second wife, while the first wife remained in China to manage family affairs. Even children born abroad were sometimes sent to China to be raised and educated. Within recent decades when Chinese overseas developed more normal family lives many elderly men still looked forward to retiring to live out their years in the ancestral home in China. Chinese veneration for their ancestors gave

COMMUNIST DESTRUCTION OF OVERSEAS CHINESE SUPPORT

these ties with the family homestead a religious as well as a filial significance.

Chinese abroad sent regular remittances home to support the clan establishment. These funds became an important source of foreign exchange for
China. They also made Chinese with relatives abroad the rich families in their communities who owned most of the land and business. Before the war with Japan Overseas Chinese owned about one-half of the real estate in Canton. They were large investors in Hong Kong business and property. The managers in China of these investments, particularly in land, became a special class of individuals who often were hated by the tenants.

Near the beginning of this century, as China awoke to the realities of life beyond her borders, the Chinese who had lived abroad led in the development of their homeland. They supplied most of the funds for Sun Yat-sen's first revolution that toppled the Manchu Dynasty in 1911. Men who had been born and raised abroad returned to China to become leaders in politics, education and business. During the early years of the war with Japan they contributed large sums to finance Free China's resistance. Young Chinese from Indonesia, Malaya and the Philippines returned to China as volunteers, determined to help protect and modernize their native country.

After the Communists overran the mainland, a great many Overseas Chinese, particularly in Southeast Asia, welcomed the establishment of the new government in Peking. They were disgusted with Nationalist administrative failures and corruption. Chinese abroad, especially in Thailand and the Philippines, felt pushed around by local governments trying to protect their nationals against tough Chinese competition. Many of these Chinese took pride in the power of the new Communist regime and hoped it would help them.

The Chinese Communists were aware of the opportunity this situation offered and at first capitalized on it. Radio Peking broadcast warnings to "reactionary American-rigged governments that oppress Chinese overseas." About the same time Communist agents appeared in all large Chinese communities in Southeast Asia. They helped organize the sending to Peking of delegates. These representatives of the Overseas Chinese participated in establishing the new government. The agents encouraged Chinese abroad to send money to China for investment in the "South China Enterprises Company" -- a Communist-managed joint government and private development corporation. They also promised the Government in Peking would continue the former Nationalist policy of recognizing as citizens of China all persons of Chinese race, regardless of where they were born or lived. Publicity was given to announcements from Peking that the property and relatives of Overseas Chinese would be given special protection when the land reform program was extended to South China.

Although a large number of Chinese in Southeast Asia and elsewhere remained skeptical of the intentions of China's new government and a tiny minority continued loyal to the Nationalists, this Communist approach had great appeal. The indications were that the Communists in time would be able to organize most of the Chinese in Southeast Asia and thereby exert an economic strangle-hold on the area. It appeared that by skillful use

COMMUNIST DESTRUCTION OF OVERSEAS CHINESE SUPPORT

of Chinese abroad the Communists could develop an excellent intelligence and propaganda network.

The story of how the Communists now have muffed this opportunity, at least for the time being, can best be told in terms of a single community. It is hazardous to generalize about the present stage of the Chinese upheaval. But fragmentary reports suggest similar revolutionary procedures have been at work in most of the ancestral communities of the Overseas Chinese.

The Four Districts, known in Cantonese as "Ssu Yap," are the ancestral home of about 90 percent of the Chinese settled in the United States. These Districts are Toishan, Hoiping, Sun Wui and Hok Shan. They are located on the coast of Kwangtung Province, about 100 miles southwest of here. Toishan has a
population of about one million, of whom perhaps 40 percent depend for part or all of their livelihood upon funds remitted from the United States or property owned in the district by Chinese in America. In the other three Districts the combined population of about one and one-half million is less dependent upon outside support. Funds from America, helped build up roads, schools and homes in the Four Districts and made them more prosperous than other communities in South China.

The Communists first entered the Four Districts in October, 1949, when the Red Armies captured Canton and over-ran South China. Before that time the citizens of the Ssu Yap had little contact with the Communists who had operated as guerrillas in Kwangtung Province particularly during the war with Japan. Like many Chinese they did not so much welcome the Communists as accept them. The most common attitude at the time seems to have been one of hoping to get along with the Communist regime in the Chinese fashion, as they had done with earlier governments.

This attitude among citizens of the Four Districts toward the regime, that apparently had inherited the "mandate of heaven," was encouraged by their first experience of Communist rule. The newly-appointed Communist officials arrested a few of the more prominent ex-Nationalists and levied fines against the `notoriously rich." But the new rulers were more lenient than many had expected and residents who have escaped report that during the months immediately following the Communist take-over there was a general air of relaxation throughout the "Ssu Yap."

Apparently, the Communists wanted such a breathing period; as soon as their rule was secure they started a careful study of the internal social structure of the villages. Young Communist political workers who had arrived with the Red Armies were sent into the countryside. At first they listened more than they talked; discovering who were the dispossessed, what were the felt wants and dislikes of the community and who was raw material for leading the local revolution.

The political organizers who arrived first in the Four Districts were Cantonese. But they were soon out-numbered by young, ardent political workers who came down from the North. Chinese who have come out to Hong Kong estimate there now are more than 4,000 of these political workers in the Four Districts. About the time most of them were recruited the Communists were running short of trained political cadres needed to organize the large areas of South, West and Northwest China their armies had captured. Many of the political workers had received only a primary school education before they were enlisted. Since joining the Communists they have been intensely indoctrinated. They often lack the common sense approach characteristic of many of the more veteran Chinese Communists when they are dealing with domestic problems. Local citizens insist that these Northerners were brought in "because Cantonese don't go to extremes."

As soon as they had learned to know the villages, the political workers began organizing the "Nung Wei," or Farmers Associations. These Associations were composed of tenant farmers, farm laborers, "poor farmers" and "middle farmers." The "Nung Wei" also accepted for membership "bad elements" -- individuals who had been expelled earlier from the Four Districts for minor offences or who had run off to Canton to escape punishment for such crimes as petty theft and now returned home on the heels of the Red Army. It appears that from 30 to 70 percent of the families in a village are represented in the "Nung Wei," depending upon how much of the wealth and property was home-owned. The head of each Farmers Association usually is elected for a term of three months and efforts are made to rotate the chairmanship, evidently in order to make the members more equally responsible for the decisions and actions of the "Nung Wei." In the Four Districts these Farmers Associations have steadily assumed more power until now they act as the supreme authority in each community. The political organizers work through the "Nung Wei" in helping them "turn over the society and build the new China." Regular Communist officials in the Four Districts are reported to have told local citizens that "at this stage of the revolution" they have no authority to interfere with the actions of the Farmers Associations and the political organizers. It is significant that many of these regular Communist officials, who claim their authority is severely circumscribed by directives originating in Peking, are natives of Kwangtung Province. As an example, the Communist magistrate of Toishan was a former primary school teacher in the neighboring district of Hoiping. His assistant also was formerly a school teacher in Hoiping.

After they were first organized, the "Nung Wei" started gradually to dominate the community. One of their first campaigns was known as the "support with donations the troops in the front area." Individuals who were thought to have wealth were informed of the sums expected from them. Almost everyone contributed as asked. The few who failed to do so discovered they had violated regulations of the new government that made them liable for heavy fines. The "Nung Wei" followed up with a series of money raising campaigns. Some were to purchase victory bonds, sold by the new government in Peking. Other levies were in the form of new taxes to be paid in grain. Failure to pay was treated as a crime against the new regime. These fund raising drives drained off the cash and grain in the possession of the more well-to-do families. Recently, they have also hurt the "ordinary people"; the small shop keepers, vendors and craftsman.

About a year ago, after the "Nung Wei had acquired some confidence in handling the wealthy families and elders who formerly dominated the community, they began to "settle accounts." At public meetings all citizens were encouraged to air their grievances and the crowd -- with the quiet help of the political workers -- dispensed "justice." Many landlords in the Four Districts were required to repay their tenants ten times the rent they had collected in a year. So far the landowners have retained title to their property and remained liable for taxes. But rents have been drastically reduced and most owners are denied the right to take back land, even to farm it themselves. Money lenders who had collected interest often were forced to return it. Clan heads were required to explain their management of accounts dating back many years; all the old festering family disputes were brought out into the open for public discussion. When the head of a family was judged "guilty" he usually was required to pay a fine. Since most cash and grain already had been contributed to earlier campaigns, the "Nung Wei" confiscated clothing and household effects and divided them as directed by the meeting.

Public enthusiasm for this new order was mobilized by holding more and more meetings where political workers and local leaders talked on the philosophy of the new era and the "power and justice that is on the side of the common people." These meetings of the "Nung Wei," wherein they also discussed their local program, often lasted far into the night. Refugees from the Four Districts claim the farmers held meetings and talked so much they had little energy left for daytime work in the fields.

In February, 1951, the emphasis in this revolution changed. The public search for men guilty of past financial misdeeds continued. But now the "Nung Wei," with the energetic assistance of the political workers, took on the new job of hunting out and destroying "counter-revolutionary elements who endanger the peoples movement." The start of this new campaign followed the announcement from Peking of a nation-wide program to eliminate active and potential enemies of the regime within China. Revolutionary methods that had formerly seemed harsh to local citizens now became cruel and often bloody.

From the outset of the drive against "counter-revolutionaries" everyone was forbidden to leave his home village except on a pass issued by the "Nung Wei." A special watch was kept on every citizen listed as a "first class landlord." The individuals singled out for liquidation included most of the former intellectuals and persons of wealth and status who had failed to become enthusiastic supporters of the new order.

The procedure used for destroying these individuals in the public mind, and often physically, is known as the "People's Trial." This grim affair usually is held by authority of the "Nung Wei." The accused appear singly or in groups on a platform. Under the leadership of a master of ceremonies, members of the audience are encouraged to announce charges. The crowd is whipped into a frenzy with the help of Communist organizers planted in the group. At a critical moment the crowd is asked to recommend punishment for the accused. Some persons have been forced to kneel on heated broken stones. Others have been hung-up or beaten in turn by the entire crowd. Men who have escaped report two cases in Toishan where relatives were forced to get down on the ground and drink the blood of individuals executed. They state that some time ago the Communists announced that more then 400 had been executed in the district of Toishan.

COMMUNIST DESTRUCTION OF OVERSEAS CHINESE SUPPORT

A Chinese who had lived for 20 years in the United States retired some yearsago to his ancestral home in the Four Districts. He became a respected and honored elder who was called in to settle disputes in keeping with the old Chinese custom of using a mediator. As part of the charge that marked him for liquidation, he was accused of believing in "Feng Shui", the ancient Chinese principle that graves should be situated where they overlook water and can be reached by the winds. He also was charged with being a land owner and a public enemy.

Last June, when the campaign to eliminate opponents of the new regime had generated terror throughout the Four Districts, the "Nung Wei" began adding a new feature; they arrested or placed under house supervision selected individuals on charges that required the payment of heavy fines. The accused persons were told to ask their relatives abroad for money to pay the fine. Illiterate individuals were helped to write telegrams and letters requesting the funds. Whenever fines were paid the "Nung Wei" kept 30 percent of the money for division among its members. The remaining funds were passed on to the Communist authorities. This practice is in keeping with the present revolutionary technique of paying a reward to those who "bring a criminal to justice."

The practice is illustrated by the case of a Chinese who worked for 40 years in Los Angeles. Before the outbreak of the war with Japan he returned to live in his ancestral home in Toishan. During the Sino-Japanese War he helped organize a "home protection corps" to safeguard property in the community. When a thief stole two pumpkins from the old man's garden the culprit was caught and shot by the corps.

Recently, the relatives of the executed thief brought charges against the old man from Los Angeles. He was arrested by the "Nung Weil" hung up by his hands and beaten many times. His fine was fixed at the equivalent of US $2,000. An urgent plea for help was sent to relatives in Hong Kong. After these relatives had contributed three-fourths of the funds required, the old man committed suicide, apparently out of desperation resulting from continued persecution. Several thousand similar suicides are reported from the Four Districts. Persons whose fines have been paid once sometimes have been charged a second and a third time. The "Nung Wei" have killed a considerable number of Chinese whose fines were not paid. Individuals who have escaped from the Four Districts believe this ransom system will continue as long as the "Nung Wei" think 'there is any hope of collecting more money.

The revolution has moved at a different speed in each local, area. However, the experience of a fairly typical community will indicate the scale of this practice in the Four Districts. In a section where lived about 650 families, 82 families have been prosecuted so far for all "crimes," including those requiring the payment of money by relatives abroad. In this community the largest sum demanded as ransom money was equal to US $9,000 and the second largest sum was US $7,000. To date there have been no executions in the community. Two persons have committed suicide while waiting for ransom money to be paid. Ransom money that was paid rather freely at first now is provided much less frequently. But the revolution in this community is still young. There has been very little "mind-washing" -- the Communist practice whereby persons of doubtful loyalty have their thoughts improved. In the schools

COMMUNIST DESTRUCTION OF OVERSEAS CHINESE SUPPORT

"self-criticism groups" have not yet been organized. One primary school teacher, who welcomed the Communists with enthusiasm, has now taken to the hills and become one of the few anti-Communist guerrillas in the area.

Recently, Communist officials in Canton and Peking have begun receiving protests from Chinese abroad, particularly in Hong Kong. However, the senior Communist officials, who once maintained close contacts with events on a village level, seem to have become much more remote. South China is far away from Peking and the leaders of the new government appear to be preoccupied with other affairs, including the Korean War and the development of Manchuria and North China. They are also accustomed to hearing complaints when the rough tools of the revolution destroy the fabric of an earlier society.

There have been earlier instances when the Communist-led revolution also has gotten out of hand. In parts of Shantung Province in 1946 they carried through a land reform program that was so bloody and destructive the Communists still refer to it as one of their major mistakes. Shantung, however, was fairly remote from the rest of the world and few persons outside of China learned of these Communist excesses. In South China now the Communist techniques themselves have advertised their character abroad.

It is difficult to envisage all of the consequences that will follow from this development of the Communist revolution in South China. But there are certain immediate implications that deserve attention. Although the ransom racket has brought a few extra funds to China for the moment it has also literally killed the golden goose. It is doubtful that the ransom techniques have yielded as much foreign exchange as Overseas Chinese would normally send home in an average year. And with their relatives in China gone they will have no reason for sending money to their ancestral homes in the future.

The political implications are apparent in this British Colony of Hong Kong. Two years ago the great majority of Chinese here welcomed the new Communist regime on the mainland. Now the great majority appear to be more loyal to the integrity of this place as a British Colony than many of the foreigners here.

The reaction among Overseas Chinese was suggested by the words of the Chinese owner of a large rice mill near Bangkok. He told me "The Communists have killed my whole family, including my grandmother. They all lived in our ancestral home near Swatow. My family never hurt anyone -- and look what happened to them." The Communists in China now have made a personal enemy of this Overseas Chinese. Since they killed his family, the Red regime lost all hold over him. This man who formerly was not interested in politics now is convinced the Communists seek his destruction. However, at present there is no indication that his opposition to the Communists is being organized.

FOREIGN AFFAIRS
AN AMERICAN QUARTERLY REVIEW

JULY 1952

FORMOSA TODAY

By Albert Ravenholt

THE IMMEDIATE PROBLEM that confronts Formosa is military. Last winter the Chinese Communists completed construction of a string of airbases along the Fukien coast on the mainland opposite the island. These bases are backed up by a network of airfields-including many built by Americans during the war-stretching across the interior of China to the foothills of Tibet. The new Communist airbases have been stocked with petrol and lubricants, and equipped with radar and antiaircraft guns. The Communists also have kept near at hand the thousands of junks and other craft they assembled for an invasion of Formosa before the U.S. Seventh Fleet moved in to protect the island in June 1950.

If the Korean war ends without a settlement that includes provisions for Formosa, the Chinese Communists may shift a substantial portion of their strength south. Their high command can then choose between launching a full-fledged invasion of Formosa or putting the Chinese Red Air Force, reported to number about 1,6oo combat planes, to work on the island. The Red Air Force can now stage out of relatively secure bases deep in the interior and strike against American planes and ships that have only limited air warning facilities.

In anticipation of possible Communist attack against Formosa, the United States is working with the Chinese Nationalists to organize a defense of their island refuge. A U.S. Military Assistance Advisory Group has been functioning on the island officially since May 1, 1951. During the fiscal year ending June 30, 1951, it supervised the use of about $78,000,000 worth of military aid. The Mutual Security Program for 1951-1952 included an additional appropriation of roughly $217,000,000 to provide military aid to Formosa.

In addition to enlarging several Formosan airfields and modernizing other installations, the American effort has aimed chiefly at reorganizing, training, arming and otherwise rehabilitating the Nationalist military establishment. These Nationalist forces number nearly 650,000 men. They include roughly 90,000 in the Air Force, some 50,000 in the Navy and about 20,000 in the Combined Service Forces. Political officers and garrison troops account for about 120,000. The remaining 370,000 can be classed as ground forces.

But these figures suggest a much stronger force than actually can be mobilized for action. There are several regiments of infantry in the Air Force, used to guard airfields, and the Navy includes a force of Marines. There is a superabundance of officers, including more than 125 admirals and

1,600 generals. Many of the troops suffer from disease, particularly tuberculosis. When the Red Armies completed conquest of the mainland in 1949, the Nationalist soldiers best able to evacuate to Formosa were often the older men assigned to rear area service units near the ports. There is no working retirement system; the Nationalists lack the funds to pay for pensions and instead transfer old soldiers to less active service such as cooking. Each year the entire military establishment grows that much older.

From among these forces the American military advisors are encouraging the Chinese to select the 300,000 who are judged to be potential combat effectives and organize them into a modern fighting force. To accomplish this a drastic reorganization of the Nationalist military is required. Infantry, artillery and armored forces have operated as semi-autonomous units, without training in the combined operations that are so essential for the defense of Formosa's coastal plain. Each branch of the service is jealous of its identity. Old personal rivalries that cost so many battles on the mainland are still much in evidence; but now the generals are all crowded together on one island.

Morale within the Nationalist forces has been hurt by the expanding activities of a corps of political officers under the command of President Chiang Kai-shek's elder son, General Chiang Ching-kuo. Two of these political officers are assigned to each company where they manage political indoctrination and report on the activities of all officers and men. Many Chinese officers complain that a number of their comrades have been imprisoned without trial on charges made by these political officers and that the system generates suspicion and intrigue. Official explanations state that these political officers are needed to counter Communist attempts at subversion, but responsible American and Chinese officers believe that more effective and less destructive methods to insure loyalty can be devised. The activity of political officers is closely related to the practice of political interference with the military. Officers still are promoted or demoted on occasion without the previous knowledge of their superiors. In practice there is no single clearly defined chain of command -- a basic requirement for morale and loyalty. The Generalissimo apparently lacks confidence in a single subordinate command structure and tends to balance one group in the military against another. The resulting duplication of responsibility is another reminder of the military practices that proved so destructive on the mainland.

American efforts to improve upon this military structure are handicapped by the fact that the members of the U.S. Military Assistance Advisory Group are only advisors. They screen Chinese requests for military aid and demonstrate use and maintenance of the new equipment in training. They are helping improve the inadequate

diet of Chinese troops and supporting the development of combat rations and improved uniforms. But their suggestions usually are ignored when they affect the crucial personal relationships within the Nationalist military structure. Chinese generals sometimes admit the soundness of American recommendations and then confess their own inability to alter existing arrangements; each of the senior Chinese military leaders is so much a prisoner of his old loyalties and accumulated obligations that none is able to cut across the channels of influence and make drastic changes. These considerations have led some responsible Chinese and Americans to conclude that the military humbug that has plagued the Nationalists for so long can be eliminated, and the combat potential of the Chinese soldier realized, only when an American is placed in command. In the absence of such an arrangement, they feel progress could be made by sending Chinese Nationalist forces to Korea, where it would be possible to reorganize and train them in combat situations tinder United Nations command.

Even such measures, however, would provide no adequate answer to the strategic problems posed by the threat of Communist attack on Formosa. These strategic considerations can, I think, be summarized as follows:

1. The Nationalists alone never can organize and support a permanent defense of Formosa against the kind of total attack the Chinese Communists can launch if the Korean war ends. This will be the situation even after the United States has outfitted the Chinese forces as now planned.
2. Since the United States has determined that the Chinese Communists must be kept out of Formosa, at the very least for the period that America is responsible for the defense of Japan, it is a minimum requirement that the U.S. Fleet and Air Force continue to participate in the protection of the island and the 100-mile-wide strait that separates it from the mainland.
3. The Nationalists can make only "token" invasions of the mainland, unless they receive American protection, supply and military support, including troops. Such action automatically would involve America in full-scale war with the Chinese Communists and perhaps with the Russians.
4. Although the Nationalists continue to use the myth of an early return to the mainland to bolster their own morale and enlist support abroad, the most sincere proponents of this line of action at present are the native Formosans, who see it as a means of ridding themselves of an unwelcome tax burden.

II

In many respects the island of Formosa is one of our planet's more attractive garden spots. Almost three-fourths of the land surface is covered by extremely rugged mountain ranges that rise abruptly out of the Pacific and, near the east coast, reach a height of 14,000 feet. Most of the approximately 9,000,000 civilians, including about 8,000,000 native Formosans, live on the lush subtropical plain that skirts the west coast of the 270-milelong island. This naturally rich island was systematically developed by the Japanese after they were ceded Formosa by the terms of the Treaty of Shimonoseki in 1895. As part of their pioneer colonial effort, the Japanese introduced a system of public health, and built railways, roads and a hydroelectric power system. They started a sugar industry that achieved a prewar peak production of more than 1,000,000 tons per year. Farmers were taught to use improved seed and fertilizer. Before the last war there was a popular saying on Formosa that the island produced enough rice in one year to feed itself for three; the surplus was shipped to Japan. The Japanese also developed Formosan production of superior varieties of oranges, pineapples and bananas. They organized production of tea, camphor and fish and built cement and paper making plants.

When their police measures failed to keep the rebellious Formosans in line, the Japanese introduced universal primary education as a method of inculcating allegiance. All they sought was to help supply Japan's needs for labor, food and raw materials, but, incidentally, their program also developed for the Formosans the highest material standard of living that is available to ordinary citizens anywhere in the Far East, with the possible exception of Japan itself. Whereas the ordinary Chinese farmer on the mainland usually goes to bed shortly after sundown because he cannot afford to burn an oil lamp, the Formosan farmer stands a good chance of having an electric light bulb in his house. Instead of the straw sandals so commonly used on the mainland, the Formosan wears rubber shoes. Unlike his cousin across the Formosan Strait, an ordinary Formosan expects to own a bicycle. Island farmers haul their heavy goods on ox-drawn wagons with pneumatic tires that carry a ton and a half-a great advance compared to mainland peasants who usually depend either upon wooden wheelbarrows or their own backs.

This prosperous economy suffered substantial war damage. Before V-J Day brought an end to hostilities, American submarines had sunk the Japanese ships that carried fertilizer to Formosa. Our bombers destroyed large areas in several cities, burned railway yards, and, by attacking dams and power facilities, reduced electricity production to one-third of the prewar level.

At the end of the war the United States assisted in the repatriation of all the Japanese administrators, engineers, technicians and businessmen who had managed the island. They with their families numbered about 300,000. The Nationalists, who had difficulty finding enough men to govern the newly liberated coastal cities of China and Manchuria, sent to Formosa only a small number of first-rate technicians. These few, however, did a superior job of patching up essential facilities. The Nationalist Government also dispatched to Formosa a group of loot-hungry officials. The activities of these men, combined with the policy of milking Formosa to feed the mainland, further depressed the standard of living, and in February 1947 goaded the Formosans into open revolt. The uprising was put down by troops brought in from the mainland. Observers on the island at the time estimate that between 5,000 and 10,000 Formosan leaders were hunted out and killed in an action that has left a deep scar, despite the later execution, by the Nationalist Government, of the governor responsible for the slaughter.

When the spectacular Communist victories in 1949 drove the Nationalist Government off the mainland, Formosa was poorly prepared to absorb the influx of refugees and troops crowding the LST's that arrived from Shanghai and Canton. However, the Nationalists came equipped with the desperate determination to survive. And they brought to Formosa many of their ablest administrators, whose energies formerly were dispersed from Manchuria to southwest China.

Within the last two and one-half years these underpaid officials have made significant progress in reassembling the tattered ends of their government. They have introduced new vigor and effectiveness into the

Formosan provincial administration and carried through some important reforms. One of the most effective of these is the land-reform program which has denied the Communists an opportunity to organize rural discontent. All rents have been reduced to a maximum of 37.5 percent of the main crop, and tenants have received written land contracts and achieved security of tenure. The program is now in its second stage, with the sale to tenants of public land confiscated from the Japanese. The third and final phase of the program calls for government purchase of large private land holdings and the sale of these properties to tenants. The returns on this effort are already apparent in falling land prices, as capital moves to invest in business and industry. More working capital is now in the hands of actual farmers, and there are greater incentives for production now that peasant families retain a larger share of the proceeds of their labors.

The Chinese have been greatly aided in their efforts at reconstruction and development by a rather unique American aid program. The United States effort, organized originally under E.C.A., and now under the Mutual Security Administration, has developed along three distinct lines. Through its commodity program the American M.S.A. mission finances and supervises importation of critical items such as fertilizer, textiles, bean cakes and replacement parts for industry. As a rule these items are sold on the market and most of the proceeds are used to finance the Chinese Government's deficit. As a second phase of the American aid effort, the United States Government, through M.S.A., finances the employment by the Chinese of the services of the J. G. White Engineering Company to assist industrial rehabilitation and development. The results of this effort have become very evident during the last year. The railway system has been repaired, and daily tonnage hauled is more than twice what it was at the end of 1949. Two and one-half years ago there were about 5,000 spindles operating on Formosa; late last year this number had been increased to more than 95,000. In 1951 the island's plants produced 104,000 tons of chemical fertilizers -- an amount far short of consumption needs, which are more than 500,000 tons, but a great improvement over the previous year.

The most distinctive feature of the American aid program has been its support of the Chinese and American Joint Commission on Rural Reconstruction. This Commission, composed of Chinese and American agricultural specialists, was first established under the provisions of the China Aid Act, passed by Congress in 1948. The members of the Commission initiated their efforts on the mainland during the last hectic months of the civil war. However, it is only on Formosa that they have had the time and opportunity to implement a comprehensive program of helping Chinese farmers use more modern methods. The program has affected almost every phase of Formosan farm life. The specialists have worked with local officials to organize self-supporting public health stations in the villages. Improved seed, pesticides and purebred breeding stock have been made available to farmers. Island-wide programs have been carried out to vaccinate cattle against the dread rinderpest, and hogs against cholera. Formosan farmers are being taught new methods and attitudes toward their work and community through illustrated pamphlets, posters and a rural newspaper. Many of these efforts are channeled through the Farmers Associations that were established by the Japanese as a control and distribution mechanism, but now are gradually being converted into member-managed cooperatives. There is mounting evidence of the effectiveness of this kind of aid. Last year Formosa produced the largest rice crop in its history-more than 1,500,000 tons. This crop, which was partly achieved at the expense of a reduced sugar acreage, left a small surplus for export. The island now carries more than 1,800,000 hogs compared to 1,300,000 two years ago -- important news to Chinese who value pork as much as Americans do beef. The Commission has found that social change to insure more equitable distribution of beneafits is a necessary counterpart of any comprehensive attempt to increase farm production. In keeping with this discovery they are now working to improve rural credit facilities to prevent money lenders from syphoning off returns from increased production.

III

Despite these substantial achievements, the pressure of the military and governmental burden periodically threatens to wreck the Formosan economy and start runaway inflation. The heavy taxes levied, particularly on Formosan farmers, meet slightly more than one-half of the total internal expenditures on the island. To date the Nationalists have covered part of the deficit by selling gold bullion, and public property such as houses confiscated from the Japanese. The remainder has been financed largely through the sales proceeds made possible by American economic aid. In the fiscal year ending June 30, 1951, E.C.A. allocated more than $97,000,000 for economic aid to Formosa. The Mutual Security Act for 1951-1952 provided almost as much again. However, the new barracks, roads, bridges and runways demanded by the present military program on Formosa all must be paid for in local currency. And the Chinese have very little gold bullion left to meet a financial emergency. The indications are that unless military expenditures are reduced, for example by training more effectively for productive work the several hundred thousand military personnel who are unfit for combat, only increased American aid can save the Nationalists from resorting to printing more money.

Without the present military load most economists agree that Formosa could be both prosperous and self-supporting. This would be especially true if capital were available to develop Formosa's great hydroelectric power and industrial possibilities. However, long-term prospects must take account of the rate of population growth. The records indicate that there were about 2,000,000 persons on Formosa when the Japanese took the island in 1895. Since then the native population has increased about fourfold. The present birth rate is more than 42 per 1000 and the death rate is less than 11 per 1,000. And yet the island has only 2,000,000 acres of arable land and all of it is cultivated. Rice production per acre per year is higher in Formosa than anywhere else in the Far East; the average yield is about five times as high as it is in the Philippines. There are limited opportunities for further expanding productivity. But, as one American agricultural scientist expressed it, "We can begin to see the ceiling that is feasible with presently known methods." A few of the Chinese leaders are concluding that if they are to avoid a falling standard of living and with it growing discontent, they must somehow limit the rate of population growth. In approaching this problem the Chinese have received no assistance from the United States Government or its representatives on Formosa.

Within the last two and one-half years the Chinese Nationalists have made only rather halting progress in evolving more democratic methods of government. But the obstacles to the growth of democracy include more than lack of faith in a popularly elected government among many senior Nationalist leaders; Formosa is desperately short of democratic experience and education. When the Nationalists retreated to Formosa in 1949 the ranks of their government and army were infiltrated by a large number of Communist agents. Chinese on the island, whose families remained on the mainland, also were easy marks for Communist blackmail. As a consequence, the Nationalists acted hurriedly and sometimes ruthlessly to stamp out Communist activities, arresting and interrogating some thousands of suspects. They captured and executed some real Communist agents and frightened others off the island, but they also intimidated and imprisoned many individuals who appeared to be innocent. At present several thousand persons are in jail, where many of them have been held for more than a year and a half without benefit of public trial. For the great majority of Chinese on Formosa the fearful feature of this situation is the lack of legal protection for the ordinary citizen. He can be arrested at night by a squad of military police, tried by a military court-martial and sentenced, with little opportunity for appeal. Once taken into custody, the ordinary Chinese is in effect at the mercy of the garrison headquarters. A person may be arrested because he actually is subversive. He can also be picked up because someone who wants his job or property has denounced him as a Communist to the authorities. Responsible Chinese officials state that within the last two years much progress has been made in correcting such conditions, and that no civilian now can be legally arrested without a civil police warrant. To the extent that this regulation is enforced, it should provide the civil authorities with a record of individuals who have been arrested by the various secret police organizations and make it possible to trace persons who disappear. The Cabinet has ruled that defense counsel must be allowed in military courts and that the accused must be permitted the presence of his family and material witnesses during the trial. And the cabinet also has decided that all cases of alleged violations of economic regulations must be dealt with by civil courts rather than by military tribunals.

However, there is still no civilian board empowered to review and rule on the cases of all persons arrested. In the absence of such a board, with supreme authority, and the means to make independent investigations, the garrison headquarters, the special police and several secret police organizations exercise enormous power. Many Chinese feel that with the added security from Communist attack made possible by American participation in the defense of Formosa there is no adequate justification for this lack of due process of law, which tends to discourage even constructive criticism of the Government. They are particularly disturbed by the lack of respect for civilian authority demonstrated by police and garrison officers.

The absence of effective rule by law and resulting limitations on freedom of expression were reflected in the elections held on the county and municipal levels throughout Formosa last year. The elections started in the southern sections of the island where there was considerable freedom to campaign and vote. Indications are that about one-half of the offices in that area were filled by relatively fair elections. But when it became apparent that a great majority of Formosans were winning office, the Kuomintang Party machine stepped in and so managed the elections that their candidates were chosen for most of the offices in northern Formosa. In some districts where its man was not elected, the Kuomintang continues to exercise indirect control either through the police or by placing a party man in the same office with the local official. Some Nationalists have justified this practice on the grounds that there are few local Formosan leaders experienced in managing public affairs.

This approach to the elections, however, reflects a much deeper political conflict within the Nationalist regime; the senior leaders are not agreed upon what kind of government they should develop. A number of Chinese leaders would like to see the creation on Formosa of a genuinely democratic society with protection and opportunity for the individual. These men include several members of the Cabinet, and the Governor of the island. But they lack a commonly agreed-upon, clear-cut program for applying the political principles they have learned from the West. Most real authority on the island, however, belongs to another group that can best be identified as the Kuomintang Reform Committee. The 16 members of this policy-making body of the Kuomintang were appointed by Chiang Kai-shek in his capacity as Director-General of the Party. Most of these men subscribe to the principle of democratic government, but tend to think of it as an objective to be attempted after they have liberated the mainland. Meanwhile, they are working to make the Kuomintang a more efficient and disciplined party. Some of their actions suggest they believe the mainland was lost because their control was not sufficiently thorough. It is significant that the Kuomintang Party reforms, announced in July 1950, adopt as one of the principles of organization the system of "democratic centralism." This permits open discussion in party meetings, but requires that once a decision is reached all members must obey. Therein it is similar to Chinese Communist Party practice.

These conflicting ideologies are developing among a people who have only a vague conception of democracy. Japanese education made the Formosans literate and taught them technical skills, orderliness and respect for authority. It did not encourage appreciation for nonmaterial political and cultural values. And today a large proportion of the young people on Formosa adopt the principle that might makes right. Chinese educators working on the island since 1945 have been too poor and powerless to modify these attitudes substantially. They also have been handicapped by the activities of secret police informers who report on students and teachers in the schools. The present educational facilities are not equipped, financed and staffed in a manner that enables them to turn out young men with the technical qualifications needed to manage the Formosan economy at its present rate of productivity. There is even less evidence that young Chinese are being trained to carry forward the fine traditions of synthesizing Chinese and Western thought and science that have been built up during the past century of our contact with the Orient. So far the great economic, military and political leverage possessed by the United States on Formosa has not been used to encourage constructive political, intellectual and scientific development of a long-term character. The essential question for all Chinese, whose illusions of the "New Democracy" have been shattered by the harsh realities of Communist rule, is whether Formosa holds any promise for the future of their race. It is already apparent that the determining factor will be, not the international legal status of Formosa and its Chinese Nationalist Government, but the opportunity available on the island for ordinary Chinese to express and realize their hopes. The first need of the Chinese today is for an acceptable ideal that offers a demonstrable alternative to their presently inadequate experience. Formosa today does not provide this. Within the last 18 months Communist land-reform tactics on the mainland have alienated large elements among the more than 10,000,000 overseas Chinese who live in Southeast Asia. But many overseas Chinese leaders are afraid to make trips to Formosa to organize anti-Communist resistance for fear they will be imprisoned because of old personal and political differences with senior Nationalists on the island. Some of China's ablest thinkers and leaders, who have escaped from the Communists to Hong Kong, are not permitted by the Nationalists to enter Formosa. Most of the Chinese students, professors and businessmen in America are reluctant to return to the island. The businessmen see no adequate legal protection for their enterprise. Students and professors whose skills are needed on the island see little prospect of being able to do worthwhile work. The Nationalist Government, which fled from the mainland, scorned and some times hated by the people it had ruled, has not yet won a substantially different reputation with a significant number of Chinese, particularly on the mainland. As the Communists proceed with the liquidation of the unconverted officials, intellectuals and gentry who once were the link between the Nationalist Government and the Chinese people, this becomes even more difficult. Communist efforts also are aided by systematic reeducation of the young, rewriting of the history books and capitalizing upon the national prestige they have won as a result of the Korean war. And yet, when viewed in a longer perspective, Formosa has many of the physical prerequisites for building one of the most attractive societies in the Far East. For example, it is estimated that at least 15 years of intensive effort, including heavy capital investment, would be required to bring the Philippines to the same level of development. The high productivity and extensive use of modern scientific farm methods as applied to Asian conditions suggest Formosa could make an almost ideal demonstration area for showing other nationals in the Far East how to improve their agriculture.

It is to some of the Chinese leaders and thinkers whose values most closely harmonize with those of the West, however, that Formosa suggests the most significant possibilities. Like most Chinese they have a keen sense of history. They are convinced that if all the significant elements of the Chinese people are fitted to the Communist mold, their race will lose many of its finest values. In order to avoid such a loss to world culture and to offer their people an alternative standard for judging life, they feel it is essential that there be maintained outside of Communist domination an area where Chinese civilization can carry forward its great traditions. If Formosa is to be used for this purpose, they are convinced that the United States must more skillfully and firmly use the power that is ours to insure healthy development. It is now apparent that if our concern for the defense of Formosa stops merely with the prevention of invasion it prejudices the democratic case throughout the Far East, and at the same time jeopardizes the military effort itself. We are forced to make certain that the total economy is sound. Active American governmental and private interest in the administration of justice under the rule of law on Formosa is necessary if we really want the Chinese people to be on our side. In order to provide non-Communist Chinese leadership for the future, efforts must be launched now to train up young men and women with the necessary qualifications. If blunders are to be avoided, it will be necessary to provide American diplomatic representation with enough support to permit courageous and sustained action in dealing with the Chinese situation. Charges of interference in the internal affairs of another country beg the essential issue; in the minds of the ordinary citizens of Formosa the United States is primarily responsible, for the presence on their island of the Nationalist Government. In their minds the decisive question is whether our interference has been in their interest.

POST SCRIPT *When this article, FORMOSA, was published in FOREIGN AFFAIRS in July 1952, President Chiang Kai-shek immediately ordered the Ministry of Foreign Affairs to translate it into Chinese. This was promptly done, with at least one copy provided to each member of the Kuomingtong Central Committee and a special meeting of the Central Committee was held to discuss the article. K.C. Wu, Governor of Formosa, gave an autographed copy of the Chinese translation to Albert. Soon thereafter, it happened that Formosan police practices changed so as to require a warrant from civilian police before any civilian could be arrested in Formosa. This and related changes helped transform Formosa (Taiwan) into the democratic and open society it has become.*

AS A WELL-RECOGNIZED EXPERT ON ASIAN AFFAIRS, and Asian correspondent for the Chicago Daily News and the American Universities Field Staff, Albert helped write speeches for Adlai Stevenson during his presidential campaign in 1952; and in March 1953 he accompanied Stevenson and party on an extensive fact finding tour in Asia, described in this AUFS report

Adlai Stevenson's Journey:
What Price an Effective Political Opposition.

c/o United States Embassy,
Manila, Philippine Islands

Mr, Phillips Talbot
American Universities Field Staff
522 Fifth Avenue
Now York 36, NY,

31 March 1953

Dear Phil,

Adlai Stevenson's trip tbrough the Far and Middle East and Europe promises an early test of whether the United States at this poriod can develop a political opposition that in responsibility and effectiveness equals the dimensions of our worldwide involvement. As a consequence his travels assume a special significance in the areas of understanding they open up for him and his associates. His Journey also illustrates some of the questionable practices for educating our national leaders that Americans have fallen into, particularly with the postwar expansion of air transportation. At stake is really the issue of whether we can have worthwhile competition of ideas in the formulation of foreign policy at the damestic political level.

The Group that started west across the Pacific with Stevenson early In March included four other members, Walter Johnson, Chairman of the History Department of the University of Chicago, was responsible for insuring that the group gained a broad and balanced understanding of critical problems in each country they visited and tbat this information was organized for future use. Johnson had served as chairman of the organization that secured Stevenson's nomination at the Democratic National Convention in Chicago last summer and managed much of the research during the campaign, Barry Dingham, publisher of the Courier Journal in Louisville,KY, traveled with "the Governor" as a veteran advisor and observer. Bingham's wide experience included a tour of duty as Director of the ECA Mission to France. William McCormick Blair,Jr., in his capacity as executive assistant, helped determine where Stevenson and the party went and whom they saw. Blair is a Chicago attorney whose experience includes wartime service in India,, Burma and China. Alliam Attwood, the European Editor of Look Magazine, made detailed arrangements for the party and kept them working an the series of articles Stevenson is writing for the Magazine. In return for those articles Look pays all expenses for the trip plus a substantial fee.

ADLAI STEVENSON'S JOURNEY

After Stevenson had visited in Honolulu with Admiral Arthur Radford Commander-in-Chief of the Pacific, the group flew on to Tokyo, where they arrived on March 10, 1953. In Japan Stevenson made a special effort to learn the attitudes of Japanese political leaders and intellectuals toward the United States and rearmament. In addition to briefings by U.S. Government specialists, he saw Japanese political leaders and other prominent individuals. Johnson and other members of the group meanwhile sought out intellectuals, professors, writers, businessmen and newsmen for discussions. In his speech given in Tokyo Stevenson emphasized the need for patience in building democracy; he implied that confidence must not be lost in the institutions because they failed to bring quickly all the hoped-for results. In Kyoto on the 13th, the Stevenson group visited Buddhist temples and shrines and took tea with one of the abbots and his senior monks, They had break-fasted with students at Amherst College House at Dooshisha University and heard young Japanese express their fears for the resurgence of extreme rightism in their country, their preference or Marxism over Fascism in Japan and their dissatisfaction with unemployment among college graduates that last year left nearly one-half of them without jobs. Enroute Stevenson bad stopped for a surprise visit to a cotton textile factory.

After the party arrived in Pusan, Korea, on the 14th they were briefed and dined at the American Embassy and enjoyed a presentation of Korean dancing and singing. The next day while Stevenson visited prisoner of war camps and ROK training centers, Johnson talked with Korean educators, officials of UNKRM and other foreign specialists. Enroute to Seoul the following morning the group visited a RGK officer training school. They were entertained in the capital by President and Mrs. Syngman Rhee and suffered the consequences experienced by so many foreigners when they first taste Korean food. They also talked with news correspondents covering that war-shattered country.

In Korea Stevenson's chief concern was with understanding the military problem. In addition to briefings by General Maxwell Taylor and his staff, the group spent a day at the front and another day with the U.S. Navy operating off the east coast of the Koreas. The experience convinced Stevenson that he had been right during the campaign last fall in opposing then an enlargement of the Korean War.

Upon the party's return to Japan, Stevenson went into the countryside to explore conditions among farmers and the progress of rural reform with Wolf Ladejinsky, the U.S. Agricultural Attache who has done so much to further land reform in non-communist Asia. After a few other talks in Tokyo the group flew to Formosa on the Morning of March 20th. The Chinese Nationalist leaders entertained them with their usual skill and hospitality and Chiang Kai-shek gave Stevenson a detailed accounty of his objectives and hopes. While Stevenson visited with Chinese governmental leaders and saw Nationalist troops in training, other members of his party talked with U.S. Embassy and MSA specialists and Chinese educators. The Chinese and American Joint Commision on Rural Reconstruction took the Democratic Party leader and his group into the countryside to visit a Formosan farmer, a Farmers' Association, a hybrid hog farm and other projects. On the morning of the 22nd, the Stevenson party flew into Hong Kong for four days of dioscussions on the problems of that British Crown Colony, trade with the Communists and internal developments on the

Communist mainland. He and his group talked with knowledgeable foreigners who have been studying Chinese Communist developments, including American and foreign diplomatic observers, military attaches, newspaper correspondents and several business leaders. In addition to the U.S. Consul General and a reception at the American Club, Stevenson visited British defences facing the Communists in the New Territories. He also took time for a liesurely look at a teeming life in several of the Colony's Chinese business districts, visited a fishing village and enjoyed the scenery along Hongkong's island-studded coast. As the deadline approached for the first of the series of magazine articles that Stevenson had promised Look, he and his group began the difficult job of pulling together their impressions and research into an appropriate article. Stevenson insisted upon writing the article and other members of the party usually could only outline ideas and facts for his use. This placed a demand upon Stevenson's time that limited the number of persons he saw in Hongkong and on his four day visit to the Philippines. On the evening of their arrival here American Ambassador Raymond Spruance gave a dinner for the group. The guests included Foreign Secretary Joaquin Elizalde and Nacionalista Party leaders Senator Jose Laurel and Ex-secretary of Defense Ramon Magsaysay. Discussions with these and other prominent Filipinos were continued the next day. They were resumed in the summer capital of Baguio, where President Qurino gave a Sunday luncheon for Stevenson on the 29th. (Quirino later criticized Ambassador Spruance's guest list on the grounds that it included too many opposition party Nacionalistas. The President apparently had not troubled himself to learn that two leading members of his own Liberal Party had failed to use their invitations to dine at the American Embassy residence.) While in the mountain retreat Stevenson completed the first magazine article; just in time to make the issue wherein Look had advertised that it would appear. Meanwhile, here in Manila, Johnson continued his energetic search for facts and news to round out the Governor's understanding. On the ovening of the 30th, after a visit to nearby Los Banos Agricultural College and a press conference at the residence, the Stevenson group flew on to Singapore en route to Saigon for a six-day visit in Indo-China. Thereafter, their journey will take them to Indoneisia, Thailand, Burma. India, Pakistan, the Middle East and several countries in Europe before they return in mid-summer to Illinois.

As this schedule illustrates, the Stevenson group was more conscientious than most American leaders who fly out for a "quick survey of the Far East". Although on the avorage they visited a new country every week or less, several members of the group were exceptionally well qualified to learn the most from their experience. Stevensen's own intellectual curiosity set an unusually high level for their explorations. Unlike so many of the traveling American generals, congressmen, columnists, radio commentators and others who practice strategic soothsaying, this group had read some background materials on the countries they visited. Enroute they eagerly acummulated additional books and articles. Each member of the party had collected his omn list of personal contacts. While they accepted the official briefings offered by the United States embassies, consulates, MSA and military missions, they also sought out independent sources. By doing so they were able to avoid somewhat the dangerous cycle whereby American leaders traveling abroad get their information from the same sources who supply the U.S. government departments and agencies in Washington, D.C., and indirectly most of our magazines, newspapers and radio stations. This system accounts partially for our national failure to develop more meaningful criticism of our foreign actions; the same American officials who make the mistakes provide most of the data upon which their work is evaluated. Because of Blair's firm guidance, the Stevenson party avoided many of the formal dinners and cocktail parties that usually sap the energies and fog the minds of American VIP travelers in Asia.

Despite these efforts, this pattern of exploration promises to give the Stevenson group primarily a first-hand knowledge of many of the leading personalities in non-Communist Asia, a mass of assorted facts and impressions and glinpses of some of the major problems confronting this region. The Democratic leader and several of his principal advisors now can visualize the almost infinite complexity of the problems created for us by the extension of American national interests to Asia. On this basis they can make some useful suggestions to Democratic leaders in Congress. But Stevenson is under great public and political pressure to provide simple and easy answers to problems that confront us in Asia. The Look magazine articles will necessarily be largely a reportorial account of his travels, although the editors expect much more in view of Stevenson's reputation for intellectual integrity and sagacity. If he accedes to numerous requests and writes a book on the trip, Stevenson cannot avoid discussing the major foreign issues that confront us. As the head of the Democratic Party he will be expected to speak with authority on the problems that affect American relations with more than one-half of the hunan species and to take a clearcut stand on such questions when they become of national interest.

It will be difficult for Stevenson and his group to accomplish this in a manner that continues his record of generally superior performances. After making this trip they will not be adequately prepared to formulate the inde endent foreign policy ideas that an effective and constructive political.opposition now demands. Their Group lacks the time, the specialized talents and the detailed and yet digested information necessary to evaluate realistically the activities abroad of the United States government and offer the American people useful alternatives. The small research staff now working with them in the Democratic Party headquarters is concerned primarily with domestic political policy. It lacks the facilities to do worthwhile work in the foreign field.

Postwar experience in the Far East indicates that many of our policy mistakes and the failure of the American people to understand the basic difficulties confronting them in Asia result from this blind spot In our political institutions. Despite the importance of recent historic events in this regicn and the tortured American response to them, there has been very little meaningful competition of ideas in our political discussion of them. The great MacArthur debate was fought in a verbal wonderland; the contestants played for the emotional favor of the American audience but rarely mentioned the fundamental strategic, political and human questions at stake. The life of an opposition political party depends strongly upon finding fault with the administration in office. Unfortunately some Republican leaders before last November generated mythical issues wherewlth to belabor the party in power when the Democrats are vulnerable to very real charges of negligence and failure of foreign policy in this region that went unmentioned. Rarely did political criticism "become a spur to more effective national action in this area. These failings among some Republican members of Congress result partly from the fact that they lacked the dependable independent sources of significant information needed by a political opposition dealing effectively with our worldwide involvement. Unless this problem is overcome the Democrats likewise may find it expedient to use petty fault finding and vindictive personal attacks to destroy their political opponents.

The growing tendency among American newspapers, magazines and radio stations to go to Washington, D.C. for foreign news, rather than relying upon independent sources abroad places a premium upon any statement by a political leader, it makes the quality of Congressional debate an index to the level of curiosity about foreign problems among many Anericans. With the increased dependence of so many foreign countries upon United States Government decisions, the expressions of our Congressional leaders have become a major guide whereby many Asians judge American motives and objectives. And the failure of the U.S. Congress to develop more realistic debate of our policies abroad has led some Asians to doubt our capacity for leadership. An Asian ambassador to Communist China who participated in the crucial negotiations in the early fall of 1950 that failed to keep the Chinese Communists from intervening in Korea once asked me why no senator supporting the administration had made an understandable statement then of the U.S. Government's aims. He said that if this had been done it would have facilitated the task of limiting the Korean War. Although defeat is forcing the democrats to reexamine their policies and rebuild their party, they are not creating the instruments that would permit their opposition to significantly stimulate a more effective United States foreign policy. Attention so far has been focused largely upon the domestic reasons for their defeat. The dimensions of the problem that post-war expansion of American activitles abroad poses for our political parties is not fully appreciated. There are independent sources wherefrom information could be collected to evaluate U.5. Government actions abroad. Those include knowledgeable private citizens such as businessmen, scholars newspapermen, missionaries and technicians who have accummulated valuable experience and insights that now often remain unused. Their information would not be as complete as that provided by U.S. Government sources; there would be important omissions concerning events in Communist countries. But it could be better digested and more objective than the mass of fragmentary bits of information and overlong reports that now often clutter up our official collecting agencies. A small but highly skilled staff would be needed to assemble and evaluate such information for congressional and other leaders who want dependable material from independent sources to incorporate in their speeches and guide their actions. If the staff were able to "farm out" research to scholars and bpecialists, additional resources would be available to them.

A small group of men who had a sense for fundamental trends in the areas of American concern abroad sometimes could anticipate coming trouble and through such a staff insure that at least some political leaders were better qualified to comment intelligently when the need arose. There are comparatively few specialists with such capabilities. The precarious state of Democratic finance, and the uncertainty of working for a political party suggest the development of such a new institutian in our political life may require special government or private funds. Such an institution seems to be needed, however, if Stevenson or every future opposition leader, is to effectively fulfil his role in the field of foreign policy. Within the next faw years the United States will make decisions of momentous consequences for the future of Asia and our relations with these peoples. Do we intend to get along with the Chinese Communists as long as they remain within their own borders. Should we embark upon the many years-long struggle that a serious attempt to liberate the more than 470 million Chinese from Red rule would require? What kind of defense arrangements can be made for the Western Pacific that will not reinforce the political power of local military cliques and submerge the prospects of democracy? To what extent does a healthy American economy depend upon the accomplishments of the economic development programs now under way in Asia. Only informed political debate can hammer out the real alternatives that confront us abroad in terms of our total domestic capabilities and willingness to pay the price demanded by each. Such discussion also could help shift popular attention from the obvious daily foreign events to the more significant problems and clarify for Americans the decisions that they must make.

Sincerely,

Albert Ravenholt

AMERICAN UNIVERSITIES FIELD STAFF

FAR EAST
(CHINA)
AR-9-'58

THE GODS MUST GO!

By Albert Ravenholt

Hong Kong
November 22, 1958

CHINESE PEASANTS on the mainland are digging out the graves of their forebears and sawing up the heavy wooden coffin planks for use in building communal pigsties. Meanwhile, the ancestral tablets are being pulled down and converted to such odd purposes as the sides and tailgates of farm carts and walls for new grain bins. All of this, if we are to believe the Communist press, is part of a national effort to dispense with the "vestiges of a feudal and capitalist superstructure." Reverence for the past and the numerous religious beliefs and practices of the people now are all to be "actively" eliminated, and not simply left to "wither." For some of us who have lived intimately with the Chinese before this "new era" it seems that something more basic is being attempted. The Communists are seeking to remake the Chinese personality. The passive acceptance of life as it is, often associated with Taoism, must be rooted out. The dualism, with its concept of cyclical harmony, of which yang and yin are the symbols, is to go. In its place the Red leaders would raise the martial male spirit. The aim is a man, necessarily shorn of much humanism, who is persuaded that he can master his environment, his neighbors, and himself.

The movement launched in the countryside last spring to "reform funeral customs" and encourage "thrifty burials" is avowedly designed to release even greater resources for the "leap forward" campaigns in agriculture and industry. Those who have explored on foot the countryside around Chungking, Shanghai, and other metropolises can readily appreciate the urge to halt the crowding of grave mounds upon the tiny farm plots. The Communists argue that not only did the tombs cause a serious wastage of land, but also they impeded the merging of individual farms into collectives, and now into communes, and the construction of irrigation canals. A survey of burial practices conducted in Shantung Province since 1956 is described in the Peking Jen Min Jih Pao or People's Daily. In the 18 hsian (township) and chen (smaller administrative unit) that was selected as representative of lowland and mountainous administrative districts three per cent of the land suited to cultivation was found devoted to tombs and sepulchral purposes. In the suburbs of one town mentioned, better than seven per cent of the land was so set apart.

The Communists calculated that throughout Shantung roughly 700,000 acres of arable land was given over to graves and related use, depriving the inhabitants each year of 625,000 tons of grain and its equivalents in tubers that could be grown on this soil. They estimated that almost 1,000 acres were being lost annually to farming purposes as new tombs were constructed. The figures for Shantung are suggestive of the situation throughout other regions of China, though the more densely populated provinces, such as Kwangtung and Kiangsu, tended to devote an even larger percentage of land to graves.

The area taken annually for tombs in Shantung tallies in a rough way with what we know historically of such tendencies on the part of the people. History also gives us precedents for the Communist action. Except for the founders of the Ming Dynasty, who rose to power in 1368 A.D., and the Manchus, who seized control in 1644 A.D, each emperor starting a new dynasty tried to erase the tombs of the previous rulers. Across the land this was matched by a general blasting or leveling of graves covering desirable agricultural land. Exemptions were given for the tombs of some local heroes and graves less than five generations old claimed by relatives -- after a longer period the spirit of the departed was believed to have sunk so deeply into the ground that it could not return to trouble the living descendants.

With their passion for statistics the Communists are equally thorough in calculating the cost of funerals. They reason that the wood used each year for coffins in Shantung alone would be enough to build 200,000 dwelling units (clearly simple houses) or provide ties for 11,200 miles of railway. And these were usually the better timbers since elderly peasants, particularly in the interior, prided themselves on their coffins. In Yunnan Province of Southwest China it was not uncommon to enter a home where the grandfather had supervised the building of his own coffin out of planks sometimes four to six inches thick and two feet wide and then had had it placed in a prominent position in the house while waiting to use it. Funeral clothes in Shantung, the Communists report, absorbed more than three million yards of cloth and nearly 800 tons of cotton for padding. Family spending for ceremonies, food, and other necessities for the deceased in the next existence, reached a total equivalent to a skilled technician's pay for 25 million days of labor. The Communists state that the "obligations imposed by such feudal funeral rites and customs" meant hardships and "even bankruptcies" for entire families. Their findings in Shantung correspond to the traditional experience of peasants in much of China for whom these ceremonial demands were certainly burdensome, although they were made mandatory by the pressure of convention and clan and community sanctions.

Interwoven with these funeral rites common throughout most of rural China was the worship of spirits of the dead and local gods who originally represented departed individuals. In classical times these cults had been associated with the great deities of heaven and earth to whom the emperors led the people in paying personal reverence. This was the rudimentary religion of the Chinese people; among the uneducated, Confucianism, Taoism, Buddhism, Muhammadism, and Christianity were in varying degrees superimposed upon and adapted to it. Faith in the power of these spirits was among the elements that buttressed filial piety. And this pantheon of the peasant, tied to him by kinship and folklore, entailed continuing obligations. Not only did he sweep the graves and burn Joss before the tablets of his direct ancestors, but he also ministered to a host of heroistic gods that were expected to watch over the community. If offended, these spirits were believed capable of ruining crops, bringing sickness to animals and men, and otherwise thwarting human aspirations.

In Nan-an Hsien, or county, of Fukien Province the communists recently conducted another of their studies. Here they discovered that celebrating the "birthdays of the gods'" had deprived the community of 940,000 working days annually, consumed 2,900 tons of grain, and cost the equivalent of 1,530,000 man days pay for a skilled industrial worker. At least twice every year each family would observe the "birthday" of one of its special clan gods or the occasion when the god "went to heaven to make reports." A procession was then held, a banquet spread and theatricals staged, often with hired players. As in other provinces of China, the demands of "face" compelled even impoverished peasant families to spend for these festivities and entertain guests. Similar pressures moved peasant families to burn Joss sticks and candles twice within each lunar month before the household shrine of their particular god and sometimes pay homage to community deities whose "houses" (temple-shaped clay structures usually one to three feet high) were spotted along country roads. Such gods also were entitled to offerings of rice cakes and other "treats" when something special was desired of them. Altogether it was a religion which offered the peasant a psychic refuge from his fears and lent variety to his existence. But this was achieved only at the expense of assigning nature such powers as to leave mere man helpless before it and constrained to search for redress through the intercession of spirits that must be propitiated. Clearly, this system of belief was incompatible with the grandiose schemes the new rulers in Peking have designed for this ancient land.

Employing that relentless capacity for compulsion they can bring to bear, the Chinese Communists today are systematically rooting out the religious scheme of life of the peasant. According to the mainland press, the "struggle to break down superstition" carried on during the summer has been spreading to "every corner of the country." Although it is less spectacular than the massive concurrent campaign to weld 500 million Chinese farmers into People's Communes, this attack upon their most intimate beliefs must affect the peasants at least as deeply. So far there have been no reports of major violence by peasants resisting this destruction of their religious practices and symbols. As with so much of the Communist revolution in China this may be traceable to the use of an ingenious method of compelling the people themselves to wreck the old order and thus, through personal experience, learn to revere it less as their own values inevitably are altered. It is also still possible that drastic tampering with man's inmost concerns may produce scattered explosions or mass civil disobedience. But when we consider the totality of forces within which the Chinese peasant is caught, we must recognize that we are receiving a glimpse of a people for whom choice among alternatives may be a vanishing concept.

The initial attack in this nation-wide campaign to eradicate traditional Chinese folk religion has been against the graves. In Chekiang Province on the East China coast, "shock brigades" of Communist-led youth last spring began giving "scientific explanations that dead men were like blocks of wood; they were unable to bring prosperity to their descendants." Some 20,000 young Chinese cadres there were engaged in moving graves to less desirable land. In Liaoning Provinces of Manchuria, the Communist press reported, 25 per cent of the tombs had been moved off arable land by July. In Shantung the Communists claim the "masses are reforming the old funeral rites and customs of their own accord or are proposing such reform." Slogans expressing this demand include: "Let us compete with heaven; let us save land from graves and tombs; let us fight against nature; let us rely not on the gods and heaven, but on our own hands, for more production." The time-honored Chinese concern with feng-shuis of choosing a site for the dead as well as the living that harmonizes with the currents of "cosmic breath" in the community, is now being denounced. No longer will this customary search for a location that overlooks water and is freshened by the winds be permitted to guide the discerning. Instead, the "consciousness of the masses" allegedly prompts them, while leveling graves, to chant such phrases as, "If there is any feng-shui at all, the Communist Party and the co-operatives will be enough feng-shui."

Burial practices are being revamped in keeping with this new "consciousness." Use of thick planks for coffins is prohibited; coffins are manufactured from thin boards, or are simply frames covered with woven reeds and plastered with mud. The dead are interred in the least arable hillsides or in other out-of-the-way places. But the Communists evidently are not satisfied with this. They are preparing the people, particularly near the larger urban centers, for erection and use of public mausoleums. Poems, attributed to ordinary peasants that extol such a change are printed. In time, when public acceptance is more assured, the Communists want to introduce cremation as the standard practice throughout China. Even the new leaders in Peking, however, seem reluctant to push openly and "massively" now for a practice that so radically violates the old Chinese faith in death as a stage of "suspended animation" that does not entirely preclude the possibility that the soul might again return to the body it once inhabited.

The rites linked with this belief in the continuing influence of departed ancestors are similarly being altered by new "scientific" considerations, In Fukien, it is reported that a meeting of the People's Congress of Chenshan Hsiang agreed to combine celebrations of birthdays of the gods in one annual occasion for the entire community -- it is to be observed on the sixteenth day of the twelfth month of the lunar calendar. One village was reported to be saving enough by this new ceremonial practice to build six small irrigation projects. In Kweichow Provinces one of the most tradition-bound regions of Southwest China, the mainland press cites a mass campaign to pull down ancestral tablets and replace them with pictures of Mao Tse-tungs Chairman of the Chinese Communist Party Achievements by rural communities in making ancestral tablets taken from private homes and clan shrines into wagons and building material are praised in the press. News accounts describe images representing local deities being tossed into the crude communal smelters for conversion into roller and ball bearings for farm carts and equipment. Burning of incenses chanting of the liturgy, and other worship of the gods are said, officially, to be performed by "very few people." In any event, it would be difficult to continue these practices since Joss papers, incense, and the like are disappearing from mainland shops. Also popular and government pressure inhibit open display of faith in the old gods.

THE GODS MUST GO

The Communists claim that they still support filial piety. They are opposed, however, to the idea of a soul. "A man dies just as a lamp goes outs" they say, and it is superstitious to burn Joss sticks for him." Likewise, kowtowing before the graves of ancestors is discouraged, It is all a "struggle" between "the advanced and the backward," they insist, and the entire focus of concern and satisfaction of the people now must be upon the present. There are exceptions to this intensive insistence upon demolishing regard for the departed -- "heroes of socialist constructions" outstanding "fighters in the Red Army," and such folk are to be appropriately exalted by the community with graves that can become public shrines. Thus, performing rites in behalf of the new faith emanating from Peking becomes the only means to veneration in the old tradition,

Eradication, or at least severe modification, of Chinese folk religion is a mandatory step in such convulsive technological progress as the Chinese Communists are engineering. Modern health and sanitation are hardly compatible with popular faith in the healing power of spirits. The rice borer, that costs China some millions of tons of grain annually, cannot be controlled by burning incense before the shrine of a local deity. Nor can the watering of fields be left to the whims of Yu Shih, the mythical god who is known as the "Master of Rain." Long before the Communists became potent on the scene, Chinese scientists and educators, impatient to introduce the blessings of the twentieth century, had wrestled against this "accumulated prejudice." Western Christian missionaries, who contributed so much to the growth of China's intellectual class during the past century and provided most of the modern medical education, never were able to make theirs a "faith of the masses." Chinese life was too integrated, The peasant could not adopt a new religion without also altering his entire scheme of existence, and, to some extent, that of his neighbors.

The "religious superstitions of the masses" also are a bar to Commmnist political objectives. Some of the most stubborn opposition the new regime has encountered was organized by religious sects and secret societies associated primarily with Taoism and Buddhism. The authority of these groups in the popular peasant mind stemmed from their power with the same spirits whose favors were judged so crucial. With such a "mass base" destroyed by the open attack on religion launched this year, the Communists could reason they were eliminating the foundations for future opposition. The great T'ai Pling Rebellion that nearly unseated the Manchu Dynasty in the mid-nineteenth century was inspired by a new political creed based in part on a local version of Christianity -- a principal rebel leader lost out in the imperial examinations and then took to studying early translations from the Bible. Believers in Taoism also were active in the rebellion; they furnished much of the organizing talent. Now, the Communists, who long studied the T'ai Pling revolt as a guide to their own, must be quite aware that it, like most major upheavals in Chinese history, was linked to a popular conviction that the ruling dynasty no longer enjoyed favor with the gods and could be deposed. It would be contrary to their natures for Mao Tse-tung and his associates to leave untouched such a potential source of appeal for an opposition.

THE GODS MUST GO

For the Chinese of today and tomorrow this scrapping of customs and beliefs that have been honored for better than 25 centuries means more than a parting with the past. The individualism and family-oriented loyalties of this civilization are rooted in an awareness of ancestral links. In the minds of the peasantry, there was the added faith in associated spirits that gave each person a sense of special guardianship; and harmony with the rhythm of nature was much to be desired. While Confucians, Taoist, and Buddhist teachings influenced this folk religion at various periods, they did not capture it, but rather each enriched it with added insight. The Chinese peasant thus had a legacy of humanism and tolerance of which his extraordinary sense of humor was a most delightful indication. Its submergence now in the service of the modern gods of blast furnaces and communal farms would be a loss not only for the Chinese but for all of us.

AMERICAN UNIVERSITIES FIELD STAFF

CHINA
AR-8-'58

PEOPLE'S COMMUNES
China's Peasants Take "The Ultimate Step"

By Albert Ravenholt

Hong Kong
October 23, 1958

CHINESE HISTORY records some cataclysmic events, but none, if we are to trust available accounts, have shaken the traditional life of the peasant like the recasting of his existence now under way. Throughout the land he is being rushed into "people's communes" and shorn of that familial economic security which has been his traditional guide to living. Since the Emperor Shih Huang Ti first unified the "Middle Kingdom" under the state of Ch'in in 221 B.C., launched his immense water-control schemes, and began building the Great Wall, collection of taxes in cash or kind (particularly grain) and exaction of corvees have been prime requisites for dynastic vigor. Were the same emperors who gave their names to successive dynasties, their scholars, eunuchs, and other administrators to return now, they would undoubtedly look with envy upon what is being wrought by the new rulers in Peking. For, surely, never before have the Chinese toiled as they do today, nor have they ever been taxed with such utter thoroughness. And, with the present organization of some 500 million peasants into communes, the new regime aims to assure itself of a continuous malleable human work force, one which subsists with the minimum of expense and "lost energy for unproductive effort."

According to the Communists, these communes are the final form into which they will mold Chinese society. The form itself, they add, should not be mistaken for the ultimate expression of communism when each person will be provided for according to his needs. Until this goal is achieved, rations from the communal kitchen and all other such necessities "will be available to each according to his performance." It is too early to judge whether the Chinese peasant will have any capacity but to accept this drastic remaking of his life, irrespective of how deeply it violates his instincts. Evident, however, are several internal and external implications. The Central People's Government and the Communist Party that manages it seem to feel themselves nearly omnipotent at home. The speed with which the communes are being created is a startling index of the effectiveness of the cadres at all levels of society. With the recasting of its people into communes, Red China moves considerably beyond that stage of social engineering reached by other communist states -- with all this implies in that part of the world which deifies Marx and Lenin. While such monumental internal change will tend to discourage Peking from involvement now in a major war, limited hostilities, as the fighting over the offshore islands, seem useful for justifying an even greater speedup on patriotic grounds. If the Communists can succeed with the communes, it is difficult to visualize any early internal miscalculation that can unseat the new power on the ancient dragon throne.

To appreciate the enormity of the change the Communists now are working, we must examine the experience of the Chinese peasantry within recent years. The Red Armies that completed their campaigns of conquest on the

PEOPLES COMMUNES

mainland of China in 1949 were drawn from the peasantry and the soldiers were ideologically fired with promises of land and justice for their families. Initially the Communists capitalized upon the hunger for both to systematically shatter the old rural social structure. Along with, and sometimes even in advance of the Red troops came the Communist cadres-- those intensively indoctrinated young men and women assigned responsibility for "turning over the society" and shaping the rural scene to a new purpose. In each "liberated" village all residents were classified. The cadres usually identified a few who were rated as landlords or rich farmers. Normally, not many more fell into the category of "middle farmers." The great majority were rated as "poor farmers" or "farm laborers," and these were organized into the "farmers associations," or Nung Hui, as they were known in South China.

Under incessant tutelage, prodding, and lecturing by the cadres, and with the use of the massive psychological group and community pressure the Communists in China have perfected, these "farmers associations" became the new ruling power in the community. And it was these Nung Hui, with their regularly rotating chairmen and their identification with the mass of local citizens that made the revolution, but always there was behind-the-scenes guidance from the Communist-schooled cadres. It was the "farmers associations" that organized the "settling-of-the-old-accounts" and "wiping-of-the-slates-clean" campaigns -- requiring landowners to return excess rentals, moneylenders to refund high interest collected -- and in other ways stripped the formerly prominent families of wealth and status. When Red China embarked on the "liquidation of counter-revolutionary elements" early in 1951, these same "farmers associations" held the "peoples trials," where selected individuals were denounced, sentenced, and executed or punished -- with all citizens sometimes required to share in beating the one who had been condemned.

The land redistribution that followed classification of all properties did give land and, in large areas of China, also awarded titles to the peasants. In facts many Chinese who had flocked to the cities went home to their native villages, if only temporarily, to insure getting their parcel of the soil that has been so prized in this civilization. Then, soon after this nation-wide reshuffling of property ownership, came the organization of peasants into "mutual labor teams." These demanded a sharing of the work load and were handy as a device for easing the peasants into collective farms. Significantly, this pooling of land, livestock, and manpower into collectives was achieved only gradually over several years. And the peasants retained an identifiable individual interest in the collective, at least theoretically, based upon contribution in land, equipment, and animals. Their share in the produce of the collective was calculated primarily according to "labor contribution" -- after taxes, state purchases, allocation for modernization, reserve and other deductions had been made from the collective's crop, the peasant family still received a proportionate share that "belonged" to it. Also, peasant families on the collective farms continued to cultivate their own garden plots, to raise their own pigs and chickens (fed largely with household waste), and otherwise to further their family economic interests within this new environment.

PEOPLES COMMUNES

Although a few single and more heavily taxed farms remained, the creation of these collectives which absorbed the bulk of the peasantry, plus the organization of scattered state farms, was a traumatic experience and it engendered criticism even within the Communist Party. It went against the grain of Chinese peasant values, and the cadres, who were following Communist directives, encountered stubborn resistance, some sabotage of production, and occasional peasants who simply refused to remain in collectives. They had to work literally day and night to generate enthusiasm for the new system.

Coincident with creation of the mutual labor teams and the collectives, peasants in the villages were given a strong dose of what the Communists term "new social consciousness." The new marriage laws for instance, radically altered not only the status of women but internal family relationships as well. During the first year of the "struggle" to secure its implementation in
what was then the "Central-South Administrative District" comprising six provinces, the Communist press reported more than 10,000 women had committed suicide. Evidently they were caught between the pressures of the women's organizations, that in each community examined a wife's compliance with the law's demands for equality, and the embedded customs of the home, including the now prohibited concubinage. The All-China Federation of Women, which assumed special responsibility for implementation of the marriage law, was only one of the mass organizations that increasingly tied the peasant to directives from Peking. The "Aid-Korea-and-Resist-American-Aggression" campaign made its demands, often in the form of contributions, of everyone. Constantly in the villages there were the "self-criticism meetings," the lectures, wall posters, and particularly the schooling of the young in new attitudes toward the values their parents had taken for granted. But, despite all the innovations in education and rural leadership patterns, the single family unit remained the basic group wherein Chinese lived their lives, sought security, and planned for the future. And there were hints that an uneasy equilibrium was being achieved between the new institutions the Communists had engineered and the traditional Chinese search for satisfaction within the family.

The respite from induced change that followed completion of collectivization in 1958 proved only a brief "breather." Last autumn Red China embarked upon so massive a country-wide effort to expand irrigation that it staggers the imagination. As part of the "leap forward" campaign in agriculture, almost every able-bodied peasant man and woman not critically needed elsewhere was mustered out with a hoe, a shovel, wheelbarrow, carrying basket, or cart drawn by a mule or draft cow. Office workers, professors, and officials were sent into the countryside to join in the work. A Chinese friend from here, who traveled to Peking to visit his doctor son, found him working eight hours daily in the hospital and then going out to "labor for the people" with a hoe for three hours every day.

Symbolically, Mao Tse-tung, who is concurrently chairman of the Chinese Communist Party and head of the government, and Premier Chou En-lai were photographed lending a hand to the "labor brigades" constructing the Ming Tombs Reservoir outside of Peking. The bleak, cold, and, in parts of China, wet winter was traditionally a period when Chinese peasants hibernated. It was a time to repair tools, to weave cloth, to earn a bit of extra income doing odd jobs, or simply to rest, But last winter the typical labor team marched to the work site, sometimes with a mouth organ accompaniment, at about five o'clock in the morning and returned after sundown too exhausted to do much but sleep. The cadres who pushed the peasants so relentlessly even argued with them about whether they should be allowed one day of rest in each month.

When this phase of China's "Three-Year Campaign of Suffering to Build a Glorious Future" was ended last June, the Communists announced achievements that challenge belief. They now claim to have supplied water to more than an additional 65 million acres by building new irrigation canals and systems, repairing and extending old works,, and providing reservoirs. (This is roughly 50 times the acreage being irrigated by the Columbia River's Grand Coulee Dam, America's biggest man-made water barrier.) Not all of their announcements give identical figures, although they approximate one another. But the latest compilation states that irrigation now covers roughly 163 million acres, or 59 per cent of China's farmland. They also report draining, during the past year, some 34 million acres, or about one-half of the land "chronically subject to water logging." In a manner characteristic of the regime, they add that this "herculean achievement" is only a step in the direction of a grand effort to harness China's rivers that is to culminate, eventually, in the control and use of the wild, and now largely wasted, waters of the giant Yangtze. For the peasants, completion of these extraordinary construction tasks only served as a prelude to this summer's intensive push to expand food production. Nature was generous in sparing the mainland natural disasters, in the form of major floods and droughts, that habitually visit China where the moisture-conserving tree cover on the mountains has been long since stripped off. Travelers now report that for the past several years tree planting has been given so much emphasis that vast expanses of once regularly deforested slopes are turning green with young pine seedlings. Vital for this summer's crops was the moderate, well-distributed rainfall which meant that only the plateau country of Yunnan and Kweichow in Southwest China, sections of Manchuria, and Shensi and Shansi Provinces suffered from light early drought. The thoroughgoing utilization of human labor was directed to dredging fertile mud from pond bottoms to stimulate the rice plants and to the employment of every available plant nutrient. Some 32 billion tons of manure were gathered and applied, the government asserts. The Communists, who in their first Five Year Plan virtually ignored chemical fertilizer in their obsession with establishing heavy industry, have now discovered their error. Roughly 100 European ship charters were arranged this year by Peking chiefly to import chemical fertilizer. And Communist officials now talk of needing to produce 20 million tons a year which is almost ten times the present estimate of local production and imports combined.

Communist claims of expanded agricultural production defy acceptance at face value. Cotton production, they say, this year reached 3.5 million tons with an average yield of 534 pounds per acre -- roughly double last year's output and yield. Soybeans, peanuts, rapeseed, sesame, sunflowers and other oil-bearing crops are reported to have totaled 20 million tons, or 40 per cent more than the 1956 peak outputs on 76 per cent of the previous acreage. Average soybean yield is placed at 1,148 pounds per acre. The fishing industry is supposed to have boosted its output to 8.2

million tons, or two and one-half times last year's harvest. In considerable measure this resulted from increasing the area of fresh-water fish ponds from 1.5 million to 5.75 million acres, On their experimental fish ponds, the Communists announce, they have secured a combined yield of 30 tons per acre of all forms of marine products. Shellfish, common to the South China coasts are supposed to have been adapted to North China waters, and the production of seaweed for human consumption substantially expanded,

It is in the basic grain and tuber crops that Communist China makes her most grandiose claims and in this category increased output will have consequential results. The wheat harvest this year is reported at 39.5 million tons, 67 per cent above 1957 [for domestic and foreign effect the Communist press adds that this is 2.93 million tons more than the United States produced]. They say further that their average wheat yield this year jumped from 721 pounds to 1022 pounds per acre. But two hsien, or counties, in Honan Province are reputed to have produced an average of better than 3,400 pounds per acre on more than 100,000 acres; thus, as the Peking press gleefully points out, bettering Denmark's record in the West by 113 pounds per acre. The early rice crop this year is reported to have totaled double the 1957 outputs or 40 million tons, while the semi-late rice crop was 40 per cent above last year for a harvest of 56.5 million tons. The late harvest on fields producing two rice crops has yet to be gathered and tabulated, but the Communists are equally optimistic about it. And the production of millet, tubers, sorghum and minor crops is also up* Communist newspapers now are carrying official estimates of a total grain and equivalent (four tons of tubers equal one ton of grain) production for 1958 of 350 million tons--"90 per cent more than last year." The 1957 crop of 185 million tons of grains and equivalents compared to 132 million tons during 1950 (the first year the Communists were in power)s and a pre-Communist peak of about 150 million tons, These claims -- to put it mildly -- are well beyond what past experience in agriculture elsewhere suggests is possible. Not only does this avowed Chinese acceleration in production place in the shadow the great farm revolution of America during the past 20 years, but it makes the efforts of the Soviet Union in agriculture look a bit miserable. However, while experienced observers here doubt the complete veracity of announcements from Peking, every person I have spoken with who has come out of Communist China recently is convinced that this past summer has witnessed the growing and harvesting of the most bountiful crops ever. And if the figures for increased irrigated acreage alone are taken as a guide, it is reasonable to expect an increase over last year's harvest of some 50 to 60 million tons of grain and equivalents. The most improbable claims are those for the early rice harvest; the Communists report that they have pushed yields 122 per cent above last year to a national average of 3,340 pounds per acre. The mainland press abounds with accounts of fantastic production achieved on tiny areas, such as 146 tons of wheat grown on one experimental plot of little more than an acre in Honan Province. Women are reported to have worked in 24-hour-a-day relays to feed fertilized water through these patches of wheat, separate the stalks to let in sun and air, and otherwise follow up deep plowing with greenhouse practices and all conceivable yield-boosting measures. Observers here are led to believe that the amazing Communist claims, particularly on test plots, are intended to disabuse the peasants of their old assumptions regarding attainable results. The psychological foundation is thus created for pushing future output even beyond the present evidently remarkable agricultural record.

The men who make the major decisions in Peking seem to have determined upon moving the peasantry into communes shortly after midsummer when they saw the promised bounty of this year's harvest -- China's bumper production affords them a "margin" to offset the losses in farm produce such a drastic change may bring. But the very character of the "people's communes" suggests their creation is an attempt to overcome obstacles the Communists have encountered in their efforts radically to increase production while remaking China. The first public hints that the Communists had such a national enterprise in mind came early this year. The Peking press and some North China provincial publications pictured the advantages of the larger collectives for organizing labor brigades and otherwise speeding work on the more ambitious water-conservation projects. A year earlier in a campaign to dig wells and construct small irrigation systems, particularly throughout areas north of the Yellow River., most opportunities for creating additional irrigation units within the land area controlled by a single collective had been exhausted. Also evident was the insatiable demand for more raw human energy once China's manpower became organized and disciplined -- as it is now. It is the major item for capital investment the Communists can marshal. With a population of some 650 million increasing by an estimated 15 million plus annually, if the economic treadmill thus created is to be outpaced, labor performance per human consumption unit obviously must be accelerated.

Pilot communes, by giving form to ideas the Communists apparently have been examining for several years, now are providing guides to the transformation being worked among China's peasantry. The Weihsing, or "Satellite," commune created last April 20 in Suip'ing Hsien of Honan Province is among the first and most publicized in the Communist press (another of their early communes is named "Sputnik"), This "Satellite" model for China's future society incorporates 27 former "agricultural producers' co-operatives," otherwise known as collectives, composed of 9,369 families. Other early communes include as few as 2,000 households, although the average membership for the North China area seems to be about 7,000 families. Each commune absorbs the functions of one or several hsiang governments, the lowest formal administrative unit. In theory at least, the communes are designed to fit natural geographic formations, such as a watershed, and thereby facilitate efforts to make nature serve the new order. Like their comrades in other communes, the 43,265 Chinese in Weihsing are parts of a local "agro-industrial complex" managed by a Communist Party elite that aims for self-sufficiency in manufacturing the tools, fertilizers, building materials, clothing., and other major requirements previously purchased outside, while producing every more in surplus farm products for delivery to the state. With its own nurseries to take the young, schools and "red universities" to educate them, mess halls to feed workers, and "happiness homes" providing for oldsters, the commune serves to supplant the family with a larger loyalty and an even tougher taskmaster.

The essence of the commune concept is a more total and efficient control over and use of labor. In place of the former labor teams, peasants --

both men and women -- now are grouped in platoons, companies, battalions, and regiments or brigades. Wherever manpower is needed within the commune they are shifted accordingly; the Communists say they want an "all-around-gifted-person." A battalion of women workers may devote one week to transplanting rice seedlings and the following week be marched out to join other battalions carrying earth on a dike construction job. The decision as to where and when to employ these peasant forces -- avowedly "organized along military lines" --is made according to the size of the task -- the Communists have been emphatic in warning against overly centralized direction. Priorities are fixed in keeping with the commune's role in serving national production targets.

Presently, as part of its "leap forward" campaign in industry, Communist China is seeking to double its 1957 steel production by achieving an output of 10.7 million tons for 1958. In regions where iron ore and coal are found in relative proximity, thousands of small "blast furnaces" and "steel smelters" reportedly are being constructed. Mobilized peasants are manning these crude "factories day and night, thereby giving their commune its rudimentary "industrial base." Often pig iron produced in such scattered workshops is shipped to more modern central plants for further processing. Across the country an effort now is underway to mechanize" farm equipment by fitting all wheeled vehicles with ball bearings. The mainland press blazons accounts of how many thousands of vehicles were fitted with bearings within a week or two after the "peasants rushed to join the communes." Admittedly2 some of the bearings may last only a few months, but the Communists blithely cope with this difficulty by telling the peasants to melt down the worn bearings and cast them over again. It is all in keeping with the principle: "To make do with available things. Small factories are to be built first and then gradually expanded."As collective farms are merged into communes, agricultural production also is reorganized with an emphasis upon "rationalization" and larger units. Lands within a commune judged the best for growing rice because of availability of water for irrigation are so allocated; the Communists insist that this possibility, within the larger scope of the commune., permits a sounder adaptation of crops to suitable soil-types than the former practice when a collective sought to produce its basic grain requirements irrespective of location. Each commune is reputed to be creating one or several farms for hog and poultry raisings bee keeping., cattle breeding and specialized projects such as silk production. Every commune is also to conduct its own agricultural experimental work, seed selection2 and pest control -- this is the era "when the people can do everything. Clearly, such a thorough reshuffling of agriculture and especially of the fragmented farms of China holds the hazard of critically upsetting the productive cycle. Communist instructions to the cadres repeatedly emphasize that these changes in farm layout and cropping patterns must never be pushed faster than is possible without damaging prospects of achieving their production targets. In practice it may take several years for a commune to so concentrate each type of farming.

"To make full use of labor power," explains the Communist press., "to enable women to play their full part in field work and to insure that there is no waste of labor time to men and women, the farm co-operatives [communes-in-the-making) must be not only organizers of production but also organizers of the way of life; not only do they have to collectivize labor further, but also to organize the collective way of life," In this effort the commune kitchens play an important role, Communist writers calculate that these common mess halls, now numbering 310,000 in Honan Province alone and already feeding 71 per cent of the population, achieve a ten per cent saving in peasant grain consumption, Established frequently in the larger homes that in an earlier day belonged to landlords, these communal dining facilities also provide a neat means of insuring that only those who work eat -- rations for each person are delivered to the communal kitchen. Along with the communal nurseries that take in the youngsters, laundry units and sewing brigades where elderly females readily find a place, these kitchens are the means to "liberating" women for "labor in production." In describing the new opportunities for field work by women in East China's Kiangsu Province a Communist writer states: "On the average one of them [formerly] could only work six or seven hours. Also, because the time for meals was not fixed, the time for them to go to and leave work was not the same for everyone. It often happened that workers lay idle waiting for the start of work, and at least one hour every day was wasted. After establishment of mess halls, the attendance rate can be raised generally by 10 per cent, the number of hours spent in work increased by 20 to 30 per cent and working efficiency by 40 to 50 per cent."

For the peasant the commune means the end of his private garden plot on which., with his customary applications of animal manure and human "night soil," he had relied for much of his livelihood. Sweet potatoes, taro, water chestnuts, green leafy vegetables to be dried or salted away for the winter, turnips,, squash, melons, and the innumerable other vegetable crops that gave variety and nourishment came from these tiny plots. The sow that a peasant family traditionally kept in order to raise her litter on scraps from the table and garden now goes to the pen kept by the communal mess hall where it is fed every waste, including the dishwater. (The Communists apparently discovered that in some collectives grain had found its way to animals being fattened for individual family tables.) The three to a dozen hens that a Chinese family frequently kept as scavengers must follow the pigs into a communal coop. This "communal-izing" of livestock and poultry became mandatory once eating centered upon the communal kitchen. So far, a family may be permitted to retain a few fruit trees for itself. Evident, however, is a determination not only to deny opportunity for family economic activities, but also to insure that the peasants' non-working hours are available for other pursuits.

Within each commune the Communists are creating a militia. All able-bodied men and women between the ages of 18 and 45 are eligible and for certain duties the age limit can be extended up or down. In practice the militia is built around the veterans of the Red Army, who may number five to six million men, and the new conscriptees with three years of service (the first class of whom will begin returning to their homes this year). Next in line for intensive military schooling are the cadres or activists who provide the Communist "yeast" and direction within the commune. Thereafter, the militia training will be extended to other "advanced groups2" presumably the more technically skilled. Weapons, perhaps in limited numbers, are being issued to this communal militia with much fanfare. The Communists may see the communal militia as a means toward a numerical reduction in the "People's Liberation Army," without denying Peking an abundance of trained military. Such a reduction in the Red Army, whose strength is now estimated at two and one-half million men, would be economically advantageous and could enhance Communist China's efforts to court neighboring Asian nations. But the militia seems to have an even more crucial role in providing the "firm steel ribbing" of the entire communal system. It was within the Red Army that the Chinese Communists first perfected their techniques of "mind washing" and demonstrated their capacity for converting illiterate peasants into dedicated and sometimes furious champions of the revolution Mao Tse-tung led. However, as was demonstrated with the Chinese soldiers that surrendered in Korea, including many former Nationalist troops, this indoctrination does not necessarily stick with the first wash. The communal militia will be entrusted not only with the maintenance of order but also with assisting in the endless re-education in which the cadres, wall newspapers, mess-hall radios, touring drama troups, study meetings, and "red universities" all have a part. Meanwhile, the militia also are assigned to "unify" their efforts with the labor brigades to insure maximum "work discipline." Booming brass gongs, the throbbing of drums, and sputtering firecrackers in the villages, so the reports read, are now signaling the "rush" of the peasants to enter these communes.

Shansi Province, which established its first commune in mid-August, is scheduled to amalgamate all of its 20,000 or so collectives into 800 or 1,000 communes by the end of the autumn harvest. Across the border from there, in Kwangtung Province, the "overwhelming majority" of peasant households, according to the Communists, are expected to be in communes by the end of this month. Throughout mainland China the roughly 700,000 collectives, plus the state farms, and stubborn peasants who have held out as individual cultivators, are slated for similar treatment this autumn or early this coming winter. Notably, the communes are being extended almost simultaneously to the areas of the "national minorities" that were given gentler and more gradual treatment during the earlier Communist reworkings of Chinese rural life -- only the remoter hinterland of Tibet seems to be a partial exception. From Lanchow comes a report that 502000 households of herdsmen and peasants of the Kannan Tibetan Autonomous Chou [Region] recently "Joined people's communes with great jubilation." Trial communes have been established among the Miao, Yi. and other tribes of Yunnan, while the Mongols also are finding their herds and co-operatives assembled into communes.

The national campaign reached the Shanghai suburbs with creation of the "July First People's Commune" on that date. It is larger than the average, incorporating 22,297 households and merging the functions of six hsiang governments and one chen (small community). In the pattern the Communists are employing elsewhere, these families were assembled in "big blooming" and "big contending" meetings where the entire matter of joining the commune supposedly was publicly debated. The limitations of the small co-operatives was "exposed" and the superior features of the people's communes publicized. The resulting "group thinking" agreed that the lead indicated by the Communist Party was correct and justified organization of the commune into 12 production companies and 110 production teams. Appropriately2 a prominent comrade issued a "combat order" on deep plowing and manure collection to insure that wheat "satellites" will be "shot into the sky next year." Of note in these experiments the Communists are making on the periphery of the larger cities is the merging of agricultural and industrial units in a single commune. During a recent visit to the new modern steel center at Wuhan, Mao Tse-tung is reported to have urged the plant managers to seek out an agricultural commune with which they could join. Although they apparently have not yet sorted through the method, the Communists seem determined in time to fit their industrial population into communes comparable to those in the countryside. A few scattered and usually secondhand accounts by travelers from the mainland tell of peasants "simply sitting down and refusing to work" when they got the word about the communes. But these occasional reports are inadequate as a basis for judging acceptance of the undertaking and it is still too early to measure the consequences for China. Some of the more serious problems are apparent not only from occasional mention in the Communist press, they are also revealed by the very environment in which communes are established. Throughout North China peasants entering communes are confronted with the critical question of how to keep warm this winter. In these colder regions a family sleeps and spends their indoor daytime on the kang. This raised clay platform covering up to one-half of the main living quarter is built over the winding flue which carries smoke from the kitchen fire to the chimney -- an ingenious arrangement in a land where fuel has been terribly scarce. Now cooking is done in central kitchens, where the Communists claim they save fuel. But the kang will then be cold. Clearly, the weather can become an argument for moving the peasants into dormitories (a practice about which the Communists have said little), and the establishment of dormitories can serve as an indirect means for encouraging birth control, should it be desired.

Far more critical is the question of the peasants' original investment in the collectives which now are incorporated into the communes. The Communist press makes no mention lately of privately owned lands; the implication is that they already belong to "the people." Regulations for the commune specifically state that a peasant's house may be torn down if it interferes with scheduled development and he and his family assigned living space elsewhere. From Liaoning Province in Manchuria a correspondent for the People's Daily in Peking writes: "Horses and carts, farm implements, and fishing nets not yet paid for will be converted into investment in the co-operative [commune-in-the-making] and there will be no further repayment." Actually, the issue remains unresolved. The same writer adds, "For building of the farm and to realize Communism, the peasants at the time of the merger voluntarily expressed their readiness to write off debts due them by the co-operative for horses and carts given up." From other provinces the Communist press cautions that it will be three or four years, and, perhaps, five or six, before these possessions of the peasants "become the property of all the people." But it appears that the intended compensation for the peasants is ideological: "The Party organs should place the trend of thought of the commune members under their control at all times." In the few communes where complete state ownership has been achieved, the peasants became outright wage laborers. They can still seek eligibility for a bonus, but the requirements include "working at least 28 days per month." And it is evident that the peasants are to receive little more than a meager subsistence. The satisfaction with which the authorities officially view the new order is indicated in a revealing account: "Co-operative cadres report that in the past they had either to beat drums and gongs or to go here and there before they could hold a meeting and direct work. Now they can simply make an announcement in the mess halls, and everything turns out all right."

The capacity of the Chinese Communist state to enforce such regimentation ultimately will depend primarily upon the quality of their internal organization. It alone can save them from a disastrous miscalculation which could cripple Chinese agriculture as did forced collectivization during the early thirties in the Soviet Union. Peking must depend, too, upon the skill and political trustworthiness of the cadres to bring enough of the peasants into willing co-operation so that the recalcitrant ones find no substantial haven among fellow malcontents; a commune providing virtually all of its own needs could conceivably also assert its independence of the "central authority." Specialists in Russian affairs generally agree that Joseph Stalin settled for a compromise with the peasants which placed them formally in collectives but left them significant prerogatives as family economic units. His successors in the management of the Soviets have gone farther in trading consideration of peasant aspirations for expanded agricultural output.

Students of communism who look at China through Russian experience tend to overlook one basic difference -- the vastly greater and more highly disciplined organizational resources of which the leaders in Peking can dispose. This is chiefly a product of the differing processes that brought communism to power in the two nations. Russia's Bolsheviks numbered roughly 200,000 when they made their revolution., and most of these had joined the Party within the preceding year. Having captured the major cities and lines of communication, they imposed their government and system of life upon a huge and for the most part sparsely settled land mass. By contrast, in 1949 when the new government was established in Peking, the then some five million members of the Chinese Communist Party had been schooled, tested, and selected for doctrinal loyalty and organizational capacity -- the hard core had been formed over two decades. And the process goes on among the 12 million members today as well as among the several times that number who help perform the Party's work. Long before capturing total power this Party had perfected techniques for "going inside of society" and refashioning it to their ends. Now, aided by the authority a totalitarian state possesses, this method that the Chinese Communists have developed is being put to its severest test.

Should Communist China accomplish her purpose of welding the peasantry into communes without engendering critical resistance, the returns in sight are such as to tantalize even the relentlessly hardheaded leaders in Peking. They can, then, with confidence born of example, claim the mantle of ideological leadership within the communist orbit. In consequence, they can be expected to exert an ever-widening influence not only in the affairs of communist states but also among smaller Asian nations searching for a formula. Measured in terms of sheer power, such a total marshaling of the Chinese offers the Communists increasing latitude for choice internally. The rest of us are bound to feel it, once one-fourth of the human race is so organized.

PEOPLES COMMUNES

Some years ago when opportunities for such conversations were not unusual among correspondents working in China, I asked Chou En-lai just what basic changes they would make in Chinese life if he and his comrades came to power. He replied with a disarming candor that made the listener skeptical: "We will make China over from a family-centered into a community-centered society." Little did I then appreciate how literally this would be attempted and with what unforeseen prospects of accomplishment.

FOREIGN AFFAIRS

AN AMERICAN QUARTERLY REVIEW

July 1959

THE CHINESE COMMUNES: BIG RISKS FOR BIG GAINS

By

Albert Ravenholt

WITHIN THE PAST YEAR Communist China has incorporated some 550,000,000 of its peasants into "people's communes." Now, after a winter and spring of "tidying up" these communes and examining their performance in the face of peasant resistance, the Communist Party has shown this is no mere experiment. The rulers in Peking are committed to them for "transforming rural society through socialism to Communism." A single commune today manages the total activity of several thousand peasant families -- sometimes more. Their crops are planted, harvested and stored, or sold to the state, as dictated by the commune. Men and women in a labor platoon may shift from farming to mining coal or processing beans into soya sauce. But the decision is not theirs -- it is made by Communist commune managers. They determine how long the peasant will work and his meager compensation. The commune drills him in its "people's militia," selects the movies he is to see, decides what schooling his child shall receive and the gods he may acknowledge. It likewise may tell him when to demolish his house and where he then will live. For these communes are "more than the organizers of production, they are the organizers of a new way of life."

One can hardly overestimate the importance of this monumental human enterprise to the future of Red China. The increased productivity demanded of the communes and the bitter but passive peasant opposition will determine whether the Chinese Communists can rapidly transform their ancient land into an industrial and technologically modern state. Much of the character of the "people's democratic dictatorship" that now governs nearly one-fourth of mankind can be discerned in this grim new institution. Its blueprint for the future is here most concisely delineated. Within that part of the world that takes Marxism-Leninism as its bible the communes are the chief Chinese claim to ideological inventiveness. And the balance of influence between Peking and Moscow will inevitably reflect what happens in the communes.

Neighboring Asians searching for a formula that can guarantee them speedy progress watch this device for harnessing Chinese manpower with a certain frightened fascination; its success could offer them an example while also posing the greatest single threat to their continued national existence. For the United States and the Western world the tempo of change in Asia with which we must cope may be read in the rapid creation of these Chinese communes and their pace of evolution.

THE CHINESE COMMUNES: BIG RISKS FOR BIG GAINS

As an arrangement for mobilizing human energy, the communes recall the massive corvees that Chinese emperors used to dig the Grand Canal and construct the Great Wall and the coolies who in a modern day chipped the Burma Road out of mountain rock. But today China's rulers, who are digging a second Grand Canal farther inland to link the Yellow and Yangtze Rivers, have become more thorough and total in their demands. No longer is only one of two persons conscripted from each family and sent off for labor service. Rather, the entire society is organized for such performance at home. In the process the Chinese are toiling as these sturdy, patient people never have done before, despite centuries of bending their backs under the carrying pole or over the paddy field. During the past winter shock teams of peasants have labored as much as 36 to 48 hours at a stretch without sleep in furious and often desperate pursuit of production targets. Their rewards are the water conservation works they have extended, the crude blast furnaces erected in the countryside and the rich mud dredged from pond bottoms to fertilize this summer's next "leap forward" campaign in agriculture. And all of this has been done for the benefit of the state, or the "whole people" as the Peking press would phrase it.

Seldom if ever has a comparable portion of the human species experienced so traumatic a recasting of its existence in such a brief time span. The familial economic security that was the core of the Chinese peasant's social system is now denied him, although the biological family is to continue. The Chinese farmer, his wife and working children eat in a communal mess that also has taken his sow, nearly all his chickens, denied him most garden produce and commandeered the family cooking pots. Infants are cared for during the day in communal creches. Older people who now have no one to look after them at home can enter communal "respect-for-the-aged" establishments. Although the communes are the form in which Red China's rulers say they will cast their future society, they repeatedly emphasize that this must not be mistaken for Communism. Now only the first "germ" of Communism is available in the form of free food at the communal mess. For the peasant, the critical point is that full provision "for each according to his needs" as defined by some idealistic Communists must wait for the indefinite future. Meanwhile, the meager cash wages depend very much upon the ardor of his labor; commune workers may be classified into eight grades. They can also strive for a bonus. To emphasize this point the Central Committee of China's Communist Party last winter categorically denounced "equalitarianism," or demands for equal sharing, as a "petty-bourgeois trend" that will "adversely affect the development of socialist construction." Somewhat obliquely the Chinese Communists admit that their cadres made a number of mistakes during the great "push" last autumn to bring up to 120,000,000 families into communes. The election in April of Liu Shao-chi to succeed Mao Tse-tung as chairman of the People's Republic of China may well be related to a desire inside the Party to tighten control and minimize the "unscientific" haste with which communes were organized. It left Mao Tse-tung, who remains chairman of the Party and the preeminent Chinese Communist, free to cope with the far-reaching theoretical implications of the communes. The younger Liu Shao-chi and his fellow Party stalwarts meanwhile are afforded a firmer hold on the administrative mechanism. The Communist leaders seem to have concluded that the success of their daring venture with the communes depends greatly upon the sensitivity of their organization to events in the countryside. They need to know quickly and accurately just how far and in which direction the peasants can be pushed, and when a bit of relaxation becomes essential. For they are taking great risks. As the peasant has been stripped of the opportunity to realize most of his old social and family values he has also lost many compulsions for performance. And the despair and indifference reported by Chinese who have worked in communes could be turned against the regime. Also, the very speed with which the cadres marshalled the rural populace into communes suggests how rapidly they can run off the track if a mistake is made at the top. China lacks the "margin for error" in untapped raw land and natural resources that cushioned Soviet Russia's collectivization during the 1930s. Instead, with her population now burgeoning by an estimated 15,000,000 annually, China still is painfully at the mercy of nature for the crop yields that are the key to these grandiose Communist schemes.

II. WHY THE CHINESE COMMUNES?

The compulsions that led Red China to create the communes can best be grasped by examining the dilemma in which the new rulers found themselves in 1957-the final year of their first Five Year Plan. By then they seem to have realized that even with Russian and East European Communist assistance they could not, at the pace they were then moving, build a modern economy in this generation. Instead, they were caught between a growing need for capital formation and the mounting demands of a population expanding rapidly because of new emphasis on mass sanitation and public health. Mao Tse-tung and his cohorts also were impatient to catch up technologically with Japan and the West. The means to accomplish this could be generated only through increased agricultural collections from the peasants and capitalization upon China's vast human power so far only partially employed. If the sacrifices exacted from the peasants were not to be compensated for by better food and some consumer goods, new and more efficient organizational devices and tighter controls would be required.

Yet, at this very time the Chinese Communists were encountering opposition in the countryside approximating in character that which had forced Stalin to compromise with the Russian peasants during his ruthless collectivization drives. The Chinese peasant's yearning for land and justice had been the motive force on which the Communists rode to power before 1949. It had also been the means through which they "turned over" the old rural society during the first years of their rule. Cadres organized the poor and middle peasants into Farmers Associations that staged "settling of old accounts" meetings, stripping landowners and other prominent families of wealth and status. These Associations managed the "people's trials" where enemies of the new regime were condemned-sometimes beaten to death, sometimes given the opportunity to "reform through corrective labor."

Once the land had been redistributed and peasants given titles, the Farmers Associations served as instruments for organizing "mutual labor teams" through which the entire community shared in planting and harvesting. These in turn became a convenient device for bringing the peasants into cooperatives where they kept the titles while pooling their land, tools, work animals and labor, and collecting a proportionate share of the produce. In the more "advanced" communities these were converted

THE CHINESE COMMUNES: BIG RISKS FOR BIG GAINS

into full-fledged collectives that owned the means of production and paid the peasants according to work points they earned. This was accomplished only through endless "explanation and discussion" meetings often lasting far into the night, constant group and official pressure organized by the cadres and a final crash program in 1955-56. And the process required six years.

Collectivization alone, however, proved not enough. The cadres, novices to agriculture, had given only erratic direction to introducing mechanization, extending irrigation and other innovations. In keeping with an early Chinese Communist inclination to throw all resources into heavy industry at the expense of agriculture, the first Five Year Plan had almost ignored the great need for building chemical fertilizer capacity. By late 1956 peasants were balking, partly in protest against the heavy state collections of grain but also in disgust with the bookkeeping complexities and jealousies the system encouraged. Some peasants simply walked out of their cooperatives. Others were held in the collectives by promises from the cadres that there would be no further reorganization of the peasants at least for a decade. While valuing the land reform, peace, order and certain other innovations which the Communists had brought, the peasants generally felt they had had enough. Peking had not succeeded in "remolding" their values.

III. THE "GREAT LEAP FORWARD"

It was in this setting that Mao Tse-tung less than two years ago launched a "thaw" period -- the famous movement to "Let one hundred flowers bloom, Let one hundred schools of thought contend." When, however, the Party felt the extent and violence of the opposition thus released it clamped on controls far tighter than before. It set in motion a nation-wide "rectification and reindoctrination" campaign that reached almost every person in China, including the peasantry. It was the fierce discipline and propaganda of this movement that made possible the first "leap forward" campaign which began in the autumn of 1957. This was the start of a country-wide effort to expand irrigation on such an enormous scale that one has difficulty in visualizing it. Normally, winter has been a period when Chinese peasants rest, repair their tools, weave cloth and earn a bit of extra income with other handicraft occupations. Now it became a time when every man and woman not urgently needed elsewhere was mustered out to move dirt. In platoons they marched out at sunrise singing or to the accompaniment of simple musical instruments. They employed the traditional Chinese methods-transporting earth in baskets, mule carts and wheelbarrows and breaking rocks by hand with hammers.

The Communists now calculate that in the year beginning October 1957, irrigation was extended to an additional 80,000,000 acres. They admit that some of the dikes were hastily thrown up and need rebuilding. Also, this figure includes renovation of ancient water control systems constructed in imperial times that had fallen into disuse or silted up. But if the achievement is anywhere near that claimed, it is an organized human effort without parallel. During the same period the Communists claim to have reforested some 66,000,000 acres of the barren mountain-sides that for centuries made China a land of floods and erosion.

THE CHINESE COMMUNES: BIG RISKS FOR BIG GAINS

That winter of exhausting labor served only as an initiation to the 1958 "leap forward" in agriculture. Some 32 billion tons of manure were spread, according to Communist figures; they exhumed garbage pits, dismantled fireplaces for the ashes and ripped off old straw-thatched roofs to make compost. Peasants who were required to demolish old graves and spread the contents as fertilizer were shaken to the depths of their ancestral veneration. Massive coffin planks were sawed up for use in farm tools, for fencing and as firewood. Deep plowing and close planting became the rule. Weeding was made an honored national occupation and intellectuals and bureaucrats were mustered out of the cities to help.

The results claimed by the Communists exceed anything that experience elsewhere suggests is possible. Whereas a continuing annual increase in agricultural output of 6 to 8 percent is judged extraordinarily good in countries applying advanced technology, the Chinese Communists calculate that they boosted their output of grain and its equivalents by 90 percent in 1958. They claim a production of 350,000,000 tons of grain and root crops (tubers are converted at four tons to one ton of grain) as contrasted to 185,000,000 tons in 1957. (The figure for 1950, the first year of Communist power, was 132,000,000 tons compared to a pre-Communist maximum production of about 15,000,000 tons.) Cotton production is supposed to have increased from 1,6¢0,000 tons in 1957 to 3,500,000 tons in 1958. Although some of these figures appear to reflect over-enthusiastic crop estimates by Party cadres, travelers returning from the mainland late last summer agreed that China had its most bountiful crops ever. The great extension of irrigation coincided with a summer when adequate and rather evenly distributed rainfall reached most regions, and China was spared destructive typhoons at critical seasons.

The promise of this bountiful harvest gave the Chinese Communist leaders courage and opportunity to organize the peasantry into communes since it offered a margin of safety that they evidently felt would carry them through the inevitable period of dislocation. The basic decision appears to have been made by Mao Tse-tung and his associates in late July or early August. The formal move to bring the peasants into "people's communes" was made on August 29 at a meeting of the Central Committee of the Communist Party. The official announcement came on September 10, when the Chinese people learned of this "irresistible" development of the commune idea. The previous April the Communists had merged a few collectives into rudimentary communes, using temporary common kitchens or canteens established during the push to build irrigation works. These had served as pilot projects where organizational techniques were tested. Communist publications had carried a few articles on the advantages enjoyed by larger collectives; these, at least in retrospect, could be taken as hints of the thinking in Peking. But this was the extent of public forewarning. Even today the Chinese Communists do not buttress their decision with justifications traced to Marx, Engels or any other member of their philosophical pantheon. According to Peking, the communes are simply a "reflection of the objective law of development.

Once the word was out, the peasantry felt the consequences with phenomenal speed. For most peasants three to thirty days were required for incorporation into communes. The time depended primarily upon how conscientious the cadres were in making the move "spontaneous." "Big blooming and big contending" meetings were held day and night, with peasants encouraged to speak "frankly" of their criticisms and objections. Then cadres relentlessly showed them how mistaken were their thoughts. At the politically propitious time, to the accompaniment of "firecrackers, booming brass gongs, and the beating of drums," a collective or cooperative "voluntarily" joined with its neighbors. By mid-November Peking announced that 740,000 cooperatives and collectives had been amalgamated into some 26,500 communes. According to the Communists, they held 98 percent of the rural population -- a claim that may be nearly accurate. Within approximately two months virtually all cooperatives, collectives, state farms and remaining individual farmers, except in Tibet and among some other national minorities, were organized into communes. There is an awesome audacity about this Chinese Communist effort, suggesting their organizational resources, their capacity for venturesome innovation and their apparent feeling of near omnipotence at home.

Doubts about the permanence of the communes were resolved in December 1958, when the Central Committee met in plenary session at Wuhan, the new industrial and steel center on the Yangtze River. Evidently the meeting was devoted almost entirely to the communes, and to making clear that the move was irreversible. The resolution published following the session calls for a very gradual and experimental extension of communes into the cities, where, it states, "ownership by the whole people"state ownership-already is well advanced, conditions are more complex and "bourgeois ideology" is still fairly prevalent among former capitalists and intellectuals. Otherwise, the Party spelled out detailed measures for correcting excesses committed by the cadres in the first rush of commune organization. It called for tightening management at all levels. This most authoritative Communist document to date describes the communes as a "morning sun" above the horizon of East Asia and possessed of "immense vitality."

IV. COMMUNE ORGANIZATION

With usual membership of 5,000 families; since their geographical size is determined by water sheds and topographical features, communes on the lowlands may contain up to 10,000 or more families and those in the mountains may include as few as 2,000 households. This compares to the earlier cooperatives and collectives that each held 100 to 200 families. The commune also absorbs local government administrative functions. The most common type of commune includes one or several hsiang, which correspond roughly to a midwestern American township but usually are more densely populated. These are being grouped into hsien or county federations of communes, apparently a transitional step toward a second type of commune, one which encompasses an entire county. Since Red China today is divided into slightly less than 2,000 counties, excluding some areas of national minorities, it is probable that the number of communes may be considerably reduced from its present total of 26,500.

Within each commune the chairmanship usually is taken over by the former official of the corresponding level of local government. But the commune chief and his staff now also plan and direct agricultural production and negotiate contracts for sale of produce to state purchasing agencies. They integrate all construction of irrigation systems, roads and housing; they also develop industry, which is usually small scale and designed to

THE CHINESE COMMUNES: BIG RISKS FOR BIG GAINS

meet commune needs for consumeritems. Research stations, schools, kitchens, propaganda and security organs are under their control. Each commune is divided into administrative chu or districts designed to fit the productive functional units. Under the new system of "military organization" peasants are grouped in regiments, battalions and platoons. This is apart from the communal militia, which appears to have more political than military significance. Organized around a core of Red Army veterans, it affords the authorities an added instrument for imposing their will. While emphasis is upon integration of all functions in the commune, there are repeated admonitions from Peking to keep the Party distinct so it can retain its "objectivity." Actually, one of the chief purposes of the communes is enhanced Party control of the peasants. This is accomplished by bringing so many more of the peasants' activities under supervision of Communists working through the commune management and "seeding" Communists in at lower levels.

While the commune radically remakes the existence of the peasant, it affects his wife even more. For one of the chief Communist objectives is to expand the labor force by "freeing" women to work in the fields. To this end the communes are creating a system of creches and kindergartens. Some of these charge mothers for tending their children, but the fees are low. Originally, some cadres simply took the children away from parents and even discussed "migration of children" to neighboring counties to remove them from home influence. But parental reaction was furious. Now Party directives decree that parents must be allowed to take their children home at night.

They also stipulate that mothers should be permitted to breast-feed their infants in communal nurseries when they are working nearby. The Communists state that their eventual goal is a system of boarding schools for all children-an educational arrangement which will largely free the young from parental control.

THE CHINESE COMMUNES

The communal kitchens and mess halls are likewise designed to get more women to work while also enabling the regime to limit food consumption and restrict it to those serving the aims of the new society. Often established in the homes of former landowners, these messes now tend to become the new centers of community life. When the communes were organized, one of the inducements which the cadres offered peasants was the promise of free food in the communal mess for everyone, and all they could eat; in the collectives there had been frequent trouble over who was entitled to take home how much food. But in many communes sweet potatoes are the only food that has been abundant so far and the Chinese traditionally regard these as the poorest of food. They are now often served with a thin gruel made of rice or millet. This dietary emphasis may result from a deliberate Communist effort to encourage consumption of a bumper crop of sweet potatoes that otherwise would spoil. But in the peasant mind it is aggravated by the miserable vegetables that communal kitchens so often serve. When the communes were formed the messes were to take over the garden plots on which peasants grew the cabbage, turnips, squash, beans and other vegetables they dried or salted away to provide a large and vital portion of their diets. Many communes evidently ignored the care of these vegetables. The Communists now are relenting and

THE CHINESE COMMUNES: BIG RISKS FOR BIG GAINS

allowing individual peasants a "small" garden. The pigs that Chinese kept as scavengers were turned over to the communal mess and remain there to be fed largely on potato peelings, dishwater and scraps. But the peasant now has been permitted to take back a few of the chickens he was compelled to surrender last fall. Since he has no fire at home and cooking pots have all been collected, such produce presumably must be prepared at the communal kitchen where others will be waiting to share it.

Contrary to some published accounts, the Communists have not generally moved men and women into separate barracks. Instead, Peking repeatedly insists that the "new" family will be kept intact and "liberated" from its old "economic" compulsions. The marriage law introduced by the Communists eight years ago and enforced with all the fervor that organized women can generate did much to equalize status between the sexes. Now that the communes are releasing them from the homes and kitchens it can be expected that Chinese peasant women will be no more restricted than their men. Within the communes a vast construction program is in progress as entire villages are relocated in order to centralize the labor forces near production sites. In the process, many houses are torn down and some families are required to double up. They are also compelled to share household furniture and some personal possessions with fellow commune members. Since land titles and tools not already delivered to the collective now go to the communes, the concept of private property virtually has lost its meaning for the Chinese peasant.

Most acutely of all, the peasant today feels the relentless pressure to work ever harder. The day in a typical commune begins with drill at sunrise-the Communists are systematically toughening all of China's population, and city dwellers as well as peasants are required to get out for morning calisthenics. After a quick breakfast, men and women march off in platoons to work in the fields, in a primitive "factory" or on construction. There they are under the constant supervision of a commune regimental commander or other cadres. Usually these commune officials are exempted from manual labor as a mark of status. Each platoon is urged to compete with the next platoon in "labor emulation drives." The winning platoon is entitled to carry a banner and may paint a "sputnik" on its mess hall door. Sometimes there is also the promise of meat or a similar delicacy several times each month for the outstanding platoons. In the push of the "leap forward" campaigns the cadres were mustering even the children to weed or to move earth. Now the Communists have ruled that only children over nine years of age are allowed to work to "learn productive habits." One-half of each day is supposed to be reserved for schooling, although there are complaints that some cadres reduce class time to two and three hours daily. Older people also are expected to contribute their labor; women may be assigned to sewing teams or charged with baby-sitting in a communal creche while the older men are out driving the birds away from the ripening grain fields. Throughout the past year and a half the cadres have been so demanding that the Chinese a peasant, accustomed though he is to strenuous labor, has begun to give in physically. Due partly to the inadequate diet, men and women on labor platoons are reported working themselves to exhaustion. The Party has now decreed that every person is entitled to at least eight hours daily for sleep and four hours for eating and (actually largely non-existent) "personal" life.

V. THE COST OF HASTE

The disruption of rural life resulting from such a drastic reorganization was aggravated by the efforts of the Communists to reach their 1958 steel production target of nearly 11,000,000 tons--roughly twice the output for the previous year. Coincident with the launching of the communes, they realized that this could be achieved only by extraordinary measures. So in this era when "people's science" wedded to brawn and will power supposedly can do almost everything, the peasantry was ordered to erect native blast furnaces and haul coal and ore by any means available. According to Peking, these shock tactics produced the required quantity of iron and steel; little is said about the quality, although it probably can be used in commune blacksmith shops for making simple farm tools. But the agricultural costs were great. Figures released by Peking admit that peasants ordered out to make steel failed to harvest 10 percent of the grain crops. Travelers report seeing cotton standing unpicked in the winter snows of north China; and there is reason to believe that much of the crop harvested may have rotted due to improper threshing and storing. Throughout Chinese cities last winter the customary grain rationing was more stringent than before. Some urbanites were compelled to stand in queues to buy bean curd, that commonest of all protein staples. Vegetables for sale were scarce and occasionally spoiled. All reflected the disorganization of farm supply and transportation; the rail system was severely dislocated in the great push to make iron and steel.

During its spring campaign to "rationalize" the movement, the Party explicitly designated specific communes to produce vegetables for the urban market. Early talk of converting communes into "agro-industrial complexes" is being modified--there is to be less attention to iron and steel and more on cotton industries. Communes are to devote at least 90 percent of their manpower to agriculture during peak periods and must not again leave crops in the field. But the drive to work ever harder is to go on. This year the plan calls for increasing production of grain and equivalents by 50 percent above 1958. Cotton output is scheduled to go up from 3,500,000 to 5,000,000 tons.

Simultaneously steel production is to increase by another 65 percent and the Chinese are called upon to mine an extra 220,000,000 tons of coal, All of this must be accomplished primarily through the sweat of the peasants.

The very organizational mastery of the Chinese scene that enabled the Communists to engineer these profound changes also generated the opposition that now could cripple their schemes -- the so far largely non-violent anger, sense of hopelessness and frustrated resentment of the peasants. Essentially, it was the character of the Chinese Communist Party that made possible what has been accomplished so far. Its top leadership had remained united, with rare exceptions, for a quarter of a century. All key positions today are held by men and women who chose the hard life of guerrilla warfare in the mountains for many years before there came the promise of official power and personal advantage. Some 5,000,000 members had been toughened and indoctrinated in the Party

THE CHINESE COMMUNES: BIG RISKS FOR BIG GAINS

before they seized power. Presently, the party membership of 12,000,000 is being expanded to include more peasants and women as a means of further leavening the communes. All are schooled in the disturbing new science of "going inside of society" and shaping it to the Communist image. So thoroughly have the Communists shattered China's old family and social institutions that the peasant has lost his former lust for life and worst. The concept of "face" which once was such a powerful social prop virtually has vanished. No longer can the peasant expend himself to provide for the future economic wellbeing of his family or for his own old age. His children are not taught to venerate elders and the familial security and respect from his grandsons that a peasant once dreamed of achieving in his latter years now is hardly even a mirage. He knows, too, that the prospect of his descendants sweeping his grave and paying homage at his tablet in the clan shrine are minimal since all such "feudal customs" are being abolished by the state. Even the gods who were his refuge and source of support in times of personal and natural disaster are now proscribed.

Though he is denied the satisfaction of values which have been imbedded in his culture for some 35 centuries, the peasant has not in general accepted those offered by the new order. The Communists moved too rapidly and ruthlessly. They insisted upon such total verbal conformity that prospects for genuine reeducation of this generation of peasants have not yet been realized. The result is a mass of peasantry who "labor without heart." On major construction and industrial projects where cadre supervision is most effective, passive resistance and "unseen sabotage" among the peasants may not be critical. "Civil disobedience" is hard to gauge. But the price of anything like a genuine peasant enthusiasm for agricultural performance within the communes will be a revamping of present policies, particularly those affecting the family. Unless the Party becomes more responsive to the "human element," the entire system of people's communes might be a success organizationally and yet bog down in actual performance. China's demographic dilemma and the narrow margin on which Chinese agriculture must perform mean that the consequences of a short-fall could be critical.

The forcible shifting of the Chinese peasantry into communes raises several international issues that will condition much of the future development of Asia. What will remain of the ideological bonds that tie together the nations of the Communist orbit in the face of such a divergence in internal social organization? Will the Soviet Union and Eastern Europe accept the Chinese contention that at least for Asia the communes offer the right instrument for effecting a rapid transition from socialism to Communism? How will Peking accommodate its ideological propaganda to the fears that such regimentation will surely awaken among its neighbors? China's manner of suppressing the revolt in Tibet already is convincing many Asians who have been oriented toward neutrality that the values they hold dear are far removed from those fostered by the Chinese Reds. Thinking Asians, however, are concerned by the fact that their underemployed manpower is their country's major unused capital resource. They are impressed with Red China's material achievements by the use of sheer manpower -- her massive public works, her canals, irrigation schemes, roads, railways, mines and reforestation. They will be assured by Peking that the communes are what make all this possible. And there will be increasing demands in the lands bordering China for the West to produce equally effective means for them to engineer their own physical progress.

Chicago Daily News   Monday August 24, 1959

Trouble in the Communes
Bitter Peasants Force Easing Of China's Farm Plan

Rules Relaxed to Allow Eating in Own Homes

Here is another significant report on Asia by Albert Ravenholt of the Daily News Foreign Service. Ravenholt in recent weeks has made first-hand observations in Communist-dominated areas in Asia which have sharpened his intimate knowledge of today's fast-paced developments in the Orient.

BY ALBERT RAVENHOLT
Daily News Foreign Service

HONG KONG - Red China is backtracking on a key issue in its massive organization of 500 million peasants into communes. Families formerly forced to join communal messes now are allowed to return to cooking eating in their homes.

This retrenchment in the gigantic rural scheme launched nearly a year ago was forced upon the rulers in Peiping by passive resistance of the peasants.

Resentment at such utter regimentation of the family life had led the peasants to sabotage agricultural production. Combined with droughts and floods that alternately ravaged extensive areas of mainland China this summer, these stubborn peasants threatened to cripple Peiping's second five-year plan.

However, Chinese Communist leaders after a secret meeting have just reaffirmed they have no intention of abandoning the basic commune system.

Rather, granting of permission for the embittered peasants to eat at home is "a step backwards so we can take two forward" on the road to communism, the Red leaders say.

EVIDENCE so far is favorable to Liu Shao-chi, newly chosen chairman of the people's government in Peiping; Premier Chou En-lai, directing the administration; Mao Tse-tung, who as head of the world's largest Communist party remains the preeminent Chinese Communist, and their associates.

This group continues in sufficiently intimate touch with the rural scene to ease up on pressure just when the peasants have been pushed to a kind of despair that could be disastrous for Red China.

But it also appears that these same Chinese Red leaders are in a tight spot domestically. They could find useful a relaxation of international tensions such as an Eisenhower-Khrushchev meetng might encourage.

Reds Admit Crop Claims Exaggerated

The stage was set for releasing the peasants from commununal mess halls when Peiping early this summer began admitting obliquely that last year's claims for unbelievably bumper crops were grossly exaggerated.

TROUBLES IN THE COMMUNES

Peiping's announcement last autumn, that it had doubled the national output of grain and tubers in one year of the "great leap forward campaign" violated the lessons of practical agricultural experience elsewhere. And when Red China last winter imposed the severest rationing yet, it was apparent that something was radically wrong with more than the transportation and distribution system that Communists named.

IT IS NOW clear that the culprits were the local cadres, "kann pu," as they are known in Chinese. These are activists, often young men and women, responsible for engineering the Communist revolution among the peasantry in the countryside.

More than a year ago they were assigned impossibly high production targets on collectives where they then worked.

At harvest time many of these cadres reported filling or overfulfilling their quotas, making for fantastic national totals.

REAL TROUBLE started when the Communist government began collecting its percentage of grain for the state. On the basis of claimed yields this left many peasants without enough to eat just when they were being corraled into communes.

Furthermore, communes established from September to November last year required the peasants to surrender their pigs, chickens and gardens to communal mess halls.

But rarely did any new communal mess hall give the sort of tender concern to these household livestock and vegetables that a peasant had known when he benefited directly from his own effort.

Consequently food in the communal mess halls last winter and spring generally was so miserable that it stirred intense peasant disgust.

Sometimes it left farm famiies too undernourished to keep up with shock brigades and platoons laboring in the fields and on public works.

Classify Peasants in 3 Categories
Announcement that the peasants now may leave the comnual mess halls if they wish has come piecemeal, beginning with a statement in late June by Vice-Premier Teng Tzu-hui, whose special concern is Communist agriculture.

This leading Chinese Comnunist official claims the peasants can be classed into three different categories regarding communes.

FIRST are bachelors, young women and newly married persons whose status welcomes the communal mess halls as saving them trouble and expense.

The second group are families with many adult healthy members who earn numerous work points under the Communist system and can take or leave the communes.

The third group are families vith many infants and older nembers unable to work, who are penalized by the communal mess system and determined to eat at home.

Also in this third group, according to the Communists, are comparatively better off families who want better food than the communal messes serve.

RECENT instructions from Peiping to party workers in the countryside now emphasize that they must do nothing to prevent peasants from leaving

TROUBLES IN THE COMMUNES

communal mess halls. Peasants are now entitled to take their grain rations home for cooking.

Equally important, peasants are again permitted to keep their own pigs, chickens and garden plots.

Communal messes are to be converted into canteens where bachelors and others can eat if they wish and breakfast and lunch can be served during rush planting and harvest seasons.

Later, according to Communist leaders, peasants can be attracted back to communal mess halls by improving the quality of food offered.

No Peasant Family To Be Penalized

One hint of the critical importance of this move is contained in the Peiping admonition that no peasant family is to be penalized in its rating for work efficiency in the comnunes for withdrawing from communal mess halls.

Orders from Peiping also required that there must not be any reduction in the supply of commune food staples to peasants who withdraw from communal mess halls.

This is a key point because once the peasants no longer are dependent upon eating in communal mess halls, they are also less vulnerable to regimentation by Communist party cadres.

THIS major reversal of Chinese Communist policy after less than a year of trying to fit China's patient, abused peasants in the world's most total form of state-controlled communism does not mean that the rulers in Peiping have abandoned their ultimate objectives.

But it does mean that more than ever before, since their government was established a decade ago, the Chinese Communists are compelled by the sheer toughness and resentment of China's peasants to make a major concession.

MEANWHILE, however, the Peiping press has failed to explain one critical point.

Last autumn, in a hectic drive to make iron and steel output reach their targets, the Chinese Communists collected pots and pans throughout the land and melted them down in crude blast furnaces along with other scrap and native ore.

Now peasant families who once again are permitted to eat at home literally must find a pot to cook in.

AMERICAN UNIVERSITIES FIELD STAFF

EAST ASIA SERIES

RED CHINA'S FOOD CRISIS
Communist Agriculture Crippled by
Massive Revolutionary Changes

By Albert Ravenholt

Hong Kong
January 1961

LETTERS SMUGGLED OUT of North China tell of near starvation among peasants in the "wheat granary" above the Yellow River. They estimate that one in five of the population over fifty-five years of age may not survive the winter. A Chinese lady doctor who escaped to this Colony from the mainland reports her patients in Kwangtung Province suffering from widespread and increasingly severe dropsy (edema) due to malnutrition. The Peking press announces that the country has experienced the worst natural disasters in a century. Communist China which has exported rice, soybeans, and eggs to the Soviet Union and non-Communist bloc countries, now has trade missions here that have just made an emergency purchase of 350,000 tons of Australian wheat after buying a nearly equal tonnage of Burmese rice. With a haste that suggests far more than ordinary urgency, Red China is arranging for ship charters to bring food and is seeking to learn what quantities of Canadian grain may be available for export from British Columbia ports. Now Mao Tse-tung has announced a far-reaching "rectification" movement in the world's largest Communist party; China's food crisis is becoming the pivotal issue around which vital domestic and international political decisions revolve. For the first time since the victorious sweep of the Red armies over a decade ago, the chronic dilemma of feeding her people is compelling the men leading a revolutionary crusade avowedly aimed at shaking the world to modify their programs.

Red China's furious industrialization, which is the key to her bid for forcing acceptance as one of the three dominant world powers may now need re-examination and new plans; it must take account of reduced means for buying capital equipment abroad and the imperative demand for chemical fertilizer production at home. Americans approaching the world under a new administration in Washington are confronted with the question of whether the "Trading with the Enemy Act" should be set aside to permit sale of surplus grains and corn to Communist China, a sale that Peking is unlikely to seek and might reject if proffered.

This publication is one of a continuing series on current developments in world affairs written by associates of the American Universities Field Staff. It is distributed by the AUFS as a useful addition to the American fund of information on foreign affairs. AUFS associates have been chosen for their skill in collecting, reporting, and evaluating data. Each has combined long personal observation and experience in his foreign area with advanced studies relating to it.

ALBERT RAVENHOLT, the author of this report, has for more than 15 years specialized in the affairs of the Far East. Based in Manila, he is studying and writing about Philippine affairs. He also reports on Southeast Asia in general and, from Hong Kong, on developments in Communist China, and evidence of passive peasant resistance, the farmer's only recourse amidst the authoritarian controls the new dynasty has forged.

RED CHINA'S FOOD CRISIS

A student of Chinese history is reminded that over the past 37 centuries rarely has a dynasty long survived continued disaster on the land. Just as the emperor was symbolically the first farmer of the realm who at the spring planting rites to propitiate the gods of the elements sought their bounty, so the most vital functions of his administration concerned themselves with the harvests. It was the need to harness water -- at least so some historians reason -- that first gave the special authoritarian character to the Chinese state in its cradle along the Yellow River. And it was chiefly a mastery of superior agricultural techniques that permitted the Han peoples to multiply so that today they constitute one-fourth of the human species; over several thousand years they displaced the native aboriginal tribes, first throughout the Yangtze River Valley, then along the smaller river basins of South China and in time through the most fertile stretches of the Southwestern and Western frontiers and Manchuria.

It is intriguing to consider that throughout these intervening centuries the Chinese peasant altered but slightly his system of farming. And the crops he grows today are much like those his forebears planted some 22 centuries ago when the Great Wall was begun -- two notable exceptions are cotton and sweet potatoes -- Cotton growing seems to have moved into China from Borneo and the Philippines about 600 years ago. The sweet potato was carried into Asia by Spanish and Portuguese merchants and priests who had found it in the Americas. Equally consequential is the special contribution of Chinese agriculture to the biological vitality of her people which still makes them by and large the sturdiest and most persevering workmen in Asia. The crops that the peasant grew in his scheme of predominantly subsistence farming provided a dietary balance remarkably complete -- on the average about 98% of the food consumed was directly from the vegetable kingdom.

Garden Plot Farming

China's total land area is only slightly larger than that of the United States including the new states of Alaska and Hawaii; the figure most frequently used is 3,768,726 square miles although this will need modification as the boundaries are delineated in the Himalayas and elsewhere. Roughly one-ninth of this area is cultivated and the land suitable for farming lies chiefly near the eastern and southern coasts, along the river basins that reach back toward the Tibetan plateau and on the North China and Manchurian plains. Much of the land that actually is cultivated is in belts of near marginal rainfall. While the alluvial soils of the great Yangtze River Valley and some of the smaller river basins and the loess formations of Northwest China are amenable to agriculture, much of the land from which peasants have wrested a living would make an Illinois farmer quit in disgust. And yet, on this relatively inhospitable landscape

China's population has multiplied to number now some 700 million, according to Peking's statistics.

Early in this century Wisconsin's pioneer soil scientist, F. H. King, found peasants in Shantung Province supporting 240 persons, 24 donkeys, and 24 pigs on the equivalent of a 40-acre Midwestern farm. He calculated that Shantung had an average annual rainfall of only 25 inches on a land area nearly equal to that of Wisconsin with its annual precipitation of 31 inches. This Chinese province today holds a population in excess of 48 million, or 12 times that of the Badger State. A comparison made with the more hospitable sections of China, such as the Chengtu Plain in the far west of Szechuan on the borderland of the Tibetan mountain ranges or the Pearl River Delta in the south, yields even more dramatic examples of how intensively the Chinese have employed their land.

The essential principle in this system of farming was its economy, in use of land, in conservation of soil fertility and water, in the husbanding of animal and human manure, the composting of refuse and ashes from the kitchen and selection of farm animals giving the highest returns for calorie intake. Within the limits of knowledge then available, only terraced agriculture could have enabled the Chinese to maintain productivity in the regions of heavier rainfall. It prevented erosion and the leaching out of soil nutrients in the paddy fields of dominant wet culture rice areas that with their winter wheat crops yielded well over one-half of China's grains. All available plant food was returned to the fields, as on the lush Chengtu Plain where the 2,200-year-old irrigation system yearly had its waters diverted while mud was dredged up from canal bottoms and ponds and carried in baskets to fertilize the next crop. The nitrogen balance was maintained. Careful collection of human liquid and solid excreta from the cities and its transportation by cart and sampan to the fields was combined with regular use of legumes in rotation. A labor intensive system of farming that required hand transplanting of rice seedlings permitted an overlapping of crops; by starting the second crop in the seedbed before the first was harvested a growing season that otherwise would have allowed only one rice harvest in some regions was made to produce two.

Although such intensive culture never was duplicated in the wheat, millet sorghum, soybean, and corn sections, there was the same meticulous attention to the growing of subsidiary vegetable crops. The Chinese preference for the young, succulent, leafy plants that are quick-cooked in oil so as to preserve the maximum of nourishment and conserve fuel lent itself admirably to the peasant's need to use every square foot of land. And the several kinds of cabbage, as well as melons, turnips, large radishes, squash, spinach, mustard and clover leaves, all permitted him to expand his food resources at little expense to the production of grains. With the introduction of the sweet potato and other tubers -- which remain second choice dietary items for the Chinese-the output of basic starches was pushed up the slopes of formerly unused land. Now the tea bushes, mulberry trees that fed the silk worms, tung oil plantations, and fruit orchards had to compete for space with cultivated annual crops on sites readily subject to erosion.

This maximum use of China's arable plots was accomplished at great expense to the total ecology. Throughout the hinterland hills and mountains were denuded, except for small groves of trees protected by Buddhist monasteries and forests in nearly inaccessible mountain fastness. Fuel was a constant problem for the peasant, unless there was a small coal mine nearby. Twigs, grass, and leaves were gathered from the hillsides, often by children, to burn along with the dried roots of field crops. In spring it was common to see the slopes burned over so the ashes would wash down upon the fields. The resulting erosion by water and wind has rarely been equaled in man's abuse of what nature has provided him. Chinese civilization with its focus on life in the courtyard, whether rural or urban, seems to have missed that regard for preservation and enjoyment of the uplands, trees, and mountains apparent in Japan. The consequences can be seen far out in the East China Sea. Long before the shore line comes into sight, the blue waters of the Pacific are muddied to a reddish brown by the silt carried down by the mighty Yangtze, especially during the flood season.

Dynamics of Chinese Population Growth

Nature, its use, and human procreation, already had begun to get seriously out of step long before the Communists captured power in China. With a remarkably intensive and productive yet technically static agriculture, the only readily available Chinese response to population pressure was to cultivate more land. By the mid-20th century the 269 million acres under cultivation represented about all the land fit to till. The only important exception is Manchuria, the great frontier for migration of Chinese peasants during the past five decades. In the Northeast perhaps another 15 million acres could be put in crop. But the growing season is short and the grains adapted to the climate are not among those most needed in China- -this area merges from the soybean belt into the sorghum, millet, and barley region. Throughout the past century Chinese in the south and east responded to pressing need for employment and food by emigrating to Southeast Asia, the Americas, and in smaller numbers to the Pacific islands which they could enter. Many traveled on the "coolie ships" that before World War H carried their annual human cargoes to provide workers for the Malayan tin mines, rubber plantations there and in Sumatra, Viet-Nam, and Thailand and the growing Chinese role in trade throughout the "Balkans of Asia." Their remittances home helped pay for China's annual average prewar imports of some two million tons of food.

Export of population provided only a temporary solution to the Chinese dilemma. The other was the vast disorganization of life brought on by 23 years of civil strife and the Sino-Japanese War. Total casualties of this "bitter" era in China will never be known. But some 14 million young men were conscripted into the Chinese Nationalist armies alone during the struggle with Japan. Of these some 3 million remained to be accounted for on V-J Day. Among the 11 million missing must certainly be included the deserters who no longer would accept the miserable rations of most armies that marched across the land. But countless others had been left to die by the wayside, had succumbed to malaria or been lost in the battles where medical facilities were rarely within effective reach of the front lines. In the Chinese Red armies and the Japanese puppet forces several million more men had served, with equally scant statistics on mortality.

The war also took its civilian toll. When the Chinese Nationalists breached the Yellow River dikes in 1938 to block the Japanese advance, they flooded farms and homes in large portions of East-Central China. Anyone who watched refugees fleeing before the successive Japanese offensives against Chinese bases of resistance could not but wince at the price paid in lives for this desperate effort at national survival. As the Chinese civil war reached its climax in 1948-49 Chinese fought Chinese- -brothers or fathers were sometimes on opposing sides -- on a scale rarely recorded. In the bloody battles for the Central China Plain in November and December of 1948 over a million men were in combat. And the next spring a nearly equal number were in the Red armies alone that pushed their offensive south across the Yangtze. The revolution exacted a terrible human price, as in February 1951, when Mao Tse-tung announced the "liquidation of counterrevolutionary elements." In some South China communities the victims included 1% to 1.5% of the population.

As the Communists imposed their hard new order upon China they also brought stability, and the greatest resurgence ever in population growth. During the past decade they have added a degree of sanitation and preventive medicine such as this ancient land never experienced before. While admittedly crude and often inadequately supplied with drugs, clinics today are an accepted part of the rural scene. Tens of thousands of nurses with rudimentary knowledge work in the villages. And there is great emphasis upon maternal and child care. The "germ warfare" campaign that during the Korean War mobilized Chinese to denounce America, also afforded the opportunity to engineer a nationwide hunt for flies, dogs, rats, and other "enemies of the people." The results are evident primarily in a falling rate of infant mortality. Communist figures on this score deserve skeptical treatment; for some major urban centers such as Shanghai they claim a figure that compares favorably with Singapore's infant mortality of 45 per 1,000 live births under the age of one year, while admitting that in rural areas it is still often well over 100. But there is an undeniable and radical improvement witnessed by foreign observers over the pre-Communist period when disease, various forms of infanticide, and ignorance permitted less than one-half of the infants to survive in sampled rural communities of West China.

Such energetic public health measures -- they include also the publicly respectable study and use of ancient Chinese herbal and other remedies -- are now producing their first demographic results. A graph depicting China's population increase from the Manchu imperial census of 1741 until the Communists took their first census in 1953-54 and reported 582 million inhabitants on the mainland, would show an average annual growth rate of about .6%. The figures based upon the imperial tax census and other sources are not exact. There have been periods when the population remained nearly stagnant. Other epochs like the internal peace following establishment of the Ching Dynasty in 1644 and general introduction of the sweet potato witnessed a more rapid increase. But a net annual average gain of slightly more than .516 is indicative of China's past capacity to provide for an expanding population with existing resources and knowledge.

Although Peking today is minimizing attention to population growth- -it might raise some embarrassing questions at this time of admitted food shortages --fragmentary data available indicates the inhabitants of Communist China now may be increasing at a net annual rate of 2.5% to 316. Startling as these figures are, they are lent authenticity by comparison with known patterns of increase among Chinese in relatively controlled environments where modern health facilities have been introduced and accurate statistics are available. Singapore, where the great majority of the 1.5 million inhabit-ants are Chinese, has a net annual increase of 3.5%. The native population of Formosa has multiplied more than four times since Japanese administration was established on the Island in 1895. And Formosa's present annual rate of increase approxi mates that of Singapore. It is this biological and cultural propensity for procreation that is credited with pushing the mainland population to approximately 700 million -- an increase of 118 million since the 1953-54 census. Indications are that for the near future China may need to cope with an annual increment in population of some 18 to 20 million. [Western demographers and statisticians understandably regret Peking's secretiveness on details of its population count. But those who dismiss the 1953-54 census figures do not always make adequate allowance for Communist extension of administrative authority from the traditional level of the hsien or county government down into the villages.]

Errors in Red Planning

When establishing their bureaus in Peking and starting their planning, Red China's leaders appear to have counted upon the enshrined advantages of "socialism" coupled with efficient administration to enable them to cope with China's resource -population dilemma. Only such reasoning would permit of a rational explanation for their decision to "follow the path of the Soviet Union" in vital allocations of investment resources. And during the first four years of their regime -- despite the drains of the Korean War -- experience tended to confirm these assumptions. Internal peace alone permitted a substantial restoration of agricultural production; the late civil war imports of food including American-supplied grain and cotton were compensated for with enhanced domestic output. Meanwhile, rapid extension of China's railway network enabled them to shift grain about the country to meet regional needs and tap traditional food surplus areas such as the Red Basin of Szechuan, on which the Chinese Nationalists had based their Government during the war with Japan.

The extent to which Peking is committed to employing a surplus from the land to finance its grand schemes for industrialization and modernization can be traced partly in export figures. During 1959--the most recent year for which relatively complete statistics are available- -China's exports to the Communist countries exceeded the value of one billion US dollars. Roughly three-fourths of this was composed of products from agriculture. The Soviet bloc has received some 55% of about 900,000 tons of soybeans shipped yearly -- in 1959 these soybean exports increased by 7016 tons. Nearly one-half of approximately two million tons of rice and other grains exported in 1959 likewise went to the Communist countries. That year exports included some 250 million US dollars worth of animal and poultry products, such as fresh frozen meat, mostly pork, large shipments of eggs in and out of the shell, hides and skins, etc. During recent years Chinese rice has been bartered for Ceylonese rubber. Indonesia has taken rice from China and Hong Kong in some years received 20% of its rice from the mainland. Exports to Europe annually of 40,000 to 50,000 tons of peanuts, 11,000 to 14,000 tons of tung oil, as well as soybeans, have paid for industrial equipment and chemicals, including fertilizer. Tea exports, including 14,000 tons in a year to Africa, have financed Chinese Communist credits. It is primarily the products of Chinese agriculture that paid for the mushrooming political influence of Peking throughout the emergent new nations of the underdeveloped world.

RED CHINA'S FOOD CRISIS

Policy Toward the Peasants

Red China's revolutionary policy toward the peasantry has aimed both to generate such surpluses for export and to engineer a vast social reshuffle that would serve the political purposes of Peking. Ruthless curtailment of consumption has been a key to this policy with the evident expectation that a remaking of rural life in time would facilitate rapid modernization of farming and expansion of output. The first objective proved relatively simple for the Communists with their extraordinary organizational mastery of China. But it has now been pushed to, and possibly beyond, its ultimate limit. In neighboring Kwangtung Province the adult monthly ration is now reported to be 25 pounds of unhusked rice, or its equivalent in tubers. (The Chinese rate four pounds of tubers as equal to one pound of grain.) Cooking oil which also serves a vital dietary function is so scarce that some accounts credit this with affecting eyesight; a monthly ration of three ounces is reported from some districts.

Lassitude among the peasantry resulting from the meagerest of subsistence rations has been compounded into resentment of the regime by the destruction of the peasant's old way of life that was climaxed by marshaling the farmer and his family into communes 28 months ago. No venture in recorded human history has quite matched the extent and thoroughness of this change. Essentially, it has served to transform the highly individualistic family-oriented and largely subsistence economy of the Chinese peasant into a scheme of activity where Communist managers dictate all efforts: they determine the type of meals to be served for breakfast in commune mess halls; methods of child care in the improvised nurseries; when and how rice seedlings are to be transplanted and the time for harvesting. Theoretically, a commune that today disposes of the life activities of anywhere from 10,000 to 50,000 persons, should be an extraordinarily effective device for introducing technical innovations. No longer need the Chinese peasant be persuaded to adopt techniques for improving production, he can simply be ordered, on threat of being denied his ration. And he can be made to work to and sometimes beyond the limit of human endurance. China's present tragedy and the specter that stalks Mao Tse-tung's empire is that in practice this has not worked out as planned.

The Cadres

The engineers of change throughout China's rural scene have been the cadres (kan pu), those fanatically indoctrinated, harsh young harbingers of the totalitarian future numbering several million. They it was who followed the conquering Red armies to "turn over the society." First, they classified all peasants in gradations from landlords to rich peasants, poor farmers) and farm laborers. Then the mass of more dissatisfied including tenants and rural laborers were assembled into "farmers associations" that destroyed the gentry and others who had held status under the old order through "wiping slates clean" meetings where excess rentals and interest were returned, "land reform," and "people's trials." Under constant guidance and prodding from Peking, they successively took the peasants into "mutual labor teams," co-operative farms and collectives. They alternately cajoled, lectured, threatened, and sometimes pleaded with the peasants to "follow the new way." When, late in the summer of 1958, Peking announced the "irresistible nationwide demand" of the peasantry for joining the communes -- about which few had ever heard before -- the cadres staged the "big blooming and big contending" assemblies. There peasants had to argue themselves and each other into this new order where they exchanged a measure of independent action for a place in a labor brigade and a seat in one of the new communal mess halls.

The cadres also were charged with insuring peasant use of new technology in agriculture; they have made one really great contribution in reforestation. But the very thoroughness of the authoritarian controls they had forged permitted of some disastrous consequences. In 1956-57, when the planners in Peking apparently realized that China must secure an almost immediate jump in farm output to meet her ambitious targets, the word went down that this would be achieved with maximum mobilization of human labor. The "Great Leap Forward" resulted, preceding by a year and continuing with establishment of the communes. While there was renewed attention to digging more mud from pond bottoms and streams for fertilizer, making compost, etc., and the abortive backyard blast furnace campaign, the emphasis was upon extending irrigation systems and water control. The aim was to intensify use of and enlarge that portion of China's arable land which is double -cropped- -about 60% --while also bringing water to dry regions. The arguments for this were strong. For example, Japanese experiments in North China during World War II had shown that wheat production could be doubled by only irrigating at the two stages when the plants were 11tillering" and "booting." Claimed achievements for this human mobilization are extraordinary by any standard; Peking reported that water had been brought to an additional 80 million acres. But it is now apparent, and inferentially admitted by the Communist press, that much of this rush irrigation construction was faulty. Hastily thrown up dikes often did not withstand the next summer's rains. Fragments of evidence suggest the water table over much of the North China Plain has been seriously disturbed. And alkali is beginning to blight fields irrigated without adequate soil surveys and provision for drainage.

Simultaneously, Chinese agriculture was crippled by one of those curious abortive ventures that only so efficient a totalitarian regime could be caught in. Someone in Peking -- and it must have been at the highest policy level -- became persuaded that China could greatly boost its crop yields by close planting. Roughly stated, the idea was that by spacing rice seedlings two inches apart instead of 14 to 18 inches, as has proven most effective in much of Japan and the Philippines, yields could be comparably multiplied. The peasants scoffed at this, but the cadres insisted. And substantial areas of China's best land was so planted. To give a special impetus to this "leap forward" campaign, Peking had set impossible production targets; they were broken down into specific quotas for which each cadre was held accountable. Nature was unusually friendly to China in 1958 and most of the land was spared both drought and devastating floods. Under relentless pressure to perform, cadres throughout much of the countryside reported meeting and even over-fulfilling their targets. And Peking made the unbelievable announcement that total production of grains and tuber equivalents had reached 350 million tons. This total claimed harvest for 1958 contrasted with the announced output of 185 million tons in 1957 and a pre-Communist peak production of 150 million tons.

During the winter it became obvious to the new rulers that close planting was, as the peasants had argued it would be, a mirage; the grain stalks grew green and close but the heads were mostly empty. Not until the next summer did Peking evidently realize fully the disturbing fact that the cadres had often grossly over-reported actual production in their areas. Once state collections of grain had been made on the basis of reported harvests, many peasants were left little to eat. Although the crops had been good, they had nowhere near equaled the announced returns. And yet, Mao Tse-tung's great venture into the communes had assumed a substantial surplus that would carry China through the inevitable disruption of production such a total reorganization on the land entailed. Peking today is still caught in the toils of this national blunder. With all of the political considerations that a totalitarian state links with announced targets and production, the Communists apparently have yet to get their statistics back onto a realistic basis. So many careers are at stake in a thorough reassessment of figures that have been falsified on such a scale. And yet, the Red planners must work from statistics. But these hardly afford a dependable basis for forecasting actual deliveries or calculating amounts that can be realistically exported and leave enough to sustain the burgeoning populace.

Natural Calamities

Within the past two years China has experienced two inferior harvests. The announced figures mean little, since the Communists themselves continue to revise the totals. But the dominant factor, which is still the weather, generally is known. And the search for enough food to go around is apparent. Actual production of grain and tuber equivalents in 1959 may have been nearly 200 million tons. This is an educated estimate since Peking claimed a 1959 harvest of 270 million tons, after reducing their announced 1958 output by an even 100 million tons to 250 million tons. By last midsummer Communist China seemed headed for a moderately prosperous agricultural year, with possibly a 10% improvement in output. Then the elements turned against the land, its peasants, and the regime. Early in August Typhoon Polly dumped 12 inches of rain in one day on the most productive regions of Manchuria and a second typhoon flooded the Sungari River basin. Some of the soybean crop that did survive is moldy and the beans small and uneven. Meanwhile, a severe drought in the North China Plain has compounded the moisture shortage and reduced water table inherited from 1959. Peasants in the four provinces nearest the capital are in truly desperate straits, according to all information available. The late rice crop in the Yangtze Valley and South China last autumn was good enough to compensate, but only in part, for disaster in the North. Peking now reports that more than one-half of the total cultivated land in China suffered "natural calamities," including locust plagues, during the past year. The Communists may want to employ this disaster to help bring their statistics into line with reality and justify even more stringent rationing -- this would appear practical only with favored elements such as the Red army and the bureaucracy. But it does appear that some food-growing areas produced hardly any harvest. As reports are sorted out in Peking and more accurate statistics assembled, there may be further disturbing news. Most critical of all is the ugly fact that a large proportion of China's 550 million peasants are weakened by overwork and malnutrition; stringent past rationing and distortion of the traditional diet through disorganization resulting from creation of the commune kitchens reduced resistance to a dangerously low ebb.

Communist Alternatives

As the authorities in Peking learn the full extent of the disaster in which they and the Chinese people are embroiled, they are attempting solutions the regime knows and trusts. Even they must now be recognizing that the failures of Communist agriculture to produce as planned relate to apathy among the peasants and growing "passive resistance." Peasants are reported working as instructed by the cadre and when the young arbiter of the new order turns his back the farmers may quit weeding and even sabotage the commune effort. Stealing of sweet potatoes and grain intended to feed pigs is increasing as are complaints about commune chickens and hogs eaten surreptitiously. The first remedy the Communists are attempting is a restoration of private garden plots to enlist peasant willingness to work and produce emergency food for next spring. These plots are tiny and sometimes include the borders between fields and along roadsides. In one commune of Shansi Province the maximum allowed a family measures about 30 by 35 feet. Since the cadres have twice before given plots and then commandeered the produce, the peasants are mistrustful. As an emergency measure, tens of thousands of the new bureaucrats favored by the regime are being ordered to the countryside to help grow vegetables and winter grains. Fancy experimentation with mechanization in the communes is discouraged and the hoe is again the honored tool, with penalties imposed if it is lost or broken.

Peking's present purchases of wheat and rice abroad can provide only a minimal relief for the food needs of great coastal centers such as Canton and Shanghai and the most critically affected cities of North China. These purchases must be made primarily with credits accumulated from earlier agricultural exports. The Australian wheat bins are reported "nearly cleaned out" by the present sale, leaving Canadian wheat the primary available source under present political and financial arrangements. Nikita Khrushchev's admissions of the past summer's failures in Soviet agriculture suggest Russia has little food to spare, even if the transportation were available. As the possessor of the world's really great stocks of surplus wheat, corn, sorghum, and other foods that a large proportion of the Chinese people now desperately need, the United States will be compelled during the next few months to make some difficult decisions. Action must be prompt if actual shipments are to reach China as the food shortages become more acute in the traditional "famine months" of late spring and early summer. Red China's ferocious posture of hostility toward America creates both enormous problems and also opportunities for a United States policy that seeks to use its food to ease acute human need on an enormous scale and to bridge at least partially the abyss of hate that is the heritage of the greatest revolution of our time. But to succeed any such enterprise must be managed with the greatest of skill and patience.

Within the dark labyrinth of the "Central Authority" that rules Red China this now undeniable crisis in their affairs is impelling a vast and yet only partially discernable reshuffling. Caught in the strait jacket of t heir own tortured philosophy, the senior Chinese comrades are trying to sort out where they actually are and a more viable course of action for the future. Fertilizer, and the need to produce this on an enormous scale as related to the present emphasis upon heavy industry, with all this implies for international political posture, is now an unavoidable issue. Consumer goods are also essential to sustain the peasants and induce them to want to work. And the very structure and management of the communes has to be overhauled.

There are three innovations that make a major difference in Asian agriculture: water, improved seed, and chemical fertilizer. Red China has expended herself to the limit to provide the first. Seed selection is encouraged and Peking has a core of able scientists who have been helped by the Russians. But this cannot be done rapidly. And certainly the cadres with their obtuse devotion to "politics must lead" are ill-equipped to manage delicate hybridizing of seed such as spurred the great jump in American corn yields. Chemical fertilizer offers the quickest and greatest means to expanding output on the land. But of this China is miserably short, due in substantial measure to insignificant attention to constructing fertilizer capacity during the first Five-Year Plan (1952-57). The mainland now uses some three million tons of chemical fertilizer annually, of which about one-half is imported. But if China is to provide for its present and anticipated population, yearly chemical fertilizer needs are of the order of 40 to 45 million tons; Peking today admits it should have 20 million tons. The consequences of revamping industrial plans to build such capacity would substantially alter Red China's role in world affairs. For the men who today manage the "good earth" it is not a simple choice to forgo their dreams of revolutionary grandeur in favor of such provision for production by the peasants, that traditional basis for Chinese survival, individually and nationally, in a land affording only the slimmest margin for error.

AMERICAN UNIVERSITIES FIELD STAFF

EAST ASIA SERIES
Volume X, No. 4
(Communist China)

THE HUMAN PRICE OF CHINA'S DISASTROUS FOOD SHORTAGE

A Refugee Doctor Describes His Patients.

by Albert Ravenholt

Hong Kong
May 1962

"ALMOST THE WORST THING THAT CAN HAPPEN to a woman in China today is for her to learn that she is pregnant," the refugee Chinese doctor explained with a dispassionate calm that revealed a compassion for his people worn nearly to exhaustion. "Not enough food is available for her to nourish herself and the fetus - should the child be born alive, it has little possibility of survival. The mother's breasts usually are dry. Even if she gets to a hospital there will be no milk; most infants die within the first few months - When it happens many mothers are relieved. Although they love their children so much, the Chinese mothers don't know where they would find cloth to keep the baby warm or how they would provide nourishment. Very few drugs from Russia are now available and the Communist government is spending most of its foreign exchange to buy wheat in Canada and Australia. So we had few medicines to treat maternity cases. Also, endemic malnutrition now makes most Chinese vulnerable to infection. We find the symptoms in every province where I have worked; both the very young and the older people have been weakened until their prospects for survival are poor."

With these words Dr. Stephen Wang, the thirty-four-year-old devout Chinese Christian medical practitioner who has just reached this British Crown Colony summed up the tragedy of his people and his own sense of hopelessness in trying to combat it. Within recent months a number of doctors have come to Hong Kong from the mainland in the flood of refugees. They include men whose work had taken them into the vast reaches of northern or western China as well as those who had worked in the more accessible southeastern coastal regions. Their experiences and findings largely confirm each other. The story they tell is of suffering from lack of food on a scale difficult for the outside world to comprehend. Under-nutrition now has become so, widespread in China that it is crippling the capacity of people to work. It also is curtailing the rate of population growth among nearly one-fourth of humanity, as infants die and undernourished women cease to menstruate.

Despite their bold pronouncements, it is evident that the rulers in Peking now recognize the dimensions of the disaster in which they are involved. Before the end of June they are scheduled to have imported some nine million tons of food grains, which are used largely to feed the great coastal cities. Their massive schemes that were to make Red China an industrial giant within a generation and place it technologically on a competitive level with the other great powers are being scrapped. Industrial imports during the past 18 months have been cut by more than one-half as the Central People's Government spent some $600 million of its limited foreign exchange buying food abroad. The statistics of this

HUMAN PRICE OF CHINA'S DISASTROUS FOOD SHORTAGE

planned economy are such that when the National People's Congress finally met in Peking this spring -- after failing to assemble last year -- no budget for the past or current year was presented to the 1,027 delegates.

As the "good earth" waits upon the weather at this height of the famine season before the first harvests are gathered in midsummer, the balance of influence between Peking and Moscow within the Communist world hinges increasingly upon the crops now being planted. In domestic affairs, Mao Tse-tung and his comrades have been compelled to abandon most of the harsh features of the Communes they initiated three and one-half years ago to marshal the peasants to labor for the state. In a bid to overcome passive peasant resistance in the countryside they have given back to the farmers their private garden plots. And the "free markets" that appeared as desperate city folk bartered for food from the rural areas now officially are encouraged. The entire design of internal Chinese communism as it affects particularly the land is being radically altered as the regime seeks its own survival despite the grumblings of the people. But the fate of China will depend largely upon the harvests; unless they are bountiful, the creeping starvation that now affects the health of so large a portion of the population could make a mockery of all plans.

The Making of a Doctor in Red China

It was natural for Stephen Wang, born in Shanghai, and raised in Shantung, to decide that he should become a doctor. His father belonged to that great tradition of Christian medical practitioners in China who led in introducing the scientific Western healing arts in many provinces The home the young man grew up in was shielded from some of the roughest vicissitudes of recent Chinese history. His was a Chinese Christian family, content with modest middle-class economic circumstance and largely devoted to service, enjoying religious music and intellectually committed to the Western concepts of freedom. Like many Chinese Christians, Stephen's family also was only partly aware of the seething social discontent that in pre -Communist days fired the demands for a change in the management of public affairs.

Stephen was preoccupied with his premedical studies at St. John's University in Shanghai when the Red Armies captured that great trading metropolis at the mouth of the mighty Yangtze River in the late spring of 1949. Although he thinks of himself as having been quite a dreamer who paid scant attention to politics, he like many of his fellow students was relieved at the departure of the Chinese Nationalist Government, which fled first to South China and then to Formosa. They knew little of the Communist leaders and plans, but trusted that the new regime offered hope of affording China a brighter future. While the Communists soon organized their youth league among the students, St. John's remained relatively unaffected by the Communists during the first few years; students continued to wear Western clothes and enjoy American music and foreign dances.

Shortly after the Communist take-over, Stephen applied for entrance at Peking Union Medical College, the Rockefeller -established foremost center for medical teaching and research in China. When there was a delay in his acceptance at Peking, the young man enrolled instead at the

HUMAN PRICE OF CHINA'S DISASTROUS FOOD SHORTAGE

Cheeloo University College of Medicine in northern Shantung. Supported by ten Christian denominations in Great Britain, the United States, and Canada, with its degrees accepted at Toronto University, it was one of the leading centers of Western learning in China. When Stephen entered the Medical College 300 students were matriculated there. By 1953 when the Communists completed their reorganization of all private education, Cheeloo had become a state university which included Shantung Medical College with 2,000 students enrolled, some of whom had formerly studied at other institutions. During the first years, however, standards of medical education remained at the relatively high level they had been before. The original faculty was left largely intact. Subscriptions were continued for Canadian, American, and British medical journals and there was energetic attention given to supplying microscopes and other laboratory equipment. In Anatomy classes four students worked on one cadaver, often they were provided with the remains of executed Nationalists. In fact, the Communists insisted the Shantung Medical College must accept much enlarged responsibilities . And the able new director sent from Peking, who had studied in Germany and Russia, had scant contact with the students since he also was in charge of seven health districts in east China.

Red China's entry into the Korean War in the winter of 1950-51 was the signal for a vigorous acceleration of thought reform among the medical students. There were innumerable meetings, chiefly at night, where students denounced America in the "Aid Korea and Resist U.S. Aggression" movement and also "cleansed" themselves by making confessions. All were required to volunteer for service in the war. But the Communists left most of them to continue their medical preparation, sending only one hospital group from the then Cheeloo University to serve with their forces on the Korean Front. It was only in 1957, after Stephen had graduated, that the faculty and students felt the full force of the harsh new order imposed by the Communists. The previous year Mao Tse-tung had invited criticism of the regime with a typical Chinese flourish, urging that "A Hundred Flowers Must Bloom and One Hundred Schools of Thought Contend." After an initial hesitation intellectuals here as elsewhere in China had joined in a massive denunciation of rigid Communist authoritarian practice that clearly frightened the leaders in Peking. All of China was compelled to undergo a tortuous "rectification movement" designed to expose and destroy critics of the regime. It proved a major turning point in modern Chinese history, as the Communists followed this with the "Great Leap Forward," inauguration of the Communes, and a new terror directed against all who failed to conform. Chinese Christians now became a particular Communist target.

After capturing power in 1949, the Red leaders had sought to incorporate into their "democratic front" the Christians who largely composed an educated and professionally skilled minority. Protestants were compelled to participate in the "Three Self Movement" specially designed to sever their ties with foreign Christian missionary groups and mold the teachings of Christ to suit Communist purposes. Initially, the rulers in Peking sought to destroy the Roman Catholic Church in China; only later, when it coincided with their interests in Latin America and elsewhere, did the Communists work to create a Chinese Catholic Church independent of Rome. By 1957-58 the Communist leaders appear to have concluded that they had failed to subvert totally the Christian minority. Although some had become the servants of the new order, a hard core of Christians remained who were not vulnerable to the political blandishments directed from Peking. When the regime forsook blandishments for persecution, these Christians took it as a trial of their faith. And the Party now began to remove them from positions of influence in Chinese life where they might garner support.

When Stephen entered Cheeloo University roughly one-third of the students were Christians. In ever-growing numbers they were quietly arrested and sent off to ''Reform through Labor'' camps chiefly in Manchuria-rarely were they heard from again. Following the great "rectification campaign," the faculty at Shantung University Medical College became demoralized and terrified. Many of the ablest professors were Christians. Some of them committed suicide when they felt the pressure of persecution, particularly when they were denounced in rigged student and faculty confession assemblies. Others simply disappeared. And a tough new policy of ''elevating politics" became the guide in teaching medicine. The seven-year training for doctors was reduced to five and courses of study condensed as the Communists became obsessed with numbers as the criterion of progress.

Health and Medicine Under the Communists

Stephen had been graduated several years before his university experienced this ruthless attempt to impose the new order; however, he had kept in touch with classmates and through them learned of the fate of their colleagues. He credits his own survival during this tumultuous era primarily to his personality and habits - By instinct he is more of a reflective student than a man of action. Thus, he joined only rarely in the tense discussions of politics and the "new thought" of Mao Tse-tung. When he did so, his remarks usually concerned technical matters subject to less dispute. His deep commitment to the Christian faith afforded him a "hidden anchor" denied many educated Chinese cut adrift from their moorings by the destruction of the old society. Already he was discovering that "Everyone in China acts a part on the great stage erected by the Communist Party." He recalls, "I was learning that what you profess publicly and what you do and say among intimate friends are two different things - they had to be if we were to exist."

In Shanghai the young doctor had joined the Parasitology Institute of the China Medical Academy; he had sought the position stating bluntly that he would only work in the field of his special interest. Because of the shortage of doctors he believes the authorities may have made an allowance for him that otherwise would have been denied. But Stephen's work was not limited to Shanghai. As a specialist concerned particularly with schistosomiasis japonicom and filaria he has been almost constantly on the move during the past seven years, gathering data and helping design control and eradication programs in the provinces of Szechwan, Anhwei, Hunan, Fukien, Shantung, and Kiangsu. His salary was equivalent to US $38 per month and no per diem was allowed for travel, only reimbursement of direct expenses for tickets. But he was afforded a unique opportunity to observe both the design and development of Communist medical services and the consequences for the health of the Chinese people of recent tragic food shortages. In his own quiet way he

HUMAN PRICE OF CHINA'S DISASTROUS FOOD SHORTAGE

was able to appraise the changing character of the Communist regime as former revolutionaries accustomed themselves to power and privilege.

Stephen's findings can best be communicated by concentrating on his knowledge of Fukien, one of the several provinces with which he became intimately familiar. Fukien, the mountainous coastal ancestral homeland of most overseas Chinese in the Philippines and the more recent settlers in Malaya and Thailand, rarely escaped a local epidemic in the years before the Communists arrived. Malaria was endemic among the population of some 12 million, particularly in the north. Although typhus was little known here, plague, cholera, small pox, and typhoid were frequent hazards to the inhabitants. Filaria was a problem and so to a lesser extent was schistosomiasis. Gastrointestinal diseases, particularly bacillary and amoebic dysentery, were chronic, and tuberculosis an ever-present threat. But Fukien did not suffer from the grinding pressure of population upon the available farm land as did many provinces in the north. Traditionally, the coastal population had added to its income and diet by fishing in the straits opposite Formosa. And in pre-Communist days remittances from Chinese relatives abroad had supported numerous families, particularly near the larger cities.

The Communist design for remaking the health of Fukien's inhabitants was largely the work of a woman, Chou Ying, who had served as a nurse at the wartime Red Capital in Yenan. Following the Communist "liberation" she had become the director of public health throughout the province. Her husband belonged to that privileged and potent elite in Red China known as the "Lao Kann Pu." He was an old and trusted cadre of the Party by virtue of having been one of the Communists on the "long march" that in 1934-35 led them several thousand miles from Kiangsi Province in south China to their World War II base near the borderlands of Mongolia. A ranking veteran of the civil war, he now had become the Red Army commander of the Fukien military area. Such husband - and-wife teams who reinforce each other within the power structure are a characteristic feature of Communist China's ruling class today.

The public health organization this determined woman built in the province aimed at a massive attack upon a few selected major diseases with the limited trained personnel available. As ultimately developed after 1955, this was organized around a Public Health Section in the government of each of the 60-odd hsien, or counties. In such a hsien there was a public health hospital, usually staffed by two doctors, ten "assistant doctors'' who had received a three-year short course in medicine after graduation from middle school, and perhaps two dozen trained nurses. Associated with the hospital in each hsien was a clinic for "traditional Chinese medicine" where three or four practitioners of the ancient Chinese healing arts, including specialists in acupuncture and herbs, worked with their apprentices. Each hsien also had a preventive clinic staffed with some 20 to 30 "assistant doctors" and nurses, reportedly patterned after a Russian system, who worked in the field in close co-operation with the rural People's Communes. The skeleton staff for this organization was partly inherited from the days of the Nationalist Government; it was now augmented by private practitioners forced to enter government service and the new graduates of the greatly expanded medical schools.

HUMAN PRICE OF CHINA'S DISASTROUS FOOD SHORTAGE

This entire health organization was energized by vigorous support and ample funds from above, such as had never been available during the pre-Communist era. Direction came from the Division of Public Health of the provincial government in Foochow which maintained its own institutes in fields such as epidemiology, public health, and parasitology, and which supported its own hospitals, and a large tuberculosis clinic co-operating with hsien TB pavilions. During the past three years Fukien has made substantial progress in medicine and doctors in Foochow now are doing advanced heart and brain surgery. Vaccines are available in abundance from the new factories established for their production during the past decade. The foremost of these in Peking pioneered in developing inexpensive mass methods for making and transporting vaccines; performance here was crippled after 1958 when the able director committed suicide following the "One Hundred Flowers" movement. More recently other factories, in Wuhan, Shanghai, Dairen, and Chungking, have begun making vaccines for China's population of some 700 million.

The campaign to improve the health of Fukien's inhabitants employed the mass mobilization techniques perfected by the Communists. Its first concern was with plague and cholera. Teams of "assistant doctors" and nurses helped by middle-school graduates given a short course on vaccinations were sent into every village. Peasants who were suspicious or fearful of modern medicine were mobilized by the Party cadres and everyone was compelled to be vaccinated. Simultaneously, a province-wide campaign was launched to exterminate rats and fleas, with school children delivering their daily quota of rodents to their teachers. Since this campaign was completed three years ago, there have been several small outbreaks of cholera, but the incidence of these diseases, as well as of small pox and typhoid, has been brought substantially under control.

Eradication of malaria also has been a major feature of the Communist health program. With their substantial medical organization allied with the control over the countryside by the Party and the Army, the provincial health authorities were able to carry through a spraying program affecting all houses – Mosquito –breeding places were largely cleaned up and water-control methods adapted to minimize the hazard. Until recently quinine and paludrine have been readily available for clinical treatment of all diagnosed cases of malaria. Occasional outbreaks of polio were countered with vaccine brought from Russia. For light cases the Communist administration relied upon treatment with acupuncture, with some apparent effect. Intensive organization of the population made possible identification of cases of once prevalent filaria and treatment with locally manufactured "hetrazen." Schistosomiasis japonicom was substantially reduced in Fukien by killing the snail that serves as median host and treating infected cases with tartar emetic. But in Anhwei and Kiangsu, by contrast, Stephen found that this crippling disease was still far from being under control. Parasite infestations, such as hookworm and ascaris, remain endemic in Fukien. Amoebic and bacillary dysentery are still so prevalent that the health services can do little more than treat them clinically. As in much of Asia, tuberculosis has been the most stubborn medical problem in Fukien, and neither enough drugs nor sanitarium facilities are available for treating this much feared disease.

HUMAN PRICE OF CHINA'S DISASTROUS FOOD SHORTAGE

Consequences of Starvation

Were it not for the under-nutrition that during the past 18 months has severely sapped the energy and resistance of the Chinese people throughout the land, Stephen feels that Fukien, like several other provinces where he worked, would have been well on the way to solving some of its most acute health problems. However, with the steady deterioration in the diet of all ordinary Chinese a host of otherwise manageable diseases have begun to take a terrible toll. Today edema, sometimes known as dropsy, is encountered almost everywhere in China. This disease, which is directly traceable to inadequate nutrition, manifests itself through accumulation of fluids that leads to bloated limbs and bodies and in the terminal stages may bring on heart failure; not infrequently peasants so affected and yet compelled to labor in the fields collapse and sometimes die on the spot. Most Chinese patients Stephen had observed, who superficially appeared to be "in good flesh," actually were afflicted with edema.

An ailment that Stephen and his medical colleagues identified as "nutritional hepatitis" he calculates now affects 40% of the population of Fukien. Classmates in Hunan Province reported that they encountered this condition in up to 90% of the inhabitants of some communities in China's great ''rice granary." In Shantung and several other provinces of north China, where food shortages are even more acute and the right to gather mountain grasses and bark from selected trees for grinding into meal is jealously sought, this condition is more advanced inpatients observed. Sufferers most frequently have an enlarged liver with impaired related functions; their doctors attribute this to the near absence of all protein and sugar in the diet. Even bean curd, the protein staple that has contributed so much to Chinese vitality throughout the centuries, today is rarely available; in Fukien the ration is one four by three inch block of bean curd per month for each person. The Chinese Communists are trying to overcome this shortage by encouraging peasants to plant vegetables in their own garden plots-this former critical source of fresh foods and vitamins had been ignored during the tumultuous days of regimenting farmers to join Communes. But a rural subsistence economy, once it is so totally disorganized, is not readily restored and Stephen's medical colleagues on the mainland so far had found scant evidence of a resulting improvement in the health of the populace.

The women of China betray their undernourishment in ever greater menstrual irregularity. Both in urban and rural areas even women in their twenties are ceasing to ovulate. Among those who give birth, prolapse of the uterus is commonly observed. Rare is the mother who now has enough milk in her breasts to suckle a newborn infant. And wet nurses, who formerly were readily available in China, have almost disappeared. In one of Shanghai's better hospitals specializing in pediatrics during the past year the mortality among live-born infants has been roughly one-third during the first three months. Children who do survive on the diet of coarse gruel with a few vegetables and a little soybean milk often show the miserable symptoms of rickets. And evidence of chronic amino acid deficiency and beriberi is a routine finding by practicing physicians. Doctors confronted with such cases in the hospitals try to give palliative treatment with the few vitamins available. But they find themselves almost helpless to deal with the basic problem which reflects lack of an adequate caloric intake and deterioration in the quality of the diet, as food reserves are buttressed with the ground roots of bananas, water weeds, and similar "fillers."

No accurate statistics on births have so far been kept for Fukien Province as a whole. But Stephen and his medical colleagues observed a general pattern. Six years ago they joked about how rare it was to have a young female patient who was not pregnant. Now there is a marked decline both in the number of pregnant women and young children seen on the streets. Although they are not making public propaganda about it, the Communist authorities are taking energetic steps to establish abortion clinics, particularly in the larger cities such as Shanghai, and nurses are being specially trained to staff them. Legally, abortions are available and often free to any family that has five or more children. In larger urban centers shortage of food and pressure for women to work are leading to an acceptance of this practice, despite the significance Chinese families traditionally attached to having large families to carry forward the Confucian tradition. In rural areas, however, peasant women still resist acceptance of abortion; many believe that the Communes are temporary, that eventually they may regain possession of the land and then the ancient advantage of having more hands to till their fields will again apply.

Although the continuing preoccupation with the search for food by individuals and state organizations now takes precedence over all other concerns and topics of discussion, doctors on the mainland are concluding that the fundamental difficulty results from overpopulation. The failure of the Communist Government to solve the agricultural problem during the past three years has fortified this conviction. Among their colleagues, medical men in China do discuss the implications – They have read in foreign journals about the contraceptive pill developed in America and now being tested. But most are dubious about its practicality in China; six years ago when the authorities in Peking officially encouraged birth control the attempts of the doctors to induce the peasants to accept the use of contraceptives met with miserable failure. Now many doctors are convinced that only surgical sterilization, once a family has its quota of children, will prove effective for curtailing the population. Such drastic measures they can only visualize being effected provided the Central Committee of the Communist Party faces up to the issue and recants its earlier condemnation of the few independent- minded Chinese leaders, such as the venerable educator, Ma Yin Chu, who sought to call attention to China's demographic dilemma. For the present they feel the rulers in Peking are too occupied with setbacks besetting the economy and Party to plan far ahead.

A Personal Quandary

Stephen only made the decision to leave China reluctantly. Sometimes he still feels that his escape to the free world should be a source of shame; so many of his fellow Chinese Christians whom he left behind are continuing to pay a heavy price for their faith. To the regime they are suspect and are subject to innumerable penalties. But he had come to the conclusion that ahead lay only stagnation and suffering for his people that he was powerless to remedy. While the Communist authorities still demonstrated energetic concern for pioneering in creating new health services Stephen experienced a measure of professional and personal satisfaction despite other ruthless and fearful aspects of the regime. With the failure of their gigantic gamble on the Communes and the growing preoccupation with individual survival, however, he found corruption and inertia creeping up the political hierarchy.

In contrast to their attitude three years ago when they drove the peasants in ''shock brigades" to labor sometimes day and night on the massive and hastily designed irrigation and road-construction projects, the cadres now had begun to fear "the masses." And so many of the directives from above had proven patently unsound that few of the Party functionaries now trusted in the infallibility of Mao Tse-tung and his senior comrades. Within the Communist Party, faith in the orthodox teachings also is being shaken by the new campaign against Nikita Khrushchev who now is denounced as a deviationist from the teachings of Marx and Lenin. For the criticism of the Soviet Russian example so recently glorified from Peking opens a ''Pandora's box" of other questions about Communist tenets -- Even many of the "Lao Kann Pu," or senior Party members, betrayed the beginnings of demoralization. Some who had been sternly self-disciplined and spartan in their habits now were resorting to corruption to insure more food for their families and privileges for their children. And others were taking concubines. A favored class is emerging that reminds Chinese of earlier harsh dynasties that also maintained themselves at the expense of the people.

While he sees no indications that the Communists will learn adequately the lessons of these disasters (they are "imprisoned by their own distorted understanding''), Stephen also does not expect that the present Chinese Nationalist Government on Taiwan offers a viable alternative – Traveling in Fukien and elsewhere he found that with the recent easing of controls more Chinese were listening to foreign radio broadcasts, including those beamed to China by the Voice of America, the British Broadcasting Corporation, and stations on Taiwan. A few of the peasants and some former businessmen did hope that Chiang Kai-shek would return. But Chinese intellectuals and professional groups remained disenchanted with the Nationalists. And their discussions of alternatives focused on the United States. In their desperation many intellectuals argue among themselves that they would welcome a third world war. Most see themselves powerless to alter the character of what some describe as the "cruelest regime since the dawn of civilization," because it stops at nothing to achieve its purpose. Meanwhile, the sense of humor and tolerance once so indelibly associated with Chinese character is being erased. And the stark struggle for existence hardens the essential character of the individual.

Caught in this quandary, Stephen chose a personal solution by escaping to Hong Kong. He came, according to his own view, not just for personal survival but to make something of himself. He feels there must be a way whereby he can give expression to his profession and beliefs, despite all the handicaps that confront a refugee here. For today it is easier to escape from the Chinese Communist dictatorship on the mainland than to find anywhere to go in the part of the world that calls itself free. The British authorities in the Colony have begun deporting refugees back to

HUMAN PRICE OF CHINA'S DISASTROUS FOOD SHORTAGE

Red China -- they are deliberately trying to discourage the influx that creates great problems of employment, housing, and public services. No nations have shown a willingness to accept Chinese refugees in significant quantities. So, like many refugees here, Stephen finds it wiser not to give public details of just how he succeeded in entering. He remains still too confused over all that has happened in recent weeks and the shock of being among people who speak and act freely to sort out his personal problems of support and career. Instead, he quotes the Bible about planting one grain of seed and trusts that his faith will carry him through the period ahead, as it has done before in difficult circumstance.

AMERICAN UNIVERSITIES FIELD STAFF
SERIES

EAST ASIA

Vol. X No. 5
(Communist China)

RED CHINA'S SAGGING INDUSTRY
Peking Forfeits Early Modern Great Power Prospects

by Albert Ravenholt

Hong Kong
July 1962

THE SMOKELESS FACTORY CHIMNEYS that today mark Red China's vast new urban complexes are the symptoms of more than a nearly stalled economy; they symbolize a dream of industrial competition with the West that has gone aglimmer. Even if and when Communist China manages to pull itself together, fully assesses the disaster in which it is involved, and gives effect to its new priorities, the consequences of unsound direction and misspent resources will be stubborn to overcome. For the present the tortuous revamping of China's industry-now only dimly perceived from the outside-will mean an even more restricted consumption for that nearly one-fourth of the human race ruled from Peking. But the implications reach far beyond its frontiers. There will be less with which to offer economic and technical aid to such developing lands as Cambodia and Burma. And Mao Tse-tung's political appeal may be tarnished in the process. The Red Chinese will hardly be able to push so vigorously their once ambitious schemes for capturing markets for manufactured goods in Southeast Asia and elsewhere from the Japanese, the Europeans, and the Americans. The political- strategic implications are even more consequential. Without creation of a sophisticated heavy industry, once so dear to the hearts of the Red Mandarins, any success of theirs in exploding a nuclear device will be of limited worth. For they will lack the capacity to build substantial military delivery systems of their own. And both within and without the Communist orbit Red China's actions and role will reflect the agonizing reshaping of its industry now in progress.

How is it that Red China which only recently seemed on the threshold of entering the great power industrial league now finds itself in such desperate straits? When the present period of turmoil is sorted out this question may challenge scholars of modern Asia as few have. One fact emerges clearly now: only a regime as politically omnipotent and administratively efficient as that which the Communists engineered in China during the past 13 years could have committed mistakes on such an enormous scale. The causes behind these monumental blunders must be searched for in the mental recesses of the chung yang (or central authority) that made itself heir to China's imperial traditions. Most among the 180-odd members of the Central Committee of the Chinese Communist Party had scant knowledge of modern economies. And when power finally became theirs after the long years of civil war they did not attempt a systematic search for alternative foreign experience that could guide their efforts, as did the Japanese after the Meiji Restoration in the late 19th century. Instead, they settled for "following the path of the Soviet Union"-and much of this proved unfitted for China. But most of all, the Red leaders became the prisoners of their own ideology. During the decades when they struggled to survive and then to conquer all of China, a miscalculation in policy-as happened several times-would manifest itself quickly and, no matter what the cost, prompt correction would be provided; it was all charged to the price of success in the revolution. However, once all power was theirs, the latitude for error expanded immensely. Today the consequences are evident on a scale that is shaking the self-confidence of Chinese Red leaders who had come to believe that they were "historically anointed" as have been few men in a land continuously conscious of its past for the previous 35 centuries.

Faulty Planning

The start of Red China's present troubles traces back to decisions made shortly after the Central People's Government was formally established in Peking on October 1, 1949. Like so many of Asia's contemporary officials and intellectuals, the Chinese Communist leaders were mesmerized by the blast furnace, the assembly line, and similar features of industrial advance in the West and in Japan. When Mao Tse-tung shortly after his triumph made his first announced tour of the Soviet Union, it must have made an indelible impression on him. Here was the ruler of the most populous state on earth whose previous experience with applied modern technology was limited largely to the comparatively crude semi-handicraft factories constructed in the Chinese hinterland during the Sino-Japanese War. He was only vaguely acquainted with the larger textile and metal-working industries that had appeared in such centers as Shanghai and Manchuria. According to available information, the Russians gave the Chinese Red leader a thoroughly impressive tour. He was taken through the huge industrial centers where harnessed energy moved cranes, spun lathes, rolled steel plate and tubing, and stamped out parts. And Mao Tse-tung returned home convinced that his regime had but to follow the Soviet example; it must have appeared to him that the Chinese even could profit by accelerating the application of Russian methods.

Within the Chinese Communist hierarchy there were few in a position to urge consideration of alternative plans for development. The very concentration after 1927 upon building Communist power in the countryside meant that the Red leaders had been isolated from learning about modern scientific and technological progress. Yet, the nature of the revolution they engineered had given them such complete authority that more informed Chinese, those understanding the character of contemporary industry, were at best relegated to the role of advisers who could prepare lengthy briefs but who could not ensure acceptance of their views. All were agreed that theirs would be a planned state economy with priorities and schedules determined in Peking. In practice, the ultimate decisions in this controlled design for China's material future were made by men who had little experience of such matters and relied largely upon their interpretation of Marxian ideology. They were motivated also by a Chinese "mechanical inferiority complex" that had accumulated during the past century as a people who traditionally thought themselves superior culturally to all others was inundated by the steamships, weapons, and mass-produced consumer goods that represented Western and Japanese dominance in China. This state of affairs the new rulers in Peking were determined to redress.

RED CHINA'S SAGGING INDUSTRIES

Such emphasis then in planning its future denied Red China several shortcuts to progress that might otherwise have been discovered through a more discriminating examination of Western technical experience. Had greater attention been given to the new industrial role of plastics, fiber glass, and lighter metals such as aluminum, Red China might have spared itself part of the costly investment in building an iron and steel industry. It can be argued that Red China missed an opportunity to skip some of the rudimentary industrialization steps taken by earlier advanced economies. The heady preoccupation with quantity rather than with quality and efficiency led to needlessly expensive design of electric-power development. And there was clearly inadequate attention to providing replacement parts for China's already existing railway and other transportation systems, for its plants whose equipment had come originally from Japan, Europe, and the United States, and for its handicraft industry.

The fundamental error made by the Chinese Communists, however, was in designing an industrial blueprint and economic plan unsuited to China's needs at this stage. They evidently failed to take account of the basic differences between Russia in the 1920's and the "Middle Kingdom" in the 1950's. Also, they must have grossly overestimated possible expansion in Chinese agricultural production with more intensive application of traditional methods. Unlike the Soviet Union 30 years earlier, China did not possess substantial areas of fertile unused or little used farm land. Unexploited fisheries and forestry resources were negligible or virtually inaccessible in China. And known mineral resources were not of a character easily or cheaply exploited. The capital to finance and the raw material to supply industry had to come chiefly from agriculture. And on the land population already pressed relentlessly upon the available food productivity. Despite these facts, the Peking planners designed a grandiose scheme for the future that committed all potential resources in sight overwhelmingly to creation of a heavy industry base centered on steel, machine tools, coal, electric power, and base metals. Their light industry plans looked largely to agriculture for materials such as cotton to supply textile production partly for export. The extent to which agriculture was neglected is indicated by the provision in the first five-year plan launched in 1952 for the erection of only 200,000 tons of chemical fertilizer manufacturing capacity-a small fraction of the fertilizer needed annually by just one of China's provinces.

At the outset the Chinese Red leaders were spared realization of the mistakes they had made. Re-establishment of peace and order after a quarter century of civil and international strife permitted Chinese farmers to resume their intensive cultivation of the "good earth." Irrigation and drainage ditches were cleaned out and restored. Millions of peasants were mobilized to erect massive public works, including new dikes to curb the Yellow River on the scale of those built by the most vigorous of the emperors who used corvée labor. The Communists proudly claimed that they brought irrigation to some 80 million acres. Now many of these water conservancy works are proving to have been carelessly constructed; water is undermining some dams and seeping out through unlined canals to ruin once fertile fields with alkali. Particularly on the North China Plain, a hastily conceived large canal system appears to have upset the water table so vital to the agricultural cycle. But throughout the first nine years of Communist rule, expanding farm production and exceptionally efficient state collection of almost every bit of surplus did provide the regime with exportable agricultural produce. Soybeans, frozen pork, dried eggs, peanuts, tea, and grain were among the items shipped in surprisingly large tonnages to the Soviet bloc countries and elsewhere. China began paying with shipments of rice for imports such as rubber. Hong Kong, at the time, lived substantially upon purchases of vegetables, meat, and grain from the mainland; the British Crown Colony even imported such delicacies as frozen pheasants from Manchuria and melons from Central Asia.

Headlong Industrialization

Their earnings abroad the Chinese Communists committed chiefly to investment in heavy industry at home-an exception was made for foreign exchange devoted to expanding Peking's political influence in the underdeveloped countries of Asia, Africa, and Latin America. The results were physically impressive as old industrial bases in Manchuria and East China mushroomed over the landscape and major new cities were created as at Wuhan and Pao-tow, at the petroleum capital around Lanchow, and beyond in the remote Northwest. Within the first decade of their rule, the Communists roughly tripled China's railway mileage. A railway line was laid across the deserts of Outer Mongolia to connect through the capital, Ulan Bator, with the Russian Trans-Siberian system. Railroads were pushed through the mountainous passes to tap the resources of the interior Southwest and Northwest, including Kweichow, Szechwan, Kansu, and even the fringes of the Tibetan plateau in Tsinghai. Coal production was given equal emphasis and by 1960 Peking claimed an annual output of 425 million tons, roughly a fivefold increase from their starting base. Two-thirds of this coal was produced in Manchuria and in North China where the great Kailan Mines that once helped feed Japanese industry have been partially mechanized and expanded. Production was also developed in most other provinces as the planners sought to encourage a regional dispersal of their industrial base and provide alternative sources of household fuel.

Energy from electric power claimed an almost equally important role. By early 1960 installed generating capacity totaled roughly 9.5 million kilowatts. Some 82% of this was thermal capacity which was emphasized during the first five-year plan; only with the start of the second five-year plan in 1958 did generation of hydro power become important with the completion of the first major dams such as those on the vast Yellow River scheme. It was in 1960 that Peking announced a steel output of over 18 million tons. Admittedly, the portion of this produced by many small blast furnaces was of inferior quality. And the big steel centers at Anshan, Taiyuan, Tayeh, Chungking, as well as the two giant new industries at Wuhan and Pao-tow, produced chiefly manganese steel and silicon steel. But within a decade it seemed that Red China had come to rival Japan and some developed European countries as a nation with its own substantial heavy industry.

The extent to which heavy industry had claimed a priority upon available funds, material, transport, and labor is suggested by the published figures on increases in production. During the period of the first five-year plan, China's output of finished steel - the "vital link" in the Communist scheme - increased at an annual average rate of 34%. Yet, one-fifth of the steel used by the expanding machine industry was im ported. Peking claims that throughout the first three years of the second five-year plan steel production expanded on the average of 5 1% annually. The announced increases in the output of electric generating equipment are equally impressive. Official Communist publications state that in 1957 China manufactured generators with a capacity of 198,000 kilowatts. In 1958 generator production had increased to 800,000 kilowatts and in 1959 to 2,150,000 kilowatts, as new plants came into production. For modern industry as a whole Peking's figures indicate a better than 207o annual increase in output during the first five-year plan. And the fragmentary statistics available suggest this rate of industrial growth was accelerated during the initial years of the second five-year plan.

Price of Miscalculation

This compulsive marshaling of China's skimpy resources to the creation of heavy industry has now proved a trojan horse threatening the very stability of Communist rule in China. Over the past year and one-half there have been increasing signs that all was not going well with Peking's plans. But the last three months have seen vast sections of industry on the mainland practically come to a halt. A few examples are suggestive of the process at work. In Canton which has become the industrial center of South China more than 800lo of all factories are closed down; some of these are being dismantled for removal into the more secure interior as the Communists prepare for a possible Chinese Nationalist landing along the coast. Many other plants, however, simply are standing idle. Recent travelers through the Central China industrial centers around Wuhan-once the prize show place of Red China for foreign visitors-saw smoke from only very few of the chimneys on some 150 factories. Reports indicate that the new steel industry there is operating at less than 25% of capacity. Arrivals from Shanghai state that "almost all factories are closing down." And plant managers there are telling the workers, "Those of you who have relatives in the countryside, go there." Some of the largest textile mills in the metropolis have laid off three-fourths of all their employees. In North China locomotives are drawn up along the tracks, where it is possible to see that they have been cannibalized for parts to keep other engines moving. Even loaded freight trains are stalled on railway sidings, and passenger trains that once moved on meticulous schedules now usually run far behind. River boats on the mighty Yangtze are reported unable to negotiate the passage through the gorges at Ichang for lack of boiler pressure. As one sector of China's industry closes down the crippling effects extend to others. And there is even less of such formerly scant consumer goods as cloth to satisfy the needs of the populace.

A symptom and partial cause of this "industrial brownout" is an apparent 50% drop in coal production within the past 18 months; a great many plants including thermal electric power generating stations are without fuel. Raw material shortages extend to virtually every category of industry from cotton for the textile mills to copper for manufacturing electric wires. More than a simple shortage of supplies, however, is affecting industry. The once so highly publicized "Great Leap Forward" has begun to take its toll. Red China is paying the price for "letting politics rule the factories" and for ignoring both the counsel of its own qualified engineers and the Russian technicians, many of whom went home in disgust. The speed-up of production as party cadres vied with each other during the past hectic years to meet the often impossible targets has left a record of burned out bearings and drive shafts, hastily welded gears that now have cracked completely, and overheated steam pressure systems. Near the great blast furnaces at Anshan in Manchuria the surrounding mines have yet to repair most of their electric cutting tools and a large percentage of the dump trucks are broken down with no spare parts in sight. Although controlled, the Communist press gives glimpses of the plight of factory managers throughout the land. Faced with their own factories' difficulties, they are rejecting shipments from other plants because the lathes they receive are unworkable or the steel they had depended upon for making parts is of such inferior quality it cannot be used. And the bogged down transportation system leaves them little choice but to try and manufacture parts locally that will make do, at least for the time being.

Belatedly, a managerial reshuffle is underway in mainland industry with the once all-powerful factory party committees being told to confine themselves to political matters -although by their Marxian interpretation almost everything involves politics-and let the engineers determine how to operate the plants. However, restoring an effective system and performance to China's industry may prove almost as difficult as its initial creation. For once a planned economy gets so far off the track, the designers at the top must first learn the real facts before they can issue sound new directives. Doctored statistics presented partly in the new language of communism have become a tortured part of the way of life in China. So many careers are at stake that it is proving difficult for the Red leaders themselves to discover the actual situation, as witnessed by the failure of the National People's Congress meeting belatedly in March at Peking to announce a budget for last year or for this year.

Role of the Peasant

China's internal crisis now, however, reflects more than a gigantic and almost -hard -to -believe mismanagement of its industrial effort. Basic to its present travail and the immense suffering of the people is a breakdown in agricultural production that vitally affects prospects for the present rulers. [See _Red China's Food Crisis_ (AR-1-'61), an AUFS publication.] Although so largely ignored by the planners in the allocating of investment resources, Chinese farmers performed remarkably well during the first nine years of Communist rule. They took in their stride, without significantly curtailing production, the shattering experiences of "turning over the society," "land reform," and "liquidation of counterrevolutionary elements," that transformed the old order in the villages. Aided by their near total organization of Chinese rural life, the party cadres marshaled the peasants successively into "mutual labor teams," co-operative farms, and collectives. While the farmers grumbled and sometimes stubbornly resisted such recasting of their lives, they went along with the promises from the party that this would be the "final innovation." When the process was completed about 1956-57, Chinese rural folk had reached an uneasy accommodation of sorts with the regime and a considerable proportion felt that they were better off than they had been before the Communists arrived.

The driving compulsion of Mao Tse-tung and his colleagues to accelerate even more rapidly China's heavy industrialization appears to have been the overriding consideration in their fateful decision of 1957-58 to push the peasants into "people's communes." The record crops of 1958, when the weather proved exceptionally friendly, undoubtedly encouraged the regime to take this hazardous step. And their extraordinary past success in remolding Chinese society lent them confidence. But several events of the time also must have persuaded the party leaders that they were again warranted in resorting to "ideological initiative." The rulers in Peking by then had concluded that despite Russia's contribution toward the erection of 140-odd selected key industrial plants and credits that had financed purchases of equipment particularly in Eastern Europe, assistance from abroad was not proving as substantial as they had hoped. And the communes were designed to wring even greater savings from agriculture by further curtailing consumption through such extraordinary devices as the "public kitchens." Simultaneously, the communes would serve to capitalize China's raw peasant manpower and harness it to the purposes of the state. The national campaign to erect tens of thousands of "backyard blast furnaces" that followed immediately upon creation of the communes in the autumn of 1958 expressed this concept. Throughout the land men and women, both old and young, were set to constructing crude furnaces, often from locally made brick packed with earth. With the simplest of hand tools they labored through the long harsh winter, hacking out coal and ore and moving it in baskets and wheelbarrows to their new local "plants." And the party cadres, acting under urgent orders from Peking to show results, kept "shock brigades" of peasants at this task both day and night, even when it meant leaving un-harvested crops in the fields to lodge in the snow.

This time the Communists, however, had miscalculated. Their past successes in engineering revolution had made many arrogant and careless about basic human motivation. They had lost sight of one key secret of their earlier successes: that any major social change to be achieved rapidly must appeal to "felt needs" of a significant number of those affected. Yet, the communes were so designed and managed as to violate the basic instincts of all the peasantry. The new order in the countryside erased even the fiction of private ownership of property that had been retained in the collectives where each farmer supposedly owned a share based upon his contribution in land, animals, and tools. Now all of this was "voluntarily" donated to the state, although cadres in several regions tried to temper the move by suggesting there might eventually be some financial adjustment. And the farmer was reduced in his own mind to the role of a regimented rural laborer, with all that this implied in the traditional Chinese pattern of cultural values. Likewise, destruction of family stoves for conversion into "fertilizer" -a Chinese mud stove contains some ashes among the bricks-and collection of cooking utensils for melting into scrap struck at a foundation of rural emotional security. For the very prospect of bettering their simple diet through work, economy, and the ingenuity that everywhere marks a good housewife was denied the family. The commune kitchens offered no compensating attractions; rather, they soon fell prey to the difficulties of such group enterprises, including the failure of the managers to preserve the vegetables that are so vital a part of the Chinese winter diet. The voluble propaganda about "liberating" women for work in the fields hardly deluded the peasant who now came home with a tired wife to a cold <u>kang</u> (sleeping platform) and could see his young children only by fetching them from a commune nursery.

RED CHINA'S SAGGING INDUSTRIES

Now began the passive resistance of the peasants to the regime, a resistance which has grown to such proportions it is threatening the entire structure of Communist authority in China. "Working by the rule book," or carrying out the exact orders received from above but as slowly as possible and often in ridiculous detail, has long been a device employed by workers without access to other means of enforcing their will. But never has it been used on the scale that it is today in China. When applied to agriculture, the consequences are disastrous for production. Intensive farming is essentially an art; no one field needs identically the same care as the next and the planting cycle must be adjusted to the elements. Cadres who bossed the commune labor brigades and work teams rarely possessed a knowledge of crops and livestock that commanded the peasants' respect. Today they are the miserable agents of the hated changes, caught between the hostility of country folk and the demands from higher authorities.

Peking's press has sought to blame unfriendly weather over the past three years for the declining domestic farm production, while glossing over opposition in the countryside. And there is no disputing that "natural conditions" have been less auspicious than during the bumper harvest year of 1958. This year, again, China is afflicted with intermittent drought and flood that appear to rule out the bountiful crops so desperately needed. On the great plains north of the Yellow River a dry and windy spring prevented the grain heads of the winter wheat from filling out fully. Scattered reports now suggest this harvest may be only three-fourths of normal. In the Yangtze Valley, from the great "rice bowl" of Hunan to Kiangsi and coastal Chekiang, torrential floods in May drowned out much of the first planted rice. Similar calamities affected important regions of Fukien and Kwantung provinces. For reasons which are yet unclear Szechwan in the far west, the province that with its fertile soils and 65 million people fed the Chinese Nationalists during the Sino-Japanese War, also appears to be suffering from food shortages-scattered reports suggest that locusts may have destroyed some crops.

Reports are still too few to estimate with certainty China's agricultural output for this year. But it is now apparent that the food problem on the mainland will be at least as acute as it has been in the recent past. During the last 18 months the Communists have imported some nine million tons of food. This was composed chiefly of wheat shipments from Australia and Canada, lots of barley and other grains from Western Europe, and some sugar-possibly of Cuban origin-from Russia. A significant portion of the imports was purchased on credit and the remainder paid for with Peking's foreign-exchange reserves, which now appear to be nearing exhaustion. For the rulers in Peking one dilemma that will confront them as winter approaches is meeting the nutritional needs of the great cities, the army, and the vastly expanded government service, who have been fed lately so largely with imported grain.

Among the mass of the populace indications are of a possible further decline in their restricted diet, which already has made diseases stemming from malnutrition endemic throughout most of the land. Recent Communist gestures of permitting the peasants to eat at home and cultivate their own garden plots-in Kwangtung Province the average private family unit measures about 15' x 15' - have eased the shortage of vegetables. But the vitality of the people has been so sapped by undernourishment that even if the peasants were willing, they could not duplicate the "heroic labor performance" of the early years of the Great Leap. And commune production of main crops from grain and cotton to sweet potatoes, peanuts, and soybeans remains crippled by recent events. It is improbable that the reported 20 million factory workers and urbanites ordered back to the rural areas this spring "to reinforce agriculture" will prove a major asset. These extra mouths are resented by peasants in widespread areas. Many are discontented rootless folk like those who stormed into Hong Kong some weeks ago when border controls were temporarily eased. Their temper can be judged by the acts of a mob of nearly ten thousand who at that time demonstrated in Canton, booed the Communists Vice Mayor, overturned police cars, and only were disbursed by army troops using rifle butts.

New Priorities

While struggling to cope with such immediate crises, including refusals by some of their provincial governments to make state deliveries of grain, the Red rulers are sorting out a new pattern for industry. After such painful lessons the needs of agriculture have finally been given top priority. Secondary attention is being accorded to light industries that can produce consumer goods needed by the peasants and calculated to tempt them into working. In contrast with earlier practice, heavy industry and capital building has been cut far back. Construction of many factory buildings has been halted halfway. Once politically glamorous heavy industries are being ordered to return to the farmers land that had been commandeered for plant sites-the press carries numerous complaints that some factory party committees refuse to give up the land because they want to grow crops there to feed their own staff.

Production of chemical fertilizer has now been made the most urgent task of the industrial managers. In 1958 official figures indicate that China's output of fertilizer was about 12 million tons. That year the Communists imported almost 1.5 million tons, largely from Western Europe and North Africa. During 1959, imports rose by 200,000 tons and domestic output expanded by a claimed 575,000 tons. The following year recorded imports dropped by 40% while expansion in domestic production increased almost as much. This was the peak period. Within the past 18 months China's manufacture of fertilizer may have declined by one-half, as the industry experienced the consequences of the general slowdown in transportation and coal miners were too ill-fed and discontented to maintain output. Imports were limited to the 1959 level as foreign exchange and shipping were shifted to acquiring food grains. In any event these fertilizer tonnages are a fraction of China's needs. The Communist leaders have stated that they want to produce ZO million tons per year. A more adequate figure would be 45 million tons annually-the island of Formosa now uses more than twice as much when calculated on the ratio of fertilizer to land under cultivation. Creation of such an enormous chemical fertilizer industry is no simple task; the plants begun since the priority was first recognized last year can at best add another one million tons of annual manufacturing capacity by the end of 1963. Present manufacturing facilities are still concentrated at the pre-Communist centers of production near Nanking and in Manchuria. The Communists have encountered repeated difficulties with the new plants started at Canton. Reports on the fertilizer plants at Kaifeng, and in Chekiang, Kweiyang, and Anhwei provinces are too fragmentary to permit evaluation. As yet there is no evidence that Red China has constructed a urea plant, although the North China coal deposits would make this promising. Nor is the natural gas in the remote Northwest being used for fertilizer manufacture. There are indications that their desperate need for chemical manufacturing plants is prompting the Chinese Communists to seek a new accommodation with the Japanese. Meanwhile, Overseas Chinese in Southeast Asia are being urged each to pay for a ton of fertilizer that the Communists promise to give to their relatives on the mainland with permission also to use it on their private garden plots. But such arrangements are palliative; they do not solve China's needs on the massive urgent scale that circumstances demand.

The nature of the difficulties confronting the Communists as they seek to correct their misspent efforts and revamp industry to meet now undeniable needs of agriculture is suggested by the Loyang tractor plant, which is China's prize effort in this field. This factory was designed to manufacture annually 10,000 track-type 48 drawbar horsepower diesel tractors made on a Russian model-the Chinese do not now produce a rubber-tired farm tractor. Last year the factory at Loyang actually turned out about 8,000 tractors. But the communes where these comparatively crude, heavy-built units have been sent encounter endless troubles in keeping them running. Steel used to make the links and pins in the tracks often proves to have been faulty. The rollers that carry the tracks soon wear out, even when the mechanics do remember to lubricate them daily. Repair facilities and stocks of spare parts have yet to be established and there are long weeks of waiting for replacements when a machine breaks down in the field. Operators who understand how to handle and maintain such equipment in China are very few. And all the political lectures by the now weary and harassed party cadres on the new importance of agriculture as the "first wave" of the national future prove of little use in making the machines - or the men - perform.

AMERICAN UNIVERSITIES FIELD STAFF

EAST ASIA SERIES
Vol. IX No. 3
(Communist China)

THE NEW CHINESE "RED" CATHOLIC CHURCH

A Brief History of the Church in China
Before and After the Communist Take-over

by Albert Ravenholt

Hong Kong
March 1961

SINCE EMERGING FROM THE CATACOMBS OF ROME, the Catholic Church has experienced its full measure of harsh persecutions. With the possible exception of Muslim suppression of Christianity in North Africa some 11 centuries ago, however, it is doubtful whether followers of the faith ever have known so intense and thorough a regimentation as that now under way to compel Catholics in China to worship as prescribed by Peking. More than three million Chinese Catholics have been shorn of all organizational ties with the Vatican. They are permitted to profess their beliefs today only on condition that such Christian teachings also embody Communist tenets laid down by Mao Tse-tung -- a "patriotic" church is being constituted to serve the ends of the new Chinese revolutionary crusade. Communist success after a decade of ceaseless persecution, "study", and forced "confession," in enlisting participation of otherwise admirable Chinese priests in this effort, at the price of automatic excommunication, is becoming a measure of the Red regime's imposition of its ideological stamp upon one-fourth of humanity.

While Chinese Catholic leaders, still at liberty to work, thus are forced to suit their open efforts to mesh with Communist purposes, a "silent" struggle goes on beneath the surface. No people perhaps is more skilled at hiding true feelings behind a facade of acquiescence than the Chinese. Some years ago the Minister for Public Security in Peking reported discovering nearly 200 caves in neighboring Hopei Province used by "counterrevolutionary elements" under the name of the "Catholic Church." Today, particularly in North and East China, there still are small groups of workmen in factories and other urban centers who shun the churches sanctioned by Peking and secretly worship in keeping with their former Catholic practices; the communes that marshaled peasants under new collective control 30 months ago have severely curtailed such opportunities in rural regions. Occasionally a priest, compelled to seek "productive employment," may surreptitiously visit his former parishioners while officially making his rounds to repair bicycles. But the penalty for such independent Christian practice is harsh. And young people are dissuaded from following the faith of their elders by all the ruthless molding of opinion of which the new rulers are masters.

The new Communist emphasis upon creating a "kept" Chinese Catholic Church rather than erasing Catholicism[1] relates to Peking's vastly expanded international goals. As the Chinese Red leaders foster their influence in Cuba and elsewhere in Latin America, as in Africa and adjacent areas of

*See Christianity and the Chinese Communists (AR-17-'53), AUFS publication.

Asia, they evidently are finding that Christianity also must be given altered attention. It is convenient to present the appearance of greater religious tolerance at home and there may be advantages to be gained from seeking to pose as true protectors of the faith abroad. Just as the Buddhists have their "model" temples in Shanghai and Peking to show the visiting believers, so foreign Christians who come to China must be encouraged to accept the best about the new order. And Catholics are assured that they will be sanctioned provided that the Vatican and its influence is excluded -- the messianic nature of Chinese Communism readily accommodates itself to this interpretation. It is an index to the towering ambition of the men in the Central Committee of the Chinese Communist Party that they presume to accomplish such a revamping of the Church as no major East European Communist government has managed. And the very nature of the Catholic experience in China facilitates this extraordinary enterprise.

The Church in Pre-Communist China

On the eve of the Communist triumph in China the Catholic Church was an institution to be reckoned with, despite the small fraction of the populace who were avowed Christians. While ministering to some 3,300,000 Chinese Catholics, the Church also maintained a vast program of educational and social services. According to the _Annuaire de L'Eglise Catholique En Chine 1949_, there were 3 universities, 189 middle schools, 1,500 primary schools, and 2,243 rural schools with an enrollment of 320,000. The Church managed 216 hospitals, 781 dispensaries, 5 leprosaria, 254 orphanages with 16,000 orphans, 29 printing presses, 55 reviews, 1 observatory, the largest library in Shanghai, 2 museums, and an ethnological institute. The priests active in the Church numbered 5,788 of whom 2,698 were Chinese and the nuns totaled 7,463 including 5,112 Chinese. Three years earlier the somewhat fragmented missionary organization for China had been replaced by a regular hierarchy established by the Holy See.

Like the Chinese Protestant churches whose combined membership was one-fourth that of the Catholics, this Christian establishment was the product of the "most ambitious missionary enterprise since the conversion of Europe." The Catholic Church was really the "fruit" of the third major Christian effort in China. Chinese classical civilization was in its "golden age" when the Nestorian Christian priest, A-Lo-pen, in 638 built his first church in the imperial T'ang capital of Chlang-an near the modern Sian. Along with Buddhism, which had reached the "middle kingdom" from India not long before, the Nestorian teachings derived from the Syriac version of the Christian scriptures served to broaden the Chinese intellectual and philosophical horizon. For six centuries the Nestorians preached their faith and established their congregations, particularly among Chinese in closest contact with Central Asia.

The newer and more dynamic and yet curiously rigid European tradition of Christianity first reached China with the aid of the Mongols. Having driven back Islam, consolidated their Eurasian empire and opened overland trade routes to the West, the hard-riding nomads of the steppes now with cool discrimination searched for a religion to buttress their rule. Kublai Ehan in 1269 invited the Pope to send a hundred of his most accomplished Christian priests to the great assembly in Peking that was to weigh the merits of all the great faiths. The learned men from Rome proved less than equal to the opportunity; rare was the medieval European who could match in subtlety of wit and argument a Confucian scholar or Buddhist monk. But despite this failure and over the vigorous opposition of the Nestorians, European Franciscan and Dominican missionaries led by John of Montecorvino were able to construct churches in the capital and elsewhere in China before the end of the century, converting perhaps 100,000 Chinese. Collapse of Mongol rule in the next century disrupted the caravan routes to Europe. The Ming Dynasty established on the Dragon Throne in 1368 energetically sought to restore traditional Chinese values and eradicate foreign influences. Both the Catholic and Nestorian churches soon were submerged, leaving hardly a trace of their religions.

The modern Christian era in China opened in the late 16th century with the new Society of Jesus pioneering one of the historically most intriguing human ventures of which we have record. For the Jesuits came "within reach" of their aim -- the conversion of the imperial family that would have made Christianity the official religion of China, with all the far-reaching consequences this implied. Fired by the missionary zeal of Francis Xavier, who had given his life in a futile attempt to enter the "Forbidden Kingdom," and guided by the astute observations of Matteo Ricci, the Society correctly appraised the Chinese social and intellectual scene. Only by making Christianity respected by the Chinese scholar -official elite did the Jesuits conclude that they could triumph. To this end the new corps of missionaries mastered the Chinese language, studied the classics, garbed themselves in Mandarin dress and cultivated the curiosity of the officials in the new scientific knowledge of the West. They reformed the Chinese calendar upon which depended state ceremonial functions and the all-important agricultural cycle. While managing the Bureau of Astronomy and schooling the young princes, the Jesuits pursued their purposes amid the intrigues of the Court and won sanction and protection for their fellow missionaries, who built churches in nearly every province and baptized roughly 300,000 Chinese Christians.

Had missionary activities in China been left entirely to the Jesuits, the ultimate role of Christianity in the Orient might have been vastly different. But Franciscan and Dominican priests who had come to the Philippines with Spanish conquistadores from the Americas were determined to participate. They finally forced an entry to China over Jesuit objections, bringing a far more doctrinaire and nationally - identified missionary effort, closely allied with the competition for trade and influence of European powers opening sea routes to the Far East. These fellow missionaries soon condemned the Jesuit practice of permitting Chinese converts to honor their ancestors in the Confucian tradition. The resulting feuds undermined the Church's extraordinary position in China. Commissions of inquiry dispatched by the Vatican to investigate the "rites controversy" antagonized the Emperor. Dissolution of the Society of Jesus in Europe and elsewhere by 1773 completed the debacle, as the full authority of official persecution was turned against Chinese Catholics.

The 19th century decay of the Chinese empire that opened the way for carving out European spheres of "extraterritorial" influence also facilitated a much expanded Christian missionary movement. Backed by all the prestige of Western technical power, both Catholics and Protestants were able to appeal to Chinese who had become dissatisfied with the old classical order. As an example, young Chinese unwilling to endure the system of arranged marriages found in Christianity a sanction for individual choice. Discovery of such opportunities by churches in Europe and America led to sending thousands of missionaries to China. And the twenty-fold increase in baptized Catholics before the outbreak of World War II was evidence of the devotion with which the Church's representatives spread the gospel.

Despite the reappearance of the Jesuits, whose Society was restored in 1814, the Church never again was able--and possibly did not seek--to win and mold an elite that could guide Chinese society out of this "era of chaos." Individually, a few priests, like the great Jesuit scholar Pierre Teilhard de Chardin, attempted a synthesis of Christianity and science that would enhance the acceptability of their religion among Chinese scholars. In common with the Protestants, who had schooled a much greater proportion of the modern-minded Chinese doctors, teachers, and engineers, the Catholics failed to offer substantially adequate solutions to the most acute problems of Chinese society. As impatient younger Chinese discovered this "social bankruptcy" of otherwise morally attractive Christians, they turned elsewhere for their answers and the Marxists were afforded their great opportunity. The continued Catholic dependence upon a large contingent of foreign priests and nuns made the Church especially vulnerable in a time when virtually all Chinese were motivated by a desire to see their ancient land restored to its rightful dignity in world esteem.

The Communist Triumph

The first year of Communist rule following the 1949 victory in the civil war almost convinced some Christians that the new regime meant its promise of religious freedom spelled out in the "Common Program." But this proved to be only a lull while the Red leaders consolidated their power. Almost coincident with the start of the Korean War, Christians in China began to feel the special consequences for them of the new order. Peking's design was particularly harsh for the Catholics; while Chinese Protestant churches had been classed as "progressive elements capable of reform," the Catholic Church seemed destined to be broken. The first targets were the foreign priests and nuns. In a campaign that mounted in fury after Chinese "volunteers" entered the Korean War, these foreign missionaries were accused of crimes ranging from the murder of infant orphans to espionage and organizing counterrevolutionary movements "under the cloak of the Legion of Mary." During the next four years accusation meetings, imprisonment and torture, "people's trials," and deportation under humiliating circumstances became the lot of these foreign Catholics. There were martyrs who died in prison and others who were expelled after serving part or all of their terms. The campaign served to eliminate from the Catholic Church this vital core of the organization and left the Chinese clergy on their own.

Meanwhile, all schools, hospitals, printing establishments, and other religious institutions, except some of the churches, were taken over by the new regime. Investment in land and urban property to support their work in a time of disastrous inflation made the Catholics vulnerable to the massive "turning over of the society" through which the Communists proceeded to destroy support for the old order. All Catholic publications were screened, along with Protestant religious books, and any that offended the new teachings of Marxism-Leninism and Mao Tse-tung's interpretation of these were burned or reduced to pulp to manufacture paper for a very different kind of propaganda. Chinese priests often were subjected to even harsher treatment than their foreign counterparts, and, but for the exceptional few who escaped to Hong Kong, they had nowhere to go. During the anti-Catholic terror those who died, were imprisoned or otherwise deprived of their freedom, numbered several hundred. Particularly in the rural areas, many were compelled to cease their religious work and seek lay occupations. Illustrative was the treatment of Kung P'in-mei, Chinese Bishop of Shanghai. After his arrest in late 1955, the 150,000 Catholics in Shanghai had to join in a series of mass accusation and indoctrination meetings where they "cleansed" themselves of all ties with such "imperialist intriguers" and publicly endorsed the new "justice."

The "Patriotic" Church

Throughout the first six years of this Catholic persecution the Vatican increasingly was cast in the role of an "imperialistic instrument at the service of the American warmongers." Articles and editorials in the Communist
press sometimes delved deep into the more murky periods of Church history to prove that the Papacy ever had been ready to sacrifice religious principles in pursuit of political advantage. Readers were treated to an intensive dose of Marxist interpretation of Christian development. First word of a possible schism came from remote Szechuan Province in the West--far from the centers of Catholic strength. There, late in 1950, an obscure priest issued a call for a church reform campaign. With energetic support from the Red press this was given national publicity and in time similar resolutions were reported from Tientsin, Tsingtao, Tienshi, Nanking, and other communities with important Catholic populations. In Canton 400 Catholics were credited with holding a symposium and signing a manifesto to be carried from house to house so that all Church members might endorse the demand for such a reform movement.

It was not until June of 1957, however, that this movement was able to generate sufficient support to assemble 240 Catholic bishops, priests, nuns, and lay members in Peking to found the "Patriotic Association of Chinese Catholics." Guided and encouraged by the Religious Affairs Bureau of the Central People's Government, this organization now formally began to chart a new course for Chinese Catholics. A bishop returning to his diocese of Hsienhsien reported on the decisions of the Congress: "We can maintain with the Vatican ties that are solely and strictly religious but we must sever all political and economic relations. The Vatican is certainly a small state, but it has its political positions; it sides with capitalism against the Socialist system, and it is the enemy of the Socialist line followed by the new China. So we must take our position on the side of the Chinese people and analyze carefully the orders and decrees coming from the Vatican. We shall obey implicitly those which relate to strictly religious questions concerning doctrines to be believed and ecclesiastical rules to be observed, but we absolutely refuse to obey those which impede our Socialist construction. It is quite correct and by no means sinful to act in such a way."Catholic study circles throughout the land were convoked on instructions of the Religious Affairs Bureau. In these gatherings the decisions of the Congress became the basis for a re-education of Church members. A priest from the Diocese of Peking is reported to have told his flock: "Although we should not have, like many, any political ambitions, we must however examine ourselves, to ensure that the imperialist poison, which in the past so profoundly marked our ideology, does not continue to influence us so that we still have feelings of resistance to the Socialist system and to the leadership of the Communist Party . . . . 11 Certain Catholics might ask, he added, "If you priests do not submit to the orders of the Pope how can the followers obey you?" But it was not, he explained, a question of knowing from whom the orders came. It was a matter of seeing 11 . . . if the orders are just or unjust. We must not obey unjust orders. Shall we claim that we must obey orders which force us to oppose the Government?"

Indoctrination in the new role assigned Catholicism was intensive. That year 51 priests in Shansi Province "with the support of the Provincial Bureau for Religious Affairs" began a course of political indoctrination which was to last for 80 days. At Huhohate, the capital of Inner Mongolia, 26 women catechists were summoned for "collective learning." In Shanghai some 4,000 Catholic laymen, including 1,000 students, participated with the 80 priests and nuns in indoctrination courses that lasted for several months. Lectures continued for ten hours in a day. It was reported that throughout the "study course" priests were held in semi-internment and that a portrait of Mao Tse-tung sometimes was hung in front of the altar and the crucifix. The "graduates" were given a four-hour tour of an anti-religious exhibit. In March of 1958 the New China News Agency announced that conferences of Catholic representatives which also served as forums and study meetings had been held in 26 provinces, municipalities, and autonomous regions "to undertake Socialist study and propagate the resolutions" of the Congress held the previous year in Peking.

The following month Chinese Catholics officially moved more openly toward schism; they began consecrating bishops without Vatican permission, thus incurring automatic excommunication. That April two bishops were consecrated at Wuhan, the new industrial complex of cities on the middle Yangtze River. In July of 1958 Roman Catholics in the Diocese of Foochow in coastal Fukien Province "elected" a priest named Lin Chuan to succeed the Spanish bishop Monsignor Theodore Labrador, who had been expelled from China. "Elections" of bishops frequently climaxed intensive "big blooming and big contending" meetings where opposition to such a step was aired and then relentlessly argued down. The Communist press went to considerable pains to explain that because a priest had been selected by Catholics in his diocese to serve as their bishop he could not possibly become less of a Christian for lack of sanction of this action by the Pope.

Official response from the Vatican came in the form of an Encyclical Letter by Pope Pius XII dated June 29, 1958. The Pope appealed to Catholics throughout China to "remain unflinching and without blemish." He condemned the "crime" of consecrating bishops without permission of the Vatican. But the time had passed -- if it ever existed -- when the movement could be stopped.

As *L'Osservatore Romano* said the next spring when the dimensions of this enterprise became apparent, "Roman Catholics in China face the choice of schism or the catacombs." No longer was it simply a matter of distinguishing between a "political vatican" and a "religious vatican."

Initially, the Chinese Catholic priests who had led in the creation of this independent church frequently were individuals whom their religious colleagues outside of China judged to be opportunists, or at least men anxious to preserve their own persons. But among the 32 bishops that have been consecrated to date in China are now numbered many able and attractive priests whose lifelong devotion has been to their Church and propagation of the Christian faith. The conclusion is inescapable that for these priests who have experienced the trials of their faith during the past decade participation in building an independent Chinese Catholic Church has seemed the only available solution, personally and nationally.

AMERICAN UNIVERSITIES FIELD STAFF

EAST ASIA SERIES
(Communist China)

FEUD AMONG THE RED MANDARINS

How Kao Kang and Jao Shu-shih Challenged their Comrades

by Albert Ravenholt

Hong Kong
February 1964

THE ACTUAL MANAGEMENT OF POWER inside the elite hierarchy of revolutionary veterans who rule Red China is among the least understood of crucial elements today shaping world events within and without the Communist orbit, for since establishing their Central Peoples Government on October 1, 1949, the Chinese Communists have continued the practice, evolved during earlier decades of civil war, of quietly making key decisions behind the scenes. Even a few insights concerning how these distant and discreet masters of one-fourth of humanity deal with each other and their most critical differences can be revealing. Only once during the past 15 years has there been a major challenge within the more than 17-million-member Chinese Communist Party to the leadership of Chairman Mao Tse-tung and his trusted associates. That was a decade ago when Kao Kang and Jao Shu-shih were deprived of all titles and authority. Both were men of consequence; among the determined engineers of Red victory in China, they held numerous positions and were included in the 180-odd members of the Central Committee of the Chinese Communist Party. More potent was their role in the Political Bureau – which may number from 15 to 17 and is the real chung yang, or central authority, that now molds China's destiny.

Peking's announcement at the time of their disgrace was brief and hardly hinted at implications that extended to the very structure of Communist rule throughout the land. Later it was publicly stated that Kao Kang had committed suicide and Jao Shu-shih had been expelled from the Party and was occupied within "reform through study," that now-classic Chinese Communist procedure for inculcating orthodoxy. For those who are students of China's contemporary history this was a less than adequate explanation, even as these events receded from popular attention. Seminal political episodes have a way of unveiling themselves at a later date, and so it was with this incident. Among refugees who have found their way from the mainland into this British Crown Colony is a Chinese scholar who for purposes of this Report shall be known as Cheng Shih. He was present at the meeting in Shanghai of Communist and "democratic" leaders when Marshal Chen Yi, now Red China's Foreign Minister, revealed the "crimes" of Kao Kang and Jao Shu-shih. This meeting took place some three weeks before there was any suggestion of these developments in the Communist press. Chen Yi began his account to the assembled group numbering between 40 and 50 at about seven o'clock in the morning, halted for a ten-minute break, and continued until one o'clock in the afternoon. Such closed sessions where unpalatable facts are bared before key leaders are a regular feature of Chinese Communist rule. The internal evidence of Chen Yi's presentation, his character as a rather forthright military person, and Cheng Shih's own broad experience lend this account credibility.

FEUD AMONG THE RED MANDARINS

Despite the lapse of a decade, the inherent drama of this meeting and its discussion subject conveys an indication of the magnitude of the considerations at issue.

Marshal Chen Yi was no stranger to the group assembled that morning at the headquarters of the City Committee of the Party in the onetime German Consulate General in the former French Concession. As commander of the Third Field Army, his were the Red columns that in the climactic civil war offensive of April and May 1949 vaulted the mighty Yangtze River in full flood and "liberated" Nanking, Shanghai, and China's richest hinterland. Following consolidation of nationwide Communist authority, this became part of the East China Regional Peoples Government which included the provinces of Kiangsu, Chekiang, Fukien, Kiangsi, Anhwei, and Shantung, with a population at that time of about 160 million. The real power behind this structure was managed by the Chinese Communist Party's East China Bureau of which Chen Yi was second secretary. He was subordinate in rank within the East China Bureau only to the first secretary who was also Chairman of the East China Regional Peoples Government -- Jao Shu-shih. Although Jao Shushih still retained these positions, he had been absent from Shanghai for most of a year, since he transferred to Peking to head the organization division of the Chinese Communist Party.

Chen Yi began his presentation to the meeting with the words: "A very important development has occurred in our Party. Kao Kang and Jao Shu-shih have been in conspiracy against the Party." He then went on to state that the guilt of Kao Kang had been "beyond imagination." Kao Kang's position was possibly even more important than that of Jao Shu-shih, for he had been Chairman of the Northeast China Regional Peoples Government that embraced Manchuria. As concurrent first secretary of the Northeast Bureau of the Party, Kao Kang had been the virtual "boss" of an area with some 40 million inhabitants that held China's greatest natural resources and produced much of her soybeans and other agricultural exports. Due to intensive Japanese development, particularly after 1931, Manchuria possessed China's principal heavy industries, complete with extensive electric power generating facilities and a vast railroad network linked to the Trans-Siberian Railway. Within the past year Kao Kang, while retaining his official positions in the Northeast, had left this "land north of the Great Wall" to become Chairman of the State Planning Commission in Peking and also to fill other consequential positions.

The "crimes" of which Kao Kang had been guilty, according to Marshal Chen Yi, were substantially those of violating basic tenets. First, as the Marshal reminded his listeners, the Chinese Communists had always insisted that the Party must be supreme. But Kao Kang had long opposed allowing Party commissars control when army units were under his command. This difficulty stemmed from the earliest years in Shensi Province where Kao Kang is reported to have been born in Hungshan Hsien in 1892. Fragmentary biographical records indicate that after studying at the Sian Normal School, Kao Kang became a clerk in the Yenan Hsien Party headquarters of the Kuomintang. Following the 1926-27 split between the Communists and the Kuomintang, Kao Kang 0went into the countryside and joined Red irregulars under General Liu Chih-tan. When General Liu was killed by provincial militia in 1934, Kao Kang succeeded to command, organizing the local base of Communist power that in time became the Shensi-Kansu-Ninghsia Border Area. It was here in the mid-1930's that he welcomed Mao Tsetung and other exhausted survivors of the "Long March" from the distant Kiangsi Soviets.

According to Marshal Chen Yi, Kao Kang had been guilty of creating similar Party-Army friction after moving to Manchuria in 1945. At the time of the Japanese surrender in August and September 1945, the Chinese Communists were almost without a following in the Northeast. Among the cadres sent into Manchuria to organize Red power it is reported that there were 17 leading Communists who went from Yenan, including the now Defense Minister Lin Piao, Peking's Mayor Peng Chen, Li Fu-Chen, Kao Kang and others. Blocked from taking the overland route through the Great Wall, first by the Japanese and later by Chinese Nationalist and United States forces, these key Communist leaders traveled instead to the Shantung Peninsula and in junks crossed the 70-mile-wide mouth of the Gulf of Chihli to land on the Liaotung Peninsula near Dairen. Communist success in taking over the Manchukuo puppet army numbering perhaps 400,000 men and in collecting weapons from the Japanese Kwantung Army then surrendering to the Russians provided the base for Red power there. Marshal Lin Piao commanded these forces that later became the Red Fourth Field Army. The first secretary of the Party in the Northeast then was Peng Chen, and Kao Kang only ranked third in the political hierarchy. After the disastrous Communist defeat by able Nationalist Generals Sun Li-jen and Chen Ming-jen in the first battle of Szepingkai in May and June 1946, Peng Chen was blamed and recalled to the Red capital in Yenan. It was then that Kao Kang moved up to become the top Chinese Communist in Manchuria.

The second "crime" for which Marshal Chen Yi held Kao Kang responsible was phrased in these terms: "We all respect our Chair man Mao." But he charged that Kao Kang used to say: "I am a foreign educated Communist" -- referring to his 1936 trip to study in Russia. Kao Kang reminded others that Mao Tse-tung was only a "native Communist." The Chinese terms he employed -- Yang Kung and Tu Kung -- also can be used so that the "native" implies a dull person. Kao Kang had told his listeners that when Mao Tse-tung and his fellow veterans of the "Long March" arrived in Yenan they were "beggars in rags" with nothing to eat. Kao Kang reportedly said, "If I did not take him in then, where would Mao be today?"

Throughout his speech Marshal Chen Yi was careful to credit Kao Kang with major contributions to their cause, including great competence in the economic sphere. Kao Kang was recognized for developing the coarse hand-woven woolen cloth which the Communist leaders often wore at Yenan and which also proved valuable for Red troops braving the North China winters. When Kao Kang took over in Manchuria, however, his appetite for recognition was unhindered. According to Chen Yi's speech, at that time few people in Manchuria ever heard of Chairman Mao Tse-tung. Instead, they were required to line up, sometimes with flowers, and shout three times, "Long live Chairman Kao Kang!"

The third "crime" of which Kao Kang was accused involved the employment of the immense assets he controlled as Chairman of the Northeast Regional Peoples Government to bargain with the Central Government in Peking.

Chinese often use the term Kwan Nei for the regions of China inside the Great Wall and Kwan Wei for the lands that lie beyond this great man-raised barrier. Kao Kang was charged with demanding the sacrifice of Kwan Nei for Kwan Wei and in effect building up the Northeast as an independent region. Furthermore, Kao Kang set aside orders from Peking on grounds that "they cannot be applied in the Northeast." More serious was his attempt to utilize these advantages for his own personal power. When the leaders in Peking were considering a reshuffle of the Central Government, they sent an important comrade to Manchuria to solicit Kao Kang's opinion on the selection of the several vice-chairmen and the cabinet. When asked his own desires, he is reputed to have assured the envoy "I don't care for high position or title," and then added that if they really sought his frank opinion all he wanted was to be Vice-Chairman of the government and concurrently Premier. Implied was his aim to succeed to the highest office in China and meanwhile to fortify his power for this purpose.

Kao Kang's fourth "crime" was failing to practice the principle of "government getting close to the people." Instead of mingling with ordinary folk and listening to their ideas, the Chairman of the Northeast Regional Peoples Government usually was bureaucratic, "acting like a warlord." His fifth "crime" was not being the good Party man, good soldier, and good scholar suggested by his public image. Marshal Chen Yi reminded his listeners that in the spring of 1949 Kao Kang delivered a speech before the assembled cadres of the Northeast entitled "To Whom the Glory Belongs." This later became required study for cadres throughout China. In this speech Kao Kang reportedly classified Party members into three categories —those who were 100% for the people and service; those who were half for the people and half for themselves; and those who were all for themselves. Kao Kang pleaded for all cadres to be 100% for the people. Chen Yi told the meeting that not only was Kao Kang really all for himself, but it was discovered that he had not actually written the speech. Rather it was the work of his secretary, although Kao Kang took the credit. The Marshall then added that he supposed many at the meeting would wonder whether he wrote all of his own speeches. He admitted that his secretary did help, but unlike Kao Kang the ideas were those Chen Yi himself outlined to the secretary.

Normally, the Party did not interfere with the private life of members, the Marshal explained: "a good Party man should be so devoted to his work that his private life would be normal." Kao Kang's sixth "crime" was failing to abide by this standard. A big, husky man with a smallpox-scarred face, he had used his position in the Party and the Government in the Northeast to indulge in libertine pursuits. According to the accusation, in the Northeast, Kao Kang had compelled - attractive women, both single and married, to submit to his attentions. And these women had scant recourse since he was the supreme political power in the region.

As the Red leaders in Peking received increasingly disturbing reports concerning Kao Kang's management of the Northeast and encountered difficulties in gaining acceptance there of government decisions, this was informally discussed within the close-knit group who make the major decisions. Kao Kang was an old and trusted comrade and they decided to deal with the problem by inviting him to take up new responsibilities in the capital, while retaining his positions in the Northeast. It was after transferring to Peking, Marshal Chen Yi said, that Kao Kang entered into conspiracy with Jao Shu-shih. Mention of Jao Shu-shih, who had held such power in East China made the group assembled that morning in Shanghai even more tensely attentive. They were aware of the long-smoldering rivalry between the military and political chieftains of their region, a rivalry dating from the bleak winter of 1940-41 when the Communist New Fourth Route Army was attacked in the central Yangtze River Valley by Chinese Nationalist forces. General Yeh Ting, among the ablest of the early Communist military leaders, was captured. His vice-commander, General Hsiang Yin, was killed and the Red troops scattered in an incident that signaled the virtual collapse of the Nationalist- Communist alliance against the invading Japanese negotiated four years earlier after the kidnaping in Sian of Generalissimo Chiang Kai-shek.

In the following reorganization of the New Fourth Route Army, General Chen Yi, who had led the first of its ten columns, moved upto command. The political commissar of the New Fourth Route Army, Liu Shao-chi, returned to Yenan; remaining close to the center of power, Liu later became Chairman of the Central Peoples Government and second in authority only to Mao Tse-tung. The key post of political commissar went to Jao Shu-shih, then only thirty-six years old and a native of Nanchang in Kiangsi Province.

A short, dark, quick-witted professional revolutionary with a ready sense of humor, Jao Shu-shih had joined the Communist Party while still a university student in Shanghai. After studying in France, where Chou En-lai, Chen Yi, Teng Hsiao-ping and other leading Chinese Communists had organized a branch of the Party after World War I, Jao returned to become a labor agitator in Shanghai. During the great purge of leftist political workers that followed the Nationalist-Communist split in 1926-27, Jao Shu-shih escaped, reputedly with a Russian assist, to the United States. For several years he "studied" in America, England, and Europe and returned to China to go underground during the period of the "Long March" in the mid- 1930's. In 1946 he told Albert "In America I was studying democracy."

The competition between Chen Yi and Jao Shu-shih, as, respectively, the military and political chiefs of the New Fourth Route Army, had been acute even during the lean years while they managed guerrilla resistance to the Japanese and fought off Nationalist forces on their flank and rear. As the Marshal detailed the "crimes" of Jao Shu-shih, it was evident that he did so with feeling. According to Chen Yi, a good Communist must have "all thought for the Party" and not cultivate private friends and enemies. Yet Jao Shu-shih had done just this. The Marshal mentioned as the most flagrant case that of Huang Yi-fung who was removed in 1952-53 as Minister of Communications of the East China Regional Peoples Government and dismissed from the Party. Huang had served under Marshal Lin Piao throughout the civil war in Manchuria, but during World War II he had been chief of staff to Chen Yi in the New Fourth Route Army. Chen Yi now informed his listeners that all the allegations published in the Jen Min Jih Pao and the Hai Feng Jih Pao against Huang that led to his dismissal were "absolutely false." They were concocted by Jao Shu-shih, he said, because of the old rivalry dating from the

Sino-Japanese War. (Later, Huang Yi-fung was reported exonerated as having been a victim of Jao Shu-shih and reinstated in the Party.) Further evidence cited of Jao's personal proclivities was the keeping of his daughter as a student in Paris after the Communist "liberation" of China. She did later return to China, but already she was a "typical Paris citizen."

Jao Shu-shih's second "crime" was described as that of being a "typical defeatist." The Marshal explained that even in fighting a guerrilla war it was not necessary to always remain in hiding-there were opportunities for attack which should be exploited. But Jao Shu-shih always wanted to retreat, and so the New Fourth Route Army lost many opportunities for inflicting a defeat upon the enemy. Chen Yi hinted at bitter wrangles within the command of the New Fourth Route Army, describing how Jao Shu-shih refused to endorse his more aggressive battle plans. "Suppose I had got no support from Yenan," he added, "what then?" This defeatism, Chen Yi said, became particularly evident in Jao Shu-shih's actions during the Korean War. As Chairman of the East China Regional Peoples Government, Jao had ordered many factories evacuated from the coastal area to Central China. He was reported to have said, "In case Chiang Kai-shek or the United States attack Shanghai, then all is lost." As a result, Chen Yi said, there was confusion and great economic loss, and demoralization spread to the staff, who became fearful of the United States and the Kuomintang on Taiwan. An exception to this was Shanghai, the Marshal said, where he held the position of Mayor.

Jao Shu-shih's third "crime" was in the "sphere of thought." Although he held the highest position in East China, Jao was accused of being a "typical capitalist." According to Marshal Chen Yi, Jao Shushih repeatedly told members of his staff that the two greatest leaders in history were Abraham Lincoln and Franklin Roosevelt. Chen Yi said that while he might agree that these were great men, it was important not to forget Marx and Lenin. Great men could be produced in any country, he said, and unfortunately the men Jao named were only Americans, which confused the "thought of the staff." Chen Yi added that Jao had told him the best "living method" in the world was the American method. It was all right for him to say that "to me," Chen Yi explained, but not to the staff. There were after all many ways of living, the Marshal emphasized, like the Russian, the Chinese, or the American. As a Chinese, he had always supposed that the Chinese way was best. The fourth "crime" of which Jao Shu-shih was accused concerned his method of using power. Everyone must obey the orders of the Central Government, Chen Yi emphasized. Although Huang Yi-fung had been charged with creating an "independent kingdom," it actually was Jao Shu-shih who had done this in East China. He had employed his official and political control over more than one-fourth of China's population and the most developed industrial, commercial, and shipping facilities outside of Manchuria to pursue independent objectives. When orders from Peking did not mesh with his purposes, Jao Shu-shih had ignored them. (After the "Jao case," Chen Yi conducted an intensive personal *investigation of* the government in all of the provinces of East China and replaced many officials.)

In 1953, as the leaders in Peking became increasingly concerned about Jao Shu-shih's independent proclivities, they discussed the problem within the membership of the Political Bureau. While retaining his posts in East China, Jao was asked to come to Peking and there was named Minister of Organization of the Party. In the daily management of Communist Party affairs, the Minister of Organization is next in importance to the Secretary General, holding greater authority than the Minister of Propaganda. Within the Chinese Communist Party, which at that time was approaching a membership of ten million, this position afforded Jao Shu-shih substantial scope and held the promise of access to even higher positions.

Both Jao Shu-shih and Kao Kang took up their new responsibilities in Peking at approximately the same time in 1953. Although they had been intensively occupied with managing the great authority hold respectively in the East China Regional Peoples Government and the Northeast China Regional Peoples Government, neither was a stranger to the elite hierarchy governing from Peking; for, throughout three decades of intimate association in pursuit of a common revolutionary goal under harsh circumstances, the leaders of the Chinese Communist Party have come to know each other intimately. The closest Western equivalent in terms of personal association would be one of the professional military establishments, but engineering a revolution requires much greater mobility and commitment to a common philosophical orientation than is demanded in a more bureaucratic and static organization. A source of strength for the Chinese Communists is a sense of accumulated confidence among the top leaders who have taken each other's measure. This contrasts with the wide diversity of experience, including that of expatriates with little knowledge of their comrades at home, among the men who assembled in 1917 to make Russia's Bolshevik Revolution.

In Peking, Kao Kang and Jao Shu-shih soon found they had much in common and were reported often in each other's company. Although they both continued to exercise power in the Northeast and East China, such authority clearly would not be everlasting. The Chinese explain this with a phrase: "When you take the tiger from the mountain he is finished." Evidently, Kao Kang and Jao Shu-shih jointly decided to fortify their regional bases of individual strength. According to Marshal Chen Yi's account, they began quietly shifting staff so as to place men personally loyal to them in additional key positions and otherwise to favor those two vital regions of China. They may have hoped thereby also to further their own careers within the Central Government. The Marshal emphasized that if the plans of Kao Kang and Jao Shu-shih had succeeded, China would once again have faced the ancient problem of fragmentation into semi-autonomous districts. The earlier Kuomintang-dominated Chinese Nationalist Government had been crippled by diffuse centers of real power. Such was the underlying pattern of authority that rent China during the destructive era following the overthrow of the Manchu Dynasty in 1911, when rival warlords fought each other. The history of every dynasty since Chin Shih Huang Ti first unified the empire in 246 B.C. records this unending tussle between central authority and centripetal forces of regionalism and personal ambition throughout this vast and geographically fractured land.

"Fortunately for our Party," Marshal Chen Yi elaborated, "there were members who showed true loyalty." As Kao Kang and Jao Shushih developed their "anti-Party clique" this was reported to other key leaders in

FEUD AMONG THE RED MANDARINS

Peking. When the evidence became such as to convince the majority within the Political Bureau, Kao Kang and Jao Shu-shih were separately invited early in 1954 to meetings where they were confronted with the charges. Such a full meeting of the Political Bureau of the Party brings together the men who really make essential decisions in Communist China, including Mao Tse-tung, Liu Shao-chi, Chou En-lai, Teng Hsiao-ping, Peng Chen, Lin Piao, Chen Yun, Chen Yi, Li Chingchuan, Li Fu-chen, and other less active "honored revolutionaries" like Chu Teh. As his senior comrades detailed the accusations to Kao Kang, he refused to admit any fault. Instead, Kao Kang reportedly pulled a pistol and threatened to commit suicide in front of the assembled group if they did not trust him. According to Marshal Chen Yi's reported account, when Kao Kang lifted the gun toward his own head the man sitting alongside struck his elbow and the bullet went into the ceiling. As Chen Yi recounted the event he was clearly shaken. Contrary to all Party rules, Kao Kang had brought a gun to the meeting and endangered the lives of others present. The Marshal emphasized that the Party expected a member when faced with an accusation either to disprove it or admit his mistakes. Kao Kang also refused to submit himself to judgment by the most senior of his Party comrades.

Kao Kang's dismissal from all of his posts and expulsion from the Party soon followed. The New China News Agency reported in September 1954 that he was formally relieved as Chairman of the Northeast Regional Peoples Government by the 34th meeting of the Communist Party's governing council. The resolution formally confirming his expulsion from the Chinese Communist Party came much later; it was officially reported to have been adopted on March 3 1, 1955. Although stripped of all position and authority, Kao Kang was left his personal liberty. Until he did commit suicide somewhat over a year later, Kao Kang was reported living the life of a broken man in Peking, occasionally drinking heavily and otherwise betraying a loss of his sense of purpose. Jao Shu-shih when confronted by his fellow members of the Political Bureau with the accusations of his "anti-Party activities" reportedly confessed. He likewise was removed from all his positions, and his formal expulsion from the Party was announced with that of Kao Kang. Rumor has it that Jao Shu-shih suffered from some symptoms of hysteria at the time. More recently, he has been reported living in the countryside near Nanking, devoting himself to reading and such pursuits as Chinese opera. While he has been ousted from all participation in authority, the Party evidently still looks after him. It is revealing that Jao Shu-shih's father, Jao Ssu-ch'eng, a former schoolteacher, remained as Vice-Governor of Kiangsi Province until he died in August 1958 at the age of seventy-six - some four years after his son's disgrace. The fate of Jao Shu-shih lends credence to the Chinese Communist Party maxim: "Self criticism must be heavy - sometimes very heavy - but the punishment can be light."

A Special Report in the WORLD BOOK YEARBOOK, 1965

AWAKENING THE LAND
How Land Reform in Formosa is Creating a Better Life

By

ALBERT RAVENHOLT

LEE CHUN-SHENG, a 67-year-old Formosan farmer, can neither read nor write. But Elder Brother Lee, as he is known, is a happy man. He confidently tends his crops and rears his family in Nantou County on Formosa's garden-like west-central plain. He owns 31/4 acres of land, which he tills with the aid of his four sons.

His younger brother, Lee Chun-ho, who is 58, is even more prosperous. Younger Brother Lee owns only 21/2 acres, which he works with two of his three sons, but he earns additional income by buying pigs from other farmers, fattening them, and trucking them to market. His new, two-story, concrete home dominates the old courtyard where the crops are dried. Ducks and geese wander about, and healthy grandchildren play together. An electric fan helps cool the house; a radio brings music and news into the home.

All across the Formosan countryside today there are signs of a vigorous prosperity comparable to that which the Lees enjoy. Modern brick houses are replacing the traditional thatched huts. Almost every farmhouse has electricity. Radios and sewing machines, once virtually unheard of, are commonplace. Many farmhouses now have electrical appliances such as rice cookers; some even have refrigerators. Mechanized farm equipment and up-to-date food processing plants are increasingly evident.

Elder Brother Lee, once a victim of a harsh tenant system, works rice paddy he owns under land reform.

AWAKENING THE LAND

So rosy was the economic outlook in Formosa that the United States government in 1964 announced that it would end its economic aid to the island in 1965. After 15 years -- and 1,400,000,000 U.S. dollars -- the island economy was ready to stand on its own feet.

A System of Virtual Slavery

TO GRASP THE TRUE SIGNIFICANCE of this transformation, one needs to look back. For over 4,000 years, the people of Asia have been chiefly farmers. They have always looked to the land for life, but the earth has been more cruel than kind. Peasants, charged with feeding more than half the human race, farmed with sticks and shovels. They grubbed at worn-out soil. They suffered under drouth and pestilence. And, to top it all, they were shackled in virtual slavery by a tenant-landlord system that wrung - from them most of what they did produce.

The story of the Lee family of Formosa -- coming as it does at a time of exploding population and emerging nations -- has a profound significance for the world. The Lees have been swept ahead by social and economic changes that may be applied to many other parts of the world. These changes -- loosely described as "land reform" -- constitute a remarkable chapter in modern history.

The Lee story really begins back in 1948 in Washington, D.C., where the U.S. Congress passed the historic "China-Aid Act." Intended mainly to bolster the Chinese Nationalists against the communist threat, the act nonetheless specified that for every nine U.S. dollars spent on Chinese military strength, at least one dollar must go to improve the economy of hard-pressed rural areas. To administer this program, a Joint Commission on Rural Reconstruction (JCRR) was set up. It was staffed by three Chinese commissioners and two American commissioners.

But before the JCRR could make a significant impact upon Chinese agricultural life, communist armies overran the mainland, and President Chiang Kai-shek and his Chinese Nationalist government withdrew to Formosa. So it was Formosa, not the mainland, that was to become the scene of this dramatic story.

We saw that we had two major tasks," said Chiang Moulin, the late chairman of the JCRR. "First, we had to break the economic and social obstacles that had blocked any chance for the peasant to get ahead. Then, we needed to introduce better farming methods that would assure greater, more dependable harvests."

The shift of scene from the mainland to Formosa brought both advantages and disadvantages. More than 2,500,000 mainland Chinese suddenly were superimposed on the economy of an estimated 7,300,000 Formosans. The Formosans, although largely of Chinese ancestry, had problems of their own. As far back as 1683, when Formosa became a prefecture of China, the Formosans had been victimized by officials appointed from faraway Peking. Special taxes exacted by these imperial mandarins eliminated many small landowners, forcing them to work for others. Hence, there emerged on Formosa a large landlord class which took a portion of every harvest. For 200 years, tenant farmers worked the land of others, keeping little for themselves.

AWAKENING THE LAND

Formosa Is Ceded to Japan

IN 1895, FORMOSA WAS CEDED to Japan as part of the booty of the Chinese-Japanese War. Japan began at once to develop the island as an agricultural granary to supply its own industrial empire. The Japanese built new irrigation canals, stepped-up fertilizer production, and developed better seed varieties. They built new processing plants, railroads, and seaports.

Production of tea, rice, bananas, and pineapples increased. Mineral production boomed. But the lot of the Formosan peasant changed little. Elder Brother Lee remembers those days well.

"We were farming with our father and Middle Brother," he said. "Together, we worked 10 acres, but we paid seven-twelfths of all we produced to the landlord. We had barely enough left to live on, but we had no choice. We did not own the land, and pressure for land got greater and greater."

Perhaps life for the Lees under the Japanese would have been better had not the population of Formosa grown as it did. In 50 years of Japanese rule, the number of Formosans increased from 2,000,000 to 7,300,000 -- over three and a half times! Credit for this population growth must go largely to modern public health programs, medical facilities, and doctors trained by the Japanese. It was a great achievement, but it intensified an already critical overpopulation problem in Formosa because the total of cultivated land remained fixed at about 2,153,000 acres.

"We could only have moved to the sea or the mountains," a county official says in describing their dilemma. As the population grew-, ever more tenants competed to farm the same land. Landowners pushed rents higher, sometimes up to 70 per cent of the main crops. They also bought out smaller farmers when bad weather or family misfortune forced the latter to sell. Toward the close of the Japanese period, 68 per cent of the farm families on Formosa lived under a system of tenure.

Formosa was restored to China in August, 1945. Paradoxically, this at first made life even more difficult for farmers suffering from disrupted shipping, bombed-out railroads, and lack of fertilizers. Japanese administrators and technicians were sent home. They were replaced by Chinese officials, who now saw a chance to enrich themselves after lean years in the wartime capital of Chungking. Formosans had at first welcomed the mainland Chinese as liberators, but disillusionment turned to anger, and by February, 1947, it sparked an uprising that was suppressed with bloodshed.

Economically hard-pressed, tenant farmers became even more clearly "second class citizens." They hesitated to speak out in their dealings with landowners who often were the only available moneylenders. Formosa was developing bitter rural discontent similar to that which had given rise to communism in mainland China.

By 1949, Chinese Nationalist leaders, having learned a bitter lesson from their earlier reverses on the mainland, were ready to try new ideas. To revive production, and at the same time ease mounting social unrest, the provincial government led by then Governor and now Vice-President Chen Cheng put into effect the program of land reform originally planned for the mainland. The joint Commission on Rural Reconstruction was revitalized, and a radical yet simple three-stage program was set up. As a first step, rents were to be reduced. Second, public land was to be sold to tenant farmers. Third, limits were to be set on how much land landlords could hold, and the surplus-to be purchased by the government-was to be subsequently resold to the tenant farmers.

The first step was taken in 1949. All farm rents were chopped to a maximum of 37.5 per cent of the annual main crop. (A photograph of the period shows a tenant farmer with his "37.5 per cent bride"- the girl he had been waiting for and now could afford to bring home with the extra cash retained from the crop.) Tenant farmers were guaranteed security by providing them with written leases for a minimum of six years. No family could be ousted from the fields it tilled without cause.

With JCRR assistance, more than 4,000 local officials and young people, including students, were recruited for intense educational "short courses." They then fanned out into the countryside to spread the word. Public meetings were held to explain the program. Posters, pamphlets, and mass media such as
radio and newspapers were used to mobilize public enthusiasm before opponents of land reform could organize resistance. The volunteers supervised the writing of new land leases, especially those involving illiterate farmers. Since only a few Nationalist government officials owned land on Formosa, there was little political objection to the action at the top.

Going After the Tenants

CRUCIAL TO THE SUCCESS of the program were locally elected land commissions. These commissions, on which tenants and farm laborers held the majority of seats, arbitrated disputes between landowners and tenants and among tenant farmers themselves. Because the commissions were composed of neighbors who knew each others' affairs intimately, they were able to act quickly and with a minimum of political involvement. The few problems they could not solve were referred to the courts. Some charged that this first step in land reform was high-handed. But Dr. Tang Hui-sun, chief of JCRR's Land Division, had a simple, compelling answer. "When you are fighting a civil war, who do you want on your side? The few who are landlords, or the many who are discontented tenants?"

Dramatic results followed. By the end of 1949, more than 370,000 leases had been signed and registered with village officials. Tenant farmers, who now knew they would be on the same land the next year, built pigpens and dug compost pits. Some planted fruit trees and green manure crops that could be plowed under to enrich the soil. Other developments were almost as revealing. Prior to reform, there had been considerable speculation in farmland. Now, however, with returns from farmland stabilized, families with wealth looked for alternative sources of income. This encouraged a more modern business attitude in the towns.

In 1951, the government initiated the second part of its program. Government-owned land was put up for sale to the tenant farmers. This land, involving almost one-fifth of all the farmland on Formosa, had been acquired by the government in 1945 as former enemy property. Only a part of it was held back for sugar plantation management. The price per acre was fixed at two-and-one-half times the value of the annual main crops. It could be paid for in semiannual installments spread over a 10-year period. Within two years, 121,953 farming families had bought 155,610 acres of government land. Income from these land sales in turn produced a much needed source of government revenue.

Meanwhile, provincial officials and JCRR specialists had launched a massive survey of available land and its potentials. All privately owned agricultural land was registered. This land in turn was classified as to productivity. By April, 1952, the task force assigned to the job had compiled and organized all the data on 6,600,000 "Land-Record and Landownership Cards." It was a large undertaking but well worth the effort, for the painstakingly gathered information became the basis of land reform legislation which was drafted the following month.

The Provincial Assembly, where Formosa's landowners were well represented, was offered an opportunity to comment. Then the draft was submitted to the Legislative Yuan of the Chinese Nationalist government. On Jan. 20, 1953, the Yuan, after great deliberation, passed three related laws. One provided for the transfer of government enterprises to private ownership; a second authorized the provincial government to issue land bonds in kind -- redeemable in crops -- and the third was the "Land-to-the-Tiller" Act.

In the Land-to-the-Tiller Act, the Nationalist government gave scrupulously fair consideration to the rights of landlords who had obtained their holdings legally under the prevailing land system. Every landlord was entitled to keep approximately 7.5 acres of irrigated land, or 15 acres of dry land. This he could continue leasing to tenants on terms provided earlier by law. All land in excess of these amounts was bought by the government.

Under the program, the landowners received 30 per cent of the purchase price in shares of stock in government-owned corporations which, under the act now became private enterprises. The remaining 70 per cent due the landowners was paid in commodity bonds representing stipulated quantities of rice or sweet potatoes and bearing 4 per cent annual interest. The bonds were redeemable in cash or kind to guard against currency inflation. They were payable semiannually over a 10-year period. Tenant farmers were then offered this land at the same price paid by the government and on the same terms -- 4 per cent interest in 20 installments spread over 10 years. Under the new act, 194,823 farmers bought 354,612 acres of land. By the end of 1953, more than three-fourths of all the agricultural land on Formosa was being cultivated directly by owners. The remaining one-fourth either continued to be rented -- thus providing a "ladder" for new farmers to get started toward eventual ownership of their own land -- or it was used for government enterprises such as the Taiwan Sugar Corporation, schools, experimental stations, or similar projects.

To understand what all this meant to the average farmer, let us turn again to the Lees. At the close of World War II the three Lee brothers were still working the original 10 acres their father had rented. When local political pressures compelled them to give up this land, they pooled their meager resources and bought 1 1/4 acres of land. Next, they managed to rent an additional two acres of privately owned land. In a third, separate plot, they also leased 2 1/4 acres of government land. This was the extent of their holdings when the Land-to-the-Tiller Act was passed.

"Since we were really cultivating these fields ourselves," Elder Brother Lee explains, "we had the first right to buy them under the act. When the land reform program was completed, we owned approximately six acres. These we divided into three equal parts. But later, when our Middle Brother decided to give up farming and go into business, he sold his shares to us. As for me," Elder Brother goes on, "I was allowed 10 years under the law to pay for my new fields. But I paid for them in six. We made good money raising pigs for several years, and I thought the safest thing was to pay for my land."

New Business Ventures

NOT ALL FORMOSAN LANDLORDS were happy to part with their fields. For generations, land had been the most trusted investment, both as a status symbol and as a prized possession to be passed on to the children. But now, with rentals from land either stabilized or nonexistent, families with wealth to invest had to look elsewhere for alternatives. Many former landlords embarked on new ventures. Some joined with the new entrepreneurs who were remaking the faces of Formosa's cities. A Taipei stock exchange soon appeared, trading shares in the corporations now controlled by former landlords. Within a decade, Formosa was manufacturing most of its textiles, though it continues to import raw cotton, especially from the United States. New glass plants, plastics factories, brick kilns, metal fabricating shops, and electrical manufacturing firms sprang up and absorbed capital and talents in often highly profitable pursuits. Thus, a new class of citizen -- the businessman -- was born on Formosa.

Simultaneously, the old-type tenant farmer had disappeared. Farmers were now secure on their lands and were fortified with new incentives. Still, only one-half of the goal had been achieved. The new landowners now needed a knowledge of more scientific farming methods. A most crucial need, too, was credit and marketing. In a society where interest on private loans often exceeded 40 per cent annually, the farmer still risked becoming a victim of the moneylender. To avoid this, the JCRR began reorganizing the Farmers Associations. These had originally been established by the Japanese and acted as rural banks as well as suppliers of seed, fertilizer, and mill rice. Most, however, were financially unstable. Also, they were controlled by city merchants. Ordinary farmers had little authority in their management. Now, however, they were redesigned into genuine cooperatives. Only families that earned more than half of their income from farming were allowed to vote. Association managers and their staffs were given thorough training. Proper accounting procedures were introduced. Experts from provincial government headquarters audited each cooperative's books every six months. In addition, JCRR grants and loans helped pay for new rice hulling machines, peanut and soybean seed granaries, fertilizer and rice warehouses, and orange-packing plants.

In more personal terms, the Lees again serve as examples of what has taken place. Both brothers are among the 7,503 members of the Tsao Tun Township Farmers Association which is located in a bustling, brown-plastered building on the edge of town. Its 15 directors and comptrollers are elected every three years. But every November, about 90 per cent of the members assemble for two days to talk over association business. They also approve the budget for the coming year's operations.

Formosa's First Mass Market

THE ASSOCIATION'S ACTIVITIES are many. It serves, for example, as a bank. "I have on deposit cash equal to 105 U.S. dollars," says Elder Brother Lee. It earns him interest at the rate of 4 per cent annually if he leaves it for one month, and twice this rate of return when left for six months. As a member, he is entitled to borrow at a somewhat higher rate of interest from total deposits in the association. These deposits are equal to about $825,000.

Behind the association's main headquarters is a warehouse. There the Lee brothers and other members of the cooperative trade rice for fertilizer. There, too, they sell their jute and buy farm equipment, such as Elder Brother Lee's new paddy-field marker which enables him to transplant rice seedlings in straight rows.

The warehouse also has a merchandise department where farmers can buy pesticides, bicycles, or even electric rice cookers, the latter priced at $12, Lately, the department has been selling on installment half a dozen small electric refrigerators a month which cost the equivalent of $274. "They still cost more than I can afford," says Younger Brother Lee, "even though the women at home would like one." But already farm families are providing Formosa's first mass market for consumer durables, sometimes manufactured by their former landlords.

Profits earned by the Tsao Tun Township Farmers Association annually have totaled the equivalent of $26,000. Thirty per cent of this went into a sinking fund. The cooperative is building a new $70,000 headquarters. An 11man cooperative extension staff includes three veterinarians who vaccinate pigs and water buffalo, and a manager of the livestock breeding farm that specializes in artificial insemination of sows. Two 4-H Club directors guide 850 boys and girls belonging to 49 clubs. Among the club members is Younger Brother Lee's bright and eager 20-year-old third son. "I work in the daytime reading irrigation water meters," he says. "On weekends and in the mornings and evenings I am out in the field helping my brother to see if we can set a rice production record." He would like to try for a college education when another brother returns from army service.

New ideas move through this network into the bosom of the family. A home economics supervisor from the Farmers Association visits with housewives, showing them how to save costly fuel by rebuilding the open Chinese kitchen stove, preserve vegetables, and cook more nutritious, yet simple meals. Four extension specialists explore fields in the township daily for opportunities to give technical help. In the evening, they meet with adult farmers in village "agricultural discussion groups."

A Source of Pride

FORMOSA'S FARMERS take a great deal of pride in their production records. Over the past decade, island output of rice has increased 40 per cent to above 2,100,000 tons, leaving a surplus for export. Sweet potato production has increased 50 per cent, and the harvest of peanuts even more. Pineapple production tripled, and the area growing citrus fruit has increased nearly threefold. New crops now being canned and exported, such as mushrooms, earn Formosan farmers $7,000,000 annually. A growing Chinese taste for milk has aroused interest in dairy farming, especially among 4-H Club members who have returned from visits to America. Modern milk pasteurization plants have begun bottling milk from black-and-white Holsteins that graze on the dikes between the tiny fields and on new pastures planted on the hillsides. Unlike most of the burdened lands of South and Southeast Asia, rural Formosa has reached that dynamic stage where it can now digest new forms of technology.

AWAKENING THE LAND

The results of these new ideas can be seen in the fields of Elder Brother Lee. His first crop yielded a return of 2 1/2 tons of paddy rice per acre, and the second crop was almost as much. A winter crop of sweet potatoes and beans, however, was killed by unusual frost. jute, first inter-planted with rice, was stripped and sold for cash, cucumbers and other vegetables were grown for family use and as feed for pigs and poultry. "Even though I don't write it down, I have a pretty good idea of what we make," Elder Brother Lee admits. He calculates that the annual crops yielded a gross cash return equal to $1,160. Chemical fertilizer, which island farmers use intensively, was the largest single expense. It cost Lee $149. Other major operating costs were for taxes -- which are high, he thinks -- insecticides, and irrigation fees. These totaled $174. Labor is the biggest factor in growing rice. If paid for, it would have cost Lee the equivalent of $286, even at the prevailing rural wage of one U.S. dollar per day. But since he has grown sons, the family can till the paddy fields, transplant rice seedlings, weed, and harvest largely with their own manpower, or, if the occasion demands, by exchanging work with their neighbors.

A High Living Standard

LIKE FARMERS IN MANY OTHER LANDS, the Lee brothers calculate their income as much by their standard of living as in cash. Food for the family is chiefly homegrown, and the Lees eat well. Daily caloric intake on Formosa rivals Japan's, the highest in Asia. Meat, especially pork and fowl, or fish appear on the table almost daily. Clothing is simple, yet ample, and becoming more colorful as women buy the new prints. Rubber raincoats are replacing the traditional straw capes among farmers. By choice, the Lees still go barefoot in the paddy fields, but they own rubber boots. The old rural fear of illness has relaxed. "We trust and use the modern drugs and doctors," they say, referring to the health stations and centers which have been established on the island with help from JCRR and the provincial government.

Education has a new importance. All seven sons of the two Lee brothers completed primary school and two attended middle school, although the cost still bars the children of some farmers. Since they can read and write and manage figures, the sons help their fathers in business calculations. They study the rural magazine *Harvest*, published fortnightly in Taipei, and glean ideas on crops and animal care from extension pamphlets. Unlike the cities, rural Formosa has little juvenile delinquency. Young people are productively and satisfyingly involved in many of the affairs of the community.

Elder Brother Lee measures his lot in life by contrasting it with that of his father. Farming is still hard work from sunrise to dusk, but the rewards are vastly greater. "Someday, I may lighten the work a bit," he says, "by buying one of those new little tractors to replace the water buffalo. But not yet." Mechanization will become more practical as the provincial government, with JCRR assistance, helps farmers trade land and rebuild dikes so they can consolidate fragmented holdings and simplify cultivation. Lee and his neighbors feel they could make more money out of poultry and pigs if there were a large packing plant in Tsao Tun Town to stabilize prices and manage marketing.

Good farming and cautious use of his income since land reform have made Elder Brother Lee a man of solid financial means. At today's prices, his fields are worth $9,750, or almost $3,000 per acre, based on Formosan dollars which have an official exchange rate of 40 for one U.S. dollar.

Another measure of the prosperity that has come to Formosa is the annual average income of its farming families. Between 1952 and 1964, it has more than doubled. To help make this possible, the JCRR has spent some $7,100,000 in grant aid and roughly the equivalent of $127,800,000 in counterpart funds -- Chinese currency generated by the sale of U.S. farm surpluses like cotton on Formosa and partly used for loans that financed irrigation construction.

A New Way of Life

Formosa has become Asia's agricultural "showcase," a kind of pilot plant where ancient civilization and Western techniques have combined to provide a new way of rural life. Formosan agricultural specialists, invited to many Asian, African, and Latin-American countries under technical cooperation arrangements, now are demonstrating modern rice growing methods in Liberia, Libya, and the Ivory Coast. Nations in many parts of the world send their own agricultural experts to Formosa to see an agricultural miracle in operation. Many take home with them ideas on land reform and crop production to put into use in their own countries.

Although political institutions on Formosa leave much to he desired, rural communities have achieved social and economic democracy. For the Lee family and its neighbors, the hard old days are a fading memory. The better life, to which land reform was crucial, holds out a promise to emerging peoples in many parts of the world.

AMERICAN UNIVERSITIES FIELD STAFF

EAST ASIA SERIES
Vol. XIV No. 3
(Communist China)

THE RED GUARDS

by Albert Ravenholt

Hong Kong
April 1967

"We are Chairman Mao's Red Guards,
The vanguard in the cultural revolution.
United with the masses we go into battle,
Vowing to wipe out the black gang.
We dare to criticize and to struggle,
And we ceaselessly make revolution and rebellion.
We dare to criticize and to struggle,
And we ceaselessly make revolution and rebellion,
So that the old world may be thoroughly crushed,
And the revolutionary regime may stay red for
ten thousand generations,
Red for ten thousand generations."

Thus goes the concluding verse of "The March of the Red Guards," which was reportedly composed by students of a middle school attached to the Central Conservatory in Peking late last summer as the movement gained momentum. Sung by the Red Guards as they paraded a million strong through the capital's immense "Square of Eternal Peace," these words lent impetus to a curious, romantic, and frightening convulsion.

For over ten months China has been experiencing a shattering though guided ferment as part of a "Great Proletarian Cultural Revolution" that evinces both nihilism and xenophobia. Initially conceived of and adroitly engineered as shock troops in an internal struggle for control and direction of authority over nearly one-fourth of humanity, the Red Guards have launched forces and ideas strange to the Chinese totalitarian state, and in time they may help wreck the very orthodoxy they were designed to fortify. Meanwhile, more has been revealed than just the depth of dissent among the Red Mandarins, for the succession to control at the top, the character of communism for China, and China's world role have all been questioned. Despite eighteen years of the 1nost massive indoctrination of a people ever attempted, it is now apparent that Chinese youth remains 'Largely confused, bitter, thwarted in their careers and personal. ambitions, and increasingly cynical about the purposes to which they have lent their enthusiasm. After the odd official ploy of keeping all students out of schools, colleges, and universities since June 1966, it is unlikely that returning them to the classrooms now offers a real solution.

Only an ability to read Mao Tse-tung's mind could fully account for the appearance and role of the Red Guards. Yet, enough is known to allow a reconstruction of seemingly decisive events. in January 1958, Mao, who was then sixty-four years old, told a visiting Asian diplomat that he was thinking of retiring as Chairman of the Chinese People's Republic

Government. Winters in Peking were too cold, he explained, and he disliked the snow and dust storms that whistled down out of Mongolia. He was tired of the ceremonial performances expected of a chief of state, especially attendance at the interminable formal dinners for visiting dignitaries; they left him little time to think. He wanted to compose poetry -- despite the official scorn for such classical pursuits, Mao writes in his version of the old style with a brush -- and he also allowed that the climate and food in Central China's great Yangtze River Valley, including his native Hunan Province, suited him much better than Peking.

For Communist China, 1958 proved a seminal year. Mao's overriding faith in the triumph of man's harnessed brawn over nature -- for which there have been numerous imperial precedents, such as digging the Grand Canal -- was applied in the "Great Leap Forward." The populace marched out by the tens of millions to build dams, drain swamps, plant trees, speed up industry, and erect "backyard blast furnaces," all to insistent mobilization and indoctrination by cadres. The weather was kind and the crops extraordinarily abundant that summer -- as the countryside benefited in many regions from the cumulative effects of eight years of peace following more than three decades of war and turmoil. When, in September 1958, China's half a billion peasants suddenly discovered in their "big blooming and big contending" meetings that they were being herded into "People's Communes," the Maoist millennium seemed almost at hand. Voices of dissent within the Party were drowned by official reports of fantastic achievements, as one factory or province outdid the next in its claims of surpassing production targets.

In this euphoric atmosphere, the Central Committee of the Chinese Communist Party met in plenary session at Wuhan in December 1958. The meeting evidently concerned itself chiefly with assessing results of the three-month-old commune venture, and measures were adopted for correcting some obvious excesses in the headlong creation of the communes. For example, cadres often ignorant of agriculture commanded the "labor brigades" and "labor platoons -- in which peasants and their wives were marched to the fields at sunrise and told where to plant, hoe, and weed. A resolution published after the session called for extending the commune system to the cities, but only gradually. Communist publications discussed uniting the cities with their surrounding rural regions in virtually self-sufficient communes, where urban and rural folk would exchange products and share labor. Otherwise, the Central Committee accepted Mao's retirement as Chairman of the Government, which opened the way for his designated heir-apparent, Liu Shao-chi, to move up to this position in January 1959. For Mao, the culmination of his life purpose was near. With the massive recasting of Chinese rural life under way, and the commune pattern now delineated for the cities as well, he had proved himself the great modern innovator of Marxism-Leninism. While he retained the Communist Party chairmanship, he could now contentedly watch comrades whom he had promoted in the hierarchy take over the reins and carry on his work.

As so often happens when a giant expects to pass along his vision intact, the heirs had other ideas. It was not that they disowned the premises of Chinese communism as evolved over thirty-two years. Rather, they were caught up by events and trapped in circumstances of the Party's own creation. As the men responsible for ruling the country, and also now for managing the economy to an extent never before attempted anywhere, they began to realize that possible disaster loomed before them. Even today the outside world is only dimly aware of how close Red China was to coming apart at the seams in the years from 1959 through 1962. Peking officially blamed the crisis on a succession of "natural calamities," but this was a canard. It is true that the weather was unfriendly in localized regions -- as in the late summer of 1961 when a succession of typhoons hit Manchuria, ruining most of the soybean crop -- but what really brought the Communist regime to its knees was the gross mismanagement of the Great Leap Forward combined with peasant anger against the commune system, which prompted the sabotage of production, killing of cadres, and rural upheaval. Malnutrition became so widespread that disease took a frightful toll. Rioting and other expressions of discontent threatened Communist authority in many big cities, and even the Red Army was driven by dissension. The "central authority" was able to maintain control only by massive imports of five to six million tons of wheat annually (chiefly from Canada and Australia) to help feed the urban population, the military and the bureaucracy.

In the face of such compelling considerations, the government and the Party backtracked from the heady experiments of 1958. "Politics must rule" and "people's science" were replaced in the factories and railways with more professional management by engineers. Bold promises to surpass Great Britain and Japan were set aside as Lie emphasis shifted from the building of heavy industries to supporting agriculture with such vital but neglected essentials as chemical fertilizer production. The problem of adjustment was compounded by the withdrawal of Russian technicians, the termination of Soviet economic and military assistance, and the beginning of the Peking-Moscow split. On the land, many commune innovations, such as common kitchens, infant nurseries, and "happiness homes" for the aged, were abandoned as concessions to the peasants. Management was decentralized primarily to the level of the production team, corresponding approximately to the former village unit. Even more important, peasants were given the use of their private garden plots, again allowed to raise their own pigs and chickens, and granted permission to sell much of the produce in "village free markets." These adjustments - although made unevenly according to the dictates of necessity and initiative by Party leaders in each region and province - enabled Red China to begin restoring production and to survive the grim emergency in the late spring and early summer of 1962. Codified and officially sanctioned during the Central Committee's plenary session of September 1962, this "new path" emphasized agriculture as the basis for China's economic rehabilitation, but several years were required for the regime to sort out its distorted statistics and resume more systematic planning. Economically, this proved a period of gradual but consequential progress, with expanded production of electric power, petroleum, chemical fertilizers, and other technical supports for farming - plus the manufacture of nuclear bombs. Although rationing of some essentials continued, the diet improved greatly, with private production providing an abundance of vegetables, pork, and poultry for consumption and for export to Hong Kong and other foreign markets.

It now seems apparent that Mao took little part in these detailed decisions to return China to more pragmatic management. Fragmentary reports indicate that he was away from Peking much of the time and that, disengaging himself from routine decision-making, as he had done several times earlier in his career to allow leisure for reflection and writing, he had sought favorite retreats. At Hangchow, he used a specially constructed villa in the hills which skirt the west side of the lake; and in Shanghai he took over the former French Club, chiefly because of its excellent indoor swimming pool. He also visited at Wuhan University as the guest of President Li Ta (now purged). Both Chinese officials and visiting foreigners frequently had to travel out of Peking for an audience with the venerable Red sage.

Just when Mao Tse-tung decided that "his" revolution was being betrayed is unclear. Bits of information suggest that he only gradually realized the extent to which his grand design for the People's Communes was being relegated to the back shelf, for organizational charts were largelyretained while the focus of decision-making shifted and cadres practiced the Communist genius for ideological double-talk. Certainly, as a student of China's long history, Mao was well aware of how earlier dynasties had quickly settled into patterns of privilege for the new elites, thus abandoning the public ideals for which they had avowedly pursued power. And he has long been especially alert to the critical importance of youth's formative experiences. Like so many other Chinese who as students joined in the May Fourth Movement of 1919 protesting against the awarding of German holdings in Shantung to Japan under the terms of the Treaty of Versailles, he knew the indelible effect of "learning by making revolution."

The course of Chinese fortunes abroad was probably as decisive as domestic developments in Mao's decision. In the deepening differences with the Soviet Union he must have read more than a simple fracturing of the faith joined with the emergence of national self-interest. When the Russians stubbornly refused to fall in line with Mao's interpretation of Marxism-Leninism, despite the deposing of Nikita Khrushchev, the differences could no longer be explained as the fault of a few misguided individuals. Instead, the entire fabric of "revisionism" had to be held accountable. And were not these same trends already under way at home in China? In the face of Peking's repeated threats of intervention, the Americans were steadily expanding their role and build-up in Vietnam, while Chinese setbacks in the Afro-Asian world were also humiliating. Having lost ground to both the Chinese Nationalists and the Russians in Africa, Red China simultaneously watched its revolutionary role fade in Latin America. The bloody abortive Communist grab for power in Indonesia on October 1, 1965, was soon compounded by the Chinese back-down from its threatening posture towards India, which followed concerted American and Russian pressure.

Mao has had a partner without whose collaboration what he was to attempt would have been impossible. Lin Piao is that rare phenomenon, a genuine military genius, with all that this implies in the grasp of essentials and organizational skill. Born in 1907 in the central Yangtze Valley province of Hupei, he has been a committed Communist since' the age of eighteen. A graduate of the fourth class at Whampoa Military Academy (which was established with Russian help to train Kuomintang and Communist officers during their coalition in the early 1920's), Lin joined in the Nanchang uprising of 1927 that saw the birth of the Red Army. Already a veteran of innumerable military engagements during Chiang Kai-shek's campaigns of suppression in the early 1930's against the

THE RED GUARDS

Chinese soviets in Kiangsi, Lin led the First Army Group as an advance force on the "Long March" through southern and western China". to the Yenan refuge near Mongolia. Wounded while fighting the Japanese along the Yellow River in the late 1930's, he went to Russia for medical treatment, and there, the Chinese insist, Lin helped design the defenses of both Leningrad and Stalingrad. Once back in the cave city of Yenan, he became president of the Party School while also training Red Army staff officers. It was Lin Piao who went into Manchuria with some 2,000 cadres upon Japan's surrender in August 1945 and within three years created twelve armies totaling 800,000 men, chiefly outfitted with weapons of the defeated troops -- Japanese, puppet government, and Chinese Nationalist -- taken with Russian co-operation. When the last 680,000 Nationalists surrendered after the October 1948 battles below Mukden and Lin moved through the Great Wall against Tientsin and Peking, the Red Army possessed the military preponderance that was to prove decisive in the civil war.

Lin's performance since he was made Defense Minister in 1959 has made some informed Chinese ask whether he will inherit the revolution and become their "Red Napoleon." He first instituted a thorough reorganization of the People's Liberation Army (P.L.A.) at the top. Marshal Peng Teh-huai, who had led the Chinese People's Volunteers in Korea, went out as Minister, and others dismissed included the Chief of General Staff, General Huang Ko-cheng, and the Directors of Military Training, the Political Department, and Rear Services. This was far more than a mere change in the command structure, for with these men also went plans for transforming the P.L.A. into a more technically proficient, professional military service primarily concerned with national defense. Lin was aided by his new Chief of Staff, General Lo Jui-ching, who over the previous decade had been the architect and head of the immense and dreaded Kung An Pu, or Ministry of Public Security, managing China's omnipresent police, secret police, and "reform through labor" camps, which were reported to have held nearly thirty million at their peak.

After 1959, the P.L.A. became an ardent participant in the Great Leap. Military trucks were used to move coal and iron ore and air force planes to rush spare parts for industry from one part of the country to another. There was a great increase in the use of both troops and demobilized veterans as pioneers in remote regions like Chinese Turkestan. The abolition of all designations of rank two years ago was explained as a return to the "comradely spirit" of military democracy identified with the early guerrilla period, but the internal remaking of the military establishment was more consequential. The terrible hardships experienced by the populace from 1959 to 1962 generated confusion and discontent among the troops, and the cure applied was an intense ideological indoctrination of the military, fortified by a great extension of the role and authority of political commissars.

On the surface, the Party appeared to be assuming a larger role in the P.L.A., as was initially true; but, actually, the enterprise was pursued with such vigor that the military became the most important avenue to training for membership in the Chinese Communist Party. The public idolization of the virtues of "the good Red soldier" was equally significant. In massive campaigns such once obscure troopers as Lei Feng and Wang Chieh, who had lost their lives in service to the cause while fortunately leaving detailed diaries, were presented as models for youth. Although conscientious in the performance of duties, they were shown to have accomplished much by ritualistic study and the daily application of "The Thought of Mao Tse-tung." The vastly expanded role of the P.L.A. in publishing, radio, film production, dramatics, and other popular propaganda ensured that this message got across. It was from this base that the "P.L.A. method" for energizing performance with intense ideological commitment was steadily widened to selected sectors of industry and agriculture. In effect, as Lin Piao reshaped the two-and-a-half-million man military establishment, he was making it "a party within the Party." Older "heroes of the revolution" were moved into semi-retirement to allow ever greater roles for younger disciples, whose mission Lin elaborated publicly in his definitive pronouncement of September 1965 on Red China's commitment to mobilize the "countryside" of Asia, Africa, and Latin America against the "cities" of Western Europe and North America.

Even a Communist elite as closed as that of Red China at the top is not immune to the role of personalities, motivated by their individual experience and aspirations. Through this period several individuals have acted in a manner which illustrates how human they are after all. Chiang Ching achieved her special stature by being Mrs. Mao Tse-tung. Accounts concerning her formative years differ in detail, yet there is sufficient evidence to explain both her insecurity and ambition. Slim, standing about five feet four inches, and handsome in a hard sort of way, according to those who have seen her, she was born fifty-four years ago near Tsinan, the provincial capital of Shantun, into a family in very modest circumstances. When she was about twenty years old and meagerly educated, she found employment in Shanghai at the Tien Tung Movie Company as a bit actress under the name Lan Pin, earning the equivalent of US$14.00 a month. At the time this was a forbidden profession for respectable Chinese daughters -- Left-wing writers and actors were dominant at the studio, and she was caught up in this atmosphere, marrying one of them, Tang La. They were divorced within a year. Poor and lonely, she left the big city, making her way by rail, mule cart, and on foot to the new Communist capital of Yenan, in about 1936.

As a student at Kan Tse Ta Hsueh, the anti-Japanese resistance university, Chiang Ching soon won the special interest of its leading lecturer, Mao Tse-tung. Perhaps a bit maliciously, some Chinese say that the other female students were "ugly" and she submitted her paper in the evening for the teacher's correction. Mao's first wife had been executed by Nationalist warlords at Changsha, as had his brothers, while the second Mrs. Mao, also known as Ho Tze-cheng, had suffered a nervous breakdown following childbirth on the Long March. At this time she was in Russia for medical treatment. (Her eldest son, Mao An-ying, was later killed during the fighting in Korea; a second son, Mao An-ching, studied in Russia and is reported specializing in nuclear science.) Those who should know say that when Mao Tse-tung first asked the Central Committee for a divorce from his second wife it was refused, partly at the insistence of Marshal Ho Lung, the colorful ex-bandit chieftain turned Communist guerrilla leader. Then, when the Central Committee finally did give its assent to Mao's divorce and re-marriage to Chiang Ching, there reportedly were conditions: she must never hold political office -- as do the wives of many prominent Chinese Communists-and even leadership in the All China Federation of Womer was forbidden her. Chiang Ching bore Mao two daughters who later studied at Peking National University (Pei Ta), where they are reported to have been treated like "young mesdemoiselles."

Another attractive girl came to Yenan several years later, but one from a radically different background. Wang Kuang-mei's family, in Tientsin, was one of the "eight big houses" of North China. An ancestor who managed the imperial salt works near Shanhaikwan had built up one of the country's great fortunes. At Catholic Fu Jen University in Peking she had been chosen "Flower of the Institution" in recognition of her beauty and wit; and upon graduation, like many students from Peking during the Sino-Japanese War, she joined the guerrillas who brought her to the Communist cave city headquarters. There, like Chiang Ching, she met a "senior comrade," Liu Shao-chi, who apparently without difficulty divorced his wife to marry her. It is children by the earlier wife who have recently been denouncing Chairman and Mrs. Liu. Wang Kuang-mei has borne Liu Shao-chi several children. Now forty-six years old and standing about five feet one inch, she has become a bit plump, but those who know her say that she is still graceful and "very much a lady."

Once Liu became Chairman of the Central People's Government, Wang Kuang-mei assumed an active public role. She became a member of the Executive Committee of the All China Federation of Women, and two years ago she was the guiding influence in launching the "Four Clean Movement," emphasizing the "cleansing" of past patterns of thought, financial ties, relatives, and personal habits. As the first hostess of the land, she was prominent in the reception of such foreign visitors as the senior Madame Sukarno, and while accompanying Liu on his visits as chief of state to Burma, Pakistan, North Vietnam, Cambodia, and Indonesia, she attracted both attention and favorable comment. The evidence available fails to substantiate recent wall-poster charges in Peking of her scandalous behavior abroad and the bringing home of suitcases full of perfume and other luxuries.

In contrast, although Chiang Ching usually remained in Peking when Mao Tse-tung was on extended trips to other regions of China, she had no known public role. Like nearly all members of the innermost Chinese Communist ruling group, Mrs. Mao and Mrs. Liu lived in the 'tightly restricted enclave of the Chung Nan Hai in the Forbidden City, once the exclusive domain of the imperial family and their retinues of concubines and eunuchs. For all of their long revolutionary association,' it can hardly have been cozy neighborhood.

Among the individuals who came to compose Mao Tse-tung's cabal, one other merits special mention, Chen Po-ta. When I myself met him in Hong Kong two decades ago, I unfortunately lacked the prescience to realize that his role would one day be so crucial. Short, rather fat, and rarely given to humor, his appearance belies his brilliance. Nor is he eloquent on the platform. The story is told that when he returned from Russia and was teaching under an alias at Chung Kuo College in Peking in the early 1930's, he let slip the admission that he really was the author Chen Po-ta - only to be accused by his students of an impersonation. However, the pen of this largely self-educated writer, born sixty-two years ago in

Fukien Province, has had a major influence upon the character of Chinese communism. Early in his career he was a pamphleteer and political muckraker, and his books, like The People's Enemy: Chiang Kai-shek and China's Four Big Rich Families, which detailed the misdeeds of the Kungs, the Soongs, and their allies, did much to discredit the Nationalists among Chinese intellectuals. After the guerrillas brought him to Yenan, following the outbreak of the Sino-Japanese War, Chen moved in close as Mao's political secretary, lecturer at the Party School, and chief of research, shaping long-range Communist policy. He progressed steadily as a manipulator of power, becoming a full member of the Central Committee in 1946, editor-in-chief of Red Flag, the Party's theoretical journal, in 1958, and finally a Politburo member at the Central Committee meeting last August. At present he ranks fourth in Red China, after Mao, Lin, Piao, and Chou En-lai. As the real author of much of "The Thought of Mao Tse-tung," his ideas are being imprinted upon the minds of an entire generation of Chinese-and upon many others as well.

The Great Proletarian Cultural Revolution

Few political ventures in our time have matched the dimensions of the gamble that Mao Tse-tung -- aided and encouraged by intimate associates whom he trusted -- embarked upon late in 1965. At the age of seventy-three, he set about retrieving the revolution's "true" mission'. This was to be accomplished over the objections of the vast majority of the lao kan pu, or veterans of that enormous ruling elite, the twenty-million-member Chinese Communist Party. Yet, he wanted neither to wreck the organization itself nor to destroy many of its leading figures. Instead, he aimed at employing the techniques for compelling individuals to "remake" their thinking through the "brainwashing" and "struggle" sessions that have been such a distinguishing feature of Chinese communism. Formerly these had been used against the Chinese populace, which despite its immense numbers was relatively vulnerable to coercion by the highly organized power-holders, but now these methods were to be utilized against the very men who held office and were skilled in such manipulation.

It was from within the People's Liberation Army that this massive enterprise was initiated. Chen Po-ta emerged as chairman of the inner group guiding the Great Proletarian Cultural Revolution and, for the first time, Chiang Ching appeared on stage as vice-chairman and concurrent adviser to the P.L.A. (For still unexplained reasons, Chief of Staff Lo Jui-ching dropped from public sight at this juncture.) Significantly, the first salvo was fired in Shanghai, where Mao and Lin Piao had consolidated a power base. It came as an attack in the Wen Yi Pao upon Wu Han, the Vice-Mayor of Peking, for a play that this historian and former professor at Tsinghua University had written, entitled The Dismissal of Hai Jui. The theme of the play was the courageous battle against corruption waged by an official within the Ming Dynasty's official court, who returned to the peasants land which had been grabbed by greedy officials. The play was condemned because it depicted a representative of a "former exploiting class" as capable of acting in the interests of the masses.

THE RED GUARDS

In a pattern that was to become characteristic, the same charges were next printed with great fanfare in the <u>Liberation Army Daily</u> in Peking. Only later were they repeated in the <u>Peking People's Daily</u>, the official Party mouthpiece. By December 1965, Wu Han was confessing his errors. The denunciation of Tien Han, another playwright, followed, and in time almost the entire roster of China's prominent writers had been condemned. Although the attacks recalled the "rectification campaign" which followed Mao's invitation for criticism in his "Let a Hundred Flowers Blossom and a Hundred Thoughts Contend" in 1957, the target was still narrow. There is evidence, however, that reveals the hand of that thwarted actress, Mrs. Mao, who was at last having her say in cultural matters. Even that paragon of cultural-political fence-sitting, Kuo Mo-jo -- who is in his mid-seventies and has been Peking's champion of everything from "Supporting the American Negroes' Struggle Against Discrimination" to the Chinese "Committee for World Peace" -- had by spring 1966 to make his public self-criticism.

Meanwhile, the study of "The Thought of Mao Tse-tung" had taken on a fervor never known before in China. In November 1965, Defense Minister Lin Piao announced that the military would become the pacemaker of "politics in command." He stated that for 1966 their chief assignment was to "regard the works of Mao Tse-tung as the highest instructions on all aspects of work over our whole army." The three-by-six-inch, 312 page book, with red waterproof-plastic cover, Quotations from Chairman Mao Tse-tung, was printed in tens of millions of copies. Cadres, young people, railway and bus conductors, and interpreters for visiting trade delegations all carried the volume in their pockets and conspicuously read it aloud to anyone around. While many newspapers and magazines closed down as their staffs experienced "struggle for reformation of thought" and reorganization, those that continued to publish carried banner quotations from Mao across the front page. Both Peking's domestic and foreign broadcasts began programs with lengthy quotations from Mao. It was indoctrination on a scale that inundated the senses.

Schools, colleges, and universities - which were closed in June 1966, supposedly for six months of "curricula reform" - became the objects of very special attention. At such institutions as Pei Ta in Peking, foreign students were transferred to special hostels outside t~ city or encouraged to return home. "Work teams," officially representing the Party but often with P.L.A. support, were sent into all institutions to investigate their faculties. While unauthorized outsiders were excluded, truckloads of peasants and workers arrived on campuses to demonstrate, and professors were then hauled before these staged meetings and made to confess deviation from Mao's teachings. Explanations and self-justification were rarely condoned. Many were compelled to do menial jobs and wear dunce caps proclaiming: "I am an anti-Party intellectual"; while directed mobs on the campuses were often carried away by hysteria, prompting violence and beatings on such a scale that official publications had to urge caution. The announced aim was to forestall the danger that these institutions would train "bourgeois students," who would in turn betray Mao's revolution. As the heated sessions progressed, with the "masses" criticizing the scholar; the compulsion was for all faculty who would remain to conform with Education Minister Ho Wei's pronouncement: "Development of China's part-work part-study and part-farming part-study is a. great victory for Mao Tse-tung's thought." By midsummer the dismissed academic leaders included outstanding men in at least eighteen Chinese colleges and universities. Many of them had been presidents of their institution who had also often served as Party secretaries.

A political bombshell exploded on June 2 and 3, 1966, with the oblique public announcement of a reorganization of the Peking Party Committee. Out went Peng Chen, Mayor of the capital and for four decades an intimate comrade of Mao's; Vice-Mayor Wu Han; the editor of the People's Daily, Teng Ho, who was also secretary of the Peking Party Committee; Fan Hsiang, one of China's leading women and a prominent Communist writer; and Tien Han, the noted playwright and author of Red China's national anthem, who had been attacked earlier. Also sacked were the editorial boards of the authoritative People's Daily, the Peking Evening News, and the fortnightly magazine Frontline On June 4, the now reorganized People's Daily warned: "Any monster or freaks, schemers or careerists who plan to capture our bastion from within and stage in China the ugly drama of Khrushchev's usurpation of Party, Army, and State power will be knocking their heads against a brick wall, lose all standing and reputation, and end in failure."

It soon developed that those forced out in Peking were only a nucleus of the "black gang of conspirators" to be officially vilified most energetically by the P.L.A. press and mass-communications network. Somewhat sporadically, and betraying tortuous political crosscurrents beneath the surface, the campaign spread to the provinces. The chief editor of the Yunnan Daily, Li Meng-wei, was condemned for "vicious" attacks upon the Party and "deliberately and openly opposing the study and application of Mao Tse-tung's thinking." In neighboring Kweichow, Wang Hsiao-chuan, the provincial head of the Party's propaganda department and editor of the Kweichow Daily, was dismissed for "frenzied attacks" upon the Party and socialism. When subordinates are accused in China, it is often a hint that rough treatment is in store for their superiors. This proved to be the case in mid-July when Lu Ting-yi, Director of Propaganda in the Chinese Communist Party since 1948, Minister of Culture and a Vice-Premier, was ousted along with his deputy, Chou Yang. These men had wielded immense influence and their removal meant that an earthquake was sundering the Party. The elevation of Tao Chu, the hard brilliant star of Communist rule in the Central-South Administrative Region and an associate of Lin Piao's, to replace Lu Ting-yi suggested a pattern. Yet, Tao Chu, in turn, fell from grace within a few months as the inner political convulsion began cannibalizing some of its own instigators.

By the early summer of 1966, Red Guards began appearing on the streets of Peking-earlier they had been active on campuses, pasting up "big character posters" denouncing professors slated for "struggle" or dismissal. A young relative of friends of mine, who recently arrived here in Hong Kong from the mainland, participated in this extraordinary movement. "At first there were two kinds of Red Guards," he recalls "One sort wore common clothing with red arm bands; the others were in uniforms supplied by the P.L.A. Although we had been out and working for several years, I joined with my classmates from middle school and organized a band of the first kind. It was a great opportunity for anyone who was frustrated. Each band chose its own name, usually leftist, like 'East Wind, I 'Red Flag Rebels, I or 'East Wind Rebellious Group.' We were free to take on all problems not managed properly. Then, all could play at this. We could catch any teachers we had not liked and beat them. Psychologically, when you are poor, I guess, there is something in beating others down to the same level. We would stop buses, trucks, and trams and climb aboard without tickets or paying. We would tell the driver where to go and if he refused we beat him with our belts; this was usually done by Red Guards in uniform. The police meant nothing. Red Guards would ride two or three on a bicycle, contrary to Peking city ordinance."

On August 18, 1965, the Red Guards became official when one million of them, including those who had performed "Long Marches" from the provinces, paraded through Peking's "Square of Eternal Peace before Mao Tse-tung, Lin Piao, Chou En-lai, Chen Po-ta, Chiang Chi, and Kang Sheng, who comes from Mrs. Mao's hometown in Shantung and is a potent, shadowy ally with control in Party intelligence and security activities. There was now an effort to screen out of the Rei Guards any with "undesirable" backgrounds and to limit participation to children of "revolutionary classes," for in Red China the sins of the fathers are officially visited upon their children. The targets for sanctioned attack became the "black six classes," which included the families of former landlords, rich peasants, counter-revolutionaries, "bad elements," rightists, and bourgeois capitalists. Potentially, the, numbered perhaps a third of Peking's population of nearly five million.

Bands of Red Guards started a street-by- street search of hot in Peking, checking references and "historical background." Anyone arbitrarily judged "black" was liable to have his belongings seized:, furniture, furs, clothing, bedding, and books were then piled outside and either burned on the streets or hauled to public warehouses. Man a family had to beg for permission to keep a bed, comforter, and pot. Red Guards appear to have taken a vindictive delight in sacking private, libraries, for which Peking was noted. As part of the new class struggle "100 examples" for "breaking the old and establishing the new" were printed by the "Banner Defending Red Guards School of Mao Tse-tung' Doctrine" (students chose this name – formerly it had been Number 2 Middle School). A selection of these "rules" is revealing:

> (24) House-owners riding on the backs of the people and sucking blood of the people in post-liberation days, we hereby warn you despicable swine to hand over quickly all your private-owned houses to the state, since the existence of you vampires can never be tolerated in the socialist society.

> (43) Bourgeois habits of keeping crickets, fish, cats, and dogs are not allowed to exist among the Chinese people. Anyone violating this rule shall be held responsible for all consequences.

> (48) Without approval of the masses, all monsters and demons, sons of bitches of the black gang, are not allowed to receive their salaries. We must cut salaries of these old and despicable swine and give them only a subsistence allowance.

(68) The names of authors, players, and directors must at once be eliminated from all performances or literary and art broadcasts so as to block the road to personal fame and gain.

(74) The wearing of bracelets, earrings, longevity symbols and other feudal things is banned.

A furious attempt was made to implement the "rule" calling for resettling "black six class" families. Special trains were assigned and families herded aboard, often consigned to their ancestral counties and watched en route by Red Guards. The People's Communes, however, refused to accept city-folk who did not know how to farm and would be a burden on food supplies, so the hapless families were again loaded onto trains and given passes to return to Peking. With their homes already commandeered, many went to the police, pleading, "What do we do?" - but the best the police could usually offer was only another railway pass to return to the designated commune and an affidavit stating what the family's ration had been in Peking. Perhaps 50,000 persons were thus shuttled about from Peking before September 10, 1966, when the turmoil became so great that authorities published the "ten point ordinance" of restraint, which inhibited the beating and insulting of families of the "black six classes." Estimates are not available from firsthand participants in most of the other cities of China. The Red Guards, encouraged to believe themselves righteous, operated on a scale which substantially accounts for the confusion that beset China's transport and much else.

Another accomplishment of the Red Guards was reported in a New China News Agency broadcast from Peking:

On the afternoon of August 24, a revolutionary fire was ignited in the Central Institute of Arts to destroy the sculptures of emperors, kings, generals, ministers, scholars and beauties, images of Buddha, and niches for the Buddha sculptures. The revolutionary students and teachers of the Institute said: "What we have destroyed and crushed are not only a few sculptures, but the whole old world."

The masses of revolutionary students and teachers of the Central Institute of Arts, together with the revolutionary students and teachers of other fraternal schools and institutes of higher learning, such as the Peking Normal College and others who carne to support them and join their rebellion, were in high spirits. They cast out from their classrooms, studios, and storerooms the sculptures of the Goddess of Mercy, princes, the fierce-looking gods of Shu Yu and Yu Lu which they had collected from various temples in China, the stone horses and stone tigers which they had collected from paths in front of imperial tombs, and the sculptures of King David of Israel, of the "hero" David in the Bible, of the "goddess of love and beauty" Venus of Greek legends, of Apollo, and so forth, which had been purchased abroad, and they completely destroyed these by burning and crushing.

The Peking broadcast further explained:

THE RED GUARDS

After liberation, the Central Institute of Arts entirely copied the system of bourgeois institutes in the West, giving students a European bourgeois education in the arts under the control of a number of anti-Party and anti-socialist rightists. Those rightists and reactionary academic "authorities" treated the works of ancient and foreign "venerable masters" as treasures and distributed many copies to various party of the country. From enrollment to graduation, all students were required to crawl in front of these "venerable masters" to paint and worship them.

Now the revolutionary storm of sweeping away all old ideas, old culture, old customs, and old habits of the exploiting classes has swept the whole country. The revolutionary students and teachers of the Institute have carried axes, picks, and iron spikes to crush the sculptures to pieces. The wooden Buddha sculptures and niches were burned by the revolutionary masses. All the demons and monsters in this Institute of Arts were burned to ashes. [Until this happened Communist China had been justly proud of great achievements in uncovering archeological treasures of the past and in museum science.]

From August 1 to 12, 1966, the Party's Central Committee met in Peking for its first plenary session in four years. The events surrounding this curious meeting are still obscure and clouded by rumors, including reports of attempted movements by Red Army units to influence the outcome. Contrary to all past practice, outsiders were evidently admitted, and there are indications that Mao and Lin packed the gathering with a claque of Red Guards. Certainly, the results tend to confirm this suspicion. The Politburo, formally known as the Standing Committee of the Political Bureau of the Central Committee, was revamped to include Mao's nominees: Chen Po-ta, Tao Chu, and Kang Sheng. From this meeting on, Lin Piao openly and officially became Mao's "Closest comrade in arms" and designated heir. Equally crucial, the "Great Proletarian Cultural Revolution" assumed a new emphasis. Whereas formerly it had been aimed against vestiges of the old order, it was now also directed against "power holders within the Party who are taking the capitalist road" (by Chinese Communist definition this meant they were "revisionist" heretics).

Another significant development soon became apparent. Traditional mass organizations of the Party, especially the All China Federation of Women and the hundred -million- member Youth Corps, had been immobilized and partially dismantled. The "100 examples" quoted from above included a provision requiring all Youth Corps members to remove their badges, "thus uprooting that poisonous weed." The field of mass mobilization and "struggle" was now to bereserved for the P.L.A.'s chosen instrument, the Red Guards.

That their efforts were to be focused against specific targets was emphasized by Premier Chou En-lai in a speech to a Red Guards, rally in Peking on August 31. Asking them to emulate the P.L.A.'s "three main rules for discipline and eight points for attention," he said:

THE RED GUARDS

The Red Guards must be built into a highly organized and disciplined militant army with a high level of political consciousness and become the reliable reserve force of the Liberation Army.

They were to pattern themselves on an historical model: the peasant Red Guards whom Mao had eulogized for aiding revolutionary troops in Hunan from 1926 to 1928. To ensure direction, "control squads" organized with military assistance were "seeded" among the, teeming bands of youngsters on the streets. Even Lin Piao cautioned the vigilantes:

Coercion or force in the struggle against them [the "black six classes" and other rnisguided folk] can only touch their skins. Only by reasoning is it possible to touch their souls.

Yet, the reverse happened. Most of the Red Guards vented a generalized hostility and made of hate a fervent faith. They "reformed" tailors, cobblers, barbers who gave "Hong Kong style" haircuts, and street peddlers by seizing their fruits and vegetables. Some were flogged with ropes. Peking's few remaining houses of religious worship also felt their anger. While red flags appeared above the Roman Catholic South Cathedral, a carved stone cross was broken off, and statues of Christ and the Virgin Mary were destroyed. Religious pictures were ripped and windows broken. The Protestant church was also redecorated (with a bust of Mao placed in the center); a mosque was similarly invaded; and Buddhist statues were removed from parks and temples. Public signs were torn down and streets renamed, the one in front of the Russian Embassy becoming "Street for Struggle Against Revisionism."

With the military providing logistics-such as hostels, feeding stations, and some transport-Red Guards from Peking fanned out over the country to "exchange revolutionary experience" and energize new vigilante groups. From distant Manchuria and South China, other Guards hiked on "Long Marches" of a month or more to the capital, where on October 18, 1966, a reported one and a half million paraded in the Tien An Men Square. By the end of the year more than nine million Red Guards had walked or ridden into Peking, and the authorities had to turn away many because of overcrowding. Some seized the opportunity to walk off their jobs, escaping unwanted assignments; youngsters – and others not so young – left frontier construction and resettlement projects in remote Central Asia and returned home.

The confusion caused by these millions of youths turned loose upon the society was compounded as provincial, county, and city Party chiefs responded by mustering their own Red Guards. As with any mass campaign in China, some bands were merely local duplicates of groups in the capital, but far more were created to protect the authority of senior Party officials in their bailiwicks. Conflicting and undoubtedly often exaggerated "big character posters" pasted up in Peking and other cities told of bloody skirmishes as "outside" Red Guards invaded the territory of local groups. In this atmosphere of mobilized hysteria, the Red Guards had become the outer instruments for wielding power in the labyrinth of the Party hierarchy, and the men marked for destruction by Mao and his associates were by now fully alerted and determined to hold on to their own. Liu Shao-chi, Teng Hsiao-ping, the Secretary General of the Party, and their veteran appointees and associates might "bend like the bamboo" in the wind of Mao's fury, but they had no intention of abandoning either their predominant. strength in the Party or their conviction of what was sound for Communist China.

Toward the end of January 1967, when the Mao-Lin group may have felt that they were on the threshold of victory, there was a startling announcement by the New China News Agency:

> *The Taiyuan Municipal Revolutionary Committee, the new organ of power for the revolutionary people in this North China industrial city, has been set up.... This was done by the local proletarian revolutionaries, who have forged a great alliance in the course of the struggle to seize power. The Shansi Provincial Revolutionary Rebel General Headquarters [the local ad hoc umbrella under which the Great Proletarian Cultural Revolution was promoted by the Red Guards and their allies] has officially granted this organ the right to exercise power in political, economic, and cultural affairs in Taiyuan... pending general elections according to the Paris Commune principle.*

The following week in Shanghai, according to wall posters, a "Provisional Shanghai People's Commune Committee" took over all power from the former City Council and the City Committee of the Chinese Communist Party. Far to the southwest in Kweiyang, it was announced that a "Provincial Proletarian Revolutionary Rebel Command" had seized power from the former government and Party authorities. It was acting until a "Kweichow Provincial Revolutionary Committee of Mao Tse-tung's Thought" could be established, whose members should be "nominated and elected by the Revolutionary Rebels in a democratic way."

Mao and his ghost writer, Chen Po-ta, have long been enamored; of that miscarried venture, the Paris Commune of 1871, to which Karl Marx also devoted such emotional attention. Evidently, A has matter little to them that this Parisian insurrection managed power for only the brief period from March 18 to May 29, 1871, when the monarchists recaptured the capital, executed many Communards, and deported others to New Caledonia in the South Pacific. This supposedly was the firs genuine example of a "workers republic." Now, nearly nine years a engineering the People's Communes for the Chinese peasants, Mao introducing an equally drastic innovation for the cities, and one that, he had been impatient to see realized. At this stage in Red China, the inauguration of communes in cities held another attraction: it offered an opportunity for the architects of the "Great Proletarian Cultural Revolution," including the P.L.A., the Red Guards and "revolutionary rebel cadres" allied with them, to usurp authority from the regular Communist Party hierarchy.

Mao's commune venture for the cities, however, proved even more transient than the one attempted ninety-six years ago in Paris. 1n Shanghai, with its population of roughly ten million, what was intended to have been quite a dramatic commune enterprise bogged down for even in that "pacesetter" city which had become the prime Mao-Lin stronghold, the allied leaders of the new revolution were unable to agree on how to make the commune work. As confusion stalled the economy, the P.L.A. took over the management of the post office, airport, harbor, railways, newspapers, and some of the factories and radio stations. Elsewhere in China pronouncements were made about "Rebel Revolutionary Committees," but there is scant hard evidence that these were much more than paper gambits. The Mao-Lin innovators were discovering that, although no one might openly defy Mao and his teachings, Communist Party members were accomplished in the Chinese talent for cloaking actual sabotage with apparent acquiescence. They stalled, renamed their local Party machinery, and gave lip service to Mao's "Thoughts," but they hung on to position and power and made it rough for any interloper. Furthermore, Lin Piao's control over the P.L.A. proved to be not so complete as anticipated. Lin had with him most of the harsh, younger activists. He had openly denounced Chu. Teh, the eighty-one-year-old retired Commander in Chief of the Red Army, and Ho Lung; but within the upper levels of the military – particularly in Central, West, and Northwest China – respected commanders and their staffs still felt binding ties to the regular Party organization dominated by Liu Shao-chi and Teng Hsiao-ping. These loyalties were not eroded by Red Guard and wall-poster denunciations of Liu, his wife, Teng, and other veteran comrades. Instead, such juvenile political witch-hunting seems to have been interpreted as a threat to their entire generation of lao kan pu, or old revolutionary cadres.

Officially, Mao and Lin backtracked for even more compelling reasons: the economy was sagging ominously and cherished instruments of Communist control were slipping. Already in the autumn of 1966, Chou En-lai, who as Premier had stood with Mao while also urging restraint in dealing with misguided Party leaders, had warned that nothing must interfere with production. His plea proved futile. Not only did millions of Red Guards cripple China's transport and curtail output as they "struggled" with factory workers trying to keep the Guards out of their plants, but Chinese peasants also took quick advantage of conflict among Party cadres to get back some of their own. As the time approached for the annual settling of accounts in People's Communes before the Chinese New Year (the celebration of this ancient and most important holiday was officially banned this year), Peking inveighed against "economism." Peasants were parceling out among themselves commune cash reserves intended for investment in the coming year's crop. They were also extending their private garden plots and occasionally subdividing fields according to pre-1958 ownership, while state deliveries of grain were dwindling as peasants sold their own and commune produce directly to the cities. Even in the factories, contending cadres won support for their factions by raising pay scales and by other "capitalist" maneuvers.

With a volte-face possible only in a totalitarian state, the Peking press and radio called upon everyone to mobilize for spring planting. "Grasp revolution and make production" suddenly became the slogan. Throughout the winter Chou En-lai had tried to save his most valued economic administrators from the vigilantes. In February 1967, he admonished a rally: "I am not calm in my mind about the death of Chang Lin-chih" (this Minister of Coal Production reportedly died following forty days of interrogation by Red Guards); and he lectured the youngsters about the nonsense of their trying to take over the Peking Ministry of Public

THE RED GUARDS

Security. According to Chou: "The Party Centre is very displeased to see leaders made to wear dunce caps and name cards around their necks.... old leaders are an asset of the Party, there are extremely few who are really bad. Such a manner of treatment is unnecessary even toward Peng Cheng [the ousted Mayor of Peking]."

Purportedly to ensure the spring planting, the P.L.A. was ordered into the countryside to assist cadres in the People's Communes. These rural cadres supervising the peasants number roughly ten to ., every soldier in the P.L.A., so at best the P.L.A. could only concentrate upon the most critical provinces, which are in the regions with potential food surpluses. The evidence has yet to come in as to whether they can compel the cadres, who must both survive among and rely upon the peasants, to take back the "small freedoms" so cherished on the land.

A major political ground swell once set in motion has a morn turn of its own, immune even to the will of its initiators. Although the crisis confronting China's economy dictated a moratorium on political fighting, Mao, Lin, and their allies could hardly allow this without discrediting their cause, so in March and early April 1967 they narrowed heir target. The chief culprit became "the greatest power-holder who takes the capitalist path within the Party, thinks only about capitalism and talks only about capitalism. His voice is the great exposure of hi: dirty bourgeois soul." Several hundred thousand parading in Peking shouted: "He is the Khrushchev beside us." Thus were Liu Shao-chi, now being condemned for "conducting an anti-Party policy for the pas: twenty-two years," and his classic volume, How To Be a Good Communist, identified. His fellow villains included Teng Hsiao-ping, Tao Chu (who had allegedly joined their ranks), and a nucleus of other senior Party veterans. Such histrionics served chiefly to cloak the expansion of Lin Piao's military rule into traditional preserves of the Party. Although publicly dominating the arena by the sacrosanct use of Mao's name and stature, fragments of available information indicate that the Mao-Lin group still had to "capture" the majority of China's provinces. Perhaps to discourage greater union among their opponents and also to offer inducements to those who might switch camps, the "struggle" was conducted within the special bounds of tolerance that operate among China's senior Party members. Should the monumental maneuvering for control break into outright physical violence between opposing factions of the Communist Party, then it is questionable - can China remain a unified state.

Largely dispensing with the discredited Red Guards, as Mao and Lin have done, also begs the question of what to do next with the generation whose emotions they have exploited. For no longer can the youth of China, who number roughly a half of its some 780 million inhabitants, believe in the infallibility and integrity of their rulers. The frustration and hatred that Mao, Lin, and their associates have muster' in this angry "class struggle" against selected elements in the society, and their opponents could boomerang. Mao is old; Lin's health is poo and their trusted younger military allies lack even the patina of genuine revolutionary sanction. Requiring middle-school students to be tested, as they are now, upon memorizing a hundred quotations from Mao Tsetung must prove only a temporary opiate for the mental processes. In a larger sense, Mao's original betrayal of the aspirations of Chinese intellectuals to make theirs a decent society may now come back to hauunt him and his purpose.

AMERICAN UNIVERSITIES FIELD STAFF,

About the writer:

ALBERT RAVENHOLT has worked on Asia and the Western Pacific since before World War II, serving as a correspondent in China, India, Burma, Indochina, and the Philippines. In 1947, as a fellow of the Institute of Current World Affairs, he went to Harvard University for advanced study of Far Eastern history and Chinese language. In 1948 he returned to China to cover the civil war. Mr. Ravenholt joined the Field Staff at its founding in 1951 and covers large areas of Asia from his base in Manila. He has written for *Foreign Affairs*, *The Reporter*, the *Chicago Daily News Foreign Service*, and other magazines, in addition to his regular Fieldstaff Reports. Published works include reports for the *Encyclopaedia Britannica Book of the Year* and the *World Book Yearbook*, a book entitled *The Philippines; a Young Republic on the Move*, and chapters in other volumes. Although a generalist on East Asian and Southeast Asian affairs, Mr. Ravenholt maintains a specialized knowledge of Asian and tropical agriculture.

University Sponsors: University of Alabama · Brown University · California Institute of Technology · Dartmouth College · University of Hawaii
Indiana University · University of Kansas · Louisiana State University · Michigan State University · Tulane University · University of Wisconsin

EAST ASIA SERIES,

CAN ONE BILLION CHINESE FEED THEMSELVES?

by Albert Ravenholt

April 1971

Chinese Communist representatives here in recent months repeatedly have referred to theirs as a country that will soon number a billion people. They use the phrase *shih wan wan,* or literally ten, ten thousand, ten thousand. Although their comments are entirely unofficial and were made in private discussions with interested Westerners, their attitude has been one of pride, rather than an expression of concern Among the attributes of Red China's power will be a billion human beings.

This claim compels a critical look at what has been happening to the population of China. Inevitably, it also raises a host of questions. Why has the largest single ethnic component of humanity accelerated in numbers at a pace that promises this prospect? What will and can the Red Mandarins who rule from within the massive walls of the ancient Imperial City of Peking do to curb such a rate of increase? What are the implications for China's modernization, both economically and militarily? And, most fundamental of all, can the "good earth" be made to feed such numbers in time and by what means?

How Many Chinese?

The number of China's inhabitants long has prompted speculation, and hypotheses have been more available than facts concerning this "one - fourth of humanity." For the very size of the largest concentration of people on our planet fascinated scholars and officials both in the "Middle Kingdom," where regular large-scale census taking first evolved to facilitate taxation, and abroad. At the start of the twelfth century, the Chinese appear to have totaled about 100 million, according to Jacques Gernet in his intriguing account, *Daily Life in China on the Eve of the Mongol Invasion, 1250-1276*. Yet, three centuries later, as of about 1400, the population of China numbered some 65 million in the judgment of Ping-ti Ho, who, in his *Studies on the Population of China, 1368-1953*, has written the most authoritative account.

The loss of life that resulted as the "Golden Horde" of the Mongols plundered and massacred was only one of the cruel periodic checks that warfare inflicted upon the Chinese population. Late in the Ming Dynasty (1368-1644), Szechuan in the far west adjoining the mountain ranges of Tibet and today the most populous of all the provinces suffered an extraordinarily cataclysmic loss of inhabitants. The bandit chieftain Chang Hsien-chung slaughtered most residents in one *hsien*, or county, after the next. Apparently, he was a short man, since legend credits him with stretching a rope across the main street of a town and disposing of anyone unable to walk upright under it. Historians have yet to fit together a comprehensive account of this depopulation of much of China's richest hinterland. Certain it is that the idle lands were again brought under cultivation often by immigrants even from distant Canton. Possibly the costliest episode in human lives coincided with the Taiping Rebellion in the mid nineteenth century. Western estimates of those killed both by rebels and the Manchu Dynasty's repression of the uprising and related fighting have ranged from 15 to 30 million. Ping-ti Ho in his above-mentioned *Studies* cites a fearful and telling indication of the casualties of this terrible upheaval. He shows that from the imperial census of 1850 until the Communists conducted their census in 1953 there was a decline in the combined population of the provinces of Chekiang, Anhwei, and Kiangsi of over 32 million; only part of the region devastated by the Taiping Rebellion, these three provinces after a full century had not recovered their earlier numbers.

Other disasters also curbed China's population. The late nineteenth century Moslem uprising in the Northwest and the great drought and famine of 1877-78 cost at least several million lives. Another drought and famine afflicted this region of the upper Yellow River in the late 1920s. Then came the great floods of the Yangtze River, especially in 1931, that washed away entire communities. Fighting between the Nationalists and Communists in the early 1930s largely depopulated many counties in Kiangsi Province as both sides pursued a scorched earth policy. A decade later, this writer found extensive rice fields in the region still overgrown with grass. The Sino-Japanese War that began in 1937 following the earlier struggles in Manchuria was cruel to civilians and military alike. In 1938, the Nationalists blasted the dikes of the Yellow River, shifting its course south through the Huai River basin to the sea; their objective was to block the advance of Japanese armies from the north. In the process, they flooded out several millions of households and the loss of life can only be estimated. During this war, 14 million men were conscripted into the Chinese Nationalist armies. The late Dr. Chiang Mon-lin, former Chancellor of Peking National University who became Secretary General of the Executive Yuan after V-J Day, said only some three million of these survived in the armies. Some of the missing had deserted. Most of the others died of wounds or disease; many were seen to drop in the line of march along the roadside and left to themselves. In addition, there were the losses among the provincial forces, among the Chinese Communist armies who fought the Japanese in North, Central, and East China, and among the puppet troops conscripted by the occupying Japanese. Having covered eight campaigns with Chinese armies, to me Ping-ti Ho's estimate of 15 to 20 million total casualties caused by the

CHINA'S POPULATION PRESSURES

Sino Japanese struggle appears conservative. Communist figures for killed, wounded, and missing on both sides before the civil war was concluded in 1950 add up to over another three million and do not include civilian losses.

It is against this background of often chronic and depopulating warfare and natural calamities that the increase in China's inhabitants must be considered. In the preface to his *Studies,* which include investigation of numerous local histories, Ping-ti Ho writes: In the history of population growth in China, no period is more important than the two centuries from 1650 to 1850. Under unusually favorably material conditions and the benevolent despotism of the early Manchu rulers, the population apparently trebled and reached perhaps 430 million by 1850.

Major agricultural innovations preceded or coincided with this population expansion. Sorghum, or *kaoliang* as the Chinese know it, originated in Africa. When the Mongols opened trade routes from Europe and the Middle East across Central Asia, sorghum evidently was introduced to North China. As a drought-tolerant crop it proved an important staple, supplementing reliance upon wheat, barley, and millet. More consequential was the bringing of new, earlier maturing varieties of rice to China. Although rice had been cultivated as far back as the reign of the legendary Emperor Chen-Nung in 2700 B.C., these were late maturing varieties requiring in most of the Yangtze Basin almost an entire growing season to mature. From the Hindu Champa Kingdom on the central coast of what today is Vietnam, Sung Dynasty Emperor Chen-tsung (998-1022) introduced an earlier maturing variety of rice. As this became more widely propagated, it led to development of strains that historical accounts indicate could be harvested within two months after transplanting seedlings into the field -- per crop yields usually were lower than on longer maturing varieties. Several important developments resulted. Although these strains appear to have been photosensitive, in time there evolved both early and late season types. This allowed farmers to harvest at least one crop in a year when flood or drought made either end of the growing season unproductive. Aside from facilitating double cropping, in some regions with winter wheat and other grains or oil seed crops, it also encouraged expansion of rice terraces and irrigation canals onto theretofore unused and often higher ground. Although the innovations required some time to be widely adopted, there resulted both an expansion in per land unit yields and area under cultivation as Chinese farmers practiced their traditionally superior conservation of soil fertility in paddy fields, including application of animal manure and human "night soil."

The introduction of American food plants came on the heels of these innovations in rice cultivation. These new economic plant introductions to Asia, most of them carried by Spanish priests on galleons from Acapulco to
the Philippines, where Christianization and colonization were initiated in 1565, eventually numbered about 200. A few decades earlier, the Portuguese sailing around Africa also had carried a few American food plants to Goa in India, Malacca on the west coast of Malaya and even to Macao on China's southern coast. The Portuguese, however, had only limited access to the most important centers of plant cultivation in the Americas. Most consequential of these new food crops that reached China

was the sweet potato many centuries earlier the yam, *Dioscorea alata,* originating in the hinterland of northern Assam and Burma had spread southeast into Indonesia and Oceania and west through India. The American sweet potato, *Ipomoea batatas,* which usually produced more numerous and smaller tubers, traveled around the globe with remarkable speed, often following after European colonial expansion. Its advantages over the yam were many; it was easier to cultivate, matured quicker, yielded more heavily, was adapted to many types of soil and proved relatively drought resistant.

Somewhat later came the so-called Irish potato, *Solanum tuberosum,* which had originated in the highlands of the Andes. As was to be expected, this tuber found favor chiefly with farmers in the colder climates of China's hinterland from Manchuria through the Northwest to Szechuan -- by contrast the sweet potato was grown primarily in the warmer regions of the Yangtze Valley uplands and South China. Corn and peanuts likewise became important crops for Chinese farmers beginning in the seventeenth century. Like the other introductions, they encouraged clearing of forested mountainsides to allow planting of these crops that yielded comparatively greater tonnages of staple food under soil and climate conditions less favorable than those demanded for rice and wheat.

Scholars who have differed over whether corn and sweet potatoes first reached China overland from the Southwest via Yunnan or by sea along the east coast will be alert to recent scientific discoveries in India. In the mountain valleys of the eastern Himalayas, usually between 4,000 and 6,000 feet, Indian researchers have found primitive type corn plants resembling the ancestors of corn in the Americas. Related type corn plants have been reported from the Patkoi Mountains between India and Burma and the uplands of Laos. This accumulating evidence suggests that corn actually had two ancestral homes on our planet rather than only one in the Americas as formerly assumed. The more primitive type corn plant from the Sino-Himalayas never was developed to become economically important like the one from the Americas, but it could account for the early Chinese historical references to corn entering the Empire over the mountains from the Southwest. It is possible, too, that a confusion of description between yams and sweet potatoes -- a mistake that still persists in Western supermarkets -- explains early Chinese references to this type of tuber, i.e., the *Dioscorea alata* or others of the same genus originating in Southeast Asia, as also being introduced over the mountains from the Southwest to become an additional source of food.

Population and the Communists

True to traditions of earlier new dynasties in China, the Communists, after establishing their Central Peoples Government in Peking on October 1, 1949, concentrated upon consolidation of their rule-albeit with revolutionary dimensions-and rehabilitation of the war-ravaged economy. As was to be expected of a vigorous regime, one of their first national concerns was a census of the inhabitants. Some foreign observers have found fault with the enumeration of the population as of the 24-hour period between midnight of June 30 and midnight of July 1, 1953; it has been argued that it was not a true census in the technical definition of such an exercise, that the two and one-half million officials, students, Party cadres, and others mobilized for the task may have been influenced by extraneous political considerations and incomplete details have been made public. Yet, there is no disputing that this was by far the most comprehensive, best organized, and meaningful tabulation of the Chinese in over a century, and possibly on record. This writer is persuaded that the Communist officials came as close as they could to an accurate enumeration with their adjusted total of 582,603,417, which usually is rounded out to 583 million Chinese.

What has become of China's population over the subsequent 18 years must rate as the world's greatest demographic mystery. Officials in Peking have been reluctant to release exact figures, although individual leaders periodically have made reference to China's numbers. Lack of exact data may have contributed to this hesitation. More consequential, however, was the long continued dispute within the *Chung Yang,* or Central Authority, over the critical issue of whether curbing their rate of population increase was necessary and in their national revolutionary interest. Like some other disciples of Karl Marx, the Chinese Communists upon seizing power assumed that socialism somehow speedily would solve the problems of production. And during the early years of Communist rule this almost seemed possible; redistribution of land gave peasants a new incentive to improve farming practices while peace for the first time in decades allowed restoration of irrigation systems, extension of railroads and roads and reapplication of the Chinese genius to productive pursuits. Inevitably, it also encouraged the Confucian concern for fortifying the family by providing numerous male descendants although the political order had changed, ancient social values still dominated in the countryside. Despite the evident prosperity of Red China during the early and mid-1950s, a number of Democratic League leaders who had joined with the Communists to create the new regime cautioned that population control was essential to generating capital for industrialization through savings from agriculture and for raising living standards. Their spasmodic efforts were countered by other leaders, both Communist and non-Communist, who refurbished Sun Yat-sen's arguments advanced four decades earlier that China must compensate with numbers for what she lacked in technology. This view triumphed with Mao Tse-tung's dictum, which became gospel with the Great Leap Forward after 1957, that "people are capital" -- the more you have the faster you can develop, provided they are properly motivated and organized, whether in labor brigades or "peoples communes," and so made to produce more than they consume.

Two other developments had a major effect upon population growth. First was the Communist prohibition of infanticide; it was lent authority by the sense of moral righteousness enveloping the revolution in its early days of ascendancy. Missionary and other doctors who worked in the densely inhabited rural regions like the Chengtu Plain of Szechuan before the Communist victory found infanticide a little discussed yet prevalent practice. Even in the great city of Shanghai before World War 11 several hundred newborn infants were abandoned on the streets in a single night. Second was the immensely successful Communist effort in sanitation, public health, and preventive medicine, which must rate as their greatest single physical achievement to date. National enterprises, including the "Anti-U.S. Germ Warfare Campaign" during the Korean War, involved the entire population in massive campaigns to "eliminate " -- in practice radically to reduce -- flies, dogs, rats, and other pests. "Peoples Organizations," such as the All China Federation of Women, and national groups of students and workers joined with Party cadres to insure effective vaccination for infectious diseases and, with the help of "street committees," enforce public health as China never had experienced before.

Demographic consequences of such enormous effort necessarily involve conjecture. It seems realistic, however, to accept the official assumption that from the 1953 census through the summer of 1958 China's population increased at a net rate of approximately 2.5 per cent annually. This is the figure that Premier Chou En-lai and other leaders on several occasions during this period mentioned to visitors as the basis on which they were planning. When contrasted with what similar reductions in infant mortality and morbidity accomplished elsewhere in Asia, the figure appears conservative. After the peasants of China were corralled into Peoples Communes in the grim and tumultuous autumn of 1958, this picture changed radically. The rural populace now turned against the regime they felt had betrayed them by depriving them of their land and livestock. Peasants sabotaged production and frequently fought the cadres enforcing the hated new measures that included commune kitchens and other radical changes in rural life. The calamity was compounded through the crop years of 1959, 1960, and 1961 -- the "three bad seasons" -- when the weather, so critical for much of Chinese agriculture, caused both drought and floods in differing regions. For example, in the late summer and fall of 1961 unseasonable typhoons virtually wiped out the Manchurian soya bean crop, vital for cooking oil and protein. Famine again plagued localized regions, and malnutrition became a national problem.' Although China now became a major importer of food, including over five million tons of wheat annually chiefly from Canada and Australia, this helped mostly a few cities. During these years, certainly the birthrate was curbed -- protein deficiencies disturbed female ovulation as reported by doctors from a number of regions -- and the death rate climbed as those weakened by inadequate diets succumbed to diseases they otherwise might have resisted. It seems probable that for the fiscal years ending June 30, 1959, 1960, 1961, and 1962 China's population increased annually by perhaps 1.5 per cent.

By the summer of 1962, the reforms had begun to work for which former Chief of State Liu Shaochi, Communist Party Secretary General Teng Hsiao-ping, and other pragmatic leaders since have been pilloried. Incentives, though modest, had been restored to the peasants; their private garden plots, the right to eat at home, raise their own pigs and chickens, and sell surplus produce on free markets. Commune management had been decentralized to the production team, usually corresponding to the former village unit, where accounts also were kept so farmers could see the harvest with which they were credited and what share went to controlled state purchases. Agriculture became the "leading sector" and the headlong rush toward overnight industrialization was abandoned. For the first time, production and distribution of chemical fertilizer became a key concern of top officials in Peking. And more modest, practical water control schemes were emphasized. As the industrial sector also responded to rational management policies, prosperity brought an easing of circumstances for all Chinese, although rationing continued. The health of the populace improved greatly. Predictably, and this was indicated by fragmentary reports, the rate of population increase climbed, probably averaging an annual increment of again 2.5 per cent through the summer of 1967.

During the prosperous era of the early and mid 1960s, a new demographic influence became important. With Mao Tse-tung on the sidelines of power and his theory of "more people, more development" discredited, for the first time there was an approximation of unity among the leaders in office about the importance of curbing China's rate of population increase. Even in the 1950s there had been crude attempts to popularize birth control, without, however, full official backing or reliable contraceptives. Throughout the early 1960s doctors who came out to Hong Kong from China usually reported their truly effective means was abortion and its consequential use was limited to the cities. Peasants who expected some day to recover ownership of their land and were disenchanted with the social experiments of the new regime generally refused to pay attention to proposals of limiting family size and held to their Confucian convictions. Beginning in the cities during the 1960s, the Communists applied more compelling techniques. Young people aspiring to become good Communists were firmly advised they must marry late and then only with Party approval, so they could dedicate their all to the revolution. Factories began intensive indoctrination of workers in family planning. Control over housing, maternity leave, and the numerous other compulsions an authoritarian state commands were employed. Where the Communist health authorities originally had doubted the effectiveness of intrauterine devices and the pill, they now began serious research, small scale manufacture, and testing of these methods of birth control.

These promising beginnings at curbing population growth might have yielded earlier and far more significant results but for the riotous "Great Proletarian Cultural Revolution" that engulfed China starting late in 1966.1 Convinced that "his" revolution was being betrayed by "power holders within the Party taking the capitalist road," Mao Tse-tung and a few key intimates led by his wife, Chiang Ching, joined forces with the Red Army to first discredit and then destroy the existing government and party structure. Indications suggest Mao was prompted partly by the Sino-Soviet split of the early 1960s which he read as evidence of the "revisionist tendencies" of the Russian leaders. Their example, he concluded during the mid-1960s, was being followed by Central Peoples Government Chairman Liu Shao-chi and most of his senior comrades in office -- Mao had stepped down as Chief of State in 1959, retaining his title as head of the Party but not control of its organization.

Consequences for China of this internal ideological and power struggle were traumatic as millions of Red Guards made "long marches" across the land to demonstrate in Peking and factions struggled violently for control of cities and provinces. Mao and the Red Army, led by his anointed heir, Marshal Lin Piao, formalized their triumph at the Party Congress in the spring of 1969. They have yet to recreate a complete national Party organization, officially adopt the promised new constitution, or create a new civilian government. Instead, with the exception of a few centers such as Shanghai, China today is ruled by the military who increasingly are assuming concurrent civilian titles. Many of the idealistic, young Red Guards, after their heady taste of power in helping wreck the former order of rule, have been banished to remote frontiers of Manchuria and Inner Asia to "learn from the peasants." Here they share in the harsh tasks of building roads, canals, and other public works with hoes, wheelbarrows, and baskets on bamboo carrying-poles and construction methods in use since the emperors first diked the Yellow River to keep it within bounds some 30-odd centuries ago.

As Red China has returned to more normal ways over the past two years, the decision makers in Peking have devoted increasing attention to curbing population growth. Propaganda for limiting births now is national and pervasive. The "barefoot doctors," who as briefly trained medical first aid personnel are the rural extension of Mao's new "peoples medicine," are supposed to indoctrinate every peasant family. Reports indicate that the pill is being manufactured on a very large scale as the health authorities shift away from primary reliance upon abortion, IUDs, and encouragement of late marriage -- evidently many young folk who tramped over China during the Cultural Revolution "exchanging revolutionary experience" also found time for other pursuits as they were thrown together in hostels and exhilarated by their new roles.

Condoms have become abundantly available in most communes. Occasionally, according to incidental information which carries at least the spirit of truth, they are put to odd uses. Recently, a young couple who tried to escape to Hong Kong by swimming from a nearby coastal commune strapped inflated condoms around their waists and one of them lost his life before he drifted ashore in this Colony. An escapee from another commune in Kwangtung reported a revealing incident. The "barefoot doctor" had distributed a stock of condoms to their production team. The wife of one farmer boiled her share and fed the soup to her husband. When the "barefoot doctor" returned some 14 weeks later, she berated him because she was pregnant again.

	POPULATION GROWTH IN COMMUNIST CHINA	
1953 July 1,	National census-official	583,000,000
	Health services rapidly and effectively expanded after abolition of infanticide. Redistribution of land to the peasants plus peace allowed great improvements in water control and other encouragement to expanding agricultural output. Extension of railways and roads greatly improved distribution and average Chinese diet best within memory of most.	2.5 per cent annual increase (semi -official)

1958 July 1,	China's Estimated population	659,611,000
	Creation of Peoples Communes, resented by the peasants who often sabotaged production, combined with three bad crop years in 1959, 1960, and 1961, drastically reduced food and other farm production. Local famines and malnutrition over most of China increased, especially infant mortality.	1.5 per cent annual increase (estimate based on refugee doctors)
1962 July 1,	China's Estimated Population	700,087,000
	Restoration of peasant incentives with private plots, free markets, etc., plus national emphasis on agriculture, much improved diet, though rationing continued. Effect of first major national attention to birth control was inhibited by start of Cultural Revolution in 1966.	(reports comparing health and food with early 1950s)
1967 July 1,	China;s Estimated Population	792,084,000
	Cultural Revolution continuing, limiting effectiveness of birth control activities. But delayed marriage, and increased abortion in the cities.	2 per cent annual increase (estimate based on official hints, refugee observations)
1970 July 1,	China's Estimated Population	840,567,000
	Maximally intensive nationwide birth control program begun with implementation of Fourth Five Year Plan in 1970. Barefoot doctor's clinics very effective.	China's intensified birth control program parallels USAID'S P/FP assistance program to the LDCs.
	Compiled by Albert Ravenholt	

Note: Readers of *Krushchev Remembers* will recall that, in 1959, Mao Tse-tung told the Russian leader China's population then numbered 700 million.

CHINA'S POPULATION PRESSURES

As is apparent from the above figures, a calculation of population growth in Communist China involves many assumptions and judgment of complex factors at work. Possibly the best comparative yardstick available is offered by the demographic behavior of other predominantly peasant societies under comparable conditions of health and nutrition. Students of Latin America may be particularly qualified to contrast these influences and the Islamic world also offers leads. While Confucianism and Roman Catholicism differ greatly as religions, their pro-natalist influence upon the family of a predominantly peasant and substantially subsistence economy has some common effects. A key question, of course, concerns the efficiency of a totalitarian state in enforcing new familial patterns and values. However, China's methods of internal rule have been radically altered over the past two decades. Let me quote from that astute "China watcher," the veteran Jesuit, L. La Dany. In an article entitled "China: Period of Suspense" published in the July 1970 issue of *Foreign Affairs*, he wrote:

The situation inside of China is utterly different from that of a few years ago, and observers of the China scene have the feeling that the methods used before the cultural revolution are no longer valid. The reason is not the scarcity of information coming out of China; information was almost as scanty in some periods before 1966. The reason, not grasped by all, is that the country is no longer the unified country it once was. A few years ago it was enough to study the directives issued by Peking; it could be assumed with fair certainty that orders from the center would be carried out in the provinces. This is not true today, when Peking is ceaselessly complaining about lack of implementation, about "words not followed by deeds." It might be thought that now, with the military in charge of the administration of the country, discipline and strict unity would have returned; but this has not happened. Today it is necessary to follow the attitudes and the development of each of the 29 provinces and equivalent administrative areas. They react in different ways to orders from Peking.

Red China's capacity to curb its population growth is likewise hostage to such fragmenting of official management. Even the most dedicated among Peking's planners must filter their purposes through this labyrinth of shifting political alignments; similarly they are handicapped in securing exact information. As the figures in the table indicate, a projected 2 per cent annual increase throughout this decade will push China's population to over one billion by 1980. Should birthrates be brought below the presently estimated 35/1000 annually, it is at least equally probable that the death rate will decline below its presently estimated 15/1000 annually as China's population increasingly is composed of younger people and health services continue to improve. Radically effective acceptance of abortion, as has happened in some East European countries, will be difficult to encourage among the peasantry. And the immense size of China makes the mechanics of any enterprise time-demanding before it can take effect. Hence, although their expectations may prove premature, Chinese Communists who speak of a population of one billion evidently are viewing the future realistically.

CHINA'S POPULATION PRESSURES

Food for One Billion

While Chinese publications occasionally refer to the 20-year-old figure of 106 million hectares (one hectare equals 2.47 acres) of farm land, there appears to have been an increase of about eight million hectares cultivated chiefly in Manchuria, Northwest China, and Tibet for a total of approximately 282 million acres. Growing enough on this roughly 12 per cent of China's land surface that now can be cultivated to provide for the vast and burgeoning population has become the overriding economic preoccupation of her rulers, most of whom are new to the task. Although less publicized than past grand enterprises aimed at speeding material progress, the military who today manage affairs have inaugurated a new "leap" in agriculture. Presumably, this is in response to a realization, at least in part, of what the country lost in economic headway after 1958, when the Great Leap Forward, creation of the Peoples Communes, and harsh weather brought disaster, and again following 1966, when the country was caught up in the convulsions of the Great Proletarian Cultural Revolution. As we have seen above, during these dozen years the population expanded by perhaps 180 million. Yet, because the military won power under the symbol of Mao Tse-tung and a return to his "true" path of revolution, they cannot easily disown the blunders that created these setbacks since Mao personally was the architect. For "the great helmsman" still is there, more firmly entrenched and deified than ever before and committed to the efficacy of ideological molding of human beings over mundane material incentives for insuring performance for production. They are a bit like men who are riding down an escalator, found they were headed in the wrong direction and have turned to run up, without being able to admit they got onto the wrong moving staircase.

What kind of China is it where this grave and potentially cataclysmic contest between population and food is under way? This land has changed remarkably since the Peoples Republic of China was proudly inaugurated on October 1, 1949 amidst the triumphant euphoria of the greatest revolution of our time. Today, except for a few familiar veterans like the durable and effective Premier Chou En-lai, most former officials have disappeared along with the government they led. The constitution for a new design of government has yet to be announced, although the Chinese Nationalists on Taiwan have released what they claim is a draft smuggled out of the mainland. The Chinese Communist Party, once the largest of its kind in the world with over 19 million members and disciplined traditions dating back to its founding that hot July night in Shanghai in 1921, also was shattered by the Cultural Revolution. What remains of the Party is soon to celebrate its fiftieth anniversary. Lao kan pu, the respected older cadres formerly thought even beyond the reach of criticism, are rarely heard from. Many have been banished to May Seventh Cadre Schools for "re-tooling."

Only within the military, formally known as the Peoples Liberation Army, has a Communist Party continued to exist. And it is from this nucleus that a new national party is to be created. For a Communist state to be self-respecting must have a governing Party, supposedly with civilian authority supreme. In practice, the courts and procurate almost have ceased to function, as have the police and once feared security agencies that lost out in the struggle to the military. No longer heard from are the Red Guards, who with their "small generals" in 1966 and 1967 stormed across the country and wreaked vengeance upon targets of their choice from innocent peddlers to the Ministry of Foreign Affairs and museums with ancient treasures that were judged symbols of a feudal order. Their utility spent in discrediting former Central Peoples Government Chairman Liu Shao-chi and most of his senior civilian comrades, these self--righteous youngsters are among the 20 to 25 million youths assigned for life to labor in the villages and pioneer on the frontiers or sent to military farms that have replaced state farms. As the technical universities now reopen, only those will be eligible as students who have worked in the rural areas for at least three years and are above 20 years of age. The military is omnipresent, controlling through the Revolutionary Committees administering the 29 provinces, special districts, and three separate cities of Shanghai, Tientsin, and Peking. Red Army political commissars are usually in key positions superior to their opposite commanding officers.

The blueprint adopted to meet China's pressing needs for food and other farm produce is the "draft of the program of national agrarian development" that Mao Tse-tung reportedly wrote with his own hand in 1955. The First Five Year Plan, begun in 1953, was showing encouraging progress. Mao could dream confidently and did so in his introduction to the book *Socialist High Tide in Chinese Villages*, although the Party Central Committee later modified his targets. A few figures illustrate his vision of what China would be like on the land by the late 1960s. In North China, average annual production of food grains was to increase from 150 catties (one catty equals 1.1 pounds) per mou of one-sixth acre to 400 catties. This meant that the short growing season regions of Manchuria and Northwestern China where sorghum, millet, and wheat predominate would boost production from 990 pounds per acre to an average of 2,640 pounds per acre. For Central China, where winter wheat and other second crops can be grown, the average increase would be from 280 to 500 catties per mou. While in South China, where it is possible to raise two crops of rice and sometimes a winter oil seed or other crop, Mao's program called for an average increase from 400 to 800 catties annually per rmou. Four catties of sweet potatoes or other tubers are calculated as equivalent to one catty of food grain.

Equally ambitious targets were set for most industrial crops. Cotton yields were to rise to the equivalent of 660 pounds per acre. Average yields of soya beans, of which China is the world's second largest grower, were to double or triple depending on the region and reach 2,640 pounds per acre and thus surpass the United States average. Likewise, peanut yields were to increase and average up to 3,300 pounds per acre. Illiteracy was to be eliminated in some 200,000 villages where about 80 per cent of all Chinese live. Preventable disease was to become a burden of the past, both among humans and livestock; epizootics like rinderpest formerly might cost the rural economy several million work animals in a year. Although Mao in his draft had apparently forgotten to mention chemical fertilizer, the Central Committee set a target of 15 million tons annual domestic production by the late 1960s-this presumably was based upon a 20 per cent nitrogen content. The forested area of China, excluding Tibet and Central Asia, was to increase 130 per cent by planting trees on 250 million acres. Most crucial was Mao's promise that "natural disasters caused by water or drought will have been substantially eliminated. In practice, this visualized effective water control with irrigation and some drainage for swampy areas covering roughly one-third of China's cultivated acreage.

As China embarks on her Fourth Five Year Plan (1971-1975), these objectives, often originally scheduled for achievement by the end of the Third Five Year Plan in 1967, essentially remain the national goals. That this is so even though there was a three-year hiatus before the start of the present Plan suggests how much the agrarian economy went awry during the Second and Third Five Year Plans and the Cultural Revolution. At the height of the Great Leap Forward fervor in 1958, fantastic accomplishments were announced, such as the promise that irrigated acreage would be doubled by 1962. These grandiose claims later were scaled down. Over ambitious projects, however, had led to some disastrous mistakes. Like India and Pakistan, China failed to construct adequate drainage canals to complement irrigation works in regions of marginal rainfall. The consequences were predictable; over vast areas of the North China Plain alkali percolated up to whiten the surface and often deaden the fields. A tragic by-product of relaxed control in the countryside during the Cultural Revolution was unlawful peasant cutting of trees planted earlier on barren hillsides and as windbreaks for fields -- a commendable Communist objective has been to halt the centuries-old encroachment of the Gobi Desert sands upon the farm lands of Northwestern China and Western Manchuria by planting shelter belts.

China's New "Rural Economic Policy"

Enormous effort is now being invested in correcting these errors and expanding agricultural production to meet the relentless demands of China's increasing population and her requirements for modernization. First in importance are the furiously implemented projects to expand water conservancy and reclaim additional land for cultivation with tens of millions laboring on these jobs this past winter. Over much of the North China Plain the water control systems that must also keep the turbulent Yellow River within its dikes are being redesigned. Irrigation canals are being lined to minimize seepage and now water is applied to fields more expertly. Salts are being washed out of the soil as drainage systems improve, often with the help of pumping from deep wells. Throughout China the emphasis appears to be on numerous smaller scale irrigation works and drainage canals that can be largely engineered and built with local talent and labor. Probably the most dramatically effective are the extensive pump schemes for lifting water from major rivers -- as a rule, these are cheaper to construct per area benefited than gravity systems. Three regions lead the country. In the Pearl River Delta of Kwangtung Province the one million acres irrigated several years ago with electric-powered pumps is being expanded. In Central China's Hunan and Hupeh Provinces adjoining the mighty Yangtze River and around the Tungting Lake these fertile alluvial soils are benefiting from similar pump installations. The third region where massive pump irrigation is allowing effective water control is chiefly in Kiangsu Province, where soils around the mouth of Yangtze likewise promise maximum returns from reliable irrigation and drainage. Other existing systems also are being expanded. For 2,200 years the Tukiangyen irrigation system has led the waters of the Min River out of the Tibetan foothills down to irrigate the Chengtu Plain in western Szechuan and make t among the most productive farm regions man has created. Some two million laborers now are reported to have enlarged this system more than three times to water 466,000 hectares.

Equally consequential is the extensive terracing of hillsides to convert largely unproductive slopes into fields where fertility can be stabilized. This is the ancient technique upon which the great agricultural civilization of Asia primarily depended -- it spared them declining like the Mayas of Central America whose corn fields eroded until the soils had lost so much fertility they no longer could sustain the population. Now, China's terracing often is combined with Indian type "tanks" to trap rain water on the hilltops for release onto the fields below during the dry season. Scattered reports by refugees who have come out of Tibet suggest that along with harsh Chinese rule has come possibly a 50 per cent expansion in cultivated acreage on the "roof of the world," with other crops being introduced to supplement traditional reliance upon barley as the chief staple. Scholars differ as to the total potential for so adding to China's cultivated area. Probably the best estimates derive from observations made by the National Geological Survey of China in the 1930s. These suggest that in the southwestern provinces of Yunnan, Szechuan, Kweichow, Kwangsi, and mountainous regions of Hunan a total of perhaps 20 million hectares of additional cultivated land can be reclaimed by those costly methods. A vital consideration is that these areas have both the rainfall and longer growing season to reward such investment with greater harvests.

A key practice making Chinese peasants traditionally the best farmers on earth, before the coming of Western agricultural science, was their ingenuity in maintaining field fertility. Hence, their intense concern with "night soil," or human excrement, that they conserved and utilized as was not matched elsewhere. Collected each morning from the cities and villages in the large wooden tubs of the "honey carts" and hauled out onto nearby fields, this liquid excreta maintained the balance of nutrients in the most intensively cultivated fields. Theoretically, "night soil" today is to be divided between commune fields and private plots. However, repeated admonitions to the peasants suggest it is difficult to insure against a farmer pouring the richer mix on his own garden plot and only delivering a watered down portion to the common fields.

Even more than in pre-Communist years, the pig is becoming China's pre-eminent farm animal. And the Chinese preference for pork seems to be almost secondary to the pig's role as a converter of scraps and crude feed into manure. The national goal is to raise one pig for each person in every commune, and there is talk of increasing this to one animal for each mou of land cultivated, or 1,710,000,000 -- a distant prospect. While the commune production team may keep and breed the sows, at least a portion of the piglets are advanced to individual farmers to rear. A contentious issue is whether they can be slaughtered by the farmer or must be sold back to the production team, which also is supposed to receive the manure.

Chemical fertilizer is new to most Chinese farmers, and, as we have seen, even many Communist leaders were slow to grasp its critical value. Fragmentary reports suggest China may now be manufacturing about eight million tons annually -- this also is calculated on a 20 per cent nitrogen basis. Figures similarly calculated for imports reach about 6.5 million tons annually, although the volume actually is smaller since it includes urea containing about 46 per cent nitrogen. Largest among the foreign suppliers is Japan, with Western Europe as a secondary source depending upon prices and freight rates.

There are several puzzles in China's chemical fertilizer production. Elsewhere in the world usually the cheapest source of nitrogen is natural gas. Yet, China appears to be making little use of recent major discoveries of petroleum and natural gas in Central Asia and Manchuria. Natural gas may be being utilized for this purpose in Szechuan. A possible explanation is the transportation required to bring large tonnages to the principal consuming regions of Eastern China.

Present emphasis is upon building small fertilizer plants, usually of about 20,000 tons annual capacity, for each *hsien*. And Shanghai has won kudos for manufacturing 100 such plants. Curiously, the mainland press refers to most of these small plants as producing ammonium bicarbonate, evidently with coal as the chief raw material. Relatively small shipments of phosphate have been imported from Morocco and the Middle East, and there has been scant attention to developing the large apatite deposits in North Vietnam, but adjoining Kwangsi Province is reported producing phosphate fertilizer. Like most of the more moist regions of Asia, the soils of South and East China generally are believed to be deficient in phosphorus, especially for rice growing. China can produce potash as a by-product of her extensive coastal solar salt industry, and there may be substantial deposits in Szechuan. Fundamental is the fact that the present targeted annual output of 15 million tons of chemical fertilizer is only a fraction of China's needs. To approximate rates of application found economic in Japan, Taiwan, and Southeast Asia will require a yearly production of roughly 100 million tons.

Use of improved varieties, especially of wheat and rice, now rates renewed and more rational attention. Provincial radio broadcasts repeatedly emphasize that communes must expand planting of short-stemmed types and officials frequently are reported holding regional telephone conferences to push this campaign. As chemical fertilizer becomes more available, these shorter plant types acquire greater promise since they can carry the heavier heads of grain without lodging. While China has indigenous short varieties, this is also a key characteristic of introduced "Mexican" type wheat that is proving so productive in India and Pakistan and of the new rice plants bred at the International Rice Research Institute in the Philippines. Communist China is believed to have acquired these varieties through Nepal and Pakistan, although as in other countries they have been given local names. Interest in better varieties extends to other crops. Like Italy except on a much larger scale, China is planting hills and even entire mountain slopes to higher-yielding chestnuts; chestnut flour is excellent for humans and the nuts also provide a superior feed for hogs. Scattered references in mainland publications indicate comparable emphasis on planting better mulberries, walnuts, persimmons, citrus, and other famous Chinese fruits.

Tachai is the model for this transformation of the countryside; the example during recent months is being imprinted upon the public mind with all the thoroughness Peking's national propaganda commands. Located in Hsiyang Hsien, east and south of the Shansi Provincial capital of Taiyuan in the mountains forming the boundary with Hopei, Tachai was an impoverished village where 75 families farmed 132 acres when China came under Communist rule 22 years ago. The village's credited achievement tells much about how rural life is to be remade. Most emphatically it is "do-it-yourself," with almost superhuman dedication and sweat moving rock and earth rather than reliance upon outside assistance. As with nearly everything in China, the ideological dimension is vital. The slogan is *i-ta-san-fan;* one enemy is struck while three are opposed. The first are class enemies who have infiltrated among the cadres or otherwise found means to misguide, and the latter three are fear of hardship, fatigue, and difficulties. Chen Yung-kuei, the peasant who led in rebuilding this mountainous community, has become a member of the Party Central Committee and travels about China to teach others.

Utilizing such methods, Tachai reportedly has transformed both its inhabitants and landscape. The people have been "remolded" to give their utmost. Despite storms and other setbacks, the hillsides were terraced, trees planted, and water trapped above to be let down as needed. Since 1952, credited grain yields have more than quadrupled to reach 1,000 *catties* annually per mou (equal to 6,600 pounds per acre) in this region where wheat, millet, corn, and sorghum predominate. That production claim, which is more than twice the target for North China, has become a goal toward which communes elsewhere strive. Coastal Chekiang Province southeast of Shanghai now claims to be approximating this per land unit output as an annual average. As every farmer knows, however, calculating accurately average yields, especially when several crops annually on the same field are included, can be confusing. And wishful thinking easily can enter into tabulations. Regularly, the question arises whether the grain measured was wet or dry or at what percentage of moisture content. Nevertheless, Tachai is important for exemplifying what can be attempted.

Equally revealing is the new pragmatism Peking is allowing in encouraging the peasants. Early on the heels of the Cultural Revolution incentives were abjured as the authorities cautioned curtailment of private plots for farm families to a maximum of 5 per cent of the cultivated land and inhibited free sales of produce. Now these controls are eased. Recent discussion in the mainland press tends to confirm reference in the draft Communist Constitution released in Taipeh assuring peasants possession of both their private plots and houses. Peasants also can reclaim additional small scraps of wasteland for their own use. More startling, Chinese publications are beginning to suggest a distinction between rich and poor should be allowed, provided it results from productive labor. Just how far to ease restraints in these directions is the conundrum confronting the predominantly military decision-making organs in each province. Apparently, many cadres in the communes, bewildered and frightened by the ideological shifts during and after the Cultural Revolution, also have turned enthusiastically to farming their own private gardens, fish ponds, and small orchards. This threatens a return to the very bourgeois tendencies the Cultural Revolution was to erase. Therefore, the conflicting instructions that go out from the Revolutionary Committees to the communes, admonishing against "capitalism" yet emphasizing the essential requisite of promoting production.

CHINA'S POPULATION PRESSURES

This odd mix of intense ideological mustering of rural Chinese to gigantic labor coupled with "small incentives" for the present brings results. The claimed harvest for last year of 240 million tons of grain and tuber equivalents at four to one probably is not greatly in excess of performance. The weather was comparatively friendly and nearly everyone important seems to have realized that performance on the land must take precedence. However, it was accomplished at the expense of reducing acreages devoted to other crops. It appears that China's soya bean harvest, which in the mid-1950s reached about ten million tons annually, may have dropped below seven million tons, and the planners seem concerned also for other industrial crops. Tung Yueh, who as a technical specialist for 35 years analyzed rural trends for the United States Agricultural Attache' Service, has done a significant study of China's agricultural trade. He found that since commercial contact with the West began, except for times of warfare, exports from agriculture regularly exceeded imports. Tea, silk, tung oil, tallow, hides, and hog bristles, along with soya beans and other oil seeds, paid for most of China's imports of textiles, petroleum products, medicine, machinery, and much else. Today, while China has become self-sufficient in vital sectors like textiles and petroleum, the same need to export farm produce persists if she is to modernize. Now, it is primarily export of agricultural commodities -- from pigs and ducks to vegetables to herbs, woolen rugs, and canned Chinese food shipped to this British Colony -- that pays for wheat imports.

As we look ahead to the time when the Chinese will number one billion, it is theoretically possible for them to feed themselves, providing the diet remains as it traditionally has been, one wherein animal protein is at a minimum and at least 90 per cent of all food comes direct from the vegetable kingdom. China's present ratio of roughly three persons per acre of cultivated land is not excessive by the standards of intensively developed Asian agriculture. Taiwan, which has probably the highest average caloric intake in the Far East, feeds about seven per cultivated acre; Japan's calculation is complicated by great imports of fish catch and foodstuffs. This performance requires a literate farm population and alert acceptance of new technology plus all the vital inputs at hand from irrigation water to fertilizer, insecticides, and the complex infrastructure for processing, transportation, and marketing. Whether Red China can create these in time is questionable. Despite heroic achievements for which the Communists can claim just credit, they also are handicapped on the issue of incentives. The Chinese farmer, like his counterparts everywhere, after all is an artist who with the raw stuff of soil and water and weather creates according to his instinct. The revolution, which has made China over the past two decades the most massive social experiment ever attempted, has yet to fashion Mao Tse-tung's "new man" on the land. On this centenary of the creation of the brief and urban Paris Commune that China's Red rulers have chosen as their inspiration, the old pragmatic human ways still persist so stubbornly among the peasants that one wonders whether they ever will be fundamentally altered.

BIBLIOGRAPHY

Buck, John Lossing, *Land Utilization in China,* University of Nanking, 1937. Reproduced by The Council of Economic and Cultural Affairs, Inc., New York, 1956.

Coursey, D.G., *Yarns-An Account of the Nature, Origins, Cultivation and Utilisation of the Useful Members of the Dioscoreaceae,* Tropical Agriculture Series, Longmans, Green and Co., Ltd., London, 1967.

Gernet, Jacques, Daily *Life in China on the Eve of the Mongol Invasion 1250-1276,* translated by H.M. Wright, Ruskin House, George Allen & Unwin, Ltd., London, 1962.

Grist, D.H., *Rice,* Tropical Agriculture Series, Longmans, Green and Co., Ltd., London 1953, 3rd Ed. 1959.

Heissig, Walther, *A Lost Civilization- The Mongols Rediscovered,* Thames and Hudson, London, 1966.

Ho, Ping-ti, *Studies on the Population of China, 1368-1953,* Harvard East Asian Series, Harvard University Press, Cambridge, Massachusetts, copyright 1959, second printing 1967.

King, F.H., *Farmers of Forty Centuries* (or Permanent Agriculture in China, Korea and Japan), edited by J.P. Bruce, Jonathan Cape, London, 1927, 4th impression 1949.

Schwanitz, Franz, *The Origin of Cultivated Plants,* Harvard University Press, Cambridge, Massachusetts, 1966.

Wrigley, E.A., *Population and History,* World University Library, McGraw-Hill Book Company, New York and Toronto, 1969.

China News Analysis, weekly newsletter, China News Analysis, Hong Kong, relevant issues 1967-71.

China News Summary, published by U.K. Regional Information Office, Hong Kong, mimeograph, relevant issues 1967-71.

AMERICAN UNIVERSITIES FIELD STAFF

East Asia Series
[AR -2-78]

WHOSE GOOD EARTH?

Health, Diet, and Food Production in the People's Republic of China

by

Albert Ravenholt

OVER THE PAST DECADE OR SO, China has imported on the average four to five million tons of wheat a year -- some 10 percent of its consumption, a little less than 10 percent of the global wheat trade. It has been a net exporter of rice. Its potential impact on world markets, should there be a significant shift in its degree of self-sufficiency, is obviously momentous. Outsiders have been in a poor position to appraise China's agricultural performance, although that is to some extent changing because of the regime's increasing openness, its entry into FAO (of which the Soviet Union is still not a member), and, perhaps, Landsat imagery. For a writer and a farmer who first began observing Chinese agriculture in 1941, returning in summer 1977 to visit experiment stations, communes, and orchards in the People's Republic of China was a special experience. Having been a correspondent in China during and after World War II, the land and its people command particular affection, and since 1950 I have sought to follow events in the Chinese counmtryside from information filtering out to Hong Kong, Tokyo, and elsewhere. Inevitably, it is hazardous to generalize about so immense an enterprise as the cataclysmic events that have shattered that ancient civilization and recast the lot in life of nearly one-fourth of the human species. Yet, my recent observations, comparing visually, on the ground, what is happening in the Chinese countryside today with pre-revolutionary conditions in the same areas, compel conclusions.

With the caution that the statements which follow are oversimplified, this writer submits, first, that a great deal of nonsense has been reported and written about Communist accomplishments in agriculture by individuals who should know better, even though they may lack earlier experience in China. Second, the Communists since they captured power at the close of the Civil War in 1949 have made major physical advances -- most notably in sanitation and public health -- that spurred population growth, although at great cost in human liberty. Third, the diet of ordinary Chinese farmers now appears adequate in calories and inferior in cooking oil and protein to what it was in 1941. Fourth, should weather on the Eurasian Continent deteriorate, China could rapidly become the greatest drain of all upon the world food budget.

Perceptions: Establishing a Baseline

Travelers in China move into a unique world largely isolated from contact and outside information except such fragments of fact their Communist hosts think should be made known. Except for "special guests" judged disciples of Mao Tse-tung's ideology, all foreigners are carefully guided and monitored to prevent unsanctioned contact, a purpose simplified by the lack of language facility of most visitors from abroad whose dependence upon their official interpreters leave some resembling a flock of sheep seeking their herder.

Our group of horticulturists and fruit growers started its 15-day tour in Peking. We first flew to Sian and visited the Wei River Valley, then to Honan and the Yellow River Plain, by train to Hunan in Central China, and on by train to Kwangtung and out to Hong Kong. Except for Peking, this writer first came to know these areas of China in 1941 and visited them repeatedly in subsequent years. Chinese agricultural scientists did their utmost with their meager means to make us welcome and left us wishing that somehow we could help them more in the face of their discouraging handicaps.

Why should competent and sometimes leading agricultural scientists and observers visiting China often have come out with misleading and over-optimistic accounts of developments in the countryside? The answer is important, for the ability of the Chinese to feed themselves in the future is far too vital an issue to allow propaganda to replace sound judgment: there is no legitimate room here for careless proponents for or against the Chinese Communist system.

The first reason for errant reporting appears to be ignorance among most visitors to China of what agriculture was traditionally. Even among foreigners who lived in the old China, including scholars, only a small minority ventured outside the cities and their compounds enough to experience life as it was lived by ordinary peasants. Innocently, some travelers today ascribe as a Communist achievement the intense cultivation of every little plot of arable land and the conservation of nutrients for return to the soil.

A second cause of confusion is the failure of the government of the People's Republic of China to publish meaningful annual statistics on yields, total harvest from each of the major crops, and otherwise enlighten their own citizens and the world of real food availability.[3]

Confusion is further compounded by the language barrier. During visits to commune production brigades I was repeatedly puzzled at the differences in figures on yields presented, in Chinese, in briefing sessions by the vice-chairmen or other "responsible persons" of the governing revolutionary committees and the translated figures then given in English by our official escorts. The problem proved to be primarily the interpreters' lack of familiarity with agricultural units and terminology: horticulture, they readily admitted, was for them a most unfamiliar subject.

The Communists are, however, anxious to magnify their achievements in the eyes of foreign visitors, and they do employ statistics that fortify this objective. As an example, they regularly use 1949 as a base year for calculating advances in production on the grounds that the People's Republic of China was formally established on October 1, 1949. As anyone who was in China in 1949 will know, using this as the base year in most regions is not realistic. East, Central, South, West, and Northwest China were all engulfed by the military campaigns that concluded the civil war. When the People's Liberation Army launched its offensive south across the

WHOSE GOOD EARTH?

Yangtze River on April 20, 1949, the Communists had 84 armies in position on the north bank. With millions of men engaged in combat across the face of much of China, and with transport and food commandeered, there was scant opportunity for anyone to keep meaningful records, except in Manchuria and North China. Many fields were forced into idleness and crops curtailed on others, so the 1949 production is not a representative yardstick for pre-Communist yields.

Much is made of Tachai, the model commune in Shansi Province where mobilization of manpower, terraced mountain slopes, and resources were mustered to maximize production and publicize an example of achievements by politically motivated peasants. A United Nations report mentions corn harvests at Tachai of 8 to 10 tons per hectare (one hectare equals 2.47 acres), which is equivalent to 125 to 158 bushels per acre. This certainly is an achievable yield. However, it is misleading as a general indication of farm production in North China. According to responsible Chinese Communist officials, average corn yields in neighboring Shensi Province, which has generally better soils, are equal to 76 bushels per acre, or about 5 tons per hectare. (It is a bit like suggesting that Michigan farmer Roy Linn, Jr.'s 1977 harvest of 352 bushels of corn on one acre, or the equivalent of about 22 tons per hectare, is indicative of the crops grown by most American mid-western farmers, when they would be more than happy with a crop approaching one-half of this yield.) That average corn production in Shensi Province from 1937-1945 was 280 *shih chin* per mou or equivalent to 2,100 kilos or a little over 2 tons per hectare -- less than one-half the present average yield -- puts the Tachai commune achievement in even clearer perspective.

Her relative isolation from the international community during the past 28 years, it has been difficult to gain a factual understanding of affairs in the Chinese countryside. When the Red Armies triumphed in China three decades ago, it was with the aid of peasants who were promised land in return for supporting the revolution. Once the Communists were in power they implemented a land redistribution program, usually parceling out the cultivated areas within a village according to the number of adults in each family. In a number of areas the new peasant-owners were given titles confirming possession of their prized plots. During the nine years following establishment of the People's Republic, Chinese agriculture made major progress. For the first time in half a century in some regions there was real peace and order in the countryside. Chinese farmers restored irrigation canals, dredged mud from pond bottoms onto the fields and, often with the help of sons returned from the wars, reclaimed idled fields.

In September 1958, however, there issued from Peking the sudden announcement that all peasantry was to be grouped in peoples' communes, about which until then few had heard. Peasant bitterness and sense of betrayal expressed itself in production sabotage which, combined with unfriendly weather over the next three years, brought massive starvation to many regions and nearly toppled the regime. Yet, today, among the carefully reported trips of foreign visitors to China's communes, there is no single candid account of this period. Farmers reveal their attitudes only in how they do and do not till the Good Earth that in some locations has known such assiduous husbandry for 45 centuries.

WHOSE GOOD EARTH?

Health and Population Growth

Chinese villages, with their weathered houses and earthen walls, crooked lanes, and partially cobbled streets, looked as drab in 1978 as they did three and one-half decades ago, although the graves, clan shrines, and temples are virtually all gone. But there is a fundamental change; in the same communities one feels there now must be about twice as many people as before. This is the result of the greatest single physical achievement of the new Communist order which has truly revolutionized public health and sanitation.

Human excrement, or "night soil" as it is more politely known, has been critical for maintaining fertility of Chinese fields throughout recorded time. The *mao fang* or open pit latrine was almost omnipresent in the countryside and indelibly imprinted upon the senses of everyone who has squatted over one. Here the feces accumulated to the delight of some very healthy flies until the season when the farmer chose to haul the night soil to his field in wooden tubs. In the cities with their surrounding "green circles" this was a continuing routine. On the canals the sampans that carried fresh vegetables into Shanghai and other cities hauled back the night soil to the farmers. In Chengtu, capital of the most populous province of Szechuan, men pulled "honey carts" through the streets early in the morning, stopping at each house to ladle out from the *mao fang* the night soil to be sold later that day to surrounding farmers who were expert at detecting any dilution. A partial list of the fecal-borne diseases suggests the implications; bacillary and amoebic dysentery, typhoid and paratyphoid, enteritis and diarrhea, cholera. schistosomiasis, ascariasis and the hookworm, ancylostomiasis. Nearly 80 percent of the population of Canton alone were estimated to be infected with clonorchiasis, due in part to the marvelously economical planning of fishpond owners who placed public toilets conveniently to feed their carp, which then were often served raw as a delicacy.

Improved toilets appear to be almost everywhere in China today. Naturally, these are not flushing facilities in the countryside, nor in the cities except at a few hotels and modern buildings. Rather, they are concrete lined troughs and pits, often with screen over the window openings. In a city such as Sian, every evening families place their excrement-filled wooden buckets on the pavement in two or three locations per block. After daytime traffic has left the streets, tank trucks collect the contents. Use of trucks allows hauling to greater distances from the cities -- at intervals along the roads concrete and covered cisterns are used to store night soil until it is needed on the land. In smaller communities night soil still may be hauled by humans pulling wooden tubs on carts, but nearly everywhere it appears to be accumulated in covered concrete pits. [4]

Provision of piped water into the villages and enforcement of sanitation regulations inhibiting contamination of wells has been as vital for public health as the improved management of human excrement. Widespread use of DDT, which was the preferred insecticide in agriculture although it is now being replaced with organophosphates and other chemicals, also has helped reduce the fly population as well as control malaria by killing the mosquitoes. This in part may explain a noticeable reduction in the bird population, which also was curbed by the mass campaign to

286

kill the sparrows. Cats always were rare in China and more so now. Dogs have been eliminated, with a few exceptions, and thus are not available to spread rabies or any of the other 65 diseases they share with man. (It was not possible to get a clear account of whether dogs were eaten in a time of food shortage or merely a luxury no longer to be tolerated.)

Rats were omnipresent in the Old China and sometimes so bold they would gnaw through a mosquito net at night to disturb the sleeper at an inn. Even during World War II, rats following movement of grain after the harvest carried the lice and fleas that brought plague. The Communists have organized several mass campaigns to kill rats -- presumably these were not sabotaged as before by enterprising individuals who then bred rats to sell the tails. Although reliable statistics are not available, examination of granaries and other buildings on communes suggests there has been a significant reduction in the rodent population.

The massive organization of street committees in the cities and production teams in the countryside that facilitates political control of the population has also provided an efficient means to vaccinate against smallpox and some other communicable diseases and to curb schistosomiasis in Central and South China. Paramedics, many of them middle school students, were mobilized and trained to carry out this national program soon after the new authorities established power in 1949.

Continuing this preventive health program in the villages has become the responsibility of the barefoot doctors, who administer first aid and treat simple illnesses with both modern and traditional medical methods. One of the most obvious improvements has been a great reduction in skin disease, especially among children. Rural folk have access to a network of common clinics and provincial hospitals that commonly utilize acupuncture for anesthesia and otherwise capitalize upon indigenous resources. Production teams are proud of the member-financed health insurance that enables farm families to pay for such services. Although some modern types of antibiotics are in short supply and hospital facilities may appear crude by Western standards, they are a marked improvement over the medical facilities that existed in pre-Communist China and rarely were available in the rural areas. For the peasants it is important that similarly effective measures appear to have curbed epizootics of rinderpest, hog cholera, and other communicable livestock diseases.

The demographic revolution inaugurated by this effective and massive improvement in sanitation and preventive medicine combined with rudimentary clinical care is on a scale difficult to visualize and assess. Morbidity and mortality statistics in the Old China were at best available in sample surveys.[5] Typhoid, dysentery, and cholera ranked with smallpox, tuberculosis, and measles as the leading causes of death in the north.

As is the case in much of the non-modern world, infants and children were the most frequent victims of this mortality pattern, making it necessary for a family to have many babies in order to insure that a few survived to adulthood. Since male children were so essential to the Confucian concept of immortality through the family, this further fortified emphasis upon procreation -- the original grounds for taking a concubine was to provide descendants for one's uncle. However, in times of critical food shortage or among the most impoverished families drastic measures were taken to curb the number of mouths to be fed. In the fertile Chengtu Plain of Szechuan, where an irrigation system has functioned almost without interruption for some 2,300 years, when a family had all the children it could feed, a newborn infant might be destroyed by one of the grandmothers who hit its head on a stone, smothered, or drowned the baby. In Shanghai such infants were abandoned in the streets and in Kwangtung they often were left in a basket in the markets, where the mother hoped someone would take the child, in effect, for adoption.

After establishment of the People's Republic the new Marriage Law in 1950 gave legal equality to women, abolished concubinage, and led to rapid elimination of infanticide as the young enthusiastic Communist cadres preached the benefits of the New China where there would be enough for all to eat. Similar fervor fortified their early mass efforts to enforce the initial sanitation and vaccination programs. When expedient, popular compliance with essentially sound public health measures was prompted by all the persuasive methods an authoritarian state can command. Between 1951 and 1953 the "anti-U.S. germ warfare campaign," triggered by charges that the United States was resorting to bacteriological means in the Korean conflict, was made the occasion for galvanizing the entire populace into killing flies and other insects. As the death rate, especially infant mortality, dropped drastically, a few independent-minded Chinese leaders warned of the danger of population pressure, but these warnings were brushed aside in the heady atmosphere of the early years of Communist triumph. Socialism, they evidently assumed, would rapidly solve China's problems of food production. During the early and mid-1950s, moreover, performance by Chinese peasants tilling their own fields with improved irrigation and under conditions of peace and order fortified these expectations with bountiful crops. The pro-natalist Confucian value system was reinforced by a conviction prevalent in the minds of important Chinese leaders of this century, like Sun Yat-sen, who argued China must make up with numbers of people for what she lacked in industrialization. It was in this context that Mao Tse-tung, with the immense authority of a successful revolution and civil war behind him, evolved the principle that "people are capital" and the more you have the faster you can develop the country, provided they are effectively organized. It was a short step intellectually to inaugurating the "Great Leap Forward" in 1957, when tens of millions were marched to massive public works and much else, and the following year to the momentous decision creating the "Peoples' Communes."

The population growth spurred by these public health achievements is as yet only partially perceived. The best available base figure is the national census conducted during the 24-hour period between midnight June 30 and midnight July 1, 1953, for which some 2.5 million officials, students, party cadres, and other personnel had been recruited and trained to carry out this task. While purists sometimes argue that there are mistakes in the management of the census, the evidence indicates it was the most complete and accurate the new government could accomplish. The tally, rounded to 583 million, corresponded to the estimates of some of the most experienced China observers.

WHOSE GOOD EARTH?

The growth in population since 1953 has often been a subject for speculation and dispute. Nikita Khrushchev in his recollections reported that in 1959 Mao Tse-tung told him China's population numbered 700 million. Actually, I believe it only passed this mark in summer 1962; the terrible food shortages following creation of the Peoples' Communes meant that from the winter of 1958-59 to the summer of 1962 many women stopped menstruating, and mortality increased greatly, especially among infants. With importation of grain to feed coastal cities and restoration of agricultural production, the most radical features of the communes were moderated. Incentives were restored in part for the peasants through private garden plots and free markets. The rate of population increase moved up to where it had been in the 1950s, or about 2.5 percent annually. Pragmatic policies of the time under the leadership of Chairman Liu Shao-chi, Premier Chou En-lai, and Communist Party Secretary General Teng Hsiao-ping had just begun to show results in birth control by 1966, when China became embroiled in the Great Proletarian Cultural Revolution.

These political events had important consequences for China's population policy and action. The birth control program begun earlier slackened during the Cultural Revolution while the cadres were preoccupied with political in fighting and peasants returned to older ways, including desire for more children to provide security in old age. A lack of consensus on population policy was evident among the senior Communists until Chairman Hua Kuo-feng's leadership was assured. Even today visitors to Peking are given widely varying figures for China's total population. Some are told it is 800 million, some are informed it is 900 million and others that it is 950 million; my own calculations put it somewhere between the last two estimates.

During the past six years, as the necessity for more drastic food rationing became increasingly apparent, government officials at all levels have recognized the urgency of birth control. Measures now being enforced would be judged draconian in any other society. Women are forbidden to marry before the age of 24 or 25, depending upon local option, and men before the age of 28. When we questioned doctors, as in Honan, about premarital sex and illegitimate births they were aghast; such activities are not tolerated in the New China where a marriage must be sanctioned by the local Revolutionary Committee. Tubal ligation is recommended for a woman who has had three children, and often two. We observed two such operations done under acupuncture anesthesia. Contraceptives appear to be nearly universally available and knowledge of their use effectively disseminated. In 1973, the then Minister of Health, Li Hsu-hsien, stated privately at an international conference that she believed China's birthrate was 25 per thousand and the death rate 7/1,000, a rate of increase of 1.8 percent. Two years later a leading Chinese official of the World Health Organization estimated China's birthrate had dropped to 16/1,000. Clearly, the present Chinese leadership recognizes the demographic implications of an immense population of which well over one-half is under the age of 21.

For the People Food Equals Heaven": Diet and Nutrition

This classical Chinese proverb, min yi shih wei Cien, is as compelling for the Communist rulers of today as it was for the mandarins of old who jealously sought to retain the "mandate of heaven." Probably no society on earth historically has been so occupied with insuring this most basic of human needs, nor so zestfully devoted to enjoying eating and measuring the quality of life by this yardstick. [7]

Chinese think of food in two categories. Fan is usually prepared from wheat, millet, sorghum, or buckwheat, possibly with ground corn mixed in the north, and rice, frequently cooked with sweet potatoes, especially in Central China and the south. Ts'ai refers to the almost innumerable variations in cooking vegetables -- China has the world's greatest variety -- often blended with bean curd, bits of meat, pickles, and possibly seafood. In addition, soybean products -- a major source of protein -- are considered Ts'ai.

In the Old China, only the rich and powerful ate dishes of pure meat or fish, except on special occasions like Chinese New Year when ordinary folk might feast. This reflected the basic nutritional fact of China, that 98 percent of food eaten came direct from the vegetable kingdom. Popular awareness of this was expressed in the phrase "mandarins eat meat." For the less affluent, there were inexpensive options for sampling a small bit of meat or seafood along inland waterways and in the coastal communities. They were chopped and mixed with the vegetable fillings in the boiled dumplings called chiao tzu or pan fried to become kuo Cieh. A similar stuffing might be covered by a ball of dough and steamed to become pao tzu, or a bit of meat or seafood blended with vegetables and noodles and fried to become ts'ao mien or cooked with soup stock to become Cang mien. For the abstemious or less affluent these could be eaten either as snacks or an entire meal at noon or in the evening, the flavor enlivened with selections of chopped ginger, chopped garlic, shredded radish, soya sauce, hot oil made with chili peppers, sesame, or peanut oil, and numerous other seasonings.

Of necessity because of burgeoning population pressure the People's Republic has concentrated upon providing the Jim, or staple component of the diet. The model production brigades we visited were quick to emphasize that they are growing enough to supply the basic ration for their members, plus meeting their quota for state grain purchases. They were less definite about revealing what proportion of the ration was provided by grain and how much was supplied by the less desirable sweet potatoes, potatoes, and other tubers (four kilos of tubers are the equivalent of one kilo of grain in the ration).

Economies in the use of grain are apparent in North China. Only the favored elite and visitors eat white man Cou or steamed bread. The general population must make do with a staple that is dark brown, and rather heavy and may include ground bran, barley, sorghum, and other rough grains. In Central and South China all the rice we saw was rough milled; the bran had been removed and the grains were lightly polished. Brown rice, with its greater protein and vitamin content, generally is not eaten, although this may reflect the methods of milling?

Inferior ts'ai, however, is now the most critical food problem for the Chinese. Tofu, which is the curd, was traditionally the most important single source of protein in the diet. Along with other foods made from soybeans in the Old World, it was normally abundant and cheap. Poor people especially relied much upon the curd, which might be dried (tou fu kan) or fermented. They also drank soy milk (tou chang), and ate bean sprouts (tou ya), cooked green immature seeds as a vegetable and seasoned with soy sauce (chang yu). Mature seeds were pressed to produce oil used for cooking, lighting, and industrial manufacture, while the residual bean making noodles and bean curd, a repair shop with two lathes, a blacksmith forge, and a small hog-raising farm,[10] Although their orchard never would make a living for a fruit grower in New Zealand, Japan, or the United States, they were growing good millet and sorghum, called kaoliang. Their excellent horse and mule farm reflects[11] the exceptional leadership of this brigade.

China is more abundantly endowed with varieties of vegetables than any other country and traditional skills -- cutting, seasoning, and cooking them -- probably are without peer. The art of growing these many vegetables is a distinguishing feature of the East Asian civilizations; an equivalent capacity for cultivating intensively and productively small plots of land to yield a maximum of edibles is largely lacking in Southeast and South Asia. Much of the traditional physical vigor and sustained working endurance Japanese, Koreans, and Chinese must be due to their diets which combine an abundance of cheap protein with this wealth of vegetables. Significantly, in Northern and Western China where corn is grown, failure to utilize lye or lime in its preparation evidently restricts its nutritional value. When China's peasants were dispossessed of their property with creation of the People's Communes two decades ago, food shortages that overtook the land resulted partly from peasants abandoning cultivation of their gardens and slaughtering the pigs since they had become the property of the state. Recovery of agricultural production after 1961-62 also resulted in part from the then pragmatic decisions of Liu Shao-ch'i, Teng Hsiao-p'ing, and their associates to restore use of private garden plots to peasant families and encourage free markets where they could sell their produce.

As the Great Proletarian Cultural Revolution gathered momentum after 1966, Mao Tse-tung, as part of his campaign to recapture power, charged that this pragmatic policy in the countryside betrayed the revolution and was a step toward bourgeois capitalism. With Mao's consolidation of control and political power accorded the radicals, free markets largely were abolished -- this happened only gradually in some regions because political infighting between actions left the peasants scope to barter with the people in towns until the new authority was firmly in place. Most serious was reduction in the land allotted for private garden plots. Formerly, in most areas of China, private gardens were allowed about 5 percent of the cultivated area. After the Cultural Revolution these areas for growing family food were drastically reduced. In Kwangtung, we were informed that private plots now are allowed one-half of one percent of the cultivated area of the production brigade. The intensive crowding of these plots, creating a multistoried effect with numerous vines, vegetables, spices, and medicinal plants, suggests the pressure farmers feel in augmenting their food supplies.

In the fields, peasants were simultaneously finding it less advantageous to grow more soybeans than needed for their own immediate consumption, even in the North China and Manchurian regions where the plant does well. Officially, the state insisted upon purchases of oil rather than beans in most instances. This was intended in part to avoid transporting beans to the cities from which the residue oil cake then must be shipped back to the countryside. After farmers were corralled into People's Communes in 1958, the private enterprise incentives that had encouraged them to grow soybeans for sale through free markets to towns and villages ceased to operate. Meanwhile, during the following years of desperate food shortages all emphasis was focused upon inducing the radical new mechanism of the production teams and brigades to grow just enough of the basic grains and tubers people needed to fill their stomachs. As China recovered in the 1960s and began expanding agricultural production, a pattern had been set. Instead of raising soybeans as a single crop, which was the practice formerly in the main growing areas, soybeans became an inter-planted crop. This is how we saw most of them grown this past summer in North China; a row or two of soybeans would be grown between corn rows or inter-planted with other crops, while crops like cotton retained their single field dominance. Although the soybean originated in China supposedly some 26 centuries ago and has had a vital dietary role, the People's Republic has accorded it only limited attention in research and plant breeding and without the incentive of a free market farmers show scant interest in expanding production.

In addition to soybeans, the other chief sources of cooking oil in the past were rape seed, sesame, peanuts, cotton seed oil, miscellaneous crops such as sunflower, plus lard, a little tallow, and limited use of fish oils along the coast. It appears that commune production brigades, in order to meet the state purchase quotas of grain and cotton, hemp or ramie, where these are designated to be grown, have given these crops priority in allocation of available fields. The compulsion to grow sufficient staple grains and tubers to provide the rations for their members also has been important. As an result, these other oil crops also now are chiefly planted as an intercrop and their yield is subordinated to the staples. As with the soybean, so with most of these oil crops, problems of where and how to extract the oil have hindered production in this era of drastic social and economic remaking of the countryside. The seed cake remaining after extracting the oil is considered useful only for feeding livestock or use as fertilizer. China so far has not developed the modern oil extraction, packaging, and transportation facilities for managing large-scale distribution of a perishable commodity like cooking oil.

Irrigation

Standing on the dikes of the Yellow River at Hua Yuan K'ou, 15 kilometers northeast of Chengchow, the provincial capital of Honan, one gains a sense of the enormous stakes. Here, in 1938, the dikes were breached and the river changed course shifting its mouth some 600 kilometers to the south of the Shantung Peninsula as part of a deliberate effort to slow the southward march of the Japanese armies coming from Manchuria and North China. An estimated three million peasants were flooded out with an inestimable loss of life. In 1946-47 the return of the Yellow River to its old northerly course became a major concern of the United Nations rehabilitation efforts, and today it remains a challenge as female labor teams unload boulders from railway boxcars atop the dike and energetic young cadres explain the mistakes in the 106 meter high San Men Dam built with Russian assistance between 1957 and 1960. One-half the storage capacity of the vast reservoir already has silted up and there are schemes to correct this by tunneling through rock on the north side and opening gates for sluicing out the silt. On a smaller scale the Huai River and other drainage basins have been similarly made over, and the Grand Canal has again been tied into a complex water conservancy network. The main stream of the Yangtze has yet to be controlled, except chiefly for diking and water storage in the T'ungt'ing Lake region of Central China. Otherwise, wherever earth and rock can be moved to harness water the Communists have capitalized upon their mustering of human labor to enlarge and refine China's ancient engineering enterprises.

Such improvement of water control has allowed two major changes in Chinese agriculture; shifting north the areas where rice can be grown and improved double-cropping. Especially in North China, this has been combined with field consolidation and planting of windbreaks that reduce problems with the wind deposited loess soil and rapid evaporation of moisture. Where the necessary water to provide 11,000 cubic meters per hectare per crop can be delivered on the North China Plain and South Central Manchuria, rice now is being grown. This allows the Chinese to benefit from the advantages of anaerobic cultivation which releases a larger portion of nutrients locked in the soil, especially in more acidic regions. The model commune that has reclaimed land from the 1938 to 1947 bed of the Yellow River at historically memorable Hua Yuan K'ou reports a yield now of 385 kilos of paddy rice per mou, equivalent to 5,775 kilos per hectare. In addition they claim that on most of their land they can harvest, with the benefit of irrigation, 265 kilos of winter wheat per mou, equal to 3,975 kilos per hectare, or 58 bushels per acre.

Related to this northward shift of staple grain crops has been much of the plant breeding program. Between 85 and 90 percent of China's annual wheat production is winter wheat grown roughly between the Yangtze River to just beyond the Great Wall-the spring wheat belt reaches further north into Manchuria, Inner Mongolia, and irrigated oases in Central Asia. In addition to seeking disease resistance and dwarfing characteristics, which shift utilization of nutrients from stalk growth to grain production, plant breeders have sought spring wheats with a shorter growing season and winter wheats with greater temperature hardiness. Yields still are modest, especially on the non-irrigated fields, and are variously reported from scattered communes to be ranging from 1,058 kilos per hectare, equal to 15 bushels per acre, up to 2,500 kilos per hectare, or about 36 bushels per acre. Since 1962, China has supplemented its domestic wheat production by importing up to five million tons annually.

It was a pleasure to see some of the fine sorghum and millet varieties developed. A field of Chengchow Green Number One near the Yellow River was expected to yield 300 kilos of millet grain per mou, or 4,500 kilos per hectare. A new variety of sweet potato, the Hung Tsu, was reported to be yielding 4,500 kilos per irrigated mou in 4 months, or about 67 tons per hectare. In Central and South China there is a similar emphasis upon multiple-cropping and breeding rice varieties with a shorter growing season, plus other desirable characteristics. In Hunan Province, the heart of the immense Yangtze Valley and one of the most fertile regions in China, a special effort has been made because this was the birthplace of the late Chairman Mao Tse-tung. Moreover, the new Chairman, Hua

Kuo-feng, made his mark from 1949 to 1972 as the political boss of Hunan. The average yield for the province is reported by officials to total 400 kilos per mou from 2 crops, or about 3,000 kilos of paddy rice per hectare per crop.

Fertilizer

Fertilizer has been and remains the greatest single physical input problem for China's agriculture. Conservation and return of nutrients to the soil has been fundamental throughout history to the maintenance of agricultural productivity in China. The best available calculations indicate China may now be returning to the fields better than two million tons of true nitrogen annually, or the equivalent of about ten million tons of ammonium nitrate. The potassium content in human excrement is about 35 percent that of true nitrogen and the phosphorus content roughly 16 percent. Aside from conserving nutrients, night soil has the advantage over chemical fertilizer of not requiring transport over long distances since it is utilized locally and farmers are accustomed to its application.

Yet chemical fertilizers are also needed, and the slowness to develop production capacity illustrate the curious amateurishness that periodically has dominated decisions about agriculture within the chung yang, or "central authority," of the Chinese Communist Party and the government of the People's Republic. When the outline of the First Five Year Plan was made public in 1953, providing for the construction of only about 200,000 tons of annual fertilizer production capacity, it was apparent that someone had miscalculated. Evidently, the political leaders, without technical experience themselves, overrated what could be accomplished with mobilization of manpower and simple improvements, reflecting largely the ideas that gained dominance during the years of hibernating in Yenan from 1937 to 1945. It was only after three years of terrible food shortages when, in 1962, the late Liu Shao-ch'i, as Chairman of the government, and his political partner, the tough minded Teng Hsiao p'ing, as Secretary General of the Party, restored some incentives to farmers that the value of chemical fertilizer was officially acknowledged. Unfortunately, the government chose an unconventional solution that proved a disastrous failure; they would build "backyard" fertilizer plants in each county, utilizing natural gas in the few communities where available and otherwise coal. These appear to have been intended to employ an ammonium carbamate process. Producing nitrogenous fertilizer like urea from coal is a sophisticated chemical engineering task. It proved impractical with the crude equipment and limited skills available in most hsien. But by 1966, when this was becoming manifest, China was embroiled in the Great Proletarian Cultural Revolution. It was not until the early 1970s, therefore, that scientists and engineers won full acceptance for their view that China must build modern chemical fertilizer plants, much as is done in the rest of the world. But two decades of time had been largely lost, while China's population continued to grow.

Although for most years in this decade China has imported between 4 and 6 million tons of chemical fertilizer (calculated on a 20 percent nitrogen basis), it is necessarily a small factor. Contracts for building major fertilizer complexes have been negotiated with the French, the British, Japanese, Dutch, and, most recently, the Americans. The largest single contract is with Pullman Kellogg of Houston and their Dutch associates for building eight urea plants each designed to produce half a million tons of fertilizer annually. On a 20 percent nitrogen basis China appears now to be producing annually approximately 30 million tons -- ammonium nitrate has 20 percent nitrogen, whereas urea contains about 46 percent nitrogen. Included in this total figure also are limited quantities of phosphate, which the Chinese have been slow to develop, and potash. Most of these plants are located deep in the interior, chiefly near natural gas deposits in West, Northwest, and North China, and Manchuria. Foreign engineers who have worked on construction report several problems. Aside from difficulties of securing parts and tools and the language problem, they have been compelled to contend with local political struggles over whether "red or expert" is best and even with some Chinese technicians who insisted the "Thought of Mao Tse-tung" would allow them to operate equipment faster than the rated speed.

Once a fertilizer factory is in production, the greatest problem is transportation. The Communists have extended and improved China's rail network, as with the double-tracking of the Pinghan. Road construction into the countryside, however, is rudimentary. While there are more trucks in rural China now than after World War II, most transport still is by animal and human-drawn cart. Even the limited number of tractors introduced especially in North China for plowing appear to be used at least as much for hauling wagons. This very limited construction of a rural road system is in keeping with the Communist philosophy of emphasizing local self-sufficiency. However, it creates major problems of distribution -- some chemical fertilizer plants have had to close down while waiting to move out accumulated production. Experience in Japan, Taiwan, and the Philippines indicates that for intensive multi-cropping such as China is attempting, annual chemical fertilizer requirements are of the order of 1.5 tons per hectare on a 20 percent nitrogen basis. For China to produce and distribute approximately six times the chemical fertilizer now available will require a technological revolution of major proportions plus a commitment for many years of national resources to agriculture on a scale not in sight.

The chemical fertilizer problem becomes even more acute when exploring options for expanding China's cultivation. Officials now say that 12 percent of the land area is cultivated and use the figures of 106 or 107 million hectares. This writer believes the actual cultivated area is about 114 million hectares. Theoretically, the largest available area for reclamation where rainfall is sufficient is in Southwestern China. Those most knowledgeable about these soils estimate that perhaps up to 20 million hectares could be added to the cultivated area here with massive terracing of mountain slopes and construction of irrigation systems. The second most promising area is in Manchuria where several million additional hectares possibly can be brought under plow. But these soils will require very heavy applications of nitrogen, phosphates, and potash to make them productive even for wet culture rice. While the Chinese aver they will provide an important part of this with pig manure, their present hog population of 260 million is still far short of the announced goal of the 2 billion needed, at the ratio of one for every mou, which is still not adequate for supplying the required soil nutrients.

Farmer Motivation

Ironically, restraint upon the Chinese farmers' skills and initiative in service of a political theory creates the greatest handicap crippling agriculture and also offers the new leaders their most available opportunity for expanding production. Time wasted in production teams arguing about whether a family's night soil had been devoted to their private plot or gone to the brigades' fields could be better employed. Peasants are forbidden to leave their production brigade or even travel away from the commune without the permission of the revolutionary committee. Once this is granted, it is still extremely difficult to secure the special ration tickets needed to eat anywhere else. The lethargy observed among production teams in the fields contrasts oddly with the traditional physical vigor of work style in the China of old. While this may partly reflect dietary deficiencies, the national work-to-rule attitude evident also in so many factories that are obviously inefficient and overstaffed now has become a concern of officials at the highest level. It is questionable whether only raising wages in this land of comparatively stable prices will prove an adequate remedy. The tortuous ideological circuses, when everyone condemned first one deposed national leader and then the next for setbacks in agriculture due to entirely different causes, are no longer creditable, even among the cadres. China's leadership still has an opportunity to evolve a genuinely scientific and productive method of solving problems in the countryside. Meanwhile, China's best hope of feeding herself even meagerly resides in the traditional skills and wit of her extraordinary farmers.

NOTES

1. Ours was a group of 21, all American and including 5 women. As members of the International Dwarf Fruit Tree Association, we have an intense interest in the proliferation of ideas, dwarfing rootstock, improved varieties, and other innovations leading to growing compact fruit trees and more productive, profitable orchards. The "guru" of our Association is the Swedish-born and widely traveled Dr. Robert Carlson, professor of horticulture at Michigan State University, who worked for three years to arrange this trip.

2. Farmers of Forty Centuries, written by Dr. F.H. King, University of Wisconsin professor and chief of the Division of Soil Management of the U.S. Department of Agriculture, after his trip through East Asia in 1909, remains the best preparation for understanding the economic foundation of the civilizations of Japan, Korea, and China.

3. This type of economic paranoia is not uncommon in the Communist world. The suggestion that such vital statistics are being withheld for reasons of national security hardly makes sense. Russian and American satellite

photography today allows remarkably accurate monitoring, which, combined with weather reporting and other sources of intelligence, limits severely the options for hiding knowledge of any major crop disaster. Thus, it is the Chinese and the world intellectual and scientific community that is most handicapped by China's secrecy regarding the state of her agricultural production.

4. Although we did not see this, we were informed that in several of the larger cities, including Shanghai and Peking, the sewage system is designed to pump human excrement into the rural areas for distribution.

5. In his classic Land Utilization in China, J. Lossing Buck includes a table indicating the role of fecal-borne disease in relation to other selected causes of mortality the figures are chiefly indicative of conditions in North China and would be different in the south and southwest where malaria and schistosomiasis were much more prevalent.

6. This titanic struggle for power within China lasted for nearly five years and eventually returned Mao Tse-tung to control, this time with his wife Chiang Ch'ing emerging as a prominent figure. The turmoil barely subsided when, in September 1971, China and the world were shaken by the news that Marshal Lin Piao, the Minister of Defense and Vice Chairman, who according to the new Constitution was Mao's designated successor, had died in a plane crash in Mongolia after attempting the assassination of the "great helmsman." Chou En-lai and his associates struggled with heroic patience and persistence to return the country to normalcy before he and Mao died in 1976. It was well into 1977, with Chiang Ch'ing and her "Gang of Four" set aside, before the new Chairman, Hua Kuo-feng, could pursue more pragmatic policies as evidenced by restoration of Teng Hsiao-p'ing to the senior leadership.

7. A returning Sinophile is bound to note a sad decline in the standard of eating available to many ordinary Chinese as well as visitors to the hinterland. In Peking, Canton, and reportedly in Shanghai some once-famous restaurants remain and approximate the old culinary performance. These, however, are very much the exception. In hotels, restaurants, and on trains where foreigners are taken, cooking and serving generally are sloppy; although ample and good ingredients may be used, skill in preparation and seasoning compares poorly with the Old China, and dishes often are placed on the table cold by comrades, or Cung chih, who care little about service.

In cities, towns, and villages tens of thousands of restaurants, noodle shops, teahouses, and other modest eateries have disappeared. Since state enterprises have supplanted private business, such small, often family ventures were eliminated and the private initiative they mobilized was sacrificed. Stringent rationing of staple grains, cooking oil, vegetable proteins-including bean curd, meat, and fish also inevitably would have crippled commercial eating establishments.

It is essential to realize that private profiteering, including boarding of grain that sometimes caused suffering in Old China, also has been eliminated. In the New China when food supplies are skimpy, they appear to be equally shared, except for a favored small elite of officials and party cadres who are the only stout persons seen.

8. Much of the fun in life for ordinary Chinese has been lost with the disappearance of most of the roadside stalls, small eateries, and teahouses. It is indicative that the Szechuan provincial capital of Chengtu formerly had more than 500 teahouses, including the gathering places for merchant guilds, such as both the official and unofficial gold bar dealers. With hands up each other's sleeves they would bargain by finger pressure so that other merchants would not know the highest price bid or the lowest offered. Similar transactions, including sale of pigs and poultry, usually with oral bidding, were conducted in other teahouses, in between sipping the green or red tea, munching peanuts, pumpkin and melon seeds, and visiting with friends. Today such establishments, where a few remain, are shells of the former boisterous, busy, and vital centers of community activity and news. One searches almost in vain throughout Canton for the dim sum shops that specialized in numerous types of steamed dumplings (served usually from morning through noon). In the towns and villages of North and Central China it is difficult to find the few simple shops that still offer one of the world's finest breakfasts: tou chang, or soya bean milk, with yu Viao, an elongated fritter of flat or twisted dough, and shao ping, individual unleavened bread usually baked with sesame seed. Even the simplest tsung yu ping, or onion pancakes, and lobo sze ping, baked radish patty, hardly are available. And the hsiao mi shi fan, or millet gruel, is equally hard to find. Following an inquiry at one of the remaining market eateries, an older attendant looked around to see who might be listening and said, "Oh, so you remember what it was like before," and shook his head with a wry smile.

9. China appears not to have introduced rubber roller rice hullers in substantial numbers. These are manufactured mainly in Japan and their use is spreading rapidly throughout Southeast Asia because they permit recovery of at least another 20 percent of edible grain from the paddy rice, even when the bran is removed.

10. Rural emphasis today is upon inducing every family to raise two pigs annually to capitalize upon table scraps and to produce manure for the fields. Usually the hogs are sold to state agencies; the export of trainloads of live pigs to Hong Kong provides an important part of China's annual earnings of US$1.7 billion from the British Crown Colony. In the regions of China we visited, better boars are being used for breeding. Occasionally, one sees an old type swaybacked Chinese sow with her teats dragging on the ground. These native pigs were prolific and, at the present state of China's development of agricultural science, gradual up-breeding indigenous stock is probably a sounder strategy than replacing them with foreign breeds that offer more efficient feed conversion ratios.

Chickens appear to command a low priority and there is little evidence of either improved egg and meat breeds or a modern feed industry; they are still raised chiefly as scavengers. Ducks, and to a lesser extent geese, have rated attention both in breeding and feeding. Again, they are a valuable export item to Hong Kong where they go live and dried, smoked, salted, or canned to overseas Chinese communities in Southeast Asia. Beef, mutton, and dairy products have been important in China's diet chiefly in the North and Northwest, which has been influenced by the nomadic Mongols and other minorities. Limited quantities are shipped to the cities and a few special herds are maintained there to supply this largely hotel demand. Although China's wastelands offer potential for livestock raising, it is alien to their Han cultural tradition.

11. Chinese in general always have abused their draft animals and fed them miserably, and this was as true in the Old China as in the New. At this production brigade, however, the mares being bred to an ass for producing mules were in splendid flesh and the young colts were quick and healthy.

FOREIGN AFFAIRS

AN AMERICAN QUARTERLY REVIEW

APRIL 1951

THE PHILIPPINES: WHERE DID WE FAIL?

By Albert Ravenholt

AMERICANS who have assumed that in the Philippines we did a model job of starting a colonial people toward independence and prosperity are now experiencing a rude shock, and there are others to come. Less than five years after the establishment of the new Asian nation, our hopes —and those of the Filipino people—have been met with the emergence of something acceptable neither to us nor to them.

It is now evident that the Philippines do not have an adequate foundation for developing democracy under their own leadership and with their own resources. Mismanagement, corruption and failure to enforce needed reforms have destroyed public confidence in the Government and contributed to a breakdown in administration and economic life. Possibly more than anywhere else in the Far East, society in the Philippines is coming apart at the seams. Internal developments in the Islands make it unrealistic to think of the Philippines as a secure military base for the United States and its allies at this time. In view of the need for a viable American position in the Pacific and Asia we now are being forced to improvise answers to these fundamental problems.

The Communist-led Hukbalahaps are the most dramatic symptom of the social disease that affects all levels of life in the Philippines. These guerrillas have set aside government authority in some of the richest rice-growing areas on the main island of Luzon. Their strength now is expanding rapidly on the smaller southern islands. The major Huk attacks have been carefully timed and well coordinated. From their mountain bases they have struck simultaneously at widely separated Constabulary posts. Wherever they succeeded in killing or dispersing the defending garrison, they usually looted government offices for money and documents and seized all arms. They also made off with medical supplies commandeered from hospitals and stores. During such raids the guerrillas have killed a number of wealthy landowners and suspected police informers.

In retaliation the Philippine Constabulary has wiped out entire villages and sometimes learned later that the Huks actually were elsewhere. The majority of the combat units of the armed forces of the Philippines, numbering about 37,000 men, today are tied down battling the Huks. But so far they have failed to "settle the dissident question." Instead, during the last three years the Huks have welded themselves into a force resembling the early Chinese Red Army. Their regular troops are believed to number between 10,ooo and 15,000 men well-armed with light weapons. An equal number of partly trained men are reported to be in an organized reserve. In addition, the Huks have thousands of sympathizers in the rural and urban areas who assist the guerrillas in maintaining a superior intelligence network.

The small corps of senior Huk leaders-including their Supremo, Luis Taruc-are avowed Communists. However, many of the guerrilla soldiers are boys still in their teens who left the farm because of wretched rural conditions. Others are veterans of the war against Japan who resented the U. S. Army's failure to award them the back pay and recognition given many of the more politically respectable guerrilla units.

So far the Huks have avoided large-scale planned attacks upon Americans and American installations. The available evidence suggests that their leaders do not want to arouse American attention and action at this time. However, should they choose to do so, it would be possible for the guerrillas to isolate our major Air Force base at Clark Field. At present it is frequently necessary to ship supplies from the port of Manila to Clark Field in truck convoys to guard against bandits. Several of the other and now inactive military bases which we have leased in the Philippines would be equally vulnerable to guerrilla attack. Should United States troops garrisoning our bases be forced into combat with the Huks there is the danger that the Communists could exploit the struggle as evidence of "American imperialism" among their nationally sensitive countrymen. It is with this in mind that thoughtful Filipino army officers have discouraged suggestions of direct American military participation in the war with the Huks.

This Hukbalahap movement meanwhile is capitalizing upon several unhealthy developments in the postwar Philippine society. They are helped by the popular fear and hatred in the rural areas of the Philippine Constabulary---the 7,000-man national police force. In some districts Constabulary commanders are paid substantial sums by large landowners in return for collecting rents and guarding property. Some landlords complain that Constabulary officers in their areas have taken over and are collecting most of the crop for themselves. There is substantial evidence to indicate that the Constabulary usually has seized considerably more rice from the farmers than have the foraging Huks. On paper, the Constabulary last summer was incorporated into the armed forces of the Philippines and is slated for reorganization. But prosperous Constabulary commanders also acquired political power and regular Filipino army officers schooled in the American military tradition have been prevented from cleaning up the force.

It is estimated that after Japan's defeat perhaps half a million weapons were held by private individuals in the Philippines. Additional arms were left in poorly-guarded surplus dumps turned over to the new government. There thus was an unlimited supply of weapons for criminal elements and those at loose ends due to unemployment and postwar dislocations. The Huks have outfitted themselves from the same sources. To date no adequate effort has been made to gather in most of these weapons. Some of the surplus dumps now are owned by politically powerful individuals who have sold arms to Communist China and other buyers.

At the root of the Hukbalahap problem, however, is the dissatisfaction generated by the growing numbers and poverty of the Filipino farm families who constitute almost three-fourths of the population. Within

THE PHILIPPINES: WHERE DID WE FAIL?

the last 10 years the population of the Islands has increased by 25 percent, but agricultural production has not yet reached its prewar average. Meanwhile, the "sharkskin gentry class," which includes roughly 1 percent of all Filipinos but controls most of the wealth, has taken a larger slice of the returns for itself.

Land in the Philippines, as in many other Asian countries, long has been the safest investment. With the steadily rising price of land it has become almost impossible for an ordinary farmer ever to buy the land he farms. Meanwhile, the growing population has created more tenants competing for the same land; thus the large landowners who usually dominate the local courts have been able to dictate their own terms. As a consequence the laws reducing land rents passed by the Philippine Congress since the war have not been enforced. In large areas the tenants who by law should be paying not more than 30 percent of their crops as rent actually are delivering more than 70 percent to the owners. The latter frequently are the only source of credit. Interest rates on loans in some of the richest agricultural areas are between 100 and 200 percent per year. Many tenants are so deeply in debt that they have no hope of ever getting out from under this burden; they are in effect the property of the person whose land they work. As a general rule, farm productivity per man is the lowest in provinces with the highest rates of tenancy, and the Hukbalahaps are most active in those provinces.

The Philippines have large areas of potentially rich, underdeveloped land, particularly on the southern island of Mindanao. According to law some of these areas are supposed to be open for homesteading. Land registration, however, is so confused and is so infected with corruption that many small farmers who "proved up" their homesteads in 1935 still have not received title. They are unable to sell their land or use it as security for a loan. Meanwhile, individuals with political and financial power have laid claim to large sections of the public domain that are permitted to lie idle. Consequently, even the few tenant farmers with the necessary capital to move onto and develop new land often encountered insuperable difficulties.

The abuses of this system of land ownership are made more destructive because of the primitive character of Filipino agriculture. Some of the larger sugar, pineapple and hemp plantations have applied modern methods to production. But the ordinary Filipino tao lives and farms almost the way his ancestors did 100 years ago. Average annual rice production per acre in the Philippines compares unfavorably with most other countries in the world despite the naturally rich soils. The ordinary farmer does not use commercial fertilizer or improved seed such as have enabled Japan and Formosa to produce bumper crops for many years. He is ignorant of modern methods of controlling pests and plant disease. His storage and marketing facilities are primitive and wasteful. Irrigation and drainage methods that have been common practice in China for centuries are used only on limited areas. The Filipino tenant farmer who is part of this system lacks both the knowledge and incentive to grow the additional food which he and his country require to maintain even the present low level of livelihood.

We Americans have a direct share of the responsibility for some of these conditions. When our administration was first established in the

THE PHILIPPINES: WHERE DID WE FAIL?

Philippines we recognized the Spanish land grants. Thereby title covering large sections of land and entire towns was awarded to families and religious orders originally granted only tax collection rights over that area by the Spaniards. Many Filipino families working this land once had been farmerowners. Our action legalized a process that had gone on for more than a century and gave the tenants no compensation for land they had once owned. During several American administrations a beginning was made toward buying up large estates and reselling them to tenants. But the program never was implemented on a broad scale. After the Commonwealth was established in 1935 Filipinos with property used their growing political power to block reforms.

The abuses of this system would have been less severe if we had made certain that Filipino agriculture was modernized and the productivity of the average farmer steadily raised. But our policy of emphasizing agricultural research and education while failing to insure extension of improved methods to ordinary farmers made the pressures of a rapidly growing population both politically and technically destructive.

The present government of the Philippines has done an even poorer job of building up agriculture. Although farming is the most important source of livelihood and accounts for more than one-half of the national income, only about one-fourth of one percent of the budget for the fiscal year 1951 was appropriated to the Department of Agriculture and Natural Resources. The agricultural scientists trained during the American administrations are growing old; and because of the lack of opportunity, few young Filipinos are coming up to take their places. The Government has attempted to increase food production by creating a number of corporations to grow and distribute agricultural commodities. These corporations have absorbed and sometimes wasted large appropriations. They have hampered healthy agricultural development and made only a limited contribution to increased production.

Low agricultural productivity and miserable living conditions are partly responsible for the unhealthy state of labor in the larger cities where the Communists are making a major bid for support. Lack of opportunity on the farm pushes a growing number of young people to the cities. But the industrial revolution has not yet reached the Philippines and there is no expanding demand for a large labor force. Many of the young people from the farms join the unemployed who now number about 1,000,000 out of a total population of roughly 21,000,000. The pressure of these unemployed has kept wages for common labor in Manila at from one to three dollars a day---although the cost of living is almost three times as high as it is in Chicago. Hundreds of thousands of seasonal workers on the large plantations receive less than one dollar a day; the average wage for these workers is below their prewar real income level.

Labor unions in the Philippines still are at the mercy of government and management interference, racketeering of labor leaders and other abuses. Collective bargaining as developed in this country is almost unknown. A Court of Industrial Relations, largely dominated by the same interests which control the Government, has power to decide all questions that arise between employers and employees. The Court in effect dictates the amount a firm must pay in wages. This has encouraged the development of "labor lawyers" who collect a percentage of the pay raises workers gain

THE PHILIPPINES: WHERE DID WE FAIL?

as a result of hearings before the Court. The practice has hampered the development of responsible union leaders. The failure of Filipino laborers to earn a living wage and their inability to see hope for the future have convinced an important segment of them that the Communist promise of violent revolution offers them their real opportunity.

The potential young leaders who might cope successfully with these and other basic problems are being warped by one of Asia's most destructive educational systems. Unless an adequate remedy for this situation is devised in time all other attempts at helping the Philippines appear doomed to ultimate failure, despite the fact that a fervent desire for an education is part of the American heritage in the Islands.

The first shipload of American schoolteachers who arrived in the Philippines in igoi opened public schools in the rural barrios where they taught the three R's--often after the stern fashion of the late nineteenth century. They and other teachers who followed .established English as the common language of instruction, trade and government. In so doing they for the first time enabled ordinary Filipinos, whose native tongues include eight languages and more than 80 dialects, to communicate throughout the Islands. (The use of Spanish under the previous regime was limited to a small group of officials, clergy and landed gentry.) By 1940 the American efforts had raised the literacy rate in all languages, including English, to 48 percent.

In 1940, however, the Philippine Commonwealth enacted a law requiring the National Government to finance all primary education. It was essentially a political move aimed at winning popularity, and no additional funds were made available at the time to replace former local and provincial contributions. The budget problem was met by cutting class time for all students in half. Since then, and partly as a result of the war, there has been a rapid decline in the quality of education.

The ordinary child in the rural areas who attends school does so half time for four years. His instruction is in English-a foreign language usually not spoken in his home. The average primary school student does not learn enough English to use the language, and those who do not continue their studies usually forget all except a few phrases. Because instruction often is not related to the student's need in daily life it tends to become a ritual.

A few statistics suggest the kind of schooling children receive in the Islands. Most of the primary schools have only one book for every three students. Many high schools use one book for every seven students. Funds supplied by the United States through the War Damage Commission were used to rebuild most of the schoolhouses destroyed by the war but not to equip them adequately. Less than one-half of the elementary school teachers have professional training. A teacher whose salary is listed at $50 per month may be three and four months behind in receiving his pay. The available schools and teachers fall far short of meeting the needs of the growing population. The low quality of elementary education is reflected in the work done by older students. The average student in one of the better colleges in the Philippines has the equivalent of a fourth grade knowledge of English From his textbooks and lectures he absorbs only a smattering of each course.

THE PHILIPPINES: WHERE DID WE FAIL?

The effects of this development have been made more serious by the postwar commercialization of education in the Philippines. Private colleges and universities have become one of the most profitable businesses in Manila. Last year one of the larger universities earned a profit of nearly $5,000,000 for its stockholders. Shares in these schools can be purchased on the market. A number of successful college presidents ride in luxurious automobiles. These profits in education are earned only at the expense of the students, many of whom work long hours to pay the fees. Classes are overcrowded, most of the professors are poorly paid, and students usually are graduated regardless of scholarship, provided they have paid the necessary tuition. Among the 296 colleges and universities registered in the Philippines only about six meet American standards. Filipino educators who have tried to establish and enforce educational standards that would prevent racketeering by private schools were blocked by political pressure.

With the development of these profit-making schools has come a distorted emphasis on education. Only one out of ten secondary school students is enrolled in agriculture and vocational courses. The thousands who are receiving degrees in law and other professions promise to add to the present white-collar unemployment and provide none of the technical personnel necessary for Philippine development.

These ills of the society are reflected in the character and performance of the Philippine Government and the Philippine economy. Within the last six months Filipinos have discovered that their government is nearly insolvent. The National Treasury was forced to hold up payment on government checks until revenues accumulated. Public construction projects were discontinued for lack of funds. The Government, which had accumulated a deficit of $260,000,000 since the end of the war, had almost exhausted its available resources and borrowed beyond the legal limit from its own banks.

Lack of realistic planning and some very fancy corruption contributed to this financial crisis. But the major cause was the failure of the Government to collect an estimated 60 percent of the revenue due. The tax collection system has disintegrated to the extent that Government revenue agents are employed by private firms to fill out their tax returns. Some of the biggest tax evaders are defended in court by the law firms of powerful senators. A junior Treasury attorney who is too energetic in prosecuting a tax case may lose his job, or find the senator has brought other forms of pressure against him and his family. These practices now are so widespread that the enactment of additional tax measures by the Philippine Congress provides no assurance in itself of a substantial increase in revenue.

Within the past year the Philippine Government has been forced to impose severe import and exchange controls to protect its fast-dwindling foreign exchange reserves and minimize the flight of capital. During the last six years the United States Government has paid out more than $1,700,000,000 in the Philippines. These funds included disbursements by the War Damage Commission, military agencies, the Veterans' Administration and the Reconstruction Finance Corporation. These dollars financed an import boom that flooded the cities with new automobiles and other expensive

THE PHILIPPINES: WHERE DID WE FAIL?

American consumer goods. Only a small percentage of these funds were used to finance basic development. With the present tapering off of United States governmental disbursements the Philippines face an increasingly difficult foreign exchange position. No likely early expansion of exports can bridge the gap and only a drastic imposition of more severe controls will be adequate. Such action requires a measure of government efficiency and honesty not now in sight.

These developments prompted the dispatch to the Philippines last summer of the United States Economic Survey Mission headed by Daniel W. Bell. Members of the 29-man mission avoided most of the dinners and cocktail parties that so often sap the energies of American investigators abroad. With the help of some very able and public spirited Filipinos they made a comprehensive survey of economic and financial problems in the Islands. The report which was submitted to President Truman last October summarized their findings in part with the statement: "The basic economic problem in the Philippines is inefficient production and very low income." Specific recommendations stated what action would be needed to stimulate the development of a healthy economy. The Mission proposed that the United States extend technical assistance and provide $250,000,ooo to help finance a program of development extending over a period of years.

An agreement signed in Baguio on November 14,1950, by Philippine President Elpidio Quirino and E.C.A. Administrator William C. Foster committed the Philippine and American Governments to a joint effort aimed at implementing the recommendations of the Economic Survey Mission. The Agreement stipulated that as an initial step the Philippine Government should promptly enact a new and adequate tax program, adopt a minimum wage law and through a joint resolution by the Philippine Congress indicate approval of the recommended social reforms and economic development measures. The United States promised to provide technical assistance, particularly in the fields of taxation, revenue collection, social legislation and economic development. Both Governments agreed to review the present trade agreement, including the often criticized Philippine Trade Act of 1946, better known as the Bell Act. A bilateral pact to be negotiated later is to amplify the terms of the new program. Meanwhile, the E.C.A. has established an office in Manila and dispatched several specialists to assist in drafting the necessary legislation.

The Mission Report and the Agreement provide a realistic foundation for initiating an attack upon the Philippine social and economic problems. But they leave unanswered the key question of how it will be possible to generate the required Filipino cooperation. There is an enormous popular demand among Filipinos for the kind of American assistance that will really enable them to improve their livelihood. The available evidence indicates that if American actions are of demonstrated value in giving the ordinary citizen a better break the charges that the Americans are infringing on Philippine sovereignty will fall flat.

Any adequate program of reform and development, however, will conflict with the privileges, interests, and sometimes rackets of several of the more powerful political and financial groups in the Philippines. In the past these groups have successfully blocked efforts at breaking their hold. They are also a vocal segment of society and can be expected to try

THE PHILIPPINES: WHERE DID WE FAIL?

to make use of Filipino nationalism as a shield to protect their selfish positions. Firm and sustained action by the United States in cooperation with constructive-minded Filipinos will be necessary to overcome this initial hurdle. It is doubtful, moreover, whether the program now projected will be adequate to enable the Philippines to develop into an .independent and economically and politically healthy democracy. No substantial provision has been made to help solve the fundamental problem created by the breakdown of the educational system. The Filipinos have borrowed extensively from the United States, but too often in the form of the gadgets and other superficial appurtenances of our culture. They seem to have missed some of the essential American spirit. This is particularly needed in the Islands because they lack a highly developed indigenous culture such as is found in many other Asian countries. The Philippines are predominantly a Roman Catholic country and the Church plays a cultural role; but only recently has it taken a progressive interest in promoting social improvement. If the Philippines are to be helped to a genuinely better future it will be necessary for American private leadership to participate in a broad way along with our Government.

The success or failure of our new Philippine venture will in creasingly affect our position elsewhere in the Far East. If Japan is to remain independent of China and Russia she will need to develop sources of raw materials, particularly food, outside th Asian mainland. The Philippines have a great potential production, and in return will need Japanese capital goods if they are to progress industrially at the same time that they develop their agriculture. The Filipinos, however, have bitter memories of the war. They will insist upon guarantees to protect them fron becoming an economic satellite of Japan. No country in the Far East today is militarily defensible unles it is in good health socially, economically and politically. We can expect the Filipinos to become worthwhile allies to approximately the same extent that they achieve something which they think worth living and fighting for. In this they need our help. Most Asians have not yet had it demonstrated to their own satisfaction that a foreign nation can help them add substantially to their welfare. In the mounting struggle for the friendship and cooperation of the Asian peoples the skill and effectiveness with which Americans contribute to a better life for the ordinary Filipino will be of immense consequence.

Albert Ravenholt interviewing Filipino Workers

THE CHICAGO DAILY NEWS, August 1958

Filipino Birth Rate One of the Highest

25 Million to Double in 22 Years, and Strain Resources

BY ALBERT RAVENHOLT

MANILA, P.I. Filipinos now are increasing their population by 3 percent every year placing this predominantly Christian republic among the faster growing countries in the world.

In this corner of Asia such a rapid expansion of population is matched by the new state of Malaya, where the British introduced effective sanitation standards.

Only Formosa, with its annual increase of 3.75 percent, has a higher rate of population growth in the Far East. And there roughly 12 million people already are living on little more than 2 million acres of cultivated land.

For The Philippines the accelerating growth among its 25 million citizens means that there will be more than twice that many within the next 22 years. The resulting demand for the bare essentials of food, clothing, and housing strains the resources of almost every family.

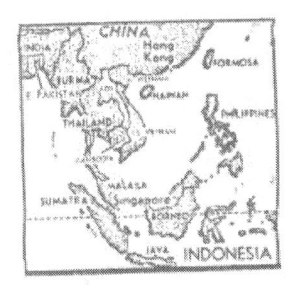

On a national scale it means that there is little saving for the capital investment that is so vital to modernizing this underdeveloped land.

Yet, the present rate of population growth in the Philippines, Malaya and Formosa, points to the drastic expansion that can be expected in neighboring Vietnam, Cambodia, Thailand, Burma and Indonesia as and when they experience peace and public health.

Gigantic Asian Surge in Making
All of Southeast Asia appears on the threshold of a gigantic population surge that will transform its 180 million inhabitants into one of the world's potent new economic and political power factors.

As in most less developed lands, statistics here have often been based upon estimates.

Until a few months ago Philippine officials planned on the assumption that their population only was growing by 1.9 percent anually. This figure was arrived at by comparing the 1948 census to that of 1939.

U.N. specialists and Filipino statisticians, in a recent scientific investigation, discovered that the population really was growing by a yearly figure of 3 percent.

FILIPINO BIRTH RATE ONE OF THE HIGHEST

Death Rate Drop Chief Reason

The population spurt in these islands results primarily from a drop in the death rate - the birth rate has remained almost constant at somewhat more than 40 per 1,000 members of the population annually.

With the help of the U,.S. economic aid mission here, some 1,300 rural health units now are offering modern advice and assistance to expectant mothers and their new. born infants. These units include mid-wives with modern training who are setting aside many old superstitions concerning birth.

Among former beliefs of village folks was the myth that the umbilical cord should be cut with a rusty piece of iron or a seashell.

American Public Health specialists also have assisted The Filipinos in an energetic and highly successful camaign to control malaria.

The vast changes brought by antibiotics and other new drugs have been even more radical in underdeveloped countries than in the United States, where modern hospital facilities are so generally available. As these have become cheaper and more widely distributed, protection against many of their most feared infections has been available even to poorer Filipinos in rural areas.

The resulting improvement in health is evident not only in greater vitality among Fillipinos and extended life among the adults, but in a rising survival rate among the newborn infants.

And in this predominantly Roman Catholic land, where families pride themselves on many children, the indications are the future will bring an even faster growth in population.

Pressure Shows In Jammed Schools

Already the pressures are beginning to tell. This year the Philippines is adding 7,000 new classes in the elementary schools - and this will take care of little more than one-third of the additional new Filipinos.

Some 3 million children of school age are not studying, due largely to the lack of school houses, textbooks, teachers and budget.

Mounting population is felt in pressure on the land. A tenant farmer with three sons tries to divide the 7 acres he tills in central Luzon among two of his descendants, hoping the third one can find a job in Manilla. And from this results the growing underemployment among Filipinos who may work only four months every year and the burgeoning force of fully unemployed now variously estimated at 1 ½ million to 2 million.

New Filipinos 'Drag' on Economy

Because ordinary Filipinos have never achieved adequate buying power this boost in population fails to spur mass consumption, manufaciring and employment, as it does in the United States.

FILIPINO BIRTH RATE ONE OF THE HIGHEST

Instead, the new Filipinos tend to become a "drag" upon the economy. Yet, the Philippines is fortunate compared with overcrowded India or China. Here less than two-thirds of the available land is cultivated.

Perhaps the toughest problem confronting Asian and American officials or specialists hereabouts is that of discovering how static economies such as that of the Philippines can be made dynamic, U.S. aid has yet to be designed to find and exploit "breakthrough points" that would enable this country to mobilize most of its latent human and other resources.

But the "march of the babies" is beginning to be felt. And unless techniques for dynamic economic development are fashioned the political gains here may be erased by a sinking standard of livlihood.

AMERICAN UNIVERSITIES FIELD STAFF
SERIES

SOUTHEAST ASIA

Vol. X No. 8
(Philippines)

A NOTE ON THE PHILIPPINES

The Land, the People, and the Politics

Albert Ravenholt

Manila
March 1962

WHEN CITIZENS OF A NEW ASIAN NATION begin moving ahead rapidly under their own management, as Filipinos are doing today, their experience and efforts assume a wider relevance. For much of the underdeveloped world is plagued with the problems of how to engineer progress amidst all the uncertainties that follow independence and reflect a rising pattern of expectations among a burgeoning populace. In the Philippine Republic these problems are being attacked while the political process remains wedded to representative government. Although democracy has its handicaps and its frustrations, the regard for rule by law and its protection of the individual and his property are of more consequence. Despite a social system embodying great inequalities in wealth and opportunity, the Filipinos have been able to select new leaders through the ballot box when they felt the need - During the presidential election in November 1961 voters throughout the Republic rejected a narrow nationalism that identified itself with "Filipino First." Instead, they chose a new administration committed to freeing the economy of the controls that had stifled initiative and one that promised to restore official integrity. Bolstered by such demonstrated mastery of democratic techniques Filipinos are capitalizing upon the great wealth with which nature has endowed their Archipelago. Rather than feuding among themselves they are looking outward toward neighboring lands to share in building a viable regional identity. How is it that in spite of all the obstacles they have faced during the past two decades of war and uneasy independence, Filipinos have afforded themselves this advantage?

Experience and environment have joined to shape Filipino character. Geography of the Islands formerly encouraged a regionalism that defied delineation of a national prototype. Now it is being overcome by radio, modern transport, and mobility. The 7,100-odd islands in the Archipelago are scattered over some 1,200 miles between Formosa and Borneo. They offer great contrasts in terrain and climate. The cool and rugged mountains of northern Luzon break down to form the island's tropical Central Plain, its comparatively dry and low northwestern coastal strip, and the Cagayan River Valley where rain falls throughout most of the year. The Visayan group in the center includes islands with dense jungle such as Samar; the almost treeless, razor backed ridges of Cebu; and the rich sugar-growing coastal plains of Negros. Mindanao offers landscapes like the fertile Cotabato and Agusan valleys and the Bukidnon Plateau that are ringed by sharp mountain ranges. Like most countries on the western rim the Philippines experiences vigorous action in the earth's

A NOTE ON THE PHILIPPINES

crust. Inhabitants of some smaller islands, including several in the Mindanao Sea, periodically are endangered by erupting volcanos. Except for most of Mindanao, southern Palawan, and the Sulu Archipelago, the Philippine Islands lie in the path of destrucrive typhoons that sweep from the Central Pacific around Guam toward the Asian mainland, ruining crops, wrecking houses, and inundating large ares with torrential rain.

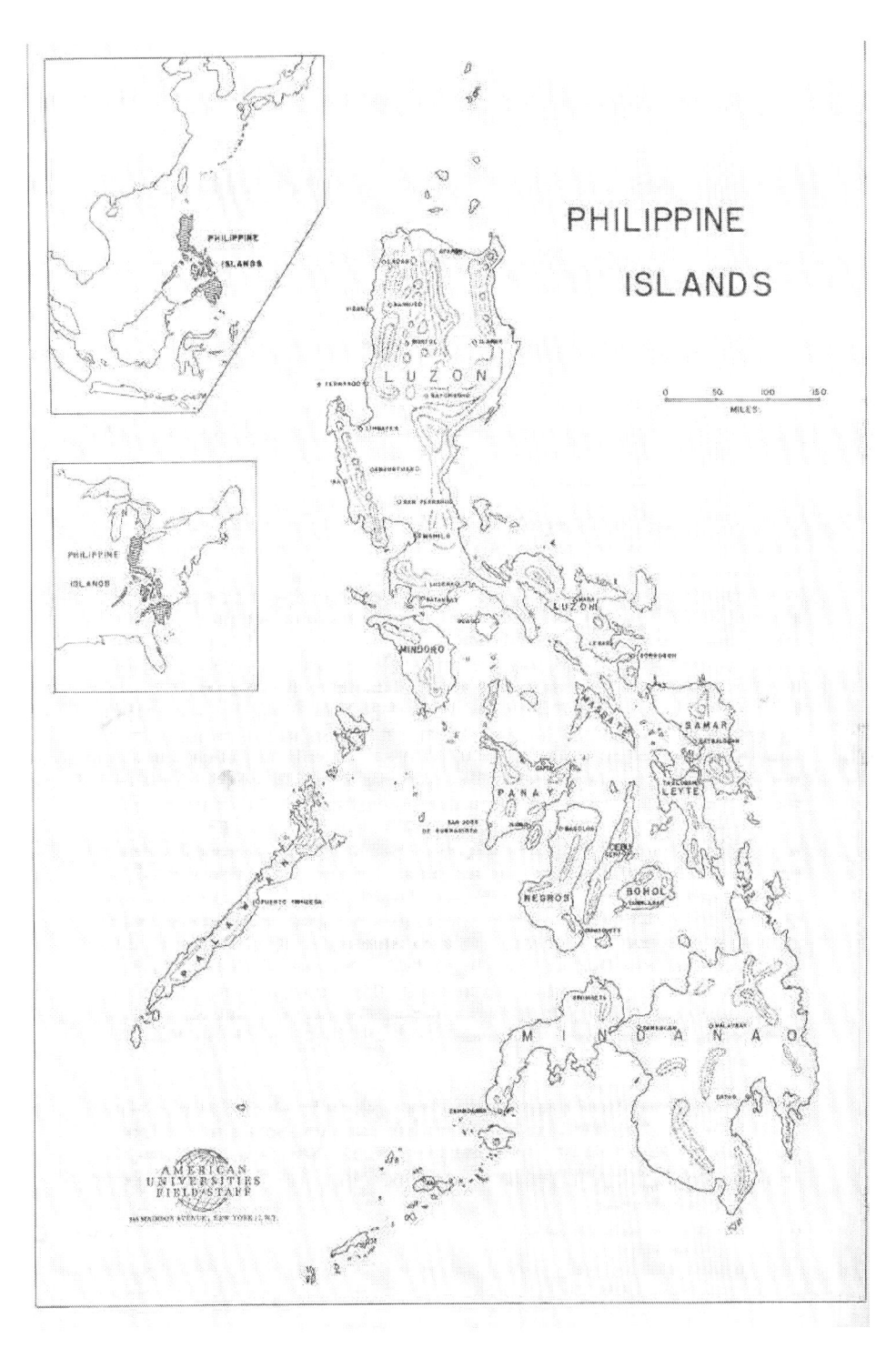

A NOTE ON THE PHILIPPINES

Although the Philippine population has quadrupled since the beginning of the century, many of the islands are sparsely settled and more than a thousand smaller isles are virtually uninhabited. Most of the nearly 29 million Filipinos are concentrated upon ten islands: they live in northwestern, central, and southern Luzon, Cebu, Panay, Negros, Masbate, Bohol, Leyte, Siquijor, Jolo, and along the coastal fringes of Mindanao. Long before the Spaniards conquered the Islands nearly four centuries ago, Filipinos engaged in water-borne trade with peoples inhabiting the countries now known as Indonesia, Malaya, Indochina, and China. In the 12th century annual junk fleets collected cargoes of cotton, timber, pearls, and delicacies like birds'-nests. Inland seas between the Islands offered highways to communication at home. Road building to facilitate internal land travel was not attempted on a major scale until the beginning of this century with the start of the United States administration; heavy monsoon rains on the mountainous centers of many islands still make highways expensive to construct and maintain.

These geographic barriers until recent times encouraged Filipinos in each community to retain distinctive cultural patterns. Although the successive waves of Indonesian, Malay, and Chinese immigrants have largely blended to form the Filipino race, important ethnographic groups remain apart. Today small Negritos, who hunt with bows and poisoned arrows and are descended from some of the earliest stock that reached the Islands, live within sight of the big runways on the United States Clark Air Force Base in central Luzon. The Ifugaos and other mountain tribes of northern Luzon have been more strongly influenced by 20th-century civilization. But their tribal laws and organizations are still in evidence and those who have been converted to Christianity often attend church in their G strings. Among the lowland-dwelling Filipinos, who form the bulk of the population, there are great regional differences in the food they eat, how they spend their money, and their treatment of strangers. The Ilocanos from the coast of northwestern Luzon are an adventurous people who settle new frontiers in Mindanao and emigrate to work in Hawaii and mainland America. The Tagalog-speaking folk, who live several hundred miles to the southeast in the environs of Manila, rarely leave home except as government officials, merchants, or engineers.

More than 70 distinct tongues are spoken throughout the Islands. And a native of the province of Pangasinan who travels across Luzon's Central Plain to Rizal has great difficulty communicating in his own language. Less than 3% of the population speak Spanish, although it was the official language in the Islands from the 16th century until the start of the American occupation in 1898. English became the language of instruction in the rapidly expanding public-school system built by the American administration, and by 1940 one in every four Filipinos claimed ability to speak the new tongue - But many used a very limited English vocabulary and only about one-half of the population had achieved a minimum literacy in any language. Wartime destruction of the public-school system and subsequent deterioration in the standards of English instruction have left their mark. While most ordinary Filipinos have never shared facility of expression in a common language, a version of Tagalog learned often through films and radio is gaining in use.

A NOTE ON THE PHILIPPINES

The Philippines is the only predominantly Christian country in the Far East, but religion has not always been a unifying influence in the Islands.

The Spaniards largely made the State the servant of the Catholic Church in what they described as their divine mission to bring Filipinos the blessings of Christianity. They brought valuable innovations in agriculture as well. European religious orders while conscripting labor to build their massive edifices also protected the peasants against the worst colonial abuses. But resentment at the friars, tactics in dealing with tenants on their landed estates helped spark the final rebellion against Spanish rule. After the United States took over the Islands the American Catholic Church sent more progressive missionaries to the Philippines. And some of the ablest leaders in the Islands today were trained in schools run by American Jesuits - However, there are continued differences over policy between the European and American religious orders. Filipino resentment against foreign domination of the Catholic Church at the turn of the century led a group of native priests to split off and form the Philippine Independent Church that now is the second largest in the Islands, although it is only a fraction of the size of the Roman Catholic Church. With United States administration came also American Protestant missionaries - They built schools and a university and established some vigorous Protestant congregations, particularly among the new professional class. Since World War II, other denominations have gained adherents and challenged the traditional churches. The most important is the Iglesia ni Cristo, a highly disciplined native church. On Mindanao and in the Sulu Archipelago the Muslim Moros have remained devoted and occasionally fanatical defenders of their faith. Critical issues are on occasion generated by these differences in belief. But Christianity has implanted a value system that is among the most basic bulwarks of the Republic.

Probably the most disruptive factor in Philippine society at present is the gulf that separates the living standard of the ordinary citizens from that of the favored few. The average Filipino lives in a rural barrio composed of nipa huts perched upon stilts and lacking all modern facilities. He may be among the more than two million who are unemployed. Or perhaps he belongs to that estimated one-half of all the farmers who are idle some seven months of each year when lack of rain on the fields halts farming. In areas such as central Luzon the problem of low farm incomes, resulting from use of primitive methods, is aggravated by a vicious tenancy system that keeps many farm families in debt to landowners and moneylenders - The new Court of Agrarian Relations is affording tenants an avenue of appeal and is beginning to moderate old abuses. But the desire to own a plot of land, if only the size of a house lot, remains a deeply felt need among Filipinos.

At the other social pole are the comparatively few almost dynastic families who own much of the rural and urban real estate. They number among them some of the politicians and control profitable businesses including dividend-paying universities - They are fond of palatial Spanish-type homes, Cadillacs, and swimming pools. Filipinos from this class casually take vacation trips to Hong Kong, Spain, Latin America, and the United States. They are now becoming "entrepreneur minded "-investing in cement plants, paint factories, and the many new

A NOTE ON THE PHILIPPINES

"packaging industries" that grew up under the umbrella of exchange controls, tax incentives, and other forms of a protected market. With this is evolving a new interest in business management. While the tendency is still for senior executive positions to be reserved for those related by blood and marriage, there is also a growing premium on technical skills. This is encouraging the emergence of more Filipinos into an urban middle class, particularly in Greater Manila which holds more than 10% of the population. Educated young Filipinos who formerly saw their greatest opportunities in seeking government employment are beginning to school themselves accordingly. The commercial middle class, however, remains chiefly Chinese. Controlling most of the wholesale and retail trade, they tend to remain culturally Chinese even after acquiring citizenship, but their children learn Filipino ways. Despite these divisive influences that are particularly active in their political life, Filipinos are an intensely patriotic people. The ordinary Filipino is fundamentally optimistic and sometimes seems almost delightfully irresponsible about the future; he has never known the pressure of preparing to survive long winters. Only recently in a few areas has he felt the grinding competition for a livelihood that results from overpopulation. His generosity toward friends is reflected in the national compadre system - and a compadre in need must be fed, lent money, or given a job regardless of personal or institutional consequences. The Filipino usually is not shackled by a sense of rigid limitations of his own status in society. Although the opportunities for advancement often are severely restricted, American education instilled great acceptance of the principle that a poor boy who worked hard could rise to the top. And social mobility lends vitality to the Re-public.

Filipinos are uniquely fortunate among the peoples of Asia in the relative wealth of unused natural resources. The Islands cover about 75 million acres - At present only 15 million acres are cultivated. And this land often is poorly managed. For purposes of comparison it is useful to realize that Formosa supports about 12 million persons at a higher average standard of living on two million acres of arable land. In addition to the land already settled the Philippines has an estimated 15 to 20 million acres of new and often rich land suitable for agriculture. When this land is irrigated climate permits the production of crops throughout the year. The Islands have a substantial stand of timber estimated to be worth more than $10 billion on the stump but it is fast being destroyed by "kaingineros" who cut and burn to plant crops and by some careless logging practices. So far no oil has been found in the Philippines, although several formations suggest its presence. Most of the coal discovered lies in thin seams and is not of adequate quality to support economically an iron and steel industry with present methods of production. The Islands have a significant and largely undeveloped hydroelectric power potential, including sites below Lake Lanao in Mindanao where some of the cheapest power in the world is produced. Iron ore, manganese, chromite, gold, copper, and other minerals are mined on an expanding scale. No complete geological survey has been made of the Philippines - But the limited explorations that have been conducted indicate there may be many rich mineral deposits yet to be discovered.

The personal skills, organizational techniques, and capital facilities needed to utilize these natural resources are beginning to appear. Despite a favorable climate and good soils, Philippine average rice production per acre per year is about one-fifth of the yield on Formosa and the Islands produce barely enough of this basic grain to meet local consumption requirements. Except in pineapple, sugar, and a few other industries, where plantation methods have been used to achieve more efficient production, similarly backward methods prevail throughout most of Filipino agriculture. The Philippines continues to import meat and dairy products although there is ample opportunity for production of these at home. There is a rich store of fibers in the Islands for which there is a growing demand in Japanese and European textile industries. But growing and processing such promising crops as ramie have only recently begun. Major crops such as the coconut are improving. Offshore and long-line fishing industries are taking a larger fraction of the catch available in Philippine waters - Great opportunities for developing chemurgic industries have been explored and tested on a pilot plant scale.

Those Filipinos who are impatient to utilize their country's resources find themselves handicapped by several national habits - The accepted merchandising practice remains one of realizing large profits upon small volume of sales - Neither the Spanish nor the American administrations made a major effort to encourage economic development. World War 11 wrecked Manila more thoroughly than any other national capital except Warsaw, and destroyed roads, bridges, sugar centrals, schools, and many other facilities throughout the Islands. The Filipinos' preoccupation with achieving independence absorbed a large proportion of their energies until their country became a republic on July 4, 1946. Until recently value patterns of political leaders largely reflected this past focus of national attention. Young men, who often dream of becoming successful politicians, still pay exorbitant tuition fees in order to study law at commercialized colleges, and graduate to find them selves jobless. But those who master technical skills are more readily employed.

A new awareness, however, is stirring in the countryside as well as among the ordinary people in the burgeoning urban centers with their new suburban subdivisions. Labor is becoming organized and increasingly effective as both an economic and political influence, although sometimes for the benefit of paternal leaders. The barrio councils that became elective six years ago are developing as an instrument for elevating new leadership from the grass roots - They have little tax power and as a result lack means to engineer substantial economic progress on their own. But the fact that Congressmen and Senators in Manila today must appeal to the chairmen of the barrio councils for support at election time reduces the power of the former provincial political bosses and encourages greater concern for fundamental problems.

It was this restlessness and demand of the people to be heard that found expression in the costly, sometimes violent, yet relatively free elections of 1961. The Nacionalista Party administration in office was determined to succeed itself. It was favored with financial support from the great majority of the business community, many of whose members were beholden for official favors in the form of dollar allocations, credit from government banks, and reparations equipment from Japan. The United Opposition included Progressive Party and Grand Alliance leaders of the 1957 and 1959 elections who had made common cause with the Liberals. They based their campaign on an appeal to the rural electorate, pleading the

A NOTE ON THE PHILIPPINES

need for greater integrity in government, an end to the exchange controls that fostered corruption, and energetic attention to improving the lot of ordinary Filipinos. Civic organizations like Operations Quick Count, that mobilized roughly 60,000 volunteers, acted to insure an accurate and rapid tally of the votes cast. When the returns were in, the Liberal Party that led the opposition had elected a president, vice-president, and six of the eight senators who were chosen at large throughout the Islands for the 24-man Upper House. Most incumbent Nacionalista members of the House of Representatives were returned to office although Nacionalista control of this body was uncertain because the Liberals were trying to win over some of its Congressmen with the powerful attractions of the patronage controlled by the administration.

Inauguration of Diosdado Macapagal on December 31, 196 1, as the fifth President of the 15-year-old Republic represented more than a victory for a younger generation of Filipino leaders. It was the second time since independence that the nation had managed an orderly transfer of power from one party to another at the behest of the electorate. The earlier shift in political control had come in 1953 with election of President Ramon Magsaysay who led the Nacionalista Party to power. This demonstrated Philippine capacity to achieve political reform through regularly scheduled elections sets the Republic apart from most new nations in Asia. While serving to elevate new leaders more responsive to popular aspirations, the elections also provide a social safety valve and fortify faith in legal procedures - Filipinos need not resort to revolution to bring change. Instead, they are increasingly learning to rely upon Constitutional processes. Despite the rising peso price of political effort and the imperfections inherent in any representative system, this encourages a stability in government that is reflected in other areas. Blessed with an open society, Filipinos are free to organize, to propagate their ideas, and so seek to remedy public shortcomings and adapt their institutions to new needs. This served to release the creative potential of the rising generation of Filipinos and fosters a growing confidence in their own capacity for effective effort. They have a shared facility of expression in a common language, a version of Tagalog learned often through films and radio is gaining in use.

The Philippines is the only predominantly Christian country in the Far East, but religion has not always been a unifying influence in the Islands. The Spaniards largely made the State the servant of the Catholic Church in what they described as their divine mission to bring Filipinos the blessings of Christianity. They brought valuable innovations in agriculture as well. European religious orders while conscripting labor to build their massive edifices also protected the peasants against the worst colonial abuses. But resentment at the friars, tactics in dealing with tenants on their landed estates helped spark the final rebellion against Spanish rule. After the United States took over the Islands the American Catholic Church sent more progressive missionaries to the Philippines. And some of the ablest leaders in the Islands today were trained in schools run by American Jesuits - However, there are continued differences over policy between the European and American religious orders.

Filipino resentment against foreign domination of the Catholic Church at the turn of the century led a group of native priests to split off and

A NOTE ON THE PHILIPPINES

form the Philippine Independent Church that now is the second largest in the Islands, although it is only a fraction of the size of the Roman Catholic Church. With United States administration came also American Protestant missionaries. They built schools and a university and established some vigorous Protestant congregations, particularly among the new professional class. Since World War II, other denominations have gained adherents and challenged the traditional churches. The most important is the Iglesia ni Cristo, a highly disciplined native church. On Mindanao and in the Sulu Archipelago the Muslim Moros have remained devoted and occasionally fanatical defenders of their faith. Critical issues are on occasion generated by these differences in belief. But Christianity has implanted a value system that is among the most basic bulwarks of the Republic.

Probably the most disruptive factor in Philippine society at present is the gulf that separates the living standard of the ordinary citizens from that of the favored few. The average Filipino lives in a rural barrio composed of nipa huts perched upon stilts and lacking all modern facilities. He may be among the more than two million who are unemployed. Or perhaps he belongs to that estimated one-half of all the farmers who are idle some seven months of each year when lack of rain on the fields halts farming. In areas such as central Luzon the problem of low farm incomes, resulting from use of primitive methods, is aggravated by a vicious tenancy system that keeps many farm families in debt to landowners and moneylenders - The new Court of Agrarian Relations is affording tenants an avenue of appeal and is beginning to moderate old abuses. But the desire to own a plot of land, if only the size of a house lot, remains a deeply felt need among Filipinos.

At the other social pole are the comparatively few almost dynastic families who own much of the rural and urban real estate. They number among them some
of the politicians and control profitable businesses including dividend-paying universities - They are fond of palatial Spanish-type homes, Cadillacs, and swimming pools. Filipinos from this class casually take vacation trips to Hong Kong, Spain, Latin America, and the United States. They are now becoming "entrepreneur minded "-investing in cement plants, paint factories, and the many new "packaging industries" that grew up under the umbrella of exchange controls, tax incentives, and other forms of a protected market. With this is evolving a new interest in business management. While the tendency is still for senior executive positions to be reserved for those related by blood and marriage, there is also a growing premium on technical skills. This is encouraging the emergence of more Filipinos into an urban middle class, particularly in Greater Manila which holds more than 10% of the population. Educated young Filipinos who formerly saw their greatest opportunities in seeking government employment are beginning to school themselves accordingly. The commercial middle class, however, remains chiefly Chinese. Controlling most of the wholesale and retail trade, they tend to remain culturally Chinese even after acquiring citizenship, but their children learn Filipino ways.

Despite these divisive influences that are particularly active in their political life, Filipinos are an intensely patriotic people. The ordinary Filipino is fundamentally optimistic and sometimes seems almost delightfully irresponsible about the future; he has never known the pressure of preparing to survive long winters. Only recently in a few areas has he felt the grinding competition for a livelihood that results from overpopulation. His generosity toward friends is reflected in the national compadre system - and a compadre in need must be fed, lent money, or given a job regardless of personal or institutional consequences. The Filipino usually is not shackled by a sense of rigid limitations of his own status in society. Although the opportunities for advancement often are severely restricted, American education instilled great acceptance of the principle that a poor boy who worked hard could rise to the top. And social mobility lends vitality to the Re -public.

Filipinos are uniquely fortunate among the peoples of Asia in the relative wealth of unused natural resources. The Islands cover about 75 million acres - At present only 15 million acres are cultivated. And this land often is poorly managed. For purposes of comparison it is useful to realize that Formosa supports about 12 million persons at a higher average standard of living on two million acres of arable land. In addition to the land already settled the Philippines has an estimated 15 to 20 million acres of new and often rich land suitable for agriculture. When this land is irrigated climate permits the production of crops throughout the year. The Islands have a substantial stand of timber estimated to be worth more than $10 billion on the stump but it is fast being destroyed by "kaingineros" who cut and burn to plant crops and by some careless logging practices. So far no oil has been found in the Philippines, although several formations suggest its presence. Most of the coal discovered lies in thin seams and is not of adequate quality to support economically an iron and steel industry with present methods of production. The Islands have a significant and largely undeveloped hydroelectric power potential, including sites below Lake Lanao in Mindanao where some of the cheapest power in the world is produced. Iron ore, manganese, chromite, gold, copper, and other minerals are mined on an expanding scale. No complete geological survey has been made of the Philippines - But the limited explorations that have been conducted indicate there may be many rich mineral deposits yet to be discovered.

The personal skills, organizational techniques, and capital facilities needed to utilize these natural resources are beginning to appear. Despite a favorable climate and good soils, Philippine average rice production per acre per year is about one-fifth of the yield on Formosa and the Islands produce barely enough of this basic grain to meet local consumption requirements. Except in pineapple, sugar, and a few other industries, where plantation methods have been used to achieve more efficient production, similarly backward methods prevail throughout most of Filipino agriculture. The Philippines continues to import meat and dairy products although there is ample opportunity for production of these at home. There is a rich store of fibers in the Islands for which there is a growing demand in Japanese and European textile industries. But growing and processing such promising crops as ramie have only recently begun. Major crops such as the coconut are improving. Offshore and long-line fishing industries are taking a larger fraction of the catch available in Philippine waters - Great opportunities for developing chemurgic industries have been explored and tested on a pilot plant scale.

A NOTE ON THE PHILIPPINES

Those Filipinos who are impatient to utilize their country's resources find themselves handicapped by several national habits - The accepted merchandising practice remains one of realizing large profits upon small volume of sales - Neither the Spanish nor the American administrations made a major effort to encourage economic development. World War 11 wrecked Manila more thoroughly than any other national capital except Warsaw, and destroyed roads, bridges, sugar centrals, schools, and many other facilities throughout the Islands. The Filipinos' preoccupation with achieving independence absorbed a large proportion of their energies until their country became a republic on July 4, 1946. Until recently value patterns of political leaders largely reflected this past focus of national attention. Young men, who often dream of becoming successful politicians, still pay exorbitant tuition fees in order to study law at commercialized colleges, and graduate to find them selves jobless. But those who master technical skills are more readily employed.

A new awareness, however, is stirring in the countryside as well as among the ordinary people in the burgeoning urban centers with their new suburban subdivisions. Labor is becoming organized and increasingly effective as both an economic and political influence, although sometimes for the benefit of paternal leaders. The barrio councils that became elective six years ago are developing as an instrument for elevating new leadership from the grass roots - They have little tax power and as a result lack means to engineer substantial economic progress on their own. But the fact that Congressmen and Senators in Manila today must appeal to the chairmen of the barrio councils for support at election time reduces the power of the former provincial political bosses and encourages greater concern for fundamental problems.

It was this restlessness and demand of the people to be heard that found expression in the costly, sometimes violent, yet relatively free elections of 1961. The Nacionalista Party administration in office was determined to succeed itself. It was favored with financial support from the great majority of the business community, many of whose members were beholden for official favors in the form of dollar allocations, credit from government banks, and reparations equipment from Japan. The United Opposition included Progressive Party and Grand Alliance leaders of the 1957 and 1959 elections who had made common cause with the Liberals. They based their campaign on an appeal to the rural electorate, pleading the need for greater integrity in government, an end to the exchange controls that fostered corruption, and energetic attention to improving the lot of ordinary Filipinos. Civic organizations like Operations Quick Count, that mobilized roughly 60,000 volunteers, acted to insure an accurate and rapid tally of the votes cast. When the returns were in, the Liberal Party that led the opposition had elected a president, vice-president, and six of the eight senators who were chosen at large throughout the Islands for the 24-man Upper House. Most incumbent Nacionalista members of the House of Representatives were returned to office although Nacionalista control of this body was uncertain because the Liberals were trying to win over some of its Congressmen with the powerful attractions of the patronage controlled by the administration.

Inauguration of Diosdado Macapagal on December 31, 1961, as the fifth President of the 15-year-old Republic represented more than a victory for a younger generation of Filipino leaders. It was the second time since independence that the nation had managed an orderly transfer of power from one party to another at the behest of the electorate. The earlier shift in political control had come in 1953 with election of President Ramon Magsaysay who led the Nacionalista Party to power. This demonstrated Philippine capacity to achieve political reform through regularly scheduled elections sets the Republic apart from most new nations in Asia. While serving to elevate new leaders more responsive to popular aspirations, the elections also provide a social safety valve and fortify faith in legal procedures - Filipinos need not resort to revolution to bring change. Instead, they are increasingly learning to rely upon Constitutional processes. Despite the rising peso price of political effort and the imperfections inherent in any representative system, this encourages a stability in government that is reflected in other areas. Blessed with an open society, Filipinos are free to organize, to propagate their ideas, and so seek to remedy public shortcomings and adapt their institutions to new needs. This served to release the creative potential of the rising generation of Filipinos and fosters a growing confidence in their own capacity for effective effort.

AMERICAN UNIVERSITIES FIELD STAFF

Southeast Asia Series
Vol. XV No. 2

(Philippines)

MIRACLES WITH NEW RICE TECHNOLOGY
Improved Varieties and Techniques Benefit Philippine Farmers

By Albert Ravenholt

Morong, Rizal
August 1967

LIKE MOST OF HIS NEIGHBORS in Barrio Lagundi, Quirino Balajadia had always been makaluma, as they say here in Tagalog, that is, by nature conservative. He hesitated to hazard on untried methods his family's food needs and the slim resources that he had accumulated by growing rice, chiefly as a share tenant, and by tending his "small poultry"; but he reluctantly agreed to become a co-operator when government technicians approached him. They wanted Quirino to multiply a new variety of rice, IR8-288-3 (locally renamed "miracle rice''), for seed purposes. Identified by most specialists simply as IR8, it is the first strain developed and released by the *International Rice Research Institute* at Los Banos, which is some twenty-five miles across the water to the south on the shores of Laguna de Bay. That was just over a year ago, and since then Quirino's world has changed. Guided at each step by specialists working with the Agricultural Development Council for Rizal (popularly known as A.D.C.R.), he and forty-six other farmers in this province became pioneers in the demanding enterprise of raising rice in a way foreign to their traditions. On his trial field Quirino won first place among the smaller farmers in the competition with almost three times his usual harvest, and he is now a committed agent of agricultural innovation.

It is too early to judge how rapidly this rice technology, which is largely alien both to the Asian and to other tropics, will be put to work. It implies more than a revolution in rural customs of cultivation, for an infrastructure of dependable irrigation, available supplies of fertilizer and modern pesticides and the credit to buy them, new rice processing, storage and marketing facilities, and much else, are also required. Intimately involved is the question of relations between tenant farmers and landowners, since incentives for the cultivator are crucial and land prices promptly reflect expanded yields. However for more than half of the human race-most of them in the underdeveloped world who rely principally upon rice as the staple crop, the implications are immense. Provided that these farmers-now often subsistence farmers can profit through joining institutions for modernizing their methods, they can become producers of a salable surplus and thus earn the cash. that will make them industrial consumers. Here in the Philippines, the national government is committed to supplanting its $60 million annual rice import with local output by 1970. More progressive local officials and private firms have an increasingly potent role-for instance, large foreign companies like ESSO are making a major contribution with their networks of agroservice centers. First in Laguna and Tarlac, and more recently in eight additional provinces, the United States A.I.D. Mission participates directly with technicians and help on supervised credit. As always though, the critical factors are still the individual farmer himself and the considerations that move him to work and change.

When they initiated their intensive rice seed multiplication program fifteen months ago, government technicians assigned to Morong had good cause to seek Quirino's co-operation. Lean and energetic, the thirty-three-year-old farmer had completed the sixth grade in school and was known in the community as quick to learn and industrious in providing for his wife and four young children. Starting in 1958 as a poultry' raiser with a borrowed capital of ₱ 300 (₱ 3.90 = $1.00), he has built up a flock of 800 layers. His savings from the sale of eggs enabled him in 1962 to buy for ₱ 3,000 a 1-hectare (1 hectare = 2.47 acres) field located half a mile from the barrio. There is water only during the wet season when this swampy area is flooded waist-high, which compels Quirino to plant the long-stemmed elon elon variety of rice which here yields about 50 cavans per hectare (1 cavan of palay, or unhusked rice, dried to 14 per cent moisture content, weighs 97 pounds).

Quirino farms another field next to the barrio road, and if used as a demonstration plot this field would attract the attention of all who passed Covering 1.1 hectares, it is the inheritance left by his father, who died seventeen years ago, to his widow and seven children. Quirino cultivates it on shares, delivering one-half of the net harvest to his mother, after deducting the cost of seed and reaping and threshing, which total about one-sixth of the crop. He agreed to devote .47 hectares of this field to the new rice variety; his co-operation being won by a guarantee by the A.D.C.R. that his crop would exceed 80 cavans per hectare, or 60 per cent more than his usual harvest. This guarantee was limited to the full amount of a promised crop loan from the Rural Bank of Morong arid was contingent upon Quirino's following a detailed farming plan incorporated in his signed contract.

Quirino's crop loan, to be applied to his test plot and approved after meticulous consultation with government technicians, totaled ₱ 152.7 Bearing interest at the rate of 12 per cent annually, it was negotiated at the local Rural Bank where the provincial government had deposited ₱ 36,000 to cover such loans. The loan was not given in cash, so there was no temptation to use the funds for other purposes. Instead, "purchase orders" issued by the bank against the loan could be traded at any one of the ten private agroservice centers in the province authorized (and supervised as to prices and quality of merchandise) by the A.D.C.R. The purchase orders issued for Quirino included IX 12.50 to cover the purchase of half a cavan of the new seed, P 50.90 for ammonium sulphate and urea fertilizer, and ₱ 89.31 for spray and systemic insecticide.

The farm plan that Quirino pledged himself to follow stipulated each step in growing his crop. On July 21, 1966, using his carabao (water buffalo) and traditional implements, he plowed a seedbed covering 250 square meters (1 square meter = 10 square feet); and three days later he harrowed the seedbed. On August 1, he soaked his rice seed for twenty-four hours in water and spread it under cover to germinate for forty-eight hours. The seedbed was harrowed again and leveled, and on August 4 the sprouted seed was broadcast densely over the raised bed. A week later he broadcast 4 kilos (1 kilo = 2.2 pounds) of ammonium sulphate 20 per cent nitrogen fertilizer over the seedbed, and this was followed three days later with a foliar spray of Sevin 85. After an interval of another week, he again sprayed with Sevin 85; and three days later, on August 24, the rice seedlings were uprooted and ready for transplanting.

Meanwhile, as stipulated by the farm plan, Quirino had begun plowing his flooded paddy field of .47 hectares on August 10. He then harrowed it three times to pulverize the clods of earth. On August 24 two 50-kilo bags of urea containing 45 per cent nitrogen were spread on the field, which was then harrowed again to work in this fertilizer. Helped by his family and neighbors, with whom labor is exchanged, he transplanted the rice seedlings on August 25 and 26. At this stage, however, Quirino reverted to the traditional way: he failed to induce his helpers to follow the recommended practice of setting the rice plants in straight rows 25 centimeters (roughly 10 inches) apart, with the seedlings similarly spaced in the rows. Instead, they were planted in approximately this spacing but in a random pattern wherever an empty spot offered in the field. This was partly the result of Quirino's reluctance to compel friends, who were "doing him a favor," to use the pegged strings and planting boards required for the straight spacing of seedlings in this "new" system. Then, too, he was being a bit stubborn. After planting he did flood the field to a depth of 3 centimeters, later leading in more water from the canal to raise the level to 5 centimeters and then 10.

Within a week after transplanting the rice seedlings, Quirino broadcast 15 kilos of Gamma BHC granules over the field. This is a systemic insecticide that is absorbed from the water throughout the plant and is especially intended to combat the rice-stem borer. Then, after another week, he followed this with a foliar spray of Sevin (government technicians both lent him a sprayer and demonstrated the mixing of the ingredients), which was chiefly intended to guard against leafhoppers, the rice bugs locally known as atangya, army worms, and a possible host of the other pests that threaten rice crops. Since he had failed to plant in straight rows, Quirino was unable to utilize a rotary weeder (which has been introduced here and which is pushed through a field) ; instead, he had to pull weeds by hand.

Because he was raising rice for seed, Quirino began going through his field on September 28, roguing[1] rice plants that showed untrue to the short-stemmed (i.e., roughly 100 centimeters high), heavy-tillering characteristics of IR8. Where the plants were off-color, betraying a nutrient deficiency in the field, he broadcast additional fertilizer, and, although it was imperfect, he continued his weeding. Under the direction of a representative of the Bureau of Plant Industry, Quirino rogued his field for a second time on November 7 and a third time twenty days later. At this stage the dike was opened and the water from the field was drained off. With a government agriculturist supervising to guard against the mixing of grain from other fields, Quirino and his neighbors harvested the rice on December 2 and 3-121 days after the seed originally had been sown. As is traditional here, they gathered the sheaves of hand-cut grain and beat the heads over a bamboo grid to thresh the rice. When the grain was measured, Quirino had produced 65.16 cavans of unhusked rice on his trial plot (a rate of 138 cavans per hectare).

His prize for achieving the highest yield among the farmers cultivating less than .75 hectares was a 4-5 horsepower Japanese Yanmar diesel pump given by the provincial government.

Quirino bought back from the threshers the one-sixth of the harvest that they had earned by their labor for P 17 per cavan. Then, after the winnowing and mechanical drying of the unhusked rice at the A.D.C.R. warehouse in Morong, he sold his crop for IM 25 per cavan of cleaned grain for a gross return of ₱ 1,588. From these funds he repaid his loan of 1R 152.71 to the Rural Bank, plus ₱ 5.75 interest. After paying his mother her share, Quirino calculated (he does not keep detailed written accounts) that he netted "a little over 1z 600" from his trial plot of the new rice. On the remaining .63 hectare of his mother's land, he had planted Consehala, an old variety, and, employing traditional methods without fertilizer and insecticide, he harvested 35 cavans. This gave him a net return of about 12 270 from a field roughly 50 per cent larger than his trial plot. His mother's field, totaling 1.1 hectares, only has water available for irrigation during the wet season, and Quirino is now an enthusiastic advocate of joining with his neighbors to install a deep-well pump that would enable them to raise two rice crops annually.

Innovations have encouraged resourceful farmers to introduce their own rudimentary mechanization, such as the gasoline engine with attached fan which this couple is using for winnowing their crop.

MIRACLES WITH NEW RICE TECHNOLOGY

Quirino was so surprised and happy with his crop during the wet season that in December 1966 he rented a .75 hectare field from his aunt and moved in his new pump to irrigate the land from a nearby stream. Planting IR8 for this palagad (dry-season) crop and utilizing the new methods he had learned-this time including the transplanting of seedlings in straight rows-he harvested 98 cavans. (Since this crop was not raised for seed, no roguing was done.) Having paid the threshers in cash, he and his aunt now have 90 cavans of their recent harvest stored in the A.D.C.R. warehouse here, against which they have taken a commodity loan of F& 16 per cavan. Quirino sagely explains, "We are waiting for the price to improve before selling." He also earned 35 cavans of grain by renting his pump to neighbors who had also planted a dry season crop of lowland rice, some of them for the first time. He could sell this rice for ₱ 20 per cavan, but he prefers to keep it in bins under his house as "a reserve for family consumption." The value of this, plus the income from the crops grown on his mother's and aunt's land, the roughly ₱ .700 he retained from growing elon elon on his own 1-hectare lowland field, and the approximately 1z 1,000 net income from his poultry promise Quirino's family an annual income of some ₱ 3,770. "This is more than double my former yearly earnings," he admits, and it is a substantial sum of money in the economy of Barrio Lagundi.

The seed grain that Quirino produced with his first crop of IR8 was purchased by the Rizal Producers' Marketing Cooperative, to which he contributed ₱ 100 and became one of the founding members. Organized under the guidance of the A.D.C.R., this cooperative includes the original forty-seven seed growers in the province. All together, on a total of 45 hectares, all planted and cared for in much the same manner as Quirino's field, they harvested a total of 5,138 cavans. Certified, treated, and attractively bagged, this seed grain is now marketed as "Rizal Seed No. One." The largest order to date at ₱ 34 per cavan was for 100 tons shipped to Burma, where it is intended to help restore production in the country that was formerly the first rice-exporting nation of the world.

Although IR8 seed has now become readily available throughout the major islands of the archipelago, the Cooperative will continue to produce it, making its own selections for guarantee of quality. Quirino is planting 1 hectare of IR8 in the present wet season, which has just begun. On another rented 1-hectare field he will also multiply C4-63, a type developed by the College of Agriculture of the University of the Philippines at Los Banos. Somewhat lower in yield than IR8, this variety is more resistant to rice blast and virus diseases, and it may prove slightly better in eating quality. The A.D.C.R. will soon distribute to seed growers a newer type called IR5, which has been developed by the International Rice Resear, Institute.

Some 30 centimeters taller than IR8, it lodges more easily; but yields can be 15 per cent higher than IR8 and the eating quality conforms more to the traditional taste. The head of IR5 grain shows above the leave which farmers prefer, unlike IR8 which was designed to produce heads below the top leaves to protect them from birds.

The dramatic effects of these meticulously supervised demonstrations which the A.D.C.R. has engineered with its seed multiplication are z "Lodge" is an agricultural term meaning to fall or beat down, as grain lodged by rain, wind, or weight of seed evident throughout this province. After witnessing the increases in yield achieved by the original 47 co-operators who started growing IR8 just over a year ago, some 600 farmers planted "miracle rice" in the dry season that began last December and January. Through rural banks and agroservice centers they had access to credit and technical inputs, for which procedures had already been standardized by the A.D.C.R. In the neighboring municipality of Teresa in this dry season, a farmer harvested; over 200 cavans from 1 hectare-for, when irrigation water is available, dry season crops usually exceed those of the wet season because of more intense sunlight. A similar record yield was achieved here on a 1-hectare field by Aurelio Pasqual, the leader of the team of government specialists from the Agricultural Productivity Commission who advised Quirino and the seven other co-operators in this municipality. These eight co-operators and 250 farmers prompted by their example planted a total of 154 hectares of IR8 in Morong during the dry season just ended; and their average harvest was 120 cavans per hectare. As the planting now progresses for this present rainy season, with water more abundantly available, there are indications that 80 per cent of Morong's 1,558 farmers, cultivating 1,333 hectares, will be planting IR8. For the province as a whole, the number may exceed 7,000 farmers trying for "miracles", with the new rice and its technology.

F.H. Soriano, the Rural Bank manager here, has observed the consequences for the community "from the inside." When the present writer visited with him, only one crop loan was overdue for payment, that of his own tenant, who evidently felt less urgency than most about settling accounts. During the dry season the Rural Bank's crop loans had totaled ₽ 16,057.30, which left a substantial unused margin of the ₽ 36,000 advanced by the provincial government. Soriano feels that some farmers had yet to learn the procedures required for securing loans and that others were reluctant to bind themselves to the stringent cultivation provisions. A surprising number of farmers, however, seemed able to find the cash for buying both fertilizer and pesticides when they saw they were worthwhile. He calculates: "In the palagad crop just harvested, the least that any farmer who planted IR8 produced was double his usual harvest. One of my borrowers got four times his former harvest; and when another farmer sold 200 cavans, he proudly told me that he was earning more money than any salaried man from his barrio."

Certainly, expanded income from the utilization of the new rice growing technology is slowing-and in some barrios even reversing the trend toward the seeking of employment by farmers in Greater Manila, which adjoins Rizal Province. Collections of taxes on real property are rising in Morong, as more cash circulates in the community; and education is almost an obsession here, with many families spending more for sending their children on to high school and college. Other farmers are showing their first enthusiastic interest in mechanization. Five centrifugal pumps are now operated by co-operative irrigation associations, and for this water service the association collects 5 per cent of a harvest during the wet season and 10 per cent during the dry season, when, of course, use is greater. New rice varieties have a shorter growing season and are non-photoperiod sensitive, which allows them to be harvester at any time of the year. Since the grain becomes available at odd season and in greater quantities, the old methods of sun-drying are no longer sufficient (freshly harvested rice may hold 26 per cent moisture and a half of this must be removed to avoid spoilage and allow proper milling). With only thirty-three mechanical rice dryers in the Philippines, there is an urgent need for the expansion of drying facilities and also for the provision of protected storage capacity. As they discover possibilities of making much more money growing rice, the farmers in Morong are beginning to buy small Japanese-made, two-wheeled tractors which cost from ₱ 5,000 to ₱ 8,000 each, and they are talking familiarly about the comparative advantages of different types of attachments. F. H. Soriano anticipates that this mechanization will demand the most consequential type of financing in order to carry through the rice-growing revolution which has already begun.

The Agricultural Development Council for Rizal

The smooth engineering of such rapid agricultural advance as this is rare indeed, either here in the Philippines or elsewhere in Asia. The design of the organization and its program, the caliber of the men who lent their talents, and the opportunities afforded initially by the new rice technology-all these together made the difference. The idea itself was the result of a visit to Taiwan by Rizal's Governor Isidro Rodriguez, in 1965. Intrigued by the thoroughgoing rural transformation accomplish there during the previous sixteen years by the Chinese and American Joint Commission on Rural Reconstruction, Governor Rodriguez returned home determined upon a similar, though more modest, enterprise. Then in November 1965, when Colonel Frisco San Juan, the director of the province's Economic Development Commission, won an election to represent the rural second district, the project gained a committed advocate in Congress. Even so, the provincial leaders realized that they must look chiefly to their own resources. Fortunately, Rizal's public revenues had more than doubled over the past four years as industries moved in and tax collections improved. Included in the 1965-66 fiscal-year surplus ₱ 14 million there was an unexpended balance of ₱ 1.2 million in the province's agricultural fund; and, after much deliberation, the Governor an the provincial board members pledged this available annual balance of five years toward a ₱ 8.7 million budget to fund the A.D.C.R. Program.

In May 1966, Dr. Orlando Sacay was induced to leave the College of Agriculture of the University of the Philippines to become executive director of the A.D.C.R. Sacay - thirty-three years old, dynamic, and athletic-is among the country's leading agricultural economists and h previously tested out his innovative ideas in what is now the Presidential Economic Staff. Governor Rodriquez made several promises to him. He would be allowed to select his own men, staff the A.D.C.R. irrespective of political considerations. (Today the staff numbers twenty-two, who have been attracted chiefly from academic pursuits.) There were to be no grants to farmers, nor would the government have a direct ha in buying, selling, or lending. This was to guard against both barrio expectations of favoritism and individual hesitancy in repaying loans to a government body. Instead, credit would be channeled through- and use to vitalize the agricultural activities of-the private rural banks, whic4 are a new institution in many communities. An exception was made for gravity-irrigation systems, and provincial funds could be lent directly to irrigation co-operatives created to build and maintain such facilities Of major importance was an agreement with the national government that nearly 300 representatives of ten official government agencies concerned with rural activities in Rizal would be directed by the A.D.C.R.

To guard against the confusion that often attends programs of the national government in the countryside, the A.D.C.R. ruled that only team members of the Agricultural Productivity Commission were to "talk to the farmer." In the eighteen rural municipalities of Rizal, the A.P.C. has thirty-four farm-management technicians, plus agronomist and others to a total of 145. When representatives of the Bureau of Plant Industry should be needed-for certification of seed, for instance-the A.P.C. team leader would call for them; in like manner, he would request help from the Presidential Assistant for Community Development when faced with a _barrio_ organizational task, or from the specialists of the Bureau of _Animal_ Industry when their skills were required. To en sure mobility, the A.D.C.R. paid ₱ 40 per month travel expenses to ea national government employee enlisted in this effort. They were assembled for retraining-for although all these technicians had paper credentials, many had never actually raised a crop of rice-and they were warned that failure to co-operate fully would lead to their removal from the province, and that no one higher up in the national bureaucracy would be able to shield them from such discipline.

Once these preliminaries were settled, Dr. Sacay and his asso- ciates determined upon a single co-ordinated program and clear implementing procedures. Their objectives were to speed development of the province's available agricultural land, expand productivity, and increase farm income, with "maximum local participation." Western Rizal Province, where it fringes Manila Bay, is urban, and it is ruggedly mountainous to the east where it reaches into the lower ranges of the Sierra Madre. In between there are only some 20,000 hectares of cultivated land, of which about half is devoted to rice (the cultivable area fluctuating from wet to dry season as the level of Laguna de Bay rises and recedes). Although yields of rice during the rainy season have averaged nearly 60 _cavans_ per hectare, only 1,500 hectares were irrigated and not all of this had enough water to grow a second crop. New types of rice and methods of cultivation developed by the International Rice Research Institute and the College of Agriculture at Los Banos in neighboring Laguna Province to the south offered the prospect of a "breakthrough." Unlike the traditional rice varieties that tended to lodge and thus rot in the paddy field when fertilized, these new strains are short-stemmed and stiff-strawed and can respond to nitrogen with radical yield increases. Also, there was available for use a greatly increased body of technical knowledge about cultivation.

As the demonstration cultivation of rice, initially intended for seed multiplication; gained momentum, the A.D.C.R. focused efforts the expansion of irrigation, the aim being to triple the irrigated area in three years. In the past, the practice in the Philippines has usual been for the national government to construct water works and charg users an uneconomically low fee. Politicians campaigning for re-el have regularly promised to excuse even these water charges, and the collection has often lagged years behind; consequently, the maintenance of canals, etc., is minimal and many irrigation systems function at a fraction of their designed capacity.

The A.D.C.R. instead fixed responsibility upon the farmers, and helped to organize them into co-operative irrigation associations. A survey had indicated the feasibility and cost of constructing a gravi system, funds were lent directly to an association.   To date, Fr 525,9 has been advanced to nine associations building irrigation canals with the help of private contractors for the watering of over 900 hectares. The average cost per hectare benefited is substantially below that fo comparable projects of the national government, and farmer-members are themselves responsible for both operation and *maintenance.* The by, a chronic source of rural friction is being overcome - that is, who decides on the allocation of water in canals when it is scarce. Another twenty-two such associations have now been organized, and their loan applications and proposed gravity systems are being screened. Pump irrigation is being expanded by the lending through rural banks of ₱ 142,800 for the purchase and installation of equipment by individual farmers and associations.

The A.D.C.R. is now turning its attention to three new programs In the remote Sierra Madre foothills of Tanay, 300 hectares owned by the municipality are being cleared. Emphasis there will be placed u the introduction of improved pastures for dairy and beef cattle in ord to build up breeding herds. A stud will be established to upgrade the quality of the horses, which still draw calesas, or two-wheeled carts, in many towns and barrios. In June 1967, 300 A.D.C.R. kits containing vegetable seeds, fertilizer, and insecticide were distributed to as many farmers; and the results of these plantings will help determine the nell step. Adapted to highland areas and capable of returning four or five times as much cash per land unit as rice, vegetables appear promising for an area with ready access to Greater Manila's roughly four milliol urban consumers. The Rizal Producers' Marketing Cooperative, bege with the forty-seven seed-growers as members, is now being enlarged by inviting in those who join the irrigation associations. Aside from buying, storing, and selling rice, the Marketing Cooperative is startin) to deal in fertilizer, pesticides, equipment, and other farm supplies. Now on the drawing board, and scheduled for construction next year, is a ₱ million Farmers' Market that would provide a wholesale outlet for retail buyers,. including both city supermarkets and the small sari sari stores that cater to barrio needs.

MIRACLES WITH NEW RICE TECHNOLOGY

Aside from the ₱ 668,759.02 in loans utilized to date for irrigation, the A.D.C.R. has lent ₱ 269,700 through rural banks to finance the purchase of farm machinery; ₱ 91,600 for production loans is outstanding, plus ₱ 30,000 for commodity loans and ₱ 60,000 for general improvements-a total of ₱ 1,120,059.02. "Start-up expenses" for vehicles, typewriters, etc., for the A.D.C.R.'s modest office adjoining the provincial capital in Pasig, amounted to ₱ 72,000; and administrative expenses for the first year, including both staff and travel allowances for national government technicians were ₱ 170,000. For the current year, the A.D.C.R. expects to reduce this to about ₱ 140,000, since much of the initial investigatory work has been completed. The evidence is conclusive that more important than the size of government budgets for rural development is a perceptive knowledge of how to use such funds, plus official support for technically skilled men to pursue freely pragmatic goals. Assured of such facilities and support, even a tenant farmer can move ahead, helped by the new technology, both for rice production and for other crops, that can now be placed at his disposal.

AMERICAN UNIVERSITIES FIELD STAFF

SOUTHEAST ASIA SERIES
(Thailand)

OF DUCKS AND GEESE AND PIGS FOR BANGKOK

By

Albert Ravenholt

March 1970

"MY REAL AMBITION was to be a doctor," Anupongs Chiewcharnvlijit explained as we ducked under the overhanging roof to look at a prize, purebred sow. "I was nineteen years old then and had just graduated from high school. I was the second in line and my older brother was already helping my father in his business, buying poultry from farmers in this part of Thailand and selling to the markets in Bangkok. But there were just too many younger brothers and sisters still to be educated -- we are six boys and two girls altogether in our family. So, I gave up my dream of a professional career. Instead, the family decided we would start farming on our own. We bought the first six *rai* (one *rai* equals four-tenths of an acre) from the former Queen. This used to be an old summer palace. When we got it, everything was jungle and nobody wanted it, so we only paid 12,000 *baht* (twenty *baht* equal one U.S. dollar) for each *rai*. We had a total starting capital of B40,000 saved by my father and grandfather over thirty years in the poultry business. It was not enough. We borrowed B200,000 from the bank at 14 per cent interest, giving the land as collateral. That's how Thai Roong Kit Farm - the name means "progress" - started. I must admit that it probably wouldn't be the success it is today except that I was one of the first two Thais -- the other was a girl -- who went to the United States on the International Farm Youth Exchange Program with your Four-H Clubs. That really opened my eyes and gave me ideas."

AnuPongs - first names are used in Thailand with or without the equivalent of "Mister," depending upon the degree of familiarity, except in formal references when both names are used, cautions matter-of-factly: "Never assume that most, or even many, Thai farmers are as prosperous as I am. They are not. Actually, many ordinary farmers even in this area have a tough time making ends meet. Like farmers nearly everywhere, we have to gamble on so many things; weather, livestock and poultry diseases, prices in the market, plus a long list of other difficulties." Yet, in spite of such hazards, Anupongs has prospered spectacularly, although only after some sobering setbacks surmounted with immense effort by him and his brothers together with shrewd mastery of the business side of modernizing agriculture. On his farm of thirty *rai* -fifteen *rai* now owned form the home farm and another fifteen *rai* are leased across the road -- he presently has 130 sows on cement-floored pig pens. They are serviced by five purebred boars; two Landrace, two Duroc Jerseys and one Large White. Three hundred small pigs from recent litters are being weaned and will be sold to other farmers for finishing and fattening at the age of ten weeks for B350 to B400 each.

Under the long roofs of the poultry houses are some of the 600,000 ducks sold each year from this farm to Bangkok. Broilers are only a side line

OF DUCKS AND GEESE AND PIGS FOR BANGKOK

and 6,000 to 7,000 are raised in each batch to be marketed in ten weeks when they are expected to weigh 1.7 kilos (one kilogram equals 2.2 pounds) and bring about B 13 per kilo. Most of the geese are kept on the rented property across the road, carefully fenced in by sheet metal hammered out of old gasoline drums. Some 40,000 geese are sold annually to Bangkok, where the chief market is to Chinese restaurants that serve them as "Peking duck." Anupongs explains: "None of our Thai ducks are really big enough for that specialized market when the roasted reddish-brown duck is served whole on the table, so they use geese instead."

Next to the roomy three-story cement house Anupongs and his brothers have built for B300,000 is the largest of the fish ponds, covering two *rai*. Like the other seven fish ponds of one *rai* each, it is partially shaded by coconut palms -- it is not easy even in this farming region to find boys who will climb fifty or sixty feet to harvest the nuts. Every five months, these fish ponds are stocked with half a million two-inch-long fingerlings of plarduk, a fish particularly popular in Northeastern Thailand. Each harvest is expected to yield about forty tons of fish, to be sold at B6 to B8 per kilo.

Anupongs keeps many of his figures in his head and, as the business manager in charge of buying, selling, and planning for this family enterprise, he has an extraordinary memory for costs. Gross monthly expenses total roughly B300,000, including wages for the eighteen full-time employees -- they receive food, clothing, and other care plus from B450 to B1,000 in cash each per month. Annual "profit" Anupongs estimates at about B500,000. "We brothers get no salary," he said. "We use the money as we all vote should be done.

Like yesterday, my older brother wanted to go to Bangkok and needed B1,000, so we voted to let him have it." Also, they are supporting their youngest brother, age 21, who is studying mechanical engineering in Bangkok. Anupongs acknowledges that they still owe the banks B400,000, "I feel a little embarrassed when I see some of the bankers at meetings of our new Rotary Club," he added. Once all such debts are paid, he calculates, they will have net assets of B1,200,000 from the nine years Thai Roong Kit Farm has been in business. At least as impressive as this solid financial success in farming, is their role in the community as agricultural innovators, sharing knowledge of new and effective methods with less fortunate neighbors. Just re-elected Chairman for Community Service of the Nakorn Pathom Rotan, Club, Anupongs also remains the leader of the Changwat, or province, Four-H Clubs, which total some 700 members each with their farming projects.

Rural Western Thailand

Nakorn Pathom, with its population of approximately 250,000, is the mercantile center for one of Thailand's richer rural regions; the western edge of the huge and fertile Bangkok Plain. Built up over eons by alluvial deposits washed down from the mountains, this Plain is extending itself out into the Gulf of Thailand at the rate of fifteen to twenty feet every year. Physically, this community has been shaped principally by the Khwae Yai and Khwae Noi Rivers starting some 300 miles northwest of here and joining at Kanchanaburi to form the Maeklong. The Khwae Noi, which won international notice through the film "Bridge on the River Kwai" has its headwaters near the Three Pagodas Pass on the Burma border. It was along this route that Allied prisoners labored for the Japanese Imperial Army during World War 11, constructing the railway to Rangoon -- it now operates only a short distance up the Khwae Noi Valley and occasionally brings Australians, English, and others visiting the graves of their relatives. As the gateway to peninsular Southern Thailand, Nakorn Pathorn also is a major junction for the railway that continues south through Malaysia to Singapore. Buses traveling every few minutes over e excellent, new, cemented highways now enable students to reach Bangkok in one and one-half hours, where formerly this trip required half a day more over often rutted and muddy roads. With such improved communications, including telephones and electricity, have come the bustle of new ideas and recently construction of a few factories that are shattering the once tranquil rural life centered on the rice paddy fields, coconuts, and mango trees that with bamboo groves dominate the landscape.

Historically, this region is of especial importance to the Thais. Recent archeological finds near Kanchanaburi are compelling a revision of earlier assumptions about Southeast Asia prehistory. Pottery shards and other evidence indicates that the foothills of the mountain ranges forming the boundary with Burma were a significant center of organized human habitation several thousand years older than was formerly believed. Thais venerate Nakorn Pathom itself as the site where Buddhism was first introduced to this land by missionaries sent by India's Emperor Asoka in the third century B.C. The vessel bearing these proponents of the faith that so pervasively has shaped Thai civilization reportedly landed at Nakom Pathom, now some fifty airline miles from the sea that has been pushed back by the build-up of alluvial land. The city is dominated by the Pra Prathorn Chedi, largest and tallest among the Buddhist stupas in Thailand, the foundations of which date back more than 1,400 years. Although modem commerce and the mechanical innovations it brings are transforming particularly Thai urban life, Buddhism remains the vital social cement that largely has enabled the Kingdom to digest imported innovations without losing its unique identity.

As farming country, the region has few peers in Southeastern Asia. Soils here share the advantages of the alluviums elsewhere in the Central Plain, without the handicaps in large areas where flooding during the rainy season from June to November is so great that only floating types of rice can be raised. Here, drainage usually is adequate to allow a much wider variety of crops. Annual rainfall of about forty-three inches requires that paddy fields also be irrigated and the old canals that take water from the rivers upstream wander irregularly over the landscape. Although ancient water-lifting wheels and other devices now are being replaced with more modern pumps, this remains primarily a one-crop rice growing area., Other significant annual crops are sugar cane, peas, tobacco, mung beans, peanuts, sesame, and corn. With improved transportation, Western Thailand already is an important supplier of vegetables and fruits for Bangkok's three and one-half million residents. Bananas of numerous kinds, the excellent Thai pomelos, chicos, a considerable variety of citrus, as well as pineapples and other tropical fruits are sold at stands along the highway. Raising papaya, jack fruit, mangosteens, durian, rambutan, santol and tamarind is increasingly a prosperous enterprise for both small and large farmers, although almost every one of these crops has its particular problems.

Beginnings of Thai Roong Kit Farm

As Anupongs recalls: "We picked this land, which was then three kilometers (one kilometer equals six-tenths of a mile) from where our family lived in town, not only because it was cheaper. We also wanted to be far enough away so that neighbors would not complain about the smell. My brothers and I worked to clear off the jungle ourselves. We hired carpenters to build the poultry houses with individual batteries to check production of each bird, using wood and thatch on the roofs -- that is cheaper and cooler. For the pig pens, we also used wood and thatch for the same reasons, but we invested from the start in cement floors. Also, we dug out the first fish pond. Right away my oldest brother and I moved out here to live. For our laying hens, we started with 2,000 Leghorns that we bought as day-old chicks for B6 each. The pond we stocked with 4,000 Chinese carp fingerlings. Our pig project was started with sixty *wieners* that we bought for B200 each. They were different kinds of crossbreds; native type mixed with Duroc Jersey, Berkshire and some Hampshire."

As he thinks back, Anupongs is convinced they were "just fortunate" that first year. He relates: "From the very start we mixed our own feed. I bought rice bran -- there are mills here that remove the oil, so we can feed more of it. We also bought broken rice that can't be exported, soybean meal and fish meal, and minerals. Also, we fed water hyacinth grown in the pond. I studied every book I could find on animal husbandry and the government agricultural extension men were very helpful and friendly. Still, we were lucky. The farm was new. There was no infection around here and we had few visitors, so we had almost no mortality among our pigs. After fourteen months, when they weighed about 180 kilos each, we sold them at the farm on a live weight basis for B9 per kilo. That allowed us to make a profit of about 40 per cent on our gross sales."

"With our chickens we didn't do so well," Anupongs continues. "We kept records on each bird. When a hen produced less than thirteen eggs per month, we culled. And, after a while, we were down to a little over 1,000 layers. Still it was hard to make money, what with the fluctuating egg prices. Also, the dogs around here would bark so much and frighten the layers out of producing. After two years, we sold out the last of our layers, and that was the end of our egg business. With the fish we were just learning our way, and that was not an expensive venture."

The second year, Anupongs and his brothers bought 200 pigs when they were about four months old. He said: "We started to have trouble with pneumonia, although none of the pigs died from it. One of the government veterinarians talked with me about vaccination. I said that we had never had any difficulty on that score -- I was still too much of a city boy. The farmers around here didn't really know about vaccination then; some of them believed if you vaccinated your pigs they would die. That lot of pigs we sold when they were about twelve months old and weighed roughly 150 kilos each. We sold the pigs here at the farm at B7.50 to B8 per kilo live weight, making a profit of about 20 per cent of gross. That's how we paid off the first bank loan."

OF DUCKS AND GEESE AND PIGS FOR BANGKOK

With such encouraging returns, Anupongs decided they would double their operation the third year. They bought 400 pigs aged about four months for B200 each. "We made a critical mistake," Anupongs realized later. "We got our young pigs from many different farmers. I think that's partly how the infection got in here. It only started slowly, with a few of our pigs not wanting to eat, then getting sick and a few would die. When the pigs got to weighing about 80 to 100 kilos, then they really started dying. The whole area around here had the same thing happen -- the farmers said 'the Gods hate us.' And the veterinarians came in and told us we had hog cholera. Then we started vaccinating and still the pigs died. I can even now remember the smell, when we hauled the dead pigs out and burned them. The pigs that were still alive and big enough, we sold them right away and cheap, just to get them to market. Every time we sold a pig, we would sacrifice to the gods, giving a chicken or otherwise sharing. At least it helps in your mind. More than sixty of our pigs died and I guess we lost at least B50,000 that year. And I learned that we didn't know enough."

shows two prize Landrace sows kept, like all his pigs, in clean and dry cement-floored pens under

they are noisy, geese are kept on rented property across the road. Fresh water hyacinth from local canals is here being fed to make up green portion of their diet.

OF DUCKS AND GEESE AND PIGS FOR BANGKOK

International Farm Youth Exchange

It was during this period of travail that Anupongs encountered the opportunity that has radically changed his life. As he remembers, "That is when I met Donald Mitchell, who was from Pennsylvania. He had been about six years in Thailand working on agricultural extension with the U.S. AID Mission in Bangkok, especially on Four-H Clubs. I was the first member of our Four-H Club here who continued out of school and he came to see my project. He told me about the exchange program and helped me be selected, along with one Thai girl who has continued in the government service. They paid all the expenses and, in June 1963, we flew by way of Hong Kong, Tokyo, and San Francisco to Washington, D.C. -- it was the first time I had ever been out of Thailand. We had our orientation at the National Four-H Club headquarters near Washington, D.C. At that time I knew very little about the United States or what farming outside of Thailand was really like."

"They sent me first to Kansas," Anupongs recalls vividly. "The first farm I went to was that of Lester Jackson near Fort Scott. It was a big farm, about 1,500 acres and they had about 800 head of beef cattle on pasture. That's where I learned to drive tractors and plow. I even operated a Caterpillar D-8 bulldozer, clearing land and filling gullies. Most important, my host was a veterinarian. So, we talked about animal diseases -- that was very useful. I also saw some research on pigs. It was with that family I learned to play chess and also the accordion." Anupongs continues today to exchange letters with the Jacksons, relating his own experiences and learning from them of farm and family events back in Kansas. The second family he lived with managed a dairy farm with twenty Holstein cows that he learned to milk. As Anupongs said, "I felt that was really not my business -- I couldn't see it in Thailand. At the third farm where I stayed near Conway, I learned about wheat and how to operate a combine. I like heavy machinery."

Midway in their American tour all the International Farm Youth Exchange Program participants met in Madison, Wisconsin. "There were 143 of us altogether," Anupongs recalls. "That included eighty-four men and fifty-nine women from forty-four countries. For one week we just talked, getting to know each other and where we came from and what we did at home. We also had organized discussions, exchanging ideas on our program and how the experience could be more useful. At the same time, we had a chance to look around and learn a little at the University. It was fall, and I swam in the lake. After Madison, I went to Lansing, Michigan. I stayed with a family who were not really farmers, but one of their boys was very active in Four-H and wanted to come to Thailand. So, for three weeks, I taught him some of the language. Then I went to a dairy farm near Belding. They had over 100 cows and a modern milking parlor, plus fifty pigs. I drove the tractor and helped make silage."

Anupongs was particularly impressed with the farm auctions he attended in Michigan. "At first I thought the auctioneer talked way too fast," he admits. "Your system in the United States is different; the auctioneer *raises* the price after each bid. Here in Thailand, he waits for the buyers to bid the price up, like at the daily poultry auctions in Bangkok. I also visited a slaughter house in Michigan and saw how they made sausages. The last family I stayed with was near Bay City. The father worked for the Chevrolet plant, although I only went through the Pontiac factory. I suppose it was what you would call a part-time farm. Many places in the United States I gave speeches; to Rotary and Lions Clubs, Parent Teacher Associations, and Girl Scouts. By then my English had become more fluent. You know, I first learned English from the tourists who would come here to visit the temple. I also picked up some from hitchhikers who came through here from Southern Thailand. Sometimes, I would invite them home and they would stay with me for a week or so. A couple of them were engineers and, at the start of our farm, they helped me design better buildings and make other improvements."

His American program ended as winter began with cold and snow in Michigan, and Anupongs' thoughts were again on the tropical warmth of his homeland. He decided, however, that he could afford out of his own pocket to add enough on his return ticket to travel through Europe. With the list and home addresses of his fellow Exchange Program participants as a tour guide, he traveled by bus for three weeks around England, then to Holland, Belgium, Luxembourg, Switzerland, and Germany. Some fifty kilometers from Rome, he visited an Italian fellow delegate who raised sheep and pigs. Likewise, in Greece, Turkey, Iran, and India, Anupongs was welcomed into the homes of fellow delegates he had met in the United States. He said, "Always we were talking, about different ways of farming, exchanging ideas on disease, feed rations. I got home here in February 1964, just in time for Chinese New Year."

Starting Anew At Thai Roong Kit

When Anupongs returned home, he found his brothers and father had encountered continued difficulties on the farm. "While I was in the States," he said, "our pigs got foot and mouth disease. Some of them could not stand, so they couldn't come and eat. And again we lost money, although not so much. Many people here wanted me to talk about my experiences in America and show slides, but I could only do that occasionally. We had too much to do on the farm. I made up my mind we couldn't just copy what I had seen in the United States —we had to adjust it to our situation and the market. People around here did not think we could make money any more on pigs, but I was convinced there was a way. From the United States I got the idea of using higher protein and dry feed mostly. Also, besides vaccination, we had to incorporate antibiotics in the feed. That's something it is never worthwhile buying cheap, especially in Thailand where some of these are phony. It's a better investment to buy the very best direct from reliable importers. Using this system, we bought 500 wiener pigs that we raised ready for market in 1965. But the price was down; we got only B6 per kilo and our feed costs had been quite high. My conclusion was that our feed conversion ratio was too poor."

It was this finding that convinced Anupongs, in 1965, that they must keep their own sows and produce an improved breed. "We bought one English Large White boar - purebred -- from Kasetsart University when it was three months old for B3,000," he related. "This I bred to our native sows. Still, I was not satisfied. So, I selected the best females from that generation and crossed them back to the Large White boar. This gave me a bigger sow, and we saved only those that produced a litter of at least ten pigs. And the feed conversion ratio proved better. Also, we decided to go into chickens again, but this time with broilers. We started 1,000 chicks of the native type crossed with the imported heavy breeds. Then we found the feed conversion with these was not so good, so we shifted to a cross between Conniss and White Rock. Those chicks cost us B5.50 each when they were one day old. The American military bases in Thailand were being built up then, and we sold 1,500 of those broilers through an Australian dealer in Bangkok supplying the U.S. forces. But his prices were too low, so I told him, 'My father is a poultry man and he can do better on selling for us.'

It was this basic lesson, first learned on his trip to the United States and Europe, concerning the importance of feed conversion ratios, that has guided Anupongs since then in his hog development program. Although he has kept a few of the upgraded, crossbred native sows, which generally are more prolific, the great majority of his breeding stock now consists of hybrids of imported breeds. "I also maintain purebred lines," he added, "both to replace my own sows and sell to others. I can sell a two and one-half months old purebred male Landrace for 131,000 and a female for B800. Our major program aims to produce young pigs that we sell to other farmers for fattening when they weigh eighteen to twenty kilos at B350 and B400 each - our neighbors also are learning the advantages of better feed conversion ratios. We are trying now for five litters from a sow in two years. If we discover that a sow regularly produces less than six live pigs per litter, we sell her. Ultimately, our goal is to have 500 sows. That should make us among the biggest hog farms in Thailand, if not the largest of all."

Unlike many of the smaller farmers who raise pigs in this region, Anupongs, is not worried about marketing even his full-grown hogs; he is not at the mercy of the Bangkok monopoly that, through controls on most slaughtering and retail sales of pork, periodically depresses prices paid to producers. "First of all, I am big enough so I can bargain better," he explains, "and I keep on top of market conditions. When prices are low in Bangkok, I sell my full-grown pigs to other provinces. For this you should have enough to make up a truck load. The trouble with the small farmers is that they fail to work together and organize a real cooperative for their marketing. When prices are good, they don't care - it's only when prices of pigs are down that they get concerned and then it's too late to do much about it."

As the brothers have built up their broiler operation to 6,000 to 7,000 birds per batch, they also have become more efficient. The price of the day-old chicks, which are a cross between White Rock and Conniss, is down to B5 each. For every 100 they buy, the hatchery actually gives them 104, so, with an average loss of six birds per hundred, they figure a mortality of two per cent. This now allows them a profit of B6 to B8 per bird, sold at the age of ten weeks, when they average 1.7 kilos and bring B 13 per kilo.

Duck raising is planned to bring birds to market at the two seasons when there is a peak demand in Bangkok; Chinese New Year and the autumn Moon Festival. For each of these seasons, Thai Roong Kit Farm aims to sell 300,000 ducks. Day-old ducklings are bought from hatcheries for B I each. These are kept on the farm for the first twenty days when the ducklings are most delicate, and the mortality usually is about 10 per cent. Then,

OF DUCKS AND GEESE AND PIGS FOR BANGKOK

Anupongs turns over many of the ducks to smaller farmers, who each contract to *raise* 1,000 to 1,500. Anupongs provides feed, medicine, and supervision and pays the farmers B 1 per month for two months for each duck. Any that die of disease are a loss for his account-the contract farmer must bring in the head and legs of the dead duck. Other ducks that disappear are charged to the farmers' accounts at B4 to B5 each, depending upon size. Feed per duck costs from B5 to B8 to *raise* it to a weight of one and one-half kilos. Since ducks sell for B 12 per kilo just before Chinese New Year and B7 a week after this great season of celebrating, success depends very much upon keeping an accurate eye on the lunar calendar that regulates Chinese feast days.

The *raising* of geese likewise is managed primarily with an eye to the Chinese New Year and autumn Moon Festival markets. Day-old goslings are much more expensive, costing from B5 to B 15 each, although the mortality of about 5 per cent is lower. After being held twenty days in the brooders on the farm, when the goslings are old enough to eat grass and glean leftover rice in the paddy fields, Anupongs turns over many of these to contract farmers on similar terms to those arranged for ducks. When they have consumed about B10 worth of concentrated feed and are about three months old, these geese weigh from three and one-half to four kilos each. Just before the holiday seasons, they can be marketed for B50 to B60 each, while ten days later the price usually drops to roughly one-half. Although Chinese restaurants in Bangkok and elsewhere serve these geese the year around as "Peking duck," entertainment outside of the home falls off substantially between festival seasons.

Planning Ahead

While Anupongs and his brothers already have created a consequential farming business, they are restlessly planning ahead. And each improvement on the farm is carefully designed to fit into an over-all plan. To insure an abundance of fresh water for their pigs, poultry, and fish, they have drilled three wells, each to a depth of about 120 meters. The average cost was B 15,000 for drilling a well plus B5,000 for each pump and B4,000 for each motor. This year, they invested B30,000 in a large elevated concrete storage tank that provides water under pressure throughout the farm. Their most recent acquisition is a new six-ton Mercedes Benz truck that cost B150,000. It is especially assigned to hauling raw material for feed from wherever this can be purchased advantageously. Rice bran is brought from a mill twenty-two kilometers away that extracts the oil by solvent process, and broken rice is purchased from a number of the larger rice mills. Another investment is B100,000 in a diesel-powered long chassis Land Rover serving multiple purposes, including carrying Anupongs on nearby business trips -- he still rides the bus into Bangkok -- collecting scrap fish that are ground and mixed with rice bran for feeding fish in the ponds, and hauling ducks and geese to contract farmers.

Anupongs is now studying the possibility of building a commercial feed mill to replace the small hammer mill and mixer he uses and selling their own brand of ready-mixed feed to farmers in the region. He reasons: "Our production of corn in Thailand has been going up so fast. We have an annual crop of 1,750,000 tons. We have now become one of the world's

OF DUCKS AND GEESE AND PIGS FOR BANGKOK

important exporters of corn, shipping out about a million and a half tons a year, mostly to Japan, Taiwan, Singapore, Hong Kong, and Malaysia. Why should we not convert that corn into feed and hogs here at home? And then we can export the hams and bacon, when we produce more than we need. That way we would also make more money than we do just shipping out the corn. Thai farmers will buy commercial feed when they know it is reliable and they see they can make money feeding it to their pigs. And here I can show them what can be done."

As operations at Thai Roong Kit Farm have proliferated, the brothers have found it necessary to specialize. While the eldest brother travels frequently with their father, buying and selling poultry, he lives at the farm and, as the only married member of the partnership, his wife cooks and keeps house for Anudat. At the age of twenty-four, Anudat comes next after Anupongs. He has taken charge of chickens, ducks and geese. Yangyong, who is twenty-three years old, is responsible for the pigs, especially the sows and their litters. And twenty-two-year-old Wotiwat gives particular attention to the fish. Whenever necessary, the brothers may "stand watch" to help out a sow about to deliver a litter to insure that none of the small Pigs is crushed or care for a batch of new ducklings when bad weather threatens to create problems. While their business operations are separated from the father's trading activities, they have yet to think in terms of more formal corporate organization. Anupongs' family typifies a phenomenon that accounts in part for Thailand's modern progress as contrasted with some of her neighbors in Southeast Asia; assimilation of the Chinese who in turn have come to feel themselves as Thais. Born in Thailand, Anupongs' father is of Chinese ancestry. His mother is a Thai, and the family identifies itself very much with the Kingdom, sharing both concern for Thailand's national future and pride in its accomplishments. Though Anupongs is quick to capitalize upon business opportunities created by occasions like the Chinese New Year celebrations among the large Chinese community in Bangkok, he thinks and talks like a Thai and I did not find him keeping records in Chinese or calculating on an abacus, as frequently happens among Chinese. The fact that the family has chosen farming as their endeavor is also at variance with traditional Overseas Chinese emphasis upon trading and similar commercial pursuits. Rather, Anupongs' drive is directed toward adapting to his homeland the best of the modern ideas he gleaned on his International Farm Youth Exchange Program tour and proving that in Thailand they can farm as productively and profitably as anywhere.

ENCYCLOPEDIA BRITANNICA YEARBOOK, 1987

The Philippines:
Is Democracy Restored?

BY ALBERT AND MARJORIE RAVENHOLT

Albert and Marjorie Ravenholt have made Manila their base since soon after World War 11, he as a foreign correspondent and associate of the American Universities Field Staff International, and she as an area consultant on the Philippines and Southeast Asia. Albert Ravenholt wrote the feature article "The Philippine Republic: A Decade of Independence" in the 1957 Britannica Book of the Year *and a subsequent book,* The Philippines: A Young Republic on the Move.

MODERN REVOLUTIONS have a cruel way of cannibalizing both their leaders and the ideals that originally generated them. As 1986 drew to a close, it was not yet clear whether this would be the fate of the extraordinary popular revolt that had elevated a once house wifely widow, Corazon Aquino *(see* BIOGRAPHIES), to the presidency of the Philippines. With an almost fiesta-like mobilization of "people power," the Filipinos deposed a dictatorship that had robbed the now 40-year old republic of its zestful political life and plundered its economy. This nation of 7,100 islands, guarding the Pacific approaches to Southeast Asia, had paid dearly for the years of tyranny. Two-thirds of its 56 million citizens were impoverished, many had suffered in prisons, some had been murdered, and others had fled into exile. In February 1986, as the lunar new year inaugurated the Year of the Tiger, hundreds of thousands of students, nuns, and entire families of ordinary people, armed only with prayers, flowers, and food, turned back the tanks of the despot who aimed to steal his reelection as president. In a demonstration of nonviolence that sent ripples of hope throughout the lands where dictators ruled, Filipinos displayed a depth of commitment to democracy that surprised even themselves. For those who value human liberty and champion the rights of the individual, it was one of the most positive and stirring events of modern times.

It was not, however, a universally popular upheaval. Over the past 15 years, thousands of students and other dissatisfied or fearful young people had taken to the hills. Joining the New People's Army (NPA), which operates under the outlawed Communist Party of the Philippines (CPP), they established a growing alternative authority. By 1986 these insurgent forces ruled between one-third and one-half of all Philippine territory. Even on the outskirts of Greater Manila, it was a rare fishpond owner who did not pay tax to this rival government. Ambushing Philippine Army patrols, enforcing vigilante justice in the countryside, and indoctrinating recruits with teach-ins, the insurgents continued to extend their reach. In December 1986 their open organization, the National Democratic Front (NDF), negotiated a cease-fire with the new national government.

THE PHILIPPINES: IS DEMOCRACY RESTORED

The leaders of the insurgents are doctrinaire Marxists, as they define their ideology. They boycotted the February 7 election in which incumbent Pres. Ferdinand E. Marcos and his vice-presidential candidate, Arturo Tolentino, were defeated by a united opposition led by Corazon Aquino and now Vice-Pres. Salvador,P. Laurel. The Marxists had refused to join the protests triggered by the assassination of former senator Benigno Aquino on Aug. 21, 1983. They were absent from the almost religious massing of "people power" that brought Marcos's rule to an end. Only belatedly did the Communists and their ideological allies acknowledge that they had made a tactical blunder. They now seek credit for initiating popular resistance to the Marcos regime. Meanwhile, insurgent Muslim Moros in Mindanao and the Sulu Archipelago and Kalinga and Apayao tribesmen of the northern Luzon cordillera have agreed to a cease-fire that could lead to a political settlement of their grievances.

Many besides the Filipinos have a stake in the outcome of this drama. Neighbouring countries -- Indonesia, Malaysia, Singapore, Thailand, Taiwan, Japan, South Korea, even China -- all look with nervous concern at what is happening in the Philippines. For these neighbours, peace in the region is a prerequisite for their military presence into the Philippine Archipelago. For own internal progress. Nor do they want an expansion of the Soviet Americans the quandary is particularly acute. For nearly half a century, beginning in 1898, the Philippines was under the American flag. There the U.S. made its most sustained effort to foster democracy among another people. The two largest U.S. military bases outside North America, Clark Air Force Base and Subic Bay Naval Base, are both on Luzon. On a more human level, an almost familial relationship has evolved between Filipinos and Americans, who shared combat against the Japanese in World War 11 and grew to be comrades in many of life's important arenas. It is not within the range of realistic options for the United States to walk away and leave the Filipinos to a hostile fate.

Fate of a Nation.
Countries and peoples, much like families, experience life in cycles; periods of setback and discouragement alternate with times of exhilaration and hope. It was exhilaration and hope that marked the "time of Magsaysay," as ordinary Filipinos call the events of 30-odd years ago. Then the country had a larger-than-life president of boundless energy, scrupulous honesty, and a compelling faith in the common man. A former World War II guerrilla chieftain, Ram6n Magsaysay used his shrewd judgment of men to cleanse government of corruption and restore faith in the electoral process. Picking up the tasks barely begun by the first two presidents of the republic, Manuel Roxas and Elpidio Quirino, he proceeded to rebuild the society from the chaos left by the Japanese military occupation in World War 11.

Yet new nations are especially vulnerable to the unexpected. Magsaysay was killed on the night of March 17, 1957, when his airplane crashed on a mountain in the central island of Cebu. Leadership of the Philippine republic passed to the incumbent vice-president, Carlos P. Garcia. A product of provincial politics, Garcia, who was reelected in November 1957 on the Nacionalista Party ticket, declared a "Filipino First" policy that started the nation on the path of manufacturing for import substitution rather than building an agricultural and industrial system that could compete in the world market. Self-styled Filipino nationalists, profiting at the expense of consumers, jealously campaigned against the foreign commercial participation that might have forced them to become efficient. Despite its great advantages -- privileged access to the U.S. market; English as the language of education and government; a corps of highly educated technocrats; vast natural resources -- the Philippines fell far behind such less favoured neighbours as Taiwan, South Korea, Hong Kong, and Thailand.

Diosdado Macapagal, elected president on the Liberal Party ticket in 1961, abolished most foreign exchange controls and attempted to open up the economy, despite stubborn resistance within the Congress. The most notable accomplishment of his administration, however, was enactment of the Land Reform Code, which benefited tenants cultivating rice and corn. In every congressional district or province proclaimed a "land reform area," all tenant farmers -- who usually had been share cropers, dividing the net harvest after the cost of threshing 50-50 with the landowners -- were entitled to shift to leasehold with the start of the next agricultural year. For former tenant farmers this Land Reform Code proved a boon, though not all of them have taken advantage of the purchase option, and the procedures for securing titles are complex. However landless labourers, who were not provided for in the code, have suffered; the new owner-farmers usually have proved less generous to rural labourers than the paternalistic, semifeudal *hacenderos* who preceded them.

Enactment of the Land Reform Code set in motion critical political changes, especially in central Luzon. This region had spawned pre-World War II socialist and Communist movements that joined forces against the Japanese occupiers as the Hukbalahap guerrillas. After Japan's defeat, the "Huks" were denied recognition, back pay, and veterans' benefits by the U.S. Army board sitting in Manila. Bitter and ripe for Communist propaganda, the Huks rose in revolt in 1948 against the often oppressive Philippine government forces. It was only after Magsaysay, who became secretary of defense in 1950, began disciplining the Philippine armed forces while offering land to guerrillas who surrendered that the Huks were defeated and their supremo, Luis Taruc, turned himself in.

As tenant farmers became owners, the Huk organizers who had retained their roots in central Luzon turned to new ventures. Beginning in 1964, escalation of the conflict in Vietnam resulted in vastly expanded activities and personnel at the Clark and Subic bases. The former Huk organization became a mafia-type operation, smuggling, dealing drugs, selling protection, and controlling filling stations, taxis, bars, and a huge gambling casino patronized by U.S. servicemen. In reaction against this profiteering, the more idealistic revolutionaries broke away and founded the NPA with its own Maoist-oriented CPP. Virtually forsaking central Luzon, they followed the early Chinese Red Army pattern of moving into inaccessible mountainous regions, like the Sierra Madre of Luzon, the hinterland of Samar, and the vast interior of Mindanao.

After Ferdinand Marcos was elected president in November 1965, some Filipinos who worked intimately with him felt that he showed great promise, though older politicians recalled that, while still a law student, he had been convicted of murdering his father's political opponent, Julio Nalundasan (the Supreme Court later reversed the decision). There also was controversy concerning Marcos's claim to be a much-decorated wartime hero, which U.S. Army records failed to substantiate. As chief executive, Marcos emphasized building infrastructure. During his first administration and after his reelection in November 1969, new roads were built and neglected ones surfaced, long-stalled bridge construction was completed, rural electrification was extended, harbours were improved, and irrigation systems were expanded. However, technocrats working with the Marcos administration soon discovered that the project proposals most readily endorsed for action were those promising lucrative contracts for the president's cronies.

Martial Law.
The social dynamite that still threatens to tear the Philippines apart was planted with Marcos's proclamation of martial law, effective at midnight on Sept. 21, 1972. Announced justifications included what he subsequently acknowledged was a faked ambush of then Secretary of Defense Juan Ponce Enrile (see BiOGRAPHIES); insurgent moves by the NPA, then numbering only a few hundred; and deteriorating peace and order. The real reasons lay deeper, however. A new political movement, Statehood USA, threatened old-line politicians in the elections scheduled for November 1973. A constitutional convention presided over by former president Macapagal had introduced a resolution that would prohibit any previous president from being reelected. Marcos saw to it that 12 of the elected convention delegates were imprisoned, along with hundreds of opposition politicians and journalists from closed newspapers, and most of the remaining delegates were so intimidated that by early 1973 they produced a constitution that allowed Marcos to remain in office with enlarged powers. The Congress was disbanded, and portions of the chambers where the Senate and House of Representatives had met since 1916 were converted into a museum.

With the proclamation of martial law and the 1973 constitution, which was approved by a casual "show of hands" plebiscite, Marcos ensured that he could remain in Malacalyang Palace. He subsequently amended this constitution twice: in 1976 to provide for a prime minister and in 1981 to accord the presidency enhanced powers, somewhat after the French model. An interim Batasang Pambansa (National Assembly) was chosen in 1978 and given limited legislative functions. At the outset some aspects of martial law were popular with many Filipinos. A reported one-fourth of Manila's adult male population had carried weapons or hired private bodyguards, and their vendettas were often settled in public places; now many of their weapons were confiscated by the military, as were the weapons of private armies linked to provincial political dynasties. Much of the press had become irresponsible and corrupt, and a significant number of the members of Congress had become champions of special interest groups often linked to their own families. Businessmen were relieved to have strikes ended (though they learned later that Marcos could mandate successive cost-of-living allowances and in time would force them to pay into a fund purportedly established to provide housing for urban employees). Marcos gained support in the countryside by proclaiming the entire Philippines subject to land reform on annually tenanted rice and corn lands. He created a Ministry of Information and asserted control of the media. The armed forces were given greatly augmented powers and expanded rapidly.

Opposition to martial law first developed among middle-class Filipinos. As the courts were politicized to serve the interests of the fraternity of power holders around the president and his prominent wife, Imelda Romualdez Marcos, that faith in the legal process so essential to fair government dwindled. The extension of Mrs. Marcos's authority as governor of Metro Manila and concurrently as minister of human settlements, her frequent foreign excursions as ambassador extraordinary and plenipotentiary, and her blatant spending at home and abroad intensified the discontent.

Perhaps inevitably, unrestrained power in the hands of a political cabal and the military had led to growing abuses. Surveillance of persons opposing the regime became routine, and recourse to legal protection was not available. Some who were only suspected of opposition were hustled off to prison. Torture became frequent, partly the vicious product of according unsupervised power to enforcers at all levels. "Salvaging" became the euphemism for the murder-by the military, police, or hired goons of someone who had been arrested and never brought to trial. Military sweeps in the countryside became the occasion for soldiers to help themselves to chickens, pigs, and sometimes the daughters of rural families. There were some officers who maintained strict discipline and were viewed by the people as protectors. Unfortunately, they were rarely rewarded by their superiors.

A Traumatized Society. In the social pressure cooker created by martial law, every feature of the economy and of daily life was affected. Traditionally, three-fourths of the people relied on farming and fishing. As the population grew to its current total of 56 million-eight times what it was in 1900-pressure on resources became acute. Formerly, most fanning was carried on in the lowlands, but now at least half of all rural households are on slope lands, where leaching of soil nutrients and erosion are exacerbated by intense rainfall during the southwest monsoon. Subsistence fishing declined as dynamiting and poisoning to trap fish destroyed breeding waters. Seventy percent of the population, urban and rural, is officially classed as living below the poverty level of a monthly income equivalent to $110 for a family of six, and just over half the population suffers from minor to severe malnutrition.

Rice is the basic staple of Filipinos, except for a corn-eating minority in the central Visayan islands. The Philippines imported rice throughout the early part of the 20th century. Except for Thailand, Burma, and southern Vietnam, which have extensive well-watered alluvial soils, the other countries of Southeast Asia also have been rice importers in modem times. These shortages began to diminish after the establishment of the International Rice Research Institute (IRRI) by the Rockefeller and Ford foundations in 1962. Located on land adjoining the University of the Philippines College of Agriculture at Los Bafios, some 65 km (40 mi) southeast of Manila, IRRI has developed numerous new varieties of high-yield rice and greatly improved methods of cultivation. The Philippine government's "Masagana 99" program of the early and mid-1970s encouraged adoption of the improved technology by assuring rice farmers of adequate credit. Credit was occasionally misused by agents who had to approve loans, and rural banks have yet to collect some of the payments. Yet the results were so successful that in normal years the Philippines is more than self-sufficient in rice and the problem is to keep prices from dropping so low as to discourage farmers. As elsewhere throughout Asia, there is a constant tug-of-war between city dwellers who want cheap rice-and government officials sensitive to their demands-and the farmers.

Sugar production has been an important sector of Philippine agriculture since the Chinese first introduced cultivation of the sweet cane in the 14th century. During and after World War 1, U.S. technical and financial interests helped create a modern sugar industry. When the U.S. Congress began regulating the sugar industry in 1934 by assigning quotas to producing areas, the Philippines was accorded its share, and this market share was protected in the independence legislation. By the 1960s the islands were supplying between I I and 12% of all sugar consumed by Americans, at prices usually above those of the world market. After the Marcos administration took office, the Philippines encountered difficulty in meeting its U.S. sugar quota, now augmented by part of the unfilled Cuban and Puerto Rican quotas. Against the advice of its National Economic Development Agency, the Philippine government sanctioned construction of 18 new sugar mills and 3 new refineries.

The failure of the U.S. Congress in 1973 to renew the Sugar Act that had stabilized the industry for 40 years was a disastrous blow to the Philippine economy, though initially the undependability of an open market was masked by a rise in world prices caused by poor growing weather in several producing areas. The Marcos administration concentrated all sugar trading for export in the Philippine Sugar Exchange, a subsidiary of the Philippine National Bank, and later in the Philippine Sugar Commission and the National Sugar Trading Agency headed by Marcos's former classmate Roberto Benedicto. For a time these monopolies profited at the expense of growers and millers, but as world sugar prices plunged from almost 40 U.S. cents per pound in 1980 to less than 5 cents in 1984, attempts at support fell short. Mills and *hacenderos,* accustomed to living on credit, went bankrupt. Bacolod City, the capital of Negros Occidental once noted for its high living, became a depressed community.

Directly or indirectly, the sugar industry had supported some five million Filipinos, or nearly 10% of the population. Now the monocrop haciendas became scenes of destitution as starving workers marched into the cane fields and took over plots to plant sweet potatoes and other food crops, Insurgent agitators and compassionate priests joined in demanding a new social order. But crop diversification and a change in the semi feudal economy can come only haltingly; even able planters are reluctant to believe the new government of President Aquino when it tells them large-scale sugar production has no real future in a world where corn sweeteners and other substitutes are taking over the market.

Coconuts traditionally have been the main source of livelihood for nearly one-third of the Philippine population, and the archipelago has supplied more than 60% of the coconut products moving in world commerce. But despite the vital role of coconuts in its agriculture and export earnings, the Philippines has not pursued scientific research on cultivation, production, and utilization of this "tree of life." Meanwhile, coconuts have been losing out to other sources of vegetable oil; only coconuts for direct consumption or for specialty export items have maintained their market share.

The Marcos administration initiated a program for the coconut industry that may have begun with positive intentions but degenerated into a racket that impoverished small growers throughout the country. Eduardo Cojuangco, one of the wealthiest of Marcos's cronies and a first cousin of Corazon Aquino, had traded part of his agricultural land holdings in central Luzon for control of Bugsug Island off the eastern coast of Palawan. There he started large scale production of hybrid seed coconuts. To finance farmers' purchases of these seed nuts, an export levy was imposed on all copra, and the funds were deposited in the United Coconut Planters Bank, which Cojuangco and his group (including Enrile) controlled. To further clinch their monopoly, this group and its allies bought or otherwise gained control of the mills that processed copra and

THE PHILIPPINES: IS DEMOCRACY RESTORED

exported oil and copra meal pellets for livestock feed. The hybrid coconut seed was an inferior type, but even so the monopoly reaped huge profits. Emmanuel Pelaez, former vice-president and now ambassador to the U.S., was shot by goons for speaking out on behalf of coconut farmers. At the same time, the price of vegetable oils in world markets was declining drastically, and poverty spread through the coconut-growing regions.

The situation was made to order for Communist organizers. They did not usually discuss Karl Marx or even Mao Tse-tung. Instead, they talked about the low prices farmers received for their coconuts compared with the world price, and the implication that greedy officials were stealing the difference caught on. The NPA has grown strong in the coconut-growing communities, where their alternative government operates openly. Similarly, in the Muslim-dominated regions of Mindanao and the Sulu Archipelago, where coconuts are also the main cash crop, the machinations of the so-called Coco Bank group have contributed to discontent and rebellion.

Timber, including the renowned Philippine mahogany, is another once-valuable source of foreign exchange in decline. In the 1950s and 1960s fortunes were made exploiting easily available stands close to water, but only a few companies made a conscientious effort to preserve the forests for sustained yield. Corrupt senior officials of the Bureau of Forestry allowed clear-cutting without reforestation, and during martial law timber concessions were allotted to relatives and other favourites of the Marcos clan with scant regard for forest protection. Mrs. Marcos ordered 25-year forest concession leases canceled on trumped-up charges, and these areas sometimes became grab bags for local politicians, who sent their tenants to become slash-and-bum squatter farmers. As a result, this may be the last generation of Filipinos to see a virgin tropical rain forest.

Quandary of the Young.
While the nation's economy deteriorated, problems of employment were compounded. At least one-fifth of the employable adults are jobless, and another two-fifths are under employed. Roughly half of the population is under 21 years of age, and of these 28 million young people, 10 million to 12 million are out-of-school youths who cannot afford to attend high school or college, even if they qualify. They rarely have steady employment, so there is scant opportunity for them to learn skills. The result is apathy and, sometimes, anger.

The Spanish made little progress in encouraging education during the 300-odd years that they controlled the islands, but the Americans instituted a radical change. They brought in teachers who quickly trained more teachers to staff the public schools that were established throughout the country. Once Filipinos saw that those who learned English and earned a diploma were given the jobs in government and business, they avidly took to education. The tradition of education as the largest government enterprise was reinforced after the commonwealth was established in 1935 and has continued since independence.

As of 1985, over nine million students were enrolled in public elementary schools and some 490,000 in the much more expensive private schools. Government secondary schools had just under 2 million, while private secondary school students numbered about 1.3 million. There were 319 government-supported colleges and universities with total enrollment of about 230,000. Private colleges and universities numbered 838 with a total enrollment of 1,274,000, and the best private universities, often managed by religious orders, are comparable to the better schools abroad.

Despite this enormous educational industry, only two-thirds of the population, at best, is functionally literate. The new constitution to be submitted to a plebiscite in 1987 mandates the development of Filipino as a national language, but neither it nor any of the eight major regional languages offers significant access to technical, scientific, or historical knowledge. It is a rare individual who can get ahead without mastery of English. In reality, the Philippines is a two-class society divided between those who do and those who do not possess effective command of spoken and written English.

As the economy deteriorated and opportunities for employment shrank, an ever greater number of Filipinos began to seek opportunities elsewhere. Those with suitable skills sought to participate in the boom in the oil-producing countries. Employment agencies mushroomed in Manila as an estimated 750,000 Filipinos went to the Middle East. Another 165,000 or so are seamen. While British immigration laws allowed, Filipinas were in demand as domestic help in London, where about 10,000 are still employed, and Filipinas also found work as amahs, cooks, and housemaids in Hong Kong and Singapore, where the Chinese now preferred to work in factories or shops. Filipino technicians and hotel staff could be found throughout the region, from Sabah in East Malaysia to Guam and the Pacific island states. The remittances from these migrants became the country's largest single source of foreign exchange, bringing an estimated equivalent of $1.5 billion annually.

In the minds of Filipinos, however, the great land of opportunity has remained the United States. In 1985 alone, some 47,000 received U.S. immigrant visas, and the total since the proclamation of martial law is 480,000 legally admitted immigrants. Well over a million Filipinos are officially present in the U.S., and at least another 500,000 are probably there illegally. Filipinos are now the second largest Asian component of the U.S. population, after the Chinese, and another 500,000 are registered on the computers at the U.S. consulate general in Manila awaiting their turn to enter. Some 16,000 Filipino doctors were practicing in the U.S. at last count, and several thousand Filipino nurses go to the U.S. each year.

In contrast, no regular annual immigrant visas are issued for the Philippines, and the quota for foreign nationals seeking permanent residence is 50 per country per year; non quota residence admissions are available to those who marry Filipinos. Under the Marcos regime foreigners were forbidden to be executives or to work in any enterprise involving mining, fishing, forestry, agriculture, or other natural resources, and they were excluded from numerous other forms of employment, except as consultants specifically allowed by presidential order. The new draft constitution prohibits foreigners from practicing any profession. A foreigner is not allowed to acquire land, even a house lot. After the proclamation of martial law, the Marcos-dominated Supreme Court ruled that any property acquired by Americans in the Philippines during the 27 years after July 4, 1946, had been acquired illegally, thus negating land titles issued under a 1946 constitutional amendment allowing Americans to own land. Most severely hurt were thousands of Filipinos who had become U.S. citizens through military service or residence and who now lost property they had saved to buy in their ancestral home. Later Marcos gave special exemption to Filipino-Americans

THE PHILIPPINES: IS DEMOCRACY RESTORED

and to Americans resident for at least 15 years, but by then most owners had disposed of their properties at bargain prices. This attitude toward foreign land ownership has put the Philippines at a disadvantage in attracting foreign investment.

For those who remain at home but lack influential connections, the struggle to make a living is intense. With roughly one-fourth of Greater Manila's eight million inhabitants living in shantytowns or slums, it is common to find teams of youngsters sorting through garbage containers, trash piles, and dumps throughout the city. In desperation, unemployed youths enter a life of crime. Syndicates of purse snatchers are often in league with collectors of lagay, the squeeze money jitney drivers and many others pay. After the Marcos regime fell, the extortion money extracted in return for issuing licenses to taxi and other professional drivers was reduced, but the gangs of racketeers that dominate Manila's harbour have yet to be eliminated.

An intriguing new underground industry that has emerged during the past decade and now involves between 450,000 and 500,000 Filipinos is panning and digging for gold, using the crudest methods and frequently without any legal claim. The Philippines was a major gold producer before World War 11, but the mines were wrecked during the Japanese invasion. By the war's end both knowledge and men had been lost, although old-timers still told tales of rich, lost veins. This began to change after 1973, when the U.S. hatted gold sales at $35 per ounce. As the price skyrocketed, the lure of gold reached into remote barrios, holding out an opportunity for the unemployed. Today gold panning is a major activity in at least 20 localities. Conservatively the free-lance panners and miners recover one-half to one gram of gold a day, worth $6 to $12, and in the jungles of eastern Mindanao the occasional schoolboy becomes a peso millionaire. The best estimates are that over $1 billion in gold annually is extracted and smuggled out of the Philippines, where government regulations prohibit private trading in the metal.

Surreptitious export of gold is not new to the islands. During the two decades when Marcos was chief of state, a major effort was made to locate the gold and other valuables buried by the Japanese when they were facing defeat in 1945. A special recovery unit of the military focused on this search, and a mint that smelted and refined gold was established in Quezon City. Estimates vary as to how much of this gold Marcos and his associates removed from the country, but some who have done considerable research calculate that its present value would be worth more than the nation's foreign debt.

Benigno ("Ninoy") Aquino. The decision of former senator Benigno Aquino, known popularly as Ninoy, to return to the Philippines from the U.S. on Aug. 21, 1983, was to prove fatal to him and, in time, to the Marcos dictatorship. By fateful coincidence, it was 12 years to the day since Aquino had escaped assassination when he was delayed in arriving at a Liberal Party rally at the Plaza Miranda, where grenades tossed on the platform killed and wounded a number of candidates. The son of a prominent family in central Luzon and possessed of notable energy and wit, he had been the youngest correspondent to cover the Korean War. He had married Corazon Cojuangco, the attractive and well-educated daughter of one of the richest men in the Philippines. Like him, she was from Tarlac, where both families held sugar and rice lands. In the pattern of young, politically ambitious Filipinos, he was elected, in succession, mayor of his hometown, governor, and senator.

THE PHILIPPINES: IS DEMOCRACY RESTORED

Throughout his career as a provincial politician, Aquino had played the rough-and-tumble role that survival demanded. He used his own armed guards and made deals for support with local power brokers, who in some Tarlac municipalities included former Huks. This was part of the charge brought against him when, under martial law, he was tried by a military court, refused to defend himself on the grounds that the court lacked civil jurisdiction, and was convicted of murder and treason and sentenced to death. Imprisoned for seven years, Aquino became a changed man, reading and thinking, evolving ideas on nonviolence based on the writings of Gandhi and others. For 40 days he went on a hunger strike. When he suffered cardiac problems, Marcos authorized his leave to go to the U.S. for surgery. He spent three years with his family near Boston, studied at Harvard, lectured, and visited abroad, including the Middle East.

Reports that Marcos was critically ill prompted Aquino's supporters to urge him to return. Although strenuous efforts were made to disguise the president's illness and his American physicians have been reluctant to talk, it appears that Marcos had a kidney transplant early in August 1983 and that it was less than successful. In mid-August members of the Cabinet reportedly said Mrs. Marcos had told them to prepare for the succession. In that time of acute political tensions, the Philippine chief of staff (and an old Marcos associate), Gen. Fabian Ver, took extraordinary security precautions. Military men met the China Airlines flight bringing Aquino from Taiwan, and he was separated from accompanying newsmen, led down an outside service stairway, and shot in the head from behind before he reached the tarmac. Rolando Galman, a small-time gangster, was shot at about the same time, before or after he was pushed from a nearby waiting van. In subsequent hearings and at a staged trial, the government tried to make the case that Galman was a Communist agent sent to murder Aquino, but this farce was so crudely managed that it only reinforced the belief that Aquino's murder had been ordered by the highest authority. A new trial was ordered after Corazon Aquino took power but, mean while, some of the original 26 defendants, including General Ver, had left the country. Radio Veritas, the Roman Catholic broadcasting station, made its reputation on August 21. While the Marcos intimidated media tried to ignore the assassination, Radio Veritas was giving an eyewitness account. Ten days later nearly two million mourners followed Aquino's funeral cortege through Greater Manila. Shocked and angered by the flagrant murder of Marcos's most outspoken political opponent, who had become an idol to many young people, the nation at last began to stir.

The Price of Abusing Power. Officially Marcos had abolished martial law in January 198 1, but he had retained powers to issue commitment and preventive detention orders, and he kept in force the presidential decrees and letters of instruction through which he had controlled the society. Relatives and cronies continued to receive favours, and opponents were targets of the military. At one stage "secret marshals" were authorized to kill on sight-supposedly they were after gangsters, but innocents also suffered. Claudio Teehankee, appointed chief justice by Mrs. Aquino and one of the few jurists who had defied Marcos, said later in a public address:

During those 14 years [1972-86], we were a nation lost in the woods of history. In place of truth reigned falsehood, dis-information, outright deception and fraud. Justice, freedom, equality became mere words used to cover crime against human dignity and basic human decency. Public office lost all concept of public trust and public accountability-lost was the distinction between what belonged to the state and what belonged to the servants of the state. They behaved as though they had received the mandate of heaven to rule, rather than to serve, and no individual rights, freedom or liberty was large enough or precious enough not to be cast into the sacrificial flames of the most capricious of all authoritarian gods -- that of national security. Every excess and abuse of power -- every disregard of the sacredness of human life and liberty-every suppression of free expression-was premised on national security, even though it involved nothing more than the ruler's perpetuation in office and the security of relatives and some officials in high positions and their protection from public exposure in the press of their acts of venality and deception in government.

These were years of systematic undermining of the national will . . . of systematic looting and plunder of the economy. And it seemed to matter little which came first, the bankrupting of the national treasury or of public morality, we ended up bankrupt in both.

In an effort to give credibility to his government, Marcos called elections for mid-May 1984 to replace the interim legislative body with a full-fledged National Assembly. Every device was used to ensure that Marcos's Kilusang Bagong Lipunan (K.BL; New Society Movement) would win; candidates were given lavish funds, public works were manipulated to their advantage, and in some districts newly emerged private armies were employed to register voters and to see that they got to the polls and cast properly marked ballots. Fortunately, the National Movement for Free Elections (Narnfrel) was allowed to function, mobilizing volunteers across the country as private poll watchers who also participated in the tabulation of results. The opposition won one-third of the 182 members elected to the assembly, although Marcos had the power to name another 30. While the election left the KBL in control of the legislature, the opposition learned that the elective process, scarred by fraud and violence though it was, could be used to gain an independent voice in national affairs.

In November 1984 Marcos survived another health crisis and began recovering some of his earlier vitality; he may have had a second kidney transplant, although the nature of his illness has been carefully concealed. Meanwhile, the mismanagement of government and abuses of power were coming home to roost. There was a massive flight of capital out of the country as, one after another, the crony companies went bankrupt and the owners moved both their wealth and themselves abroad. As a result, the government institutions, like the Government Service Insurance System into which civil servants pay their retirement funds, no longer could provide savings for capital investment. Having borrowed recklessly abroad, the Philippines was now compelled to adopt the austerity program set by the International Monetary Fund before foreign private lenders would agree to roll over loans. The political circus was ending.

Marcos remained intransigent. He refused to retire General Ver as chief of staff, despite the popular conviction that Ver was involved in the Aquino assassination. The general, who used military intelligence funds casually for political and personal purposes on behalf of the Marcos family, seemed to have become the president's "security blanket." An indication of Marcos's fear of elimination was his stubborn refusal to have a vice-president. At this juncture the Roman Catholic Church and the U.S. government asserted themselves. The church, which claims slightly over two-thirds of Filipinos as communicants, was prompted to open

THE PHILIPPINES: IS DEMOCRACY RESTORED

criticism of the Marcos regime both by the outraged consciences of its leaders and by pressure from within. As for the U.S., the Aquino assassination had focused American attention on the calamitous drift in Philippine affairs. Particularly disturbing to the U.S was the deterioration in the armed forces.

The U.S. loss of confidence became evident with the visit of Sen. Paul Laxalt (Rep., Nev.) to Manila in October 1985. Laxalt was not a specialist on the Philippines, but he was a close personal friend of Pres. Ronald Reagan, and when he told Marcos that the old political shell game had ended, no one in Malacayang could doubt his word. About two weeks later, on November 3, Marcos announced that he was calling a "snap" election for president and vice-president on Feb. 7, 1986. He seems to have calculated that he could neutralize domestic and U.S. pressure to clean up his government by staging his own reelection. Apparently he assumed that enough votes could be bought to ensure his victory.

Commitment to Democracy. Marcos had underestimated the determination of Filipinos to win their freedom. Reluctantly, Corazon Aquino, the widow of the slain senator, agreed to stand for president provided a million Filipinos signed a petition requesting her candidacy. Her supporters reasoned that she would attract sympathy and, as a female, she was less likely than a man to be murdered. Two cousins, Joaquin ("Chino") Roces, a former publisher, and Jesus Marcos ("Tuting") Roces, former vice-mayor of Manila, took the lead in organizing the Cory Aquino for President Movement, with the former serving as the first chairman. Within a few weeks they and their co-volunteers had collected 1.3 million signatures. Salvador Laurel, the scion of a prominent political family, also wanted to be a presidential candidate, but after intense jockeying and the intervention of Manila's archbishop, Jaime Cardinal Sin, a Unido PDP-Laban coalition was formed with Laurel as Mrs. Aquino's vice-presidential running mate and yellow as its colour. Unido (United Democratic Organization) was Laurel's party and the only one in the coalition registered with the Commission on Elections (Comelec) and therefore authorized to have watchers in polling booths. PDP (Pilipino Democratic Party) was headed by Aquilino Pimentel, a Mindanao politician, and Laban (Lakas ng Bayan or Strength of the Nation), established by Benigno Aquino, was the umbrella for several groups of varying strength and ideology.

It was an extraordinary campaign. On one side was the professional political machine of President Marcos, his vice-presidential candidate, Arturo Tolentino, and the KBL party organization. They were never short of money, and they dominated the electronic and print media. However, their campaign was handicapped by Marcos's lack of vitality. Marcos also was burdened by nearly two decades of promises that he had failed to keep, while his family and cronies conspicuously enriched themselves.

The turnout among wmen and young Filipinos, many of whom had never known a real election, struggled to protect the balloting.

The contrast with the Cory Aquino campaign was startling. She was the first woman ever to seek the Philippine presidency. Initially shy, this mother of five children soon gained support with her engaging simplicity. When Marcos denigrated her competence, she challenged him to come out and "stand up like a woman" to debate. Her organization, managed by leading independent businessmen and committed priests, depended on volunteers who gave their labour and paid their own way to the immense rallies that filled Manila's historic Luneta Park, facing Manila Bay. Equally vital was the performance of Namfirel, led by modem-minded businessman Jos6 Concepcion and banker Vicente Jayme. With roughly 500,000 volunteers, Narnfrel belatealy won from Comelec the role of representing the public with poll watchers in some 90,000 precincts. Still, the old political machines manipulated registration, and many voters in opposition strongholds were disenfranchised.

Election day, February 7, was tense. By law the police and military are required to keep their distance from the polling booths. In many communities violence erupted as hoodlums tried to upset peaceful polling; most strong-arm tactics were on the KBL side, although the opposition occasionally tried to also.

estimated 27 million eligible voters approached 90%, but not all of them succeeded in casting a ballot. Media coverage was exceptional; nearly 900 foreign journalists and cameramen joined the domestic press to provide graphic accounts from major cities and a few rural areas. Marcos had specifically invited a U.S. congressional delegation to observe the voting, and a larger international contingent of observers joined in visiting provincial voting precincts.

As an older Filipino politician explained: "There are two ways you cheat on elections. One is when the votes are cast and the other is when they are counted. Marcos is depending mostly on the latter." After votes were tabulated in view of the poll watchers, including representatives of both political parties and Narnfrel, the ballot boxes were taken to the municipal and city treasurers. Canvassing of the total vote was done at the provincial and chartered city level, and returns were transmitted to Comelec. This cumbersome process took days to complete, and Comelec, which was packed with Marcos appointees, used the opportunity to tamper with the final tally. On the basis of that tally, the National Assembly proclaimed Marcos and Tolentino as winners, to the consternation of most Filipinos and much of the world. Narnfrel, meanwhile, had been tabulating results based on reports from its watchers around the country, and Father James Reuter and his associates in the Catholic Broadcasters Association were sending tabulated voting returns to Namfrel from their nationwide network of radio stations and mobile transmitters. Both tallies showed that massive manipulation had not prevented Aquino and Laurel from gamering over 58% of the votes.

People Power. Faced with the National Assembly's proclamation of Marcos's reelection, Aquino and Laurel led a prayer rally at the Luneta and adjoining Rizal Park on February 16, where some two million people massed in protest. They then traveled to the southern islands to mobilize passive resistance, including a boycott of companies controlled by the Marcos cronies. The Catholic bishops' conference issued a blunt denunciation of terror and cheating aimed at thwarting the people's will.

Meanwhile, a drama was being played out within the Philippine military. Months earlier several groups with a shared aversion to the corruption and favouritism of the Marcos-Ver regime had been preparing secretly for a change. One was led by Minister of National Defense Enrile and his younger associates, who had grouped men and weapons in the Cagayan Valley of northeastern Luzon. Another was RAM, the Reformed Armed Forces Movement, composed primarily of younger officers. A third consisted of retired generals and colonels who wanted to restore professionalism to the armed forces and end the Communist-led insurgency. These groups and others had been quietly planning a coup. The announcement of the election led them to postpone their moves, but when they saw that Marcos intended to remain in power, they prepared for action.

THE PHILIPPINES: IS DEMOCRACY RESTORED

One plan was to cross the Pasig River in assault boats with the help of collaborators in the Presidential Security Command, kidnap President and Mrs. Marcos, General Ver, and their immediate associates, and proclaim a new, predominantly civilian government. Only hours before this plan was to be initiated, Col. Gregorio Honasan, Enrile's chief of security, learned that a double agent in the Presidential Security Command had betrayed the plot to General Ver's son, and a trap had been arranged. As Marcos's people and Ver prepared to mobilize troops to capture the defense headquarters at Camp Aguinaldo, Enrile invited Gen. Fidel Ramos, the vice-chief of staff, commander of the Philippine Constabulary, and a West Point graduate, to join him in support of the truly elected government. Enrile and Ramos later moved across the highway to the constabulary headquarters at Camp Crame, where, with some 400 soldiers, they made their stand.

For a time it seemed that the Marcos-Ver forces would succeed in destroying the defectors -- the telephone lines remained open between Marcos and Enrile. Then Cardinal Sin appealed over Radio Veritas for the people to protect Camp Crame, and they came by the hundreds of thousands, blocked the tanks, prayed for the soldiers to join their peaceful revolution, and kept vigil through three nights. As a steady stream of army, air force, and navy units joined General Ramos-a count he reported regularly on Radio Veritas-Ver became a general with few troops to command. An untold story was the role played by commanding officers' wives, who in several critical instances persuaded their husbands to ignore the orders to move their troops against the revolution. In this confused period, Marcos's followers succeeded in wrecking the transmission towers of Radio Veritas, forcing it to broadcast on a weak signal from a borrowed station.

The revolutionary forces soon recouped by capturing, with limited bloodshed, the government's Channel 4 and the crony-owned Channel 9, leaving the Marcos forces without television coverage.

Aquino was in Cebu City as the struggle was coming to a head in Greater Manila. She flew back to Manila, and it was decided that she would take her oath of office. At the Club Filipino in a Greater Manila suburb, she was duly and simply sworn in as the seventh president of the Philippines on Feb. 25, 1986, with Laurel, Emile, Ramos, and other supporters at her side. A few hours later, with his popular following melting away, Marcos proceeded with his own inauguration at Malacahang Palace, guarded by troops from the mobs that threatened to storm in. It was a sad final gesture by a man who could have had an honoured place in his country's history. Instead he desperately sought any face-saving opportunity to stay and avoid mob vengeance. In a transpacific telephone call to Senator Laxalt in Washington, D.C., Marcos got the final word to "cut and cut clean."

Late on February 25 Marcos telephoned Enrile and requested him to ask the U.S. ambassador, Stephen Bosworth, for help in leaving. That night the Americans arranged for four helicopters to carry Marcos, his family, servants, and close cronies to Clark Air Force Base, but they had such mountains of luggage that some of them had to travel by road. President Reagan had offered asylum in the U.S., and early the next morning the escapees and tons of their personal effects were loaded on two U.S. Air Force planes for the flight to Guam and, after a layover, to Hawaii. In arranging their departure, the U.S. government undoubtedly saved the lives of Marcos and his wife, for the crowds that broke into the palace grounds that night were lusting for blood. The action also helped minimize the cost in life and property, which inevitably would have risen if the power struggle had been prolonged. Marcos later suggested that the Americans kidnapped him and that all he had wanted was to go home to his native province of Ilocos, but in fact he knew where he was going on each leg of the journey.

A New Era. The Aquino-Laurel government is avowedly revolutionary. The National Assembly was disbanded, govemors and mayors were replaced with appointed officers, and Marcos's 1973 constitution was replaced by a Freedom Constitution incorporating selected elements of previous statutes. Some of Marcos's presidential decrees remain in force. Meanwhile, President Aquino also rules by decree, though with comparative restraint. The judiciary is being revamped and cleaned up, and new institutions include a Human Rights Commission to investigate past misdeeds of police and security agencies (but not the NPA). A board of respected retired generals is screening the military for those who have abused their positions or illegally enriched themselves. Most of the generals Marcos kept on past retirement age have been retired, and nearly two dozen younger officers have been promoted to general rank. A Presidential Commission on Good Government under former senator Jovito Salonga is screening the business empires accumulated by the Marcos clan and cronies and sequestering some of the properties. The PCGG has only begun to recover small portions of the immense wealth the former ruler, his family, and his favourites shipped abroad, often under covert identities.

In a plebiscite scheduled for Feb. 2, 1987, Filipinos are to decide whether to adopt the new constitution drafted by a 47-member Constitutional Commission appointed by President Aquino. In its essentials, this draft constitution contains many of the provisions of the 1935 constitution. One change is that presidents are limited to a single six-year term. There is a distinct separation of powers between the executive, the judicial, and the legislative branches, and the latter will again be composed of two houses, a 24-member Senate and a 250-member House of Representatives. Senators can serve a maximum of two six-year terms, and representatives will be limited to three consecutive three year terms. A comprehensive Bill of Rights seeks to guard against future repetitions of the abuses perpetrated by the Marcos dictatorship. Capital punishment is abolished, and no person may be imprisoned for debt or nonpayment of poll tax. Independent commissions are provided for the civil service, elections, and audit. Two autonomous geographic regions are created-for the minority tribes of the northern Luzon cordillera and for Muslim areas of Mindanao and the Sulu Archipelago-each to be governed according to an organic act passed by the new congress. That congress is to be elected on the second Monday in May 1987.

The Aquino government has made an encouraging beginning, but it confronts enormous problems. The Cabinet is less than unified; most ministers had not worked together before and joined the coalition chiefly to defeat Marcos. Several Cabinet members have already set their sights on campaigning for the 24 at-large Senate seats to be filled in May 1987, and some have presidential ambitions. The New Armed Forces of the Philippines are upgrading their organizations professionally. At year's end Rafael lleto became the new minister of defense; this low-key retired former vice-chief of staff, who served as ambassador to Iran and Thailand, is a graduate of West Point, fought with the U.S. Army in World War 11, and transferred only in 1950 to the Philippine Army, where he organized the rangers. Gradually factionalism among the military is being reduced and deficiencies are being corrected, but there are differences between the military and some civilian Cabinet ministers on tactical deployment.

Moro soldiers of the southwestern islands are being paid 1,500 pesos (approximately $75) upon 'enlistment and given uniforms, weapons, training, and other compensations, apparently with funding from Islamic sources abroad. The NPA in some areas has done even better; in addition to the same 1,500 pesos paid to the enlistee, an extra 1,000 pesos is given for goodwill to neighbours who will be deprived of the new recruit's, assistance. Official estimates of 23,500 to 26,000 hard-core armed NPA troops understate reality. Armed insurgents have been operating virtually where they choose, capitalizing on frustration among the young and offering a Communist vision of Utopia. Through the NDF, which serves as their political umbrella, the NPA and CPP negotiated a cease-fire with the government early in December 1986. The insurgents' demands for a coalition government, integration of their troops into the national armed forces, and removal of U.S. military bases were rejected. Instead, the insurgents were urged to seek their goals through the parliamentary process, raising the issue of legalizing the Communist Party. The government has not provided meaningful opportunities for those who surrender, and regional Communist commanders ruthlessly block followers who want to return to the government side. The Communists have recouped their fortunes and expanded their power since their low point, when they boycotted the elections and the "people power" revolution of February 1986, and they now use flamboyant public relations to further improve their image. Within the government, leaders have disagreed on how to cope with this growing insurgent challenge that commands both guns and votes. Now that political negotiations are beginning, they must resolve their differences.

It was unrealistic to expect that Corazon Aquino could fulfill all the popular expectations that her victory generated. Nevertheless, many Filipinos feel let down. Few recognize that the civil service had become so demoralized and mired in bad habits that long, sustained effort will be required to make it effective. Corruption has been curbed only in some ministries and government agencies. Dramatic gestures of public redress, such as President Magsaysay's Presidential Complaints and Action Commission at Malacafiang Palace, through which any citizen could appeal to him, have not been implemented. The Tanodbayan, designed to function as an ombudsman, is itself bogged down in bureaucracy and busy with the new trial of those accused in the slaying of Benigno Aquino. Government banks are just beginning to turn over foreclosed properties for distribution to the landless. The desperate desire of at least two-thirds of all Filipino families to own a home with a lot where they can grow some food has yet to be met, although housing construction could be a major source of jobs.

The challenge confronting President Aquino and her administration in dealing with the Philippines' pressing needs and raising funds, chiefly abroad, demands inspired leadership. This first woman president of the republic is surrounded by a trusted inner circle that, observers report, sometimes shields her from realistic awareness of the fundamental problems of rural Filipinos. She cannot do everything. Like other national leaders, she must pick and choose among the innumerable demands for her attention. Neither is wisdom easily attained by equally hard-pressed Cabinet ministers who have little time to think beyond the immediate future. Like most governments in the less developed world, that of the Philippines was not designed for development; it is primarily an administrative structure. Filipinos who care about their country are challenged as never before. Passionately concerned civilians joined with like-minded military to make the February revolution. The task ahead is less dramatic yet tougher. How Filipinos cope with the tortuous problems of their society will decide whether their mustering of popular action to topple a truculent dictatorship was a transient, though glorious, historical episode or a major step in the building of a prosperous and genuine democracy.

AMERICAN UNIVERSITIES FIELD STAFF

SOUTHEAST ASIA SERIES
Vol. IX No. 6
(Philippines)

DAIRY FARMING IN THE ASIAN TROPICS

Promising New Industry for Idle Uplands

by Albert Ravenholt

Grassland Farms
San Miguel, Bulacan
December 1961

VICENTE ARANETA is making one of the chief purposes of his life the development of a modern dairy industry in the Philippines. And the sleek Holsteins and Jerseys that graze in lush pastures here along the foothills of the Sierra Madre Mountains testify to his success after 28 years of costly and often discouraging experiments. Every morning and evening some 200 cows are milked in the modern eight-place Surge milking parlor. The milk is stored in stainless steel refrigerated tanks and once every 24 hours is trucked 46 miles to Greater Manila for sale. The 500 gallon per hour milk plant that Vicente now is building in the suburbs of Manila will use a Dutch process to sterilize and bottle the milk so it can be kept for several weeks without refrigeration, thus permitting a reduction in price to bring it within the budget of ordinary Filipino families. The implications of all this are far-reaching. A modern dairy industry would mean that several million acres of now idle upland s in these Islands and much larger areas in neighboring lands of Southeast Asia could be made profitably productive in a manner that enriches the soil while conserving it against erosion. Given proper management and adequate credit facilities, there would be the promise of abundant new opportunities - for large and small farmers and of much-needed quality protein for the national diet.

A Wisconsin or upper New York State dairy farmer looking at what has been accomplished here at Grassland Farms might understandably be tempted to trade his operation for one such as this. Consider the economics of this venture. Starting six years ago with abandoned upland rice fields in a region that has a seven-month-long dry season, Vicente has built up 275 hectares (one hectare equals 2.47 acres) of improved pastures that also can be cut and stored, he owns another 397 hectares yet to be developed. Pasture development has cost about 150 pesos (three pesos equal one US dollar) per hectare on land originally priced at 200 to 300 pesos per hectare. Using improved grasses that are fertilized, such as Alabang X imported from India and Townsville Lucerne brought from Australia, the farm can carry three to four cows per hectare throughout the year. This is accomplished with a mixed program of grazing, haymaking, and grass silage; a domestically produced concentrate and imported mineral supplement is fed particularly to milking cows. (With installation of pump and sprinkler irrigation, which is expensive and difficult to secure here, the number of cows maintained per hectare could be doubled.) On this feed Vicente's Holsteins now are producing an average of better than 7,000 pounds of milk annually and the Jerseys are giving more than 5,000 pounds of milk per year with a higher butterfat content. Although these production figures do not yet equal those of prize herds in Europe and America. This output being achieved in a country that now imports 91% of all dairy products consumed that have an annual value of some US$24 million. In addition the Philippines also is a major importer of beef and other meats, production of which offers a natural side line to dairy farming. A 1.5 million peso milk plant under construction near Manila is designed with sufficient capacity to absorb production from the dairy-farmers-to-be Vicente hopes will follow his example.

Costly Education

Existence of such proven opportunities in dairying raises the question of why more farmers have not ventured in such a locally noncompetitive field; the only other modern dairy in the Islands is the Hardie Farm of the Jose Yulo enterprises at Canlubang, 25 miles southeast of Manila. The answer can be found in Vicente's painful years of apprenticeship and experimentation. Even as a boy this vigorous, hefty Filipino pioneer refused to accept the judgment of "impossible" when applied to farming in the tropics. Born the fifth son of the first Filipino Secretary of Justice and Finance to serve in the American administration here, Vicente early was encouraged to join in the new cause of introducing modern science to agriculture. As teen-age boys, he and his late brother Ramon three times had the winning entries in the annual national egglaying contest; they introduced White Leghorns and Rhode Island Reds when the experts at the College of Agriculture at Los Bafios insisted only a cross between imported fowl and the native or Cantonese type of hen would survive. Since then many other Filipinos, including several matrons prominent in Manila society, have taken up the challenge and today nearly every egg and meat type bird known in the West is being raised successfully in these Islands.

Vicente's introduction to dairying came in 1931 when he accompanied his mother to Spain and France for a rest following the death of his father. Wherever the twenty-one-year-old Filipino traveled in Europe, he studied farm techniques unknown in the Islands. He was impressed in Madrid to find milk delivered to their hotel for one-twentieth of the price it cost in Manila. Correspondence with Clarence Eckles, pioneer dairyman and author of Dairy Cattle and Milk Production, led Vicente to inquire whether Holsteins would thrive in the Philippines. He was assured that they did well in Cuba and should adapt to these Islands if properly fed. Vicente ordered a Holstein bull from Carnation Farms near Seattle, Washington, and returned home to Manila in time for its arrival in February of 1933.

A family friend who had attempted managing a dairy near Manila with cows periodically imported from Australia tried to dissuade the young man. "Your European and American type dairy cattle soon will die," he was told. "And those that don't die will not reproduce." But Vicente already was committed, although his original plan to upgrade native cows proved impractical because the Holstein bull was too large for breeding. Instead, he imported four Holstein cows from California. Two of these died upon arrival and those remaining suffered from retained placenta. Vicente's formal schooling had emphasized commerce and law, but now he was avidly educating himself on every aspect of dairying. He is delighted that the book, Diseases of Cattle, which he purchased for one dollar from the Department of Agriculture in Washington, D.C., enabled him to solve this problem. Meanwhile, another seven Holsteins were imported. When four of these died, Vicente's brothers refused to continue to help in financing the experiment. Using funds he had inherited, Vicente, alone, went ahead and brought in another 11 Holsteins; within 14 days after arrival nine of these were dead of Texas fever. "That Was almost the end of my dairying, 11 Vicente recalls. "But the importing firm shared the loss and helped me insure future shipments of cattle with Lloyd's of London until one month after arrival. After that mortality continued, but we always lost them more than one month after the cattle were landed!" Before World War II Vicente imported about 150 Holsteins and Jerseys -- the latter were brought in when he concluded that native cattle included some Jersey strains. These cows cost an average of US$300 each delivered and 50% to 80% of successive shipments died within a few months of arrival.

By 1937 after numerous discouraging feeding trials Vicente hit upon the practice he now considers most essential for maintenance of the health of dairy cows brought into the tropics from temperate climates. He began feeding them a sea kelp preparation, marketed under the trade name of *MAN-AMAR*, imported from San Pedro, California. He explains that surface soils in the moist tropics are subject to more rapid erosion of trace elements than those of the temperate zones. Also, there is lacking in these ever-warm climates the frost action that speeds the breakdown of basic rocks and releases mineral elements each spring. Since cattle from temperate climates inherit nutritional needs not naturally supplied in the lowland tropics, these must be met by feeding the cattle kelp that has taken up minerals from the sea, or something with equivalent nutrients. Only then can the animals fully use the various types of protein concentrates and roughage with which he had been experimenting.

Once this breakthrough on feeding had been achieved, Vicente soon solved the problem of inducing his dairy cows to reproduce. He found that the lack of green feed and disturbance to the animals' normal routine on long sea voyages affected the ovaries, causing large cysts to form around these organs that inhibited breeding. After doing intensive research on animal anatomy and studying all veterinary journals available, Vicente evolved his own corrective treatment. By massaging the ovaries and irrigating the troubled area he reduced the cysts. Success of the treatment was demonstrated when his imported cows began giving birth regularly to healthy calves and ceased to be troubled with retained placenta.

Other Trials with Imported Breeds

Vicente's achievement is even more remarkable when it is measured against unhappy government experiments here during this period. The first American administrators to arrive in the Archipelago at the turn of the century were determined to provide a supply of fresh milk. In 1903 eight Jersey cows were landed in Manila and another 58 Jerseys and six Holsteins arrived the following year. The condition of these milk cows can be judged from an official report dated 1906: "It was necessary for the young milk calves to be fed with canned milk because they became thin and died of gastritis." During the next three and one-half decades repeated attempts were made with government financing to introduce foreign breeds of dairy and beef cattle and upgrade native animals originally brought by the Spanish from Mexico and China. After unfortunate experience with imported Ayrshires, Shorthorns, Herefords, Angus, and Galloways, the then Bureau of Agriculture began crossing these with indigenous animals. Later, emphasis shifted to introducing Indian breeds. These included Red Sindhis, Sahiwals, Tharparkars, Nellores, Ongoles, and several less known types. Indian cattle did prove fairly adaptable to the Philippines and crosses with native stock added a larger frame and some greater milk capacity that was chiefly important for raising better calves. Once rinderpest, surra, hemorrhagic septicemia, foot-and-mouth, and other epizootic diseases then plaguing the animal industry here had been brought under control, these importations of foreign breeding stock facilitated increased local production of beef. But until the outbreak of World War II respected agricultural scientists continued to insist they had proved that dairy cattle from temperate zones could not be adapted to these Islands.

Wartime Losses

Throughout the years of Japanese occupation Vicente kept his herd of Holsteins and Jerseys that now numbered 120 head on his 52 hectare Hacarin Farm some nine miles north of Manila. "They really saved our lives," he recalls. "I sold milk in the city and earned enough to feed both the cows and our family." Although importation of mineral supplements was halted, sufficient trace elements already had been passed through the manure onto the soil of his farm to sustain the animals. Vicente had encouraged neighboring small farmers to begin milking their carabaos that are kept chiefly for cultivating rice paddies. With improved feeding these water buffalo could be induced to yield a quart or two of milk daily containing 8% to 10% of butterfat. This he purchased and processed for blending with milk from his own herd. His milk delivery route included the Santo Tomas University internment camp where he supplied the children of American prisoners; twice Vicente was slapped by Japanese guards. When the Emperor's troops began preparing for the Allied landings in these Islands late in 1944, they seized Vicente's entire herd and drove it north into the mountains of Luzon. The last Vicente heard his cows had been strafed by U.S. Air Force planes during the fighting and he believes they probably provided a meal or two for a regiment of hungry troops. Filipino farmers all suffered. Nearly a million cattle were lost, reducing the national population to some 430,000 head. And more than one-half of the carabaos so vital to the agricultural economy had been destroyed during the fighting, leaving only about 1,300,000 draft animals to till fields throughout the Archipelago.

Pioneer Instinct

In the opinion of most associates among prominent Filipino families, Vicente is a sport, given to spending his money on radical experiments when he could buy good land, farm it with tenants raising sure crops like rice and sugar cane, and enjoy the income. But, as Vicente explains, "That would not be any fun at all. " And he is fortunate in having a wife and children who share his enthusiasm. Late in the war he had written a book published at his own expense and entitled, *We Can Have a Dairy*

Industry in the Philippines. It summarizes his findings and urges national attention to dairying. In October 1945, roughly one month after the close of World War II, he began rebuilding his dairy herd, importing ten cows from California. This foundation stock since has been augmented with Holsteins and Jerseys brought from Europe, Australia, and America and a few Herefords imported just to prove that with proper feeding and care they can do well here.

At Hacarin Farms the following year he started the Araneta Institute of Agriculture, training young Filipinos in the care of livestock -- the site proved too remote and the Institute since has been moved into Greater Manila and come under the management of his brother's family. So far Vicente concluded he had demonstrated: (1) that dairy cattle from temperate zones can thrive here in the tropics even at sea level and give eight to ten lactations; in Indonesia before the war Dutch farmers had kept dairy cows in the cool highlands; (2) these supposedly delicate, highly bred cows could reproduce regularly and the calves grow into healthy animals with dependable milk production reflecting their genetic heritage. He also discovered, as have farmers in California and elsewhere, that cows fed primarily on a diet of concentrates did not maintain their vigor as long as those given a substantial quantity of roughage. But to make dairying a national industry he was convinced it would be necessary to develop cheap domestic feed and this meant primarily good pastures.

To provide the land necessary for extensive pasture development Vicente began soon after the close of hostilities to acquire the properties that today compose Grassland Farms. While Hacarin Farms was turned over to a real-estate firm for subdivision, experience gained there with tropical grasses was applied here beginning in 1956. Initially, Vicente was much impressed with Tropical Kudzu (Pueraria javanica), Lespedeza Sericea and Centrosema pubescens, all rapidly spreading legumes. But he found that in central Luzon they would not tolerate heavy grazing. Guinea, Napier, Para, Molasses, Sudan, and Rhodes grasses all have been planted at various times. For making silage he has come to favor Sorghum Almum and Sweet Sorghum, which have proven drought resistant and yield a high tonnage. His two favorites today are Alabang X (Polinia fulva), that here yields 80 to 100 tons of fresh nutritious grass per hectare annually without irrigation, and Townsville Lucerne, which produces about 60% of this tonnage, but has the advantage of being a highly palatable legume. During the rainy season precipitation here averages about 80 inches so fertilizer is applied lightly after each of some five cuttings for hay or green feed. Fields used for pasture, of course, are naturally fertilized, but Vicente is careful to rotate grazing. During the dry season he favors shed feeding with grass, hay, or silage to guard against hoof damage to the roots of his grasses; chief exception to this are the 50 hectares now provided with sprinkler irrigation from the 22 storage dams constructed to hold runoff water in the ravines.

On the 275 hectares planted to improved pasture-hay-silage crops Grassland Farms now is supporting more than 700 head of cattle; feeds purchased outside are limited to mineral supplements and Philippine produced concentrates including bran, copra meal, brewers' grains, molasses, and corn. In addition to the present milking herd of 200, stock on the place includes dry cows, calves, less promising bulls that have been castrated and are being raised as steers, and some 180 beautiful heifers fed chiefly on grass since the age of three months. Improvements, aside from roads, fences, and the milking parlor with its connecting holding pens, include three loafing barns, a well-equipped machine shop and power plant, and a full complement of tractors and farm equipment. Some 50 men are employed on the operation including those tending the 218 pigs in the hog farm, which specializes in raising purebred white Danish Landrace. Drawing on frozen stocks flown in from the United States, artificial insemination is used on more than one-half of the cows. On his monthly gross of about 30,000 pesos from milk sales VJ cente makes a modest profit despite the considerable overhead which is partly devoted to public education. Meanwhile, he is building up his pastures and breeding herd and in time will have an increasing number of animals available for sale.

While pioneering as a dairyman, Vicente also has been active on other agricultural frontiers. In his farm machinery plant on the outskirts of Manila where tractors and other imported equipment are assembled he designed and developed the ARA-WHEEL. This is an attachment fitted on the outside of the rear wheels on a tractor that directly tills the soil in a flooded rice patty. In 1948 he ventured into the growing of ramie as a textile crop and later helped organize the first ramie decorticating central and spinning mill in the Islands. Active in the Soil Science Society, the 4-H Club Advisory Council, the Knights of Columbus, and other public groups, he has been instrumental in shaping Filipino thinking on many fronts. His greatest governmental contribution was in helping design and secure passage of the Congressional legislation establishing the Agricultural Credit and Cooperative Financing Agency in 1952. It is the principal farm credit and co-operative marketing organization in the country and since returning to serve as its administrator two years ago Vicente has been vigorously involved in the enormous task of affording ordinary farmers a better break and encouragement for expanding production of basic crops.

DAIRY FARMING IN THE ASIAN TROPICS

These prize heifers raised at Grassland Farms show the lines of good breeding and promise to better the production records of their dams (below) which are grazing in a mixed pasture of Tropical Kudzu and sugar cane.

Scientists at the Alabang Stock Farm of the Bureau of Animal Industries show the growth of the grass "discovered" there after it had been accidentally introduced from India with an importation of cattle.

DAIRY FARMING IN THE ASIAN TROPICS

Wide-ranging Interests

As a most unusual member of the comparatively small group of privileged families that inherited financial dominance in the Islands from the Spanish period, the development of Vicente's social thinking is significant. The most telling contribution to his education came in March of 1950 when Vicente and his son, Freddy, were captured by bandits in Cavite Province. While Freddy was sent home with a note demanding 100,000 pesos ransom, Vicente was taken to a hideaway in the mountains. During the time required to pay over the money and negotiate his release there was an intimate opportunity to discover the reasons for such social unrest. "I learned then," Vicente remembers, "why they were so unhappy with the landlords. As tenants they even had to share the firewood they collected with the owner or his manager." Since then while he remains a tough-minded businessman, Vicente has become convinced that economic progress and national prosperity can come only if it is linked to basic social change.

In engineering a more healthy agricultural society Vicente believes that dairying can have a creative role. The average small farmer is limited to cultivating about two hectares of rice because this is all the land that a family with carabao can prepare for planting during the critical portion of the rainy season. By shifting to grass farming and dairying Vicente calculates that the same family with carabao power can manage a ten-hectare farm; carabaos can be used for the entire rainy season to plant improved grasses that become a permanent crop. "The beauty of dairying," he advises, "is the progressive improvement of the soil through natural fertilization." Vicente would start such a family with five milk cows. He calculates that 10,000 pesos in capital would be required for cows, pasture improvement, fencing, a simple barn with hand pump, and other essential equipment and not including the cost of land. Such farmers would need to be grouped in a community where they jointly produced 300 to 500 gallons of milk daily to justify a refrigerated collection center. To begin with, his model family could expect an annual gross from milk sales of about 6,000 pesos of which one-half would be return for labor; this is four to five times as much as a rice tenant farmer can earn now. And as Vicente remarks with a sweeping gesture toward idle, rolling hills covered with worthless cogon grass, "The land lies there waiting."

But the obstacles to such innovation are enormous. At present the credit facilities necessary to finance such integrated development do not exist. Nor is there yet available the seed and planting material required for extensive establishment of improved grasses. More critical is the problem of securing land for small farmer s at prices they can afford to pay even on reasonable terms. Although most of them have made no substantial improvements, the owners of tracts adjacent to Grassland Farms now are asking 1,250 to 1,500 pesos per hectare, basing this price upon Vicente's demonstration that such land can be made attractively productive. The custom of leasing land for long-term fixed rentals has not been established and many of the owners look upon property chiefly as a speculative investment that also affords status. Vicente feels the only solution may be a substantial boosting of the land tax that now is very low and sometimes uncollected to compel owners to embark upon production or sell. While such problems await solution, Vicente is working with the Bureau of Animal Industry to have more Filipinos trained as dairy farmers. A project now under negotiation with the Danish government provides for the importation of 1,000 milk cows to be located in Mindanao and cared for during the initial five years by farm families from Denmark; Filipinos working with them would later take over management. The College of Agriculture at Los Bafios, now convinced that dairying can be sound in the Islands, is negotiating for a large tract of public land nearby and foreign assistance to establish its own large-scale milk farm. In the United States Vicente has been seeking financing for larger imports of Holsteins, Jerseys, and possibly Brown Swiss and already he is bargaining with farmers who have prize herds for sale. For as Vicente believes so devoutly, "It's the dairyman who really makes a good farmer -- he has to in order to make his cows give him a living."

INDIA'S BOVINE BURDEN
Dairy Cooperatives in a Tradition-ridden Society

By Albert Ravenholt

Anand, Gujurat, India
December 1966

THE SOFT THIN LIGHT OF DAWN over Western India was lifting the fog from Valasan village as the women lined up to deliver the milk newly taken from their buffaloes to the collection station. Women, girls in their teens, and occasionally boys brought milk in brass pails and pots, balanced on their heads or tucked under their arms. Some carried only one or two quarts; but each delivery was carefully measured, the amount was recorded by the Co-operative Society's clerk, and a sample was taken for testing to determine the butterfat content. Then each woman moved on, often joking gently, as rural folk do with a neighbor, to accept from the Society's cashier payment for the milk which had been delivered and tested the previous evening. The cash they pocketed seemed small - frequently only a rupee or two (1 rupee=US$.14); yet, the implications are immense for the lives of these simple Indian farm families, for their village that is moving toward modern ways, and for the entire subcontinent now stricken with famine in large regions, even while burdened with some 270 million often useless cattle and buffaloes - or nearly one-third of the world's bovine population.

Kaira District Co-operative Milk Producers' Union, Ltd., Anand, in which Valasan is one of 549 member societies, includes altogether 110,000 farm families. It is a remarkably successful dairy in a land where most other co-operatives are either paper organizations or run from above. Its trade mark "AMUL" -- for Anand Milk Union, Ltd., which also means "priceless" in Sanskrit -- has become such a symbol of quality throughout India that its butter, processed cheese, baby powder, and other products are regularly sold-out in great city stores. An economic method for rapidly expanding India's critically inadequate milk production is being demonstrated here. Although milk and the numerous dishes made with it are more crucial to the Indian diet than to almost any other, a daily average of only five fluid ounces per capita is now available, as compared with the daily consumption per capita of 35 ounces in the United States, 38 ounces in Denmark, and 54 ounces in New Zealand.

Of even greater consequence is the evidence that fair and effective marketing is a key to inaugurating the scientifically guided renovation of attitudes regarding livestock, and much else, so long overdue in the minds of India's farmers. Despite the discouraging experience of many who have attempted innovations in agriculture on the subcontinent, the Indian farmer is not immune to change. Once he discovers that altered methods of animal care and cultivation are within his reach and will return benefits for his family, he will adopt new practices. These may include a more rational approach to livestock management-a problem that is becoming just as acute as the problem of India's human population, which now numbers over 500 million and is increasing by some 12.8 million annually.

INDIA'S BOVINE BURDEN

Near noon on November 7, 1966, I stood on New Delhi's Connaught Place, puzzled at the sight of bearded, long-haired, ash-smeared, and nearly naked sadhus who had joined with women, some with babes in their arms, and others to carry banners protesting against the slaughter of cows. The newspapers that morning had barely mentioned the planned demonstration, and none of us in the journalistic community had expected much more than a feeble public gesture, recalling the ancient veneration of the cow which had seemed to be fading. Instead, by the time demonstrators reached the Lok Sabha (the House of the People, or Lower House, of Parliament) they had become a mob, estimated to number some 120,000. Urged on by Swami Rameshwaranand, they tried to storm into the Lok Sabha. Police opened fire on the crowds, and the army was called out. Seven were officially reported as killed and some 200 were injured, though these figures were supplied later and were adjusted several times.

Thwarted in their attempt to enter the Lok Sabha, the mobs turned to burn buses, mail trucks, and the scooters of government employees. They broke into and set fire to the offices of All-India Radio and attacked the residence of Kamaraj Nadar, the potent political chieftain of the Congress Party. More than a thousand of the Sadhus were reported imprisoned that night and Mrs. Indira Gandhi, the Prime Minister responded by dismissing her Home Minister, Gulzarilal Nanda, and soon rearranged her cabinet. Across India, one after another, the Hindu holy leaders announced a "fast unto death" unless the Union Government in New Delhi capitulated. Already confronted with a rash of student riots that forced the closing of several universities, wrecked trains, and resulted in other violence (reflecting rising prices, shortages, unemployment, and deep-rooted frustrations), responsible leaders now faced a new dilemma. With general elections scheduled to begin in mid-February 1967, nearly all political parties except the Communists were campaigning for the amendment of the Constitution to allow the central government to prohibit cow slaughter throughout the nation. This is now a responsibility of the states, and seven states and three union territories (of the sixteen states and twelve union territories) have forbidden the butchering of cattle.

The veneration of the cow is almost as old as Indian history. Like the early civilizations of the eastern Mediterranean, the Indians of antiquity deified the bull, partly as a symbol of fertility. Repeated Aryan invasions across the northwest barrier of the Hindu Kush and the lower ranges into the Indus Valley gave an added dimension. Originally relying substantially upon their herds for a livelihood, Hindu religious influence turned the invaders toward vegetarianism. Milk products, in all their many forms, became vital protein components of the diet.

Cooking was done with ghee, or clarified butter made from soured milk or cream. The cow gave all these and also produced the male calves which could be castrated and raised as bullocks to become draft animals, tilling the fields and pulling carts along dusty roads. And so the cow is "Kamadhenu," representing the bountiful mother who gives all to mankind. For the Hindus she also symbolizes

Lakshmi, the goddess of wealth, and acquired a sacred place in the pantheon.

Other Asians and Westerners alike have difficulty in appreciating the emotional attachment Hindus -- particularly in the rural areas -- feel for cows. In much of North India, including the Ganges River plain, cows are often stabled in the farmer's house. He likes to be able to see the cow when he first awakens in the morning. Fresh cow manure is carefully collected, usually by the women or young girls of the family, then mixed with their bare hands and shaped into cakes that are slapped onto walls or placed on roadsides to sun-dry. This is the chief kitchen fuel throughout most of India
and a primary reason for the lack of fertility of her fields. Cow manure is also used for plastering the smooth interior walls of the home, occasionally being mixed with straw as a binder. The smell permeates most villages. Cow urine is likewise prized by many Hindus, and in some rural regions it is drunk fresh and warm from the animal as a treatment for coughs. Cow urine is also drunk by some devout Hindus, even when they have moved to the cities and become prominent there. Indeed, one leader of note is reputed to have offered it to a foreign visitor.

It is this emotional attachment to cows-fortified by religion, sanctioned by tradition, and joined with Hindu vegetarianism, that causes the abhorrence of the slaughter of cattle. Instead, in Old and New Delhi, say, a Hindu often feels himself acquiring merit by feeding bananas, or whatever else he should happen to have at hand, to one of some 8,000 unclaimed stray cows which wander the local streets. There are much larger numbers loose in other cities, including Calcutta and Bombay, where they help themselves to vegetables in the markets, obstruct traffic, and move amidst the urban bustle with a supreme nonchalance that mere men might well envy. A crucial question is what should be done with such cattle when the cows are nonproductive and the bullocks overage for use as draft animals (one of India's leading dairy specialists has calculated that there are at least 80 million useless cattle in India). Orthodox Hindus argue that they should be retired to gosadans, or homes for aged cattle, and state governments and other institutions are supposed to have actually established thirty-six of these <u>gosadans</u> holding 500 animals each (bulls are only allowed in after being castrated) during the second Five Year Plan. However, these "retirement farms" are but a fraction of the number realistically needed, and many of them are actually little more than enclosures wherein animals are left to starve. The available pasturage is inadequate, especially in the dry season, and budgets permit buying little fodder. Nor have most of the orthodox and wealthy Hindus who champion this solution been openhanded with financial assistance.

An ordinary Indian farmer, trying to survive with his family on three acres of land, faces an unhappy choice when either his cow is too old to give milk (or bear another calf) or his bullock can no longer pull the plow -- and this is particularly so when he is a Hindu or lives in one of the ten states where slaughtering cattle is forbidden. Unable to afford keeping and feeding such an animal, he may some night quietly drive it down the road, well past another village, and trust that it does not return. Cattle freed in this manner do much damage to crops in the largely unfenced fields. Or he may follow the example of farmers I learned about in southeastern Uttar Pradesh. Encumbered with a useless cow, a farmer there will secretly lead it out at night into the jungle and tie the animal to a sturdy shrub -- trusting that a tiger will finish it off - neither solution is sanctioned by orthodox Hindu mores.

The political ramifications of this veneration for the cow are far reaching. They were spelled out at a session in New Delhi of the South Asian Correspondents Association during December 1966 by Professor Balraj Madhok, President of the Jan Sangh, the political party of rightwing Hindu orthodoxy which has shown steadily growing power at the polls during the past three elections. In the February 1967 vote it hopes to become the opposition to the Congress Party in a yet undetermined number of state governments (where most real political power resides), either alone or in possible alliance with the Swatantra Party, which speaks for conservative, free-enterprise business and large landowners. Professor Madhok disowned all responsibility for alleged improprieties.

An elementary fact of animal husbandry in India suggests both the dimensions of the dilemma there and some of the opportunities: that is, buffaloes numbering some 60 million provide two-thirds of the nation's milk, as contrasted with one-third of the milk supply produced by about 210 million young veterinarians said: "This is the result of farmers being able to cull by slaughter their unproductive buffaloes." For the Hindu proscription against butchering cattle does not generally extend to buffaloes, which are the animals of less sentimental importance. Other factors also weigh in the above equation on milk yield. Except in some wet-culture rice areas, particularly in Southern India, buffaloes are judged too slow to be widely used as draft animals. They also lack a hump behind the neck, useful for holding the yoke, and are less tolerant of the summer daytime heat-the rice farmer compensates for the buffalo's deficiency in participation in the New Delhi riots; instead he blamed "goondas_[gangsters], Communists, and the Congress Party," and claimed that they were maneuvering to discredit the Jan Sangh. Professor Madhok argued vehemently, however, for amending the Constitution to empower the Union Government in New Delhi to forbid butchering cattle everywhere. "A ban on cow slaughter was always a sign of freedom in the past," he insisted. Such action by ten state and territorial governments to date is to him evidence of accomplishment since the British departed and India became independent nearly two decades ago. For a professor of history, he seemed oblivious to both scientific findings concerning livestock on the subcontinent and the apparent increase in cattle by 6 per cent or more annually. Instead, he insisted that India is short of bullocks and cows: "The best animals are being butchered [presumably by Muslims], so we support the ban and any one for it." The Jan Sangh is not alone, for within recent weeks one political candidate after another has announced support for amending the Constitution to protect the cow (including all scrub cattle); and Congress Party leaders in the Union Government have responded byprohibiting cattle butchering in New Delhi and some other regions directly controlled by the Center. In private, some Indian politicians admit that this is irrational, especially at a time when they cannot feed their human population and must import 11 to 12 million tons of grain annually, chiefly from the United States. Yet, for them it is somewhat as though an American candidate were asked to campaign against

INDIA'S BOVINE BURDEN

motherhood and the female franchise in the Middle West - it's hardly the way to get elected.

Dawn at the temporary milk collection center of the Valasan Co-operative Society finds members bringing their small containers of buffalo milk. The scene is repeated daily at dusk.

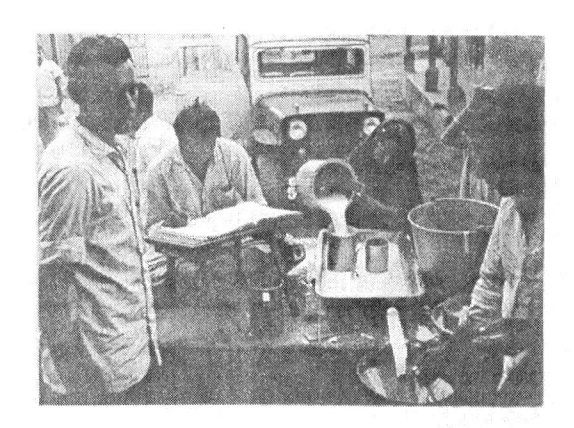

All milk is measured, the volume recorded, and a sample taken for butterfat testing by the Co-operative Society's clerks.

At each collection, payment is made for previous delivery.

INDIA'S BOVINE BURDEN

Rational Opportunities

As would be expected of scientists, India's modern dairymen, veterinarians, and other animal husbandry specialists are both frustrated and occasionally embittered over such political "Neanderthalism." Many are doing superb work, vital for India and significant for agriculture throughout the entire Asian and tropical worlds. The subcontinent's dozens of breeds of cattle, and more especially the seven breeds of buffalo, offer major promise for upgrading livestock throughout this immense region. Better herds -- both government and private-hold breeding stock that combines both adaptation to warmer climates and resistance to pests and diseases, such as temperate cattle can never possess, with some impressive tropical records for milk production. Although all animals require improved feeds for maximum performance, most of these breeds can survive on inferior fodder with small supplements of protein concentrate. The incorporation of Indian blood strains in the development of Santa Gertrudis beef cattle in the Southern United States and Mexico is only one indication of many possibilities.

An elementary fact of animal husbandry in India suggests both the dimensions of the dilemma there and some of the opportunities: that is, buffaloes numbering some 60 million provide two-thirds of the nation's milk, as contrasted with one-third of the milk supply produced by about 210 million cattle (this total figure for cattle is based on the 1961 census, allowing for the indicated increase before and since). As one of India's concerned young veterinarians said: "This is the result of farmers being able to cull by slauter their unproductive buffaloes." For the Hindu proscription against butchering cattle does not generally extend to buffaloes, which are animals of less sentimental importance.

Other factors also weigh in the above equation on milk yield. Except in some wet culture rice areas, particularly in Southern India, buffaloes are judged too slow to be widely used as draft animals. They also lack a hump behind the neck, useful for holding the yoke, and are less tolerant of the summer daytime heat − the rice farmer compensates for the buffalo's deficiency in perspiration glands by letting the animal wallow in a pond at midday. Throughout much of India, therefore, male buffalo calves are often allowed to starve to death, since the farmer reasons that they are not worth the milk required to raise them. In most regions this causes a critical shortage of buffalo bulls for breeding (the period of gestation for a buffalo is ten months, as compared to nine months for a cow); and an insufficient number of bulls together with the relatively slow maturation of buffalo heifers (due partly to low-grade feed) means that in the Punjab-the homeland of the Murrah, the largest and most productive of the buffaloes-they produce their first calves at an average of age forty-five to forty-seven months. By contrast, an ordinary farmer considers a male calf the most valuable product of the cow. This calf can be castrated and raised as a bullock for draft use. Also because of low-quality feed and popular ignorance about breeding principles, the average cow in North India throws her first calf when forty to forty-four months old, as compared with twenty-four to thirty months for first calving in North America.

INDIA'S BOVINE BURDEN

The dearth of male buffaloes means that a higher percentage of buffaloes than cows produce milk.

The choice of the buffalo as the generally preferred milk animal is in part explained by a study done three years ago in the Hissar District of the Punjab. Under the better than ordinary village conditions there, cows kept for milking averaged nearly six pounds of milk daily over approximately a 300-day lactation. The buffaloes in the District, chiefly Murrahs, produced an average of twelve and a half pounds of milk daily throughout the lactation period. Equally consequential was the comparison of the character of the milk. Cow's milk averaged 4.5 per cent butterfat and just a little over 9 per cent of non-fat solids. Buffalo's milk, on the other hand, averaged just under 7 per cent butterfat and nearly 10 per cent non-fat solids. Thus, by keeping a buffalo, an Indian farm family could produce almost four times asmuch of the _ghee_ prized for cooking as it could expect to recover from a cow. Like the rural folk in the Philippines and elsewhere in Southeast Asia, Indian farmers often remark that buffalo milk has "more taste," although cow's milk is reputed to make a softer and more desirable curd. Indian farmers took pride in serving me sweetened tea with buffalo milk that was so rich that small globules of butter floated on the surface. Among the advantages that have made so many Indian farmers prefer the buffalo for milk production is its evident ability to better utilize coarse fodder. Experiments indicate that the proportion of cellulose digested by the buffalo during the first forty-eight hours after eating can be as much as twice that of the cow. Since improved and managed pasturage, and especially legumes, is rarely available in the villages, this has major implications. Throughout India, the fodder available for livestock is commonly the residue left after threshing grain. Near-dry stalks of jowar (sorghum), bajra (a type of millet), and corn are all carefully collected for cattle feed; and then as a rule they are put through a chaff cutter, often turned by hand, before feeding. Rice and wheat straw are also principal sources of roughage. When afarmer expects a significant milk return from either a buffalo or a cow, however, he must also include a protein concentrate. This may be provided by rice or wheat brans, peanut cakes, copra meal, the residue left from crushing mustard seed, linseed, and cottonseed for oil, or from other agricultural by-products, depending upon the locality and fluctuating prices. The common pattern throughout nearly all Indian villages, however, is one of inadequate and unbalanced nutrition for livestock, frequently approaching semi-starvation.

Such miserable animal nutrition in most of rural India is the result of backward farm practices combined with an overpopulation of cattle competing with the human population for food from the land. It is compounded by the need both to keep buffaloes for milk production and to raise cattle chiefly for draft bullocks. West Bengal, with a human population of roughly 40 million, illustrates the problem. Cultivating the state's nearly 14 million acres of arable land requires some 3,220,000 pairs of bullocks (a pair of bullocks can work about five acres), allowing for 15 per cent annual replacement. Because of slow maturation due to inadequate food, high mortality among animals, and faulty breeding, some eight million cows and calves must be kept to ensure the annual production of 420,000 pairs of mature bullocks for replacement.

Were buffaloes alone to provide each person with five ounces of milk daily, this would require in addition roughly one-half as many buffaloes as there are cattle in the state. Small wonder that West Bengal has adamantly resisted the imposition of a ban on cow slaughter, for were all useless cattle also retained for sentimental reasons, then nutrition for animals and humans alike would further decline. Actually, milk supply for consumption in West Bengal, including the huge urban complex of Greater Calcutta with its nearly eight million inhabitants, is already much below the national average, for in recent years only about two ounces daily per capita has been available. Nearly two-thirds of this has been used for the manufacture of such sweetmeats as sandesh, rosgolla, and barfi, so prized for religious and family ceremonial occasions. The manufacture of these channa-based sweets involves wasting about 38 per cent of the milk solids; and after much controversy and many court tests, this industry now has been curbed in Calcutta and nearby municipal areas.

Enforcement of the Milk Trade Control Order of November 1965, plus a higher price paid to farmers, resulted in an almost fourfold increase in procurement of fresh fluid milk for November 1966 (as compared to that of two years earlier). As it is, only 250,000 liters (1 liter = approximately 2.2 pounds) are available per day for Calcutta. Of this volume, some 135,000 liters are processed and marketed daily by the government-controlled Calcutta Milk Scheme. The milk is retailed in three grades: whole cow is milk with 4.5 per cent butterfat and sells for Rs. 1.36 per liter; toned milk with 3 per cent butterfat sells for R. I per liter; and double-toned milk with 1.5 per cent butterfat for R - 0.7 2 per liter -- Initiated by the government of West Bengal in 1949 in order to supply hospitals, the Scheme now employs 2,200 women students for two hours daily to manage booths for the distribution of fresh milk. At the present price, they estimate that it would be easy to sell four times the present volume of the above grades of milk, even while continuing to limit the manufacture of popular dairy-type sweetmeats.

Like the Bombay Milk Scheme Colony, twenty miles north of the metropolis at Aarey where some 16,000 buffaloes are kept to supply fresh milk, and smaller colonies near other Indian cities, Calcutta has a major dairy enterprise at Haringhatha. This center, which was begun in 1949 to distribute improved Hariana-breed bulls, now covers three farms totaling about 5,000 acres. A half of the animals kept there, or some 8,000, are Murrah buffaloes. They are owned by private contractors, managing herds of from fifty to sixty each and operating under government lease for the use of facilities. These Murrahs average 3,300 pounds of milk each lactation period of about ten months. The other 8,000 animals at Haringhatha are cattle, mostly Hariana cows belonging to the government and averaging 2,000 pounds of milk per lactation. At this level of production, it costs R. 0.97 a liter to produce cow's milk - which is among the reasons for continuing the government subsidy of Calcutta milk distribution.

Over recent years, however, the West Bengal Milk Commissioner, Dr. A. K. Ray Chauduri, and his able staff have been conducting experiments at Haringhatha that can have major consequences for India. Aiming to reduce milk costs by boosting production, they first tried to upgrade the Hariana breed of cows by selection. This was simpler in West Bengal because inferior animals could be sent for slaughter; yet the results were unsatisfactory. Ten years ago Australia gave them a purebred Jersey herd of ten bulls and twenty-five cows, and two years ago they received a Holstein herd of ten bulls and thirty cows. Crossing the Jersey bulls with Hariana cows, they now have 130 crossbred female offspring mature and giving milk, plus some 500 calves. These crossbred cows produce an average of about 6,000 pounds per lactation, with a butterfat content of 4 to 4.5 per cent. The cost of producing this milk is R. 0.57 per liter, or 60 per cent of the milk production costs from the parent Hariana cows. Using artificial insemination, they now have 5,200 Hariana cows bred by Jersey and Holstein bulls. While the native Hariana cow produces her first calf at the age of about forty-six months, crossbred animals calve for the first time as early as thirty months. Harianas and Jerseys are about equal in size, weighing some 700 to 750 pounds. Mature male offspring are proving satisfactory draft animals and will be used for puddling rice fields. Crosses between the Hariana and the Holstein are expected to produce larger and stronger animals, with a slightly higher milk yield but lower in butterfat content. This achievement, of course, has only been made possible by much improved care and feeding. Female calves are dehorned when young, but popular custom demands that males to be sold as bullocks retain their horns.

All animals are dewormed every year before the start of the monsoon rains and receive continuing veterinary attention. The feed consists of approximately one-half rice straw for roughage, matched by greens-chiefly legumes-with protein concentrates added. They are given a mineral supplement, which is particularly needed in the moist tropics where trace elements tend to wash out of the soil rapidly. Utilizing this method, it is proving possible to maintain up to six cows per acre of irrigated land devoted to green fodder. Such intensive and scientific animal husbandry is presently beyond the ken of an ordinary Indian farmer, but it indicates some of the opportunities for more modern mixed farming in milk- shed areas around the subcontinent's burgeoning urban complexes.

"AMUL" (Anand Milk Union, Ltd.)

The larger problem of India's increasing bovine burden must be solved where the great mass of the peasants live -- or far from the environs of cities like Calcutta with their readily available markets. It is in this context that the Kaira District Go-operative Milk Producers' Union, Ltd., at Anand acquires unique significance. The state of Gujarat has long had a custom of progressive livestock management. A prize herd of 200 beautiful Kankrej cattle, native to this region, is maintained by the Anand Agricultural Institute, and the sixty milking cows average a combined production of 660 pounds per day, in addition to the 20 to 30 per cent of the milk suckled by calves. Traditionally, this is a mixed-farming area, where cotton, rice, wheat, millet, sorghum, and tobacco are grown in relatively fertile soils that periodically suffer from a moisture deficiency. Godhra District, some sixty miles northeast of Baroda, normally receives thirty-five inches of rain annually. Three years ago, however, eighteen inches of rain fell on the District; two years ago precipitation totaled thirteen inches; and last year only eleven inches fell. Near the Great Rann of Kutch on the border of Pakistan along the Arabian Sea, near-desert conditions prevail, although districts like Mehsana, Ahmadabad, and Anand are more favored.

INDIA'S BOVINE BURDEN

Kaira District, with a human population of 1,977,540, includes 973 villages and seventeen towns in a geographic area totaling 1,641,000 acres. Literacy is comparatively high, averaging 36 per cent (twice as many men as women can read). The net rate of population increase is a bit under 2 per cent annually. About one and a half million of the population live in rural areas, and the total area cultivated is 1,342,800 acres, or about 77 per cent of the total. Roughly 100,000 acres are irrigated, chiefly from wells that tap considerable underground water sources 60 to 150 feet down. Much of the 23 per cent of land not cultivated is in community-owned Panchayat pasture, traditionally overgrazed and barren. The cattle population numbers 312,383, of which two-thirds are bullocks used for draft. Of cows over three years old, which total 40,383, only 16,506 are giving milk; and some 63,958 young stock are being raised chiefly as replacements for bullocks. The buffaloes number 423,496, of which only 3,615 are bulls over three years of age. Female buffaloes over three years old number 244,631, of which nearly 60 per cent are being milked at any one time and 175,250 are being raised as young stock. These are predominantly Surtis, which are native to this region. They are smaller than Murrahs and able to thrive on a poorer diet.

It was in this setting that the idea of the co-operative marketing of milk first took form two decades ago. Early in the centuryu villagers had begun selling their surplus milk - left over after family needs were served as a sideline to farming. This was usually managed by women. Merchants collected the milk by donkeyback or by bicycle and made ghee, sweetmeats, and crude casein (this last was first exported to Germany for the manufacture of glue). The merchants introduced the first hand-driven cream separators, and soured cream was shipped south 260 miles by rail to Bombay for churning into butter. During World War I, the Military Farms price the government paid and the money they received, and as Gujarat has a tradition of popular action born during the independence movement and given constructive guidance by the late Deputy Prime Minister of India, Sardar Vallabh Bhai Patel, whose home was in this District-a co-operative movement took root. A Department of the Indian government built a small creamery here to produce butter for troops in Mesopotamia. Then, in the years between the wars, the creamery became a small dairy school, which also experimented with making buffalo-milk cheese.

A private company, Polson's Model Dairy, opened a larger creamery in 1929, and by 1943 it was producing up to three million pounds of butter annually, again for the Defense Services. It was through Polson's and other firms that the Bombay government began buying pasteurized milk late in 1945 for its subsidized milk distribution in the city. The villagers became restive, however, as they observed the discrepancy between the two systems.

The first two co-operative societies began functioning here in 1948, shipping 500 pounds of milk direct to the Bombay government daily. They leased the old World War I creamery plant and gradually added new equipment. As more village co-operative societies were organized-there were sixty in 1953-the Kaira Union's milk shipments increased to 80,000 pounds daily for Bombay and another 13,000 pounds for Ahmadabad. But this very success created a new p-roblem: i.e., during the winter flush season more milk was available than could be disposed of in fresh form. During these months the Union was compelled to curtail collections for as many as fifteen days out of thirty. This was a severe blow to the entire co-operative concept, since few farmers wanted to return to the old method of the home manufacture of ghee that sold for low prices. From the outset, three men had led in building the Kaira Union and its member co-operative societies: Trivubandhas K. Patel became and remains the president and guiding elder aid, they would help to construct a fully modern dairy plant; while the Union was to repay the UNICEF contribution by providing milk for children. The Bombay government advanced a loan of one million rupees and made a smaller grant in return for an option on all fresh milk. The new dairy plant, erected on a thirty-acre landscaped site adjoining the city of Anand was opened by the late Prime Minister Jawaharlal Nehru on October 31, 1955, and since that time it has steadily expanded, processing in the year 1965-66 over 65,000 tons of milk. Looking ahead, the Union management has provided an installation with a capacity of handling a million pounds of milk each twenty-four-hour day (60 per cent of capacity was in use during my visit). The facilities include a fluid pasteurization capacity of 264,000 pounds a day, of which 200,000 pounds of chilled milk is shipped daily by rail tank-car to Bombay. The new spray drier can produce forty tons of statesman; Verghese Kurien, who as a Christian from Kerala had to live in a garage when he first came here, is the energetic general manager and the assistant general manager, H. M. Dalaya, who has an M.S. degree in dairying, is a refugee from Pakistan. Around them, they have gathered a talented and committed staff imbued with the concept of marrying scientific effort to the cooperative approach. At the critical juncture in the Union's emergence, UNICEF chiefly through its representative Donald Sabien proposed a solution. In cooperation with the government of New Zealand under the Columbo Plan whole milk powder a day. A rotary drier has a daily capacity of ten tons of baby food, which is neatly packaged and labeled. Tow huge churns make five tons of butter a day, while in another section of the plant 120 tons of cheese is turned out in sealed cans each month. Fifty-two tons of cheddar cheese can also be made, plus seventy-five tons of ghee, thirty tons of casein, and smaller quantities of dried buttermilk and whey powder. (content sells outside for Rs 900 per ton). Such economy is accomplished by the shrewd outside buying of such agricultural by-products as molasses, watermelon-seed cake, mango-seed kernels, wheat bran, okra-seed cake, corn gluten, rice polish, sesame cake, and even the seeds of weeds, which were formerly wasted. through its representative Donald Sabien proposed a solution. In co-operation with the government of New Zealand under the Colombo Plan whole milk powder a day. A rotary drier has a daily capacity of ten tons of baby food, which is neatly packaged and labeled. Two huge churns make five tons of butter a day, while in another section of the plant 120 tons of processed cheesew is turned out in sealed cans each month. Fifty-two tons of cheddar cheese can also be made, plus seventy-five tons of ghee, thirty tons of casein, and smaller quantities of dried buttermilk and whey powder.

Five miles from Anand at Kanjari the Union has also completed the construction of a concentrated feed plant with a daily capacity of 200 tons. Manufacturing "AMUL DAN" with 16 to 20 percent protein (according to the season of the year), they are selling this product through member societies for Rs 457 a ton (cottonseed meal with similar protein content sells outside for Rs 900 per ton). Such economy is accomplished by shrewd outside buying of such agricultural by-products as molasses, watermelon seed cake, mango-seed kernels, wheat bran, okra-seed cake, corn gluten, rice polish, sesame cake, and even the seeds of weeds, which were formerly wasted.

What all this has meant to the rural villagers can best be judged from the experience of the Valasan Milk Producers' Cooperative Society, its 640 member families and their neighbors. The Society's simple, carefully printed report for last year, begins: "Dear Member Brothers and Sisters: Our Society was started 15 years back. Since then we have published a yearly statement. It is fortunate that during these years we have collected 11,802,333 pounds of milk worth Rs 2,871,898. …. The report goes on to detail the Society's accounting for the past year, including the bonus received from the Union, interest from veterinary first-aid and artificial insemination stockmen. They are particularly proud of how their Society has also helped Valarsan Village and its 3,962 inhabitants by the discriminating use of its profits – which totaled Rs 25,058 last year. Reading through the list, illustrative items suggest the Society;s concern and growing capabilities. During the first two years they spent Rs 1,030 on common water troughs, and two years later, Rs 10,800 were contributed to enlarge the primary school. At the time of the Chinese Communist attack through Tibet on India in 1962, the Society contributed Rs 2,376 to the National Defense Fund. A large waterworks was built for Rs. 25,000 and sold to the Panchayat for Rs. 6,000 three years later. This year they will donate another Rs 11,000 to mfurther enlarge the primary school.

AMUL butter emerges from Danish-made churns to be weighed and packaged.

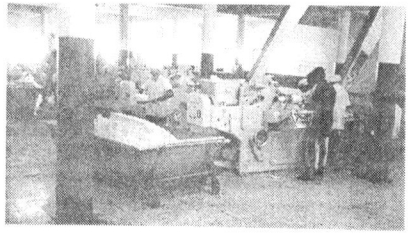

AMUL cheddar cheese ripening in cold storage warehouse is a new product.

A spray-drier produces forty tons of powdered milk daily for the Indian military.

Certainly these villagers are only starting on the long road to democratic modernization, and many necessary changes still lie ahead. For example, the Union's veterinarians who work with the villagers are still frustrated by their reluctance to let the police poison the stray dogs that make rabies a perennial threat to humans-and even buffaloes-in Gujarat. These same veterinarians also doubt that the local farmers are ready to use the loop and coil as a contraceptive for useless cattle, since they still hope that the old cows may produce male calves. (Research on this contraceptive device for cattle-financed by the Ford Foundation-has proved promising at the Anand Agricultural Institute.) It is significant, however, that although cow slaughter is forbidden in Gujarat, villagers increasingly arrange for the nocturnal disposal of useless animals by local Muslim butchers. In this way a farmer may recover Rs. 90 for such an animal and its hide-its death usually being explained as having occurred naturally.

There are a number of signs of increasing modernization. On condition that no men from their village should be present, for instance, the women of a nearby village welcomed the opportunity of attending an autopsy at Valasan on a buffalo cow which had been artificially inseminated with a colored fluid; and afterwards they wanted to know what the relationship was to the process of conception in humans. Villagers are also taking a lively interest in a new cement stall, with water trough and manger attached, which the Union has designed and is attempting to popularize as a replacement for the dilapidated sheds in which most families now keep their buffaloes - Then, too, the Valasan Co-operative Society is presently securing the use of five acres of land from the Panchayat community pasture, on which they are planting the lush lucerne legume to be utilized in boosting the milk output of their buffaloes. For the competition in milk production is catching on - to date 1,975 buffaloes in the District have produced over 4,000 pounds of milk each in a lactation. The achievement of greatest consequence so far, however, has been accomplished by Valasan's 470 Surti buffaloes, which are soon to be joined as producers by 156 buffalo heifers.

The road to modernization may indeed be a long one, but India's technologists are trying to reach a goal worth the effort -- a day when India's bovine burden will have become one of India's major assets.

Photographs by Albert Ravenholt

AMERICAN UNIVERSITIES FIELD STAFF

SOUTHEAST ASIA SERIES
Vol.XXI No.4 (Indonesia)

MAN-LAND-PRODUCTIVITY MICRODYNAMICS IN RURAL BALI

by

Albert Ravenholt

January 1973

LAST JULY, at the age of 35, I. Gusti Ngurah Ketut Muglong, a work-hardened, reserved, and direct-spoken Balinese, was elected *klian dinas* (elder) of the village of Wanayu located some eight kilometers northwest of Gianjar, seat of authority for Gianjar Regency. His neighbors evidently judged him a good farmer, but the honor also imposed responsibilities and he hardly can spare time from his efforts to secure his family's survival.

The *khan dinas'* farming activities are so dispersed much effort is lost. Reached only by a difficult path nearly four kilometers from the mud brick-walled courtyard of his home in the village lie the 25 *are* (one *are* equals 100 square meters or approximately 1,000 square feet) of *sawah*, or irrigated rice field, he owns. On this equivalent of slightly more than one-half an acre he receives an average of 300 kilograms (one kilo equals 2.2 pounds) of *bras*, or white milled rice, per crop net after the harvesters are given their traditional one-sixth share plus free meals. These yields are achieved with an improved variety of rice, *Gadis*, he began planting seven years ago with seed provided by the *kantor pertanian*, or chief agricultural extension agent, of Gianjar. *Gadis* can be harvested three and one-half months after transplanting into the field rice seedlings that have been sprouted for one month in the seed bed. Were sufficient water available from Subak Kedangan, the irrigation cooperative to which he belongs, it would be possible to grow three crops of *Gadis* annually. This summer a drought has affected much of Indonesia, including Bali, however, and even in normal years *subak* (irrigation cooperative) members are fortunate when water in their canals is adequate for two rice crops.

Nearly one kilometer from his house, also irrigated by the waters of Subak Kedangan, the *klian dinas* rents another 25 *are* of *sawah*. At the insistence of the landowner, this field is planted to *Bangawan*, a variety of rice introduced here in 1958 from the Bogor Experiment Station in Java. Like most indigenous Balinese varieties, it is also almost non-photosensitive and so can be planted at any time of the year and ripens in about 165 days. It does have the disadvantages of most *Indica* rice varieties; the stalk grows tall-up to one and one-third meters (one meter equals 39.37 inches) or more in height when nitrogen is abundant-and has a tendency to lodge with the fallen grain rotting in the mud of the *padi* field. When the owner provides his promised 50 kilos of urea, which is supposed to contain about 46 per cent nitrogen, our farmer expects here, too, to produce a net of 300 kilos of *bras* per crop after deducting the harvesters share. As a tenant, he pays 75 per cent of this crop in rent. From the two crops that can be grown in most years, therefore, 1. Gusti Ngurah Ketut Muglong expects to earn 150 kilos of rice for his family's consumption.

Renting another six *are* of dry land a little closer to his house, the *khan dinas* is able to grow yearly three crops of the white *Katela* sweet potato. With a yield of about 100 kilos (harvest weight) of sweet potatoes per *are* per crop he nets 900 kilos of sweet potatoes annually after delivering one-half the crop as rent to the landowner-the vines are important feed for his draft cow and one pig that he bought as a weanling aged two months for R1,000.00 (R400 equals US$1.00) and expects to sell when it is full grown. Other farm activities include tending four chickens, ten ducks, seven coconut trees in the village plus a few banana plants and fruit trees. When Farm work and his new responsibilities as *klian dinas* allow, he goes out to look for odd jobs near the village or even in Gianjar and then may earn R120.00 to R150.00 for a day's labor.

Despite sustained hard work, the result is a skimpy family budget. Like many farm families here, the *klian dinas,* his wife, and their two sons and three daughters aged one to seven years, usually eat only plain or sweetened bread with their native coffee for breakfast. The two principal meals are eaten at noon and about six o'clock in the evening. The family consumes two kilos of rice daily, cooked with an equal quantity of sweet potatoes, absorbing all the rice they grow, after allowing for seed, and most of the sweet potatoes. Even though their annual rice intake of 104 kilos per capita is far below the prized Balinese goal of one-half a kilo each per day, it still is above the average for the island of 94 kilos a year per person. In addition to spiced pickles and small side dishes, the diet occasionally is varied with fish and frogs caught in the canals or *padi* (rice) fields, vegetables like both the taro leaf and root and wild leaves that are collected and cooked, plus tropical fruits, such as the green *nangka,* or jackfruit, that grows sometimes two feet long and can be eaten as a vegetable cooked with coconut oil or ripe as a fruit.

Most immediate is the problem of a growing family that increasingly needs more of food and everything; the mother had tried family planning, but she now is pregnant again, apparently due to misunderstanding, embarrassment, and contradictory motives. The shortage of cash is chronic. So much must be paid for besides clothing, medicine, school supplies, and temple contributions. Annual land taxes on the 25 *are* they own are R450.00, plus a fluctuating contribution to maintain the Subak irrigation canals. Rental of the sprayer from the *kantor pertanian* costs R25.00 per day plus the price of insecticides. Urea costs about R1,500.00 for a 50 kilo sack-no phosphate nor potash is readily available commercially-and the yellowing leaves of the young rice plants in many fields are grim reminders of fertilizer deficiencies. "Every year I find myself more in debt," the *klian dinas* explains, with resignation. At present, he owes R25,000.00 borrowed from friends on which he is obligated to pay 5 per cent interest per month.

Crucible of Balinese Culture
Situated almost midway between the provincial capital and chief commercial center of Denpasar on the southern plain and still active, often mist-shrouded, 10,308-foot-high Mount Agung, eastern anchor of the volcanic mountain range forming the backbone of the island, Gianjar is in the heartland of Bali's unique culture. Wet rice cultivation's seminal role in making possible most of Asia's great civilizations is apparent here in one of its more dramatic and scenic settings where green padi fields form giant steps from seaside to mountain slope. On Bali, which

extends roughly 100 miles from east to west and 55 miles north and south, geography and climate proved propitious. Techtonic folding in the earth's crust raised such limestone ridges and plateaus as are especially apparent on the western arm and southern peninsula of Bukit. Massive volcanic eruptions over an arc of 50 miles from Mount Batukau to Mount Tjatur, Mount Batur, Mount Agung, and numerous smaller vents through eons of time laid down immense deposits of tuff and made the island appear truly "sculptured by the gods," as local legend alleges. Located between eight and nine degrees south of the equatorand at the southeastern fringe of Asia's predominantly wet monsoon climate belt, even relatively dry Denpasar receives an average of about one and one-half meters of rainfall yearly. East of Bali in the Strait of Lombok flows a powerful current marking the Wallace Line, named after the great English naturalist, Alfred Russell Wallace, where flora and fauna from Asia meet that originating in Australia and New Guinea.

Just when wet rice cultivation reached Bali remains for archaeologists and botanists to determine. It appears to have been practiced here during the first millenium of the Christian era and may have been brought from mainland Southeast Asia during the great migrations into the Pacific Island world. Elsewhere throughout this region available evidence suggests that construction of diked and especially irrigated padi fields for rice cultivation, excepting tilling of swamps and seasonally flooded river basins, was a second stage in settled agriculture. *Padi* field construction followed after the tropical rain forest had been cleared by shifting slash and burn, or swidden, cultivators. And it necessitated sufficient concentrations of population to provide both labor for such costly construction and the demand for its produce. As the late pioneer geographer of Southeast Asia, Robert Pendleton, explained to this writer nearly a quarter century ago, wet rice cultivation in diked *padi* fields was the only form of traditional agriculture that halted the otherwise rapid erosion of fertility through action of high heat and humidity on most tropical and often lateritic soils.

While fertility carried down onto the *padi* fields from slopes above in the irrigation water was helpful in selected settings such as Bali, far more consequential was the new microenvironment created in a flooded *padi* field. Particularly on the more acid soils, the pH was raised, thus "unlocking" more mineral nutrients for plant use. Given the primitive plows, harrows, and other farm implements available then and still in use throughout most of Asia, a flooded *padi* field facilitated through "puddling" a quality of soil preparation that would have been impossible with dry fields. Weeds could be more effectively controlled both at the time of tillage and because of the "head-start" achieved by rice seedlings transplanted by hand from the seed bed aged three to four weeks or older. Once they appeared, it was also easier to pull weeds from a flooded *padi* field. And some algae forming a scum in the *path* fields fixed nitrogen from the air in the water for plant absorption. Hence, at a time when crop failures elsewhere on this planet periodically prompted widespread famine and death, wet rice cultivation provided predictable yields fostering growth of population and immense civilizations in classical Asia.

MAN-LAND-PRODUCTIVITY MICRODYNAMICS IN BALI

The extent to which this ever more intensive system of farming was applied in "Inner Indonesia," namely Java and Bali, was perceptively documented by Clifford Geertz in *Agricultural Involution: The Process of Ecological Change in Indonesia. Berkeley University Press, 1963.* From the early nineteenth through the middle twentieth centuries the elastic capacity of wet rice cultivation to absorb productively increasing applications of labor in further refinement of *path* field farming astounded officials and scholars who observed this process. Dutch administrators expedited the development through construction of roads and rudimentary improvement of irrigation systems, notably as cement became building dams, siphons, water control gates, and numerous other Much of Java and Bali, however, enjoyed an advantage rarely matched elsewhere in Asia: most rivers bring irrigation water fed from alkaline volcanic debris. The rich mix of nutrients these streams carried to the *padi* fields made possible an intensity of farming and population sustenance that only the great alluvial flood plains on the Asian mainland could naturally approximate.

By a curious combination of favorable setting and accumulated skills Bali came to possess another advantage; on this enclave of Hindu civilization in otherwise predominantly Moslem Indonesia her farmers evolved practices making them extraordinarily accomplished by traditional Asian peasant standards. Varieties of rice selected were largely non-photosensitive, permitting planting and harvesting at all seasons of the year. This is in contrast to most of Asia where photosensitivity of rice varieties regulated flowering of the plant and locked farming into seasonal cycles and greater vulnerability to fluctuating rainfall. The *subak* irrigation cooperatives encouraged a quality of popular participation in the vital maintenance of canals that so often has lapsed elsewhere when central authority disintegrated. This led to better field preparation and weed control of the growing crops. Rotation to farmers of water supplied through *subak* canals also may have compelled them over centuries to select rice plant types that were least photosensitive.

Hindu farmers in Bali do not venerate their beautiful red-brown cows -- the bulls are black -- that were first domesticated from the white-legged, wild *banteng* of Southeast Asia. So, farmers here are spared the encumbrance of sacred cows that when made useless by age still compete with man for land and food in the Indian countryside. Lack of Balinese interest in milking their cows, since dairy products are not consequential in their diet, may account for this more pragmatic attitude, although some very devout Hindus here tend toward vegetarianism. Rats also are not protected in Bali as among Indian farmers who credit them with carrying *Ganesh,* the elephant trunk-nosed human figure that is their god of good fortune. Yet *Ganesh* is a favorite figure for Balinese sculptors whose art adorns the innumerable *pura,* or temples, and many puri, or palaces, of the former nobility. *Dewi* Sri, goddess of agriculture, is venerated; each *subak* maintains at least one temple and often two where offerings are made regularly to guard the crops against insects and insure a bountiful harvest, and witchcraft and other concerns with the supernatural are an intimate, vital, and colorful part of Balinese rural life. Nevertheless, the "burden of obsolete belief" weighs more lightly upon Balinese agriculture than almost anywhere in traditional Asian villages. And the near holy emphasis upon the rice plant in all its stages of growth and use insures an intensity of attention to every feature of its cultivation that has immense survival value.

Man Versus Land

Despite these exceptional advantages, time is running out for Bali and her gifted, attractive people. Ironically, the very quality and profuseness of artistic expression that pervades the society and is evident in their dances and drama, their carving not yet all cheapened and stereotyped for tourists, their weaving and painting and the grace of ordinary activity tend to mask the harsh facts beneath. Willard A. Hanna in *Too Many Balinese*[2] and *Bali: Population and Rice,*[3] has provided a detailed account of the demographic dilemma confronting this 5,600 square kilometer (2,147 square miles), lush and lovely island. A Dutch colonial census of 1930 counted a population of 1,101,393. Today the Balinese total over 2.2 million. That their numbers have only doubled during four decades is no cause for complacency; present rate of increase is calculated at 2.7 per cent annually. A crude death rate of 18-20/1,000 and infant mortality (birth to one year) estimated at well over 100/1,000 can both be expected to decline as modern medicine and drugs become more available. Even the considerable efforts at family planning now initiated through maternal and child care clinics imply protecting more effectively the health of the children now living.

Balinese farmers are affected critically by the fact that the present area of *sawah,* or irrigated rice *padi* land, totaling about 96,000 hectares is only slightly larger than it was in 1930, judging by available accounts. As Hanna has reported, this is due partly to the 1963 eruption of Mount Agung, covering more than 7,000 hectares of *sawah* and nearly ten times that area of dry land with volcanic debris. At great effort and cost this area is being reclaimed. More crucial is the shortage of water—only 68 per cent of the *sawah* now receives enough water to raise a second crop of rice. Even the rice seed multiplication station at Pegok outside of Denpasar can secure irrigation water for a second crop of urgently needed new varieties of rice on barely one-half of its ten hectares of fields. The customary irrigation systems, superb for the time when they were constructed, even with the improvements that followed the coming of Dutch administration in 1908, are now inadequate. Nealy all are constructed as "run of the stream" diversion dams; although the mountain sides are sculptured into innumerable deep ravines almost none of these have been dammed to provide storage capacity for the dry season months from late April through October. Because of the intricate system of jealously guarded water distribution between *subaks* and within each irrigation cooperative, numerous small canals parallel each other, wasting both water and land.

Springs that flow year-around at numerous points, usually below the lower escarpment on the island's profile, hint at the water resources within the mountains behind. Since many of these springs are too low to feed readily into the irrigation canals, the water they discharge is underutilized. Most promising of resources, never

significantly tapped for irrigation, appears to be the underground water table that is recharged annually from the heavier rainfall around the mountain tops where yearly precipitation frequently totals two and one-half to three meters. No survey of these resources has ever been made and Bali has no specialists in underground water geology, although Australian technicians
working under the Colombo Plan now are identifying strata that promise potable water for the city of Denpasar and the growing demands of the tourist hotels. A cursory check of wells on the island indicates water at a depth of three to 15 meters in most communities, with a draw-down of at most several meters during the dry season. While detailed survey is needed, a major underground potential lies dormant that could substantially improve irrigation and allow the main rice granary in south Bali to produce probably two and even three rice crops where now water is sufficient often only for one good crop. Until Bali's electrification is much improved, pumps could be diesel powered andwith the low lift should prove economic both for supplementary irrigation when a drought, as this past summer, dries the canals and in some areas for permanent water supply.

During the past four decades as the population doubled and the shortage of water under control limited both extension of the *sawah* and more intensive rice cultivation on existing *padis,* Balinese farmers turned increasingly to cultivating marginal uplands. The 1969 figures suggest what has happened to the landscape. Upland rice-unirrigatedwas planted on 13,758 hectares yielding about 1.3 tons of stalk *padi* per hectare on the average. Stalk *padi* includes a six- to eight-inch stem and results from harvesting with the *ani ani,* or curved thin blade, held between the fingers. Since the indigenous varieties of rice are nonshattering, grain usually is allowed to ripen fully in the field. Bound into sheaves, this stalk *padi* is dried and stored until needed in the *lumbung,* or family granary, perched on four stilts with high, rounded roofs of thatched rice straw. Dry stalk *padi* weighs about 16 per cent more than unhusked threshed *padi* that contains only the grain. Per crop yields of harvested, undried stalk *padi* from *sawah* in 1969 averaged over three tons per hectare. Most rice still is milled by hand pounding with a wooden mortar and pestle, allowing about 50 per cent recovery of *bras* from dried unhusked grain, *padi,* which is more nourishing than polished rice because it retains some of the bran. This compares with about a 68 per cent recovery of milled, polished rice from a few of the newly installed Japanese-made rubber-rollered huller mills that are operated properly.

Acreages and yields of other dry land crops also are suggestive of the great scope for improvement. In 1969, 46,513 hectares were planted to corn and yielded an average of 1.1 tons per hectare. Cassava grown on 21,281 hectares produced only some eight tons per hectare wet weight and sweet potatoes a mere ten tons per hectare on 22,729 hectares. Peanuts yielded roughly two tons per hectare (harvest weight) on 2,650 hectares and soya beans three quarters of a ton per hectare on 12,491 hectares. Coconuts had come to occupy 68,000 hectares, providing both oil and copra meal for cattle feed used in Bali and some 18,750 tons of copra for export to Java-coconut yields are difficult to calculate since nuts frequently are harvested as needed at home or for festivals. Trees show little sign of rat protection, however, which often can increase production by 20 per cent, and systematic fertilization rarely is practiced.

Although Bali's exports now are curbed by Indonesia's participation in the International Quota Agreement, coffee has become an important cash crop with 24,114 hectares planted to *Robusta* and 3,607 hectares growing *Arabica,* mostly at higher elevations. Raw red sugar is produced and cane stalks sold in the markets for chewing. Cacao, pepper, vanilla, and cloves for blending with tobacco in the favorite Indonesian cigarettes all are grown on a very modest scale, as is tobacco, cotton, and kapok.

2. Willard A. Hanna, Too *Many Balinese* [WAH-1-'72], Fieldstaff Reports, Southeast Asia Series, Vol. XX, No.1, 1972.
3. Willard A. Hanna, *Bali: Population and Rice* [WAH-4-'72] Fieldstaff Reports, Southeast Asia Series, Vol. XX, No. 4, 1972.

No figures are available on the considerable plantings of tropicalfruit trees, usually within the villages, nor on the hillsides used to pasture about 270,000 cattle. Like some 400,000 hogs, many of these cattle and water buffalo in the lowlands are kept around the villages. Livestock exports of a reported 12,000 cattle and 115,000 hogs annually to Singapore and Hong Kong are an increasingly important source of cash income for farmers and traders. Fat-tailed sheep are raised chiefly for sale to butchers who supply the vendors of *sate* skewered bits of meat broiled and dipped in hot sauce. Although lamb is preferred, the more available and cheaper goat meat is sometimes substituted. While chickens and geese are raised in Bali the pre-eminent fowl is the duck. In beautifully disciplined flocks they are marched to the *padi* fields where they consume snails and glean fallen grain after harvest-the fishy taste in duck eggs is overcome by salting. Balinese who specialize in hatching duck eggs in the Chinese-type, barrel-shaped incubator using unhusked and heated rice can determine the sex of day-old ducklings by looking in their eyes. Never to be ignored is the prized fighting cock favored by many farmers; a cock that shows real promise sometimes can be traded for one of the island's limited number of horses.

As population pressures have become ever more insistent, Balinese farmers have steadily pushed their fields further up the unstable slopes; their need for food is compounded by the emotional commitment which, as they say, makes "land a second wife." Resulting consequences for the landscape and climate are dire. Corn and other annual crops often are grown on slopes where in a few years erosion will have washed out most of the top soil. In keeping with President Suharto's order, Udayana University in Denpasar recently joined in making a regional survey for development planning by officials in Jakarta. They found that present forest cover extends over only 14.8 per cent of Bali. And this 82,880 hectares includes the 27,721 hectares devoted to coffee. Although, as Hanna has warned, all statistics must be tempered with caution, it is suggestive of the ecological process under way that the most recent previously available figures showed a total area two and one-half times larger devoted to forest reserve, ravines and wastelands, and coffee gardens. As the remaining forests become smaller, the rate of destruction also accelerates; skilled Balinese carvers require more wood for the images they sell to a growing tourist trade, cremations though now less elaborate require fuel as do the time kilns proliferating in response to a construction boom for tourists. Balinese continue to look to the forests for leaves eaten as vegetables and bark used in their native medicines. Insufficient rainfall data is available to measure the extent to which desiccation of the mountains prompts droughts plaguing Balinese farmers and denying water for the *subak* irrigation canals. Scientists at Udayana University calculate that a doubling of the forest cover to include 30 per cent of the island is required ecologically and to restore the earlier moisture pattern upon which the *sawah* and livelihood of the countryside are so dependent.

Village of Wanayu

Like most Balinese villages, Wanayu still emits a sense of tranquillity, despite the *bemos,* or small covered pickup-type motor vehicles, motor bicycles, and buses increasingly linking the community with the outside. The aerial tentacles of a huge *waringin* (banyan tree) reach down from the spreading branches to mark the crossroads that form the main streets. Opening onto these and also the side lanes are the family compounds, each entered by a gate built of two mud-brick pillars surmounted by a rice straw thatch-roofed arch and raised on a threshold of stone steps. Gates and compound walls all serve to keep in or out livestock and poultry, depending upon to whom they belong, and afford a family-centered privacy focused upon small living pavilions and the little temple raised above the bare, packed earth, the latter roofed distinctively with the durable near black thatch of sugar palm fiber. Most activity slows during the heat of the early afternoon, yet an abundance of bamboo clumps, coconut palms, and luxuriant tropical fruit trees give the village from a distance the appearance of a cool forest grove silhouetted against the glimmering green of the flooded *sawah*.

Village economic life revolves around these surrounding *padi* fields. There is neither industry nor electricity. Woodcarving, weaving, and painting provide limited part-time employment. For the 810 inhabitants of Wanayu-135 households, each with its family head-their living depends vitally upon the two irrigation cooperatives that are considered geographically part of the village. Some families do cultivate plots, both *sawah* and upland, elsewhere, and a few farmers residing in other villages also raise crops on land in Wanayu, this pattern and incidental comments by farmers suggest there is intense competition for use of any available land. In Wanayu, the two irrigation cooperatives are Subak Kedangan with canals bringing water to approximately 40 hectares of *sawah* and Subak Banjarmas that covers a slightly larger area of *padi* fields. 1. Gusti Ngurah Ketut, the venerable *klian subak,* or elected head of Subak Kedangan, has held his position since 1965. He had five years of elementary school education, served in the prewar Dutch Netherlands Indies Army and for 15 years before being elected *klian subak* held a low paid job in the public works department of the provincial government. On produce from the 70 *are* of *sawah* inherited from his father he has been raising a family of nine children and sending his eldest son to a technical school in Java. Before he was severely stricken with cancer this past summer, this broad shouldered, vigorous, and gregarious man was a true community leader, pioneering for his own and neighbors' benefit the BIMAS, which is the government-sponsored program to demonstrate the new, short-stemmed, high yielding varieties of rice first developed at the International Rice Research Institute at Los Banos in the Philippines. Introduced into Indonesia with local names, the first two varieties were identified as BP-8 and BP-5 and followed now by locally bred variants named Pelita I and Pelita II.

As the head of Subak Kedangan, I. Gusti Ngurah Ketut explained its role. The 40 hectares of sawah are cultivated by 107 farmers who own their fields and 30 tenants. He estimates that sawah within the Subak would sell for R6,000 to R8,000 per are, provided anyone were willing to sell, which is rarely the case except under duress. Annual land taxes on sawah average R25.00 per are-houses are tax exempt. Nine of the present owners acquired their fields of not over 30 are each during the land reform in 1960-they had been former tenants of the hereditary Radja of Gianjar, the family headed by the present Indonesian Ambassador to Austria, Ide Anak Agung Gde Agung. While these former tenants usually paid the government bank which was to compensate the previous owner, inflation in Indonesia during the last years of the Sukarno era made the compensation for land less than realistic. The largest landowner within Subak Kedangan today holds his allowed legal maximum of seven hectares of sawah which he inherited-he has three sons and one daughter, so this property is expected to be fragmented within the next generation. The smallest owner holds seven and one-half are and rents another 25 are of sawah in a *subak* outside of Wanayu. Since he has three daughters and no sons, his neighbors do not feel too bad about this situation, explaining "they will all go out of the compound." This attitude reflects rural inheritance practices prevalent here. Land is passed only to sons, except among the very wealthy when daughters also may share, and sometimes the daughters of ordinary folk are given the equivalent of a dowry in cash, livestock, or other portables after marriage.

Last April when I first visited with I. Gusti Ngurah Ketut, the *klian subak* was harvesting and threshing his demonstration field of 30 are of sawah planted under the new BIMAS program to BP-5. The yield weighed out at 96 kilos of unhusked grain per are, which would weigh about 80 kilos when fully dried. This yield of eight tons of padi rice per hectare is indicative of what a Bali sawah can produce per crop, given excellent management, enough water, and the required amounts of fertilizer, insecticide, etc. Had the *klian dînas* whose yields and family budget are discussed at the beginning of this Report been able to equal these yields, he would have had a per crop return from his 25 are of 840 kilos of bras, after deducting the one-sixth share for the harvesters. By proper machine-milling instead of hand-pounding, he could have increased by one-third this return of bras, allowing ample rice for his family to eat and some to sell. It is illustrative of the great potential of their sawah that awaits the full application of the Balinese rice farmers' skills. On this basis Bali should be capable of bettering the predictable production of two-crop padi fields in the Philippines that with modern management and inputs yield sufficient rice to feed 40 persons per hectare at a per capita consumption of 170 kilos of rice annually.

MAN-LAND-PRODUCTIVITY MICRODYNAMICS IN BALI

Much has been made both by Indonesians and informed foreign observers of the poorer taste and other less attractive eating qualities of the new varieties of rice, especially BP-8 and BP-5. These were originally released by IRRI at Los Banos in the Philippines as IR-8 and IR-5 and subsequently have been succeeded by varieties with better eating qualities and comparable yield performance, such as IR-20, IR-22, and IR-24, that also require more expert management in the field. The marketplace remains a revealing indicator of popular preferences within the limits of available means. Although his rice was hand-milled at home and therefore not polished white, the *klian subak* sold his bras from BP-5 for R30.00 and R32.00 per kilo when the *Bangawan* variety that has the customarily esteemed taste brought farmers here R35.00 per kilo. A frequent comment among villagers discussing rice and the new varieties is: "BP-5 is good when cooked with sweet potatoes." Necessity compels many rural Balinese to mix their rice for cooking with the much less desirable sweet potatoes-economic status of a family is judged by the proportions of sweet potatoes and rice they blend together. Given the chronic and growing shortage of rice in Bali, the insistent desire to shift from eating partly sweet potatoes, cassava, and corn to a staple of unadulterated rice and the enhanced yield potential of the new varieties, the scorn of more prosperous purists for rice that is not identical with their customary preference critically inhibits support for the "green revolution."

Despite the demonstrated advantages of the new varieties and technology, the *klian subak* remains the only farmer in Wanayu Village who systematically applied the new BIMAS program-his son-in-law, 1. Gusti Made Kenol, who farms 50 *are,* has just planted a trial plot of Pelita 1, a new variety from Bogor. And now this respected village leader is so ill he cannot walk to the fields. Yet, possibly in part because he senses life's twilight approaching, he speaks with rare candor. "Our farmers must adopt the BIMAS for all of Bali to survive," the *klian subak* insisted. "There are so many problems. Farmers still don't understand these new methods. We don't have enough water. When the insects attack, we cannot stop them. Fertilizer. Where are farmers going to get fertilizer when they don't have money to pay and the government loans are out of our reach? Still, the biggest problem is political. There is so much bad feeling between them that most of our farmers do not cooperate with each other as they need to for the program to work." Seldom mentioned today in any except intimate discussion, he was referring to the heritage of bitterness of the terrible bloodletting that followed during the months after the attempted communist coup in Indonesia in September 1965. Educated estimates place the loss of life on Bali at between 5 and 10 per cent of the adult population. It was far more than a communist- anticommunist struggle; old feuds that had festered for years and even generations were settled in the night by violence and burning. Inequality in implementation of land reform was one focus of friction. An even more bitter issue was, and still is, the ancient curse of irrigation farming; stealing of water. Walk along the canals today and an alert villager usually can show you where one farmer is drawing off water in a volume and at a time beyond his stipulated allowance, leaving less or none for the man at the end of the ditch. As population pressures increased relative to farm yields in Bali, all of these forces became more explosive, until the human volcano erupted.

MAN-LAND-PRODUCTIVITY MICRODYNAMICS IN BALI

Rural Perceptions

The farmers of Wanayu Village readily agree that Bali now has far too many people and insufficient land, especially *sawah*. What they do not share is a consensus on the solution. Hanna, in his above cited Field Staff Reports, has given a careful account of Bali's population and the family planning program that is generating sufficient publicity to make it a subject of popular discussion among farmers. Hindu Balinese must surmount far fewer hurdles than Moslems to avail themselves of family planning services. Here, male *dukuns*, the native healers who also are spiritual advisors, often act as midwives and are so depicted in wood carvings. Unlike in many Moslem communities of Indonesia, Hinduism enables male doctors in Bali to insert the intrauterine devices that public health officials recommend for rural women. One of Bali's 216 Maternal and Child Health Clinics staffed by a nurse-midwife is located one and one-half kilometers outside of Wanayu in a neighboring community. No exact statistics are available, yet it appears doubtful that in Wanayu the number of acceptors among fertile women exceeds the 12 per cent claimed for the island population as a whole.

More positive responses among younger men and women who are most interested in limiting their family sizes suggest education is vital; those who have gone to the city or to Java looking for jobs, read more, listen to radio programs, and think ahead in a larger context. Some say they are delaying marriage because they want fewer children. The great majority of farmers and their wives in Wanayu, however, are responding to keener awareness of population pressure in ways that illustrate just how time-bound rural communities can be. Whereas formerly farmers here hoped for many sons and few daughters, now their desires are reversed. They explain that because of the small plots of *sawah* cultivated by most families it is not good anymore to divide the fields among many sons. Still, it is valuable to have at least several daughters "They will marry out," one farmer said, "and then if we are sick or need money or help on the *sawah* we can depend on their husbands." While admitting that family planning is necessary for Bali, some farmers acknowledge they are "ashamed" to cooperate; children still give status as revealed by Balinese names which indicate an individual's order of birth in the family. Others fear having their wives fitted with an IUD. From fragments of information gleaned about the pill, they think it would be preferable even though more complicated to use. Curiously, the ancient Balinese taboo against twins among commoners that once led to some infant deaths no longer holds. As men who look to the land for a living, farmers here talk about other places where they can find fields or make *sawah*. During the past year, ten families emigrated to Sulawesi and Sumatra from the *desa* which includes Wanayu and nine other villages. Many of their neighbors are waiting eagerly to learn how these pioneers make out in the sparsely populated Outer Islands before deciding whether to venture. Each year, recently, more than a hundred young men left this *desa*, with a population of 5,400, to serve in the Indonesian Armed Forces. When they return home, it often is temporary; travel has enlarged their horizons and alerted them to more attractive opportunities elsewhere. Aware of Bali's booming tourist industry, Wanayu families do not see it offering substantial opportunities for themselves and their children; even some vegetables for the hotels are being imported from Java when they could be grown on this Island.

Providing food and employment for the anticipated doubling of Bali's population by the end of this century must be accomplished chiefly in the countryside. Seeking an economic solution primarily through tourism promises to prove a tragic mirage that, as Hanna has explained, will doom this unique civilization-attempts at this already generate resentment among concerned Balinese. As it has for centuries, the *sawah* remains the key to Bali's economic future. Improved cultivation of the uplands, especially with fruit and other tree crops, also can contribute substantially. It is a mistake to assume that this necessarily condemns Bali's farmers to a further and more restricted lot in a continuing process of agricultural involution. While their rice farms are miniscule by Western standards, the transformation of attitude and use of manpower and resources that many identify with industrialization can be achieved on the land and with sounder social results. Man does not need to be displaced from his familiar rural setting and shoved into an urban slum to master new skills, even though this was the prevalent pattern in Japan and the West. Herein lies the most consequential significance of the "green revolution" in the tropics that, while emphasizing rice, is including a growing number of other crops. Nature affords a modified greenhouse setting that with effective management can be almost as productive as the artificial ones created under glass in the temperate zones. Once this opportunity is realized and utilized, the emerging human prospects can look to a healthier and happier design of man's relationship to his environment.

AMERICAN UNIVERSITIES FILD STAFF   Asia   [AR-1-'78]

THE JAPANESE FARMER: WHEAT OR RICE FOR THE YEN

By Albert Ravenholt

"OUR FAMILY IS COSMOPOLITAN," my Japanese friend explained. We eat toast or some other kind of bread or rolls for breakfast. For lunch we normally have noodles, which are made of wheat, we are not so fond of the old fashioned soba or noodles made from buckwheat, especially in the north of Japan. Only for dinner do we eat rice, and less now as our diet becomes more diversified. And that is the problem of the Japanese Government and especially the ruling Liberal Democratic Party they are so desperate to please the Japanese farmers and hold their support. One of the ironies of the Allied occupation after World War II is that your American officials helped create here one of the strongest farm blocs anywhere. And now that same politically powerful farming lobby in Japan stands in the way of reducing our balance of trade surplus. They do not want to let in imports that threaten their prosperity.

Already the world's greatest importer of agricultural products, Japan, with its 116 million prosperous committed consumers, is a land where food prices and policies influence what farmers grow and how they fare in distant New Zealand, Wisconsin, and Argentina. The potency of politically organized farm groups is hinted at by the retail prices some products command. The fruit stand in the lobby of the llno Building in downtown Tokyo offers a single apple of the new sekai-ichi - meaning "best in the world" - variety for ¥1,500. With the exchange rate at the end of 1977 at ¥240 to US$1.00 that allows purchasing usually for giving to a friend an individually packaged fruit at a price of over US$6.00. Other apples are cheaper, especially in rural markets, where a single fruit may be purchased for ¥150. Although the Japanese have three varieties that many find superior to the Red Delicious, the essential reason for inhibiting importation of Washington State apples is the organized power of the growers in Aomori, Morioka, and Nagano. Likewise intriguing was Prime Minister Takeo Fukuda's explanation that Japan could only allow importation of an additional 2,000 tons of American beef for hotels because a greater import of foreign meat would jeopardize the nation's "policy of seeking food self-sufficiency." Fukuda was under pressure. Last spring in Washington, D.C. he reportedly told American officials that in 1977 Japan would have a trade "deficit" of about $700 million and thereby join with the United States as an "engine" stimulating international economic recovery. Instead, Japan this year will show a trade surplus of between $12 and $14 billion, of which more than $8 billion will be with the United States. A candid explanation of official opposition to beef imports would have included an account of the Mafia-like operations of some elements of the *eta*, or *burakumin*, who traditionally were butchers and now dominate the wholesale beef industry. These "hamlet people," about whom many Japanese talk only reluctantly, were once a discriminated minority. Now they are linked to the cattle raisers and together have political muscle within the Diet. One of the most dramatic examples anywhere of what politically inspired price incentives can do for agricultural production is provided by Japan's rice growers. Last July the government's new price paid to farmers was set at the equivalent of approximately $1,200 per metric ton for milled rice. This compares with a present world market price of $320 per metric ton F.O.B. Houston, Texas, for milled rice with 5 percent or less broken.

By contrast, in the Philippines where the government seeks to placate the numerically less important but more vocal urban consumers by keeping rice prices low, farmers get the equivalent of $263 per metric ton for milled rice. With such price encouragement, Japanese rice growers have responded enthusiastically and even some middle level white-collar city workers think they would like to return to farming if they could afford to buy land. As a result, this year despite only fair weather Japan harvested its fifth largest rice crop on record, or a total of 13,095,000 metric tons of brown rice. This will be reduced by one-sixth to one-seventh when bran and polishings are removed in milling. The crop is about one million tons of brown rice above anticipated annual consumption, and the prospect is that by next year Japan will have accumulated a surplus of about five million tons of rice. The government's quandary over how to discourage Japanese farmers from growing so much rice, while maintaining the price insuring their income and political support, leads it to many curious actions with domestic and international ramifications. This year, for example, the Food Agency is making a profit equal to $213 million on the 5,827,000 metric tons of wheat imported, in an effort to keep flour prices high enough to slow the shift away from rice consumption. Yet Japanese farmers hardly respond to the domestic wheat support price of $15 per bushel, or roughly 5 times the world market price, growing only about 200,000 tons annually.

Land of Small Fields

Japan's role in the world food budget can best be understood in the context of her agricultural history. Flying over this archipelago, which extends from just north of the Tropic of Cancer nearly to the 46th degree of north latitude, the landscape appears to have little room for the arts of farming. And so it is. Northern Honshu and Hokkaido were barely touched by Pleistocene glaciers. The total land surface-143,818 square miles or 37,348,800 hectares (one hectare equals 2.47 acres)-nearly equal in area to California, was sculpted chiefly by folding and upward thrusting in the earth's crust combined with extensive volcanic eruptions. Mountain ranges and long steep ridges predominate. They are interlaced with narrow valleys draining short rivers that empty abruptly into the sea, leaving only 16 percent of the land surface fit for cultivation. The climate is auspicious, however, as most of the island chain is warmed by the Kuroshio, or "Black Current," flowing north from the Philippines to swing east across the North Pacific. Several hundred miles of water insulate Japan from the cold winds off Siberia and North China. This contributes to an average annual rainfall of 1,600 millimeters (approximately 60 inches) that fosters a verdant countryside where the nearly 70 percent in forest exceeds the proportion of land in trees of any other modern nation.

The Oriental genius for terracing slopes and controlling water for irrigation combined with introduction of wet culture rice farming from Southeast Asia via South China near the beginning of the Christian era created the economic foundation for Japanese civilization. Early Japanese farmers also acquired other staple crops from China: millet, wheat, barley, the buckwheat that still is so symbolically important in the *soba* noodles given to new neighbors and, significantly, the soybean, which provides cheap vegetable protein and much else. Intensive gardening with an extraordinary variety of leafy and tuber plants, often also introduced from China, became an integral part of Japanese rural life, as did the fruits characteristic of Eastern Asia including the plum, peach, persimmon, the Oriental pear, and the numerous types of citrus. After about 1600 AD, when the sweet potato reached Japan via the Philippines from Central America, peasants had a high-yielding starch crop less vulnerable to drought and typhoon to guard against famine. Proximity to the sea and an early mastery of boat building and sailing skills made fish a more integral part of the diet in Japan than almost anywhere else and compensated for scant attention to raising pigs and poultry.

The unique advantage of anaerobic farming with wet culture rice had become widely appreciated and applied. By the start of the Nara Period in 710 AD, which led to a flowering of Japanese culture enriched by Buddhism, more appropriate varieties, later known as *Japonica,* evolved. Yet Japan never developed the equivalent of China's complex grain collection and transport system, which moved in immense tax-in-kind from the Yantze Valley on the Grand Canal to Peking for sustaining an imperial officialdom and large armies. Nor did Japanese rulers share the Chinese officials' supreme concern with agriculture that made mandarin officials join the emperor in the spring plowing of the first furrows. Although both cattle and water buffalo were introduced as work animals, most field preparation was done with the hoe. Except for coastal shipping, transport was primitive and goods were carried on backs of horses or humans. Even the "Tokaido" road linking the two chief centers of population on HonshuKansai and Tanto -- that became noted for the hospitality of its inns catering to travelers, was a route for moving people more than grain or goods. After the eleventh century, when imperial administration had declined and power passed to local lords and their samurai, a warrior class, agriculture suffered. Feudal preoccupation with martial arts and clan conflicts led to wars that ravaged the countryside, disrupting irrigation, draining manpower, and creating a larger unproductive elite. Rice remained the preferred staple and an important medium of exchange. Wealth was calculated in the number of *koku* (a five and one eighth bushel measure) of rice the holder was entitled to collect. Farmers themselves were often left with too little to eat. Peasants banded together in fierce uprisings that by the fifteenth century occurred almost annually in some regions of Japan.

Consolidation of power by the Tokugawa Shogunate after 1603 inaugurated an era of effective administration as power in the provinces was redistributed among some 270 loyal diamyo and their retainers. Domestic tranquility fostered reclamation of additional land from slopes and marshes and expanded irrigation. Basic to this more efficient feudal system with its strict hierarchy of status combining codes of conduct and loyalty, however, was enhanced control of farmers and their vital *koku* of rice deliveries. New land surveys insured more exact calculation of taxes to be paid. Cultivators, four-fifths of the population, were compelled to join "neighborhood associations" that made them share responsibility for payment of each other's taxes. Ordinary farmers were forbidden to buy or sell land or leave their villages and compelled to eat the simplest food, wear plain clothing, and live in modest houses. Records indicate that between 40 and 60 percent of the rice crop was taken from farmers in taxes and numerous other levies. Cotton growing was introduced about this time from China and weaving this into cloth became one of the new rural handicraft industries. Peasant families usually were not permitted to sell their goods freely, however, but instead had to deliver them at reduced prices to the monopolistic enterprises promoted by their military overseers. Population expanded and by the mid - eighteenth century totaled over 30 million. Already the new center of power at Edo, later to become Tokyo, numbered more than one million inhabitants, and the Tokugawa rulers were compelled to ease curbs on transport of grain to feed them. Population pressure combined with onerous grain collections and other exactions and restraints again brought misery to peasants, especially during famines that followed widespread crop failures in the 1780s. Infanticide now became common. Japan's tradition of violent peasant uprisings was further fortified and the urban poor repeatedly rioted, plundering rice storage warehouses and pawn shops.

Meiji Restoration and Agriculture

The modernization of Japan inaugurated with the Meiji Restoration in 1868 sought to curb consequences of Western commercial intrusion by mastering skills from Europe and America. It led to a drastic remaking of life in the countryside, as part of building a "wealthy nation and a strong army." Feudal restraints on cultivators were rapidly removed. By 1871 they were allowed to grow crops of their choice rather than those designated by military superiors. The next year official prohibitions on selling or mortgaging farm lands were removed. A nationwide cadastral survey within nine years determined area, productivity, and ownership, and facilitated issuance of titles and a new land tax fixed at 3 percent of value to be collected in cash rather than kind. It proved an efficient system for government extraction of revenue from the farmers to finance industrialization. Informal landlordism had begun during the latter period of Tokugawa decay and now was legalized, sometimes also enabling wealthier gentry to acquire ownership of formerly public communal forests. Many poorer peasants were unable to weather the shift to a cash economy with fluctuating prices for produce; borrowing money to meet expenses including land taxes that sometimes equaled one-fourth of the harvest, increasingly they lost their land. Within 60 years after the Meiji Restoration almost 50 percent of all farm land was cultivated by tenants paying usually about one-half their crop as rent.

Universal elementary education, also inaugurated in the 1870s, opened avenues for a technological transformation in Japanese agriculture. The first missions to Europe and America at the time had recognized the great advantages of applied science, with its emphasis on using fertilizer and machinery, to farming. Improved livestock and equipment was imported, a national agricultural experiment established in 1873, and six years later a factory began making similar farm machinery. As the two agricultural schools opened-later to become the College of Agriculture of the University of Tokyo and the Hokkaido University College of Agriculture-English and American instructors were employed. Much of the equipment developed for large-scale farming in North America proved unsuited to small Japanese rice paddy fields with limited road access and subsequent emphasis in instruction shifted to the German attention to soil science and use of chemical fertilizers. Other introductions, however, proved of lasting worth. In Aomori Prefecture, at the northern tip of Honshu, Protestant missionaries in the early 1870s brought apple trees from

Indiana, which became known as the "Indo" variety. Some of these trees still are bearing as part of a thriving orchard industry, although most trees have been top-worked, converting them to more desirable varieties like *Fuji*.

Among the most effective innovators were "itinerant instructors" who moved from one rural village to the next holding farm extension meetings where they encouraged interest in improved seeds and better cultivation methods. Some innovations were simple, such as placing rice seed in saltwater to float off light grains that otherwise would grow weak plants, and other improvements concerned times of transplanting seedlings and better management of irrigation water. The "instructors" stimulated creation of "agricultural discussion" and "seed exchange" societies that shared the improved strains discovered by innovative farmers and promoted deeper plowing of fields with horses. Before the nineteenth century ended farm cooperatives patterned on the German model got a start, and sought to protect cultivators from moneylenders and middlemen. As was also the case in other countries, wealthier farmers were often the most able and willing to try these new ideas and join cooperatives, which they frequently dominated. It was a time when the benefits of commercial fertilizer to augment use of "night soil" and other manure were becoming recognized. These progressive farmers also utilized imported guano, soybean meal from Manchuria, and herring meal from Hokkaido, plus nitrates from Chile.

At the time of the Meiji Restoration, Japan's population numbered just over 33 million. With a then estimated 5 million farm families cultivating about 4,489,000 hectares of land, the country was almost self sufficient in production of food for the traditional diet. With improved health measures, population expanded more rapidly thereafter and by 1900 had grown to 44,831,000. From 1868 to the late 1920s there was an almost continuous rise in the per hectare output of Japanese agriculture, combined with a shift to raising more livestock and fruit. A dramatic increase in sericulture enabled income from the silk cocoons to constitute 12 percent of the farmers' total returns. Another 1.2 million hectares were brought under cultivation, about two-thirds of this was on the colder northern island of Hokkaido where American-type Midwestern dairy farming methods proved appropriate. Japan, however, had already become a net importer of rice in the 1890s. Stimulated in part by World War I inflation, food prices escalated and in 1918 "Rice Riots" spread to many major cities. The government responded with policies that squeezed rice from the colonies in Korea and Taiwan. Koreans were compelled to shift increasingly to eating sorghum imported from Manchuria. In Taiwan (then Formosa) increased taxes and prices charged by the government monopolies in salt, tobacco, and liquor forced ever more families to eat sweet potatoes. Irrigation was extended in both Taiwan and Korea, improved rice seeds introduced and use of fertilizer promoted. By the mid-1930s Japan was importing nearly 2 million tons of rice annually from these 2 colonies, or roughly 20 percent of her domestic consumption. To guard against great fluctuations in price, trade in rice, including that from the colonies, became primarily a government operation.

Wartime Defeat and Creation of a New Rural Society

While many marvel at the emergence of Japan literally from the ashes of defeat in 1945 to become the world's third largest industrial power, few appreciate the crucial role of a radically transformed agriculture in making this possible. Understanding the political forces that govern modern Japan must include appreciation of the potent new power of farmers. Although the emancipation of women, who voted for the first time in Japan in spring 1946, is an enduring tribute to the greatest *shogun* of all, General Douglas MacArthur, as Supreme Commander of the Allied Powers, it is only the most obvious social change that impresses someone who remembers prewar Japan. It is today a land vibrant with the energies released when the ideas and pressures formerly encapsulated within hierarchical and largely traditional relationships are allowed scope and people are given ready access to world science and knowledge.Democratization in the countryside began with the land reform. When Japan surrendered in August 1945, two-thirds of Japanese farmers rented all or part of the land they tilled, paying often one-half of the . harvest in rent. At the behest of , General Headquarters of the Supreme Commander of Allied Powers, within 14 months the Diet had passed and the government promulgated enabling provisions for a sweeping change. The government purchased about one-third of Japan's cultivated land, totaling 1,956,700 hectares, including about 200,000 hectares of government land, divided into about 30 million parcels. This was resold to cultivators on terms that proved most advantageous, partly due to inflation. The new laws imposed a ceiling on individual holdings of 3 hectares, -, except for Hokkaido where this limit was set at 12. A family could retain . one hectare as tenanted land and this totaled about 10 percent of the cultivated area on which rent ceilings - were fixed. Although authority for this drastic change came from on top and was guided by experience of Japanese scholars and officials long impatient for such action, detailed implementation was the responsibility of village Land Commissions. They were elected with Land Commission membership apportioned on the ratio of five tenants to five owner-operators and landlords. Their work was supervised by the Ministry of Agriculture and Forestry through prefectural commissions. Yet the fact that locally elected farmer representatives were empowered to make such fundamental decisions, regarding the most basic rural economic resource also had immense educational consequences in fostering confidence in democratic power.

A complementary and equally vital change was the reorganization of and extension of new authority to the agricultural cooperatives. The earlier societies had been amalgamated during World War II and farmer membership made compulsory as a means of regimenting agricultural deliveries of produce. They were restructured to maximize service to farmer members who acquired full control, with non-farmers limited to nonvoting associate membership to prevent businessmen domination. By the end of March 1950 more than 90 percent of all farm families were members of at least one cooperative, of which there were a total of 34,130 providing credit, marketing, purchasing, and processing. More than four-fifths of the officers and directors had never held positions in the old government - controlled agricultural associations. An agricultural insurance system was instituted protecting farmers and their livestock and crops against disaster. Funds derived from U.S. aid sale of commodities were utilized for expanding crop loans and other credit to farmers. National leadership for these cooperatives was provided by the National Federation of Agricultural Cooperatives for marketing, the Central Bank of Agriculture and Forestry for credit, the National Federation of Mutual Insurance, and the Central Union of Agricultural Cooperatives for political lobbying. With more than five million members and nearly half a million employees, this cooperative network permeates rural life. Operations have even come to include a travel agency with more than 800 employees, now chiefly occupied with taking Japanese farmers and their families on trips abroad. It is this powerful organization of Japanese farmers that champions their cause today and enables them to bargain successfully with the giants of industry and finance.

When Japan surrendered, the population of the home islands numbered about 72 million. Soldiers were soon shipped home from far flung islands of the Pacific, Southeast Asia, and China. Civilians also were repatriated from Taiwan, mainland China, Manchuria, and Korea, and babies born to reunited families. Within 6 years the population of what remained of Japan proper had grown by about 12 million. It was a time of food shortages throughout the devastated regions of the world and rice available for export from Thailand, South Vietnam, Australia, and the United States was jealously allocated. In Japan the U.S. officials responsible for the occupation moved vigorously to spur agricultural production. The sinking of most of Japan's merchant fleet by American submarines during hostilities and destruction by bombing of many industrial areas crippled fertilizer production. Along with coal and steel, fertilizer was given the highest priority in reconstruction. In 1946 Japanese farmers had access to only 300,000 tons of ammonium sulphate or its equivalent in 20 percent nitrogen fertilizer. Within 5 years this had increased to more than 2.2 million tons. In the same period superphosphate supplies increased from 48,000 tons to 1.6 million tons and potash from 2,000 to 284,000 tons. United States assistance expenditures for fertilizer in one year totaled nearly $60 million. Pesticides were greatly improved following enactment in 1948 of a law establishing standards of quality. Agricultural research was emphasized and extension promoted while major investments were made in flood control and irrigation benefiting 1.6 million hectares of rice fields. Most dramatic of all, within 20 years of Japan's surrender her farmers, for whom tractors had been a curiosity, owned 2.5 million neatly designed and powerful little mechanical cultivators. With the bumper rice crop of 1955 Japan again was able to feed her people with this most basic of staples, even with the increase in population.

For an appreciation of Japan's agriculture now it is essential to take account of two developments. Within the past 18 years average Japanese per capita annual income has increased from about $380 and is approaching $5,000. Japanese spend some 34 percent of their income on food as compared with approximately 16 percent by Americans. Consequences in the countryside have been profound. As urban incomes leaped ahead, young people were lured off the land leaving their elders to till the fields. The rural urban income gap, however, also stimulated other changes. Japanese farmers were organized and constituted a potent base of conservative political support for the ruling Liberal Democratic Party. This resulted first in the Agricultural Basic Law enacted in 1961, committing the government to promote parity of income between rural and urban households. The aim was to foster family farms on a "viable" economic scale and assist farmers in responding to the changing market opportunities reflecting a more diversified national market. But that farming was less profitable did not mean farmers were willing to sell their land, thus facilitating consolidation into larger-scale operations. For too long they had wanted land and now it proved the most valuable thing to hold as expanding cities and affluence compounded the pressures of inflation. Instead, political pressure was used to strengthen support prices. In managing the Food Agency, which controlled rice, U.S. authorities during the occupation had introduced the parity formula for deciding the price paid to farmers. By 1960 adoption of the "Production Cost and Income Compensation Formula" provided that farm labor should be valued at the same rate as nonfarm wages. Initially, this meant fixing the price at the equivalent of about $223 per metric ton of milled rice. Within 8 years it was pushed to about $441 and steadily up until this past harvest season of 1977 when the price of milled rice was set at approximately the equivalent of $1,200 per metric ton.

Farmer responses to these price incentives were dramatic. Yields of rice had dropped almost one-third from 1942 to 1945 chiefly as a result of wartime shortages, especially of fertilizer; harvests were also reduced by a 12 percent decline in cultivated areas, mostly dry land crops, as manpower was shifted to military production. By 1950 cultivated areas had been restored to the prewar peak of approximately six million hectares. And on the roughly one-half of this area that was irrigated, rice production had surpassed the output before the war, totaling 9,652 tons of brown rice in that year. As optimum inputs of fertilizer and insecticide became available and farmers were able to mechanize first land preparation and later some harvesting and threshing, the opportunity to respond to price incentives increased. By 1967 Japan's production had reached 14.4 million metric tons of brown rice. Per capita rice consumption already had begun to decline, especially as the urban population shifted to eating more wheat products. In 1967 Japan grew two million tons of brown rice more than was consumed. Storage became a problem until the international grain shortage of 1972-1975, compounded by the partial failure of the rice harvests in South and Southeast Asia, enabled Japan to dispose of her surplus stocks.

The bumper harvest of over 13 million tons of brown rice in 1977, exceeding anticipated consumption for 1978 by nearly 1 million tons, highlights the conundrum confronting the Japanese government. Japanese scientists calculate that more than 60 percent of calories in this crop represents energy imports, chiefly of petroleum products utilized for manufacturing nitrogen fertilizer. Japanese farmers, however, also utilize the equivalent of US$170 per hectare annually for insecticide, plus fuel to power farm equipment. With a domestic support price for milled rice now roughly equivalent to US$1,200 per ton or nearly 4 times the present world market, exporting the surplus hardly offers a solution. Were this rice sold abroad at distinctly concessional prices the government would be compelled to absorb the difference rather than passing most of this cost on to the Japanese consumer as is now largely done with domestic sales. Schemes to induce Japanese farmers to retire paddy fields from rice production are gaining little acceptance, while the powerful farm lobby continues successfully to prompt the government into pushing up the support price and thus make rice growing more attractive. Meanwhile, Japanese per capita annual rice consumption has declined to 86 kilos of milled rice, which is roughly 30 kilos below average annual consumption 20 years ago, while annual consumption of wheat products averages about 32 kilos.

JAPANESE AGRICULTURE

The Japanese diet also is changing rapidly in other ways. Average annual per capita consumption of 35 kilos of fish and shellfish is the world's highest, except for Denmark. Yet it is becoming less important in the daily average protein intake of nearly 80 grams, in a diet averaging about 2,800 calories daily. Prices are being pushed up as the catch in international waters is curbed by imposition of the 200-mile fishing limit. Recently it has totaled over 10 million tons annually. The national goal is to compensate for this with large-scale aquaculture and mariculture, where Japan along with Taiwan possesses the world's most sophisticated technology. This, however, can only be accomplished gradually; during the past dozen years fish production from inland waters has slightly more than doubled to 76,645 tons. And one kilo of the prized live eel today costs the equivalent of nine or ten U.S. dollars. Instead, Japanese are shifting to becoming major consumers of poultry and animal foods. They eat more eggs than any other people except Americans and New Zealanders. Poultry and pork consumption is increasing annually at the rate of about one-half kilo per capita, and now totals about ten kilos of pork and eight kilos of poultry annually. For these the Japanese housewife pays two to three times as much as her U.S. counterpart. Beef consumption is about one-third that of pork and is curbed by high prices achieved by a manipulated market making beef almost as costly as eel. Consumption of milk and dairy products is increasing, although at 54 kilos per capita annually it is roughly one-fifth that of the United States.

It is this rapid shift in Japanese eating habits and preferences that is making her the world's largest single importer of agricultural products, with the result that only about 56 percent of the calories consumed are domestically grown. Japan's example of what 116 million people want when they become affluent is a sobering indication of what we must expect as other countries follow her example of rapid development. Soybeans remain crucial for making bean curd, soy sauce, cooking oil, and many other traditional foods plus providing protein feed for animals and fish. Domestic production now has declined to about 100,000 tons annually and imports are approaching 3.6 million tons of which the United States has been supplying between 70 and 80 percent; the Ministry of Agriculture and Forestry projects a 40 percent increase within the next 7 years. Wheat imports, with more than one-half of them coming from the United States, now approach 6 million tons and have been growing about 3 percent annually. Poultry, pigs, and cattle, both dairy and beef, take the largest imports for formula feed now exceeding 18 million tons annually. This consumption of feed has tripled since 1960 and is expected to continue growing; so that Japan's present annual imports of 15.2 million tons of corn, sorghum, and barley within 7 years will total 20 million tons. Another revealing item is the import of roughage for dairy and beef cattle. Alfalfa meal imports have been fluctuating between 292,000 and 456,000 tons annually. Hay imports, chiefly from California and Washington, have multiplied 20 times in 5 years to 62,000 tons annually. And like the New Zealand farmers making pelleted lucerne for the Japanese market, American growers in the Columbia basin of the Pacific Northwest are wrestling with regulations limiting the percentage of certain weeds allowed in bales of hay they compress for fumigation and export in containers to Tokyo.

Changes in the countryside mirror these shifts in the Japanese diet while also reflecting changing values and growing affluence. Most Japanese farmers have abandoned growing secondary winter crops; they prefer instead to seek more remunerative and pleasant work during winter in one of the factories usually located readily within commuting distance as industry is dispersed. During the past 17 years the number of full-time Japanese farm families has declined from 1,527,000 out of 5,891,000 rural households to 659,000 out of 4,891,000. The number of families primarily engaged in farming has declined in the same period from 1,950,000 to 1,002,000, while those rural families primarily engaged in non-farming employment increased from 2,414,000 to 3,231,000. It is in the context of this decline that the Japanese government is seeking a way out of its rice surplus quandary by encouraging farmers to shift away from planting to livestock raising. Japan slaughters about 14 million hogs annually, for example, and imports about 150,000 tons of pork; one-third each from Taiwan, Denmark, and the United States. Livestock offers alternative employment to farmers now growing rice, as does replacing 92,000 tons of beef imports with domestic cattle raising. It also illustrates one dimension of the stubborn facts at work in resolving Japan's trade surplus by allowing expanded imports of farm products. Domestic beef in Japan now retails for approximately Y3,000 per kilo, or about US$12.50, while imported beef of supposedly lesser quality sells for two-thirds this price. American specialists calculate that with present trends Japan can be importing another 60,000 tons of quality beef within 5 years. This, however, is precisely the market Japanese cattle raisers are looking to for expanding their opportunities, as are the powerful meat wholesalers and the Japanese officials seeking to get off the fence on Japan's surplus rice output and thus ease the burden on the Japanese consumer-taxpayer.

As rural families shifted to earning an ever greater portion of their income off the farm, earlier experience in America suggests they might sell land to fewer remaining farmers, who would then enlarge their operations. But in Japan this happens only rarely. Some of Japan's leading economists deplore the failure to "rationalize" agriculture; creating larger units with greater reliance upon mechanization and enhanced production and income per man. Japanese farmers are avid to learn about new and more productive techniques, such as the dwarf fruit trees now being demonstrated and multiplied at their excellent experiment stations. They are most reluctant to sell land, however, and for good reason. As the support price for rice has risen, so has the value of paddy fields. Prices vary greatly according to location and access to major cities as well as productivity. Even in the more remote areas-provided anyone would sell-it appears the minimum price would be Y10 million per hectare or equivalent to $16,666 per acre. In the prime apple growing region of Aomori Prefecture in northern Honshu bare slope land suitable for planting fruit trees will cost about the equivalent of $115,000 per hectare. So for the Japanese farm family that acquired fields under land reform at concessional prices three decades ago it is difficult to imagine anything more worth keeping. There is great security both economically and emotionally for a family to divide its livelihood between industrial work and farming. The recession following the oil crisis has taught them that an industrial job is not necessarily a guarantee of lifetime income. And as farmers backed by the organizational and economic muscle of Zen-noh, the huge cooperative that even sails its own ships on the world's seas to haul feed grains, they have cause for confidence.

Japanese farmers have another cause for confidence; they are relatively less vulnerable to weather fluctuations than their fellow cultivators in

most lands. Japan did experience a "little ice age" between about 1550 and 1890. The coldest spell appears to have lasted for some three decades in the middle of each century. After 1900 the climate became warmer, reaching its peak in 1960. Calculation of these climate changes is greatly helped by the records of the date when the ice first formed kept for nearly a thousand years at the temple beside Lake Sùwa at the northwest end of the Kofu Plain. During the past 17 years the climate throughout the archipelago has gradually become colder. And in winter 1976-77 ice again formed along the banks of the Yodo River near Osaka, as it last did early in the 1890s when the wild boar in Sendai and Miyago prefectures died off due to cold and heavy snow. On the big northern island of Hokkaido farmers earlier in this century experienced a poor harvest about once every four years, as late spring and early fall frosts hurt their rice and potato crops. Now they are anticipating frost problems every third or second year. As the waters of the North Pacific have become colder during the past three years, more salmon and fewer pike are caught. Japan, however, is spared the drastic weather fluctuations characteristic of the Eurasian land mass because of the surrounding seas' moderating effects. And even when the otherwise abundant rainfall is reduced farmers are protected against drought by irrigation first promoted so effectively by that great Buddhist priest-engineer, Kobodaishi, who, roughly a thousand years ago during the Nara period, traveled the countryside, designing dams and canals for farmers to build and water their fields.
(March 1978)

Acknowledgments

The author is indebted to numerous Japanese farmers, agricultural scientists, and officials who shared their knowledge. He is also indebted to:
Dr. Yujiro Hayami, author of *A Century of Agricultural Growth in Japan*. University of Tokyo Press, 1975, Tokyo;
Dr. Marius B. Jansen, who has written extensively on Japanese history;
Mr. Yoshio Kawamura, for the opportunity to read his unpublished dissertation;
Dr. Junkichi Nemoto, Director, World Weather Clinic, Tokyo;
Dr. Saburo Okita, Chairman, The Japan Economic Research Center; and
Dr. Kunio Takase, Director, Economic Research and Technical Appraisal Department, The Overseas Economic Cooperation Fund, Tokyo.
Likewise valuable were the reports on Agricultural Programs in Japan 19451951 by the Natural Resources Section, General Headquarters, Supreme Commander for the Allied Powers.

AMERICAN UNIVERSITIES FIELD STAFF: Field Staff Reports
North America Series Vol. IV No. 1 (Canada, United States)

WHO WILL GROW GRAIN FOR A WORLD FOOD BANK?
Wheat and Weather in Canada's Prairie Provinces

by Albert Ravenholt

October 1976

"SURE WISH YOU HAD COME before we had to swath our fields in order to get ready to combine before the snow flies. Our wheat this year, why it came up to here on my chest. And some farmers around here got 60 bushels of wheat per acre. Others harvested a hundred bushels of barley [wheat weighs 60 and barley 48 pounds per bushel]. Certainly, it is one of the best years we have had since moving here in 1911 from Oklahoma -- we worked with our father to break most of this prairie ground from the wild buffalo grass. That native sod was tough. Then we used five horses on a single breaking plow; hitched first two horses in front and then three behind. Sometimes two men had to hold the plow. Winters were colder then, usually with more snow than now. Lately, we don't so often have to wear a cardboard box over our heads when we go out at night to warm the air before breathing it. Why then, the temperature would stay 40 degrees or more below zero at night for a month. [Although Alberta officially is shifting to centigrade, farmers think and talk in Fahrenheit.] So, I guess you can say generally our weather has been warmer. And this summer we had about as fine weather for growing as you could ever hope for. Still, as I think over these recent years, there is something curious about the weather-it's not nearly so predictable as it was in the old days. Now, the rain, hail in some places, and temperature are so uncertain. That can be rough on us farmers."

In his eighty-second year and still robust, Frank Slavik was describing what it has been like farming for 65 years here some 80-odd miles southeast of Edmonton in the northernmost tier of Canada's grain belt. Although he no longer rides a tractor, he works with sons and nephews supervising field and elevator operations. For consumers concerned with the world's uncertain food supply his observations are vital, as they are also for grain brokers, bread bakers, and farmers elsewhere. The specter of the earth's climate cooling and pushing south the wheat belt across Northern Europe, Siberia, and Canada has begun to haunt scientists and others troubled by our planet's increasingly precarious food reserves in the face of burgeoning populations. Fertile fields of mostly deep, black soil reach over rolling hills to the horizon in all directions of this region. They are part of roughly one-third of Canada's wheat land that, it is estimated, will be lost to production if average temperatures cool 1* C below present levels.

Scholars have calculated that such a temperature decline would cost the world 40 to 50 million tons of wheat production yearly, the shortened growing season trimming crops by 12 to 14 per cent, with spring frosts coming later and autumn snow flying earlier. Probable concurrent changes in wind patterns affected by the circumpolar vortex, including the monsoons in South and Southeast Asia, could have far more disastrous consequences further south, as several eminent world climatologists have shown. Terrible famine years

WHO WILL GROW GRAIN FOR A WORLD FOOD BANK?

like 1315 and 1316 when peasants in the British Isles harvested hardly enough grain to plant again because of wet, cool weather are suggestive, as are the famine marchers during those same years in France. Also illustrative of what a "little ice age" can bring when grain fails to ripen was the starvation hroughout most of Western Europe in 1693-94 and the famine in Scandinavia in 1697 that, in Finland alone, cost the lives of one-third of the population. Only within the past century and a half has the chronic fear of famine faded in the Western World. Even then there have been extraordinary episodes like the terrible winter of 1946-47 in Western Europe, when the official ration for occupied Germany dropped below 1,000 calories per person daily.

Bumper Harvests of 1976

As it is, we are witnessing here on the Canadian prairies this autumn just how consequential good weather is for man's food supplies. From the grain capital of Winnipeg across Manitoba, Saskatchewan, and Alberta, into the Peace River country of British Columbia, spring came early. Warm, dry weather enabled farmers to get equipment into their fields promptly and thus seed in ample time. The rains came just when they should in early and mid-June, except for a drought pocket in Manitoba that extended south across the border into Wisconsin, Minnesota, and the Dakotas. The weather in July and August was hot, with just enough moisture to maximize plant growth, and the grain filled well into the head. Damage from hail and pests was minimal. Sunny skies and warm temperatures in September were a harvester's delight, in contrast to years when killing frost -- sometimes preceded by snow flurries -- came early in September, and some farmers who had swathed their wheat into windrows in the field could drive their combines only after the snow had melted the next spring.

Such friendly weather enabled Canadian farmers in 1976 to grow the greatest wheat crop in their history; a bin-busting 886 million bushels or 38 per cent more than in 1975. Total harvests of oats, barley, and rye were also up over last year and the barley crop of 475 million bushels was the largest on record. While this extraordinary wheat crop in part reflected a 17 per cent increase in sown acreage, yields per acre were the highest ever. The average promises to be 31 bushels of wheat per acre, 18 per cent above last year and 30 per cent above the 1965-1974 average -- it matches average yields to the south in the United States. Growing, harvesting, and storing this immense crop is a truly remarkable performance by Canadian farmers, proving their mastery of modern agricultural skills -- when the weather cooperates.

Around the globe reports of harvests in the northern hemisphere are of equally encouraging gains in production. Despite early reports of drought in the Soviet Union's winter wheat region, its total harvest of wheat and coarse grains may exceed 215 million tons. This will be more than 50 per cent above last year's crop and just below the record 1973-74 harvest of 223 million tons. Prospects in the United States are for a total grain harvest of about 260 million tons, including 58 million tons of wheat; this represents a slight decline from last year's record wheat harvest despite a 7 per cent increase in area sown. The corn crop of about 150 million tons is setting an all-time record. Drought in Australia and less moisture in Western Europe and Great Britain curbed their yields. Yet, the prospect is for a world wheat crop totaling perhaps more than 380 million tons (all figures are in metric tons of 2204.6 pounds). This would be 6.4 per cent above last year's 357 million tons and 2.2 percent above 1973-74, making it our earth's most abundant wheat harvest. This wheat harvest is complemented by an excellent rice crop, estimated for 1976 at 344 million tons. At that level the rice harvest would be just 2 per cent below last year's record. The chief beneficiaries are the monsoon regions of China, India, Japan, and Southeast Asia, which hold the world's greatest concentrations of population.

Abundance Creates Problems and Opportunity.

While consumers around the world have cause for being congratulated, farmers are not so confident. After the "great Russian grain purchase" nearly four years ago was followed by OPEC's multiplication of the price of petroleum, prices of grain and most farm commodities escalated. Soybeans, used principally as a protein source for original feed rather than as an item for human consumption, led the way, the price rising to $8.00 and $9.00 per bushel (a bushel of soybeans weighs 60 pounds).[1] An American president had temporarily to embargo soybean exports to stabilize prices. Japan, South Korea, Taiwan, and other major importers were frightened and some complained loudly that they were being denied one of the two most critical components of their diets -- the other is rice -- until they realized the U.S. government actually had done them a good turn by curbing wild speculation, including futures buying by large Japanese trading companies. As the price of grains rose sharply on Chicago's commodity exchange, farmers across the prairie provinces here, like so many of their American neighbors to the south, felt that expansiveness good fortune fosters. Now they could make mortgage payments, buy that new $20,000 tractor, or the $32,000 combine, and perhaps the adjoining 80 acres.

For most farmers there was just one real boom year -- the first one. After that costs quickly mounted at least as rapidly as commodity prices. First to climb were fuel and fertilizer costs, and, of course, the interest rates that banks charge on operating loans. Price tags on new equipment jumped, as did those on irrigation pipes and pumps. Land values soared, reflecting the most basic instinct of the eternal optimist, as a farmer must be. Here in mid-Canada, wheat and other grain fields that had sold for $80 to $120 per acre cost $350 and more per acre two years later. In central Illinois, northern Iowa, in the irrigated bottom land along the Platt River in Nebraska, and in Washington State's Yakima Valley, land sold for $1,700 and $1,800 an acre, not for subdivision or other speculative use, but for farming. The explanation is evident in communities like Colfax in the heart of eastern Washington's high Palouse country, the most productive dry land wheat-growing area of North America. Colfax was first incorporated in 1872 with a population of 3,000 that now has shrunk to 2,700. However, the little city is credited with the highest per capita bank deposits in the United States, including those of reputedly more than 100 millionaires. The investment they trust most is productive crop land.

The steep rise in the price of soybeans was prompted in part by the near disappearance of the Peruvian anchovy catch because of a shift in the Humbolt Current. Most of the anchovy catch goes for the manufacture of fish meal, another high-protein component of animal feed.

For the farmer and the organizations designed to assist him, and in the prairie provinces this means chiefly the Canadian Wheat Board and the United Grain Growers both headquartered in Winnipeg, the critical problem now is how to manage and market such an abundant harvest. The Canadian Wheat Board, with federal government support and working with the provincial grain pools, markets about 90 per cent of Canadian wheat for domestic human consumption and export. Since the autumn of 1973 it has aimed to guarantee producers between $3.25 and $5.00 per bushel for No. 1 Canadian Western Red Spring Wheat (13 per cent protein) delivered at Thunder Bay on the northwest shore of Lake Superior, depending upon world market conditions. World demand was a small factor in prices 40 years ago when grain exports from North America averaged about five million tons annually. Now foreign demand is of major consequence in fixing prices -- from this year's crop North America is expected to export 94 million tons, or more than three-fourths of all grain moving in international trade. Included in the total are wheat, corn, sorghum, barley and other coarse grains, plus rice. For Canada the export market has become especially vital, absorbing usually about one-half of all wheat production as grain and flour. Their most important customer has been the People's Republic of China, followed by the United Kingdom, Japan, Italy, Algeria, India, Bangladesh, and Iraq. Significant shipments also have gone to other nations of Western Europe, the Soviet Union, Lebanon, the Philippines, plus numerous smaller buyers. While the Canadian Wheat Board, partly through medium- and long-term credit arrangements, seeks to stabilize sales prices at the optimum level for producers, the United States, as the world's major grain exporter, tends to fix prices in the international markets.

The role of Washington, D.C., as the "guiding force" in determining world grain prices dates from the end of World War II, when the United States was the chief granary for feeding most of the devastated and destitute regions of the globe. For several decades numerous political careers were made or broken over issues like "parity," support prices for specific farm products, acreages set aside in the "soil bank," and crop allotments. In the process the United States government became the indirect -- through financing -- or direct owner of huge quantities of grain and other "surplus farm products." The avowed political goal was to stabilize prices, for the consumer as well as the producer, and to insure a "living wage" for the American farmer. Rejection by the U.S. Congress, during the Truman administration of the Brannon Plan, which geared price upports to family-size farms, virtually eliminated rural social benefits that might have spared turmoil in the cities during the late 1960s. Existence of large stocks of grain and other commodities at government disposal, and political interest in fostering farm prosperity facilitated the inclusion of "food for peace" aid in foreign assistance programs. Most dramatic was shipment to India of 21 million tons of grain in 1965 and 1966, after the monsoon rains there had failed over large areas.

With the advent of the Nixon administration in 1969, a new philosophy came to dominate agricultural policy that carried over into the Ford administration. Oversimplified, yet essentially reflecting this attitude, was the phrase: "Get the government out of farming and let private business take over." Several trends conspired to make it possible for the Republicans to translate this approach into action. Redistricting, following the census of 1960 and especially 1970, accelerated the shift toward an urban-based U.S. House of Representatives. This augmented the political muscle of the American Farm Bureau Federation, long a champion of "free" agriculture, as contrasted to the protectionist policy of the Grange, the National Farmers' Union, and other populist organizations. However, it was the massive wheat sales to Russia, followed by other large-scale foreign purchases of American grain and soybeans, that escalated prices. North American grain price pressures were compounded by poor rice crops throughout much of South and Southeast Asia, pushing the price of rice FOB Bangkok in 1974 above US$600 per metric ton.

In October 1974, Dark Red Northern Spring Wheat with 14 per cent protein delivered Duluth, Minnesota, peaked at a price of $5.80 per bushel, and Chicago futures for similar grades reached $5.25 per bushel. By late December 1974, Canadian Western Red Spring Wheat with 13.5 per cent protein brought $6.16 per bushel FOB Thunder Bay. These red spring wheats, like the hard red winter wheats grown in Kansas and neighboring states on into southern Alberta, are mainly used for making Bread. By contrast, the soft white wheats predominating in the Pacific Northwest go chiefly for pastries and cakes, including the Oriental steamed breads and noodles that are popular among Chinese and Japanese. Durum wheats high in the gluten-producing proteins are desired by the Italians and others for making macaroni, spaghetti, and similar beloved pastas.

For the farmer and the organizations designed to assist him, and in the prairie provinces this means chiefly the Canadian Wheat Board and the United Grain Growers both headquartered in Winnipeg, the critical problem now is how to manage and market such an abundant harvest. The Canadian Wheat Board, with federal government support and working with the provincial grain pools, markets about 90 per cent of Canadian wheat for domestic human consumption and export. Since the autumn of 1973 it has aimed to guarantee producers between $3.25 and $5.00 per bushel for No. 1 Canadian Western Red Spring Wheat (13 per cent protein) delivered at Thunder Bay on the northwest shore of Lake Superior, depending upon world market conditions. World demand was a small factor in prices 40 years ago when grain exports from North America averaged about five million tons annually. Now foreign demand is of major consequence in fixing prices -- from this year's crop North America is expected to export 94 million tons, or more than three-fourths of all grain moving in international trade. Included in the total are wheat, corn, sorghum, barley and other coarse grains, plus rice. For Canada the export market has become especially vital,

WHO WILL GROW GRAIN FOR A WORLD FOOD BANK?

absorbing usually about one-half of all wheat production as grain and flour. Their most important customer has been the People's Republic of China, followed by the United Kingdom, Japan, Italy, Algeria, India, Bangladesh, and Iraq. Significant shipments also have gone to other nations of Western Europe, the Soviet Union, Lebanon, the Philippines, plus numerous smaller buyers. While the Canadian Wheat Board, partly through medium- and long-term credit arrangements, seeks to stabilize sales prices at the optimum level for producers, the United States, as the world's major grain exporter, tends to fix prices in the international markets.

Such prices still brings demands of farmers below the border for government intervention, as they watched grain elevators across the plains being emptied. Instead, farmers rushed to plow up additional land, including more than 40 million acres of the roughly 60 million acres earlier set aside in the "soil-bank" -- much of the balance already had reverted to scrub, had become game farms, and so on. Attitudes in the U.S. Congress were reflected in what was not done. Since 1934 the Sugar Act had empowered the U.S. Department of Agriculture to determine annual anticipated consumption and set quotas for domestic beet and cane production and foreign imports. This quota system worked so well, providing farmers with an assured though modest return on their crops and consumers with a stable supply, that for over four decades the price of sugar in America increased less than any other major food commodity. In 1974 the Sugar Act with its once prized quotas was allowed to expire on the heady assumption by producers that the world had entered a new era. Many confidently expected chronic sugar shortages would keep prices between 20 to 35 cents per pound, rather than the eight to nine cents per pound customary in the protected American market, and occasionally as low as three cents per pound in the world market.

Now prices for most major farm commodities are tumbling as abundant harvests allow accumulation of stocks. *Grainews,* published by the United Grain Growers headquarters in Winnipeg, Canada, headlined the facts in its August 1976 issue: WHEAT PRICES COLLAPSE! CWB QUOTE SLUMPS 75c SINCE JULY 2. John Clark, the editor, went on to report: The Canadian Wheat Board's Thunder Bay offering price on No. 1 CWRS (Canadian Western Red Spring) 13.5 per cent protein wheat slipped to $3.95-7/8 on August 6, marking the first time top Canadian milling wheat has been quoted below $4.00 a bushel since 1973.

For farmers the prospects are ominous that the price may drop much further. Already cash prices paid for some grades of wheat on the American plains have been reported down between $2.80 and $2.40 per bushel. The United States wheat crop should total some 2,127 million bushels, of which domestic consumption takes only 845 million bushels, and exports are projected at 1,100 million bushels. The prospect is of a carryover stock of wheat in the United States next summer of 849 million bushels -- nearly equal to Canada's total 1976 bumper harvest. By comparison, the carryover from the crop harvested in 1975 was 665 million bushels, and only 339 million bushels the year before. Almost inevitably, sliding farm prices have a ripple effect on most crops -- unless government intervention in the market or a major disaster creates a

WHO WILL GROW GRAIN FOR A WORLD FOOD BANK?

demand elsewhere. With the decline in sugar prices, returns to beet growers have slumped. For most potato growers 1976 was a near-disaster year; some farmers barely recovered the cost of digging their potatoes, not having calculated the expense of growing them. Since their cost of production "plateau" has risen sharply, many farmers are worse off than before the boom of the early 1970s; a comparatively small percentage drop in prices can mean a loss on the crop; and because of the larger investment in growing it, the farmer's financial "exposure" is greater. This year in the United States, soybeans are an important exception, where an 18 per cent drop in the harvest compared with 1975-to 33 million tons has kept prices above $7.00 per bushel.

Responding to pleas from the Farm Belt, in 1976 President Ford raised the level of government guaranteed loans available to farmers for grain in storage. Most important was wheat; the loan price was raised to $2.25 per bushel, making for a target price averaging $2.29 per bushel at major terminals in the United States. In effect, this is the price at which the farmer can "sell his wheat to the government." Loan prices on feed grains also were raised modestly; most important was corn which went to $1.50 per bushel (a bushel of shelled and dried corn weighs 56 pounds). No acreage limitations currently apply to grain. By contrast, prices of peanuts and tobacco are sustained by strict limitations on the acreage farmers can plant. Rice prices in the United States are stabilized by means of a farmer's "history of allotments"; he can grow more rice but without assurance the government will provide an alternative market.

United States agricultural policy and the myriad laws and regulations that determine and implement it are a world apart from ordinary economics. Some crops, like hops, have benefited from agricultural "marketing orders" restricting what could be sold and proving highly lucrative for the growers. Two major considerations, however, merit mention. First, the present "safety net" for farmers in guaranteed loan prices for grain, despite recent increases, is obsolete since at least for most farmers, inflation has pushed costs of production above this level. Second, in 1977 the existing major United States farm legislation expires. Provisions will remain on the federal statute books to stabilize peanut prices and tobacco, which are permanent, and as authorization for supporting dairy prices without guaranteeing the level where this will function. Otherwise, most of the vast array of legislation prompted by the Great Depression and embellished during and after World War II, as the United States moved first to maximize agricultural production and then to cushion the consequences of overproduction when much of the globe recovered, will be void and no longer impede initiatives.

The combination of a renewed world surplus of grain-depressing prices and mounting political pressure for radical new United States agricultural price support legislation creates a historic opportunity. Time and forces at work offer a propitious occasion for organizing a real "world food bank"; a food reserve equal to probable foreseeable needs and yet one that is sufficiently insulated from the commodity markets to avoid depressing prices and thus discouraging farmers from growing crops. As a yardstick for calculating possible calls upon such a food bank, it is useful to keep in mind the 21 million tons of American grain shipped to India in 1965-66. This grain, incidentally, was distributed with surprising efficiency despite often primitive transportation and storage facilities. It prevented a repetition of the Bengal Famine the writer covered in 1943, when some five million persons may have starved to death -- that famine is sensitively illustrated by the Indian film director, Satyajit Ray, in "Distant Thunder." Given both population growth and probable dimensions of a future climatic disaster, an effective "ever normal granary," according to the most educated estimates, now needs to hold somewhere between 50 and 80 million tons of wheat. The latter figure is roughly equivalent to the annual combined harvest of wheat in Canada and the United States in a good year.

As Fred Sanderson of the Brookings Institution has written, "an even larger reserve... would have been required to keep real grain prices reasonably stable during the [1972 to 1975] period." Despite well-intentioned schemes seeking an international solution, as at the 1974 United Nations World Food Conference in Rome, creation of such a meaningful food reserve must be essentially a Canadian-United States enterprise-since only they have the wheat-growing capacity needed to set aside anywhere near this tonnage. The United States could also expand rice growing to accumulate perhaps two million tons annually, especially were additional acreage planted in the Arkansas-Mississippi region. Given present realities, including sensitive domestic politics ffecting agriculture, it is hardly conceivable that leaders in either Ottawa or Washington, D.C., will surrender actual control over such a food reserve to any international organization, even were funding from others available. The practical alternative is national action, it is hoped with improved collaboration across the border. For if the past is taken as teacher, it is only a question of how soon reserves in such a "food bank" will be urgently needed.

Farming on the Alberta Frontier

Just how critical weather is for the world's food is shown by Canada's and especially Alberta's crop performance. A hint of what can happen was reported in the Canadian Wheat Board's annual report for 1974-75:

... the drop in world grain production, amounting to a decrease of over 40 million tons below that of 1973, evoked fears of serious food shortages and widespread famine in many of the developing countries. These fears have been expressed before, but North American grain reserves, built up in the postwar years, had always been sufficient to meet previous production shortfalls. These stocks had declined dramatically in the preceding four years because of accelerating world consumption and were virtually depleted by the time the 1974 harvest got underway. The situation served to magnify the delicate balance between world grain supplies and requirements. For the first time in several decades, world food requirements would have to be met entirely from current production and it appeared that a grain crop greater by at least 3.5 per cent than the record 1973 harvest was needed simply to keep up with consumption trends. *(2). See Grant Cottam, The World Food Conference [GC-1-'74], Fieldstaff Reports, West Europe Series, Vol. IX, No. 5, 1974.*

WHO WILL GROW GRAIN FOR A WORLD FOOD BANK?

Explaining the drop in Canada's wheat crop from 16.2 million tons in 1973 to 13.3 million tons in 1974 -- or slightly more than one-half of the fabulous 1976 harvest of 24.2 million tons -- the Wheat Board reported:

The 1974 Prairie grain crop suffered from adverse weather conditions in virtually every stage of development from seeding to harvest. A late, wet spring delayed the start of seeding operations until the middle of May and reduced seeded acreage. Hot, dry June weather advanced crops considerably but depleted soil moisture reserves so that by early July the southern Prairies were in need of rain. Mid-July rainfall eased moisture conditions in some regions, but other areas remained fairly dry. Rain in August delayed crop ripening and the start of harvesting operations. Severe frost hit large areas of the Prairies early in September before the crop had fully matured, markedly down-grading quality. Finally, cool wet weather in early autumn delayed the completion of harvest in many areas until late in October.

The poor quality of grain harvested was as critical as the small crop. Only 38 per cent of spring wheat deliveries from the 1974 harvest qualified for the two top grades of No. 1 and No. 2 C.W.R.S. This compared with 82 per cent of these two top grades harvested the previous year. In effect it meant that under normal supply and price conditions a substantial portion of the 1974 wheat crop was good for animal feed only. For people who have lost touch with man's dependence upon nature and the weather for his food, the rolling prairies of Alberta are congenial for its recapture. Extending from the Montana border some 750 airline miles north to the 60th parallel, the province covers 248,000 square miles, or roughly five times the area of New York State, and holds less than two million inhabitants. Agriculturally, it is divided into five regions. Region one in the southeast around Medicine Hat is relatively dry and, like the adjacent region two, extending from Lethbridge in the south past Calgary, swept by very strong winds, including the "Chinooks" that, in winter, may descend from the Pacific over the Rocky Mountains and melt all snow in a couple of days. As a consequence, irrigation is vital in the south of regions one and two centers and benefits more than a million acres. Region three centers on Red Deer and Edmonton; and this Viking area is really a plateau, much of it more than 2,000 feet above sea level. Normally, rainfall is sufficient for grain crops, although frosts are a problem at the higher elevations in the foothills of the mountains to the west and in the north near Athabasca. Region four, at a much lower elevation, extends along the Peace River from the border of British Columbia. 250 airline miles northeast, to Fort Vermillion at 58.5' N. latitude. Still a homestead region for the hardy, it is the northernmost major farming area of Canada and intriguing because of abundant crops grown with longer daylight in summer, despite the short frost-free season. The remaining 60 per cent of the province comprising region five is not regarded as fit for farming, chiefly because of the soils. However, recent thinking, prompted partly by observing the bison in Wood Buffalo National Park, suggests it may offer possibilities for raising cattle on appropriate grasses.

WHO WILL GROW GRAIN FOR A WORLD FOOD BANK?

As Frank Slavik suggests, bringing this vast prairie under plow is a continuing pioneering enterprise. The late arctic explorer, Vilhjalmur Stefansson, described traveling through this region in 1908. Southern Alberta, like regions of Saskatchewan and Manitoba adjacent to the United States, was opened to settlers by completion of the Canadian Pacific Railway that, in 1885, had passed through Calgary, crossed Kicking Horse Pass in the Rocky Mountains, tunneling and bridging its tortuous way across British Columbia to Vancouver. Parenthetically, this construction also resulted in the only recorded capture of a live Sasquatch, or "Big Foot", in 1884 at Yale in the Fraser River Canyon. When Stefansson reached Edmonton en route to the Arctic via the Athabasca River, Alberta had only been a self-governing province for three years. The Canadian Northern Railway was just opening these huge tracts of fertile farm land. An era of grasslands range supporting unfenced cattle and sheep herding was being supplanted by that of the cultivator.

Although steady retreat of the Columbia Ice Field Glaciers in the Canadian Rockies during this century seems to substantiate their thesis of a warming climate, scholars who thus explain the northward shift of the wheat belt give inadequate attention to transportation. Just as on the Great Plains of the United States, so here the coming of the railways was fundamental. Before the tracks were laid the only crop a farmer readily could market was cattle on the hoof. Trains brought lumber to erect at every station the grain elevators which remain the dominant manmade feature of the landscape. Introduction of the steam tractor allowed each farmer to cultivate more "quarters" (e.g., 160 acres). Yet, the alternately muddy and dusty country roads were a hurdle to hauling grain to the elevators, until the development of oil and gas over the last three decades prompted the extension of hard-surfaced roads into many of these communities.[3]

As they plowed and planted the virgin soil, the crops farmers grew were large enough to send stories rippling across continents. In 1876, at the Philadelphia Exposition commemorating the first century of United States independence, the world championship for wheat and barley was won by the French Mission at Fort Chipewyan in Alberta's far north. In 1893, on the banks of the Peace River, another pioneer farmer, an Anglican 3. The Athabasca tar sands to the north, providing they can be extracted and moved economically, should provide virtually unlimited possibilities for paving roads in the provinces.

A missionary, The Reverend J. Gough Brick, grew the wheat that won the championship at the World's Fair in Chicago. With the opportunity to homestead 160 acres for a filing fee of ten dollars and residence "proving it up," settlers flocked in from Scandinavia, Germany, Austria, Great Britain, the Ukraine, and also from the United States, where free land was becoming scarce. One year after Alberta became a province, the Dominion government in Ottawa sent a "seed special." This two-coached train carried displays, and farmers boarded at each stop to hear lectures on better growing, cleaning, storage, and marketing of the crops, plus weed and pest control. Mormons moving into Southern Alberta late in the nineteenth century brought the soft winter wheat that came originally from Odessa. Then, in 1902, the Turkey hard red winter wheat from Kansas was introduced and proved singularly well-adapted to Alberta in the warmer regions one and two to the south that also grew durum wheat. Here in region three, and in region four along the Peace River to the northwest where the winters are harsher, the hard red spring wheats have remained dominant, especially as improved varieties have developed.

Those first seasons were bonanza years for many of the farmers. Outbreak of World War I in August 1914 escalated prices for grain, pushing wheat to 91 cents per bushel that a year earlier had sold for 61 cents per bushel. Only 177,100 acres of wheat had been seeded in 1906. By 1915, over 2.1 million acres were planted to wheat. They yielded a banner harvest, averaging 31 bushels per acre-the highest yield Alberta farmers had achieved before 1976, when the crop averaged 34 bushels per acre. In contrast to 60 years ago, today's yields are accomplished with substantial applications of fertilizer and much improved pest and weed control. The new soils of Alberta did almost as well in 1916 when the price of wheat had jumped to $1.33 per bushel; they averaged 25 bushels per acre on 2.6 million acres. Then weather and luck began turning against Alberta's farmers. In 1918, drought cut their harvests to six bushels per acre. The next year they harvested an average of only eight bushels per acre. And it was scant comfort that Alberta's farmers had planted nearly 4.3 million acres and the price had reached an almost unheard of $2.31 per bushel. The years between the two world wars were rough, especially on prairie farmers. An historical review of Alberta agriculture records:

Throughout the 1920s drought, soil drifting and grasshoppers combined to play havoc with farming on the southern semiarid lands, while varied success attended crop production in central and northern regions.... In spite of control efforts, it was estimated that in 1922, crops to the value of $1,158,813 were destroyed by grasshoppers.... The ten years between 1930 and 1940 were described by Field Crops Commissioner O.S. Longman as "the most destructive and costly grasshopper plague in the history of Alberta."

Drought often hit the same farmers who were fighting insects. Alberta's wheat harvest in 1931 averaged 17.7 bushels per acre, which is about the median yield for the 1920s and 1930s. But the price that year had dropped to 36 cents per bushel. For the decade ending in 1940 the average price received for wheat was only 59 cents a bushel. Small wonder that many farmers, and the businessmen who supplied them, reached the end of their means and strength. Some loaded their families and furniture in rattling cars or battered trucks and drove away from their land, machinery, homes, and debts.

Prospects

Three and one-half decades later Alberta's farmers, or at least those who stuck it out through the lean years, have prospered visibly. Farm buildings generally are well-kept and painted, except for those abandoned where smaller farms have been combined to make larger working units. There are now electricity and modern conveniences, along with mechanized agriculture. More than their neighbors to the east, Alberta farmers have broadened their economic base by diversification. Wheat is grown on 4.5 million acres, and barley, which does better in a shorter growing season, has moved up to be planted on 5.4 million acres. Rapeseed is increasingly important as a new crop, now planted on 1.5 million acres. With $1.4 billion worth of livestock and poultry on some 62,000 farms, the farmers have a ready market for feed grains and grass. Even before the bumper harvest of 1976, the province's annual gross farm income had exceeded $2 billion.

Yet, all this bounty results from the action of forces over which the farmers have but limited control. Prices have been steady-to-strong, due substantially to cushioning of fluctuation through the provincial grain pools and ultimately the government-funded Canadian Wheat Board. Although the Board's actions are decisive in transporting and marketing Canada's wheat abroad, its options are necessarily circumscribed by what happens to agriculture in the United States. And prosperity for farmers here throughout the past quarter-century would have been impossible without an approximate well-being on the land in the "States." Most consequential of all has been the weather. While there have been poor years-1954, 1961, 1974-there have been no disastrous years like 1918 when drought left little to harvest. It is this that farmers here emphasize as they look ahead; even if the weather does not turn colder, chronic instability in weather patterns such as those that already afflict important areas of our globe, can prove disastrous for harvests on these prairies.

Universities Field Staff International   1985/No. 36 Asia [AR-1='85]

FAITH GARDENING AND SALT FARMING

By Albert Ravenholt

The nitrogen-fixing leguminous tree Leucaena leucocephala, known in the Philippines as ipil-ipil, when incorporated into sound gardening practices and appropriate sloping land technology, can help reverse and then prevent the soil erosion and degradation in uplands throughout South and Southeast Asia. It contributes at the same time to higher yields from staple crops, improved living standards, and better nutrition for small-scale farmers.

"WE CONSIDER OURSELVES in a state of emergency; our topsoil is all going," the Reverend Harold R. Watson told me last June. He gestured toward the hillside where he and his fellow workers in the Mindanao Baptist Rural Life Center have inaugurated one of the most promising agroforestry movements of the Asian tropics. At Kinuskusan, west of Bansalan, Davao del Sur, on the large southern island of Mindanao, in a land contested by armed Moros (Muslims) and Christians, New People's Army guerrillas and Philippine Army battalion combat teams, these agricultural missionaries and scientists are demonstrating that nitrogen-fixing tropical trees, chiefly Leucaena, can husband and restore fertility to denuded soils left behind by slash-and-burn farmers. In the process, the impoverished rural family of the tropical uplands is enabled to produce enough to feed itself and begin to build a decent life.

Implications for saving what remains of tropical rain forests around the globe are immense. Ordinary small farmers using Watson's system of *FAITH (Food Always in the Home)* gardening and *SALT (Sloping Agricultural Land Technology)* farming, will no longer need to destroy the virgin forest to find fields that will sustain them. Although others in Asia, as in the Philippines, are also using Leucaena for such reclamation and improved small-farmer productivity, Watson and his co-workers have systematized these methods and are effectively spreading their use. It was in recognition of the more than 6,000 trainees and visitors who come annually to their Rural Life Center from Southeast Asia and the Philippines that Watson on August 31, 1985, received the Ramon Magsaysay Award "for encouraging international utilization of his Sloping Agricultural Land Technology to help the poorest farmers."

The scale and speed of forest destruction throughout Southeast and South Asia is accelerating at a pace difficult to visualize. This writer has flown the length of the Philippines at night near the end of the monsoon dry season and seen fires for the entire 1,200 miles. A flight over the Indonesian archipelago is almost as discouraging: the wild grasses that follow slash-and-burn are creeping steadily up the mountains. Tragically, much of both East and West Malaysia is affected. In the Kingdom of Thailand virtually no large virgin forest remains. Forty-two years ago, in first flying over and then walking through much of Burma, I was awed by the immense virgin forest that now is pock-marked by clearings left by slash-and-burn farmers, despite the fact that population pressure is modest. India, Bangladesh, and Pakistan today offer almost a moonscape as goats, sheep, and cattle are fed with foliage pulled from the limbs of trees, and in Bangladesh even mango trees may be chopped down for fuel wood. Changes in climate and shortage of water in streams and rivers during the extending dry season are predictable complaints of farmers throughout the region. The silting of rivers and ports, like Calcutta on the Hooghly, is only one of the sad consequences of the erosion of topsoil from the slopes of hills and mountains. Timber extraction, usually by land logging, is regularly cited as the first villain, and the great expansion of timber exports from Southeast Asia, especially to Japan, South Korea, and Taiwan, since the close of World War II has indeed contributed. Often easy fortunes were made by irresponsible companies and individuals who acquired timber stands near the seashore and evaded regulations for forest conservation and replanting. However, as G.E.C. Mears, the late English pioneer forester and founder of Nasipit Lumber Company in northern Mindanao, demonstrated and explained, cutting and extracting the large merchantable trees by road or rail does not need to destroy the tropical forest ecosystem. Provided residual smaller trees and ground cover are protected, especially when nitrogen-fixing trees are replanted, it is surprising to visit a cutover site four or six years later and see the speed with which the forest is reestablishing itself.

The greatest villain, in fact, is fire. Just as the white pine slash left by loggers a century ago in upper Michigan, Wisconsin, and Minnesota fed the flames of forest fires that destroyed natural regeneration, so fire has been destructive in the Asian tropics. But here the problem is compounded by insistent population pressure. There is an ancient Chinese saying that "you plow by fire." And this is precisely what millions of poor, landless rural families are doing across South and Southeast Asia. By under brushing in the rain forest near the start of the dry season and burning before the rains, it is possible to plant without plowing, so neither draft animals nor tractors are needed. Fertility provided by the ash left from burned trees provides a tempting bounty of crops of corn, upland rice, beans, bananas, squash, and other crops for a few years – until erosion and leaching have impoverished the soil. Slash-and-burn was the traditional pattern for centuries among some upland tribal peoples of Southeast Asia – the dramatic exception are the aboriginal builders of the great rice terraces of Northern Luzon who jealously protected their sources of water with forests on the mountaintops. Their conservation practices have been studied by distinguished foreign scholars and some Filipinos, but unfortunately the vast majority of Christianized Filipinos have ignored these basics. As the population of this archipelago of 7,100 islands has multiplied eight times so far in this century, the hunger for land to till has become ever more compelling. It is possible that more than one-third of the roughly 30 million hectares that comprise the land area of the Philippines, or 10 to 12 million hectares, today is largely useless (Imperata cylindrica, the "quack grass" of the moist Asian tropics) land. Cogon is usually burned early in the dry season to provide a low-yielding pasture for cattle that gain little weight. The only valuable quality of this grass that I know are the young roots, which can be boiled to make a pleasant tea.

Sometimes it is more than subsistence farming that impels small farmers to denude upland slopes. Thailand is now exporting annually about seven million tons of dried pellets made from the tubers of cassava (manioc), which traditionally was a famine food reserved in the ground throughout much of tropical Asia. Approximately five million tons a year of these cassava pellets have been going to the European Common Market as livestock feed. The cassava plant requires a well-drained site and will grow - although not ideally - in the extensive areas of soil experiencing laterization as leaching builds up concentrations of aluminum and iron hydroxides. In volume cassava pellets is Thailand's largest export and in some years earns from $400 to $600 million in foreign exchange. Although the per-hectare income is less to a farmer than he earns on crops of rice and corn, cassava brings him additional cash from the mills that chip, sun-dry, and pelletize the tubers for export. With such economic motivation small farmers are clearing ever-larger areas of Thailand's once-forested regions. Cassava is a "heavy feeder and rather than buy fertilizer farmers move to new sites, so the fields left behind have been depleted both by removal of nutrients by a high-tonnage crop and by leaching combined with erosion; what remains is essentially a wasteland.

The reverse side of this agricultural coin is equally vital; productive use of existing arable lowlands and valleys can adequately provide far more than present and foreseeable food needs well into the next century, plus ample land for export crops. The Philippines now devotes about 6.5 million hectares to growing rice and corn, often with miserable upland yields, for domestic consumption, yet they continue periodic imports which are officially preferred rather than paying the farmer a practical price for grain. Those of us who have planted the newer varieties of rice, chiefly developed by the International Rice Research Institute in Los Banos some 40 miles southeast of Manila, find that with adequate management and irrigation it is realistic to expect an average harvest of 5,000 kilograms of paddy rice dried to 14 percent moisture per hectare per crop. Provided enough irrigation water is available, it is practical to grow three such rice crops annually on the same field. On more fertile soils, such as the recent volcanics of Java and Bali, yields can readily be higher. Thus with competent drying and milling of paddy rice, one hectare can grow the desired optimum intake of 150 kilograms of milled rice per person per year for 60 people. Were farmers provided reliable irrigation and drainage plus access to required inputs, the Philippines could produce all of its human grain needs - except imported wheat - on about one million hectares, about one-sixth the land area now devoted to rice and corn. Employment in rural areas would be greater than now, when so many families are idle during six months for lack of rain, and livelihood could be greatly improved. There would remain about seven million hectares of "alienable and disposable" land that could be devoted to export crops of sugar, coconuts, bananas, pineapple and other fruits like mango, and to fish culture. Such crops plus upland corn and rice now also cover an additional 3.5 million hectares of untitled uplands. For the now nearly 56 million Filipinos this would leave about one-half of their land and some 15 million hectares that could be devoted to systematic pasture and permanent forest for many years to come.

What Pierre Gourou in his classic work The Tropical World terms "man's disastrous intervention" progresses similarly throughout most of South and Southeast Asia. With destruction of the rain forest and failure to replace it with tree crops or other sustainable agriculture, the process formerly known as laterization accelerates. The balance of the ecosystem of the rain forest maintained by the cycle of humus enriched by nitrogen-fixing trees is lost and a usually alumina- and iron-rich pebbly formation is left behind.

Thailand is the envy of many other lands because it is the largest food-exporting nation in Asia, shipping out in some years over four million tons of rice and three million tons of corn. Yet per hectare yields on the average are low. With a population approaching 50 million, Thailand devotes over six million hectares to lowland rice production, an area greater than the total cultivated acreage of Japan, which has over 120 million inhabitants and a less friendly climate. With appropriate irrigation and especially drainage in the fertile central plain, Thai agriculture can produce more than it now does on one-half of the present supposedly arable area and leave much of the kingdom for forest. It is often forgotten that Taiwan, R.O.C., which is 86 percent self-sufficient in food production and has the highest caloric intake in Asia, now supports 23 persons per arable hectare. This is more than twice the land/population ratio of Java, Bangladesh, and other struggling tropical lands with generally better soils and the potential of a year-round growing season. Sound agricultural policies could eliminate the need for new land that drives farmers into the steeper hills to seek a precarious living.

These physical constraints within which tropical Asian agriculture is evolving have been compounded, especially since World War II when "miracle" drugs were introduced, by declining mortality that is spurring a tropical population boom. Without wisely and effectively managed land reform across South and Southeast Asia, population pressure adds a powerful impetus to the hunt by the landless for fields to till in the uplands. The postwar economic transformation of Japan, Taiwan, and South Korea, that with United States assistance implemented land reform, resulted in some of the soundest, most equitable, and most productive rural societies anywhere. Malaysia's Federal Land Development Authority schemes also are proving that estate agriculture emphasizing natural rubber and oil palm can be so organized that smallholder family operations can become efficient and prosperous participants.

Designers of land reform frequently fail to recognize that "this is only one leg the farmer walks on." Land reform must be matched, as it is in Northeast Asia, with creation of sound cooperatives enabling farmers to manage irrigation, credit, processing, and marketing. Perhaps most critical of all is the provision that extension workers must not be government employees; rather, they must be paid by the farmers' cooperatives and responsible to them. In Taiwan, South Korea, and Japan, farm cooperatives have recently shown remarkable vigor in pursuing their own research on production and marketing; they are complementing and occasionally outdoing the research of universities and government institutes.

<u>Mindanao Baptist Rural Life Center</u>

Harold R. Watson and his associates at their center have the distinction of having recognized and accepted the necessity of helping the poorest farmers where they are - i.e., on the steeper uplands where almost two-thirds of rural Filipinos seek a livelihood. Second, they have recognized that the first need of this largely subsistence farmer is adequate nutrition for his family. Accumulating evidence over the past eight years compels the conclusion that by far the greatest health problem of South and Southeast Asia - excluding Singapore, portions of Malaysia, and some urban centers - is malnutrition. Unlike the great East Asian civilizations where intensive gardening is traditional, the peoples of Southeast and South Asia rarely pursued this art. Throughout these archipelagos and along the waterways of the mainland they followed instead the traditions of gathering; tropical rain forest boundaries, especially, are rich in edible leaves and pods, but this source of fresh vegetables disappears as the rain forests are destroyed. Destruction of the forest foods has coincided with loss of fisheries, both fresh-water and inshore, through poisoning and use of dynamite and other explosives. And professional fruit growing is only in its infancy as a farm specialty in Southeast Asia.

The FAITH Garden became one of the center's first efforts when it started some 14 years ago on recently acquired, abandoned wasteland. On a 100 square meter plot that was the garden that Watson, a professional agriculturist and missionary from Hattiesburg, Mississippi, first planted, he evolved a pattern of staggered vegetable production. The garden was carefully located near water and divided into three sections, with one-half of each section held in reserve for later replanting. One section was planted in vegetables that would be ready for cooking in two to four months - soybeans, mustard, pechay, carrots, cowpeas, bush sitao (long string beans), sweet corn, and tomatoes. A second plot was given over to vegetables providing food within six to nine months, including okra, cucumber, onions and garlic, eggplant, winged beans, gourds, and ginger. Vegetables that are ready for cooking in 11 to 12 months were planted on the third plot - Ceylon spinach, butter beans, pigeon peas, taro, cassava, leafy sweet potato and water convolvulus. Garden management was scheduled so that the reserved areas could be planted at the time needed to insure a continuous harvest.

The central feature was a series of raised garden beds into which were set bamboo baskets about one foot in diameter and depth. These were filled with a little animal manure and some decomposable garbage, and packed with Leucaena leaves. If no manure was available, Leucaena leaves alone were stuffed into the basket to provide nitrogen and other nutrients. After several weeks vegetables are then planted within three inches around the baskets so their roots can draw nutrients from the baskets. The compost could be removed from the basket once a year and spread around as a fertilizer. The basket was then refilled with a new mixture of Leucaena leaves and other nutrient-rich materials. The basket hole was a natural means of trapping water and was also well suited for simple irrigation with water carried in a pail. This garden system has been

Ray Watson shows how a FAITH (Food Always In The Home) garden is prepared.

proving its productive worth in an ever-growing number of barrios as farmers have observed that it works. Watson and his chief associate Warlito A. Laquihon have also written a manual explaining the techniques and emphasizing that everyone should - and with this garden can - eat a bowl of fresh vegetables daily.

Watson, speaking in his easy Southern drawl, described how and why he chose FAITH: "The toughest problem on the small farmer's place is to get protein there for improving his family diet. We tried chickens and we tried hogs. And

with both of them it was the same problem for the small farmer: how does he get his feed to maintain steady egg production and how does he compete with big farmers in shipping broilers and hogs to the far-away market in Manila? Jersey cows gave us similar problems. We had one fantastic cow that gave 19 liters of milk a day. What's a small farmer going to do with that much milk, even if he can find the feed and concentrates to make her produce at that level? We tried to cross the Indian Murrah buffalo with the native carabao, thinking we would have both milk and a draft animal. But we found you need an elephant fence to hold them in and the Indian animals are not good for plowing. Maybe the mestizos will work better. Anyway, it's a big animal and involves more investment than the small farmer can mobilize, quite apart from the fact that the Indian buffalo and the carabao certainly do not like each other to begin with and you can hear the buffalo two kilometers away complaining, bvawrahraw, wawrahraw!' "

"We have solved the needs for eggs on the farm now, I think, with ducks," Watson continued. "This is really more to the credit of my colleague Warlito Laquihon, who had been president of a small college before he joined us and had a lot of experience with ducks. Originally, we started with Muscovy ducks; they are tough, they can forage and they brood and are good for hatching eggs and much of their diet is grass. Then we looked around for egg producers and decided on the Khaki Campbells. I talked with Dick Fagan of the Philippine Rural Life Center in Cavite, Luzon, who was also the Heifer Project representative, and I believe we got 25 purebreds that he brought from the States. We started hatching our own and any which didn't look good we cropped out. For feed we used *darak* (rice bran), greens that grew in the canal, and snails. Now we have introduced the "golden snail" which originated in Brazil and feeds in the canals. The ducks like it and so do people. Rabbits are another good food source for the small farm family. Folks in the barrios may not get a litter as big as ours; instead of eight they may get four. But rabbits cost them hardly anything - mostly grass with some other greens for feed and a little rice bran or corn. They're not commercial, but they're food. And we sell every rabbit we can produce; we believe people should pay a modest price for what they receive."

"Goats have proven to be the most practical addition to the small farm here," Watson reported. "Dr. Fagan had brought in a number of milk goats through the Heifer Project. After studying them for a while and seeing how they adapted, I said, 'Dick, the Nubian is it.' And he sure helped. I was out at Fagan's center and I asked him what I would have to do to get some. He said we could get some but we would have to turn back some. Not turn back to him but to farmers, he explained. 'So you get one and you turn back two. That's Heifer Project's long-term policy.' We already had a small herd of crossbreds that we had found in South Cotabato.

"Our first problem was disease, especially tapeworm which earlier had wiped out the government's entire goat program. We found the right medicines, solved that problem, and began to teach farmers how to disbud the horns, how to milk, and how to feed the animals, which were kept on raised platforms of wooden slats if they were purebred. Our basic feed even then was ipil ipil (Leucaena) and grass with rice bran and copra (coconut) meal, plus salt and minerals. Many of our first animals died. Gradually we selected our own strains and two years ago we began breeding for both a meat type and a milk type. A farmer can keep them in a small nipa palm roofed house; he needs about 20 square feet per animal, so five or six make a practical family flock.

"We have now begun working with hair sheep, the black-bellied Barbados sheep that can stand the heat. They are meat animals and good for pasturing in rubber and other plantations because they don't damage the smaller plants like goats do. Of course they do better provided they also have some ipil ipil and other higher-protein roughage. These also we got from the Heifer Project, thanks to Dick Fagan. Especially since the sheep don't eat the bark and leaves of trees and are very good lawnmowers, I think they fit the farmers' needs and have a future here."

Sloping Agricultural Land Technology (SALT)

Watson has the directness and modesty so characteristic among rural folk. "We do not have all the answers," he stressed. "It is just a beginning ... but we do have a technology that does fit into the pattern and life of rural people within their own, the farmers' resources, financial as well as educational. What we present is a beginning, I hope throughout Asia but especially for the Philippines, to turn our eyes on one of the nation's and the world's worst problems, soil erosion and deforestation. Land degradation is an enemy to any nation - far worse than any outside enemy coming into a country and conquering it because it is an enemy you cannot see vividly. It is a slow, creeping enemy that soon possesses the land."

The mid-1970s, Watson recalled, were a low point in his life. He came from a university that "teaches high-tech," he said, but after 10 years of agricultural missionary work in Mindanao he realized "that I really did not have a lot to offer to small farmers. They would come to us and we gave them advice, a lot of quotations from universities, experiment stations.... At first I thought the small farmers, poor farmers were just a minority. Then I began to look at statistics and came to realize that they make up more than 60 percent of the farmers in the Philippines, all hill farmers, poor people. I began to see that we needed to turn our attention to them and ... to the soil on which they live and make a living. Land is not being remade.... Soil is made by God and put here for man to use, not for one generation but forever.... It takes thousands of years to build one inch of topsoil but only one good strong rain to remove one inch from unprotected soil on the slopes of mountains."

The first premise for the SALT technology, Watson continued, was simplicity. "It had to be simple enough so that we could sit down with the farmer who had no education at all and outline it to him. It also had to be a technology that could be applied to his situation, the hillsides. [And] it must be low cost, [requiring few] resources - that is pesos to put in - so that he can start with something. It must be timely and timeless."

During the latter half of the 1970s the Mindanao Baptist Rural Life Center had tried to help hillside farmers by building terraces, but the results were discouraging. Terraces frequently washed out, and the soil was exhausted. Fortunately Watson, when on home leave, had stopped in Hawaii and received from Dr. James L. Brewbaker a very small package of seeds of Leucaena leucocephala, collected by Brewbaker and his colleagues in Central America.

Watson planted the Leucaena seeds at several locations on the Center's 19 hectares. As Watson and his associates struggled to hold up their terraces, it became evident that this could best be done with living trees and that the Leucaena as a nitrogen-fixing legume was a natural on all except the most acid soil sites.

"We kept on experimenting," Watson recalled. "At first we planted one row of ipil ipil. [But] if several trees did not grow so well, you had a hole in the dike for soil to wash through. We finally settled on planting two dense rows with seeds of ipil ipil that had been soaked in water. The seeds are just dribbled in, maybe an inch apart, in two rows just half a meter apart. Two dense rows make a reliable hedge and the soil that is washing off the slope can build up against the hedge to make the terrace."

The system has now been simplified, according to Watson, to ten basic steps:

1. Prepare an A-frame instrument, preferably using a carpenter's level, and locate the contour lines across the hillside;

2. Mark the contour lines on your parcel of hilly land; the sharper the slope the closer the contour lines, although usually the best spacing is four meters between the hedges;

3. Prepare the land by plowing the contour lines; the width of each plowed strip should be one meter;

4. Plant thick double rows of ipil ipil on the cultivated contour lines;

5. Plant permanent crops in every fourth strip, with the taller ones at the base of the hill. These can be fruit trees, bananas, or coffee;

6. Cultivate alternate strips only, to prevent soil erosion while the ipil ipil are young;

7. When permanent crops are growing well, plant your non-permanent leguminous crops on the strips in between. Replant any dead permanent crop plant.

8. Trim the ipil ipil once a month and pile the leaves and twigs at the base of your crops;

9. Rotate your non-permanent leguminous crops like beans with non-leguminous crops;

10. Build and reinforce your terraces by gathering and piling stalks, branches, and rubble at the base of the ipil ipil hedges so any soil that washes down will be captured there.

Watson has four additional pointers on the practice of SALT:

1. Weed and clean the ipil ipil rows forming the hedges, as well as all the other crops;
2. Spray for insects and disease in all newly planted crops;

Pineapples are normally an erosion-prone crop. Here hedges of nitrogen-fixing Leucaena hold the soil, and tops cut back monthly provide fertilizer.

3. Leave alternate crop strips uncultivated until the ipil ipil is growing vigorously as this will help hold the soil;
4. And once the ipil ipil has matured, cultivate all of the strips.

The ipil ipil and other nitrogen-fixing trees are the key plants in the SALT system of upland farming, Watson asserts: they can fix nitrogen from the air, they grow rapidly, are deep rooted, and therefore can hold down the soil; they can withstand regular pruning, produce plenty of leaves for fertilizer and animal feed, and have plenty of other uses such as fuel wood, charcoal manufacturing, and mushroom growing.

At Bansalan and at three training centers elsewhere in Mindanao, Watson and his associates have demonstrated that SALT farming of upland assures a rural family of a regular source of cash income, as well as food, and serves as insurance against otherwise onerous credit terms, high food costs, and difficult times. One hectare of upland farmed with the SALT system and multi-cropped generated a monthly income of 1,125 pesos (equivalent today to U.S.$62) and is enough to provide the basic needs of a family of seven.

Ecologically, SALT has proven to be the answer to the deterioration and decline in productivity of upland resources. SALT methods not only restore soil fertility and enable the small farmer to grow food crops economically with reduced need for expensive inputs like chemical fertilizers: they are also culturally acceptable and applicable to most regions of the Philippines. On one hillside plot where Watson has planted corn for eight successive crops at a rate of 2.85 crops per year, the average harvest with only Leucaena cuttings as fertilizer is above 2,500 kilos of dried shelled corn per hectare per crop, which is three to five times the yield of most upland farms in the archipelago. Once the SALT is established, minimum or no tillage is recommended. Yields increase even more if farmers rotate leguminous crops like mung beans. And once tree crops of fruits, coffee, etc., have grown to suitable size, these together with the Leucaena hedges produce a sustainable agroforestry that also makes for an improved ecology, particularly since permanent trees are maintained on the crests of mountains or hilltops.

FAITH GARDENING AND SALT FARMING

For sites not suited to Leucaena, Watson and his group are testing other nitrogen-fixing trees - Glificidia Sepium, Albizzia falcataria, *Calliandra* callothyrsus, the Sesbanias and others. Watson concluded our discussions on a confident note: "If something goes wrong with ipil ipil, we have other trees we can turn to for holding up the terraces. Meanwhile we are experimenting."

[December 1985]

JOHN M. MUSSER
3080 FIRST NATIONAL BANK BUILDING
ST. PAUL, MINNESOTA 55101
(612) 222-3780

October 16, 1984

Mr. Albert Ravenholt
c/o Peter Martin, Institute of Current World Affairs
4 West Wheelock Street, Hanover, New Hampshire 03755

Dear Albert:

If I had to name the one place in the world where I would rather be next Saturday, it would certainly be with you,--but unfortunately, one does not always get his own way.

Having known you since the early "Dear Mr. Rogers" days and having met your mother in Luck, Wisconsin, I feel that I can speak with some authority. You are a man of many parts. If I were to name only three characteristics which stand out in my mind, I would say:

1. I love your curiosity, tenacity, and thoroughness in finding out about a lot to provide seed, fertilizer, firewood for peoples in the developing world.

2. I like your strong sense of integrity.
    When I would soar off into the great blue yonder and deal with generalities, your ready response would be, "Well, I don't know about that, but in the
    Punjab, I found thus and so ......"

3. You have many friends because you are a friend, and I feel this very deeply.

So, were I in Salisbury, I would want to clasp you on the back and say "Carry on".

Sincerely,

John

Albert is pictured with a bolt of the Leucaena Leucocephala tree in the Philippines, measuring 10 inches diameter in its 4th year of growth.

THE SEATTLE TIMES, Sunday, February 24, 1957

Seattlelites Help Link U.S., Orient

Ravenholts have worked for better understanding,
friendship in Far Fast since early °40's

By IRVING PETITE

ALBERT RAVENHOLT, Seattle based former foreign-news correspondent, inaugurated the movement which became ""Seeds for Democracy." He first presented the idea in an article for The Chicago Daily News in 1950. Since then Americans have formed friendships throughout Asia by the simple message of gifts of seeds.

Marjorie Severyns Ravenholt, the newsman's wife, is consultant to Asian leaders, among them President Magsaysay of the Philippines. Her advice was asked in the preparation of a law which last year assured the first elections ever held at the community level in the Philippines.

The Ravenholts, married 11 years, make extensive tours of study to the countries of Free Asia. On such tours, which sometimes extend as long as 22 months, Mrs. Ravenholt has administered several successful social-economic projects on behalf of our own or Asian governments.

Ravenholt has studied and reported on the Far East since the beginning of the Second World War., during which he served as a correspondent in China, Burma, India, Indo-China and the Philippines.

MRS. RAVENHOLT, seated, background, met with a group of information officers from Philippine-government agencies. She trained these men and women to evaluate the various governmental programs in seven provinces.

In 1947 he transferred to the Institute of Current World Affairs and helped to organize the American Universities Field Staff, of which he is an associate.

Approximately a dozen men comprise the American Universities Field Staff, each with his field of special authority. They gather information and write reports in their areas, then return to lecture and give seminars at the schools belonging to the organization. These are Tulane, Indiana, Kansas, Hawaii and Harvard Universities; California Institute of Technology and Carlton College, in Minnesota.

"Our purpose is to build up a source of significant contemporary information for the American institutions of higher education," Ravenholt says.

Ravenholt recently returned tc Seattle from a tour of four universities, then made a midwinter trip to Chicago. He and his wife now are at "Cal

Tech." He will conclude his lectures, then make another fact finding tour abroad.

Mrs. Ravenholt, a political-science graduate of the University of Washington, has held a variety of jobs in Asia while her husband has collected data. She has worked for the Asia Foundation, for the Philippine government and for the International Co-operation Administration - the latter in China before 1949 and on Formosa afterward.

THE couple met in India in 1944; when Marjorie was intelligence officer with the Office of Strategic Services and Albert was working for United Press.

Since then the two have worked together in most Asian countries. The wife's work often abets that of the husband; often she travels with him and takes photographs which illustrate his reports.

WHILE China has been Ravenholt's special field of interest for the past 16 years, he has not been able to do any first-hand study there save on the fringe of China at Hong kong, since 1950.

Of necessity, his work has been in countries such as The Philippines. He was asked to do the introductory article about the Islands for the annual edition of Encyclopedia Britannica Yearbook of 1957. His 25,000 word study was completed last year.

"The article is based on about three year's work and two main tours of duty in The Philippines," Mrs. Ravenholt says.

Ravenholt has not gained his informatron in libraries, but by going into the far islands of the Philippines. He has made friends with off-track vil lagers as well as national leaders. Reports which have resulted have no parallel in our knowledge.

Collecting the material for such reports has its difficulties. Ravenholt was for many months victim of an illness contracted in the line of duty. A wedding feast was held up two days, awaiting his arrival in the Moro country of the Southern Philippines. The food spoiled a bit during the tropical two-day wait, but he could not refuse to partake with diplomacy. His ailment resulted.

RAVENHOLT has been interested particularly in the Pbilippine Rural Reconstruction Movement which he has studied from the view point of individual farmers and from a comprehensive look at the movement.

Such reports are vitalized by a personal feeling, for the Ravenholts in tend to settle in rural Puget Sounc country and take up agricultural pursuits, eventually. One of Albert' library shelves is crowded with books on tree farming, animal husbandry, crops.

ALBERT RAVENHOLT, left, chatted with Amir Mindalano, leader of the 2,000,000 Moros in the Southern Philippines. The Moro leader was the subject of one of Ravenholt's Universities Field Staff reports.

Of the Philippines, both Ravenholts agree that there is no similar country in Asia; it's the country where Americans have had the longest, consistently responsible association.

"There's a reservoir of Americanism," Mrs. Ravenholt says. "We, like the Spanish, have made a major cultural contribution. Urban Filipinos have assumed many of our modern ways, even in food habits, musical likes, and slang.

"Most Filipinos like Americans. Particularly this is so among any who associated with American school teachers out there in the past 50 years. They have a deep, abiding affection for those teachers."

Sentimental regard is backed with practical trade, which is on the in crease, Ravenholt says.

"Eleven per cent of the sugar, being used in this country now comes from the Philippines," Ravenholt points out. "They produce the most copra (dried coconut) of any country and we are their principal market. We buy their mahogany, and also much of that which they first sell to Japan; where it is made into plywood.

"The Philippines are now the main supplier of chromite in the free world; it is used for making blast-furnace fire bricks. We buy much chromite and copper ore from them."

In 1953 the Ravenholts both helped to "cover" the Magsaysay election. At that time, also, Marjorie did an evaluation of women's organizatiow in the Philippines for the Asia Foundation.

In 1955, she did a study of the "Seeds for Democracy Program." She found it one of the strongest factors for continuing friendship between the United States and Philippines.

Mrs RAVENHOLT helped train ten information officers from eight Philippine-government agencies in 1950. She taught them to run evaluation tests on their programs and to judge their information materials.

The officers went into 30 barrios (rural communities) in seven provinces, to evaluate their programs which included health, coconut raising, agricultural credit, tenancy and other subjects.

Their years of experience have brought both Albert and Marjorie Ravenholt a special treasury of insight into peoples of the Far East. Such insight the Ravenholts are equipped admirably to translate into language which Americans can understand.

But it's a hectic life and someday the Ravenholts, now only in their mid-30's, plan to retire. What place have they picked, after all their travels?

"We like the Puget Sound Country best: There's no other place like it," the travelers agree.

U.S. Supply Convoy Climbs 21-Curves on the Burma Road!
Between Kunming and Kweiyang, China

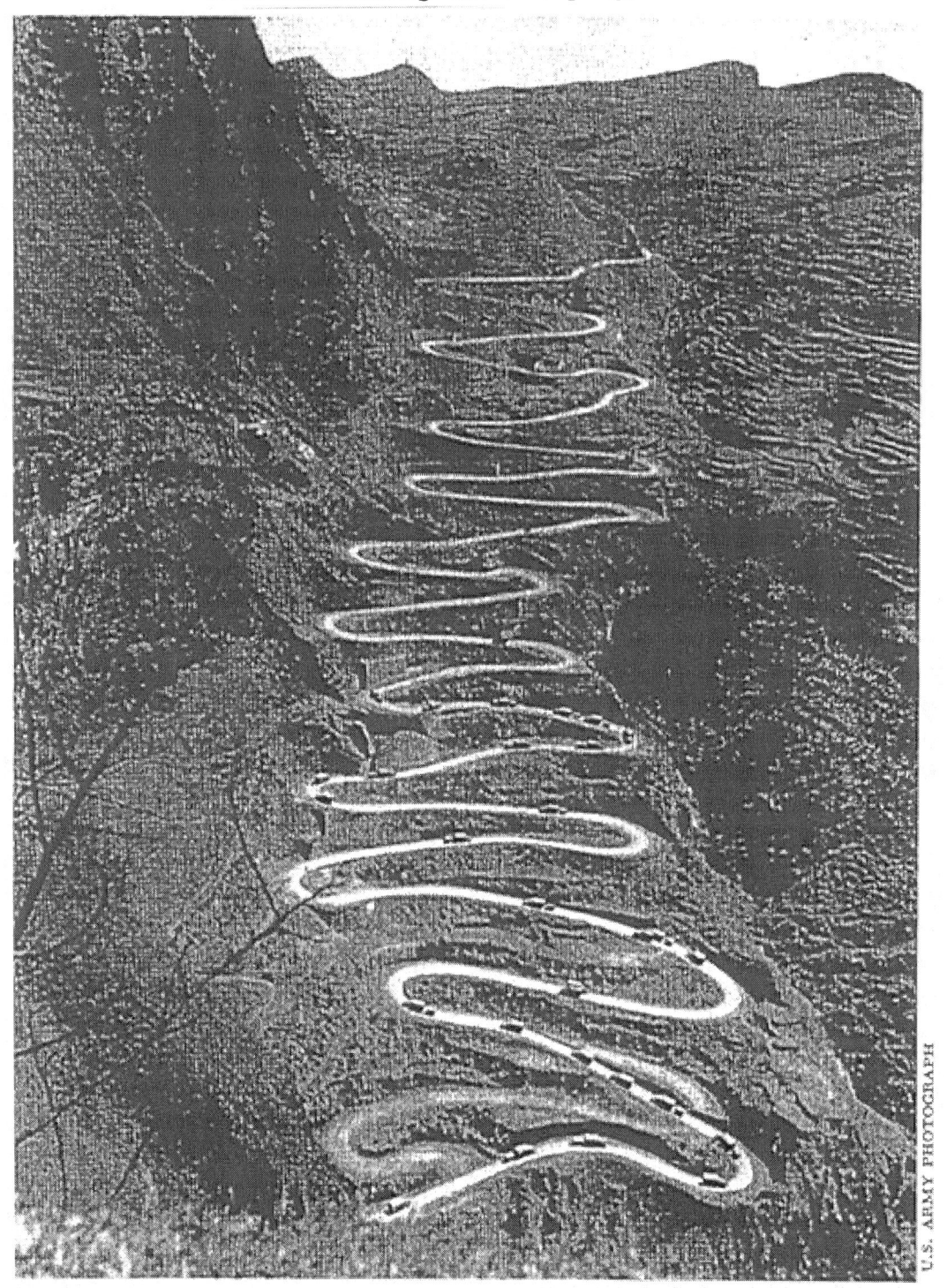

"I drove over this road more than a dozen times in 1941-45"
Albert Ravenholt, Int'l Red Cross Trucker & War Correspondent

Made in the USA
Lexington, KY
29 May 2010